BORLAND'S JBUILDER

No experience required.

BORLAND'S® JBUILDER™

John Zukowski

San Francisco • Paris • Düsseldorf • Soest

Associate Publisher: Gary Masters
Acquisitions Manager: Kristine Plachy
Acquisitions & Developmental Editor: Suzanne Rotondo
Editor: LeeAnn Pickrell
Technical Editor: Kevin Russo
Book Designers: Patrick Dintino, Catalin Dulfu
Electronic Publishing Specialist: Bob Bihlmayer
Production Coordinators: Alexa Riggs, Katherine Cooley, Robin Kibby
Indexer: Ted Laux
Cover Designer: Ingalls + Associates
Screen reproductions produced with Collage Complete.
Collage Complete is a trademark of Inner Media Inc.
SYBEX is a registered trademark of SYBEX Inc.
No experience required. is a trademark of SYBEX Inc.

TRADEMARKS: SYBEX has attempted throughout this book to distinguish proprietary trademarks from descriptive terms by following the capitalization style used by the manufacturer.

Netscape Communications, the Netscape Communications logo, Netscape, and Netscape Navigator are trademarks of Netscape Communications Corporation.

The author and publisher have made their best efforts to prepare this book, and the content is based upon final release software whenever possible. Portions of the manuscript may be based upon pre-release versions supplied by software manufacturer(s). The author and the publisher make no representation or warranties of any kind with regard to the completeness or accuracy of the contents herein and accept no liability of any kind including but not limited to performance, merchantability, fitness for any particular purpose, or any losses or damages of any kind caused or alleged to be caused directly or indirectly from this book.

Photographs and illustrations used in this book have been downloaded from publicly accessible file archives and are used in this book for news reportage purposes only to demonstrate the variety of graphics resources available via electronic access. Text and images available over the Internet may be subject to copyright and other rights owned by third parties. Online availability of text and images does not imply that they may be reused without the permission of rights holders, although the Copyright Act does permit certain unauthorized reuse as fair use under 17 U.S.C. Section 107.

Copyright ©1997 SYBEX Inc., 1151 Marina Village Parkway, Alameda, CA 94501. World rights reserved. No part of this publication may be stored in a retrieval system, transmitted, or reproduced in any way, including but not limited to photocopy, photograph, magnetic or other record, without the prior agreement and written permission of the publisher.

Library of Congress Card Number: 97-68717

ISBN: 0-7821-2135-7

Manufactured in the United States of America

10 9 8 7 6 5 4 3 2 1

Acknowledgments

First off, I'd like to thank everyone in the JBuilder Field Test Discussion Forum: Ben Matterson, Rich Wilkman, Judith Heher, Wendy Lin, Joe Nuxoll, Steven Radecki, Kevin Tien, Mike Timbol, and everyone else who offered help. Without your help, sometimes with answers to seemingly obvious questions, this book would not have turned out nearly as well. Also, special thanks go out to the JBuilder developers for creating such a great tool.

On a more personal level, I would like to thank my wife Lisa for her ongoing support despite my long hours. Special thanks to our Old English sheepdog, Sir Dudley Fuzzybuns McDuff, who celebrated a birthday during the whole process. Thanks go out to the gang at Sun, for creating Java, without which I don't know what I would have done for the last couple of years.

Finally, I'd like to thank everyone at Sybex for their hard work in putting everything together. From the beginning, thanks to Suzanne Rotondo for convincing me that one book just wasn't enough; to Lee Ann Pickrell, the ever-conscientious editor, for her thoroughness for details and for keeping the book at the proper level; to Kristine Plachy for tracking down those JBuilder betas that supposedly weren't released; and to Kevin Russo, technical editor, for his thoroughness and clear thinking. The end result is much better because of everyone's hard work. In addition, thanks go out to those behind the scenes who worked on the production of this book: production coordinators Alexa Riggs, Robin Kibby, and Katherine Cooley, and electronic publishing specialist Bob Bihlmayer.

Contents at a Glance

Introduction	xv
PART I • STARTING OUT	**1**
1 Exploring JBuilder	3
2 Employing the JBuilderApplet Wizard	25
3 Using Java Syntax	53
4 Creating a Scrolling Text Applet with Sound	73
5 Exploring AWT	95
6 Understanding Layout Management	113
7 Drawing with Java	129
8 Accessing Files	149
PART II • DIGGING INTO JAVABEANS	**169**
9 Understanding JavaBeans	171
10 Connecting Beans	185
11 Configuring the Palette	209
12 Creating Beans: Events/Properties	223
13 Creating Beans: Introspection	257
14 Creating Beans: Customization	277
15 Creating Beans: Serialization	301
16 Using the BeansExpress Wizards	321
PART III • ADVANCED SKILLS	**351**
17 Delivering Programs	353
18 Working with Menus	375
19 Creating a Toolbar	395
20 Customizing JBuilder	411
21 Debugging Multithreaded Programs	437
Glossary	461
Index	476

Table of Contents

Introduction	*xv*
PART I • STARTING OUT	**1**
Skill 1 Exploring JBuilder	**3**
Introducing JBuilder	4
Installing JBuilder	4
JBuilder Setup	6
Learning the JBuilder Environment	9
The Toolbar	10
The Component Palette	10
Status Messages	11
The AppBrowser	11
Creating a Java Program	13
Running the Applet	16
Examining the Source	18
The *<APPLET>* HTML Tag	19
Introducing Object-Oriented Programming	21
Java Object Basics	21
Methods	21
Variables	21
Inheritance	22
Are You Experienced?	23
Skill 2 Employing the JBuilderApplet Wizard	**25**
Using the Project Wizard	26
Using the Applet Wizard	29
Examining the Applet Source	32
Getting Applet Parameters	35
Using the Application Wizard	37
Examining the Application Source	39
Setting Application Parameters	42
Command-Line Parameters	43
System Properties	47
Are You Experienced?	51

Skill 3	**Using Java Syntax**	**53**
	Introducing Java Syntax	54
	Comments	54
	Keywords	54
	Identifiers	56
	Operators	56
	Working with Datatypes, Literals, and Strings	59
	Datatypes	59
	Literals	60
	Strings	61
	Declaring Classes, Methods, and Variables	61
	Classes	61
	Variables	62
	Arrays	62
	Methods	63
	Interfaces	64
	Packages	65
	Understanding Access Modifiers	66
	Using Flow Control	66
	if-else	67
	while	67
	do	68
	for	68
	switch	68
	Introducing Exception Handling	69
	Are You Experienced?	71
Skill 4	**Creating a Scrolling Text Applet with Sound**	**73**
	Getting Started	74
	Using the Override Methods Wizard	75
	Understanding the Applet Life-Cycle Methods	79
	Adding Sound	80
	Introducing Multithreading	84
	Defining the Thread Using the Implement Interface Wizard	84
	Creating the Thread	88
	Are You Experienced?	92

Skill 5	**Exploring AWT**	**95**
	Introducing the Abstract Window Toolkit	96
	Adding Components to Your Program	96
	Using Labels	97
	Using Text Fields	101
	Using Buttons	103
	Handling Events	105
	Handling Action Events	105
	Keyboard Events	108
	Are You Experienced?	111
Skill 6	**Understanding Layout Management**	**113**
	Introducing Layout Management Principles	114
	Using the *TabsetPanel*	114
	Using *FlowLayout*	116
	Implementing *ContainerListener*	118
	Using *GridLayout*	120
	Using *BorderLayout*	122
	Are You Experienced?	126
Skill 7	**Drawing with Java**	**129**
	Drawing Support in Java	130
	Using the *Paint* Method to Draw	130
	Handling Mouse Events	133
	Handling Mouse Events with *MouseListener*	134
	Handling Mouse Events with the *MouseMotionListener*	136
	Drawing from a Buffer (a.k.a. Double Buffering)	137
	Creating the Buffer	137
	Removing the Flash	140
	Changing Colors	141
	Are You Experienced?	147
Skill 8	**Accessing Files**	**149**
	Getting File Information	150
	Using a *StringWriter*	151
	Getting the File Information	152

Reading Files	154
Listing a Directory	157
Showing a Directory Graphically	158
Displaying the Tree	159
Handling Selection in the Tree	162
Are You Experienced?	168

Part II • Digging into JavaBeans   169

Skill 9 Understanding JavaBeans   171

What's a Bean?	172
What's inside a Bean?	172
Properties, Methods, and Events	172
Customization and Introspection	173
Persistence	173
What Does JBuilder Have to Do with All This?	173
Using the UI Designer	174
Dragging Components and Dropping Them into Your System	175
Bringing the Screen to Life	178
Are You Experienced?	182

Skill 10 Connecting Beans   185

Getting Started	186
Setting Up the Screen	186
Making the First Connection	188
Connecting the Buttons	192
Connecting the *Choice*	193
Connecting the *List*	194
Using the Interaction Wizard Editor	195
Using the Expression Assistant	199
Making the Final Connection	200
Are You Experienced?	206

Skill 11 Configuring the Palette   209

Setting Up the Component Palette	210
Adding from an Archive	210
Adding from a Package	213
Customizing Palette Entries	215
Removing Beans	216

Locating More Beans	216
KL Group	216
Gamelan	217
The Coffee Grinder	217
Java Applet Rating Service (JARS)	219
JavaBeans Home	219
Are You Experienced?	220

Skill 12 Creating Beans: Events/Properties   223

Creating New Beans	224
Adding Our First Bean to the Palette	226
Using the *BlueBox* Bean	228
Introducing Events	230
Notifying Listeners	232
Creating a New Tester	234
Making a Blue Triangle	237
Updating the New Tester	239
Introducing Properties	240
Working with Simple Properties	240
Working with Indexed Properties	243
Working with Bound Properties	243
Testing of Bound Properties	245
Working with Constrained Properties	250
Testing of Constrained Properties	251
Are You Experienced?	255

Skill 13 Creating Beans: Introspection   257

Introducing Introspection	258
Introducing Reflection	258
Adding the Color-Handling Code	261
Using the *BeanInfo* Introspector	264
Overriding *BeanInfo*	269
Limiting Properties	270
Limiting Events	271
Showing Off *MyButton*	272
Are You Experienced?	274

Skill 14 Creating Beans: Customization   277
        Getting Started   278
        Creating the *ShapeBox*   278
        Using the Default Property Editor   281
        Getting Shape Names as Input   284
            Creating the Property Editor   285
            Creating the *BeanInfo*   288
            Using the Property Editor   289
        Converting the Property Editor to a Selection List   290
            Using the Selection List   291
        Creating a Custom Property Editor   291
            Creating the *ShapeCustomEditor*   294
            Using the Custom Editor   297
        Are You Experienced?   298

Skill 15 Creating Beans: Serialization   301
        Learning about Persistence   302
        Creating the Interface   302
            Making the Counter Count   303
                Defining the Close Button   303
                Defining the Start Button   304
                Defining the Reset and Stop Buttons   305
        Enabling Save and Load   306
            Resetting the Thread State on Reading   309
                Restoring the Adapters   310
            Setting Up the Save Button   311
            Enabling Restoration   312
        Are You Experienced?   319

Skill 16 Using the BeansExpress Wizards   321
        Learning about BeansExpress   322
        Examining the *OKCancelBean*   322
            Adding the Bean to the Palette   326
            Using the *OkCancelBean*   326
        Working to Create New Beans and Bean Events   328
            Using the New Bean Wizard   328

Using the New Bean Event Wizard	330
Fixing Up *YesNoEventExampleBean*	332
Finishing Up the *YesNoEvent*	333
Finishing Up the *YesNoBean*	334
Testing Out the *YesNoBean*	338
Adding *BeanInfo* to Display an Image	342
Seeing the Icon	347
Are You Experienced?	348

PART III • ADVANCED SKILLS — 351

Skill 17 Delivering Programs — 353
Scooping Ice Cream	354
Creating the Applet	354
Using the Parameters	357
Creating the Scoop	359
Creating the Cone	360
Adding Action	361
Creating an Archive	367
Running *IceCreamOrder* from *order.jar*	369
Are You Experienced?	372

Skill 18 Working with Menus — 375
Getting Started	376
Using an About Box	378
Using the Menu Designer	379
Adding the *ColorChooser*	382
Customizing the *ColorChooser*	382
Adding a *FontChooser*	385
Customizing the *FontChooser*	385
Are You Experienced?	392

Skill 19 Creating a Toolbar — 395
Working with Toolbars	396
Selecting a Toolbar Button	398
Setting the Status Bar	399
Picking Files	400
Showing the Image	403
Closing Up	405
Are You Experienced?	408

Skill 20 Customizing JBuilder		**411**
	Setting the Project Author	412
	Changing the *.java* Association in Explorer	415
	Incorporating Your Own Snippets	417
	Understanding the Snippet Language	418
	Creating the Class	420
	Adding the Snippet	428
	Using the New Snippet	432
	Are You Experienced?	435
Skill 21 Debugging Multithreaded Programs		**437**
	Exploring the Debugger	438
	Creating the Producer	438
	Creating the Consumer	442
	Creating the Display Buffer	442
	Adding to the Buffer	443
	Removing from the Buffer	445
	Putting It All Together	447
	Debugging	449
	Stepping Through the Program	452
	Examining the Variables	453
	Setting Breakpoints	455
	Are You Experienced?	459
Glossary		*461*
Index		*476*

Introduction

The free Java tools you get from Sun to create Java programs are all command-line driven. You have to find a text editor in which to create your source code and then compile, package, and run programs with a series of independent programs. If you are accustomed to visual programming environments, such as Borland's Delphi or Microsoft's Visual C++, using Sun's Java Development Kit is like returning to the dark ages. It certainly gets the job done, but there has to be a better way.

Borland's JBuilder is the better way. It is a fully integrated development environment (IDE) where you can edit, compile, test and debug your programs for rapid application development. JBuilder creates 100 percent pure Java solutions and is fully Java 1.1 friendly. It supports new features such as inner classes, Java archives (JAR), Java Database Connectivity (JDBC), and Java Foundation Classes (JFC), as well as the 1.1 Abstract Window Toolkit (AWT) event model.

JBuilder also supports JavaBeans. JavaBeans is the component architecture of Java. With it, you no longer create huge monolithic applications but have only to worry about creating the ever-smaller pieces. Then, all you have to do is connect the beans to create your working programs. JBuilder is both the tool to use to create JavaBeans as well as the tool to use to connect JavaBeans.

With Borland's JBuilder you can create Java programs fast, whether by hand, with the help of the many Wizards, or by pointing and clicking. With the help of *Borland's JBuilder: No experience required*, you'll get up to speed with JBuilder even faster.

Who This Book Is For

Whether you have beginning or expert computer skills and are looking for a hands-on way to learn about Borland's JBuilder—to prepare for a job interview, to create an applet or application, to learn about JavaBeans, or just for the fun of it—this book is for you. It is a learn-by-doing book that requires only enough computer know-how to be able to point, click, and type. You don't have to be a developer or programmer, although it certainly doesn't hurt.

After you've completed this book, you will be able to do the following:

- Install and configure JBuilder

- Understand Java syntax
- Use JBuilder Wizards
- Create graphical Java programs
- Build and connect JavaBeans with and without BeansExpress
- Work with multithreaded programs
- Use the JBuilder debugger

All exercises include step-by-step instructions for Windows 95 and Windows NT 4 platforms, the only platforms that support JBuilder. Plenty of illustrations and tips accompany the instructions.

How This Book Is Organized

This book is divided into three parts. Each builds on the skills and understandings developed in the earlier sections.

Part One: Getting Started

In Part One, you will learn about the basics of Java programming in general, while exploring some specifics of JBuilder. You'll be introduced to Java applets and applications, Java syntax, and the applet life-cycle. You'll then learn about creating graphical programs, and you'll finish up by working with files.

Part Two: Digging into JavaBeans

In Part Two, you will learn about JavaBeans: what it is, how it works, and how to create your own beans. You will also learn about connecting, creating, and customizing beans.

Part Three: Developing Advanced Skills

In Part Three, you will learn about working with menus and toolbars, as well as customizing JBuilder to your liking. Part Three ends with a discussion of multi-threading in Java and using the JBuilder debugger.

Online Support for This Book

For online support at the Sybex Web site, go to `http://www.sybex.com/cgi-bin/nxrintro.pl` and click on the Borland JBuilder entry. The following are just a few of the reasons for visiting the book's Web site:

- Instead of typing in Java code for the longer examples, go to the Sybex Web site and download them.
- Check the site for additions and updates to the book, as well as information on related resources and technical developments.
- Contact the author at the Sybex site if you have any comments about the book.
- If you're looking for the perfect job, click the Job Site Links button to begin your search.

Conventions Used in This Book

This book uses the following typographic conventions:

- Monospaced font (`archiveSmall.gif`, for example) for program code and the names of files, directories, paths, methods, classes, properties, objects, keywords, parameters, and Internet URLs.
- *Italics* for variable file or directory names; that is, the portions of instructions that you can modify and still have the instructions work, such as *installdir*, meaning the name of *your* installation directory. For best results, however, use the suggested defaults.
- Bold for entries that must be typed exactly as shown (**SimpleBeanInfo**), form field settings (Set the title to **Objective**), and portions of lines that must be entered as is (prompt>**appletviewer MyApplet.html**). Also, in source code listings, some lines are highlighted in bold. This is just to focus your attention to those lines, as directed by the text.

Special information is set off from the page as Notes, Tips, and Warnings:

> **NOTE** Notes contain information that needs to be emphasized.

> **TIP** Tips help clarify the text and make you more productive with JBuilder faster.

> **WARNING** Warnings point out potential trouble spots.

I hope you enjoy using this book. If you have any comments, please contact me at the Sybex Web site.

PART I

Starting Out

PROGRAMMERS
C, C, VB, Cobol, exp. Call 534-555-6543 or fax 534-555-6544.

PROGRAMMING
MRFS Inc. is looking for a Sr. Windows NT developer. Reqs. 3-5 yrs. Exp. In C under Windows, Win95 & NT, using Visual C. Excl. OO design & implementation skills a must. OLE2 & ODBC are a plus. Excl. Salary & bnfts. Resume & salary history to HR, 8779 HighTech Way, Computer City, AR

PROGRAMMERS
Contractors Wanted for short & long term assignments: Visual C, MFC Unix C/C, SQL Oracle Dev elop ers PC Help Desk Support Windows NT & NetWare Telecommunications Visual Basic, Access, HTMT, CGI, Perl MMI & Co., 885-555-9933

PROGRAMMER World Wide Web Links wants your HTML & Photoshop skills. Develop great WWW sites. Local & global customers. Send samples & resume to WWWL, 2000 Apple Road, Santa Rosa, CA.

TECHNICAL WRITER Software firm seeks writer/editor for manuals, research notes, project mgmt. Min 2 years tech. writing, DTP & programming experience. Send resume & writing samples to: Software Systems, Dallas, TX.

TECHNICAL Software development firm looking for Tech Trainers. Ideal candidates have programming experience in Visual C, HTML & JAVA. Need quick self starter. Call (443) 555-6868 for interview.

TECHNICAL WRITER/ Premier Computer Corp is seeking a combination of technical skills, knowledge and experience in the following areas: UNIX, Windows 95/NT, Visual Basic, on-line help & documentation, and the Internet. Candidates must possess excellent writing skills, and be comfortable working in a quality vs. deadline driven environment. Competitive salary. Fax resume & samples to Karen Fields, Premier Computer Corp. 444 Industrial Blvd. Concord, CA. Or send to our website at www.premier.com.

WEB DESIGNER
BA/BS or equivalent programming/multimedia production. 3 years of experience in use and design of WWW services streaming audio and video HTML, PERL, CGI, GIF, JPEG. Demonstrated interpersonal, organization, communication, multi-tasking skills. Send resume to The Learning People at www.learning.com.

WEBMASTER-TECHNICAL
BSCS or equivalent, 2 years of experience in CGI, Windows 95/NT, UNIX, C, Java, Perl. Demonstrated ability to design, code, debug and test on-line services. Send resume to The Learning People at www.learning.com.

PROGRAMMER World Wide Web Links wants your HTML & Photoshop skills. Develop great WWW sites. Local & global customers. Send samples & resume to WWWL, 2000 Apple Road, Santa Rosa, CA.

ing tools. Experienced in documentation preparation & programming languages (Access, C, FoxPro) are a plus. Financial or banking customer service support is required along with excellent verbal & written communication skills with multi levels of end-users. Send resume to KKUP Enterprises, 45 Orange Blvd. Orange, CA.

COMPUTERS Small Web Design firm seeks indiv. w/NT, Webserver & Database management exp. Fax resume to 556-555-4221.

COMPUTER/ Visual C/C, Visual Basic Exp'd Systems Analysts/ Programmers for growing software dev. team in Roseburg. Computer Science or related degree preferred. Develop adv. Engineering applications for engineering firm. Fax resume to 707-555-8744.

COMPUTER Web Master for dynamic SF Internet co. Site. Dev. test, coord, train. 2 yrs prog. Exp. C C Web C, FTP. Fax resume to Best Staffing 845-555-7722.

COMPUTER PROGRAMMER
Ad agency seeks programmer w/exp. in UNIX/NT Platforms, Web Server, CGI/Perl. Programmer Position avail. on a project basis with the possibility to move into F/T. Fax resume & salary req. to R. Jones 334-555-8332.

COMPUTERS Programmer/Analyst Design and maintain C based SQL database applications. Required skills: Visual Basic, C, SQL, ODBC. Document existing and new applications. Novell or NT exp. a plus. Fax resume & salary history to 235-555-9935.

GRAPHIC DESIGNER
Webmaster's Weekly is seeking a creative Graphic Designer to design high impact marketing collateral, including direct mail promo's, CD-ROM packages, ads and WWW pages. Must be able to juggle multiple projects and learn new skills on the job very rapidly. Web design experience a big plus, technical troubleshooting also a plus. Call 435-555-1235.

GRAPHICS - ART DIRECTOR - WEB-MULTIMEDIA
Leading internet development company has an outstanding opportunity for a talented, high-end Web Experienced Art Director. In addition to a great portfolio and fresh ideas, the ideal candidate has excellent communication and presentation skills. Working as a team with innovative producers and programmers, you will create dynamic, interactive web sites and application interfaces. Some programming experience required. Send samples and resume to: SuperSites, 333 Main, Seattle, WA.

MARKETING
Fast paced software and services provider looking for MARKETING COMMUNICATIONS SPECIALIST to be responsible for its webpage.

PROGRAMMERS Multiple short term assignments available: Visual C, 3 positions SQL ServerNT Server, 2 positions JAVA & HTML, long term NetWare Various locations. Call for more info. 356-555-3398.

PROGRAMMERS
C, C, VB, Cobol, exp.
Call 534-555-6543
or fax 534-555-6544.

PROGRAMMING
MRFS Inc. is looking for a Sr. Windows NT developer. Reqs. 3-5 yrs. Exp. In C under Windows, Win95 & NT, using Visual C. Excl. OO design & implementation skills a must. OLE2 & ODBC are a plus. Excl. Salary & bnfts. Resume & salary history to HR, 8779 HighTech Way, Computer City, AR

PROGRAMMERS/ Contractors Wanted for short & long term assignments: Visual C, MFC Unix C/C, SQL Oracle Developers PC Help Desk Support Windows NT & NetWareTelecommunications Visual Basic, Access, HTMT, CGI, Perl MMI & Co., 885-555-9933

PROGRAMMER World Wide Web Links wants your HTML & Photoshop skills. Develop great WWW sites. Local & global customers. Send samples & resume to WWWL, 2000 Apple Road, Santa Rosa, CA.

TECHNICAL WRITER Software firm seeks writer/editor for manuals, research notes, project mgmt. Min 2 years tech. writing, DTP & programming experience. Send resume & writing samples to: Software Systems, Dallas, TX.

COMPUTER PROGRAMMER
Ad agency seeks programmer w/exp. in UNIX/NT Platforms, Web Server, CGI/Perl. Programmer Position avail. on a project basis with the possibility to move into F/T. Fax resume & salary req. to R. Jones 334-555-8332.

TECHNICAL WRITER Premier Computer Corp is seeking a combination of technical skills, knowledge and experience in the following areas: UNIX, Windows 95/NT, Visual Basic, on-line help & documentation, and the Internet. Candidates must possess excellent writing skills, and be comfortable working in a quality vs. deadline driven environment. Competitive salary. Fax resume & samples to Karen Fields, Premier Computer Corp. 444 Industrial Blvd. Concord, CA. Or send to our website at www.premier.com.

WEB DESIGNER
BA/BS or equivalent programming/multimedia production. 3 years of experience in use and design of WWW services streaming audio and video HTML, PERL, CGI, GIF, JPEG. Demonstrated interpersonal, organization, communication, multi-tasking skills. Send resume to The Learning People at www.learning.com.

WEBMASTER-TECHNICAL
BSCS or equivalent, 2 years of experience in CGI, Windows 95/NT,

PROGRAMMERS Multiple short term assignments available: Visual C, 3 positions SQL ServerNT Server, 2 positions JAVA & HTML, long term NetWare Various locations. Call for more info. 356-555-3398.

COMPUTERS Small Web Design firm seeks indiv. w/NT, Webserver & Database management exp. Fax resume to 556-555-4221.

COMPUTER Visual C/C, Visual Basic Exp'd Systems Analysts/ Programmers for growing software dev. team in Roseburg. Computer Science or related degree preferred. Develop adv. Engineering applications for engineering firm. Fax resume to 707-555-8744.

COMPUTER Web Master for dynamic SF Internet co. Site. Dev. test, coord, train. 2 yrs prog. Exp. C C Web C, FTP. Fax resume to Best Staffing 845-555-7722.

COMPUTERS/ QA SOFTWARE TESTERS Qualified candidates should have 2 yrs exp. performing integration & system testing using automated testing tools. Experienced in documentation preparation & programming languages (Access, C, FoxPro) are a plus. Financial or banking customer support is required along with excellent verbal & written communication skills with multi levels of end-users. Send resume to KKUP Enterprises, 45 Orange Blvd. Orange, CA.

COMPUTERS Programmer/Analyst Design and maintain C based SQL database applications. Required skills: Visual Basic, C, SQL, ODBC. Document existing and new applications. Novell or NT exp. a plus. Fax resume & salary history to 235-555-9935.

GRAPHIC DESIGNER
Webmaster's Weekly is seeking a creative Graphic Designer to design high impact marketing collateral, including direct mail promo's, CD-ROM packages, ads and WWW pages. Must be able to juggle multiple projects and learn new skills on the job very rapidly. Web design experience a big plus, technical troubleshooting also a plus. Call 435-555-1235.

GRAPHICS - ART DIRECTOR - WEB-MULTIMEDIA
Leading internet development company has an outstanding opportunity for a talented, high-end Web Experienced Art Director. In addition to a great portfolio and fresh ideas, the ideal candidate has excellent communication and presentation skills. Working as a team with innovative producers and programmers, you will create dynamic, interactive web sites and application interfaces. Some programming experience required. Send samples and resume to: SuperSites, 333 Main, Seattle, WA.

COMPUTER PROGRAMMER
Ad agency seeks programmer w/exp. in UNIX/NT Platforms, Web Server, CGI/Perl. Programmer Position avail. on a project basis with the possibility to move into F/T. Fax resume & salary req. to R. Jones 334-555-8332.

PROGRAMMERS / Established software company seeks program-

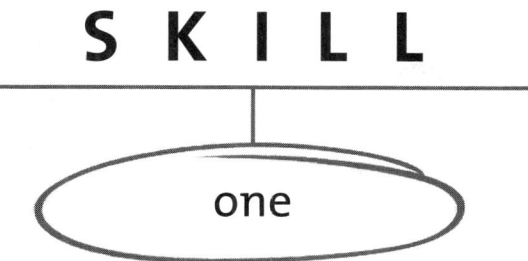

Exploring JBuilder

- ❑ Understanding JBuilder
- ❑ Installing and setting up JBuilder
- ❑ Working in the JBuilder environment
- ❑ Creating and running a Java applet
- ❑ Understanding the source
- ❑ Understanding the basics of object-oriented programming

Introducing JBuilder

JBuilder is Borland International's visual Java development environment. With JBuilder, you can quickly and easily build Java programs on your PC for delivery on any hardware platform.

Instead of using the independent, command line tools provided with Sun Microsystems' Java Development Kit (JDK), JBuilder provides a closely integrated, rapid application development (RAD) environment. With the help of the many Wizards and a rich object gallery, JBuilder helps you create applets for inclusion on your Web pages or in stand-alone Java applications.

JBuilder is also built to take full advantage of JavaBeans. Beans allows you to take advantage of small, reusable, software components to create applications quickly and easily. Instead of having to build programs from scratch, with JavaBeans you can easily integrate pieces from disparate sources to create fully functional programs with minimal effort. With JBuilder, this support is seamless.

In addition, JBuilder easily integrates with databases. With a rich set of Java Database Connectivity (JDBC) components, you can connect to any JDBC- or ODBC-compliant data source. And, the programs you create can scale from your desktop PC to an enterprise-wide database server.

All of this allows us to draw at least one conclusion: JBuilder allows you to streamline the development process, so you, the programmer, can be much more efficient. With all that said, let's install the tool and start working smarter.

Installing JBuilder

Installing JBuilder is fairly straightforward. The first release of the tool runs only on Windows 95 or Windows NT 4, so that is what we'll be working with. It's reasonable to assume that subsequent releases of JBuilder will work on multiple platforms. The installation directions that follow are specifically for Windows 95 or NT 4, because that's what the tool requires.

Before you start, you need to make sure you have enough disk space. JBuilder requires about 150MB of free space for installation. The software takes up about 100MB, but requires additional temporary space during installation. To see how much space you have available, first select the My Computer icon on your computer's Desktop and then double-click on it. Unless the icon has been changed from the default picture, it should appear as shown here.

Installing JBuilder 5

NOTE The My Computer icon is usually found in the top-left corner of your Desktop.

Double-clicking the My Computer icon brings up its folder. The folder displays an icon for each disk drive available on your system, as well as for a handful of other objects. Now, if you select the hard drive that you want to install JBuilder on, the lower-right corner of the window displays the amount of free space available on the drive, as well as the drive's capacity. On my system, the available disk drives and space appear as shown in Figure 1.1. Your computer will most definitely differ.

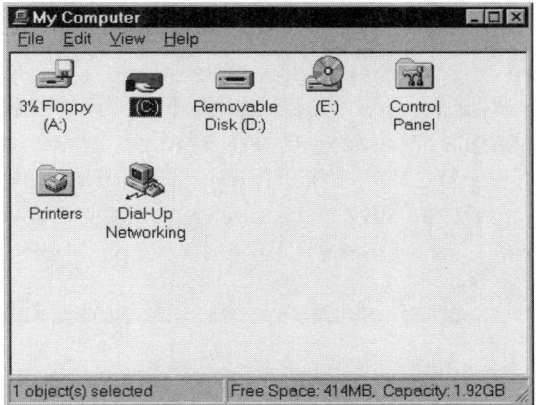

FIGURE 1.1: Checking for available free space on my hard drive

As long as the available free space is greater than 150MB, you should have enough room for the installation. If there isn't sufficient space (less than 150MB), you need to remove things from your hard drive until there is sufficient space. Be sure only to remove contents that have been backed up and you can safely delete. Random deleting could prevent your system from running properly. If you're not sure, check with someone first.

> ### REAL DISK USAGE REQUIREMENTS
>
> MB stands for *megabyte* and is about one million characters of information. If you see KB, for *kilobyte,* next to the available space you definitely do not have enough space since 1KB is about one thousand characters of information. If you see GB there, for *gigabyte,* you definitely do have enough space. A gigabyte is one thousand million (or a billion) characters of space.
>
> Although the software takes 100MB of disk space, the actual amount of space used depends upon your hard drive's *disk sector* size. A disk sector is the smallest amount of disk space that can be allocated to a file. The size of your disk sector determines how much disk space is allocated, and hence how much space is actually used. For a 2GB hard disk, the default sector size is 32KB. In other words, file space is allocated in blocks of 32KB. This translates into the JBuilder installation requiring close to 200MB of disk space (on a 2GB hard disk with the default sector size), plus even more temporary space for installation.

JBuilder Setup

Now that we've determined we have enough space, we can actually install the software. You receive JBuilder as either a single large file or segmented pieces. Either way, the setup program is called `setup.exe` and is executed by double-clicking on it within Explorer. After a little prep work by the setup utility, you will see Figure 1.2.

Selecting Next takes you to the license agreement page. Review it and select Yes to accept it. If you do not accept the agreement, you cannot install JBuilder. This takes you to the Installation Notes screen. After reading about any installation issues, select Next again to move on to the Select Setup Type window.

On the Select Setup Type window, make sure the Typical option is selected. If you're really tight on disk space you can use the Compact option, but you won't have the online help available. It saves you about 50MB. The Compact option is not recommended, though, because the online help is very beneficial.

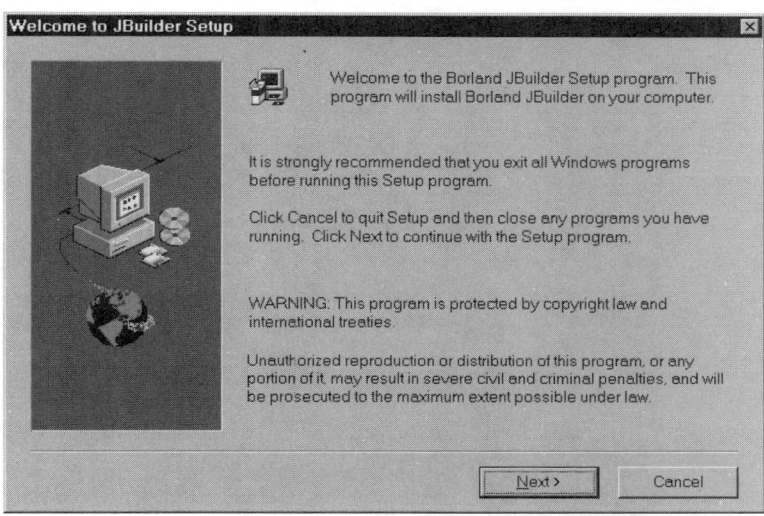

FIGURE 1.2: The Welcome to JBuilder Setup window

Once you select Next, yet again, you move to the Select Destination Location window, where you'll choose the installation location. The default location is C:\JBuilder, and in the remaining skills I have assumed you chose the default location. If you enter a different location in the Destination Directory field, you will have to translate commands to the appropriate place.

When you select Next, the system should prompt you to create the directory. If it doesn't, you are installing the software into an existing directory and could corrupt an existing application. Check which application on your machine might be using this particular directory. If possible and practical for you, move it and restart the installation; if not, to avoid corruption, select another directory. Selecting Yes starts the installation process. You can watch the setup percentage increase, as shown in Figure 1.3, until it reaches 100%, indicating the software is installed.

Once it finishes, there are still a few more steps to take before you can start the tool. The next step is to choose a folder name. This is the name under which JBuilder will appear on the system's Start menu. The default name is "Borland JBuilder," which seems appropriate, so if you're willing to go with it, you can simply select Next.

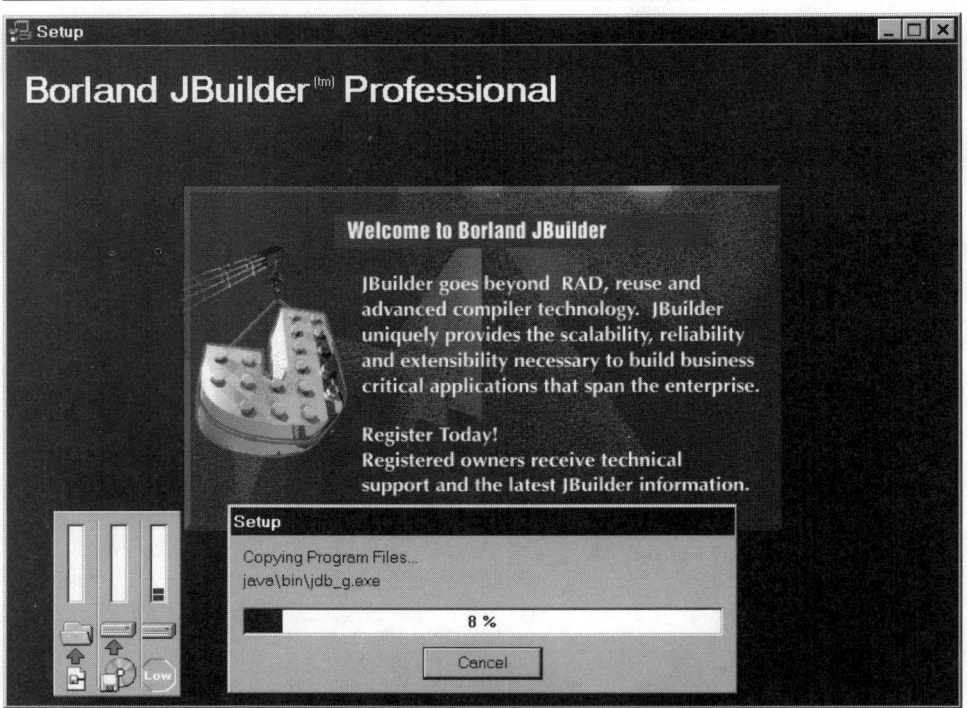

FIGURE 1.3: Sit back and relax as JBuilder installs itself

After creating the folder, JBuilder presents the Product Notes for review. These contain any last minute details that didn't make it into the documentation. Once you finish reading, select Next one more time to complete the setup process. You should see Figure 1.4 to signify you are done, indicating JBuilder's successful installation. Select OK. Congratulations!

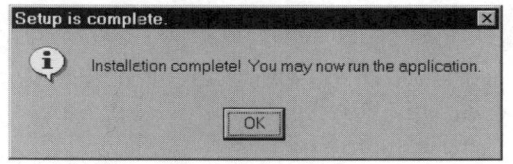

FIGURE 1.4: The Setup is Complete dialog box

Learning the JBuilder Environment

With JBuilder installed, let's start it up and learn our way around the tool. From the Windows Start icon, select Programs ➤ Borland JBuilder ➤ JBuilder.

When JBuilder starts, you are presented with its *integrated development environment* (or *IDE*). The IDE is where you build and test your Java programs (see Figure 1.5). Before jumping in and developing your Java programs, you should become familiar with the development environment. Until you're comfortable with the environment, you will spend more development time thinking "How do I ...?" instead of immediately seeing the results you are after.

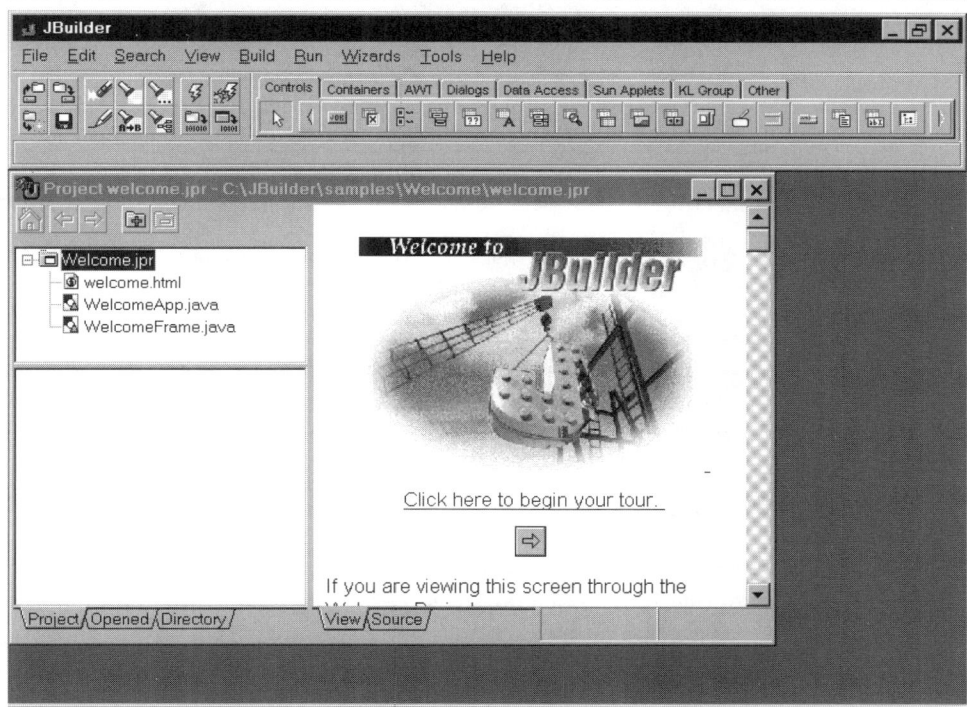

FIGURE 1.5: The JBuilder IDE, where you build and test your Java programs

The JBuilder IDE is divided into two areas, each with a number of different parts. The top area is composed of a toolbar, component palette, and area for status messages, while the bottom area contains your main workspace—the AppBrowser.

The Toolbar

Immediately below the menu bar, on the left-hand side of the window, is the JBuilder toolbar (see Figure 1.6). It consists of 14 buttons that provide access to the main development tasks. If you can't see the buttons, then go to the menu and click View ➤ Toolbar. All of these buttons provide quick access to menu bar commands.

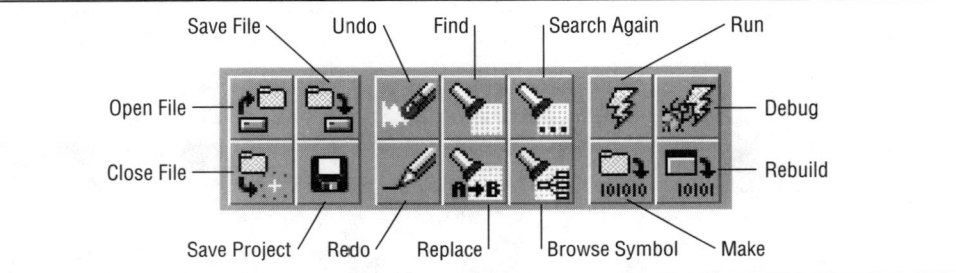

FIGURE 1.6: The JBuilder toolbar

If you ever forget which button is which, you can rest the mouse cursor on the button, and a *tool tip* will appear describing it.

 **TIP** A tool tip is a cream-colored box that describes the item's purpose. It appears when the mouse cursor dwells (rests) over an area designated with a defined tip.

The Component Palette

To the right of the toolbar, you'll find the component palette (see Figure 1.7). The component palette contains the different Bean components that JBuilder makes available. Later, when you create your own Beans, you'll learn how to add these to the palette, too.

FIGURE 1.7: The JBuilder component palette

The component palette allows you to visually create your programs. Instead of programmatically creating buttons, labels, and other visual objects, you just drag and drop objects from the component palette. This is a real time-saver when designing screens.

Status Messages

Below both the toolbar and component palette is an area for status messages. When building projects, you can watch this area for progress reports. For instance, when you compile your project, you can watch as JBuilder compiles each file within the project. After compiling a project, a good message to see is: "Compiler: Successful, with no errors." During compilation, you will also see a Cancel button on the far-right side of the status area. Clicking the Cancel button stops the compilation process before it's complete.

The AppBrowser

The AppBrowser is your main working area and is located below the status area. It consists of three different areas, or *panes:* the Navigation pane, the Content pane, and the Structure pane, as shown in Figure 1.8.

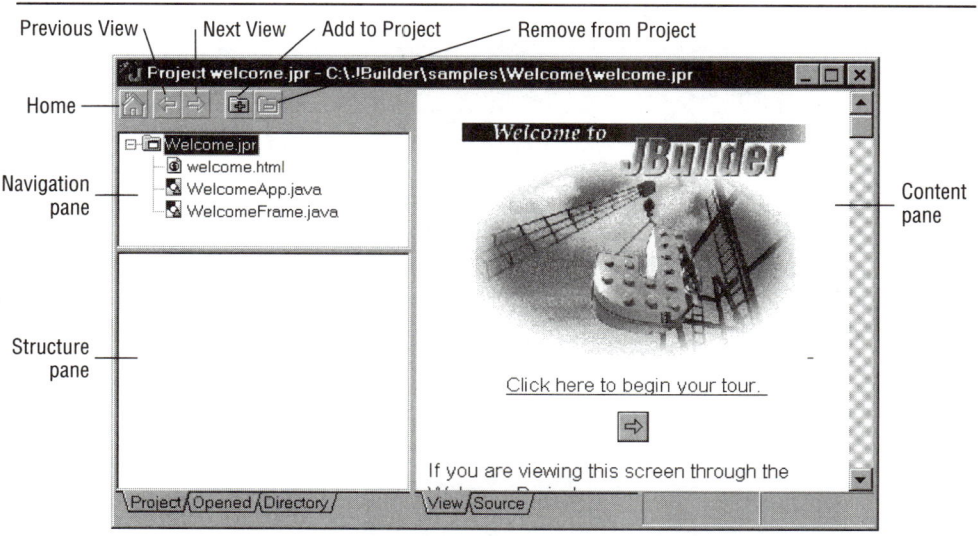

FIGURE 1.8: The JBuilder AppBrowser

TIP You may have noticed that JBuilder comes with a Quick Start Guide. You are welcome to give it a try at any time. It is always available from the Help ➤ Welcome Project (Sample) menu.

The Navigation pane, in the top-left corner, is where you'll navigate between the various files of a project. When you change files, the other panes of the AppBrowser are updated to reflect your new location. You can use the arrows at the top of the Navigation pane to return to a previous view. As an added feature, the Home icon will always return you to the top-level view of the project, in case you get lost.

To the right of the Navigation pane, you'll see the Content pane. It initially displays the source of the file currently selected. However, it is also the working area where you drag and drop component palette objects. Use the tabs at the bottom of the Content pane to switch between these different views.

Below the Navigation pane is the Structure pane. When the currently selected element in the Navigation pane is a .java source file, the Structure Pane displays the file's structure in a tree-like view. Each data member or method of the file is listed with a title and icon. The different icons are described in Table 1.1. When you select an item in the Structure pane, the Content pane moves to the location of the selected element.

TABLE 1.1: Structure Pane Icons

Icon	Description
	Class Definition with main() method
	Class Definition without main() method
	Implements interface
	Superclass
	Constructor
	Method
	init() method for applet / main() method for application
	Native method
	Primitive instance variable
	Object instance variable

TABLE 1.1 CONTINUED: Structure Pane Icons

Icon	Description
	Package declaration
	Import statement

Play around with all the different pieces of the environment to get comfortable in your new home. Once you think you know where everything is, you can move on to create some code.

One thing you should know first is that when you minimize an AppBrowser window, it doesn't appear in the window's Taskbar. Instead, JBuilder lines up the windows at the bottom of the working area of the screen with just the window  title showing, as shown here. This is useful when working with multiple AppBrowser windows open.

Creating a Java Program

We're going to create a simple example in JBuilder now, without using all the bells and whistles available. The example we create will be an *applet*. An applet is a Java program that runs within a Web page. The applet will display the words "Good Morning JBuilder."

NOTE There are two types of programs that you can create with Java and JBuilder. Java programs that run within a browser are called applets. Java programs that run outside the browser are called applications. The name *applet* implies a small application. However, applets are not restricted in size, only in security. Normally, an applet cannot access the local hard drive and can only communicate with the machine where it originated.

First, close anything that's open using the File ➤ Close All menu option.

Before we create our first applet, we need to create our first *project*. JBuilder works with a project metaphor to keep related things together. If you ever do anything that requires multiple files, you need to work in a JBuilder project. For an applet, there are two pieces necessary: the applet source file and the applet loader, which makes it possible to view it in a Web page.

To create a project, select the File ➤ Open/Create menu. This brings up the Open/Create dialog box, as seen in Figure 1.9.

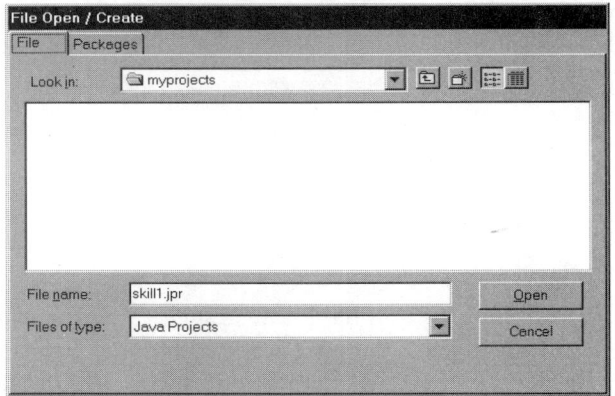

FIGURE 1.9: The File Open/Create dialog box

In the File Name field, type in the name **skill1.jpr** and press Open. This creates the file `skill1.jpr` in the default project directory and opens up the project in the AppBrowser window, as seen in Figure 1.10.

 **NOTE** JBuilder project filenames end in `.jpr`, for JBuilder (or Java) project. The default project directory is the `myprojects` directory under the JBuilder installation directory.

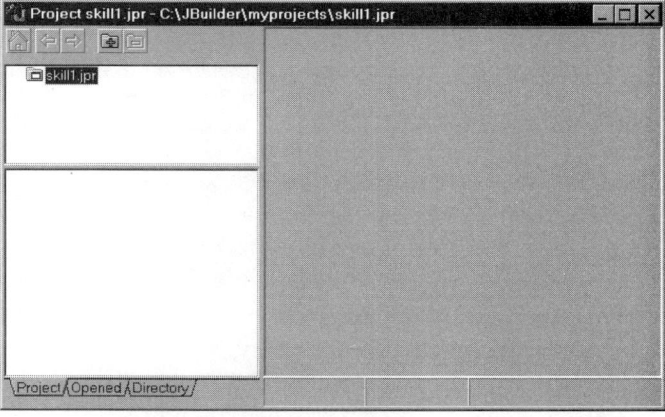

FIGURE 1.10: The AppBrowser window for a new project

Now that a project exists, you can create your first applet. The File ➤ Open/Create menu allows you to create the source file. When you select File ➤ Open/Create, the screen shown in Figure 1.11 appears. It is almost the same figure as Figure 1.9; however, because a project is open, you will see the Add to Project option at the bottom. Enter **Hello.java** in the File Name field, select the Add to Project option, and click the Open button. Because the file doesn't exist yet, *open* actually means *create;* however, the file isn't created until you save it.

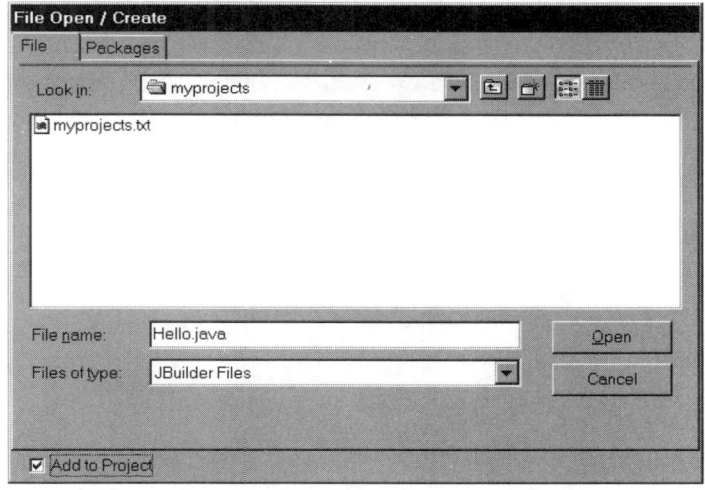

FIGURE 1.11: The File Open / Create window is where you start creating the source file.

 Be sure to check the Add to Project option before you select Open. If you forget, repeat the operation, remembering to select the Add to Project option the second time around.

In the Content pane for Hello.java, enter the following source code:

```
import java.awt.Graphics;
public class Hello extends java.applet.Applet {
   public void paint (Graphics g) {
       g.drawString ("Good Morning JBuilder", 40, 50);
   }
}
```

This is our Java program, and soon you'll see what each line means. To save it to disk, select File ➤ Save. Before we can run the applet, we need to compile it by selecting Build ➤ Make "Hello.java" (or the Build icon). If there are no typos, you will see the message "Compiler: Successful with no errors." in the status message area. Otherwise, the message will be "Compiler: Failed with errors.", and the Content pane will split in two. You can then highlight each error and correct it before recompiling. Figure 1.12 shows what would happen with the , 50 missing in the drawString call. Once you correct the error, save it again with File ➤ Save and use Build ➤ Make "Hello.java" to recompile. Once the program has been successfully compiled, it's time to run it.

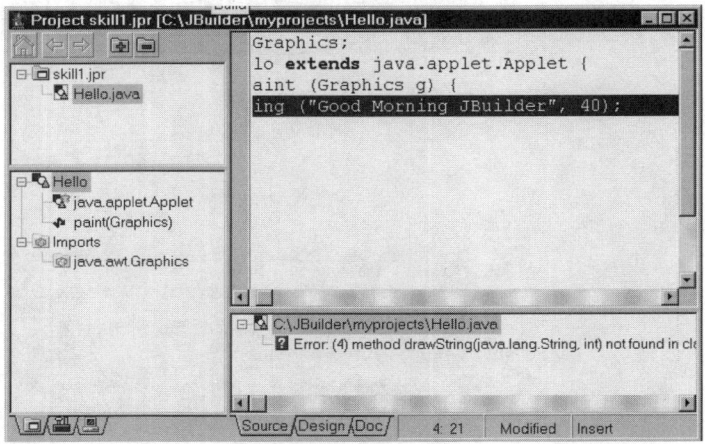

FIGURE 1.12: Compilation error for missing parameter in drawString call

Running the Applet

Because applets run within a Web browser, we need to create a file to load the applet into the browser. To create the file, select the File ➤ Open/Create command again. This time enter **Hello.html**, select the Add to Project option, and select Open.

To place anything into the Hello.html file, you need to select the Source tab at the bottom of the Content pane. This allows us to modify the contents. Place the following into the file:

```
<APPLET code=Hello width=300 height=100>
</APPLET>
```

Once you have typed that in, select File ➤ Save to save it, and Run ➤ Run Applet in `Hello.html` to run the applet. This will bring up the window you see in Figure 1.13.

WARNING If you forget to save the `Hello.html` file, nothing will happen when you try to run it. JBuilder requires that applet loader files be saved to disk before it can execute them.

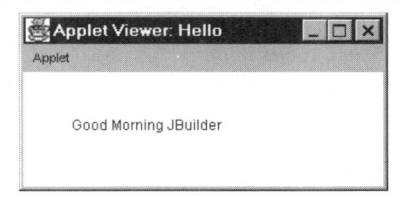

FIGURE 1.13: Running the Hello applet

NOTE The program JBuilder uses to test applets is called *AppletViewer*. This is not a full-fledged browser; it only understands the <APPLET> tag with the .html file. If you display text or images within the Web page, AppletViewer will not display them, however a normal browser like Internet Explorer or Netscape Navigator will.

If you think there are a few steps here that could be automated, there are. The Applet Wizard, which you will see in Skill 2, takes care of most of the manual steps we had to do, including the creation of the applet loader .html file.

NOTE When you compiled the `Hello.java` file, JBuilder created the file `Hello.class`. However, if you look in the directory where you saved the `Hello.java` file, you will notice `Hello.class` is not there. JBuilder places all the .class files in its directory structure under the directory `myclasses`. This structure allows JBuilder to simplify execution by centralizing access to one directory tree. If you want to run the applet in a real browser, copy the `C:\JBuilder\myprojects\Hello.html` and `C:\JBuilder\myclasses\Hello.class` files to your Web server, or just to the same directory. Then, have your browser open the `Hello.html` file.

Examining the Source

Now that we have something up and running, let's take a look at exactly what this means.

The first line of our program tells the compiler about a class called `Graphics`, in a *package* called `java.awt`.

```
import java.awt.Graphics;
```

A package is a group of related classes. In particular, the `java.awt` package is the Java Abstract Window Toolkit and contains classes that have to do with drawing and how things appear on the screen. If you come from a C/C++ background, a package is identical to a class library. Instead of having to re-create everything from scratch, you can create more complete Java programs faster by reusing the prebuilt Java packages. In fact, much of this book discusses how to reuse the predefined packages within JBuilder.

The second line of our program creates a Java *class* `Hello`.

```
public class Hello extends java.applet.Applet {
```

A class is one of those pieces that goes in a package. Because we are creating an applet, our class needs to *extend* from the `Applet` class in the `java.applet` package. This allows us to reuse lots of different pieces that are already defined for use with applets. If we didn't, our program would be much longer. If you are familiar with C++, extending a Java class is the same as inheriting from a base class in C++.

> **NOTE** Don't worry if some of these terms are confusing at the moment, they will be explained in much greater detail shortly.

Notice that the package `java.applet` and the class `Applet` are combined to form `java.applet.Applet`. We could have also done the following, with the same results:

```
import java.applet.Applet;
public class Hello extends Applet {
```

> **TIP** If you leave out the extends *classname* from the class definition, Java infers that you are extending from the `Object` class.

The rest of the source tells the program to print the string "Good Morning JBuilder" on the screen.

```
public void paint (Graphics g) {
g.drawString ("Good Morning JBuilder", 40, 50);
}
}
```

The 40 and 50 represent coordinates on the left side of the *baseline* of the string. The baseline represents an imaginary line to write on. The first coordinate is the distance from the left side of the applet's area within the browser and is called the *x-position*. The second is the distance from the top and is called the *y-position*. This is shown in Figure 1.14.

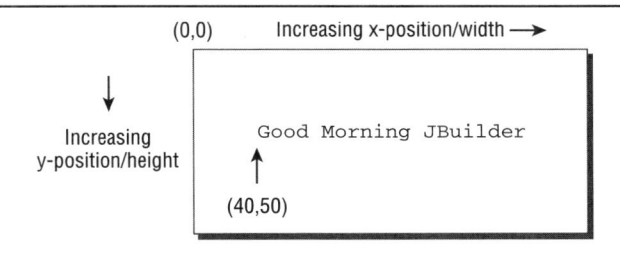

FIGURE 1.14: The Java coordinate system

> **NOTE** The Java coordinate space is measured in *pixels.* Pixels are display units on a screen. For instance, your desktop's area is probably 640 × 480 pixels, 800 × 600 pixels, or 1024 × 768 pixels. Each little display dot on your screen is a pixel.

That's all there is to it—almost. In order to display an applet, it needs to be incorporated into a Web page.

The <APPLET> HTML Tag

Applets are incorporated into Web pages with the help of the <APPLET> tag. As demonstrated previously, in the simplest case you specify the class of the applet to load and how big of an area to use within the Web page.

```
<APPLET code=Hello width=300 height=100>
</APPLET>
```

When you use the Applet Wizard later, most of the additional options are set for you. Any others are for special circumstances and require you to do extra work before you can include them, hence aren't part of the Wizard. The complete syntax for the <APPLET> tag follows. The listing shows everything that you can possibly configure for a specific applet. The actual order and capitalization of the options used does not matter, except for filenames. Table 1.2 is a key to the the listing.

```
<APPLET
   [ALIGN=LEFT|RIGHT|TOP|TEXTTOP|MIDDLE|ABSMIDDLE|BASELINE|BOTTOM|ABSBOTTOM]
   [ALT= Alternate Text - (none)]
   [ARCHIVE=filename.zip|filename.jar - (none)]
   CODE=AppletName[.class] | OBJECT=SerializedApplet.ser
   [CODEBASE=Applet Directory - (current directory)]
   HEIGHT=Applet Pixel Height
   [HSPACE=Extra Pixel Space to Left and Right of Applet - (0)]
   [MAYSCRIPT=TRUE | FALSE]
   [NAME=Applet Name - (Actual Applet Name)]
   [VSPACE=Extra Pixel Space for Top and Bottom of Applet - (0)]
   WIDTH=Applet Pixel Width
>
[<PARAM NAME=Parameter1 VALUE=Value1>]
[<PARAM NAME=Parameter2 VALUE=Value2>]
…
[<PARAM NAME=ParameterN VALUE=ValueN>]
[Alternate anything for when no Java or disabled.]
</APPLET>
```

TABLE 1.2: Option Configuration Key

Element	Meaning
[...]	Square brackets signal that something is optional
|	A list of choices separated by a separator signifies only one of the choices is to be used
[ALIGN=**LEFT**	Default values/choices are bold
[ALT= *Alternate Text*	Italics are used for specifying values
(...)	Entries within regular parentheses are assumed values when nothing is entered, and a list of choices isn't available

So, with all those options, what does it mean? Well, you normally just include the CODE, WIDTH, and HEIGHT options. If you use the Applet Wizard, though, you don't have to worry about any of this, unless you want to package up your classes into an archive.

Introducing Object-Oriented Programming

You've briefly been exposed to a few object-oriented concepts, like objects and classes. Let's dig into them a little deeper so you can get a better understanding before we move on to the bigger things.

Java Object Basics

In its simplest sense, objects are things, usually nouns if you are strictly looking at parts of speech. At any instance in time, an object has a specific state and evokes a specific behavior. An object is a specific instance of a class. A class defines what an object's state and behavior is. A class's variables define its state, while its functions, or methods, define its behavior.

To demonstrate an analogy, if the class Car existed, it might maintain state for type, color, and amount of fuel in the gas tank. If we were dealing with a specific instance of Car, the type might be Volkswagen, color might be purple with pink polka dots, and gas tank might be empty. Its behavior might be start, stop, turn, and reverse.

Methods

Methods define how objects behave. By declaring methods for a class, you create its behavior. If a class doesn't have a particular method, it can't behave in the desired way. You would have to change its behavior by defining another method. In the Car example, there would be methods for start, stop, turn, and reverse. If you wanted to be able to fill up its gas tank, you would define a method to perform the operation and then it would have the additional behavior of filling up its gas tank. If you are familiar with C++, a method is analogous to a member function.

Variables

The state of a class is maintained by its variables. By reserving space in memory, a variable stores the current state of the class.

There are three types of variables: instance, class, and local.

> **Instance variables** Maintain the attributes of a specific instance of the class, hence its name. Every object defined for the class will have its own copy of the instance variables. In the previous example, type, color, and filled gas tank amount would all have been instance variables. Every Car can have a different type, color, or filled gas tank amount.

Class variables Maintain attributes common for all instances of a class. If you ever wanted to count the number of Car instances created, you would implement this through the use of a class variable.

Local variable Variables declared to be local to some block of code, i.e., a method or a code fragment within braces ({ }). Outside of the block defined, the local variable doesn't exist.

The actual syntax for creating classes, methods, and variables is described in "Skill 3: Java Syntax."

Inheritance

Thankfully, programming has advanced to the point where everything isn't created from scratch any time you need something new. What happens now is you find something that does almost everything you want, and then you customize it for your specific environment. This allows you to take advantage of the vast library of resources already created with minimal effort. When Boeing creates a new airplane, they don't scrap the many years of effort they already spent and start from scratch. No, they start from some commonality of the last plane they created and build from there.

In object-oriented programming, this customization process is called *inheritance* and involves *subclassing* or deriving a class. Creating a subclass of an object allows you to build onto another class by altering its behavior or the state it maintains. The new class inherits all the behavior from the original and adds additional functionality onto it. Staying with the `Car` model, if we were working with various electric cars, we could extend `Car` to be `ElectricCar` and add behavior for charging. Then, the electric car would have a type, color, filled tank amount (always empty), and electric charge. `Car` would be the *superclass*, or base class, while `ElectricCar` would be the *subclass* or derived class.

Much of the time spent today is spent creating proper class hierarchies. Creating good reusable classes that are easily extensible allows everyone to work smarter. With the rich core Java class libraries and Borland's JavaBeans Component Library (JBCL), half the battle is over for you. You just need to extend their classes for your specific needs.

JavaBeans is probably another concept worth mentioning here. According to Sun, "A Java Bean is a reusable software component that can be manipulated visually in a builder tool." So, everything that appears on JBuilder's Component Palette is a component, and JBuilder is the connect-the-Bean builder tool. We'll work with Beans extensively in Part II of this book.

Now that you got your feet wet with object-oriented programming terminology, let's wrap up this skill, where we created a very simple program, mostly avoiding the niceties provided with JBuilder. In the next skill, we'll start to take advantage of these to automate the more repetitive tasks. Also, we'll learn how to customize our programs at runtime through the use of HTML parameters, command-line parameters, and system properties. All of these things allow you to alter the behavior of Java programs at runtime, without having to rebuild them.

> **NOTE** If you are still confused with all this object-oriented terminology, don't worry, as you follow the examples in the book, you will pick up more and more of it, until it becomes second nature. Also, you can look into other offerings from Sybex, such as *Mastering Java 1.1* or *Java 1.1: No experience required*, which cover working with Java objects in more depth.

Are You Experienced?

Now you can...

- ☑ use the JBuilder IDE comfortably
- ☑ create a simple applet
- ☑ understand concepts in object-oriented programming
- ☑ embed an applet in a Web page
- ☑ understand basic object-oriented topics

356-555-3398.

PROGRAMMERS
C, C, VB, Cobol, exp. Call 534-555-6543 or fax 534-555-6544.

PROGRAMMING
MRFS Inc. is looking for a Sr. Windows NT developer. Reqs. 3-5 yrs. Exp. in C under Windows, Win95 & NT, using Visual C. Excl. OO design & implementation skills a must. OLE2 & ODBC are a plus. Excl. Salary & bnfts. Resume & salary history to HR, 8779 HighTech Way, Computer City, AR

PROGRAMMERS
Contractors Wanted for short & long term assignments: Visual C, MFC Unix C/C, SQL Orade Dev elop ers PC Help Desk Support Windows NT & NetWareTelecommunications Visual Basic, Access, HTMT, CGI, Perl MMI & Co., 885-555-9933

PROGRAMMER World Wide Web Links wants your HTML & Photoshop skills. Develop great WWW sites. Local & global customers. Send samples & resume to WWWL, 2000 Apple Road, Santa Rosa, CA.

TECHNICAL WRITER Software firm seeks writer/editor for manuals, research notes, project mgmt. Min 2 years tech. writing, DTP & programming experience. Send resume & writing samples to: Software Systems, Dallas, TX.

TECHNICAL Software development firm looking for Tech Trainers. Ideal candidates have programming experience in Visual C, HTML & JAVA. Need quick self starter. Call (443) 555-6868 for interview.

TECHNICAL WRITER/ Premier Computer Corp is seeking a combination of technical skills, knowledge and experience in the following areas: UNIX, Windows 95/NT, Visual Basic, on-line help & documentation, and the internet. Candidates must possess excellent writing skills, and be comfortable working in a quality vs. deadline driven environment. Competitive salary. Fax resume & samples to Karen Fields, Premier Computer Corp., 444 Industrial Blvd. Concord, CA. Or send to our website at www.premier.com.

WEB DESIGNER
BA/BS or equivalent programming/multimedia production. 3 years of experience in use and design of WWW services streaming audio and video HTML, PERL, CGI, GIF, JPEG. Demonstrated interpersonal, organization, communication, multi-tasking skills. Send resume to The Learning People at www.learning.com.

WEBMASTER-TECHNICAL
BSCS or equivalent, 2 years of experience in CGI, Windows 95/NT, UNIX, C, Java, Perl. Demonstrated ability to design, code, debug and test on-line services. Send resume to The Learning People at www.learning.com.

PROGRAMMER World Wide Web Links wants your HTML & Photoshop skills. Develop great WWW sites.

ing tools. Experienced in documentation preparation & programming languages (Access, C, FoxPro) are a plus. Financial or banking customer service support is required along with excellent verbal & written communication skills with multi levels of end-users. Send resume to KKUP Enterprises, 45 Orange Blvd., Orange, CA.

COMPUTERS Small Web Design Firm seeks indiv. w/NT, Webserver & Database management exp. Fax resume to 556-555-4221.

COMPUTER/ Visual C/C, Visual Basic Exp'd Systems Analysts/ Programmers for growing software dev. team in Roseburg. Computer Science or related degree preferred. Develop adv. Engineering applications for engineering firm. Fax resume to 707-555-8744.

COMPUTER Web Master for dynamic SF Internet co. Site. Dev., test, coord., train. 2 yrs prog. Exp. C C Web C FTP. Fax resume to Best Staffing 845-555-7722.

COMPUTER PROGRAMMER

Ad agency seeks programmer w/exp. in UNIX/NT Platforms, Web Server, CGI/Perl. Programmer Position avail. on a project basis with the possibility to move into F/T. Fax resume & salary req. to R. Jones 334-555-8332.

COMPUTERS Programmer/Analyst Design and maintain C based SQL database applications. Required skills: Visual Basic, C, SQL, ODBC. Document existing and new applications. Novell or NT exp. a plus. Fax resume & salary history to 235-555-9935.

GRAPHIC DESIGNER
Webmaster's Weekly is seeking a creative Graphic Designer to design high impact marketing collater al, including direct mail promois, CD-ROM packages, ads and WWW pages. Must be able to juggle multiple projects and learn new skills on the job very rapidly. Web design experience a big plus, technical troubleshooting also a plus. Call 435-555-1235.

GRAPHICS - ART DIRECTOR - WEB-MULTIMEDIA
Leading internet development company has an outstanding opportunity for a talented, high-end Web Experienced Art Director. In addition to a great portfolio and fresh ideas, the ideal candidate has excellent communication and presentation skills. Working as a team with innovative producers and programmers, you will create dynamic, interactive web sites and application interfaces. Some programming experience required. Send samples and resume to: SuperSites, 333 Main, Seattle, WA.

MARKETING
Fast paced software and services provider looking for MARKETING COMMUNICATIONS SPECIALIST to be responsible for its webpage.

PROGRAMMERS Multiple short term assignments available: Visual C, 3 positions SQL ServerNT Server, 2 positions JAVA & HTML, long term NetWare Various locations. Call for more info. 356-555-3398.

PROGRAMMERS
C, C, VB, Cobol, exp. Call 534-555-6543 or fax 534-555-6544.

PROGRAMMING
MRFS Inc. is looking for a Sr. Windows NT developer. Reqs. 3-5 yrs. Exp. in C under Windows, Win95 & NT, using Visual C. Excl. OO design & implementation skills a must. OLE2 & ODBC are a plus. Excl. Salary & bnfts. Resume & salary history to HR, 8779 HighTech Way, Computer City, AR

PROGRAMMERS/ Contractors Wanted for short & long term assignments: Visual C, MFC Unix C/C, SQL Oracle Developers PC Help Desk Support Windows NT & NetWareTelecommunications Visual Basic, Access, HTMT, CGI, Perl MMI & Co., 885-555-9933

PROGRAMMER World Wide Web Links wants your HTML & Photoshop skills. Develop great WWW sites. Local & global customers. Send samples & resume to WWWL, 2000 Apple Road, Santa Rosa, CA.

TECHNICAL WRITER Software firm seeks writer/editor for manuals, research notes, project mgmt. Min 2 years tech. writing, DTP & programming experience. Send resume & writing samples to: Software Systems, Dallas, TX.

COMPUTER PROGRAMMER
Ad agency seeks programmer w/exp. in UNIX/NT Platforms, Web Server, CGI/Perl. Programmer Position avail. on a project basis with the possibility to move into F/T. Fax resume & salary req. to R. Jones 334-555-8332.

TECHNICAL WRITER Premier Computer Corp is seeking a combination of technical skills, knowledge and experience in the following areas: UNIX, Windows 95/NT, Visual Basic, on-line help & documentation, and the internet. Candidates must possess excellent writing skills, and be comfortable working in a quality vs. deadline driven environment. Competitive salary. Fax resume & samples to Karen Fields, Premier Computer Corp., 444 Industrial Blvd. Concord, CA. Or send to our website at www.premier.com.

WEB DESIGNER
BA/BS or equivalent programming/multimedia production. 3 years of experience in use and design of WWW services streaming audio and video HTML, PERL, CGI, GIF, JPEG. Demonstrated interpersonal, organization, communication, multi-tasking skills. Send resume to The Learning People at www.learning.com.

WEBMASTER-TECHNICAL
BSCS or equivalent, 2 years of experience in CGI, Windows 95/NT,

COMPUTERS Small Web Design Firm seeks indiv. w/NT, Webserver & Database management exp. Fax resume to 556-555-4221.

COMPUTER Visual C/C, Visual Basic Exp'd Systems Analysts/ Programmers for growing software dev. team in Roseburg. Computer Science or related degree preferred. Develop adv. Engineering applications for engineering firm. Fax resume to 707-555-8744.

COMPUTER Web Master for dynamic SF Internet co. Site. Dev., test, coord., train. 2 yrs prog. Exp. C C Web C FTP. Fax resume to Best Staffing 845-555-7722.

COMPUTERS/ QA SOFTWARE TESTERS Qualified candidates should have 2 yrs exp. performing integration & system testing using automated testing tools. Experienced in documentation preparation & programming languages (Access, C, FoxPro) are a plus. Financial or banking customer service support is required along with excellent verbal & written communication skills with multi levels of end-users. Send resume to KKUP Enterprises, 45 Orange Blvd., Orange, CA.

COMPUTERS Programmer/Analyst Design and maintain C based SQL database applications. Required skills: Visual Basic, C, SQL, ODBC. Document existing and new applications. Novell or NT exp. a plus. Fax resume & salary history to 235-555-9935.

GRAPHIC DESIGNER
Webmaster's Weekly is seeking a creative Graphic Designer to design high impact marketing collater al, including direct mail promo's, CD-ROM packages, ads and WWW pages. Must be able to juggle multiple projects and learn new skills on the job very rapidly. Web design experience a big plus, technical troubleshooting also a plus. Call 435-555-1235.

GRAPHICS - ART DIRECTOR - WEB-MULTIMEDIA
Leading internet development company has an outstanding opportunity for a talented, high-end Web Experienced Art Director. In addition to a great portfolio and fresh ideas, the ideal candidate has excellent communication and presentation skills. Working as a team with innovative producers and programmers, you will create dynamic, interactive web sites and application interfaces. Some programming experience required. Send samples and resume to: SuperSites, 333 Main, Seattle, WA.

COMPUTER PROGRAMMER
Ad agency seeks programmer w/exp. in UNIX/NT Platforms, Web Server, CGI/Perl. Programmer Position avail. on a project basis with the possibility to move into F/T. Fax resume & salary req. to R. Jones 334-555-8332.

PROGRAMMERS / Established software company seeks program-

seminar coordination, and ad plac ment. Must be a self-starter, ener getic, organized. Must have 2 year web experience. Programming a plus. Call 985-555-9854.

PROGRAMMERS Multiple sho term assignments available: Visua C, 3 positions SQL ServerNT Serve 2 positions JAVA & HTML, long ter NetWare Various locations. Call fo more info. 356-555-3398.

PROGRAMMERS
C, C, VB, Cobol, exp. Call 534-55 6543 or fax 534-555-6544.

PROGRAMMING
MRFS Inc. is looking for a Windows NT developer. Reqs. 3 yrs. Exp. in C under Window Win95 & NT, using Visual C. Ex OO design & implementation ski a must. OLE2 & ODBC are a plu Excl. Salary & bnfts. Resume salary history to HR, 8779 HighTe Way, Computer City, AR

PROGRAMMERS/ Contracto Wanted for short & long term assig ments: Visual C, MFCUnix C/C, SQ Oracle Developers PC Help De Support Windows NT & NetWar Telecommunications Visual Basi Access, HTMT, CGI, Perl MMI & C 885-555-9933

PROGRAMMER World Wide We Links wants your HTML & Photosho skills. Develop great WWW site Local & global customers. Send sar ples & resume to WWWL, 20 Apple Road, Santa Rosa, CA.

TECHNICAL WRITER Software fir seeks writer/editor for manua research notes, project mgmt. Min years tech. writing, DTP & progra ming experience. Send resume writing samples to: Softwa Systems, Dallas, TX.

TECHNICAL Software developme firm looking for Tech Trainers. Ide candidates have programming exp rience in Visual C, HTML & JAV Need quick self starter. Call (44 555-6868 for interview.

TECHNICAL WRITER Premi Computer Corp is seeking a comb nation of technical skills, knowled and experience in the followi areas: UNIX, Windows 95/NT, Visu Basic, on-line help & documentati and the internet. Candidates mu possess excellent writing skills, a be comfortable working in a qual vs. deadline driven environme Competitive salary. Fax resume samples to Karen Fields, Premi Computer Corp., 444 Industrial Bl Concord, CA. Or send to our webs at www.premier.com.

WEB DESIGNER
BA/BS or equivalent progra ming/multimedia production. years of experience in use a design of WWW services streami audio and video HTML, PERL, C GIF, JPEG. Demonstrated interpe sonal, organization, communicati multi-tasking skills. Send resume The Learning People at www.lea ing.com.

WEBMASTER-TECHNICA

SKILL 2

two

Employing the JBuilder Applet Wizard

- ❑ Using the Project Wizard to create a project
- ❑ Working with the Applet Wizard
- ❑ Looking at the applet source
- ❑ Displaying applet parameters
- ❑ Working with the Application Wizard
- ❑ Looking at the application source
- ❑ Setting application parameters

In the last skill, we toured JBuilder and created our first applet by hand. In this skill, we're going to let JBuilder's Wizards do much of the work for us. Also, we will learn how to provide runtime settings through applet parameters, as well as using command line options with applications.

> **TIP** Before we get started, remember to close any open projects with the File ➤ Close All menu item.

Using the Project Wizard

You'll remember from Skill 1 that when working with JBuilder, all of your work is contained within a project. If you start one of JBuilder's Wizards without an open project, JBuilder reminds you to create one with the Project Wizard, before continuing on with the Wizard you requested. Selecting the File ➤ New Project menu brings up the screen shown in Figure 2.1.

FIGURE 2.1: The JBuilder Project Wizard where you create your project

> **TIP** In addition to starting the Project Wizard directly from the File menu, you can also select File ➤ New, and then select the Project icon.

As shown in Figure 2.1, the system is asking you five questions:

- What file do you want the project saved in?
- What is the project name or title?
- What is your name?
- What is your company name?
- What is the project description?

NOTE In all the remaining skills, we are going to save our work under the `C:\Skills` directory. If you happen to be using this path for another purpose, you will need to find another place to save your work. If you do need to save your work elsewhere, you will need to translate all the skill filenames to this new location.

Fill in the dialog box, as shown in Figure 2.2, but with your own name and company.

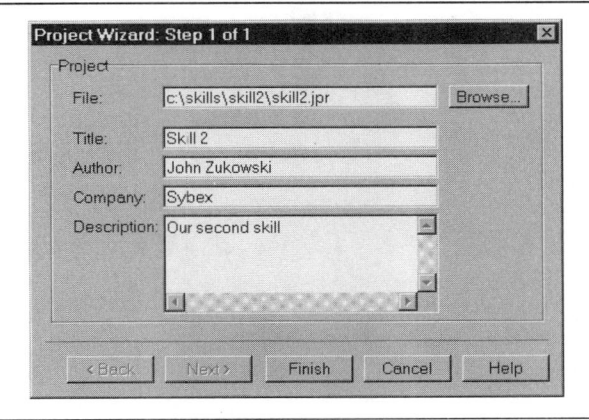

FIGURE 2.2: The JBuilder Project Wizard filled in with my pertinent information

After everything is filled in, select Finish to have JBuilder create the project file. This brings up the three-pane AppBrowser window, which will become very familiar.

Congratulations, you have now created a project!

NOTE: The Project Wizard created the file ski112.html to match the prefix of the project file, ski112.jpr. The ski112.html file retains a copy of the information you provided to the Project Wizard.

Before we go on to create anything, we need to do a one-time configuration setup. Because C:\Skills will serve as the source code base path, we should tell JBuilder to make sure it can find things there. This seems to be more of a workaround, because the JBuilder wizards do not always create things in the same location. To add C:\Skills to the default source path, select Tools ➤ IDE Options to bring up the screen shown in Figure 2.3, enter **C:\Skills;** at the very beginning of the Default Source Path entry field, and select OK. Now, for every new project, the C:\Skills directory will serve as a possible source code path, enabling JBuilder to find code when it otherwise couldn't.

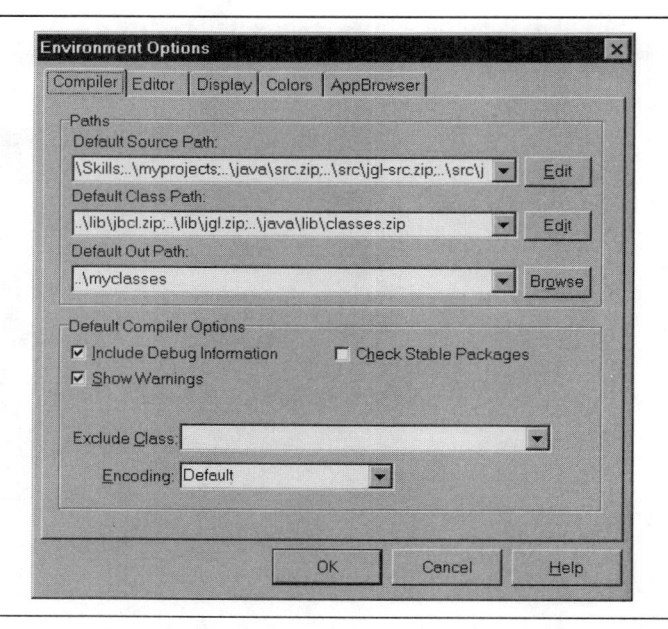

FIGURE 2.3: The IDE Options dialog box allows you to set environment options for the compiler, editor, and AppBrowser.

Using the Applet Wizard

Now that we have created a project, we can create an applet. The applet will display a message provided as a runtime HTML parameter. You start the Applet Wizard by selecting File ➤ New and double-clicking on the Applet icon.

Using the Applet Wizard is a three-part process: First, you name the applet, and then you set up runtime parameters and decide if you want an HTML page created for you. The first part, as shown in Figure 2.4, prompts you to name the applet's package and class, along with some styles we'll be using down the road.

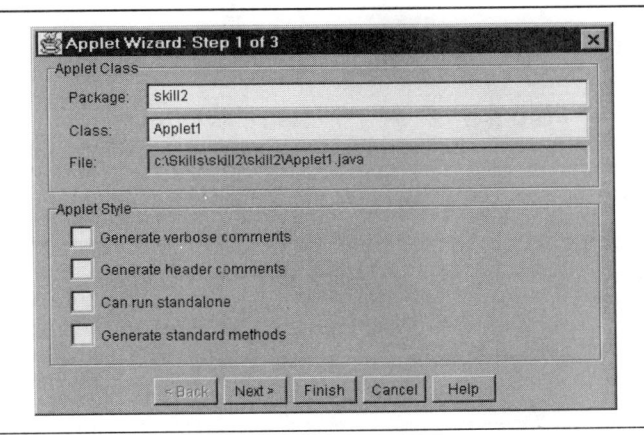

FIGURE 2.4: The Applet Wizard: Step 1 of 3; here the Wizard asks for Applet information.

We'll accept the default package `skill2`, and class `Applet1`, and select Next to move to the second part of the process.

The second part, as shown in Figure 2.5, asks you to set up any runtime *parameters* you plan to make available. Parameters allow your applets to change behavior without having to recompile the code. Our applet will display a text message provided as an applet parameter, so we need to add one parameter.

To add the parameter, select the cell under the Name title. This is where you name the applet parameter; we'll call it **message**. Now, in the first field under the Type title, tell the system the datatype of the parameter you are providing. When Java gets parameters from HTML files, they are treated as text strings. The type you select from the drop-down list determines the data conversion code that the Wizard adds to your applet. Select String as the parameter type.

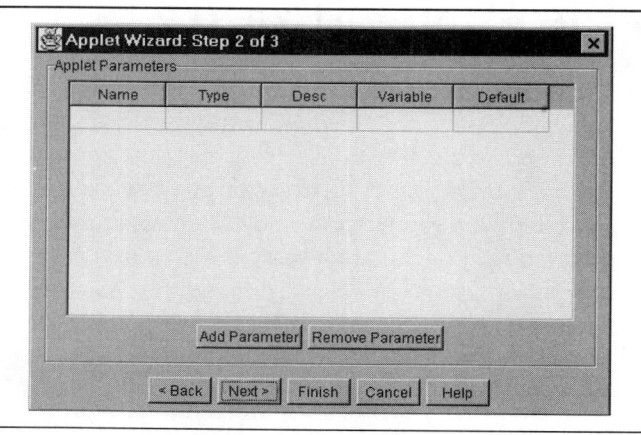

FIGURE 2.5: The Applet Wizard: Step 2 of 3; here the Wizard asks for parameter information.

> **NOTE** In addition to `String` parameters, you can select `boolean`, `int`, `short`, `long`, `float`, or `double`. The Wizard automatically generates the code to convert that parameter from a `String` to the appropriate primitive datatype.

> **NOTE** The Wizard does not let you tab between fields on this screen. If you press the Tab key while entering a parameter, you will no longer be creating an applet parameter. The form now focuses the user's input on the Add Parameter button.

The Desc field is where you provide a description for the parameter. Go ahead and enter **Text message to display** in the field. The Variable field contains the instance variable your program will store the parameter value in. This can be the same name as what's in the Name column because those names are maintained within the applet's HTML file and this is an instance variable of the class. However, to ensure that we don't confuse the two, enter **msg**. Finally, the Default field allows you to enter an initial value for the parameter. You can change this later, but for now just enter **"Good Morning JBuilder"** and press Enter. When the Wizard is done, there will be a <PARAM> tag within the `.html` file, and the Applet will contain the code needed to read in the parameter settings. All that, thanks to the Applet Wizard. Now click Next.

> **TIP**
>
> Applet parameters are specified through the <PARAM> tag within an <APPLET> tag specifying the applet to load. To define the parameter named "Publisher" with a value of "Sybex" for the applet "Book," you would use the following tags:
>
> ```
> <APPLET code=Book.class width=200 height=200>
> <PARAM name=Publisher value=Sybex>
> </APPLET>
> ```

The final Applet Wizard screen, shown in Figure 2.6, asks if you want the Wizard to create the HTML page for you. Instead of having to create an applet loader file yourself, you can have JBuilder do it for you.

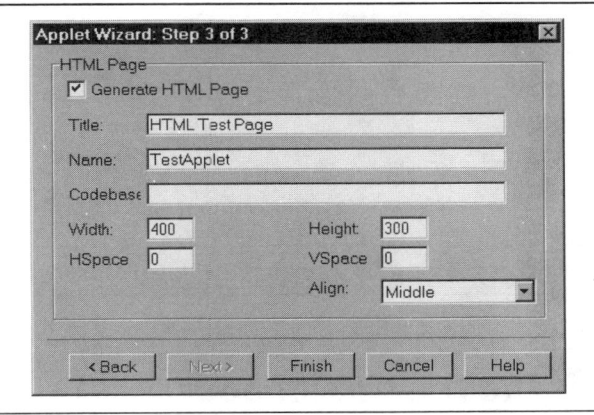

FIGURE 2.6: Applet Wizard: Step 3 of 3; here you tell the Applet Wizard to generate the HTML page for you.

We're going to leave all the default settings for this form and just select Finish to let the Wizard do its work. However, let's take a quick tour around the options before moving on. The Title field is for the HTML page's title, <TITLE>. The remaining fields each map directly to a parameter of <APPLET>, all of which were explained in Skill 1.

When the Wizard is done, you should see three files in the Navigation pane of AppBrowser: `skill2.html`, `Applet1.html`, and `Applet1.java`. To compile the applet, select Build ➤ Make Project "skill2.jpr". Although the applet doesn't do anything yet, we can run it. Before we run it, we need to remember to save everything with File ➤ Save All. Then select Run ➤ Run Applet in "Applet1.html". This brings up an empty 400 × 300 screen, as shown in Figure 2.7.

> **TIP** In addition to selecting Run ➤ Run Applet from the menu, you can right-click on Applet1.html and select Run there, too, or use the toolbar Run Button as discussed in Skill 1.

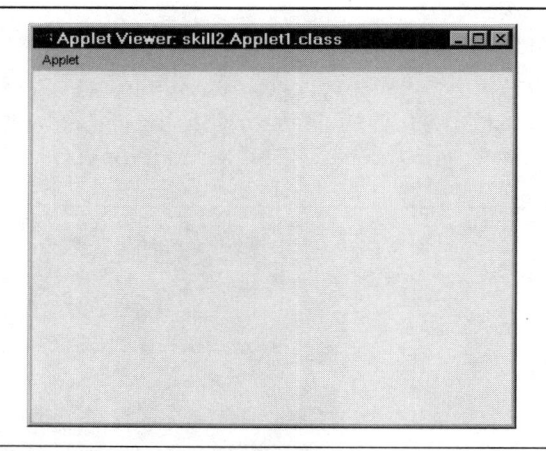

FIGURE 2.7: Running the initial applet

Examining the Applet Source

Before we display the parameter, let's take a look at the code the Applet Wizard generated for us. All that clicking and typing generated about 50 lines of code in Applet1.java. Let's break it down into code segments and take a look at the parts.

The first line comes from the Package field on the first screen of the Applet Wizard. Although working in separate packages isn't absolutely necessary, it's much simpler when working on larger projects.

```
package skill2;
```

This next set of statements is included whether you need them yet or not. They include the most frequently used packages of an applet. Remember that you either need to explicitly declare classes, like java.applet.Applet, or if you import the necessary package, you can implicitly use the class name by itself—Applet in this case.

```
import java.awt.*;
import java.awt.event.*;
import java.applet.*;
import borland.jbcl.control.*;
import borland.jbcl.layout.*;
```

On the first Wizard screen, we named our class `Applet1`. Because we used the Applet Wizard, it automatically made our class a subclass of `Applet`.

```
public class Applet1 extends Applet {
```

For the moment, we'll cover these next two statements in a cursory way since we'll be discussing both of them in much greater detail in later skills. The first statement defines something you haven't been introduced to yet—a layout manager. Briefly, *layout managers* control how Java controls are positioned on the screen. Since we aren't using controls yet, don't worry about this concept too much for now. The second statement refers to the Can Run Standalone style we didn't select on the first Wizard screen. This flag is reset at runtime based upon how the program was started.

```
XYLayout xYLayout1 = new XYLayout();
boolean isStandalone = false;
```

> **NOTE** If you select the Can Run Standalone Applet style during the first Applet Wizard step, the Wizard generates code that enables your applet to run as an application, as well as an applet.

On the second screen of the Wizard, the last field we entered was the variable name to use for the HTML parameter. As demonstrated, the variable name, `msg`, does not have to match the HTML parameter name, `message`. However, you can name the two the same, and no problems will arise as a result.

```
String msg;
```

Next is a helper routine that the JBuilder Wizard generates and uses for our Applet. You normally don't need to call this version of `getParameter` yourself because the Wizard automatically generated the getting parameters code for you. We'll look at what it does internally in just a minute. To use this feature, JBuilder automatically generates a method called `this.getParameter("message", "Good Morning JBuilder")` in this example, which asks it for the parameter setting of key; in this case, it's `"message"`. If the parameter isn't specified in the applet loader file, a default value—`def`—is used instead. That is all there is to `getParameter`.

For example, in this case, key is "message" and, if message wasn't a parameter in the .html loader, the returned value is "Good Morning JBuilder".

```
//Get a parameter value
  public String getParameter(String key, String def) {
    return isStandalone ? System.getProperty(key, def) :
      (getParameter(key) != null ? getParameter(key) : def);
  }
```

This is the constructor for our applet. The constructor is called by the system when it is time to create the Applet. Normally, activities in the constructor are reserved for one-time tasks.

```
//Construct the applet
  public Applet1() {
  }
```

However, with applets, these tasks tend to be done in the init() method that follows:

```
//Initialize the applet
  public void init() {
    try { msg = this.getParameter("message", "Good Morning JBuilder");
      } catch(Exception e) { e.printStackTrace(); };
    try { jbInit(); } catch(Exception e) { e.printStackTrace(); };
  }
```

The init method of an applet is called when the Web page containing the applet is first loaded. Here, the Applet Wizard gets the setting for our msg variable for us. If the datatype was something other than String, the Wizard would have written the Java code to convert the parameter. If no message parameter is provided in the HTML file, the value we told the Wizard to use as the default is used.

The jbInit method is called from init and is used for Java control initialization. Because this applet doesn't have any controls, you can leave the jbInit method as is. The jbInit method is not a standard Java method, but one that JBuilder introduces to make control initialization easier. If you weren't using JBuilder to automatically generate the code, this code would naturally be placed directly in the init method.

```
//Component initialization
  public void jbInit() throws Exception{
    xYLayout1.setWidth(400);
    xYLayout1.setHeight(300);
    this.setLayout(xYLayout1);
  }
```

> **NOTE** A *Java control* is a graphic, such as a button or a check box. They will be introduced in Skill 5.

And finally, we have the `getAppletInfo` and `getParameterInfo` methods. The `getAppletInfo` method shows a short information string about the applet, usually the author's name and copyright message. The `getParameterInfo` method returns a series of three element arrays, one entry for each parameter of the applet. The first element of each array is the HTML parameter name. The second is the datatype within the Java program. The third and final element is a textual description of the parameter. If you look back to Figure 2.5, we entered these values on the second page of the Wizard.

```
//Get Applet information
  public String getAppletInfo() {
    return "Applet Information";
  }

//Get parameter info
  public String[][] getParameterInfo() {
    String pinfo[][] =
    {
      {"message", "String", "Text Message to display"},
    };
    return pinfo;
  }
}
```

Unfortunately, these methods are two of the least frequently used methods around. Hopefully, through automation, they will be used more because they can be incredibly useful. The reason these methods are used so infrequently lies in the fact that neither Netscape Navigator nor Internet Explorer (Versions 4 and below) provided the means to automatically call the methods. For instance, with Netscape Navigator 3, you would expect to see this information when you select the View ➤ Document Info menu command. However, the results of neither method appear when you ask about an applet.

Getting Applet Parameters

As long as you use the Applet Wizard, this part is easy—the Wizard does the work for you. You are left with a variable of the proper datatype, even when a setting of the HTML parameter isn't provided. How easy could life be?

At some point, however, you may want to know how to do this yourself, so let's take a look at some pieces of the generated `getParameter` method:

```
public String getParameter(String key, String def) {
  return (getParameter(key) != null ? getParameter(key) : def);
}
```

and `init`:

```
msg = this.getParameter("message", "Good Morning JBuilder");
```

Here, the `init` method calls the `getParameter` helper method. It says, Get me the value of the `message` HTML parameter; if one doesn't exist, return a default setting of "Good Morning JBuilder." The parameter wouldn't exist if there wasn't a `<PARAM name=message value=...>` tag within the `<APPLET>` tag that loaded the applet.

In the `getParameter` helper routine, the Applet's true `getParameter` method is called. That version takes a single parameter, the `String`, whose value you are looking for. If the parameter exists in the `name` field of a `<PARAM>` tag, within the applet's `<APPLET>` tag, then its `value` string is returned. If the parameter does not exist, then `getParameter` returns `null`. Remember, the `<PARAM>` tag looks like this:

```
<PARAM name="message" value="Good Morning JBuilder">
```

By using the helper routine, JBuilder incorporates the necessary checks to ensure you get a valid setting.

> **NOTE** Having multiple methods with the same name but different arguments is called *overloading*. The system knows which version to call by matching the number of parameters and their type.

If the parameter datatype is anything other than `String`, the Wizard will even add the code to convert the parameter to the proper datatype. For example, if you wanted an integer and the `<PARAM>` tag was

```
<PARAM name="size" value=2>
```

then the Wizard generates the following to get the integer value of the `size` setting:

```
try {
  size = Integer.parseInt(this.getParameter("size", "0"));
} catch(Exception e) { e.printStackTrace(); };
```

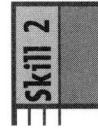

> **NOTE** The parseInt method of the Integer class takes a text string and converts it to an int.

Now, we can update our applet to actually do something with the parameter. Add the following to the `Applet1.java` source file:

```
public void paint (Graphics g) {
   g.drawString (msg, 20, 20);
}
```

Once you rebuild and rerun, the results will look like Figure 2.8.

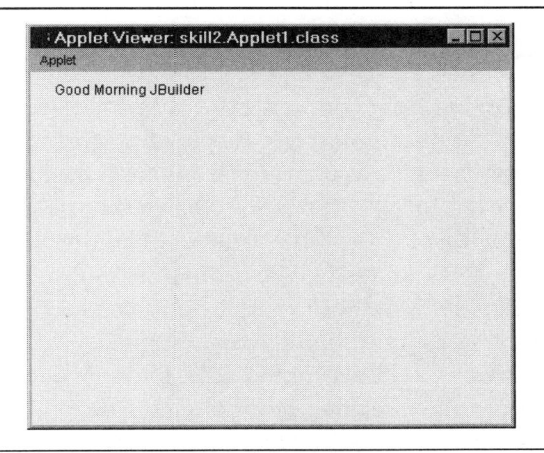

FIGURE 2.8: Applet with message parameter displayed

Using the Application Wizard

Where the Applet Wizard creates programs that run in a browser, such as Internet Explorer, you can create stand-alone applications with either the Applet Wizard or the Application Wizard.

With the Applet Wizard, if you select Can Run Standalone on the first Wizard screen, the wizard automatically generates code so your applet will run as a stand-alone application. While this sounds convincing, using the Applet Wizard to generate purely stand-alone applications is not the best alternative. Because applets are normally only given a display area within a browser, the stand-alone applet-application works within a similarly constrained area. If you are accustomed to your applications providing a menu or a status message area, the applet turned application won't have this.

The better alternative is to use the Application Wizard. With it, you can automate the creation of a menu bar, toolbar, status message area, or an "about" box. These make your program look and feel more like a stand-alone application. So, let's walk through the Application Wizard to create a frame that displays a message either from the command line or a system property.

> **NOTE** A *system property* is an attribute defined automatically for the current Java session. For instance, the location of the Java runtime environment is one of the automatic system properties.

Working from within the `skill2` project, select File ➤ New and double-click on the Application icon to display the screen shown in Figure 2.9.

From here, we can change the default package and application class name. However, to keep things simple, we are going to accept the defaults and select Next to display the screen shown in Figure 2.10. If you were to change the package or class name, the File field would automatically be updated to reflect the change. The Application style option enables automatic comment generation, which a program should expand upon.

For now, we'll accept the defaults again and select Finish. Skills 18 and 19 will demonstrate the other Frame styles available on this screen. The defaults create a class named `Frame1`. Along `Frame1`'s window title bar, the default "Frame Title" text will be displayed when the program runs.

When the Wizard is done, you should see two new files in the Navigation pane of the AppBrowser: `Application1.java` and `Frame1.java`. To compile the application, select Build ➤ Make Project "skill2.jpr". Although the application doesn't do much yet, we can run it. To do so, select the `Application1.java` file and Run "Application1" ➤ Run. This brings up an empty 400 × 300 screen.

> **NOTE** While the Applet Wizard prompts you for screen size, the Application Wizard doesn't. The 400 × 300 size is automatically placed in the generated source. If you wish to change the initial size, you have to edit the generated source code.

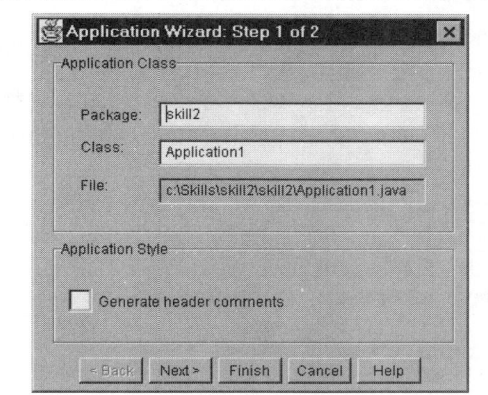

FIGURE 2.9: Application Wizard: Step 1 of 2; here the Wizard asks for Application information.

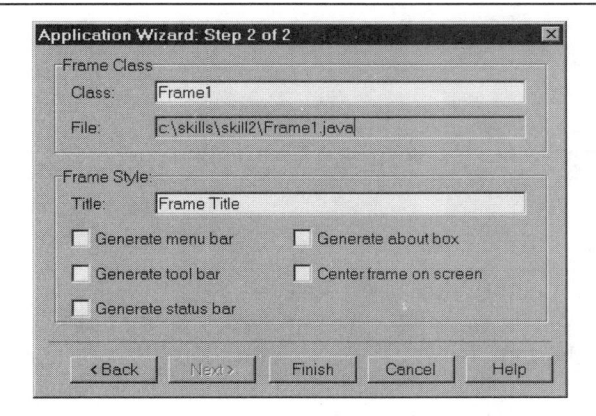

FIGURE 2.10: Application Wizard: Step 2 of 2; here you select the frame class and style.

Examining the Application Source

As with the applet, before we display the parameter, let's take a look at the code the Application Wizard generated for us. All that clicking and typing generated about 30 lines of code in `Frame1.java`. Along with the ten lines in `Application1.java`, that's the entire application.

The `Application1.java` source file represents the loader for our application, `Frame1`. The `main` method is what Java runs first for an application. This creates an instance of itself [`new Application1()`], which in turn creates a `Frame1` object [`Frame1 frame = new Frame1()`], sizes it [`frame.pack()`], and places it on the screen [`frame.setVisible(true);`]. Its impact is basically limited to this single function.

```
package skill2;

public class Application1 {
  boolean packFrame = false;

  //Construct the application
  public Application1(String msg) {
    Frame1 frame = new Frame1();
    //Pack frames that have useful preferred size info, e.g. from their layout
    //Validate frames that have preset sizes
    if (packFrame)
      frame.pack();
    else
      frame.validate();
    frame.setVisible(true);
  }

  //Main method
  static public void main(String[] args) {
    new Application1();
  }
}
```

On the other hand, `Frame1.java` does all the work, or inherits it. Initially, the Application Wizard creates a screen that displays a beveled panel. This provides the framework for the remainder of the application, which you have to fill in.

All this code should look familiar from the `Applet1.java` source. The only `import` line missing is the `java.applet` package. However, because we aren't creating an applet, this is not necessary.

```
package skill2;

import java.awt.*;
import java.awt.event.*;
import borland.jbcl.control.*;
import borland.jbcl.layout.*;
```

When you use the Application Wizard, JBuilder assumes you want a GUI application so it creates a subclass of the `DecoratedFrame` class. The `DecoratedFrame` class belongs to the `borland.jbcl.control` package and subclasses the standard Java `java.awt.Frame` class. One of the nicest things about the `DecoratedFrame` class is it automatically deals with when a user wants to close a window. Otherwise, you would have to do this yourself.

```
public class Frame1 extends DecoratedFrame {
```

If you were to subclass the `Frame` class and select the Close menu from the system menu, as shown in Figure 2.11, Java would completely ignore it. By incorporating the event handling within the `DecoratedFrame` class, all subclasses automatically handle the window Close events for you.

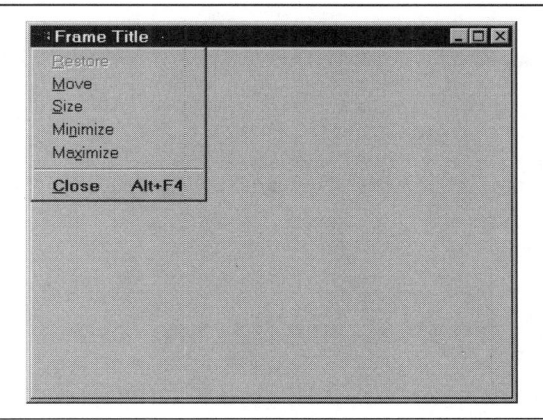

FIGURE 2.11: Microsoft's menu for closing a window

Again, saving our discussion of layout managers for Skill 6, we'll skim over these in general terms for now, but don't worry, you'll hear a lot more about these. The first two statements define the layout managers that we glanced over in the section "Examining the Applet Source." The third works its way onto the frame to make the window look more three-dimensional. You'll see how these are used in the `jbInit` method.

```
private BorderLayout borderLayout1 = new BorderLayout();
private XYLayout xYLayout2 = new XYLayout();
private BevelPanel bevelPanel1 = new BevelPanel();
```

The constructor of `Frame1` looks similar to the `init` method of our applet. It too reserves most of the initialization for the `jbInit` method.

```
//Construct the frame
  public Frame1() {
    try {
      jbInit();
    }
    catch (Exception e) {
      e.printStackTrace();
    };
  }
```

Finally, `jbInit` resizes the frame, sets the title, and places a bevel panel within the frame, as shown back in Figure 2.11.

```
//Component initialization
  public void jbInit() throws Exception{
    this.setLayout(borderLayout1);
    this.setSize(new Dimension(400,300));
    this.setTitle("Frame Title");
    bevelPanel1.setLayout(xYLayout2);
    this.add(bevelPanel1, BorderLayout.CENTER);
  }
}
```

Setting Application Parameters

There are actually two types of parameters you can use with applications: command-line parameters and system properties. Both are set in the same manner; however, accessing them is completely different. To set either the command-line parameters or the system properties, you select Run ➤ Parameters to display the screen shown in Figure 2.12. You'll see the command-line parameters discussed first, while the system properties are specified through the Java VM parameters field, discussed later in this skill. Before we explain parameters, change the Default Runnable File to `C:\skills\skill2\skill2\Application1.java`. This changes the default startup program, shown under the Run menu.

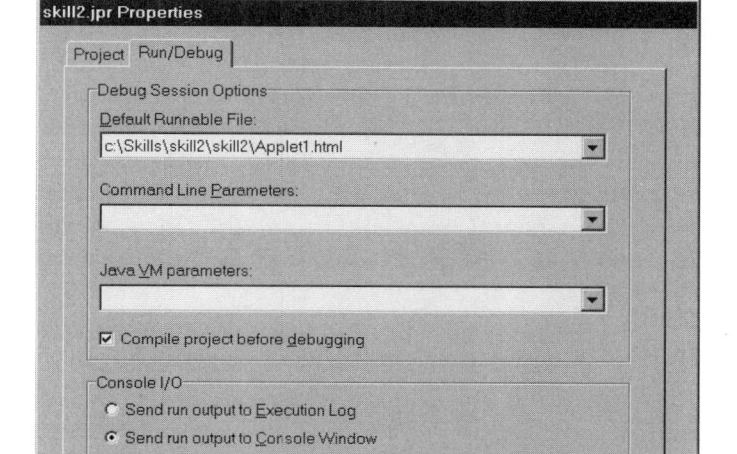

FIGURE 2.12: Select Run ➤ Parameters to display the Parameters dialog box

Command-Line Parameters

Command-line parameters get their name from the command-line compiler that comes with the Java Development Kit. Because you never see a command line with JBuilder, you need to enter parameters in via the Command Line Parameters field, as shown in Figure 2.12.

Java treats the space character as the separator between parameters, so if you enter one two three, Java treats that as three separate parameters. However, if you quote the string and enter "one two three", this is only one parameter. You'll see shortly how these differ in Table 2.1.

Let's look back at the main method of Application1:

```
//Main method
static public void main(String[] args) {
  new Application1();
}
```

Because `main` is the first thing that Java runs when it starts an application, you access the command-line parameters through its `args` parameter. To loop through all the arguments, you could create the following code fragment:

```
for (int count=0; count<args.length; count++) {
  System.out.println (args[count]);
}
```

> **NOTE** The parameter name args has no significance. You could use any parameter name you wanted. However, args is the one declared by the Wizard.

The `for` statement is one of Java's looping constructs. In this case, the loop allows you to process/print the command-line arguments individually. The processing in this case is only printing; however, more complex processing could be done if necessary.

The first thing that probably jumps out at you is `args.length`. Java arrays are objects. Every array knows its size through a `length` instance variable. You do not have to maintain it separately. Also, Java arrays are *zero-based*, so if you have a 10-element array, you access the entries with zero through nine.

To demonstrate, look at Table 2.1 to see how unquoted and quoted strings have an effect on the different settings of `args`. If the arguments are three separate strings, each is spread out among the array elements. However, if it is one quoted string, then that is only one argument.

TABLE 2.1: Command-Line Parameters Demonstration

arguments	args.length	args[0]	args[1]	args[2]
one two three	3	"one"	"two"	"three"
"one two three"	1	"one two three"	*invalid*	*invalid*

Now, to change our application to display the first command-line argument, we need to make a few changes to the `Application1` and `Frame1` classes. We need to get the argument from the command line of `Application1` over to `Frame1`. In order to do this, the first thing we need to do is get the parameter from the command line.

```
//Main method
static public void main(String[] args) {
  String msg;
  if (args.length == 0)
    msg = "Good Morning JBuilder";
```

```
    else
       msg = args[0];
    new Application1(msg);
}
```

The `if (args.length == 0)` statement checks to see if there are any arguments. You should always check for arguments before you try to access specific elements of the array because if you try to access an array outside of its boundaries you will get an exception thrown. (You'll learn more about exceptions in Skill 3.) After getting a message to display, either a default or the command-line argument, we then pass the message to the `Application1` constructor, which needs to notify `Frame1`:

```
public Application1(String msg) {
   Frame1 frame = new Frame1();
   frame.setMessage (msg);
   if (packFrame)
      frame.pack();
   else
      frame.validate();
   frame.setVisible(true);
}
```

Here we changed one line, and added one. First, we added the new parameter to the constructor. This in turn is passed to `Frame1` via a new `setMessage` method we need to create.

Now we go over to `Frame1.java` and change a few things. Because we are going to draw the message directly to the frame, we need to remove the bevel panel that it uses. First, we need to remove all mention of the bevel panel, `bevelPanel1`. Also, because `xYLayout2` is only around for the sake of `bevelPanel1`, we remove that, too.

Next, we need to add a variable to store the current message to display, `message`, and a `setMessage` method to set it. Lastly, we need to draw the string in the frame. We do this by adding the `paint` method and having it call `g.drawString`. All these changes are shown in `Frame1.java`.

Ⓒ Frame1.java

```
package skill2;

import java.awt.*;
import java.awt.event.*;
import borland.jbcl.control.*;
import borland.jbcl.layout.*;
```

```java
public class Frame1 extends DecoratedFrame {
  BorderLayout borderLayout1 = new BorderLayout();
  String message = "Hello";

  //Construct the frame
  public Frame1() {
    try {
      jbInit();
    }
    catch (Exception e) {
      e.printStackTrace();
    };
  }

  public void setMessage (String msg) {
    message = msg;
  }

  //Component initialization
  public void jbInit() throws Exception{
    this.setLayout(borderLayout1);
    this.setSize(new Dimension (400,300));
    this.setTitle("Frame Title");
  }
  public void paint (Graphics g) {
    g.drawString (message, 50, 50);
  }
}
```

If we don't set any command-line parameters and just run `Application1` (Run ➤ Run "Application1"), you'll see what appears in Figure 2.13.

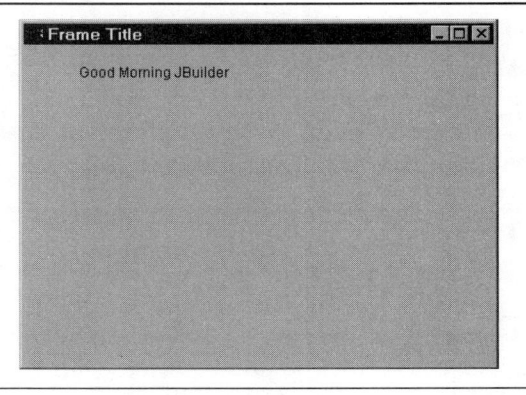

FIGURE 2.13: The new `Application1` program run without parameters

If, instead, you enter something in the Command Line Parameters field in Figure 2.12, you will see the first parameter displayed instead. For instance, if we entered `"One Two Three"` in the parameters field, you would see "One Two Three," instead of "Good Morning JBuilder," as displayed in Figure 2.13.

System Properties

System properties are more similar to HTML parameters than command-line parameters. JBuilder requires that you enter these in the Java VM Parameters field, as you saw in Figure 2.12. Each system property parameter begins with `-D` and is a key-value pair. The following demonstrates one such setting:

```
-Dskill2.message="Welcome to JBuilder"
```

The *D* in `-D` stands for *define*. The entry before the equal sign is the *key*, while the term after it is the *value*.

JAVA VM PARAMETER SETTINGS

Java VM Parameters gets its name because of other available options that can be entered in the field. These other options control settings for the Java VM. Most likely you will never need some of these options, but they are available:

> `-version` shows the current version of the Java compiler being used.
> `-ss`, `-oss`, `-ms`, and `-mx` allow you to change the available memory size (used for creating really big applications).
> `-help` shows a complete list of the options available.

Remember to select Send Run Output to Execution Log (see Figure 2.12).

A key-value pair works in the following way: you ask the system for a particular key, `skill2.message` in this case, and get its value, "Welcome to JBuilder." If it isn't set, `null` is returned. This works similarly to the `getParameter` methods we used with the applet.

```
String s = System.getProperty ("skill2.message");
```

You can also provide a default value for times when the requested property isn't set:

```
String s = System.getProperty ("skill2.message", "Hello");
```

All this works with the help of the `java.util.Properties` class. The system reads in the -D command-line options first and stores them in an internal system property table. From there the program starts in the `main` method. If the program ever needs a property, it asks the system for it, otherwise the properties are ignored.

In addition to providing system properties in the Java VM Parameters field, the system comes with a set of 21 properties already set for applications and up to 13 for applets. For security reasons, there are fewer applications available for applets. For example, while applets do not have access to where Java is installed on the user's machine, they can find out what operating system is being used. Table 2.2 lists the different properties that are available and states whether or not they are available for applets.

TABLE 2.2: Available System Properties

Name	Description	Available for Applet?
awt.toolkit	Toolkit vendor	No
browser	Browser class file	Trusted
browser.vendor	Vendor of browser	Trusted
browser.version	Version of browser	Trusted
file.encoding	File encoding type	No
file.encoding.pkg	File encoding package	No
file.separator	Platform-specific file separator	Yes
java.class.path	CLASSPATH environment variable	No
java.class.version	Java's class library version	Yes
java.home	Java's installation directory	No
java.vendor	Vendor of Java Virtual Machine	Yes
java.vendor.url	URL of Java Virtual Machine vendor	Yes
java.version	Version of Java Virtual Machine	Yes
line.separator	Platform-specific line separator	Yes
os.arch	Operating system architecture	Yes
os.name	Operating system name	Yes

TABLE 2.2 CONTINUED: Available System Properties

Name	Description	Available for Applet?
os.version	Operating system version	Yes
path.separator	Path entry separator	Yes
user.dir	User's working directory	No
user.home	User's home directory	No
user.language	User's locale	No
user.name	User's login Name	No
user.region	User's geographic region	No
user.timezone	User's time zone	No

To display all current property settings to the Execution Log, change the `main` method of `Application1` to the following:

```
//Main method
static public void main(String[] args) {
  java.util.Properties p = System.getProperties();
  p.list(System.out);
}
```

System Property Values Examples

To demonstrate possible values for the different properties, the following entries are displayed on one particular system with the `p.list(System.out)` call just shown:

```
- listing properties -
user.language=en
java.home=C:\JBuilder\java
awt.toolkit=sun.awt.windows.Wtoolkit
file.encoding.pkg=sun.io
java.version=JDK1.1.2.Borland
file.separator=\
```

continued ▶

```
line.separator=
user.region=US
file.encoding=8859_1
java.compiler=javacomp
java.vendor=Sun Microsystems Inc.
user.timezone=EST
user.name=jaz
os.arch=x86
os.name=Windows NT
java.vendor.url=http://www.sun.com/
user.dir=C:\skills\skill2
java.class.path=C:\JBuilder\myclasses;C:\JBuilder\lib...
java.class.version=45.3
os.version=4.0
path.separator=;
user.home=C:\
```

The Trusted entry in the Applet column means that the applet must be digitally signed, and the user must trust the signer in order for the property to be available. Signing code is not discussed in this book. However, you can learn more about this capability at http://www.javasoft.com/security/examples/sign/. The actual steps for the end user will depend upon the browser they are using.

Returning to our `Application1` example, if we want to display the message in the `skill2.message` property, we only need to change the `main` method to get the same results as we would if using command-line parameters. To do so, we'll replace the code that looks at the `args` parameter with code that looks at the property:

```
//Main method
static public void main(String[] args) {
  String msg;
  msg = System.getProperty ("skill2.message", "Good Morning JBuilder");
  new Application1(msg);
}
```

In this skill, we used the Applet and Application Wizard, concentrating on the basics and avoiding some of the extra capabilities that are available from the Wizards, which we'll learn about in later skills. Now that you have a feel for JBuilder, we'll take a step back and learn about the syntax of the Java language in Skill 3.

Are You Experienced?

Now you can...

- ☑ create a project
- ☑ create an applet using the Applet Wizard
- ☑ access Applet parameters
- ☑ use the Application Wizard to create a stand-alone application
- ☑ access application command-line parameters
- ☑ access system properties
- ☑ provide a list of available system properties

to R. Jones

eb Design
Vebserver &
exp. Fax
1.

C/C. Visual
Analysts/
ng software
. Computer
e preferred.
ng applica-
firm. Fax

for dynam-
Dev., test,
, Exp. C C
me to Best

are Testers
ould have 2
tegration &
mated test-
n documen-
rogramming
xPro) are a
g customer
ired along
ritten com-
ulti levels of
e to KKUP
nge Blvd.,

er/Analyst
based SQL
Required
SQL, ODBC.
ew applica-
xp. a plus.
history to

NER
seeking a
r to design
collateral,
omo's, CD-
and WWW
uggle multi-
ew skills on
Veb design
chnical trou-
. Call 435-

ECTOR -
IA
pment com-
opportuni-
-end Web
In addition
resh ideas,
s excellent
resentation
with innov-
ogrammers,
interactive
interfaces.
experience
and resume
n, Seattle,

ed software
looking for
ICATIONS
sible for its
nation, and
self-starter,
est have 2
ogramming
4.

356-555-3398.

PROGRAMMERS
C. C. VB, Cobol, exp. Call 534-555-6543 or fax 534-555-6544.

PROGRAMMING

MRFS Inc. is looking for a Sr. Windows NT developer. Reqs. 3-5 yrs. Exp. In C under Windows, Win95 & NT, using Visual C. Excl. OO design & implementation skills a must. OLE2 & ODBC are a plus. Excl. Salary & bnfts. Resume & salary history to HR, 8779 HighTech Way, Computer City, AR

PROGRAMMERS

Contractors Wanted for short & long term assignments: Visual C, MFC Unix C/C, SQL Oracle Dev elop ers PC Help Desk Support Windows NT & NetWareTelecommunications Visual Basic, Access, HTMT, CGI, Perl MMI & Co., 885-555-9933

PROGRAMMER World Wide Web Links wants your HTML & Photoshop skills. Develop great WWW sites. Local & global customers. Send samples & resume to WWWL, 2000 Apple Road, Santa Rosa, CA.

TECHNICAL WRITER Software firm seeks writer/editor for manuals, research notes, project mgmt. Min 2 years tech. writing, DTP & programming experience. Send resume & writing samples to: Software Systems, Dallas, TX.

TECHNICAL Software development firm looking for Tech Trainers, Ideal candidates have programming experience in Visual C, HTML & JAVA. Need quick self starter. Call (443) 555-6868 for interview.

TECHNICAL WRITER/ Premier Computer Corp is seeking a combination of technical skills, knowledge and experience in the following areas: UNIX, Windows 95/NT, Visual Basic, on-line help & documentation, and the internet. Candidates must possess excellent writing skills, and be comfortable working in a quality vs. deadline driven environment. Competitive salary. Fax resume & samples to Karen Fields, Premier Computer Corp., 444 Industrial Blvd. Concord, CA. Or send to our website at www.premier.com.

WEB DESIGNER

BA/BS or equivalent programming/multimedia production. 3 years of experience in use and design of WWW services streaming audio and video HTML, PERL, CGI, GIF, JPEG. Demonstrated interpersonal, organization, communication, multi-tasking skills. Send resume to The Learning People at www.learning.com.

WEBMASTER-TECHNICAL

BSCS or equivalent, 2 years of experience in CGI, Windows 95/NT, UNIX, C, Java, Perl. Demonstrated ability to design, code, debug and test on-line services. Send resume to The Learning People at www.learning.com.

PROGRAMMER World Wide Web Links wants your HTML & Photoshop skills. Develop great WWW sites. Local & global customers. Send sam-

ing tools. Experienced in documentation preparation & programming languages (Access, C, FoxPro) are a plus. Financial or banking customer service support is required along with excellent verbal & written communication skills with multi levels of end-users. Send resume to KKUP Enterprises, 45 Orange Blvd., Orange, CA.

COMPUTERS Small Web Design Firm seeks indiv. w/NT, Webserver & Database management exp. Fax resume to 556-555-4221.

COMPUTER/ Visual C/C, Visual Basic Exp'd Systems Analysts/ Programmers for growing software dev. team in Roseburg. Computer Science or related degree preferred. Develop adv. Engineering applications for engineering firm. Fax resume to 707-555-8744.

COMPUTER Web Master for dynamic SF Internet co. Site. Dev., test, coord., train. 2 yrs prog. Exp. C C Web C. FTP. Fax resume to Best Staffing 845-555-7722.

COMPUTER PROGRAMMER

Ad agency seeks programmer w/exp. in UNIX/NT Platforms, Web Server, CGI/Perl. Programmer Position avail. on a project basis with the possibility to move into F/T. Fax resume & salary req. to R. Jones 334-555-8332.

COMPUTERS Programmer/Analyst Design and maintain C based SQL database applications. Required skills: Visual Basic, C, SQL, ODBC. Document existing and new applications. Novell or NT exp. a plus. Fax resume & salary history to 235-555-9935.

GRAPHIC DESIGNER
Webmaster's Weekly is seeking a creative Graphic Designer to design high impact marketing collater al, including direct mail promois, CD-ROM packages, ads and WWW pages. Must be able to juggle multiple projects and learn new skills on the job very rapidly. Web design experience a big plus, technical troubleshooting also a plus. Call 435-555-1235.

GRAPHICS - ART DIRECTOR - WEB-MULTIMEDIA
Leading internet development company has an outstanding opportunity for a talented, high-end Web Experienced Art Director. In addition to a great portfolio and fresh ideas, the ideal candidate has excellent communication and presentation skills. Working as a team with innovative producers and programmers, you will create dynamic, interactive web sites and application interfaces. Some programming experience required. Send samples and resume to: SuperSites, 333 Main, Seattle, WA.

MARKETING

Fast paced software and services provider looking for MARKETING COMMUNICATIONS SPECIALIST to be responsible for its webpage.

PROGRAMMERS Multiple short term assignments available: Visual C, 3 positions SQL ServerNT Server, 2 positions JAVA & HTML, long term NetWare Various locations. Call for more info. 356-555-3398.

PROGRAMMERS

C. C. VB, Cobol, exp.
Call 534-555-6543
or fax 534-555-6544.

PROGRAMMING
MRFS Inc. is looking for a Sr. Windows NT developer. Reqs. 3-5 yrs. Exp. In C under Windows, Win95 & NT, using Visual C. Excl. OO design & implementation skills a must. OLE2 & ODBC are a plus. Excl. Salary & bnfts. Resume & salary history to HR, 8779 HighTech Way, Computer City, AR

PROGRAMMERS/ Contractors Wanted for short & long term assignments: Visual C, MFC Unix C/C, SQL Oracle Developers PC Help Desk Support Windows NT & NetWareTelecommunications Visual Basic, Access, HTMT, CGI, Perl MMI & Co., 885-555-9933

PROGRAMMER World Wide Web Links wants your HTML & Photoshop skills. Develop great WWW sites. Local & global customers. Send samples & resume to WWWL, 2000 Apple Road, Santa Rosa, CA.

TECHNICAL WRITER Software firm seeks writer/editor for manuals, research notes, project mgmt. Min 2 years tech. writing, DTP & programming experience. Send resume & writing samples to: Software Systems, Dallas, TX.

COMPUTER PROGRAMMER

Ad agency seeks programmer w/exp. in UNIX/NT Platforms, Web Server, CGI/Perl. Programmer Position avail. on a project basis with the possibility to move into F/T. Fax resume & salary req. to R. Jones 334-555-8332.

TECHNICAL WRITER Premier Computer Corp is seeking a combination of technical skills, knowledge and experience in the following areas: UNIX, Windows 95/NT, Visual Basic, on-line help & documentation, and the internet. Candidates must possess excellent writing skills, and be comfortable working in a quality vs. deadline driven environment. Competitive salary. Fax resume & samples to Karen Fields, Premier Computer Corp., 444 Industrial Blvd. Concord, CA. Or send to our website at www.premier.com.

WEB DESIGNER
BA/BS or equivalent programming/multimedia production. 3 years of experience in use and design of WWW services streaming audio and video HTML, PERL, CGI, GIF, JPEG. Demonstrated interpersonal, organization, communication, multi-tasking skills. Send resume to The Learning People at www.learning.com.

WEBMASTER-TECHNICAL
BSCS or equivalent, 2 years of experience in CGI, Windows 95/NT,

COMPUTERS Small Web Design Firm seeks indiv. w/NT, Webserver & Database management exp. Fax resume to 556-555-4221.

COMPUTER Visual C/C, Visual Basic Exp'd Systems Analysts/ Programmers for growing software dev. team in Roseburg. Computer Science or related degree preferred. Develop adv. Engineering applications for engineering firm. Fax resume to 707-555-8744.

COMPUTER Web Master for dynamic SF Internet co. Site. Dev., test, coord., train. 2 yrs prog. Exp. C C Web C. FTP. Fax resume to Best Staffing 845-555-7722.

COMPUTERS/ QA SOFTWARE TESTERS Qualified candidates should have 2 yrs exp. performing integration & system testing using automated testing tools. Experienced in documentation preparation & programming languages (Access, C, FoxPro) are a plus. Financial or banking customer service support is required along with excellent verbal & written communication skills with multi levels of end-users. Send resume to KKUP Enterprises, 45 Orange Blvd., Orange, CA.

COMPUTERS Programmer/Analyst Design and maintain C based SQL database applications. Required skills: Visual Basic, C, SQL, ODBC. Document existing and new applications. Novell or NT exp. a plus. Fax resume & salary history to 235-555-9935.

GRAPHIC DESIGNER

Webmaster's Weekly is seeking a creative Graphic Designer to design high impact marketing collater al, including direct mail promo's, CD-ROM packages, ads and WWW pages. Must be able to juggle multiple projects and learn new skills on the job very rapidly. Web design experience a big plus, technical troubleshooting also a plus. Call 435-555-1235.

GRAPHICS - ART DIRECTOR - WEB-MULTIMEDIA
Leading internet development company has an outstanding opportunity for a talented, high-end Web Experienced Art Director. In addition to a great portfolio and fresh ideas, the ideal candidate has excellent communication and presentation skills. Working as a team with innovative producers and programmers, you will create dynamic, interactive web sites and application interfaces. Some programming experience required. Send samples and resume to: SuperSites, 333 Main, Seattle, WA.

COMPUTER PROGRAMMER

Ad agency seeks programmer w/exp. in UNIX/NT Platforms, Web Server, CGI/Perl. Programmer Position avail. on a project basis with the possibility to move into F/T. Fax resume & salary req. to R. Jones 334-555-8332.

PROGRAMMERS / Established software company seeks program-

seminar coordination, and ad
ment. Must be a self-starter,
getic, organized. Must have 2
web experience. Programmi
plus. Call 985-555-9854.

PROGRAMMERS Multiple
term assignments available:
C, 3 positions SQL ServerNT S
2 positions JAVA & HTML, long
NetWare Various locations. C
more info. 356-555-3398.

PROGRAMMERS

C. C. VB, Cobol, exp. Call 534
6543 or fax 534-555-6544.

PROGRAMMING

MRFS Inc. is looking for a
Windows NT developer. Req
yrs. Exp. In C under Win
Win95 & NT, using Visual C
OO design & implementation
a must. OLE2 & ODBC are a
Excl. Salary & bnfts. Resum
salary history to HR, 8779 Hig
Way, Computer City, AR

PROGRAMMERS/ Contr
Wanted for short & long term a
ments: Visual C, MFCUnix C/C
Oracle Developers PC Help
Support Windows NT & Net
Telecommunications Visual
Access, HTMT, CGI, Perl MMI
885-555-9933

PROGRAMMER World Wide
Links wants your HTML & Phot
skills. Develop great WWW
Local & global customers. Send
ples & resume to WWWL,
Apple Road, Santa Rosa, CA.

TECHNICAL WRITER Softwar
seeks writer/editor for ma
research notes, project mgmt,
years tech. writing, DTP & pro
ming experience. Send resu
writing samples to: Sof
Systems, Dallas, TX.

TECHNICAL Software develop
firm looking for Tech Trainers,
candidates have programming
rience in Visual C, HTML &
Need quick self starter. Call
555-6868 for interview.

TECHNICAL WRITER Pr
Computer Corp is seeking a c
nation of technical skills, know
and experience in the foll
areas: UNIX, Windows 95/NT,
Basic, on-line help & document
and the internet. Candidates
possess excellent writing skills
be comfortable working in a q
vs. deadline driven environ
Competitive salary. Fax resu
samples to Karen Fields. Pr
Computer Corp., 444 Industrial
Concord, CA. Or send to our w
at www.premier.com.

WEB DESIGNER

BA/BS or equivalent pro
ming/multimedia productio
years of experience in use
design of WWW services stre
audio and video HTML, PERL
GIF, JPEG. Demonstrated inte
sonal, organization, communic
multi-tasking skills. Send resu
The Learning People at www
ing.com.

WEBMASTER-TECHNI

SKILL 3

three

Using Java Syntax

- Introducing Java syntax
- Working with datatypes
- Using flow control
- Declaring classes, methods, and variables
- Understanding access modifiers
- Introducing exception handling

Introducing Java Syntax

In the first two skills, we learned about the various capabilities of Java, without explaining much about the syntax of the language. Now, we'll take a look at the language so you'll be able to work through the remaining skills. If you don't grasp something right away, don't worry too much. You'll get more comfortable as you continue to use the various pieces.

The syntax of a language is called its *grammar*. It consists of the *keywords, identifiers,* and *operators* of the language, along with the rules for combining them. First, we'll look at the different pieces of the Java programming language, and then we'll see how to put them together.

Comments

First off, let's look at *comments.* You use comments to document your code, so when others read it or you look at it again in a few months, you both will have a better idea of what is going on more quickly. Java has three styles of comments. Two are inherited from C++, while the third one extends a C++ comment style.

- `//` is for single line comments and extends to the end of the line.
- `/* comment */` is for multiline comments.
- `/** javadoc comment */` is also for multiline comments; however, these are called *documenting comments.* They allow you to create documentation directly from the source code. When using JBuilder you can only look at the javadoc documentation for the system classes, not for your own. Selecting the Doc tab in the Content Pane of the AppBrowser while looking at a system class will show you the javadoc-style documentation for that class. Figure 3.1 shows this for the `DecoratedFrame` class.

Keywords

Keywords describe the words that a Java compiler will understand. Table 3.1 lists the keywords. Out of context, they don't have much meaning, but we'll learn about them as we progress through the rest of this and the remaining skills. If you've programmed in another language, most should look somewhat familiar.

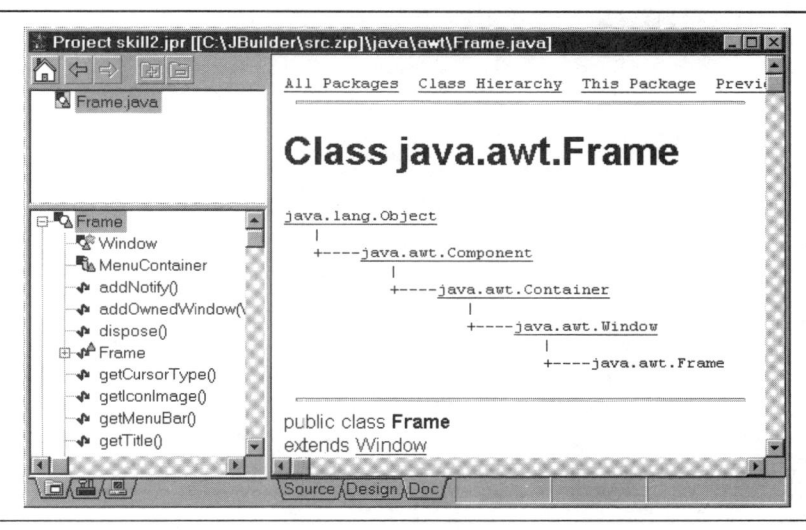

FIGURE 3.1: Looking at the javadoc documentation for a system class

TABLE 3.1: Java Keywords

abstract	boolean	break	byte	case
catch	char	class	const*	continue
default	do	double	else	extends
final	finally	float	for	goto*
if	implements	import	instanceof	int
interface	long	native	new	null
package	private	protected	public	return
short	static	super	switch	synchronized
this	throw	throws	transient	try
void	volatile	while		

* = reserved as keyword, but not used.

Identifiers

Identifiers are how Java recognizes classes, methods, and variables. They can start with a letter, underscore (_), or dollar sign ($), with remaining positions adding numerals (0–9) to the list of available characters.

Because Java uses the Unicode character set, the characters used can be outside of the typical uppercase and lowercase A–Z range. For instance, `nica` is a valid variable name. As long as your editor supports them, you can even use the ideographs found in the Asian languages in your variable names.

> **NOTE** If you are not familiar with *the Unicode standard,* it describes characters for the international community within a single 16-bit mapping. With the help of a local font or fonts, appropriate character strings get displayed. Without the font, unrecognizable garbage appears. Additional information is available from the Unicode consortium at `http://www.unicode.org/`.

Operators

Operators are used to transform identifiers and literals (see the "Literals" section) within *expressions.* Expressions are statements in which operators perform their function variables and return a value. For example, `c = a + b;` is really two expressions: The first expression takes the value of *a* and *b*, performs addition (+ or addition operator) on them and returns the sum. The second expression assigns that returned value (sum of *a* and *b*) to the variable *c*. So what's a statement? Well, a statement is a line of Java source code that ends with a semicolon. The line may span multiple physical lines within the source code. For example:

```
x = 4 * y + 8 / z;
   or
if (a < b)
   return true;
```

Java consists of operators for math operations, relational operations, bit-wise operations, and assignment operations. In addition to the operators, you can combine operations within parenthesis to create larger expressions. Let's take a look at the various operators.

The math operators, which indicate standard math functions, are listed in Table 3.2.

TABLE 3.2: Math Operators

Operator	Name	Example
+	Addition	2 + 2
-	Subtraction	18-20
*	Multiplication	6 * 0
/	Division	14 / 7
%	Modulus (Remainder)	20 % 7

You use the relational operators for comparisons. They allow you to test equality and differences, and you can combine them with logical operators to create more complex expressions. All the operators listed in Table 3.3 result in an expression that is either true or false.

TABLE 3.3: Relational/Logical Operators

Operator	Name	Example
==	Equal	s == 2
!=	Not equal	y != 0
<	Less than	b < 5
<=	Less than or equal	e <= 10
>	Greater than	x > 20
>=	Greater than or equal	y >= 100
&&	AND	(s == 2) && (y != 0)
||	OR	(b < 5) || (e <= 10)
!	NOT	!(x > 20)

The bitwise operators are on the more advanced side and work at the bit level. They allow you to manipulate the makeup of a value by examining how the machine stores it. When using JBuilder to create programs it is naturally built for, you can probably avoid the operators in Table 3.4.

TABLE 3.4: Bitwise Operators

Operator	Name	Example
&	Bitwise AND	s & 1
|	Bitwise OR	y | 2
^	Bitwise XOR	b ^ 3
~	Bitwise complement	~e
<<	Left shift	x << 4
>>	Right shift	s >> 5
>>>	Zero-fill right shift	y >>> 6

> **NOTE** If you are not familiar with bitwise operations, the *Mastering Java 1.1* book from Sybex provides a lengthier explanation.

Finally, assignment operators allow you to store values in variables. The simplest is just the equal sign (=), which stores the value on the right in the variable on the left. The others are shorthand versions of more complex operations. For instance, the += operator allows you to combine y = y + 7 into y += 7, generating the same results. This operator and the other assignment operators are listed in Table 3.5.

TABLE 3.5: Assignment Operators

Operator	Usage	Normal Operation
=	c = a;	c = a;
+=	c += a;	c = c + a;
-=	c -= a;	c = c - a;
*=	c *= a;	c = c * a;
/=	c /= a;	c = c / a;
%=	c %= a;	c = c % a;
&=	c &= a;	c = c & a;
|=	c |= a;	c = c | a;
^=	c ^= a;	c = c ^ a;

TABLE 3.5 CONTINUED: Assignment Operators

Operator	Usage	Normal Operation
<<=	c <<= a;	c = c << a;
>>=	c >>= a;	c = c >> a;
>>>=	c >>>= a;	c = c >>> a;

Working with Datatypes, Literals, and Strings

Okay, now that you know about keywords, identifiers, and operators, let's take a look at how Java manages some other things: *datatypes, literals,* and *strings*.

Datatypes

A datatype is the way that Java stores the contents of something internally. For instance, the letter 'c' is a character. Within Java, this would be stored as type `char`. A Java char is 16-bits because of the Unicode standard for international support. There are actually seven other datatypes within Java. All the datatypes are listed in Table 3.6.

TABLE 3.6: Java Datatypes

Datatype	Rule
boolean	true/false
char	16-bit Unicode character
byte	8-bit signed two's complement number
short	16-bit signed two's complement number
int	32-bit signed two's complement number
long	64-bit signed two's complement number
float	32-bit floating-point number
double	32-bit floating-point number

If you happen to come from another programming language, you may notice a few differences between Java and languages such C and C++. First and foremost, the size of an `int` is defined by the language. You do not have to worry if an `int` is

16 or 32 bits. It is always 32 bits in Java. Then there is the `boolean` data-type. Instead of having to worry if 0 is false and non-zero true or vise versa, Java defines a datatype with two distinct values as parameters. The language designers at Sun did this with you—the programmer—in mind to help reduce errors in programs.

Literals

A literal is taken quite literally by the system, kind of like WYTIWYG (What You Type Is What You Get). Specifically, a literal is a constant. The constant's datatype depends on the makeup of the content. Available literal datatypes are listed in Table 3.7.

TABLE 3.7: Literally Speaking

Literals	Possible Values	Value
boolean	true / false	true
byte/short/int	A decimal number An octal number (has a leading 0) A hexadecimal number (has a leading 0x)	11234 0123 0x8912
long	A decimal number with trailing *l* or *L*	888383L
float	A floating point number with a trailing *f* or *F*	3.14f
double	A floating point number with optional trailing *d* or *D*	3.142857
char	A single quoted character	'z'

For characters, in addition to having a single quoted character to provide value, there are nine special literals:

\'	Single quote
\"	Double quote
\\	Backslash
\b	Backspace
\f	Form feed
\n	Newline
\r	Return
\t	Tab
\xxx	Octal value of character: for example, \101 is the character 'A'

Strings

Strings are represented by a series of characters between double quotes ("), instead of the single quotes used for individual characters. A `String` is actually an object in the system, instead of just a datatype. Being an object has extra responsibilities, which gives you the ability to perform various operations on the object without the use of operators. These capabilities are available through methods, which we'll discuss shortly. One such method for the `String` class is the `length()` method. The method returns the actual length of the string. For instance, `"Hello World"` is a string. `"Hello World".length()` reports 11, because there are 11 characters within the `String`, including the space.

Declaring Classes, Methods, and Variables

With the help of our friends—the identifiers, operators, literals, and the rest—we can now start programming. With some languages, you can create stand-alone functions and global variables. With Java, that isn't the case. Everything you create must be within a *class*. Classes themselves must exist within a package. If you don't specify a package when you define a class, a default is assigned, so, initially, you usually don't need to worry about creating packages much.

Methods are usually defined next. They allow you to associate behavior with a class—what it does and how it functions. Finally, if the class needs to retain its state, this is done through variables. Both methods and variables are defined within a class.

Classes

We touched on classes briefly in Skill 1. As you may recall, a class defines the state and behavior of an object. In order to define a class in Java you start a new file with the line:

```
class SomeName
```

where *SomeName* is the name of the class to create. If you were creating a subclass of something, say an applet, the line becomes:

```
class SomeName extends java.applet.Applet
```

This says that the *SomeName* class is a subclass of `Applet`. This is how Java implements the object-oriented concept of inheritance, which we discussed briefly in Skill 1.

After you declare the class, everything else for the class goes between a series of curly braces ({}) that follow.

After you finish defining the class, you save it in a file that matches the class name. If *SomeName* represents `Bart`, the filename to save to is `Bart.java`. If `SomeName` were actually used, the filename would be `SomeName.java`.

Only classes that are public need to be saved in files that match the class name. This allows you to include support files that nobody knows about with your application and, truth be known, there is no requirement that says each class must be in its own file. Helper classes for the main class of the applet (the class that represents the applet and has the `init()` method) or the application (the class that represents the application and has the `main()` method) can all reside in the files for the applet or application. However, the Java language requires you to separate out your public classes into separate files. It is also good programming practice and enables you to find things more easily.

Variables

Variables reserve space for datatypes and classes. They can also be initialized with literals. The statement

```
int x = 7;
```

declares the variable x as an int, with an initial value of 7. To declare a variable, you define a statement that starts with a datatype, followed by an identifier. If you wish to initialize it, follow the datatype with an equal sign and a literal. Got it?

For variables that are not for the built-in datatypes, but for a reference to a class, the right side of the equal sign isn't a literal. You need to use the **new** keyword to create a new instance of the class.

The statement

```
Bart y = new Bart();
```

declares the variable y as a `Bart`, and creates a new `Bart` object. This assumes a class named `Bart` is defined somewhere.

Arrays

Arrays are another special object in Java. They allow you to store multiple variables within a single linear structure. When you create an array, you define its size and datatype. Then you can fill it to the rim with objects. Let's look at an example:

```
int x[] = new int [7];
float []y = new float [8];
```

The first thing you may notice is that the square brackets can appear on either side of the variable name. Although Java has this flexibility, you should consistently use the square brackets on whichever side is appropriate. Common practice among Java programmers is to place the brackets on the right side of the identifier.

Also, because arrays contain multiple items within a single structure, initialization is a little more involved. Instead of just setting the variable to a literal, you need to do some more work. You'll also notice the new keyword. Just like when initializing a variable to a new instance of a class, Java requires you to create new instances of arrays. The `new int[7]` part of the statement says to create a seven-element integer array. You can then fill it. On the other hand, if you know the values of the array beforehand, you can initialize it at declaration time with the help of curly braces:

```
int z[] = {100, 200, 400, 800};
```

This also allows us to mention an instance variable of arrays. Besides `Strings` knowing how big they are, arrays know how long they are. The length of an array is found via the `.length` instance variable. For the array above z, `z.length` is four.

While, technically speaking, Java doesn't have multidimensional arrays, there is nothing to keep you from creating an array of array objects. This allows you to nest multiple levels of arrays, and each level doesn't require the same size. For instance, the following demonstrates multiple dimensions of different sizes:

```
int y[][] = {{3,4}, {1,2,3,4,5,6,7,8,9,10}, {11,12,13}};
```

Methods

Methods are how we get our programs to work. A method describes the behavior of the class that contains it. You create a method by specifying the return type, method name, and an argument list. If there is no return value, you specify `void`:

```
void setValue (int x) {
   ...
}
```

If a method has a return value, you need to specify a `return` statement that returns a value of that type:

```
int getValue () {
  int value = 1;
   ...
  return value;
}
```

Interfaces

An *interface* is a special kind of class. It specifies a template for a set of methods that a class must define. To declare an interface, you use the `interface` keyword:

```
public interface Area {
   public abstract long getArea ();
}
```

When you define an interface, you do not specify the behavior of the method(s). You only specify what the method declaration looks like. That is the purpose of the `abstract` keyword. Then, when a class wants to *implement* the interface, it must fill in the details of each method of the interface:

```
public class Rectangle implements Area {
   int height;
   int width;
   . . .
   public long getArea () {
     return (height * width);
   }
   . . .
}
```

The nice thing about an interface is that every class can implement the interface differently, keeping the method declaration fixed:

```
public class Triangle implements Area {
   int height;
   int base;
   . . .
   public long getArea () {
     return (height * base / 2);
   }
   . . .
}
```

Then, you can use the interface as a parameter to other methods. Because the interface has a known behavior, you can call an interface's methods without knowing the actual class involved:

```
public void printArea (Area a) {
   System.out.println (a.getArea());
}
```

Packages

A *package* is a grouping of related classes. The core Java API provides a set of packages to work with. Each has a focused set of functionality provided by the classes within it. In other language environments, like C++, this structure may be referred to as the *class libraries*. However, some, like Ada, share the naming convention and also call them packages.

When you use any class in Java, the runtime environment needs to be able to locate it. At compile time, the compiler needs to be able to find it, too. You could reference each class with its fully qualified name—java.applet.Applet—every time you needed it. Or, you could tell the compiler where things might be—import java.awt.*—and then use just the final piece, the class name (e.g. Graphics), each time. In this case, java.awt is the name of the package within Java to reference.

In each of these cases, a package is used. The java.applet package contains classes for applets, while the java.awt package includes classes for interacting with the graphical environment. AWT stands for *Abstract Window Toolkit*, and it's important for drawing and working with user interface elements.

> **TIP** Classes in the java.lang package do not need to be imported. The compiler implicitly imports this package because its use is so fundamental. The String class is one class commonly used in the java.lang package.

You can tell the compiler about an entire package by importing it with an asterisk at the end—import java.applet.*. Or you can import a specific piece of a package by specifying the class name—import java.awt.Graphics.

> **TIP** Importing is different from the C/C++ #include keyword. Including header files in C and C++ physically incorporates the header file into the program. On the other hand, importing keeps class files separate. This greatly reduces unnecessary recompilations and leaves quite a few checks until runtime.

To better group classes when you create your own packages, the very first line of source code would be:

package *packagename*;

Then, when you build your program, JBuilder places the .class file in the *packagename* directory. For every period in the package name, a subdirectory is created. For example, the Graphics class is in the directory java\awt, with all the other classes for the java.awt package. When it's time to install your packages on a Web server, this allows you to find all the necessary pieces.

> **TIP**: If you place *packagename* in the Package field in the form for the Application or Applet Wizard, the appropriate package line is automatically included in your source file.

Understanding Access Modifiers

When classes, methods, and variables are declared, they have a certain visibility in the block they are declared in, as defined by the surrounding set of braces ({ }). However, when things are defined at the class level, classes, methods, and variables may be visible beyond the class.

In order to control who has access to classes, methods, and variables, you need to specify an access modifier when the class, method, or variable is declared. Java provides three access modifier keywords. There is also a fourth behavior when no keyword is specified. Each may be used with a class name, instance variable, or method, with similar results; these are described in Table 3.8.

TABLE 3.8: Access Modifiers

Keyword	Behavior
public	Accessible to anyone All applets must be public classes
protected	Accessible to anyone in the same package and subclasses
'friendly'/none	Accessible to anything in the same package
private	Accessible only within the defining class

> **WARNING**: The protected keyword in Java defines different behavior from the protected keyword in C++. In C++ it is only for subclasses, but in Java it is for subclasses and the same package.

Using Flow Control

If you don't mind always executing all the code you write, you can create everything with what you've learned so far. However, most people tend to develop software that alternates behavior based upon some input, whether that is the temperature, keystroke, or some other type of information.

if-else

The `if` conditional statement allows you to execute certain code based on a single condition. If the condition isn't met, nothing executes.

```
aCondition = false;
if (aCondition) {…}
```

There is also an `if/else` block that can be programmed into your code. This allows one code block to always execute; however, you don't know which one executed without looking at the condition.

```
if (aCondition) {
   …
} else {
   …
}
```

One key difference between Java `if` blocks and C/C++ `if` blocks is the condition being checked must return a `boolean` value in Java. If it doesn't, it will not compile. For example, in Java, this is not a valid statement:

```
if (1) …
```

If there is more than one condition to check, you can add another `if` statement to the `else` condition. This can go on indefinitely.

```
if (a < b) {
   …
} else if (b > c) {
   …
} else {
   …
}
```

while

In Java, the while statement repeats forever while a certain condition is true. The following example demonstrates the loop. Once `SomeStuff.x` reaches zero, increases will have the necessary count.

```
while (SomeStuff.x != -1)
  increase++;
  SomeStuff.x- ;
}
```

> **NOTE** It is possible to pass over a while loop without executing the internal statements if the condition is initially false.

do

The do loop is for those times when you need to be sure the loop executes at least once. The loop continues until the condition in the while clause is false.

```
do {
  ...
} while (aCondition);
```

for

Defining a for loop has three separate parts:

```
for (initialize; terminate; increment) {
  ...
}
```

The *initialization* part sets things up for the first pass through the loop. After each execution, the *increment* piece is run. Then, if the *terminate* condition is reached, you would be done. Frequently, you'll see a variable defined in the loop. Although the statement looks perfectly legal, you can't access the variable outside the loop statement.

```
for (int i = 0; i < 10; i++) {
  ...
}
```

switch

The switch statement is built for conditional operations with many choices, where the choices are integers. The system starts at the top, looking for matches until it finds one. If it doesn't find one, it will execute the default entry. Each choice is specified with a case keyword, followed by the value and a colon (':'). The break statement is used to prevent the execution of other check cases. In the event you want to provide behavior for when no case is matched, you use the default keyword.

```
switch (day) {
  case 0: System.out.println ("Sunday"); break;
  case 1: System.out.println ("Monday"); break;
  case 2: System.out.println ("Tuesday"); break;
  case 3: System.out.println ("Wednesday"); break;
  case 4: System.out.println ("Thursday"); break;
  case 5: System.out.println ("Friday"); break;
  case 6: System.out.println ("Saturday"); break;
  default: System.out.println ("OOPS!"); break;
}
```

If the break statement is missing, the system continues to execute code until it finds one or the end of the switch-block is reached. For example, the following will print Thursday, Friday, Saturday, and OOPS! each on a separate line, if day is four.

```
switch (day) {
  case 0: System.out.println ("Sunday");
  case 1: System.out.println ("Monday");
  case 2: System.out.println ("Tuesday");
  case 3: System.out.println ("Wednesday");
  case 4: System.out.println ("Thursday");
  case 5: System.out.println ("Friday");
  case 6: System.out.println ("Saturday");
  default: System.out.println ("OOPS!");
}
```

Introducing Exception Handling

Prior to C++ and Java, the way error handling was done in functions was usually through a special return value signifying an error, and any other value meant success. Another way it was done was an extra parameter was passed to the function. Prior to checking the return value of the function, you needed to check the parameter to see if the function performed successfully. If you forgot to check the extra parameter, the value returned could be invalid when there was an error. This lead to error-prone code, with numerous checks that were necessary but cumbersome and tedious.

Exception handling is Java's way of handling errors. An *exception* is something that alters the flow of the program. When the exception occurs, code execution is redirected, and you need to handle the exception or properly pass it along to your caller, who will be expecting it. In order for exception handling to work, you need to tell the caller when to expect an exception. Then you develop your code to handle the expected exceptions.

When you are working with something that might cause an exception, you place the statement or statements within a `try / catch` block and wait for the problem. This is called the *exception handler*.

```
try {
  // Some Statement (s)
} catch (ExceptionType e) {
  // Some error handling code
}
```

If the statements within the block execute successfully, without exceptions, the error-handling code will not be executed. On the other hand, if there was an exception in, for example, the fourth of ten statements, the fifth statement and any further statement would not execute because of this exception, and the exception handler (the `catch` block) would be executed.

If you always want something to happen, however, whether or not the statements succeeded, there is an additional `finally` block:

```
try {
  // Some Statement (s)
} catch (ExceptionType e) {
  // Some error handling code
} finally {
  // Always do it.
}
```

This block makes sure that whether or not there was an error while executing the top statements, the `finally` block gets executed.

If, on the other hand, you just want to notify your caller that you throw an exception when an error occurs, you don't need a `try / catch` block; just change the declaration line of the method to show the possible exceptions that it can throw.

This brings the compiler into the picture. To make sure everyone properly calls a method that throws an exception, the compiler ensures they are ready to handle the exception within their own `try / catch` block.

```
void stuff (int x, int y, int z) throws ExceptionType {
  // Some statement(s)
  throw ExceptionType
  // Some statement(s)
}
```

With the calling routine looking somewhat like this:

```
try {
  stuff (1, 2, 3);
```

```
} catch (ExceptionType e) {
   … // Handle Exception
}
```

There are certain types of problems that aren't serious enough to require the `try` / `catch` block. These are called *runtime exceptions*. Going beyond the end of an array is an example of a runtime exception. If it happens, an exception is thrown and the program stops. You can use `try` / `catch` blocks to handle runtime exceptions, but the system does not require them. By you handling the non-runtime exceptions, the system can almost take care of itself with the rest.

Congratulations! You now know everything you need to know to create anything you want in Java. Of course, knowing how to put all these pieces together takes practice. Now that you've learned about the language syntax and the pieces and the rules to connect them, let's move on to Skill 4 and use that knowledge to build an interactive Java form.

Are You Experienced?

Now you can...

- ☑ comment your code
- ☑ create variables
- ☑ connect variables with operators
- ☑ use Java datatypes
- ☑ create classes
- ☑ use Java arrays
- ☑ use packages
- ☑ work with flow control statements
- ☑ handle exceptions

R. Jones 356-555-3398.

PROGRAMMERS
C, C, VB, Cobol, exp. Call 534-555-6543 or fax 534-555-6544.

PROGRAMMING
MRFS Inc. is looking for a Sr. Windows NT developer. Reqs. 3-5 yrs. Exp. in C under Windows, Win95 & NT, using Visual C. Excl. OO design & implementation skills a must. OLE2 & ODBC are a plus. Excl. Salary & bnfts. Resume & salary history to HR, 8779 HighTech Way, Computer City, AR

PROGRAMMERS
Contractors Wanted for short & long term assignments: Visual C, MFC Unix C/C, SQL Oracle Developers PC Help Desk Support Windows: NT & NetWareTelecommunications Visual Basic, Access, HTML, CGI, Perl MMI & Co., 885-555-9933

PROGRAMMER World Wide Web Links wants your HTML & Photoshop skills. Develop great WWW sites. Local & global customers. Send samples & resume to WWWL, 2000 Apple Road, Santa Rosa, CA.

TECHNICAL WRITER Software firm seeks writer/editor for manuals, research notes, project mgmt. Min 2 years tech. writing, DTP & programming experience. Send resume & writing samples to: Software Systems, Dallas, TX.

TECHNICAL. Software development firm looking for Tech Trainers. Ideal candidates have programming experience in Visual C, HTML & JAVA. Need quick self starter. Call (443) 555-6868 for interview.

TECHNICAL WRITER / Premier Computer Corp is seeking a combination of technical skills, knowledge and experience in the following areas: UNIX, Windows 95/NT, Visual Basic, on-line help & documentation, and the Internet. Candidates must possess excellent writing skills and be comfortable working in a quality vs. deadline driven environment. Competitive salary. Fax resume & samples to Karen Fields, Premier Computer Corp. 444 Industrial Blvd. Concord, CA. Or send to our website at www.premier.com.

WEB DESIGNER
BA/BS or equivalent programming/multimedia production. 3 years of experience in use and design of WWW services streaming audio and video HTML, PERL, CGI, GIF, JPEG. Demonstrated interpersonal, organization, communication, multi-tasking skills. Send resume to The Learning People at www.learning.com.

WEBMASTER-TECHNICAL
BSCS or equivalent, 2 years of experience in CGI, Windows 95/NT, UNIX, C, Java, Perl. Demonstrated ability to design, code, debug and test on-line services. Send resume to The Learning People at www.learning.com.

PROGRAMMER World Wide Web Links wants your HTML & Photoshop skills. Develop great WWW sites. Local & global customers. Send samples...

ing tools. Experienced in documentation preparation & programming languages (Access, C, FoxPro) are a plus. Financial or banking customer service support is required along with excellent verbal & written communication skills with multi levels of end-users. Send resume to KKUP Enterprises, 45 Orange Blvd., Orange, CA.

COMPUTERS Small Web Design Firm seeks indiv. w/NT, Webserver & Database management exp. Fax resume to 556-555-4221.

COMPUTER/ Visual C/C, Visual Basic Exp'd Systems Analysts/ Programmers for growing software dev. team in Roseburg. Computer Science or related degree preferred. Develop adv. Engineering applications for engineering firm. Fax resume to 707-555-8744.

COMPUTER Web Master for dynamic SF Internet co. Site, Dev. test, coord., train. 2 yrs prog. Exp. C C, Web C, FTP. Fax resume to Best Staffing 845-555-7722.

COMPUTER PROGRAMMER
Ad agency seeks programmer w/exp. in UNIX/NT Platforms, Web Server, CGI/Perl. Programmer Position avail. on a project basis with the possibility to move into F/T. Fax resume & salary req. to R. Jones 334-555-8332.

COMPUTERS Programmer/Analyst Design and maintain C based SQL database applications. Required skills: Visual Basic, C, SQL, ODBC, Document existing and new applications, Novell or NT exp. a plus. Fax resume & salary history to 235-555-9935.

GRAPHIC DESIGNER
Webmaster's Weekly is seeking a creative Graphic Designer to design high impact marketing collateral, including direct mail promos, CD-ROM packages, ads and WWW pages. Must be able to juggle multiple projects and learn new skills on the job very rapidly. Web design experience a big plus, technical troubleshooting also a plus. Call 435-555-1235.

GRAPHICS - ART DIRECTOR - WEB-MULTIMEDIA
Leading internet development company has an outstanding opportunity for a talented, high-end Web Experienced Art Director. In addition to a great portfolio and fresh ideas, the ideal candidate has excellent communication and presentation skills. Working as a team with innovative producers and programmers, you will create dynamic, interactive web sites and application interfaces. Some programming experience required. Send samples and resume to: SuperSites, 333 Main, Seattle, WA.

MARKETING
Fast paced software and services provider looking for MARKETING COMMUNICATIONS SPECIALIST to be responsible for its webpage.

PROGRAMMERS Multiple short term assignments available: Visual C, 3 positions SQL ServerNT Server, 2 positions JAVA & HTML, long term NetWare Various locations. Call for more info. 356-555-3398.

PROGRAMMERS
C, C, VB, Cobol, exp.
Call 534-555-6543
or fax 534-555-6544

PROGRAMMING
MRFS Inc. is looking for a Sr Windows NT developer. Reqs. 3-5 yrs. Exp. in C under Windows, Win95 & NT, using Visual C. Excl. OO design & Implementation skills a must. OLE2 & ODBC are a plus. Excl. Salary & bnfts. Resume & salary history to HR, 8779 HighTech Way, Computer City, AR

PROGRAMMERS/ Contractors Wanted for short & long term assignments: Visual C, MFC Unix C/C, SQL Oracle Developers PC Help Desk Support Windows NT & NetWareTelecommunications Visual Basic, Access, HTML, CGI, Perl MMI & Co., 885-555-9933

PROGRAMMER World Wide Web Links wants your HTML & Photoshop skills. Develop great WWW sites. Local & global customers. Send samples & resume to WWWL, 2000 Apple Road, Santa Rosa, CA.

TECHNICAL WRITER Software firm seeks writer/editor for manuals, research notes, project mgmt. Min 2 years tech. writing, DTP & programming experience. Send resume & writing samples to: Software Systems, Dallas, TX.

COMPUTER PROGRAMMER
Ad agency seeks programmer w/exp. in UNIX/NT Platforms, Web Server, CGI/Perl. Programmer Position avail. on a project basis with the possibility to move into F/T. Fax resume & salary req. to R. Jones 334-555-8332.

TECHNICAL WRITER Premier Computer Corp is seeking a combination of technical skills, knowledge and experience in the following areas: UNIX, Windows 95/NT, Visual Basic, on-line help & documentation, and the Internet. Candidates must possess excellent writing skills, and be comfortable working in a quality vs. deadline driven environment. Competitive salary. Fax resume & samples to Karen Fields, Premier Computer Corp., 444 Industrial Blvd. Concord, CA. Or send to our website at www.premier.com.

WEB DESIGNER
BA/BS or equivalent programming/multimedia production. 3 years of experience in use and design of WWW services streaming audio and video HTML, PERL, CGI, GIF, JPEG. Demonstrated interpersonal, organization, communication, multi-tasking skills. Send resume to The Learning People at www.learning.com.

WEBMASTER-TECHNICAL
BSCS or equivalent, 2 years of experience in CGI, Windows 95/NT,

COMPUTERS Small Web Design Firm seeks indiv. w/NT, Webserver & Database management exp. Fax resume to 556-555-4221.

COMPUTER Visual C/C: Visual Basic Exp'd Systems Analysts/ Programmers for growing software dev. team in Roseburg. Computer Science or related degree preferred. Develop adv. Engineering applications for engineering firm. Fax resume to 707-555-8744.

COMPUTER Web Master for dynamic SF Internet co. Site, Dev. test, coord., train. 2 yrs prog. Exp. C C, Web C, FTP. Fax resume to Best Staffing 845-555-7722.

COMPUTERS/ QA SOFTWARE TESTERS Qualified candidates should have 2 yrs exp performing integration & system testing using automated testing tools. Experienced in documentation preparation & programming languages (Access, C, FoxPro) are a plus. Financial or banking customer service support is required along with excellent verbal & written communication skills with multi levels of end-users. Send resume to KKUP Enterprises, 45 Orange Blvd., Orange, CA.

COMPUTERS Programmer/Analyst Design and maintain C based SQL database applications. Required skills: Visual Basic, C, SQL, ODBC, Document existing and new applications, Novell or NT exp. a plus. Fax resume & salary history to 235-555-9935.

GRAPHIC DESIGNER
Webmaster's Weekly is seeking a creative Graphic Designer to design high impact marketing collateral, including direct mail promo's, CD-ROM packages, ads and WWW pages. Must be able to juggle multiple projects and learn new skills on the job very rapidly. Web design experience a big plus, technical troubleshooting also a plus. Call 435-555-1235.

GRAPHICS - ART DIRECTOR - WEB-MULTIMEDIA
Leading internet development company has an outstanding opportunity for a talented, high-end Web Experienced Art Director. In addition to a great portfolio and fresh ideas, the ideal candidate has excellent communication and presentation skills. Working as a team with innovative producers and programmers, you will create dynamic, interactive web sites and application interfaces. Some programming experience required. Send samples and resume to: SuperSites, 333 Main, Seattle, WA.

COMPUTER PROGRAMMER
Ad agency seeks programmer w/exp. in UNIX/NT Platforms, Web Server, CGI/Perl. Programmer Position avail. on a project basis with the possibility to move into F/T. Fax resume & salary req. to R. Jones 334-555-8332.

PROGRAMMERS / Established software company seeks program-

ment. Must be a self-starter, energetic, organized. Must have 2 yrs web experience. Programming plus. Call 985-555-9854.

PROGRAMMERS Multiple term assignments available: V C, 3 positions SQL ServerNT Se 2 positions JAVA & HTML, long NetWare Various locations. Cal more info. 356-555-3398.

PROGRAMMERS
C, C, VB, Cobol, exp. Call 534-6543 or fax 534-555-6544.

PROGRAMMING
MRFS Inc. is looking for a Windows NT developer. Reqs. yrs. Exp. in C under Wind Win95 & NT, using Visual C OO design & implementation a must, OLE2 & ODBC are a Excl. Salary & bnfts. Resum salary history to HR, 8779 High Way, Computer City, AR

PROGRAMMERS/ Contra Wanted for short & long term as ments: Visual C, MFCUnix C/C, Oracle Developers PC Help Support Windows NT & Net Telecommunications Visual Access, HTML, CGI, Perl MMI a 885-555-9933

PROGRAMMER World Wide Links wants your HTML & Photo skills. Develop great WWW Local & global customers. Send ples & resume to WWWL, Apple Road, Santa Rosa, CA.

TECHNICAL WRITER Software seeks writer/editor for man research notes, project mgmt. years tech. writing, DTP & pro ming experience. Send resu writing samples to: Soft Systems, Dallas, TX.

TECHNICAL Software develop firm looking for Tech Trainers. candidates have programming rience in Visual C, HTML & Need quick self starter. Call 555-6868 for interview.

TECHNICAL WRITER Pr Computer Corp is seeking a c nation of technical skills, know and experience in the foll areas: UNIX, Windows 95/NT, Basic, on-line help & document and the Internet. Candidates possess excellent writing skills be comfortable working in a q vs. deadline driven environ Competitive salary. Fax resu samples to Karen Fields, Pr Computer Corp., 444 Industrial Concord, CA. Or send to our w at www.premier.com.

WEB DESIGNER
BA/BS or equivalent prog ming/multimedia producti years of experience in use design of WWW services stre audio and video HTML, PERL GIF, JPEG. Demonstrated int sonal, organization, communic multi-tasking skills. Send resu The Learning People at www.le ing.com.

WEBMASTER-TECHNI

SKILL four

Creating a Scrolling Text Applet with Sound

- ❑ Creating the project
- ❑ Working with the Override Method Wizard
- ❑ Defining the applet life-cycle methods
- ❑ Adding sound to your applet
- ❑ Using multithreading
- ❑ Working with the Implement Interface Wizard

Getting Started

In Skill 2, we used JBuilder's Applet Wizard to create a welcome applet and JBuilder's Application Wizard to do the same in a stand-alone application. In this skill, we are going to extend the applet to scroll its message across the screen. The moving text gives us an opportunity to learn the basics of multi-threading and understand an applet's life-cycle methods.

Instead of editing the applet from the earlier skill, we'll recreate it from scratch to reinforce the skills learned earlier. After closing any open projects, select File ➤ New and double-click on the Applet icon. This brings up the Project Wizard (for Applet Wizard) dialog. Fill it in as shown in Figure 4.1 and then select the Finish button to move on to the Applet Wizard screens.

FIGURE 4.1: The Project Wizard dialog is where we enter all the pertinent information about our applet.

As you remember from Skill 2, there are three dialog boxes to complete for the actual Applet Wizard. In the first, we change the Class entry to **Billboard**, check the Generate Standard Methods option this time, and select Next. In the second, create a parameter named **message** of type **String**. Type in a description, in this case **Scrolling message**. It should be accessed by the program via the variable **message** with a default setting of **Welcome**. Select Next to move to the final dialog box. Change the title to **Scrolling Billboard**, its name to **Billboard**, and select the Finish button. Assuming everything went well, you'll notice that we're almost back to where we were in Skill 2, at the end of the Using the Applet Wizard section. All that's left is adding code to display the parameter on the screen.

Using the Override Methods Wizard

To display our message this time, instead of immediately editing the source file, select Billboard.java in the Navigation pane, then select the Wizards ➤ Override Methods menu. This brings up a screen, similar to the one shown in Figure 4.2.

> **TIP** Until you are familiar with all the different methods and their parameters, using the Wizard provides an easy way to learn the methods and their parameter lists.

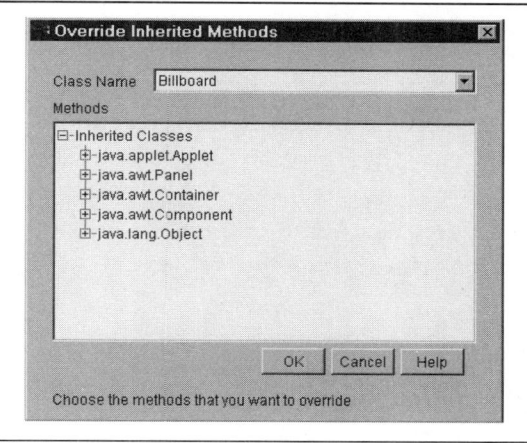

FIGURE 4.2: The Override Inherited Methods dialog box

From here, you can select which method you want to override from all of the classes that are in `Billboard`'s class hierarchy tree. Because `Billboard` extends `java.applet.Applet`, that is at the top of the list. The next entry is `java.awt.Panel` because `Applet` is a subclass of `Panel`. Below `Panel` is `java.awt.Container` because `Panel` is its subclass. `Container` is a subclass of `java.awt.Component`, so that is next. At the bottom of all this is `java.lang.Object`. Everything is a subclass of `Object`, eventually.

> ### APPLET'S OBJECT HIERARCHY: AN OVERVIEW
>
> Every program that you want to run within a browser must subclass `java.applet.Applet`. This allows the browser to know what behavior to expect when it sees an `<APPLET>` tag within a `.html` file.
>
> The immediate superclass of `Applet` is `java.awt.Panel`. By being a subclass of `Panel`, an applet gets its own drawing area. The superclass of `Panel` is `java.awt.Container`. Being a subclass of `Container` allows an applet to have other components placed inside of it and to use a `LayoutManager`. You'll visit layout management in Skill 6.
>
> Going further up the class hierarchy tree of `Applet`, the `java.awt.Component` class is next. Every graphical control in Java is a subclass of `Component`, `Applet` being no exception. Being a subclass of `Component`, an `Applet` can be grouped together in a `Container` and positioned by a `LayoutManager`. What this means is that an `Applet` can be placed within any `Container`, not just a browser. You'll learn more about `Component` in Skill 5.
>
> What does all this mean then? Well, when you define an applet, there is much behavior already defined and inherited. Frequently, you just need to override an already existing method to offer new behavior. This behavior is what defines an applet and is what the applet runtime environment, the browser, needs. If it isn't there, if you forget to subclass `java.applet.Applet`, then the browser cannot run your program.

Since we learned that `paint` is a method of `Component` in a previous skill, we can select the plus sign (+) next to `java.awt.Component` to expand its method list to look like Figure 4.3.

Scrolling down through the alphabetical listing, around ten screens worth, you'll come upon a `paint(Graphics)` entry. When you select this entry and click on OK, JBuilder inserts the framework of the method into your source.

Using the Override Methods Wizard

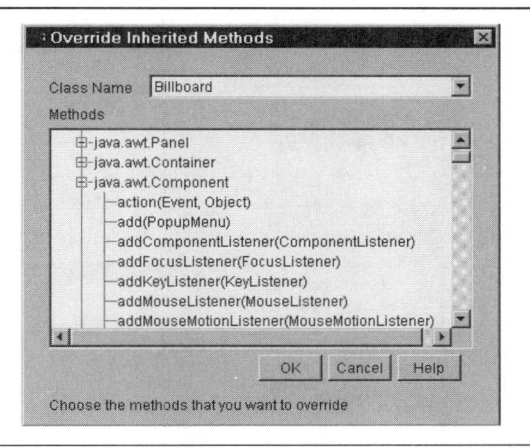

FIGURE 4.3: Component Inherited Methods list, where you select the framework of the method

> **WARNING** When using the Override Inherited Methods list, it would be great if you could type a letter and let the list jump to that listing or search for a method if you don't know exactly which class it belongs to. Unfortunately, neither of those options is available yet. Hopefully this feature will be in a subsequent release.

After selecting the OK button, the following appears within your source code:

```
public void paint(Graphics parm1) {
  //TODO: override this java.awt.Component    method;
  super.paint( parm1);
}
```

> **TIP** JBuilder adds reminders to Wizard generated code where it thinks you should add something. These are flagged with comments that begin with //TODO.

To find where this code was inserted, select the `paint(Graphics)` entry in the Structure pane of JBuilder, as shown in Figure 4.4. Once selected, the Content Pane jumps to the proper area of the source.

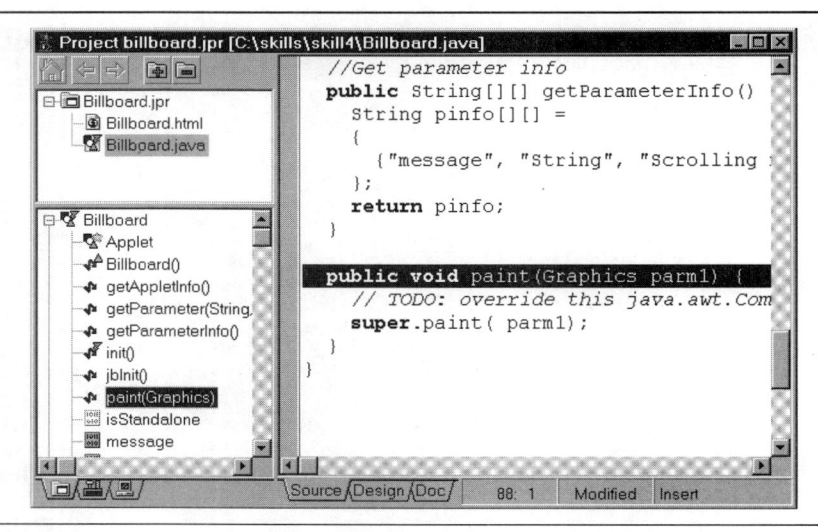

FIGURE 4.4: JBuilder Project window; by selecting an entry in the Structure pane, you can quickly access that area of the source code in the Content pane.

> **NOTE** Because the `paint` method has only one parameter, the Wizard names it `parm1`. If there were a second parameter, it would be called `parm2`. Additional parameters would be numbered accordingly.

Admittedly, for this method it would have been easier to just type out the framework. However, if you don't remember the exact parameter list for a method, you can avoid looking it up by using the Wizard. The Wizard also maintains the proper access keywords of the methods—`public`, `protected`, or `private`. You can change the method to be less protected, but if you try to make a method more protected (like making the `paint` method `private`) the compiler will complain.

Now that we have the framework, let's add the call to `drawString` to display the `message` variable. As mentioned in the previous skill, the second and third parameters are the coordinates of where to display the first. After adding the call, remember to delete the TODO comment that the Wizard added. The `paint` method should now look like the following:

```
public void paint(Graphics parm1) {
  super.paint( parm1);
  parm1.drawString (message, 20, 20);
}
```

> **TIP** If you don't like the parameter names that the Override Methods Wizard provides, you can change them to something more meaningful, by manually replacing every reference to the original name within the method with a new name.

If you save everything (File ➤ Save All), you can build and run the applet to see how things look so far. This will result in an applet that looks identical to the `Applet1` applet in Skill 2.

Understanding the Applet Life-Cycle Methods

Before we jump into sound and multithreading to set up our billboard message to scroll, we need to take a look at the life-cycle methods of an applet. The *life-cycle methods* are methods that you do not call directly—the browser calls them for you. There are four methods in the family: `init`, `start`, `stop`, and `destroy`.

> **init()** The `init` method of an applet is called once when the applet is created. For tasks that need to be done once, like loading support files, this method provides a good place to add such code. Frequently, you will load image and audio files or initialize the screen here.
>
> **start()** The `start` method is called every time the applet is visited by the user. When an applet is first loaded, the browser will call `start` after `init`. If the user leaves the applet's page to visit another Web site, the `start` method will be called again when the user returns. If the browser is *iconified*, when it is *deiconified*, the browser will call the `start` method again. To iconify a program is to minimize it to appear on the Windows Taskbar; to deiconify is to restore it to its original size. When a program needs additional threads—such as for animation—the threads are frequently started within the `start` method.

> **TIP** A *thread* is a section of code that executes independently of other sections. To maintain high interactive performance with the user, lengthy tasks are executed in separate threads. Imagine trying to drive a car and read the newspaper. Trying to do these tasks at the same time is a risky proposition. However, if there were two of you, each working in a separate thread, the tasks could easily be done simultaneously.

stop()   The `stop` method of an applet is called whenever the user leaves the Web page that contains the applet. If the user follows a link, iconifies the browser, or exits the browser, the `stop` method of the applet will be called. The `stop` method is a good place to halt the playing of sound files and the running of any extra threads the program needs. When a user isn't viewing a Web page, its applets should not be using resources.

destroy()   The `destroy` method is called when the browser removes the applet from its memory. This method could be called before the user exits the browser or if the browser needs to clear out some memory space. It is not a good idea to wait until the browser needs to clear out memory to free up resources. The system needs to use this method for certain tasks. However, you normally will not.

Adding Sound

To demonstrate when the different methods are called, we are going to have our `Billboard` play a sound whenever one of them is called. The methods for manipulating sound files are part of the `AudioClip` interface.

play()   You call the `play` method to play an audio file once.

loop()   You call the `loop` method to play an audio file in a continuous loop.

stop()   You call the `stop` method when you want to stop playing an audio file.

> **WARNING**   Java only supports the playing of .au audio files. If you want to play a .wav file, you need to convert it with a tool like SoX (Sound eXchange), available at http://www.spies.com/Sox/.

You get an `AudioClip` to play from the aptly named `Applet.getAudioClip()` method. There are two versions of the `getAudioClip` method:

getAudioClip (URL url)   To load a file from an absolute URL, use the `getAudioClip (URL url)` version of the method. The URL would be of the form `http://www.xxx.yyy.zzz/audiofile.au`.

TIP An *absolute Uniform Resource Locator* (URL) is one that contains the fully qualified location of a file, in this case an audio file.

getAudioClip(URL url, String filename) Instead of providing an absolute URL, you can place the sound files in the same directory as the applet and provide the applet's URL as a relative location to work from. Applets actually provide two URLs to work from, depending on your preferences. Using either of these URLs as the first parameter allows you to specify the sound filename as the second.

- `Applet.getDocumentBase()` provides the URL for the `.html` file that loaded the applet.
- `Applet.getCodeBase()` provides the URL for the `.class` file of the applet.

Because there are four applet life-cycle methods, we need four different audio files to play a different sound for each of them. If we place the files in the same directory as our `Billboard.html` file, we can use `getDocumentBase` to help load the files and demonstrate when the life-cycle methods are actually called.

For this applet, we'll use some sound files from the samples that come with JBuilder. From the command line, copy the audio files to the appropriate location with the following commands:

```
copy \JBuilder\samples\java\demo\Animator\audio\1.au \skills\skill4
copy \JBuilder\samples\java\demo\Animator\audio\spacemusic.au \skills\skill4
copy \JBuilder\samples\java\demo\Animator\audio\3.au \skills\skill4
copy \JBuilder\samples\java\demo\Animator\audio\4.au \skills\skill4
```

NOTE Many sound files can be acquired off the Internet. The Sound Ring at http://www.nidlink.com/~ruger/ring.html is a set of Web sites that contain audio files and provides a good starting point, if you happen to not like the available ones.

To load these files, let's make a few changes to our `Billboard`. At the top of our class definition we need to define four variables of type `AudioClip` to hold references to our sound files:

```
AudioClip one, two, three, four;
```

Because we only want the sound files loaded once, we load the four files in our `init` method. In addition, we want to play one in `init`, so we `play` one there, too. JBuilder provides a basic `init` method already for its needs, so we can add the loading and playing to the end of the existing method. The new code is in the bold font.

```
//Initialize the applet
  public void init() {
    try { message = this.getParameter("message", "Welcome");
        } catch(Exception e) { e.printStackTrace(); };
    try { jbInit();
        } catch(Exception e) { e.printStackTrace(); };
    // Load four audio files
    one   = getAudioClip (getDocumentBase(), "1.au");
    two   = getAudioClip (getDocumentBase(), "spacemusic.au");
    three = getAudioClip (getDocumentBase(), "3.au");
    four  = getAudioClip (getDocumentBase(), "4.au");
    // Play the first file
    if (one != null)
      one.play();
  }
```

> **TIP** Before calling any `AudioClip` method, it is good practice to check if the `AudioClip` reference is `null`. The `getAudioClip` method returns `null` if it fails to load the file.

For the other three life-cycle methods, we just need to play a file. Because we selected the Generate Standard Methods option in the Applet Wizard, the framework for the `start`, `stop`, and `destroy` methods are generated for us. To be a little different, the sound played in the `start` method is looped via the `loop` method. Then, the applet's `stop` method needs to stop that sound with the `stop` method of `AudioClip`, in addition to playing its own. The `destroy` method just needs to play the sound file.

```
//Start the applet
  public void start() {
    if (two != null)
      two.loop();
  }

//Stop the applet
  public void stop() {
    if (two != null)
      two.stop();
    if (three != null)
      three.play();
  }
```

```
//Destroy the applet
public void destroy() {
  if (four != null)
    four.play();
}
```

We can now save our work and try things out. As Figure 4.5 shows, the Applet Viewer tool that JBuilder uses has a few menu options to help us out. If you listen carefully, you can hear when each sound is played. You will quickly notice that Java doesn't wait for one sound to stop playing before starting another.

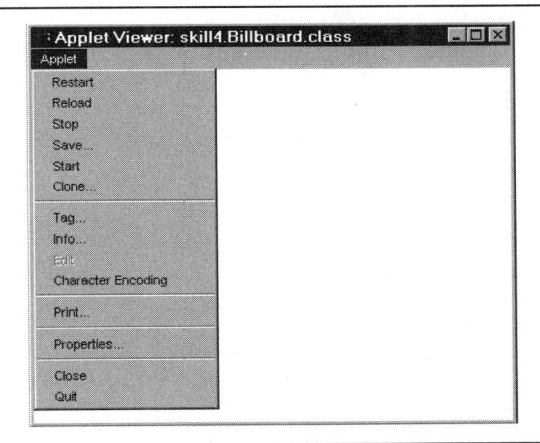

FIGURE 4.5: Applet Viewer menu where you can try out the sounds

When the applet first starts, you will hear the `init` sound and the continuous playing of the sound from `start`. Going through the menu options in Applet Viewer, the options have the following behaviors:

Restart `stop, destroy, init, start`

Reload `stop, destroy, reload .class, init, start`

Stop `stop`, if currently started

Start `start`, if currently stopped

Clone creates copy and calls `init` and `start`

Close/Quit `stop` and `destroy`

The `destroy` sound needs to be very short because the system is shutting down—it may not wait for the sound to finish playing.

Introducing Multithreading

Now that we know about the different life-cycle methods that Java applets use, we can create programs that use multiple threads to do more than one thing at once. Actually, there are many threads running in your Java program already. Most just happen to be system threads, doing their work behind the scenes, as opposed to the user threads that you control.

When programming in Java, it is necessary to get comfortable with having the system do multiple things at once. This requires special precautions so that your program doesn't step on and corrupt itself. We'll go into more depth on this point in Skills 15 and 21, but for now we'll just cover the basics to get our message scrolling.

Java has a `Thread` class to support multithreaded programming. You can create lots of threads to go off on their own to do lots of different things. In the movie *Multiplicity*, Michael Keaton's character was too busy to do everything he wanted to do, so he created copies of himself to go off and do other things, while he kept chugging along doing the task at hand. In the end, he gets more work done because the work is done simultaneously.

With Java, it works pretty much the same way: You create an instance of `Thread`, and it goes off on its own to run whatever you tell it to run. You provide what you want it to execute in a `run` method, and pass this along to the `Thread`'s constructor.

The `Thread` constructor has a parameter of type `Runnable`. As stated above, the `Runnable` interface consists of one method called `run`. Therefore, your class definition needs to `implement` the `Runnable` interface and you need to provide a `run` method in your class. The necessary framework appears here:

```
public class foo implements Runnable {
   …
   public void run() { … }
   …
   public void anyMethod () {
      Thread t = new Thread (this);
      …
   }
}
```

Defining the Thread Using the Implement Interface Wizard

Because `Runnable` is an interface, we can use the Implement Interface Wizard in JBuilder. This allows us to pick the interface name from a list, and the Wizard adds the method framework within our source file—we just have to fill in the logic. This Wizard is really helpful when an interface defines multiple methods; you won't have to type out each by hand. Selecting the Wizards ➤ Implement Interface menu brings up the screen shown in Figure 4.6.

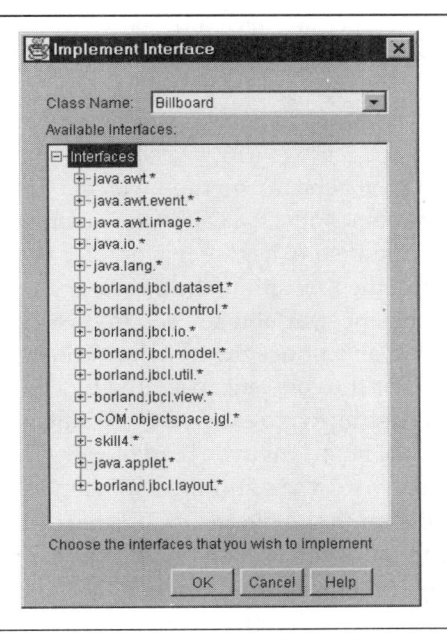

FIGURE 4.6: The Implement Interface dialog box

Here we have to locate the Runnable interface, which happens to be under java.lang.*. Selecting the + next to it reveals the entries. Select java.lang.Runnable and then OK. From there, JBuilder inserts the framework of the run method into your source and adds 'implements Runnable' to the end of your class declaration. Just providing a run method within your class definition does not automatically make the class implement the interface. In order for the compiler to properly ensure implementation, the 'implements Runnable' keywords are necessary.

Because we are creating a scrolling billboard, our thread will make the message scroll. Our run method becomes a continually executing while loop that moves the horizontal drawing position. The following code illustrates how to do this.

```
public void run() {
    while (true) {
        repaint();
```

```
        synchronized (this) {
          xpos ++;
          if (xpos >= getSize().width)
            xpos = 0;
        }
        try {
          Thread.currentThread().sleep(200);
        } catch (InterruptedException e) {
        }
      }
    }
```

Calling the `repaint` method tells the program it's time to update the screen, and it eventually results in a call to the `paint` method. After painting the screen, we need to update the display position for the next time through. Because we are increasing the x-position, the message scrolls from left to right. We also need to add an instance variable to keep track of the horizontal drawing position.

You will also notice the new Java construct, the *synchronized block*. What does this do? For the code encapsulated by the synchronized block, only one thread at a time is permitted to execute those statements. Java handles that synchronization for you with the `synchronized` block.

The keyword `this` should also be mentioned here; it is a reference to the object the method belongs to. It is basically a reference to the object. By combining `synchronized` and `this`, you're saying to use this object as the access lock. The object then ensures only one thread gets through at a time. Any object can be the lock of a `synchronized` block to serve as the gatekeeper. Also, the same object can guard multiple blocks, possibly ensuring all access is synchronized.

The `Thread.sleep` call in `run` slows down our animation so it moves approximately every 200 milliseconds. The `sleep` method has the potential to throw an `InterruptedException`, so we need to put the `sleep` call within a `try/catch` block. Basically, if something unexpected happens during the `sleep`, we will be notified by an exception. For now, we just ignore the exception.

> **NOTE** Threads could be interrupted through a handful of Thread methods, such as interrupt.

To ensure that the `paint` method doesn't try to write beyond the end of the screen, we need to control access to the `xpos` variable. Using the `synchronized (this){}` block within `run` above, and updating the `paint` routine to use a similar code fragment ensures that neither accesses the variable at the same time.

```
private int xpos=0;
public void paint(Graphics parm1) {
  super.paint( parm1);
  synchronized (this) {
    parm1.drawString (message, xpos, 20);
  }

}
```

SOME THOUGHTS ON EXECUTING SIMULTANEOUS THREADS

When multiple threads are executing simultaneously, the system could stop one thread at any time to work on another. To ensure the system doesn't leave multistep operations partially completed, you should place synchronized blocks around all code that access any shared variables of the threads.

To help demonstrate this, imagine two people depositing $200 simultaneously into the same bank account with an initial balance of $500. The end result should be a balance of $900. However, given the following sequence of events, the result could be $700 if balance access is not controlled properly:

   5:00 Person A Requests Balance
   5:01 Person B Requests Balance
   5:02 Person B Gets Balance of $500
   5:03 Person A Gets Balance of $500
   5:04 Person A Deposits $200
   5:05 Person B Deposits $200
   5:06 Person A Computes New Balance
   5:07 Person B Computes New Balance
   5:08 Person B Updates Balance to $700
   5:09 Person A Updates Balance to $700

Also, keep in mind, operations happen in milliseconds on a computer system, instead of seconds or minutes.

Well, we've done the hard part: we've defined the work of the `Thread`— however, we haven't created it yet. It's time to go back to the life-cycle methods.

Creating the Thread

We could create the thread in the `init` method and let it go on forever. However, this isn't ideal because the thread would continue to run when the user is no longer looking at the billboard. (Imagine someone looking at the front of a billboard while you are updating the back. You keep working but nobody sees your results.) Therefore, we should create the thread in the `start` method and kill it off in `stop`. This way, it will not be running after the user leaves and will be recreated when the user comes back.

Here we define another instance variable; this time called `mover`, of type `Thread`. It becomes our worker thread:

```
private Thread mover;
```

To properly initiate and terminate it, we modify `start` and `stop` a little.

```
//Start the applet
  public void start() {
    if (two != null)
      two.loop();
    mover = new Thread (this);
    mover.start();
  }

  //Stop the applet
  public void stop() {
    if (two != null)
      two.stop();
    if (three != null)
      three.play();
    if (mover != null)
      mover.stop();
  }
```

In `start`, we passed the `Thread` constructor a class that implements the `Runnable` interface. It happens to be the `Billboard` class itself—`this`—but it could be anything. After the thread is created, the `mover.start()` statement causes the `run` method of the constructor's argument to be called.

In `stop`, we added code to stop the movement thread, `mover`. If you forget to stop the thread, the thread continues to run and uses resources, even though the user has left the Web page.

And that's all there is to it. We've created an applet that does all of the following:

- Creates threads
- Plays sounds
- Reads parameters
- Scrolls a text message

If you save your work and build it, you can see what you've done when you run it. Just as you did when playing the sound file, you can start and stop your program with the menu choices. Notice that if you restart it, the message continues to scroll from where it left off. However, if you reload it, it starts back at the left margin. There you have it! The complete source follows in `Billboard.java`.

Billboard.java

```java
package skill4;

import java.awt.*;
import java.awt.event.*;
import java.applet.*;
import borland.jbcl.control.*;
import borland.jbcl.layout.*;

public class Billboard extends Applet implements Runnable {
  XYLayout xYLayout1 = new XYLayout();
  boolean isStandalone = false;
  String message;
  AudioClip one, two, three, four;
  int xpos = 0;
  Thread mover;

  //Get a parameter value
  public String getParameter(String key, String def) {
    return isStandalone ? System.getProperty(key, def) :
      (getParameter(key) != null ? getParameter(key) : def);
  }

  //Construct the applet
  public Billboard() {
  }
```

```java
//Initialize the applet
public void init() {
  try { message = this.getParameter("message", "Welcome"); }
    catch(Exception e) { e.printStackTrace(); };
  try { jbInit(); } catch(Exception e) { e.printStackTrace(); };
  // Load four audio files
  one   = getAudioClip (getDocumentBase(), "1.au");
  two   = getAudioClip (getDocumentBase(), "spacemusic.au");
  three = getAudioClip (getDocumentBase(), "3.au");
  four  = getAudioClip (getDocumentBase(), "4.au");
  // Play the first file
  if (one != null)
    one.play();
}

//Component initialization
public void jbInit() throws Exception{
  xYLayout1.setWidth(400);
  xYLayout1.setHeight(300);
  this.setLayout(xYLayout1);
}

//Start the applet
public void start() {
  if (two != null)
    two.loop();
  mover = new Thread (this);
  mover.start();
}

//Stop the applet
public void stop() {
  if (two != null)
    two.stop();
  if (three != null)
    three.play();
  if (mover != null)
    mover.stop();
}

//Destroy the applet
public void destroy() {
  if (four != null)
    four.play();
}
```

```java
//Get Applet information
public String getAppletInfo() {
  return "Applet Information";
}

//Get parameter info
public String[][] getParameterInfo() {
  String pinfo[][] =
  {
    {"message", "String", "Scrolling message"},
  };
  return pinfo;
}

public void paint(Graphics parm1) {
  super.paint( parm1);
  synchronized (this) {
    parm1.drawString (message, xpos, 20);
  }
}

public void run() {
  while (true) {
    repaint();
    synchronized (this) {
      xpos ++;
      if (xpos >= getSize().width)
        xpos = 0;
    }
    try {
      Thread.currentThread().sleep(200);
    } catch (InterruptedException e) {
    }
  }
}
```

In Skill 5, we'll learn how to do even more with Java. We'll start to learn about the various GUI controls available through the Abstract Window Toolkit (AWT) package, and we'll use them to create interactive programs.

Are You Experienced?

Now you can...

- ☑ use the Override Methods Wizard
- ☑ describe the applet life-cycle methods
- ☑ load audio files
- ☑ play audio files
- ☑ use multithreading within your Java programs
- ☑ define and create threads using the Implement Interface Wizard

PROGRAMMERS
C, C, VB, Cobol, exp. Call 534-555-6543 or fax 534-555-6544.

PROGRAMMING
MRFS Inc. is looking for a Sr. Windows NT developer. Reqs. 3-5 yrs. Exp. In C under Windows, Win95 & NT, using Visual C. Excl. OO design & implementation skills a must. OLE2 & ODBC are a plus. Excl. Salary & bnfts. Resume & salary history to HR, 8779 HighTech Way, Computer City, AR

PROGRAMMERS
Contractors Wanted for short & long term assignments: Visual C, MFC Unix C/C, SQL Oracle Dev elop ers PC Help Desk Support Windows NT & NetWare Telecommunications Visual Basic, Access, HTML, CGI, Perl MMI & Co.. 885-555-9933

PROGRAMMER World Wide Web Links wants your HTML & Photoshop skills. Develop great WWW sites. Local & global customers. Send samples & resume to WWWL, 2000 Apple Road, Santa Rosa, CA.

TECHNICAL WRITER Software firm seeks writer/editor for manuals, research notes, project mgmt. Min 2 years tech. writing, DTP & programming experience. Send resume & writing samples to: Software Systems, Dallas, TX.

TECHNICAL Software development firm looking for Tech Trainers. Ideal candidates have programming experience in Visual C, HTML & JAVA. Need quick self starter. Call (443) 555-6868 for interview.

TECHNICAL WRITER / Premier Computer Corp is seeking a combination of technical skills, knowledge and experience in the following areas: UNIX, Windows 95/NT, Visual Basic, on-line help & documentation, and the internet. Candidates must possess excellent writing skills, and be comfortable working in a quality vs. deadline driven environment. Competitive salary. Fax resume & samples to Karen Fields, Premier Computer Corp. 444 Industrial Blvd. Concord, CA. Or send to our website at www.premier.com.

WEB DESIGNER
BA/BS or equivalent programming/multimedia production. 3 years of experience in use and design of WWW services streaming audio and video HTML, PERL, CGI, GIF, JPEG. Demonstrated Interpersonal, organization, communication, multi-tasking skills. Send resume to The Learning People at www.learning.com.

WEBMASTER-TECHNICAL
BSCS or equivalent, 2 years of experience in CGI, Windows 95/NT, UNIX, C, Java, Perl. Demonstrated ability to design, code, debug and test on-line services. Send resume to The Learning People at www.learning.com.

PROGRAMMER World Wide Web Links wants your HTML & Photoshop skills. Develop great WWW sites. Local & global customers. Send sam ples...

...tation preparation & programming languages (Access, C, FoxPro) are a plus. Financial or banking customer service support is required along with excellent verbal & written communication skills with multi levels of end-users. Send resume to KKUP Enterprises, 45 Orange Blvd. Orange, CA.

COMPUTERS Small Web Design firm seeks indiv. w/NT, Webserver & Database management exp. Fax resume to 556-555-4221.

COMPUTER/ Visual C/C, Visual Basic Exp'd Systems Analysts/ Programmers for growing software dev. team in Roseburg. Computer Science or related degree preferred. Develop adv. Engineering applications for engineering firm. Fax resume to 707-555-8744

COMPUTER Web Master for dynamic SF Internet co. Site. Dev. test, coord., train. 2 yrs prog. Exp. C C Web C. FTP. Fax resume to Best Staffing 845-555-7722.

COMPUTER PROGRAMMER
Ad agency seeks programmer w/exp. in UNIX/NT Platforms, Web Server, CGI/Perl. Programmer Position avail. on a project basis with the possibility to move into F/T. Fax resume & salary req. to R. Jones 334-555-8332.

COMPUTERS Programmer/Analyst Design and maintain C based SQL database applications. Required skills: Visual Basic, C, SQL, ODBC. Document existing and new applications. Novell or NT exp. a plus. Fax resume & salary history to 235-555-9935.

GRAPHIC DESIGNER
Webmaster's Weekly is seeking a creative Graphic Designer to design high impact marketing collater al, including direct mail promois, CD-ROM packages, ads and WWW pages. Must be able to juggle multiple projects and learn new skills on the job very rapidly. Web design experience a big plus, technical troubleshooting also a plus. Call 435-555-1235.

GRAPHICS - ART DIRECTOR - WEB-MULTIMEDIA
Leading internet development company has an outstanding opportunity for a talented, high-end Web Experienced Art Director. In addition to a great portfolio and fresh ideas, the ideal candidate has excellent communication and presentation skills. Working as a team with innovative producers and programmers, you will create dynamic, interactive web sites and application interfaces. Some programming experience required. Send samples and resume to: SuperSites, 333 Main, Seattle, WA.

WEBMASTER-TECHNICAL
BSCS or equivalent, 2 years of experience in CGI, Windows 95/NT,

---

PROGRAMMERS Multiple short term assignments available: Visual C, 3 positions SQL ServerNT Server, 2 positions JAVA & HTML, long term NetWare. Various locations. Call for more info. 356-555-3398.

PROGRAMMERS
C, C, VB, Cobol, exp.
Call 534-555-6543
or fax 534-555-6544.

PROGRAMMING
MRFS Inc. is looking for a Sr. Windows NT developer. Reqs. 3-5 yrs. Exp. In C under Windows, Win95 & NT, using Visual C. Excl. OO design & implementation skills a must. OLE2 & ODBC are a plus. Excl. Salary & salary history to 8779 HighTech Way, Computer City, AR

PROGRAMMERS/ Contractors Wanted for short & long term assignments: Visual C, MFC Unix C/C, SQL Oracle Developers PC Help Desk Support Windows NT & NetWareTelecommunications Visual Basic, Access, HTML, CGI, Perl MMI & Co.. 885-555-9933

PROGRAMMER World Wide Web Links wants your HTML & Photoshop skills. Develop great WWW sites. Local & global customers. Send samples & resume to WWWL, 2000 Apple Road, Santa Rosa, CA.

TECHNICAL WRITER Software firm seeks writer/editor for manuals, research notes, project mgmt. Min 2 years tech. writing, DTP & programming experience. Send resume & writing samples to: Software Systems, Dallas, TX.

COMPUTER PROGRAMMER
Ad agency seeks programmer w/exp. in UNIX/NT Platforms, Web Server, CGI/Perl. Programmer Position avail. on a project basis with the possibility to move into F/T. Fax resume & salary req. to R. Jones 334-555-8332

TECHNICAL WRITER Premier Computer Corp is seeking a combination of technical skills, knowledge and experience in the following areas: UNIX, Windows 95/NT, Visual Basic, on-line help & documentation, and the internet. Candidates must possess excellent writing skills, and be comfortable working in a quality vs. deadline driven environment. Competitive salary. Fax resume & samples to Karen Fields, Premier Computer Corp. 444 Industrial Blvd. Concord, CA. Or send to our website at www.premier.com.

WEB DESIGNER
BA/BS or equivalent programming/multimedia production. 3 years of experience in use and design of WWW services streaming audio and video HTML, PERL, CGI, GIF, JPEG. Demonstrated Interpersonal, organization, communication, multi-tasking skills. Send resume to The Learning People at www.learning.com.

WEBMASTER-TECHNICAL
BSCS or equivalent, 2 years of experience in CGI, Windows 95/NT,

---

COMPUTERS Small Web Design Firm seeks indiv. w/NT, Webserver & Database management exp. Fax resume to 556-555-4221.

COMPUTER Visual C/C, Visual Basic Exp'd Systems Analysts/ Programmers for growing software dev. team in Roseburg. Computer Science or related degree preferred. Develop adv. Engineering applications for engineering firm. Fax resume to 707-555-8744.

COMPUTER Web Master for dynamic SF Internet co. Site. Dev. test, coord., train. 2 yrs prog. Exp. C C Web C. FTP. Fax resume to Best Staffing 845-555-7722.

COMPUTERS/ QA SOFTWARE TESTERS Qualified candidates should have 2 yrs exp. performing integration & system testing using automated testing tools. Experienced in documentation preparation & programming languages (Access, C, FoxPro) are a plus. Financial or banking customer service support is required along with excellent verbal & written communication skills with multi levels of end-users. Send resume to KKUP Enterprises, 45 Orange Blvd. Orange, CA.

COMPUTERS Programmer/Analyst Design and maintain C based SQL database applications. Required skills: Visual Basic, C, SQL, ODBC. Document existing and new applications. Novell or NT exp. a plus. Fax resume & salary history to 235-555-9935.

GRAPHIC DESIGNER
Webmaster's Weekly is seeking a creative Graphic Designer to design high impact marketing collater al, including direct mail promo's, CD-ROM packages, ads and WWW pages. Must be able to juggle multiple projects and learn new skills on the job very rapidly. Web design experience a big plus, technical troubleshooting also a plus. Call 435-555-1235.

GRAPHICS - ART DIRECTOR - WEB-MULTIMEDIA
Leading internet development company has an outstanding opportunity for a talented, high-end Web Experienced Art Director. In addition to a great portfolio and fresh ideas, the ideal candidate has excellent communication and presentation skills. Working as a team with innovative producers and programmers, you will create dynamic, interactive web sites and application interfaces. Some programming experience required. Send samples and resume to: SuperSites, 333 Main, Seattle, WA.

COMPUTER PROGRAMMER
Ad agency seeks programmer w/exp. in UNIX/NT Platforms, Web Server, CGI/Perl. Programmer Position avail. on a project basis with the possibility to move into F/T. Fax resume & salary req. to R. Jones 334-555-8332

PROGRAMMERS / Established software company seeks program-

PROGRAMMERS Multiple term assignments available: Visual C, 3 positions SQL ServerNT Server, 2 positions JAVA & HTML, long term NetWare. Various locations. Call more info. 356-555-3398.

PROGRAMMERS
C, C, VB, Cobol, exp. Call 534-555-6543 or fax 534-555-6544.

PROGRAMMING
MRFS Inc. is looking for a Sr. Windows NT developer. Reqs. yrs. Exp. In C under Windows, Win95 & NT, using Visual C. OO design & implementation a must. OLE2 & ODBC are a Excl. Salary & bnfts. Resume salary history to HR, 8779 HighTech Way, Computer City, AR

PROGRAMMERS/ Contract Wanted for short & long term assignments: Visual C, MFCUnix C/C, Oracle Developers PC Help Support Windows NT & NetW Telecommunications Visual B Access, HTML, CGI, Perl MMI & 885-555-9933

PROGRAMMER World Wide W Links wants your HTML & Photoshop skills. Develop great WWW s Local & global customers. Send s ples & resume to WWWL, 2 Apple Road, Santa Rosa, CA.

TECHNICAL WRITER Software seeks writer/editor for manu research notes, project mgmt. years tech. writing, DTP & progra ming experience. Send resume writing samples to: Softwa Systems, Dallas, TX.

TECHNICAL Software developme firm looking for Tech Trainers. Id candidates have programming ex rience in Visual C, HTML & JA Need quick self starter. Call (4 555-6868 for interview.

TECHNICAL WRITER Prem Computer Corp is seeking a con nation of technical skills, knowled and experience in the follow areas: UNIX, Windows 95/NT, Vi Basic, on-line help & documentati and the internet. Candidates m possess excellent writing skills, be comfortable working in a qu vs. deadline driven environme Competitive salary. Fax resume samples to Karen Fields, Prem Computer Corp. 444 Industrial Bl Concord, CA. Or send to our web at www.premier.com.

WEB DESIGNER
BA/BS or equivalent progra ming/multimedia production. years of experience in use a design of WWW services stream audio and video HTML, PERL, GIF, JPEG. Demonstrated interpe sonal, organization, communicati multi-tasking skills. Send resum The Learning People at www.learn ing.com.

WEBMASTER-TECHNICA

SKILL 5

five

Exploring AWT

- ❑ Learning to use the Abstract Window Toolkit
- ❑ Adding labels, text fields, and buttons to your program
- ❑ Handling action and keyboard events
- ❑ Creating a Hi-Lo guessing game

Introducing the Abstract Window Toolkit

One of the Java packages you'll recognize from previous skills is the Abstract Window Toolkit, or AWT for short. AWT provides Java with a set of simple *Graphical User Interface* (GUI) objects to work with. The Java term for these objects is *component*, because each is a subclass of the Java `Component` class. However, if you come from another environment, you may call these *controls, widgets,* or *gadgets.*

Three of these components are `Label`, `TextField`, and `Button`. In this skill, we'll use these components to create a Hi-Lo guessing game. You will learn the skills necessary to create and interact with the components, and finally, you'll be introduced to data conversion.

The remaining AWT components, `Checkbox`, `Choice`, `List`, `Canvas`, `Scrollbar`, and `TextArea`, behave similarly. Most of these will be covered in later skills, when we use the drag-and-drop GUI builder.

Adding Components to Your Program

Java's Abstract Window Toolkit (AWT) is a rich set of simple components. In addition, JBuilder provides a richer component palette with its Java Beans Component Library (JBCL). All components within the two libraries are subclasses of the Java class `Component`. The `Component` class defines the behavior and characteristics of all the other components. Methods to modify the component's display are shared by all components and appear in Table 5.1. There are actually more than 100 methods of `Component`. Most of the remaining methods will be introduced throughout the other skills; one of the methods, `paint`, has already been explored. The key thing to remember here is that every component shares this set of methods because every graphical component subclasses `Component`.

TABLE 5.1: Common Component Behavior

Method	Behavior
setBackground (Color c)	Set the background color
getBackground ()	Get the background color
setForeground (Color c)	Set the foreground color
getForeground ()	Get the foreground color
setFont (Font f)	Set the font
getFont ()	Get the font

> **WARNING** Not to confuse matters, but menu components are the exception. Although they are graphical components, they do not subclass Component. Instead, they subclass MenuComponent, which serves as the base of all menu objects.

Now that we know what a component is, we can use some to create the screen for a Hi-Lo game. The Hi-Lo game is a number guessing game. The computer picks a number between 1 and 100, and you have to guess the number with the help of clues provided by the computer. The clues tell you if the number is higher or lower. Figure 5.1 provides a general outline of what the layout for the game will look like. If you like the game, as you learn more about the Java's graphics features, you can make the screen much snazzier without affecting the game logic.

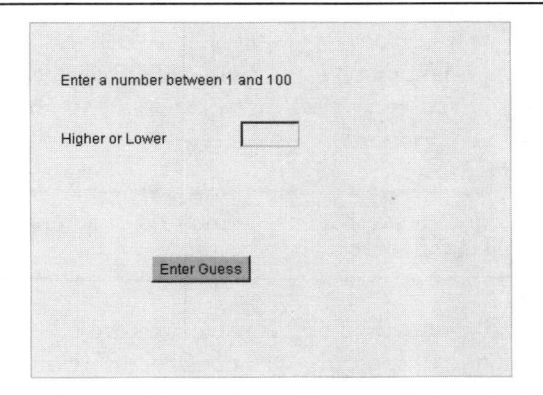

FIGURE 5.1: Hi-Lo game screen layout

Using Labels

The first component we'll look at is Label. The Label component provides a Component to display a single line of text. As Figure 5.2 demonstrates, you can change various display characteristics of labels.

FIGURE 5.2: Sample labels

Labels are used to display static or fixed text, frequently next to an input field. In our Hi-Lo game, we will need two labels, one for instructions/status and another next to the input field. When you need to create a new object, you use one of the object's *constructors* to create it. There are three constructors for the Label component.

> **NOTE** A constructor is a special method of an object that creates an instance of that object.

Unlike a method call, constructors are called through the new keyword. The following list describes the constructor's for Label.

```
// To create a Label with no text in it.
Label noText = new Label ();
// To create a Label with "Message" as its text.
Label aMessage = new Label ("Message");
// To create the same Label, aligned to the right.
// Use Label.LEFT for left aligned, the default
// Use Label.CENTER for center alignment
Label aligned = new Label ("Message", Label.RIGHT);
```

Before we can create the labels, we need to start up a new project for this skill. Go ahead and close anything that is open and create a new project through the Applet Wizard. In the Project Wizard, enter **C:\skills\skill5\skill5.jpr** and select Finish. Then, the only field that needs to be entered in the Applet Wizard is the class name. Change the default **Applet1** name to **HiLo** and select the Finish button.

Once the Wizard has completed this task, select the HiLo.java entry in the Navigation pane. Once you select the Content pane, you can update the source and declare two variables of type `Label`. These should be declared at the class level (underneath `isStandAlone`) because multiple methods will need to access them.

```
Label label1;
Label label2;
```

Now you need to initialize them. If you were not using JBuilder, you would initialize them in the `init` method. However, JBuilder keeps component initialization centralized within its `jbInit` routine, which is called by the `init` method. Within `jbInit`, initialize the first variable to be the instructions "Enter a number between 1 and 100" and the second to be "Higher or Lower".

```
label1 = new Label ("Enter a number between 1 and 100");
label2 = new Label ("Higher or Lower");
```

Instead of specifying the label's text in the constructor, however, you can do the same operation in two steps, as shown here:

```
label1 = new Label();
label1.setText ("Enter a number between 1 and 100");
```

This doesn't do anything special that the initial way doesn't. However, it does show that you can change the label's text at any time. There is even a `getText` method to see what the current text is, in case you need to check the value.

After creating the labels, you need to add the objects to the screen, so the user can see them. This is done with the help of the `add` method. Before we talk about `add`, let's discuss the `XYLayout` class the Wizard generated for the `jbInit` method.

```
public void jbInit() throws Exception{
  xYLayout1.setWidth(400);
  xYLayout1.setHeight(300);
  this.setLayout(xYLayout1);
  label1 = new Label();
  label1.setText ("Enter a number between 1 and 100");
}
```

The `XYLayout` class is a type of `LayoutManager`. The available layout managers are discussed in more detail in the next skill. However, let's go over the basics for what we are about to do next. The `LayoutManager` controls the display of components on the screen. Because Java programs are meant to work across multiple platforms and are not specific to one platform, you normally do not position objects at specific coordinates. What may look perfectly fine on one platform, in terms of size and placement, could look awful on another. This positioning is the responsibility of the `LayoutManager`.

The XYLayout is primarily a temporary layout manager. It relies on you, the developer, to provide absolute coordinates and sizes for components when they are added. It is meant to serve as the LayoutManager only during the design phase, so you don't have to worry about the details of positioning until it is important. This is how the drag-and-drop GUI builder works.

The coordinates and size for a component are specified through the class XYConstraints and passed as the second parameter to add. The component being added is the first parameter. The constraints are the second. Constraints define information specific for the layout of the component being added. In the case of the XYLayout layout manager, these constraints are specified through the XYConstraints class.

The constructor for XYConstraints takes four parameters: x position, y position, width, and height. In order to add the label1 component at position (25, 25) with a width of 300 and a height of 50, the following is added to HiLo.java in the jbInit method:

```
XYConstraints xy1 = new XYConstraints (25, 25, 300, 50);
add (label1, xy1);
```

Similar code is needed to add the label2 component at position (25,75) with width of 150 and a height of 50:

```
XYConstraints xy2 = new XYConstraints (25, 75, 150, 50);
add (label2, xy2);
```

> **NOTE** Unlike the drawString method used in Skill 4, the coordinates specified here are for the top-left corner, not the baseline. Using all four values provides a bounding box around the component.

The complete jbInit routine follows. At this point, you can save your work and run the applet to see the screen pictured in Figure 5.3.

```
public void jbInit() throws Exception{
  xYLayout1.setWidth(400);
  xYLayout1.setHeight(300);
  this.setLayout(xYLayout1);
  label1 = new Label ("Enter a number between 1 and 100");
  label2 = new Label ("Higher or Lower");
  XYConstraints xy1 = new XYConstraints (25, 25, 300, 50);
  add (label1, xy1);
  XYConstraints xy2 = new XYConstraints (25, 75, 150, 50);
  add (label2, xy2);
}
```

```
              Applet Viewer: skill5.HiLo.class
    Applet

              Enter a number between 1 and 100

              Higher or Lower
```

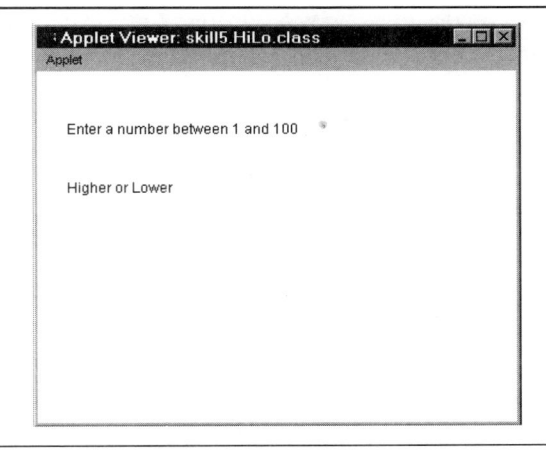

FIGURE 5.3: Hi-Lo game screen with labels

Using Text Fields

The `TextField` component is similar to the `Label` component—both provide for the use of a single line of text. Where the label's text cannot be edited, the text field's primary purpose is for the user to edit its contents.

> **NOTE** You can make a `TextField` read-only if you need to display a non-editable entry, such as a calculated total. The method to do this is `setEditable`, and it takes one parameter. If the parameter is `false`, the `TextField` becomes read-only. To return to the default editable state, use the parameter `true`.

The `TextField` component has four different constructors (shown in the following listing). Like a `Label`, you can specify the initial text within the object. However, you cannot specify an alignment. All text in a `TextField` is left justified. The other setting available to you is how long you want the `TextField` to appear on the screen.

```
// To create a TextField with no text in it.
TextField noText = new TextField ();
// To create a TextField with "Message" as its text.
TextField aMessage = new TextField ("Message");
// To create the same TextField, with a width of 20 normal characters.
TextField wideAndSet = new TextField ("Message", 20);
// To create the same TextField with no text.
TextField wide = new TextField (20);
```

If you do not specify a width in the constructor but you do specify a message to display, the message may not be fully visible. The system uses an average character width, not the actual message width, to determine how wide to make the text field. It follows, then, that you should usually specify the width yourself and pad it with a couple of characters to make sure there is enough space for the message.

> **NOTE** The length specified in the `TextField` constructor does not limit the number of characters that a user can input into the field; it only specifies how wide the object is on the screen.

In addition to the constructors, `TextField` has other routines that may prove helpful, as shown in Table 5.2. We will use the `getText` routine later in this skill, when we need to process the user input.

TABLE 5.2: Selected TextField Methods

Method	Behavior
setEchoChar (char c)	Change the input mask to c (This is helpful for password-entry fields)
setText (String s)	Change the contents to s
getText ()	Get the current contents
getSelectedText()	Get the currently selected text

For our Hi-Lo program, we need to create one `TextField` and place it next to the "Higher or Lower" label. Like the labels, define an instance variable for the `TextField`:

```
TextField textField1;
```

The next step in the `jbInit` routine is to create a `TextField` and add it to the screen. Using the `XYConstraints`, the width you set for the `TextField` determines how many characters wide it is. If you specify a height of -1, you can let the `TextField` use its preferred height. This ensures some portability of the applet. Running the applet will show the text field on the screen, as shown in Figure 5.4.

```
textField1 = new TextField();
XYConstraints xy3 = new XYConstraints(175, 85, 50, -1);
add(textField1, xy3);
```

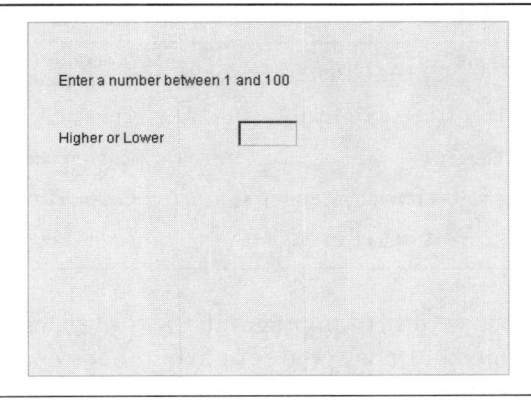

FIGURE 5.4: Hi-Lo game screen layout with text field and labels

Using Buttons

The `Button` is the next component to tackle. In AWT, buttons are used when a user needs to signal the system that they are finished with a certain action or to submit information. Buttons are also limited to a single line of text. For the button, the single line of text represents the label. Around a button are three-dimensional bevels that make the button appear pressed when selected with the mouse. This functionality is automatic, so you do not need to do anything to make a button appear properly to the user.

The `Button` component has only two constructors: one to create a button with a label and one without. Like a `Label` or a `TextField`, you can specify the initial value. The only other option is to specify nothing.

```
// To create a Button with no label.
Button noText = new Button ();
// To create a Button with "Message" as its label.
Button aMessage = new Button ("Message");
```

Like the other components, `Button` has other routines that may prove helpful; these are shown in Table 5.3. The `setActionCommand` and `getActionCommand` routines are useful in international environments. They allow you to associate a command with the button but change the label based upon the user's local environment, or locale. Then, you can identify the selected button by looking at the command, instead of the label.

TABLE 5.3: Selected Button Methods

Method	Behavior
setLabel(String s)	Change the label to s
getLabel()	Get the current label
setActionCommand (String s)	Change the command to s
getActionCommand ()	Get the current command

Back to our Hi-Lo program. User-interface guidelines tend to place action-oriented buttons at the bottom of the screen. Therefore, we need to create a `Button` for the player to signal the entry of a guess, and we need to position it below everything else. Like the other components, we need to define an instance variable for the `Button`:

```
Button button1;
```

Then we'll add it to the screen using the following code, again in the `jbInit` method. If we specify a width and a height of -1, the button will be sized to its preferred width and height. This basically means it will minimize the space around the text. Now our screen should look like Figure 5.5.

```
button1 = new Button("Enter Guess");
XYConstraints xy4 = new XYConstraints(100, 200, -1, -1);
add(button1, xy4);
```

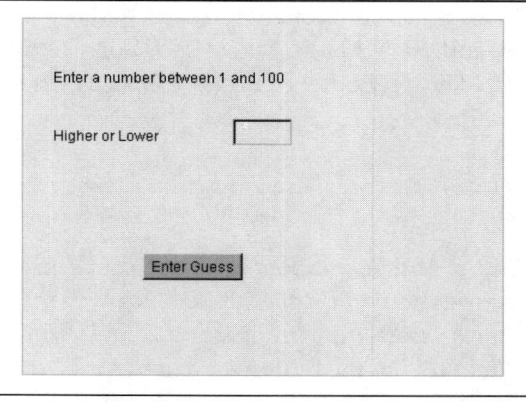

FIGURE 5.5: Hi-Lo game screen with the button, text field, and labels in place

Handling Events

OK, the screen is done, but you might notice we have a slight problem on our hands: when you type something into the text field or press the button, nothing happens. To remedy this, we need to add some code that will compare the user's input with the key number when the button is pressed. If the guess is too high, we'll change the label to "Guess Lower." If the guess is too low, we'll change the label to "Guess Higher." If they guess it correctly, we'll have the system beep and reset the program for the next round's guess.

In addition, we want to make sure the user only enters numerical input into the text field. By doing this, we can be sure that when we convert the text input to a number, there won't be any letters thrown in there.

Before we move on to handling the events though, we need to initialize the value being guessed. This requires an instance variable, `theNum`, to retain the number, `private int theNum;` a method `getNextNumber` to generate the next number to guess; and a call to `getNextNumber` within the `init` method of the applet, `theNum = getNextNumber();`. The source for `getNextNumber` follows:

```
private int getNextNumber () {
  return (int) (Math.random() * 100.0) + 1;
}
```

Handling Action Events

Events in Java are generated by the system when something happens with a component. This something could be almost anything— the user pressing a button, typing, scrolling, or choosing an entry in a list, for example. The component where the event happens is called the *source*. The event source tells anyone interested when the event happens. You just have to tell the component in which operations you are interested.

When the user presses the Enter Guess button, we need to perform an operation. In Java, the operation that deals with this is called an *action event*, signified by the `ActionEvent` class. The system automatically generates an `ActionEvent` when the user presses the button. In order to process the event, you have to tell the button you are interested in when the event happens. The process of doing this is called *listening*, and you use the `Button` class's `addActionListener` method to register this interest.

The `addActionListener` method has one parameter, which is of type `ActionListener`. `ActionListener` is an interface, like the `AudioClip` and `Runnable` interfaces seen in the last skill. Its single method is `actionPerformed`. So, when the button is selected, it calls the `actionPerformed` method of every registered `ActionListener`. This leads us to the conclusion that we need to implement the interface and register an `ActionListener` with the button.

To implement the interface, we'll use the Implement Interface Wizard. The `ActionListener` interface is in the `java.awt.event` package. When you select `java.awt.event.ActionListener` and press the OK button, the following code is added to `HiLo.java`:

```
public class HiLo extends Applet implements ActionListener {
  ...
  public void actionPerformed(ActionEvent parm1) {
    //TODO: implement this   java.awt.event.ActionListener method;
  }
```

If we create a to-do list composed of five simple steps, completing the `actionPerformed` method becomes easy:

1. Get text field value
2. Convert to integer
3. Compare
4. Change label or play beep
5. Register the listener's name

Let's go through these tasks one at a time.

1. You'll recall that we already know how to get the text field value—we use the `getText` method of `TextField`.

2. Because this method returns the contents as a string, you need to convert it to a number. The `Integer.parseInt` method converts strings to integers. If the system determines the string cannot be converted, `NumberFormatException` is thrown and the guess is ignored. Don't forget to put in your `try-catch()` block around the `parseInt` method invocation to deal with the exception.

3. Comparison is easy. Check for equality and if the guess is higher or lower than the number.

4. Once you know the status of the guess, use the setText method of Label to notify the user. Or, to have the system beep when correct, use the routine called beep in the Toolkit class. To obtain a Toolkit object to use, Component has a getToolkit method that Applet inherits.

> **NOTE** The Toolkit class provides access to information about the user's runtime environment, such as their screen resolution.

5. With one more addition in the jbInit() method to register the listener, we actually have a working Hi-Lo game.

```
button1 = new Button("Enter Guess");
XYConstraints xy4 = new XYConstraints(100, 200, -1, -1);
add(button1, xy4);
button1.addActionListener (this);
}
```

Once these five steps have been completed, the actionPerformed() method looks like the following:

```
public void actionPerformed(ActionEvent parm1) {
  String s = textField1.getText();
  int val;
  try {
    val = Integer.parseInt (s);
  } catch (NumberFormatException e) {
    val = 0;
  }
  if (val == theNum) {
    getToolkit().beep();
    label2.setText ("Higher or Lower");
    theNum = getNextNumber();
  } else if (val < theNum) {
    label2.setText ("Higher");
  } else {
    label2.setText ("Lower");
  }
}
```

> **TIP** There is no volume control support in Java. You need to adjust the volume from your system-specific volume control mechanism.

Keyboard Events

Restricting input for the `TextField` is similar to handling the button press. The listener is called a `KeyListener`. The `KeyListener` interface consists of three methods:

- `keyPressed()`—For any keyboard key that is pressed
- `keyReleased()`—For any keyboard key that is released
- `keyTyped()`—For a nonaction-oriented key that is pressed and released

> **NOTE** Action keys are function keys, arrow keys, and the like. Nonaction keys are the alphanumeric, Control, Shift, and Alt keys.

The keyTyped method is the method that allows us to restrict input. However, because we need to implement the `KeyListener` interface, all three methods need to be created. Using the Implement Interface Wizard simplifies this because we will just fill in the one method. Go ahead and use the Interface Wizard to implement the `KeyListener` interface now. It's also part of `java.awt.event`.

We want to ignore any input that is not numerical. If we check every character, we can then ignore the ones we don't want. To tell the system to ignore keystrokes, we use the `consume` method. If the text field goes through all the listeners and nobody *consumed* the event, the input character will be displayed.

> **TIP** Only input events can be consumed with `consume`. We could not reject the ActionEvent method from the "Enter Guess" button.

```
public void keyTyped(KeyEvent parm1) {
  char c = parm1.getKeyChar();
  if (!Character.isDigit (c))
    parm1.consume();
}
```

> **TIP** The `Character` class has over a dozen routines to check for different types of characters: uppercase, lowercase, alphanumeric, and white-space to name a few.

After you register the `KeyListener` with the `TextField` using the `addKeyListener` method, you don't have to worry about any more letters entered in the input field. With one final addition in the `jbInit()` method, the Hi-Lo game is complete. One more thing to mention here is adding the `KeyListener` doesn't alter the input screen; it is strictly for input validation.

```
textField1 = new TextField();
XYConstraints xy3 = new XYConstraints(175, 85, 50, -1);
add(textField1, xy3);
textField1.addKeyListener (this);
button1 = new Button("Enter Guess");
```

Here's the complete code for our Hi-Lo game.

HiLo.java

```
package skill5;

import java.awt.*;
import java.awt.event.*;
import java.applet.*;
import borland.jbcl.control.*;
import borland.jbcl.layout.*;

public class HiLo extends Applet implements ActionListener, KeyListener{
  XYLayout xYLayout1 = new XYLayout();
  boolean isStandalone = false;
  Label label1;
  Label label2;
  TextField textField1;
  Button button1;
  int theNum;

  private int getNextNumber () {
    return (int) (Math.random() * 100.0) + 1;
  }

  //Get a parameter value
  public String getParameter(String key, String def) {
    return isStandalone ? System.getProperty(key, def) :
      (getParameter(key) != null ? getParameter(key) : def);
  }

  //Construct the applet
  public HiLo() {
  }
```

```java
//Initialize the applet
public void init() {
  try { jbInit(); } catch(Exception e) { e.printStackTrace(); };
  theNum = getNextNumber();
}

//Component initialization
public void jbInit() throws Exception{
  xYLayout1.setWidth(400);
  xYLayout1.setHeight(300);
  this.setLayout(xYLayout1);
  label1 = new Label ("Enter a number between 1 and 100");
  label2 = new Label ("Higher or Lower");
  XYConstraints xy1 = new XYConstraints (25, 25, 300, 50);
  add (label1, xy1);
  XYConstraints xy2 = new XYConstraints (25, 75, 150, 50);
  add (label2, xy2);
  textField1 = new TextField();
  XYConstraints xy3 = new XYConstraints(175, 85, 50, -1);
  add(textField1, xy3);
  textField1.addKeyListener (this);
  button1 = new Button("Enter Guess");
  XYConstraints xy4 = new XYConstraints(100, 200, -1, -1);
  add(button1, xy4);
  button1.addActionListener (this);
}

//Get Applet information
public String getAppletInfo() {
  return "Applet Information";
}

//Get parameter info
public String[][] getParameterInfo() {
  return null;
}

public void actionPerformed(ActionEvent parm1) {
  String s = textField1.getText();
  int val;
  try {
    val = Integer.parseInt (s);
  } catch (NumberFormatException e) {
    val = 0;
  }
  if (val == theNum) {
    getToolkit().beep();
    label2.setText ("Higher or Lower");
```

```
        theNum = getNextNumber();
    } else if (val < theNum) {
        label2.setText ("Higher");
    } else {
        label2.setText ("Lower");
    }
}

public void keyTyped(KeyEvent parm1) {
    char c = parm1.getKeyChar();
    if (!Character.isDigit (c))
        parm1.consume();
}

public void keyPressed(KeyEvent parm1) {
}

public void keyReleased(KeyEvent parm1) {
}
```

We've now seen how to add components to a program. You should also understand the basics of event handling. For most applets, that's really all there is to it—place some components on the screen and react to user input. The key is getting your components to look right across all platforms. In Skill 6, I'll explain the `LayoutManager` in much more detail to see how Java takes care of platform-independent positioning when we work with the `TabsetPanel`.

Are You Experienced?

Now you can...

- ☑ add controls to your programs
- ☑ use the *Label* component
- ☑ use the *TextField* component
- ☑ use the *Button* component
- ☑ listen for action events to process requests
- ☑ listen for keyboard events to restrict input

PROGRAMMERS
C, C, VB, Cobol, exp. Call 534-555-6543 or fax 534-555-6544.

PROGRAMMING
MRFS Inc. is looking for a Sr. Windows NT developer. Reqs. 3-5 yrs. Exp. in C under Windows, Win95 & NT, using Visual C. Excl. OO design & implementation skills a must. OLE2 & ODBC are a plus. Excl. Salary & bnfts. Resume & salary history to HR, 8779 HighTech Way, Computer City, AR

PROGRAMMERS
Contractors Wanted for short & long term assignments; Visual C, MFC Unix C/C, SQL Oracle Developers PC Help Desk Support Windows NT & NetWareTelecommunications Visual Basic, Access, HTMT, CGI, Perl MMI & Co. 885-555-9933

PROGRAMMER
World Wide Web Links wants your HTML & Photoshop skills. Develop great WWW sites. Local & global customers. Send samples & resume to WWWL, 2000 Apple Road, Santa Rosa, CA.

TECHNICAL WRITER
Software firm seeks writer/editor for manuals, research notes, project mgmt. Min 2 years tech. writing, DTP & programming experience. Send resume & writing samples to: Software Systems, Dallas, TX.

TECHNICAL
Software development firm looking for Tech Trainers. Ideal candidates have programming experience in Visual C, HTML & JAVA. Need quick self starter. Call (443) 555-6868 for interview.

TECHNICAL WRITER/
Premier Computer Corp is seeking a combination of technical skills, knowledge and experience in the following areas: UNIX, Windows 95/NT, Visual Basic, on-line help & documentation, and the internet. Candidates must possess excellent writing skills, and be comfortable working in a quality vs. deadline driven environment. Competitive salary. Fax resume & samples to Karen Fields, Premier Computer Corp. 444 Industrial Blvd. Concord, CA. Or send to our website at www.premier.com.

WEB DESIGNER
BA/BS or equivalent programming/multimedia production. 3 years of experience in use and design of WWW services streaming audio and video HTML, PERL, CGI, GIF, JPEG. Demonstrated interpersonal, organization, communication, multi-tasking skills. Send resume to The Learning People at www.learning.com

WEBMASTER-TECHNICAL
BSCS or equivalent. 2 years of experience in CGI, Windows 95/NT, UNIX, C, Java, Perl. Demonstrated ability to design, code, debug and test on-line services. Send resume to The Learning People at www.learning.com

PROGRAMMER
World Wide Web Links wants your HTML & Photoshop skills. Develop great WWW sites. Local & global customers. Send samples

---

ing tools. Experienced in documentation preparation & programming languages (Access, C, FoxPro) are a plus. Financial or banking customer service support is required along with excellent verbal & written communication skills with multi levels of end-users. Send resume to KKUP Enterprises, 45 Orange Blvd. Orange, CA.

COMPUTERS
Small Web Design firm seeks indiv. w/NT, Webserver & Database management exp. fax resume to 556-555-4221.

COMPUTER/
Visual C/C, Visual Basic Exp'd Systems Analysts/Programmers for growing software dev. team in Roseburg. Computer Science or related degree preferred. Develop adv. Engineering applications for engineering firm. Fax resume to 707-555-8744.

COMPUTER
Web Master for dynamic SF Internet co. Site. Dev. test, coord., train. 2 yrs prog. Exp. C, C, Web C, FTP. Fax resume to Best Staffing 845-555-7722.

COMPUTER PROGRAMMER
Ad agency seeks programmer w/exp. in UNIX/NT Platforms, Web Server, CGI/Perl. Programmer Position avail. on a project basis with the possibility to move into F/T. Fax resume & salary req. to R. Jones 334-555-8332.

COMPUTERS
Programmer/Analyst Design and maintain C based SQL database applications. Required skills: Visual Basic, C, SQL, ODBC. Document existing and new applications. Novell or NT exp. a plus. Fax resume & salary history to 235-555-9935.

GRAPHIC DESIGNER
Webmaster's Weekly is seeking a creative Graphic Designer to design high impact marketing collateral, including direct mail promos, CD-ROM packages, ads and WWW pages. Must be able to juggle multiple projects and learn new skills on the job very rapidly. Web design experience a big plus, technical troubleshooting also a plus. Call 435-555-1235.

GRAPHICS - ART DIRECTOR - WEB-MULTIMEDIA
Leading internet development company has an outstanding opportunity for a talented, high-end Web Experienced Art Director. In addition to a great portfolio and fresh ideas, the ideal candidate has excellent communication and presentation skills. Working as a team with innovative producers and programmers, you will create dynamic, interactive web sites and application interfaces. Some programming experience required. Send samples and resume to: SuperSites, 333 Main. Seattle, WA

MARKETING
Fast paced software and services provider looking for MARKETING COMMUNICATIONS SPECIALIST to be responsible for its webpage, seminar coordination and ad place-

---

PROGRAMMERS
Multiple short term assignments available: Visual C, 3 positions SQL ServerNT Server, 2 positions JAVA & HTML, long term NetWare Various locations. Call for more info. 356-555-3398.

PROGRAMMERS
C, C, VB, Cobol, exp.
Call 534-555-6543
or fax 534-555-6544.

PROGRAMMING
MRFS Inc. is looking for a Sr. Windows NT developer. Reqs. 3-5 yrs. Exp. in C under Windows, Win95 & NT, using Visual C. Excl. OO design & implementation skills a must. OLE2 & ODBC are a plus. Resume & salary history to HR, 8779 HighTech Way, Computer City, AR

PROGRAMMERS/
Contractors Wanted for short & long term assignments; Visual C, MFC Unix C/C, SQL Oracle Developers PC Help Desk Support Windows NT & NetWareTelecommunications Visual Basic, Access, HTMT, CGI, Perl MMI & Co. 885-555-9933

PROGRAMMER
World Wide Web Links wants your HTML & Photoshop skills. Develop great WWW sites. Local & global customers. Send samples & resume to WWWL, 2000 Apple Road, Santa Rosa, CA.

TECHNICAL WRITER
Software firm seeks writer/editor for manuals, research notes, project mgmt. Min 2 years tech. writing, DTP & programming experience. Send resume & writing samples to: Software Systems, Dallas, TX.

COMPUTER PROGRAMMER
Ad agency seeks programmer w/exp. in UNIX/NT Platforms, Web Server, CGI/Perl. Programmer Position avail. on a project basis with the possibility to move into F/T. Fax resume & salary req. to R. Jones 334-555-8332.

TECHNICAL WRITER
Premier Computer Corp is seeking a combination of technical skills, knowledge and experience in the following areas: UNIX, Windows 95/NT, Visual Basic, on-line help & documentation, and the internet. Candidates must possess excellent writing skills, and be comfortable working in a quality vs. deadline driven environment. Competitive salary. Fax resume & samples to Karen Fields, Premier Computer Corp. 444 Industrial Blvd. Concord, CA. Or send to our website at www.premier.com.

WEB DESIGNER
BA/BS or equivalent programming/multimedia production. 3 years of experience in use and design of WWW services streaming audio and video HTML, PERL, CGI, GIF, JPEG. Demonstrated interpersonal, organization, communication, multi-tasking skills. Send resume to The Learning People at www.learning.com

WEBMASTER-TECHNICAL
BSCS or equivalent. 2 years of experience in CGI, Windows 95/NT,

---

COMPUTERS
Small Web Design firm seeks indiv. w/NT, Webserver & Database management exp. fax resume to 556-555-4221.

COMPUTER
Visual C/C, Visual Basic Exp'd Systems Analysts/Programmers for growing software dev. team in Roseburg. Computer Science or related degree preferred. Develop adv. Engineering applications for engineering firm. Fax resume to 707-555-8744.

COMPUTER
Web Master for dynamic SF Internet co. Site. Dev. test, coord., train. 2 yrs prog. Exp. C, C, Web C, FTP. Fax resume to Best Staffing 845-555-7722.

COMPUTERS/ QA SOFTWARE TESTERS
Qualified candidates should have 2 yrs exp. performing integration & system testing using automated testing tools. Experienced in documentation preparation & programming languages (Access, C, FoxPro) are a plus. Financial or banking customer service support is required along with excellent verbal & written communication skills with multi levels of end-users. Send resume to KKUP Enterprises, 45 Orange Blvd. Orange, CA.

COMPUTERS
Programmer/Analyst Design and maintain C based SQL database applications. Required skills: Visual Basic, C, SQL, ODBC. Document existing and new applications. Novell or NT exp. a plus. Fax resume & salary history to 235-555-9935.

GRAPHIC DESIGNER
Webmaster's Weekly is seeking a creative Graphic Designer to design high impact marketing collateral, including direct mail promo's CD-ROM packages, ads and WWW pages. Must be able to juggle multiple projects and learn new skills on the job very rapidly. Web design experience a big plus, technical troubleshooting also a plus. Call 435-555-1235.

GRAPHICS - ART DIRECTOR - WEB-MULTIMEDIA
Leading internet development company has an outstanding opportunity for a talented, high-end Web Experienced Art Director. In addition to a great portfolio and fresh ideas, the ideal candidate has excellent communication and presentation skills. Working as a team with innovative producers and programmers, you will create dynamic, interactive web sites and application interfaces. Some programming experience required. Send samples and resume to: SuperSites, 333 Main. Seattle, WA

COMPUTER PROGRAMMER
Ad agency seeks programmer w/exp. in UNIX/NT Platforms, Web Server, CGI/Perl. Programmer Position avail. on a project basis with the possibility to move into F/T. Fax resume & salary req. to R. Jones 334-555-8332.

PROGRAMMERS / Established
software company seeks program-

PROGRAMMERS
Multiple short term assignments available: Visual C, 3 positions SQL ServerNT Server, 2 positions JAVA & HTML, long term NetWare Various locations. Call more info. 356-555-3398.

PROGRAMMERS
C, C, VB, Cobol, exp. Call 534-555-6543 or fax 534-555-6544.

PROGRAMMING
MRFS Inc. is looking for a Windows NT developer. Reqs. yrs. Exp. in C under Windows, Win95 & NT using Visual C, OO design & implementation s a must. OLE2 & ODBC are a p Excl. Salary & bnfts. Resume salary history to HR, 8779 High Way, Computer City, AR

PROGRAMMERS/
Contract Wanted for short & long term ass ments. Visual C, MFCUnix C/C, Oracle Developers PC Help D Support Windows NT & NetW Telecommunications Visual B Access, HTMT, CGI, Perl MMI & 885-555-9933

PROGRAMMER
World Wide W Links wants your HTML & Photos skills. Develop great WWW s Local & global customers. Send s ples & resume to WWWL, 2 Apple Road, Santa Rosa, CA.

TECHNICAL WRITER
Software seeks writer/editor for manu research notes, project mgmt. M years tech. writing, DTP & progra ming experience. Send resume writing samples to: Softw Systems, Dallas, TX.

TECHNICAL
Software developm firm looking for Tech Trainers. I candidates have programming e rience in Visual C, HTML & JA Need quick self starter. Call (4 555-6868 for interview.

TECHNICAL WRITER
Prem Computer Corp is seeking a co nation of technical skills, knowle and experience in the follow areas: UNIX, Windows 95/NT, V Basic, on-line help & documentat and the internet. Candidates m possess excellent writing skills, be comfortable working in a qu vs. deadline driven environm Competitive salary. Fax resume samples to Karen Fields, Pre Computer Corp. 444 Industrial B Concord, CA. Or send to our web at www.premier.com

WEB DESIGNER
BA/BS or equivalent progr ming/multimedia production. years of experience in use design of WWW services strean audio and video HTML, PERL, GIF, JPEG. Demonstrated inter sonal, organization, communicat multi-tasking skills. Send resume The Learning People at www.le ing.com

WEBMASTER-TECHNIC

SKILL 6

six

Understanding Layout Management

- ❏ Learning the layout management principles
- ❏ Working with the `TabsetPanel`
- ❏ Working with `FlowLayout`
- ❏ Setting up a `ContainerListener`
- ❏ Working with `GridLayout`
- ❏ Working with `BorderLayout`

Introducing Layout Management Principles

Programs created with Java automatically run across multiple platforms. When you compile a Java program, the compiler creates .class files which contain platform-independent byte codes. These byte codes are understood by the Java Virtual Machine (JVM) on every platform. This is one of the key benefits of Java: "Write once, run anywhere."

> **NOTE** The instruction set understood by the JVM is defined in The Java Virtual Machine Specification document, located online at http://www.javasoft.com/docs/vmspec/VMSpecTOC.doc.html.

For visual programs, you have to do more to make everything look right on every platform. With Java, the size of a component is dependent upon which platform the user is running on. A `TextField` looks different under Windows 95, Windows NT, Macintosh, and Motif (Unix). Because of that, you should not use absolute positioning and the `XYLayout`, used in previous skills, in production programs. It works great for testing, so you don't have to worry about platform-size issues. However, in order to position objects properly across multiple platforms, you need to understand and use Java's layout manager concept.

This skill takes you through the standard layout managers provided with Java and introduces you to JBuilder's `TabsetPanel` control, a tabbed panel that allows you to pick from different component sets to display. In addition to introducing the different layout managers, the program we create will resize itself whenever you select a button to demonstrate the functionality of each layout manager.

Using the *TabsetPanel*

JBuilder contains a `TabsetPanel` component for you to create tabbed property sheets fairly easily. If you have ever changed your preferences in Netscape Navigator, you've seen the Preferences window with the tabbed panels that allow you to alter different groups of settings. Similarly, if you need to display multiple screen types worth of information, the `TabsetPanel` is JBuilder's solution. Figures 6.1, 6.2, and 6.3 show three views of a sample window. When you select one of the tabs at the top—First, Second, or Third—the displayed area below changes to display the components associated with the tab. The OK and Cancel buttons are not part of the `TabsetPanel` and are constant throughout.

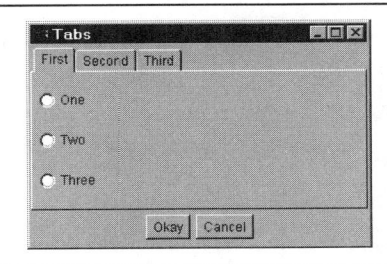

FIGURE 6.1: The settings on the First tab

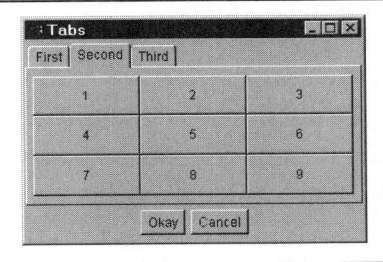

FIGURE 6.2: The settings on the Second tab

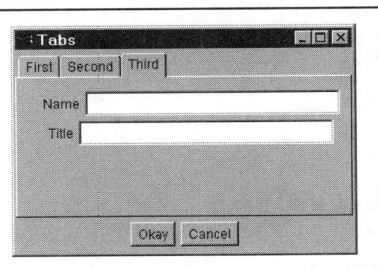

FIGURE 6.3: The settings on the Third tab

Now that you've been introduced to the TabsetPanel, let's create one. Close any open projects and create a project for Skill 6. Use the Application Wizard to create a new Project named **skill6** in the **\skills\skill6\skill6.jpr** file by selecting the Finish button. In the actual Application Wizard dialogs, select Finish to create the framework to work in. This will create an .html file named after the project, along with two source files, Tabs.java and Application1.java.

In the `Tabs` source file, we want to work with a `TabsetPanel`, so we should get rid of any mention of `BevelPanel` and `XYLayout`. Therefore, remove the two declaration lines:

```
private XYLayout xYLayout2 = new XYLayout();
private BevelPanel bevelPanel1 = new BevelPanel();
```

And remove the initialization lines from the `jbInit` method:

```
bevelPanel1.setLayout(xYLayout2);
this.add(bevelPanel1, BorderLayout.CENTER);
```

We also want the screen to size itself, so remove the `this.setSize` (but with three dots between it) in `jbInit`. Also, in `Application1.java` set the `packFrame` instance variable to `true`.

We can now replace the `BevelPanel` with a `TabsetPanel`. At the end of the `jbInit` method, create a `TabsetPanel` and add it where `bevelPanel1` was. The method should now appear like so:

```
public void jbInit() throws Exception{
   this.setLayout(borderLayout1);
   this.setTitle("Frame Title");
   TabsetPanel tabset = new TabsetPanel();
   this.add(tabset, BorderLayout.CENTER);
}
```

This creates the panel with no tabs. If you build and run the program, it will appear as shown here. Because the panel is empty, it appears rather small.

Using *FlowLayout*

To start exercising the `TabsetPanel`, we'll add the first component to it. A single component is a `Button` or a `Label`. However, you normally see multiple components grouped together. In order to group them, you need to use a `Panel`. A `Panel` is the simplest Java `Container` that can contain other components. Since a `Container` is another type of `Component`, you can embed `Panels` within `Panels`.

Every `Container` within Java has a `LayoutManager` that controls how components are displayed within it. For `Panel`, the default `LayoutManager` is called `FlowLayout`. With `FlowLayout`, every component within the `Panel` will be sized to its preferred size. Every component has a different preferred size, but it tends to be near the minimum space necessary to display it. For a Button, this would be space for the label with the adornments around it.

> **NOTE** The Applet class used in previous skills is a subclass of Panel, so it acts similarly.

When multiple components are placed within a FlowLayout Panel, they try to appear all on a single row. If there isn't sufficient space, whichever object was the first to not fit across moves down to the second row and the rest continue on the new line. Let's add a Panel with 26 buttons, one for each letter of the alphabet, to demonstrate. Adding the following to the end of jbInit will do just that.

```
Panel p = new Panel ();
for (char c='a';c<='z';c++)
  p.add (new Button (new Character(c).toString()));
tabset.add (p, "FlowLayout");
```

The for loop sets the variable c to each letter *a* through *z*. Then we create a button for each and add it to the panel. Because Button requires a text label, we have to convert the char to a String. One way to do this is with the help of the Character class, as shown above.

Another way to do this relies on the Java compiler to automatically insert the conversion code for us. If you add a String and a char together, the compiler upgrades the char to a String for you. The button label can also be defined like so:

```
new Button ("" + c);
```

Functionally, the two lines are identical.

If you run the program now, you'll see the image in Figure 6.4 after selecting the FlowLayout Tab.

FIGURE 6.4: The initial FlowLayout display state

Notice that there is now a tab visible—FlowLayout in this case. If you then resize the window, you'll see how the layout manager wraps the buttons when there isn't sufficient width to display everything across one row. This is shown in Figure 6.5.

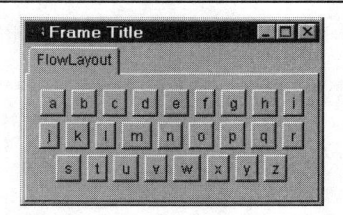

FIGURE 6.5: A narrower FlowLayout with the buttons wrapped

In addition, if there isn't sufficient height to display everything, you won't be able to see some buttons, as Figure 6.6 demonstrates. Resizing to a larger size will return the buttons—so they are not lost forever, just while the screen is too small.

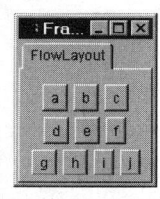

FIGURE 6.6: A short FlowLayout without all of the buttons

> **NOTE** Notice that the `TabsetPanel` sizes itself to the necessary width and height of the components within it. All tabs are the same size. So, it takes the widest components and the tallest components and makes that the size for all components.

Implementing *ContainerListener*

To have the system change the window size, we can add an `ActionListener` to every button, similar to what we did in the last skill, and call the `setSize` method of the `Frame`. We're going to do that, but in a slightly roundabout way. Because we're adding our components within a short `for` loop, the extra work may seem a bit much; however, when you are adding all your components using lots of independent statements, this skill will prove to be very helpful. Also, as we add the other tabs/screens to the `TabSetPanel`, doing things this way will require less work for the other tabs.

When you add a component to a container, a `ContainerEvent` is generated if the `Container` has a `ContainerListener` registered. The event tells the listener that a component has been added to the container. What you can do then is listen for components to be added and add the `ActionListener` (or another listener) there. This method works best when the same listener is attached to every component.

In order to do this for our example, we need to attach a `ContainerListener` to the `Panel` p, before any buttons are added. If the listener was added after the buttons were added, nothing would have been listening when the buttons were added.

```
Panel p = new Panel ();
p.addContainerListener (this);
for (char c='a';c<='z';c++)
  p.add (new Button (new Character(c).toString()));
```

Then our class needs to implement the `ContainerListener` interface. If you use the Implements Interface Wizard to add the `java.awt.event.ContainerListener` interface, the `componentAdded` and `componentRemoved` methods are added.

When a component is removed from the container (via the `remove` method) it isn't necessary to remove the listener, so we just have to fill in the `componentAdded` method. The method has one parameter of type `ContainerEvent`. The event has a child property that contains the component just added. Using the `getChild` method returns this for you. If the child happens to be a `Button`, you can then add an `ActionListener` to it.

```
public void componentAdded(ContainerEvent parm1) {
  Component c = parm1.getChild();
  if (c instanceof Button) {
    Button b = (Button)c;
    b.addActionListener (this);
  }
}
```

Now we can implement the `ActionListener` to resize the window. Using the Implement Interface Wizard again, this time for `java.awt.event.ActionListener`, we can add an `actionPerformed` method to the class. Using Java's random number generator again, we can then size the window with the `setSize` method and validate the screen display:

```
public void actionPerformed(ActionEvent parm1) {
  int width = (int)(Math.random() * 200 + 100);
  int height = (int)(Math.random() * 200 + 100);
  setSize (width, height);
  validate();
}
```

At this point, you can run your work to see what you've done. Select a few buttons to verify it works. Notice that the appearance hasn't changed since Figures 6.5, 6.6, and 6.7.

Using *GridLayout*

The next tab to add demonstrates the `GridLayout` layout manager. As the name implies, it positions controls within a grid. When you create the layout manager, you specify a size. Then, when you add objects, the layout manager fills a row at a time, from left to right, top to bottom. One key difference between `FlowLayout` and `GridLayout` is that every object within the grid will be sized the same. If there isn't sufficient space to display all the buttons, they will all be smaller.

> **WARNING** You cannot specify row-column position when you add a component with GridLayout. You must do it in row order from top-left to bottom-right, and you must fill each space in the grid, most times with a blank Label as filler.

For our example, we'll add the telephone buttons, a 4×3 grid. Creating a new `Panel` and adding the `ContainerListener` to the panel allows these buttons to resize the window, too. When you create a `Panel`, you can tell it which `LayoutManager` to use. Then, when you add the new panel to the `TabsetPanel`, you will see two tabs, as shown in Figure 6.7. By default, the first tab added is displayed.

```
// Telephone Grid
p = new Panel (new GridLayout (4, 3));
p.addContainerListener (this);
for (int i=1;i<=9;i++)
   p.add (new Button ("" + i));
p.add (new Button ('*'));
p.add (new Button ("0"));
p.add (new Button ("#"));
tabset.add (p, "GridLayout");
```

FIGURE 6.7: Our frame with the GridLayout added, but not displayed

Once you select the `GridLayout` tab, you'll see the buttons laid out like a telephone keypad (Figure 6.8). Notice their identical size. If you select a button, the window and buttons will resize, with the buttons maintaining uniform size. If the window happens to be too narrow for all the tabs of the `TabsetPanel`, two arrows will appear next to the tabs, allowing you to scroll through the different tabs. This is shown in Figure 6.9.

FIGURE 6.8: The initial GridLayout display state

FIGURE 6.9: A narrower GridLayout with arrows that allow you to scroll through the various tabs

Using *BorderLayout*

For our third tab, we'll demonstrate the `BorderLayout` layout manager. `BorderLayout` is the default layout for windows and frames. It works on a quadrant system. The window is broken apart into five quadrants. If a component is in the quadrant, it uses up its designated space. If it isn't, the other quadrants subsume it. The five quadrants are called North, East, West, South, and Center.

`BorderLayout` also has rather different sizing behavior. Controls in the North and South quadrant are the width of the container. Their height is their preferred height, just as with `FlowLayout`. Controls in the West and East areas are the height of the container (less North and South, when present). Their width is their preferred width, again as with `FlowLayout`. The Center quadrant uses up whatever is left. If there isn't enough space, something won't be shown.

Because `BorderLayout` requires this quadrant information, you need to use a different add method. This one takes two parameters, instead of the usual one, where the quadrant name is the second parameter. You may remember this from with the `XYConstraints` and `XYLayout`. The `BorderLayout` class defines five constants, one for each quadrant to be used as the second parameter: NORTH, EAST, WEST, SOUTH, and CENTER.

```
// Borders
p = new Panel (new BorderLayout());
p.addContainerListener (this);
p.add (new Button ("North"), BorderLayout.NORTH);
p.add (new Button ("East"), BorderLayout.EAST);
p.add (new Button ("West"), BorderLayout.WEST);
p.add (new Button ("South"), BorderLayout.SOUTH);
p.add (new Button ("Center"), BorderLayout.CENTER);
tabset.add (p, "BorderLayout");
```

Here we added buttons with each quadrant name. Again, creating a new `Panel` and adding the `ContainerListener` to the panel allows these buttons to resize the window, too. Then, when you add the new panel to the `TabsetPanel`, you will see three tabs, as shown in Figure 6.10. When you select the BorderLayout tab, you'll see the tab shown in Figure 6.11; and if you select a button, the window resizes, as shown in Figure 6.12.

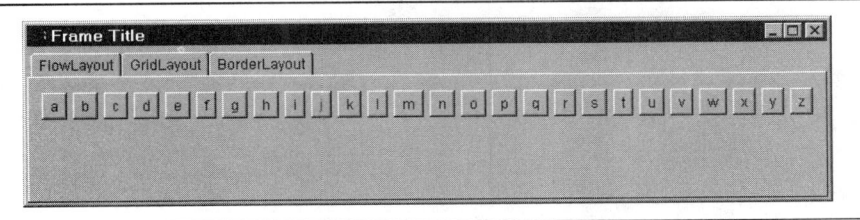

FIGURE 6.10: With the BorderLayout tab added but not displayed

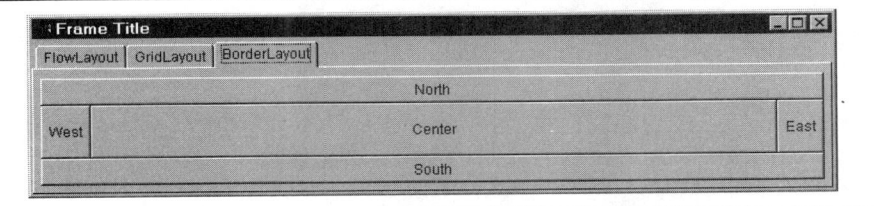

FIGURE 6.11: The initial BorderLayout display state

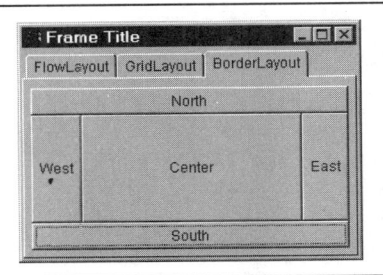

FIGURE 6.12: A resized BorderLayout after selecting a button

> **NOTE** Java comes with another layout manager called CardLayout. The CardLayout manager acts like a TabsetPanel without the tabs. If you don't want the tabs, it may be useful. However, you need some way to toggle between the different cards, hence the need for tabs and the TabsetPanel.

The following listing is the complete source code for creating the `TabsetPanel` with the different layout managers.

Tabs.java

```java
package skill6;

import java.awt.*;
import java.awt.event.*;
import borland.jbcl.control.*;
import borland.jbcl.layout.*;
import borland.jbcl.util.*;

public class Tabs extends DecoratedFrame implements ContainerListener, ActionListener {
  private BorderLayout borderLayout1 = new BorderLayout();

  //Construct the frame
  public Frame1() {
    try {
      jbInit();
    }
    catch (Exception e) {
      e.printStackTrace();
    };
  }

  //Component initialization
  public void jbInit() throws Exception{
    this.setLayout(borderLayout1);
    this.setTitle("Frame Title");
    TabsetPanel tabset = new TabsetPanel();
    this.add(tabset, BorderLayout.CENTER);
    Panel p = new Panel ();
    p.addContainerListener (this);
    for (char c='a';c<='z';c++)
      p.add (new Button (new Character(c).toString()));
    tabset.add (p, "FlowLayout");
// Telephone Grid
    p = new Panel (new GridLayout (4, 3));
    p.addContainerListener (this);
    for (int i=1;i<=9;i++)
      p.add (new Button ("" + i));
    p.add (new Button ("*"));
    p.add (new Button ("0"));
    p.add (new Button ("#"));
    tabset.add (p, "GridLayout");
```

```
// Borders
    p = new Panel (new BorderLayout());
    p.addContainerListener (this);
    p.add (new Button ("North"), BorderLayout.NORTH);
    p.add (new Button ("East"), BorderLayout.EAST);
    p.add (new Button ("West"), BorderLayout.WEST);
    p.add (new Button ("South"), BorderLayout.SOUTH);
    p.add (new Button ("Center"), BorderLayout.CENTER);
    tabset.add (p, "BorderLayout");
  }

  public void componentAdded(ContainerEvent parm1) {
    Component c = parm1.getChild();
    if (c instanceof Button) {
      Button b = (Button)c;
      b.addActionListener (this);
    }
  }

  public void componentRemoved(ContainerEvent parm1) {
    // Do nothing.
  }

  public void actionPerformed(ActionEvent parm1) {
    int width = (int)(Math.random() * 200 + 100);
    int height = (int)(Math.random() * 200 + 100);
    setSize (width, height);
  }
}
```

Congratulations! You can now create programs that will look better across all the different platforms that Java runs on. In Skill 7, you'll learn about Java's graphic capabilities and how to create smooth animation sequences.

Are You Experienced?

Now you can...

- ☑ describe layout management
- ☑ position components in a platform-independent manner
- ☑ create tabbed property sheets using the *TabsetPanel*
- ☑ use *FlowLayout* to size components
- ☑ listen for container events
- ☑ use *GridLayout* to position components
- ☑ work with frames and windows using *BorderLayout*

PROGRAMMING

MRFS Inc. is looking for a Sr. Windows NT developer. Reqs. 3-5 yrs. Exp. in C under Windows, Win95 & NT, using Visual C. Excl. OO design & implementation skills a must. OLE2 & ODBC are a plus. Excl. Salary & bnfts. Resume & salary history to HR, 8779 HighTech Way, Computer City, AR

PROGRAMMERS

Contractors Wanted for short & long term assignments: Visual C, MFC Unix C/C, SQL Oracle Dev elop ers PC Help Desk Support Windows NT & NetWareTelecommunications Visual Basic, Access, HTML, CGI, Perl MMI & Co., 885-555-9933

PROGRAMMER World Wide Web Links wants your HTML & Photoshop skills. Develop great WWW sites. Local & global customers. Send samples & resume to WWWL, 2000 Apple Road, Santa Rosa, CA.

TECHNICAL WRITER Software firm seeks writer/editor for manuals, research notes, project mgmt. Min 2 years tech. writing, DTP & programming experience. Send resume & writing samples to: Software Systems, Dallas, TX.

TECHNICAL Software development firm looking for Tech Trainers. Ideal candidates have programming experience in Visual C, HTML & JAVA. Need quick self starter. Call (443) 555-6868 for interview.

TECHNICAL WRITER/ Premier Computer Corp is seeking a combination of technical skills, knowledge and experience in the following areas: UNIX, Windows 95/NT, Visual Basic, on-line help & documentation, and the internet. Candidates must possess excellent writing skills, and be comfortable working in a quality vs. deadline driven environment. Competitive salary. Fax resume & samples to Karen Fields, Premier Computer Corp., 444 Industrial Blvd. Concord, CA. Or send to our website at www.premier.com.

WEB DESIGNER

BA/BS or equivalent programming/multimedia production. 3 years of experience in use and design of WWW services streaming audio and video HTML, PERL, CGI, GIF, JPEG. Demonstrated interpersonal, organization, communication, multi-tasking skills. Send resume to The Learning People at www.learning.com.

WEBMASTER-TECHNICAL

BSCS or equivalent. 2 years of experience in CGI, Windows 95/NT, UNIX, C, Java, Perl. Demonstrated ability to design, code, debug and test on-line services. Send resume to The Learning People at www.learning.com.

PROGRAMMER World Wide Web Links wants your HTML & Photoshop skills. Develop great WWW sites. Local & global customers. Send sam-

---

tation preparation & programming languages (Access, C, FoxPro) are a plus. Financial or banking customer service support is required along with excellent verbal & written communication skills with multi levels of end-users. Send resume to KKUP Enterprises, 45 Orange Blvd. Orange, CA.

COMPUTERS Small Web Design firm seeks indiv. w/NT, Webserver & Database management exp. Fax resume to 556-555-4221.

COMPUTER/ Visual C/C, Visual Basic Exp'd Systems Analysts/ Programmers for growing software dev. team in Roseburg. Computer Science or related degree preferred. Develop adv. Engineering applications for engineering firm. Fax resume to 707-555-8744.

COMPUTER Web Master for dynamic SF internet co. Site. Dev. test, coord., train, 2 yrs prog. Exp. C C, Web C FTP. Fax resume to Best Staffing 845-555-7722.

COMPUTER PROGRAMMER

Ad agency seeks programmer w/exp. in UNIX/NT Platforms, Web Server, CGI/Perl. Programmer Position avail. on a project basis with the possibility to move into F/T. Fax resume & salary req. to R. Jones 334-555-8332.

COMPUTERS Programmer/Analyst Design and maintain C based SQL database applications. Required skills: Visual Basic, C, SQL, ODBC. Document existing and new applications. Novell or NT exp. a plus. Fax resume & salary history to 235-555-9935.

GRAPHIC DESIGNER

Webmaster's Weekly is seeking a creative Graphic Designer to design high impact marketing collateral, including direct mail promos, CD-ROM packages, ads and WWW pages. Must be able to juggle multiple projects and learn new skills on the job very rapidly. Web design experience a big plus, technical troubleshooting also a plus. Call 435-555-1235.

GRAPHICS - ART DIRECTOR - WEB-MULTIMEDIA

Leading internet development company has an outstanding opportunity for a talented, high-end Web Experienced Art Director. In addition to a great portfolio and fresh ideas, the ideal candidate has excellent communication and presentation skills. Working as a team with innovative producers and programmers, you will create dynamic, interactive web sites and application interfaces. Some programming experience required. Send samples and resume to: SuperSites, 333 Main, Seattle, WA.

MARKETING

Fast paced software and services provider looking for MARKETING COMMUNICATIONS SPECIALIST to be responsible for its webpage, seminar coordination, and ad place-

---

PROGRAMMERS Multiple short term assignments available. Visual C, 3 positions SQL ServerNT Server. 2 positions JAVA & HTML, long term NetWare Various locations. Call for more info. 356-555-3398.

PROGRAMMERS

C, C, VB, Cobol, exp.
Call 534-555-6543
or fax 534-555-6544.

PROGRAMMING

MRFS Inc. is looking for a Sr. Windows NT developer. Reqs. 3-5 yrs. Exp. in C under Windows, Win95 & NT, using Visual C. Excl. OO design & implementationskills a must. OLE2 & ODBC are a plus. Excl. Salary & bnfts. Resume & salary history to HR, 8779 HighTech Way, Computer City, AR

PROGRAMMERS/ Contractors Wanted for short & long term assignments: Visual C, MFC Unix C/C, SQL Oracle Developers PC Help Desk Support Windows NT & NetWareTelecommunications Visual Basic, Access, HTML, CGI, Perl MMI & Co., 885-555-9933

PROGRAMMER World Wide Web Links wants your HTML & Photoshop skills. Develop great WWW sites. Local & global customers. Send samples & resume to WWWL, 2000 Apple Road, Santa Rosa, CA.

TECHNICAL WRITER Software firm seeks writer/editor for manuals, research notes, project mgmt. Min 2 years tech. writing, DTP & programming experience. Send resume & writing samples to: Software Systems, Dallas, TX.

COMPUTER PROGRAMMER

Ad agency seeks programmer w/exp. in UNIX/NT Platforms, Web Server, CGI/Perl. Programmer Position avail. on a project basis with the possibility to move into F/T. Fax resume & salary req. to R. Jones 334-555-8332.

TECHNICAL WRITER Premier Computer Corp is seeking a combination of technical skills, knowledge and experience in the following areas: UNIX, Windows 95/NT, Visual Basic, on-line help & documentation, and the internet. Candidates must possess excellent writing skills, and be comfortable working in a quality vs. deadline driven environment. Competitive salary. Fax resume & samples to Karen Fields, Premier Computer Corp., 444 Industrial Blvd. Concord, CA. Or send to our website at www.premier.com.

WEB DESIGNER

BA/BS or equivalent programming/multimedia production. 3 years of experience in use and design of WWW services streaming audio and video HTML, PERL, CGI, GIF, JPEG. Demonstrated interpersonal, organization, communication, multi-tasking skills. Send resume to The Learning People at www.learning.com.

WEBMASTER-TECHNICAL

BSCS or equivalent. 2 years of experience in CGI, Windows 95/NT,

---

COMPUTERS Small Web Design firm seeks indiv. w/NT, Webserver & Database management exp. Fax resume to 556-555-4221.

COMPUTER Visual C/C, Visual Basic Exp'd Systems Analysts/ Programmers for growing software dev. team in Roseburg. Computer Science or related degree preferred. Develop adv. Engineering applications for engineering firm. Fax resume to 707-555-8744.

COMPUTER Web Master for dynamic SF Internet co. Site. Dev. test, coord., train, 2 yrs prog. Exp. C C, Web C FTP. Fax resume to Best Staffing 845-555-7722.

COMPUTERS/ QA SOFTWARE TESTERS Qualified candidates should have 2 yrs exp. performing integration & system testing using automated testing tools. Experienced in documentation preparation & programming languages (Access, C, FoxPro) are a plus. Financial or banking customer service support is required along with excellent verbal & written communication skills with multi levels of end-users. Send resume to KKUP Enterprises, 45 Orange Blvd. Orange, CA.

COMPUTERS Programmer/Analyst Design and maintain C based SQL database applications. Required skills: Visual Basic, C, SQL, ODBC. Document existing and new applications. Novell or NT exp. a plus. Fax resume & salary history to 235-555-9935.

GRAPHIC DESIGNER

Webmaster's Weekly is seeking a creative Graphic Designer to design high impact marketing collateral, including direct mail promo's, CD-ROM packages, ads and WWW pages. Must be able to juggle multiple projects and learn new skills on the job very rapidly. Web design experience a big plus, technical troubleshooting also a plus. Call 435-555-1235.

GRAPHICS - ART DIRECTOR - WEB-MULTIMEDIA

Leading internet development company has an outstanding opportunity for a talented, high-end Web Experienced Art Director. In addition to a great portfolio and fresh ideas, the ideal candidate has excellent communication and presentation skills. Working as a team with innovative producers and programmers, you will create dynamic, interactive web sites and application interfaces. Some programming experience required. Send samples and resume to: SuperSites, 333 Main, Seattle, WA.

COMPUTER PROGRAMMER

Ad agency seeks programmer w/exp. in UNIX/NT Platforms, Web Server, CGI/Perl. Programmer Position avail. on a project basis with the possibility to move into F/T. Fax resume & salary req. to R. Jones 334-555-8332.

PROGRAMMERS / Established software company seeks program-

---

ment. Must be a self-starter, energetic, organized. Must have 2 yrs web experience. Programming plus. Call 985-555-9854.

PROGRAMMERS Multiple term assignments available. V C, 3 positions SQL ServerNT Se 2 positions JAVA & HTML, long NetWare Various locations. Call more info. 356-555-3398.

PROGRAMMERS

C, C, VB, Cobol, exp. Call 534-6543 or fax 534-555-6544.

PROGRAMMING

MRFS Inc. is looking for a Windows NT developer. Reqs. yrs. Exp. In C under Wind Win95 & NT, using Visual C OO design & implementation s a must. OLE2 & ODBC are a p Excl. Salary & bnfts. Resum salary history to HR, 8779 High Way, Computer City, AR

PROGRAMMERS/ Contra Wanted for short & long term as ments: Visual C, MFCUnix C/C, Oracle Developers PC Help Support Windows NT & Net Telecommunications Visual B Access, HTML, CGI, Perl MMI & 885-555-9933

PROGRAMMER World Wide Links wants your HTML & Photos skills. Develop great WWW Local & global customers. Send ples & resume to WWWL, 2 Apple Road, Santa Rosa, CA.

TECHNICAL WRITER Software seeks writer/editor for manu research notes, project mgmt. M years tech. writing, DTP & prog ming experience. Send resum writing samples to: Softw Systems, Dallas, TX.

TECHNICAL Software develope firm looking for Tech Trainers, I candidates have programming rience in Visual C, HTML & J Need quick self starter. Call (4 555-6868 for interview.

TECHNICAL WRITER Pre Computer Corp is seeking a co nation of technical skills, knowle and experience in the follo areas: UNIX, Windows 95/NT, V Basic, on-line help & documenta and the internet. Candidates possess excellent writing skills, be comfortable working in a qu vs. deadline driven environm Competitive salary. Fax resum samples to Karen Fields, Pre Computer Corp., 444 Industrial Concord, CA. Or send to our we at www.premier.com.

WEB DESIGNER

BA/BS or equivalent prog ming/multimedia production years of experience in use design of WWW services strea audio and video HTML, PERL, GIF, JPEG. Demonstrated inter sonal, organization, communic multi-tasking skills. Send resu The Learning People at www.l ing.com.

WEBMASTER-TECHNIC

SKILL

seven

Drawing with Java

- ❑ Drawing to the screen
- ❑ Creating event adapters
- ❑ Doing double-buffered drawing
- ❑ Displaying images
- ❑ Selecting colors

Drawing Support in Java

Java provides support for drawing through various classes—`Graphics`, `Color`, and `Image` primarily. With the help of these three classes, you can draw various shapes, images, and figures to the screen in different shades. Combining these capabilities allows you to create real-time multiuser games that can dazzle anyone. Getting this to work properly in Java, although easy once you know how, requires some extra steps—without which, even a graphic-intensive Java program leaves much to be desired.

To get started, let's create a program that draws some basic Java objects. As with all the skills, close everything first, and create a new skill to work in for Skill 7. Use the Applet Wizard to create the project and starting applet. When asked to create the project, call it **skill7**, save it to **c:\skills\skill7\skill7.jpr**, and select Finish. Then, during the Applet Wizard steps, name the class **Drawing** and select Finish.

So, what is this program going to draw? Initially, we'll have the program draw filled rectangles in black. Once we have the basic drawing done, we'll add support for stretching the rectangle as it's being drawn. Here is where you need to do some extra work in order for the program to look okay. Then we'll randomize the drawing colors.

Using the *Paint* Method to Draw

Once you've gone through the Applet Wizard, it's time to create the program. The first thing to do and understand is drawing. In Skill 5, we worked with Java controls, such as `Button` and `Label`. When you needed to use one of these objects, you created it and added it to the screen. Once it was created, it knew how to display itself.

Drawing on your own is a little different. When Java wants to update the screen, the `paint` method has to be called for the display area to update. In the case of an applet, the applet's `paint` method is called. So, because we want to draw something in our applet, we need to provide behavior in the `paint` method of our applet. First, select Drawing.java in the Navigation pane. Then, using the Override Methods Wizard, we can select the `paint(Graphics)` method of `java.awt.Component` to have an empty `paint` method added to our applet. Once you select OK, this adds the following code to the applet:

```java
public void paint(Graphics parm1) {
  //TODO: override this java.awt.Component   method;
  super.paint( parm1);
}
```

Once we have the method framework, we can add our own behavior to it. In order to draw a filled rectangle in Java, we use the `fillRect` method of `Graphics`, the parameter to `paint`. The method requires a starting point along with a width and height. Almost all drawing operations work this way. Provide the point in the top-left corner with dimensions, and tell the `Graphics` object what to do.

Instead of just drawing the rectangle with a fixed location and size, let's create four instance variables, representing two points. This will allow us to more easily support the event handling later. If we add the following line to our code after the class declaration, we'll have our two points to work with, along with initial locations:

```java
int startX = 0, startY = 0, endX = 100, endY = 100;
```

In addition to creating the variables, let's add two methods to set them. These will prove beneficial later. Each method will change the location of a point, starting or ending, to the coordinates passed.

```java
public void setStartPoint (Point p) {
  startX = p.x;
  startY = p.y;
}
public void setEndPoint (Point p) {
  endX = p.x;
  endY = p.y;
}
```

> **NOTE** The `Point` class holds the coordinates of a two-dimensional point.

Then, getting back to the `paint` routine, we can determine the top-left corner, width, and height to draw. Because Java's drawing routines want the point to be the top-left corner, we have to determine which position is lowest in both directions. The `min` method of the `Math` class performs this functionality. Then, for width and height, the difference between coordinates needs to be positive. The abs method (for absolute value) of the `Math` class performs this functionality. Putting all this together, our `paint` method will look like the following listing:

```
public void paint(Graphics parm1) {
  super.paint( parm1);
  int x = Math.min (startX, endX);
  int y = Math.min (startY, endY);
  int width  = Math.abs (startX - endX);
  int height = Math.abs (startY - endY);
  parm1.fillRect (x, y, width, height);
}
```

> **NOTE** The Math class is Java's collection of common math functions, such as trigonometric functions, a random number generator, and min/max capabilities, among other capabilities.

When we run the applet, we'll see Figure 7.1.

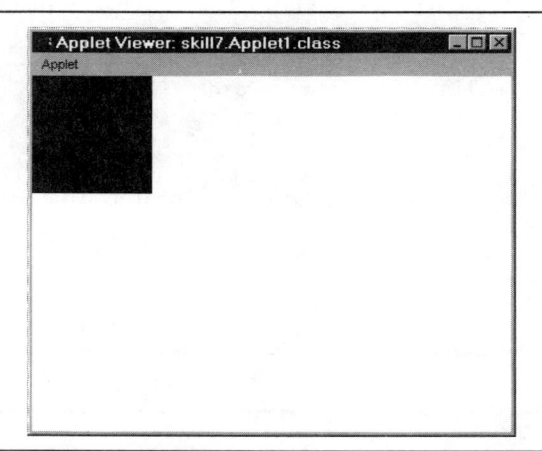

FIGURE 7.1: The applet drawing a rectangle

> **TIP** Remember to save everything with File ➤ Save All before running.

OTHER DRAWING OPTIONS

In addition to drawing a filled rectangle, there are other shapes you can draw:

- drawRect—draws an unfilled rectangle
- drawRoundRect—draws an unfilled rectangle with rounded corners
- fillRoundRect—draws a filled rectangle with rounded corners
- draw3DRect—draws a three-dimensional rectangle
- fill3DRect—draws a filled three-dimensional rectangle
- drawOval—draws an unfilled oval
- fillOval—draws a filled oval
- drawArc—draws an arc
- fillArc—draws an arc filled like a pie chart

You can try to run the program with any of these other shapes, too. Some of these methods require parameters beyond what fillRect and drawRect require. A quick glance at the Help ➤ Java Reference documentation will show the requirements. For instance, drawRoundRect allows you to specify how round you want the rectangle corners. Although all are a little different, each requires the starting drawing point in the top-left corner and the width and height to draw within, even to draw an oval.

Handling Mouse Events

Because we put all that work into drawing a fixed-size rectangle, changing its shape to coordinate with different locations is fairly easy. Although it may have seemed like quite a bit of work to draw a single rectangle, making your programs more adaptable is good programming practice. It is easier, and cheaper, for the initial designer to add in capabilities than for someone to come in later to do it. On to the mouse events.

Instead of always drawing the rectangle in one spot, our program should allow the user to specify the coordinates. The most natural way to do this is with the mouse. Pressing the mouse button signifies the *starting point*. Then you drag the mouse to another location and release the button. This new location is the *ending point*.

The methods that deal with mouse events are part of the `MouseListener` and `MouseMotionListener` interfaces. The `MouseListener` deals with mouse up and mouse down, while the `MouseMotionListener` deals with dragging.

Handling Mouse Events with *MouseListener*

We'll work with the `MouseListener` first. Table 7.1 describes the methods that are a part of the interface.

TABLE 7.1: The MouseListener Interface Methods

Method	Description
mouseClicked	For when you, the programmer, are interested in when a user presses and releases any mouse button without moving the mouse
mousePressed	For when a user presses a mouse button
mouseReleased	For when a user releases a mouse button
mouseEntered	For when a user moves the mouse into the component's area
mouseExited	For when a user moves the mouse outside the component's area

So, in order for the applet to get new drawing coordinates for the rectangle, there are four steps involved:

1. The applet needs to implement the `MouseListener` interface.
2. Its `mousePressed` method must get the new starting point.
3. Its `mouseReleased` method must get the ending point and draw the rectangle.
4. The `MouseListener` must be associated with the applet.

We learned how to implement a listener in Skill 4. Select Wizards ➤ Implement Interface, the name of the interface—java.awt.event.MouseListener in our case—and OK; then JBuilder adds the necessary source code to our program with all the interface methods empty, or stubbed out.

Define the `mousePressed` method first. Its signature looks like the following:

```
public void mousePressed(MouseEvent parm1)
```

The `MouseEvent` parameter contains the location of where the event happened. This location is available via the `getPoint` method. So, using this point, we can change the starting point with the `setStartPoint` method. The `mousePressed` method now looks like the following:

```
public void mousePressed(MouseEvent parm1) {
  setStartPoint (parm1.getPoint());
}
```

Then there is the `mouseReleased` method. Its signature looks similar:

```
public void mouseReleased(MouseEvent parm1)
```

Again, we can use the event's coordinates to change the location. This time, we change the ending point using the `setEndPoint` method. There's one more thing we have to add though. In order to update the screen, we need to notify the applet. This is done through the `repaint` method, with no parameters. The `mouseReleased` method now looks like the following:

```
public void mouseReleased(MouseEvent parm1) {
  setEndPoint (parm1.getPoint());
  repaint();
}
```

> **WARNING** You cannot call the `paint` method directly because you do not possess the reference to the `Graphics` parameter that it requires. Using the `repaint` method ensures that our applet will update the screen with the proper parameter. Otherwise, the screen will only be updated if it becomes invalid—by someone placing another object in front of the screen's area and removing it or minimizing and reselecting the applet's window.

Once we've completed filling in the methods of `MouseListener`, we need to associate the listener to the applet. Similar to associating an `ActionListener` with a `Button`, as we did in Skill 5, we use the `addMouseListener` method to associate the applet—the interface implementer—to itself. This can be done in the `init` or `jbInit` method. Keeping with JBuilder's style of having component initialization code in `jbInit`, we'll add it there.

```
public void jbInit() throws Exception {
  xYLayout1.setWidth(400);
  xYLayout1.setHeight(300);
  this.setLayout(xYLayout1);
  addMouseListener (this);
}
```

Once this is done, we can run the applet again. If you press and release the mouse at different coordinates, you will see the program draw various rectangles.

When you run the applet, you will probably notice one peculiarity. The rectangle doesn't stretch out as you move the mouse around. We can add this functionality with the help of a `MouseMotionListener`.

Handling Mouse Events with the *MouseMotionListener*

Table 7.2 describes the methods that are a part of the `MouseMotionListener` interface.

TABLE 7.2: The MouseMotionListener Interface Methods

method	description
mouseDragged	For when a user moves the mouse with a button pressed
mouseMoved	For when a user moves the mouse without a button pressed

Here we only have to perform three steps to deal with the dragging:

1. The applet needs to implement the `MouseMotionListener` interface.
2. Its `mouseDragged` method must get the new ending point.
3. The `MouseMotionListener` must be associated with the applet.

Again, we use the Implement Interface Wizard. This time selecting `java.awt.event.MouseMotionListener` and the OK button. Then, we define the `mouseDragged` method. This will look identical to the `mouseReleased` method.

```
public void mouseDragged(MouseEvent parm1) {
  setEndPoint (parm1.getPoint());
  repaint();
}
```

And we add one more line to `jbInit`:

```
addMouseMotionListener (this);
```

Once this is done, when we run the applet, the rectangle grows and shrinks as we move around with the mouse button pressed.

> **NOTE** The astute observer will have noticed that both the `MouseListener` and `MouseMotionListener` methods have a `MouseEvent` parameter. The reason there are two listener types for one event type is performance. Because the motion events happen more frequently, but the `MouseListener` methods are listened for more regularly, the two are separate. The motion events do not slow the system down when someone is listening for a nonmotion-oriented mouse event.

Drawing from a Buffer (a.k.a. Double Buffering)

At this point, the program runs fairly well. However, there are two annoyances. First, the program clears the screen when it starts drawing each rectangle. Now, this may be what you want; however, if you're creating a more sophisticated drawing program, where the user can draw a circle, square, and triangle and then print a house with a sun over it, they may be a little annoyed if things disappear as they draw each piece.

The second annoying feature you may or may not have noticed, depending on the size of the rectangles you drew, is flashing. Because the program clears the screen between each screen refresh, you'll notice a flashing between each move of the mouse. To correct this, we need to stop clearing the screen. However, we still need to remove the last rectangle drawn when dragging, so there may still be some unavoidable flashing. If we were continually drawing in the same spot, this would remove the flashing completely.

Creating the Buffer

To fix the first problem, we need to create a buffer. If all the drawing is done on the buffer, except when dragging, old rectangles will be saved. In Java, this buffer is an `Image`. In addition to needing an `Image`, you need a `Graphics` object. All the drawing operations have to do with `Graphics`, not `Image`. The way to get an

Image's `Graphics` context is through its `getGraphics` method. Once you have its `Graphics`, you can use it again to draw a filled rectangle.

So, creating three variables allows us to buffer our drawing properly.

```
Image im;
Graphics buf;
boolean dragging = false;
```

The `Image` and `Graphics` variables are initialized in the `init` method. In order to create the buffer, you need to know what size to tell it. The `getSize` method returns the current dimensions of the applet's space. As long as the applet isn't resized during operations—which is impossible to do in a browser—the buffer size is appropriate.

```
public void init() {
  try { jbInit(); } catch(Exception e) { e.printStackTrace(); };
  im = createImage (getSize().width, getSize().height);
  buf = im.getGraphics();
}
```

The `paint` method needs to be modified to use the buffer. Images are drawn with `drawImage`. So, when dragging, we need to draw the buffer and then the rectangle. When not dragging, we need to draw the rectangle to the buffer, and then draw the buffer.

> **NOTE** The drawImage method has four parameters. The first is the image to draw. The second is its x coordinate, while the third is the y coordinate of the top-left corner position. The last parameter is where the object is being drawn. As long as your class is a subclass of Component, you can place the keyword `this` there.

```
public void paint(Graphics parm1) {
  super.paint( parm1);
  int x = Math.min (startX, endX);
  int y = Math.min (startY, endY);
  int width  = Math.abs (startX - endX);
  int height = Math.abs (startY - endY);
  if (dragging) {
    parm1.drawImage (im, 0, 0, this);
    parm1.fillRect (x, y, width, height);
  } else {
    buf.fillRect (x, y, width, height);
    parm1.drawImage (im, 0, 0, this);
  }
}
```

Setting of the dragged variable is done in the MouseListener methods—mousePressed and mouseReleased. It isn't necessary to change the value within the mouseDragged method.

```
public void mousePressed(MouseEvent parm1) {
  setStartPoint (parm1.getPoint());
  dragging = true;
}
public void mouseReleased(MouseEvent parm1) {
  setEndPoint (parm1.getPoint());
  dragging = false;
  repaint();
}
```

You can run the applet now, but there is one more thing that should be added. Because we are forever drawing to the screen, it sure would be nice to clear it. Instead of adding a button or menu to deal with this, let's just have mouseClick (pressing and releasing the mouse button without moving) reset the buffer. Once this is added, your program will appear more like Figure 7.2 after drawing a few rectangles.

```
public void mouseClicked(MouseEvent parm1) {
  im = createImage (getSize().width, getSize().height);
  buf = im.getGraphics();
}
```

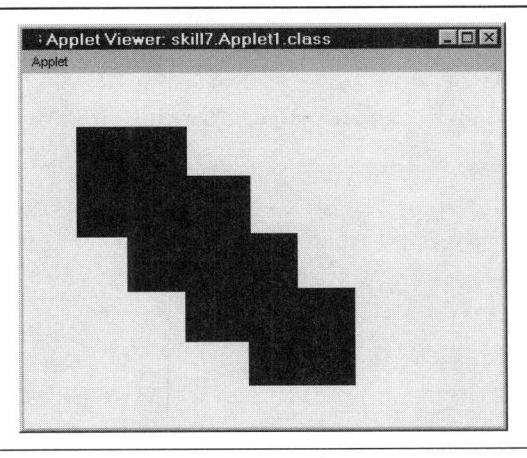

FIGURE 7.2: The applet after drawing multiple rectangles

Removing the Flash

In order to have the mouse-handling code tell the system to update the display, we called the `repaint` method. `Repaint` works by telling the system to call `update` and `paint`, thus updating the display. Herein lies the problem. The `update` method clears the screen before the `paint` method draws on it. When drawing large objects, this results in a flashing effect because a solid background is shown between screen refreshes. Because we are drawing to a buffer, which happens to be the size of the display, we can stop `update` from clearing the screen between buffer drawings. Using the Override Methods Wizard, we can select the `update(Graphics)` method of `java.awt.Component`. Changing update to only notify `paint`, without clearing the screen, results in the following source:

```
public void update (Graphics parm1) {
  paint(parm1);
}
```

DISPLAYING IMAGES FROM DISK

We actually know almost all there is to know to load and display an image from disk. With `displayImage`, we have the display part down. To load the image, however, JBuilder provides a support class, `ImageLoader`, in the `borland.jbcl.util` package. Given a `String` or `URL`, it will load the image from disk or across the network. Then, with `displayImage`, we can draw it. The `load` method has two primary varieties, the last parameter of both is where you plan on drawing the image:

- `load (URL, Component)` gets an Image given a complete URL. Because of security restrictions, it tends to be the more rarely used variety with applets. Normally, you provide the image file with the applet, and you, the developer, just need to know where the applet is installed, to use the following method.

- `load (filenameString, Component)` gets an Image given a filename string. For an application, Java will look for the file in the starting directory. For an applet, it will look for the image where the applet is installed.

So, given the file `myimage.jpg` in the directory of the `.html` file, the following tells the system to load the image from disk:

```
// Usually done in the init method
Image im = ImageLoader.load ("myimage.jpg", this);
```

The reason I said "tells the system" is because the image doesn't start loading until the system needs it, which is until you try to draw it. To ensure the image is fully loaded before continuing, the `ImageLoader` has a `waitForImage` method.

```
Image im = ImageLoader.load ("myimage.jpg", this);
ImageLoader.waitForImage(this, im);
```

There is also a variety of `load` that combines the two behaviors. The last parameter now states whether to wait for the loading to finish; the default setting is `false`.

```
Image im = ImageLoader.load ("myimage.jpg", this, true);
```

Remember that Java supports GIF, JPEG, and XBM image file formats.

TIP   For most image file animation sequences it isn't necessary to create your own program. Sun provides an applet called the Animator that supports multifile sequencing, with audio support and movement. It is available free at http://www.javasoft.com/applets/Animator/index.html. Because source code is provided, it also serves as a good working example.

Changing Colors

Working in black and white is fine if you're trying to create screen shots to include in a book. However, you probably would like to see other colors. Let's have the system change drawing colors whenever the mouse leaves and reenters the applet's space. This happens to be the `mouseEntered` method of the `MouseListener` interface.

This isn't as easy as it sounds though. All the earlier drawing operations used the default color, which happened to be black. In order for us to properly change the drawing color, this initial color value must be variable based. Although we could have done it the proper way first, as we did with the drawing points, let's look at all the extra work necessary to go back and fix up everything.

There are three steps involved in this task:

1. Create and initialize a variable to store the current drawing color.
2. Provide a method to change the color.
3. When drawing to either the screen or the buffer, use the current drawing color.

We've created instance variables for the class a few times already. This one is no different:

```
Color drawingColor = Color.black;
```

You probably noticed `Color.black` as the initial value and wondered where that came from. The `Color` class has 13 predefined colors that can be used by name. They are listed in Table 7.3. All other colors must be created manually. We'll see how to create our own shortly.

TABLE 7.3: The 13 Constants of the Color Class

black	blue	cyan	darkGray	gray	green	lightGray
magenta	orange	pink	red	white	yellow	

The method to change the variable again should look somewhat familiar:

```
public void setDrawingColor (Color c) {
   drawingColor = c;
}
```

The reason for these helper methods will become clearer once we talk about JavaBeans in Part II. Basically, creating them allows a builder tool to use them when it connects various program pieces together for us.

The third task requires two changes to the `paint` method. Because painting is done directly to the screen and the buffer, each must change colors before drawing. Add the following two lines before the if-statement, checking on the `dragging` flag:

```
parm1.setColor (drawingColor);
buf.setColor (drawingColor);
```

Now, whenever we draw, the color is reset before the drawing happens.

Now, we can actually change the color. If all the previous work was done when the applet was initially created, it wouldn't have to be changed now. Because we are going to change the drawing color when the mouse enters the applet's space, we'll use the `mouseEntered` method of `MouseListener`. However, our applet already implements the `MouseListener` interface, so we only need to add the functionality.

```
public void mouseEntered(MouseEvent parm1) {
   short r = (short)(Math.random () * 256);
   short g = (short)(Math.random () * 256);
   short b = (short)(Math.random () * 256);
   setDrawingColor (new Color (r, g, b));
}
```

The `Color` class of Java works similarly to a color computer monitor. There are three color bands—red, green, and blue—that are combined to display a particular color to the user. In Java, each band has 256 possible values—from 0 to 255. The higher the value in each band, the more of that color is shown. For instance, a value of 255 for red, 175 for green, and 175 for blue is the color pink. Unless your video mode supports a color palette of 16.7 million colors (256*256*256), when you ask Java for a specific color, you may get a slightly different one.

> **WARNING** Java requires at least a 256-color palette. If you like working in 1600×1200 mode, but can only display 16 colors with that resolution, you will not be able to run any Java programs. JBuilder might run, but a program created with it won't.

In case you missed it, we did finish the program. Let's run it again and see what we got. See Figure 7.3 for a possible screen; yours may differ. Notice that the initial drawing color isn't black. The very first time the mouse moves into the applet's area, it's reset.

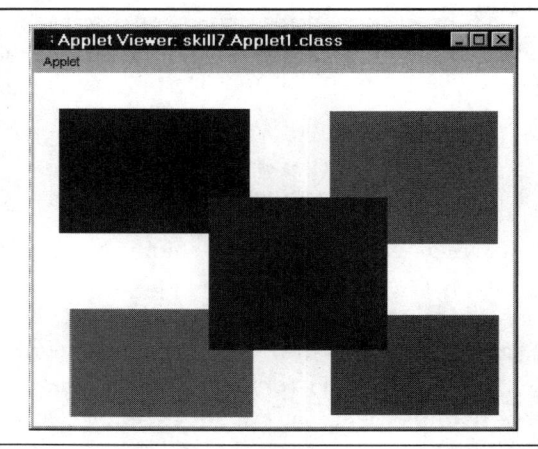

FIGURE 7.3: A black-and-white example of the multicolor applet you'll see on-screen

Drawing.java below contains the entire listing.

Drawing.java

```java
package skill7;

import java.lang.*;
import java.awt.*;
import java.awt.event.*;
import java.applet.*;
import borland.jbcl.control.*;
import borland.jbcl.layout.*;

public class Drawing extends Applet implements MouseListener, MouseMotionListener{
  public XYLayout xYLayout1 = new XYLayout();
  public boolean isStandalone = false;
  int startX = 0, startY = 0, endX = 100, endY = 100;
  Color drawingColor = Color.black;
  Image im;
  Graphics buf;
  boolean dragging = false;

  //Get a parameter value
  public String getParameter(String key, String def) {
    return isStandalone ? System.getProperty(key, def) :
      (getParameter(key) != null ? getParameter(key) : def);
  }
```

```
//Construct the applet
public Drawing() {
}

//Initialize the applet
public void init() {
  try { jbInit(); } catch(Exception e) { e.printStackTrace(); };
  im = createImage (getSize().width, getSize().height);
  buf = im.getGraphics();
}

//Component initialization
public void jbInit() throws Exception {
  xYLayout1.setWidth(400);
  xYLayout1.setHeight(300);
  this.setLayout(xYLayout1);
  addMouseListener (this);
  addMouseMotionListener (this);
}

//Get Applet information
public String getAppletInfo() {
  return "Applet Information";
}

//Get parameter info
public String[][] getParameterInfo() {
  return null;
}

public void paint(Graphics parm1) {
  super.paint( parm1);
  int x = Math.min (startX, endX);
  int y = Math.min (startY, endY);
  int width  = Math.abs (startX - endX);
  int height = Math.abs (startY - endY);
  parm1.setColor (drawingColor);
  buf.setColor (drawingColor);
  if (dragging) {
    parm1.drawImage (im, 0, 0, this);
    parm1.fillRect (x, y, width, height);
  } else {
    buf.fillRect (x, y, width, height);
    parm1.drawImage (im, 0, 0, this);
  }
}
```

```java
  public void update (Graphics parm1) {
    paint(parm1);
  }
  public void setStartPoint (Point p) {
    startX = p.x;
    startY = p.y;
  }
  public void setEndPoint (Point p) {
    endX = p.x;
    endY = p.y;
  }
  public void setDrawingColor (Color c) {
    drawingColor = c;
  }
  public void mouseClicked(MouseEvent parm1) {
    im = createImage (getSize().width, getSize().height);
    buf = im.getGraphics();
  }

  public void mousePressed(MouseEvent parm1) {
    setStartPoint (parm1.getPoint());
    dragging = true;
  }

  public void mouseReleased(MouseEvent parm1) {
    setEndPoint (parm1.getPoint());
    dragging = false;
    repaint();
  }

  public void mouseEntered(MouseEvent parm1) {
    short r = (short)(Math.random () * 256);
    short g = (short)(Math.random () * 256);
    short b = (short)(Math.random () * 256);
    setDrawingColor (new Color (r, g, b));
  }

  public void mouseExited(MouseEvent parm1) {
  }

  public void mouseDragged(MouseEvent parm1) {
    setEndPoint (parm1.getPoint());
    repaint();
  }

  public void mouseMoved(MouseEvent parm1) {
  }
}
```

Congratulations! By combining the multithreading you learned in Skill 4 with the double buffering you learned here, you now know the key features of Java needed to do smooth, steady, and multicolor animation. We'll revisit multithreading again soon to further demonstrate why it is so important to know and appreciate. But next we'll take a look at JBuilder's `TreeControl` component. We'll use it to display the current directory structure graphically and to demonstrate reading from a file.

Are You Experienced?

Now you can...

- ☑ draw within Java
- ☑ work with mouse events
- ☑ draw to a buffer
- ☑ display images
- ☑ load image files
- ☑ work with Java colors

PROGRAMMERS
C, C, VB, Cobol, exp. Call 534-555-6543 or fax 534-555-6544.

PROGRAMMING
MRFS Inc. is looking for a Sr. Windows NT developer. Reqs. 3-5 yrs. Exp. in C under Windows, Win95 & NT, using Visual C. Excl. OO design & implementation skills a must. OLE2 & ODBC are a plus. Excl. Salary & bnfts. Resume & salary history to HR, 8779 HighTech Way, Computer City, AR

PROGRAMMERS
Contractors Wanted for short & long term assignments; Visual C, MFC Unix C/C, SQL Oracle Dev elopers PC Help Desk Support Windows NT & NetWare Telecommunications Visual Basic, Access, HTML, CGI, Perl MMI & Co. 885-555-9933

PROGRAMMER
World Wide Web Links wants your HTML & Photoshop skills. Develop great WWW sites. Local & global customers. Send samples & resume to WWWL, 2000 Apple Road, Santa Rosa, CA.

TECHNICAL WRITER
Software firm seeks writer/editor for manuals, research notes, project mgmt. Min 2 years tech. writing, DTP & programming experience. Send resume & writing samples to: Software Systems, Dallas, TX.

TECHNICAL
Software development firm looking for Tech Trainers. Ideal candidates have development experience in Visual C, HTML & JAVA. Need quick self starter. Call (443) 555-6868 for interview.

TECHNICAL WRITER/
Premier Computer Corp is seeking a combination of technical skills, knowledge and experience in the following areas: UNIX, Windows 95/NT, Visual Basic, on-line help & documentation, and the internet. Candidates must possess excellent writing skills, and be comfortable working in a quality vs. deadline driven environment. Competitive salary. Fax resume & samples to Karen Fields, Premier Computer Corp. 444 Industrial Blvd. Concord, CA. Or send to our website at www.premier.com.

WEB DESIGNER
BA/BS or equivalent programming/multimedia production, 3 years of experience in use and design of WWW services streaming audio and video HTML, PERL, CGI, GIF, JPEG. Demonstrated interpersonal, organization, communication, multi-tasking skills. Send resume to The Learning People at www.learning.com.

WEBMASTER-TECHNICAL
BSCS or equivalent, 2 years of experience in CGI, Windows 95/NT, UNIX, C, Java, Perl. Demonstrated ability to design, code, debug and test on-line services. Send resume to The Learning People at www.learning.com.

PROGRAMMER
World Wide Web Links wants your HTML & Photoshop skills. Develop great WWW sites.

PROGRAMMERS
Multiple short term assignments available: Visual C, 3 positions SQL ServerNT Server, 2 positions JAVA & HTML, long term NetWare Various locations. Call for more info. 356-555-3398.

PROGRAMMERS
C, C, VB, Cobol, exp.
Call 534-555-6543
or fax 534-555-6544.

PROGRAMMING
MRFS Inc. is looking for a Sr. Windows NT developer. Reqs. 3-5 yrs. Exp. In C under Windows, Win95 & NT, using Visual C. Excl. OO design & implementation skills a must. OLE2 & ODBC are a plus. Excl. Salary & bnfts. Resume & salary history to HR, 8779 HighTech Way, Computer City, AR

PROGRAMMERS/
Contractors Wanted for short & long term assignments: Visual C, MFC Unix C/C, SQL Oracle Developers PC Help Desk Support Windows NT & NetWare Telecommunications Visual Basic, Access, HTML, CGI, Perl MMI & Co. 885-555-9933

PROGRAMMER
World Wide Web Links wants your HTML & Photoshop skills. Develop great WWW sites. Local & global customers. Send samples & resume to WWWL, 2000 Apple Road, Santa Rosa, CA.

TECHNICAL WRITER
Software firm seeks writer/editor for manuals, research notes, project mgmt. Min 2 years tech. writing, DTP & programming experience. Send resume & writing samples to: Software Systems, Dallas, TX.

COMPUTER PROGRAMMER
Ad agency seeks programmer w/exp. in UNIX/NT Platforms, Web Server, CGI/Perl. Programmer Position avail. on a project basis with the possibility to move into F/T. Fax resume & salary req. to R. Jones 334-555-8332.

COMPUTERS
Programmer/Analyst Design and maintain C based SQL database applications. Required skills: Visual Basic, C, SQL, ODBC. Document existing and new applications. Novell or NT exp. a plus. Fax resume & salary history to 235-555-9935.

GRAPHIC DESIGNER
Webmaster's Weekly is seeking a creative Graphic Designer to design high impact marketing collateral, including direct mail promo's, CD-ROM packages, ads and WWW pages. Must be able to juggle multiple projects and learn new skills on the job very rapidly. Web design experience a big plus, technical troubleshooting also a plus. Call 435-555-1235.

GRAPHICS - ART DIRECTOR - WEB-MULTIMEDIA
Leading internet development company has an outstanding opportunity for a talented, high-end Web Experienced Art Director. In addition to a great portfolio and fresh ideas, the ideal candidate has excellent communication and presentation skills. Working as a team with innovative producers and programmers, you will create dynamic, interactive web sites and application interfaces. Some programming experience required. Send samples and resume to: SuperSites, 333 Main, Seattle, WA

MARKETING
Fast paced software and services provider looking for MARKETING COMMUNICATIONS SPECIALIST to be responsible for its webpage.

PROGRAMMERS
Multiple short term assignments available: Visual C, 3 positions SQL ServerNT Server, 2 positions JAVA & HTML, long term NetWare Various locations. Call for more info. 356-555-3398.

PROGRAMMERS
C, C, VB, Cobol, exp. Call 534-555-6543 or fax 534-555-6544.

PROGRAMMING
MRFS Inc. is looking for a Sr. Windows NT developer. Reqs. 3-5 yrs. Exp. In C under Windows, Win95 & NT, using Visual C. Excl. OO design & implementation skills a must. OLE2 & ODBC are a plus. Excl. Salary & bnfts. Resume & salary history to HR, 8779 HighTech Way, Computer City, AR

PROGRAMMERS/
Contractors Wanted for short & long term assignments: Visual C, MFC Unix C/C, SQL Oracle Developers PC Help Desk Support Windows NT & NetWare Telecommunications Visual Basic, Access, HTML, CGI, Perl MMI 885-555-9933

PROGRAMMER
World Wide Web Links wants your HTML & Photoshop skills. Develop great WWW. Local & global customers. Send samples & resume to WWWL, Apple Road, Santa Rosa, CA.

TECHNICAL WRITER
Software seeks writer/editor for manuals, research notes, project mgmt. years tech. writing, DTP & programming experience. Send resume & writing samples to: Software Systems, Dallas, TX.

TECHNICAL
Software development firm looking for Tech Trainers candidates have programming experience in Visual C, HTML & Need quick self starter. Call 555-6868 for interview.

TECHNICAL WRITER
Premier Computer Corp is seeking a combination of technical skills, knowledge and experience in the following areas: UNIX, Windows 95/NT, Visual Basic, on-line help & documentation and the internet. Candidates possess excellent writing skills, be comfortable working in a vs. deadline driven environment. Competitive salary. Fax resume samples to Karen Fields, Computer Corp. 444 Industrial, Concord, CA. Or send to our at www.premier.com.

WEB DESIGNER
BA/BS or equivalent programming/multimedia production, years of experience in use design of WWW services streaming audio and video HTML, PERL, GIF, JPEG. Demonstrated in sonal, organization, communication multi-tasking skills. Send The Learning People at www.learning.com.

WEBMASTER-TECHN

SKILL 8

eight

Accessing Files

- ❑ Learning about files
- ❑ Creating temporary memory files with `StringWriter`
- ❑ Reading a file with `FileReader`
- ❑ Listing a directory structure textually
- ❑ Displaying disk structure graphically with a `TreeControl`

Getting File Information

Now that you have a feel for drawing in Java, this skill will teach you how to access the local file system. Java provides access to the file system through classes in the `java.io` package. The makeup of this package allows you to read and write bytes, characters, and objects, and share the results with any other Java runtime system, without regard for platform-specific data formats. In this skill, we'll sample the pieces of the package to get file information, read files, and display the directory structure—both textually and graphically—via `TreeControl`.

Access to the local file system in Java is restricted. Stand-alone Java applications can access it, but Java applets normally cannot. Because of this restriction, the program we'll create with this skill will be an application.

To get started, close any open projects and create a project for Skill 8. Use the Application Wizard to create a new project named **skill8** in the **\skills\skill8\skill8.jpr** file by selecting the Finish button. Once in the actual Application Wizard dialog boxes, select Next, name the `Frame` class `DirReader`, and select Finish to create the framework to work in. This will create an `.html` file named after the project, along with two source files, `DirReader.java` and `Application1.java`.

> **NOTE** Java 1.1 allows you to digitally sign applets. You then distribute the applet along with your public encryption key. If the person who receives the applet trusts you, they can register your key and give you extra permissions. These permissions could include file-system access. However, working in an applet, you shouldn't expect this to happen.

The first class to learn about when accessing the file system is the `File` class. `File` allows you to find out information about the specific file-system resource—answers to questions such as "Does it exist?", "Is it a directory?", and "What size is it?" Table 8.1 lists the information methods of `File`. There are other `File` methods that are more action-oriented and not listed.

TABLE 8.1: Information Methods of `File`

Name	Description
canRead()	Is the file readable?
canWrite()	Is the file writable?
exists()	Does the file exist?

TABLE 8.1 CONTINUED: Information Methods of `File`

Name	Description
getAbsolutePath()	What is the absolute path to the file?
getCanonicalPath()	What is the absolute path to the file, without any relative pieces in name?
getName()	What is the name?
getParent()	What is the parent directory?
getPath()	What is the directory path to the file?
isAbsolute()	Is the name absolute?
isDirectory()	Is the file a directory?
isFile()	Is the file a normal one?
lastModified()	When was the file last changed?
length()	How big is the file?

> **NOTE** One thing you may notice about all these methods is that none of them looks at the contents of the file. This means that the `File` class does not open the file. It only looks at the directory entry.

Let's create a program that displays all this information for any filename entered.

Using a *StringWriter*

To demonstrate the different methods of `File`, we're going to create a program that gets a filename from a `TextField` and calls all the appropriate `File` methods to learn about it. The information will be displayed in a `TextArea`.

> **NOTE** A `TextArea` is similar to a `TextField`, except a `TextArea` provides multiple lines for display of input, whereas a `TextField` only offers one.

As you'll find with most interactive programs, the first thing you want to do is create the user interface. Here we need a `TextField` and `TextArea`, so let's create them where the Wizard created the other instance variables of the `DirReader` class. To name them after their purpose, we can call the `TextField` **input**, and the `TextArea`, **output**. We aren't going to use the `XYLayout` and `BevelPanel` so we can delete them. The variable section now looks like the following:

```
BorderLayout borderLayout1 = new BorderLayout();
TextField input = new TextField();
TextArea output = new TextArea();
```

In order to complete the interface, we need to modify the `jbInit` method. Select the `jbInit` method in the Structure pane to move the source in the Content pane to the appropriate location. Here we need to remove the references to the no-longer-used layout and panel, and add `input` and `output` to the screen. To remove the layout and panel, remove the two lines that refer to xYLayout2 or bevelPanel1.

To add the components, use the `add` method. The `TextField`, `input`, looks best in the North quadrant, while the `TextArea`, `output`, looks best in the Center. This takes advantage of the `BorderLayout`'s constraints. We want the `TextField` to be only as tall as necessary, while letting it be as wide as possible. This is what the North quadrant of a `BorderLayout` frame does. On the other hand, we want the `TextArea` for results output to be as big as possible. That is exactly what the Center quadrant does.

The `jbInit` method now looks like the following:

```
public void jbInit() throws Exception{
   this.setLayout(borderLayout1);
   this.setSize(newDimension(400, 300));
   this.setTitle("Frame Title");
   this.add(input, BorderLayout.NORTH);
   this.add(output, BorderLayout.CENTER);
}
```

That's it for the interface for now. It isn't too snazzy, but it serves its purpose. When we get to the Reading Files section, we'll add some buttons along the bottom of the screen to differentiate functionality. For now, there is only one thing: to get the file information.

Getting the File Information

Similar to the Hi-Lo game in Skill 5, in order to get action events from the `TextField`, we need to listen for an `ActionEvent`. In order to listen, we need someone to implement the `ActionListener`. So, let's have the program implement `ActionListener` and associate it with the button. With the help of the Implement Interface Wizard, select `java.awt.event.ActionListener` and then OK. This will add an `actionPerformed` method to the source.

Now we need to call all the information `File` methods for the filename entered. By itself, that is easy, but what's the best way to get the results and send them to the `TextArea`? Java provides an in-memory, temporary file class called `StringWriter`. The class allows you to store any information in memory until you need it. When you need it, you just ask for it back via the `toString` method.

That sounds great, but how do you write to it? Well, we're actually going to sidestep that question and show you an easier way. The `PrintWriter` class has a `println` method. It prints any single argument you give it to the `PrintWriter`'s destination. By making the `StringWriter` the `PrintWriter`'s destination in the `PrintWriter` constructor, you can use `println` to display the results to a `PrintWriter`, and it then works its way over to a `StringWriter`.

```
StringWriter sw = new StringWriter();
PrintWriter pw  = new PrintWriter (sw);
pw.println ("Hello");
```

Once you are done sending the output, you display the results in a `TextArea` with its `setText` method, just like `TextField`.

```
aTextArea.setText (sw.toString());
```

The following code does what we just described.

> **TIP** Don't forget to import the java.io.* package!

```
public void actionPerformed(ActionEvent parm1) {
  StringWriter sw = new StringWriter();
  PrintWriter pw  = new PrintWriter (sw);
  File f = new File (input.getText());
  pw.println ("canRead() " + f.canRead());
  pw.println ("canWrite() " + f.canWrite());
  pw.println ("exists() " + f.exists());
  pw.println ("getAbsolutePath() " + f.getAbsolutePath());
  try {
    pw.println ("getCanonicalPath() " + f.getCanonicalPath());
  } catch (IOException e) {
    pw.println ("getCanonicalPath() unknown");
  }
  pw.println ("getName() " + f.getName());
  pw.println ("getParent() " + f.getParent());
  pw.println ("getPath() " + f.getPath());
  pw.println ("isAbsolute() " + f.isAbsolute());
  pw.println ("isDirectory() " + f.isDirectory());
  pw.println ("isFile() " + f.isFile());
```

```
        pw.println ("lastModified() " + new java.util.Date(f.lastModified()));
        pw.println ("length() " + f.length());
        output.setText (sw.toString());
    }
```

> **TIP** There is one note worth mentioning. The `File.lastModified` method returns the modification date as a `long`, twice as big as an `int`. To display it in some meaningful manner, you need to convert it to a Date: `new java.util.Date (f.lastModified())`.

Now that we've programmed the functionality, we need to listen for the events with the `TextField`. To do this, associate an `ActionListener` with `input` in the `jbInit` method—anywhere will do, but let's put the statement last: `input.addActionListener (this);`. You can now save everything and run the program. Figure 8.1 shows you a sample of the output.

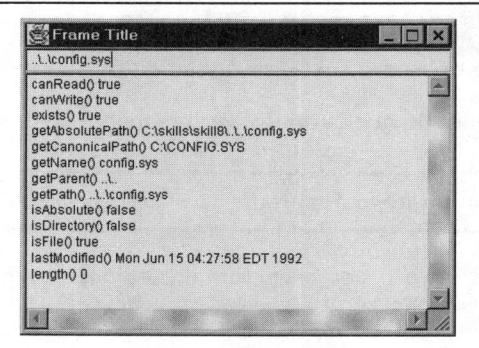

FIGURE 8.1: Getting file information. Enter different names in TextField to see different results. This screen shows the results for `....\config.sys`.

Reading Files

Once you are able to access the file information, you can find out if a file is worth reading. The class responsible for reading files is `FileReader`. Given a `File` or a filename (as a `String`), you can read the file one character at a time until you get to the end. However, just as with `StringWriter`, there is an easier way. If you want to read a line at a time, you need the help of a `BufferedReader`. Given a source, the `FileReader` in this case, we can use a `BufferedReader` to read in the contents and display them in the `TextArea`.

> **NOTE** This concept of building on an I/O class with something that offers more capabilities is called *daisy chaining*. It is very common in Java. The basic input and output classes are very simple. If you do not need extra capabilities, there is no overhead involved; if you do need the capabilities, you chain the basic class with a richer one to get more functionality.

There are a few changes we need to make in our existing program:

1. We need to add two buttons to the screen, Info and Read. This allows the user to select what functionality they want to perform.

2. We need to associate the listener with each button and remove the current listener on the `TextField`, since we don't know what action they want anymore.

3. We need to check which button is selected in the action handler. If Info is selected, we display the current capabilities.

4. If the user selects the Read option, we need to read in the file if it is a regular file.

First, let's actually do steps 1 and 2 together. We'll add the buttons to the South quadrant of the `Frame`. In order to add multiple components into one quadrant, we need to group them together. The `Panel` class provides the most common way to do this. Basically, create the `Panel`, create each button, add each button to `Panel`, and add `Panel` to `Frame`. In the middle, associate an `ActionListener` with each button. The new `jbInit` method follows:

```
public void jbInit() throws Exception{
    this.setLayout(borderLayout1);
    this.setSize(newDimension(400, 300));
    this.setTitle("Frame Title");
    this.add(input, BorderLayout.NORTH);
    this.add(output, BorderLayout.CENTER);
    Panel p = new Panel ();
    Button info = new Button ("Info");
    info.addActionListener (this);
    p.add (info);
    Button read = new Button ("Read");
    read.addActionListener (this);
    p.add (read);
    this.add (p, BorderLayout.SOUTH);
}
```

For steps 3 and 4, we update our existing `actionPerformed` method. To determine which button was selected, the `ActionEvent` parameter has a `getActionCommand` method. When the event source is a button, this tells us the label of the button selected. For the Info button, we need to check if the action command is `"Info"`. If it is, we just do what we did before.

As programmers usually do, we'll move the code we just wrote for outputting the file information into a helper method called `infoFile`. We'll write the code to read the contents of the file (we'll see it in a few minutes) in a helper method called `readFile`.

```
public void actionPerformed (ActionEvent parm1) {
  StringWriter sw = new StringWriter();
  PrintWriter pw = new PrintWriter (sw);
  if (parm1.getSource() instanceof Button) {
    String command = parm1.getActionCommand();
    File f = new File (input.getText());
    if (command.equals ("Info")) {
      infoFile (pw, f);
    } else if (command.equals ("Read")) {
      readFile (pw, f);   // code for readFile() is below.
    }
  }
  output.setText (sw.toString());
}
```

For the Read button, we check if the filename provided is a normal file, and, if so, read in the contents. The `isFile` method of `File` reports on the file status. In the case where it is normal, we daisy chain the `File` to the `FileReader`, then the `FileReader` to the `BufferedReader`. Now, when you read with `BufferedReader`'s `readLine` method, you are getting your contents from the `File`. When the `BufferedReader` gets to the end of the file, `readLine` returns `null`. This signifies there is nothing left to read. The file reading code follows:

```
private void readFile (PrintWriter pw, File f) {
  if (f.isFile()) {
    try {
      FileReader fr = new FileReader (f);
      BufferedReader br = new BufferedReader (fr);
      String line;
      while ((line = br.readLine()) != null) {
        pw.println (line);
      }
    } catch (IOException e) {
```

```
      pw.println ("Problems reading file");
    }
  }
}
```

The second phase of our program is done. It can now read the file information and read files. If we save everything and run the program, you'll see the screen shown in Figure 8.2.

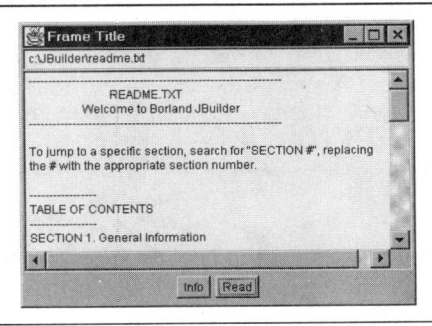

FIGURE 8.2: Reading a file. This screen shows the results for JBuilder's `readme.txt` file.

Listing a Directory

The third button we'll add to the program will allow us to get a directory listing. The File class has a list method. This returns an array of strings with one entry for each file in the current File if it is a directory. Adding the button to the screen in jbInit:

```
Button dir = new Button ("Dirs");
dir.addActionListener (this);
p.add (dir);
```

and adding code to the actionPerformed method, allows us to read the directory:

```
} else if (command.equals ("Dirs")) {
  if (f.isDirectory()) {
    String files[] = f.list();
  }
  for (int i=0;i<files.length;i++) {
    pw.println (files[i]);
  }
}
}
```

Showing a Directory Graphically

For this skill's final task, we're going to combine everything we've learned so far and display the directory structure graphically with the help of JBuilder's `TreeControl` component. In the graphical representation, if the user double-clicks on an entry, either the file information, contents, or directory will be displayed in the `TextArea`, based upon the entry type selected.

> **NOTE** The `TreeControl` is how JBuilder displays the information in the Content pane of its tool. We're going to reuse that for our own purposes. Although the Content pane displays an image next to each entry, we are only going to show a text entry.

The key to using `TreeControl` is to know all the pieces. The first thing you need is something to place in the tree. You do this with a class that implements the `GraphLocation` interface. You can do all the work and implement the interface yourself, or you can reuse the `LinkedTreeNode` class that Borland provides. Every entry in the tree needs to be a `LinkedTreeNode`. Because we want to display a reasonable value for each entry in the tree, we need to create a subclass of `LinkedTreeNode`. This also allows us to remember the `File` associated with the node and the `File` to use when the node is selected. The source for the subclass follows. Place it at the top of the `DirReader.java` source file immediately after the `import` statements. The `toString` method defines what the `TreeControl` will display for this node in the tree.

```
class ATreeNode extends LinkedTreeNode {
  File file;
  public ATreeNode(File f) {
    this.file = f;
  }
  public File getFile () {
    return file;
  }
  public String toString() {
    return file.getName();
  }
}
```

> **TIP** Don't forget to import the `borland.jbcl.model.` package!

Once the node is defined, we can build the tree. Using a simple recursive algorithm, we create a node for the `file` passed in; then if the file is a directory, we create a child node for each of its entries. This repeats forever until there are no more directories. The only thing that should appear new to you in the following code is the `appendChild` method `ATreeNode` inherited from `LinkedTreeNode`. This is how you associate a child to a node in the tree. Add the following method to the `DirReader` class:

```
private ATreeNode buildTree (File file) {
  ATreeNode root = new ATreeNode (file);
  if (file.isDirectory()) {
    String files[] = file.list();
    for (int i=0;i<files.length;i++) {
      File newFile = new File (file, files[i]);
      ATreeNode child = buildTree (newFile);
      root.appendChild (child);
    }
  }
  return root;
}
```

> **NOTE** *Recursion* is the process of breaking complex tasks down into simpler ones through a common algorithm. For instance, 6! (six factorial) is 1*2*3*4*5*6. You could program this in two ways. The first is to loop from one to six and multiply the numbers together. This is the *nonrecursive* way. The other way is to use recursion. 6! is 6*5!, but what is 5!? 5! is 5*4!. And 4! is 4*3!. Next, 3! is 3*2!. Then 2! is 2*1!. Finally, 1! is 1. This then backtracks to give you 6! is 720. Some algorithms are easier to implement recursively, while others may be *representable* recursively but are best left to the nonrecursive realm.

Displaying the Tree

Now that we can build the tree, we need to add another button to our screen. This one we'll call Tree. When the user selects it, it will create and display the tree.

```
Button tree = new Button ("Tree");
tree.addActionListener (this);
p.add (tree);
```

Creating the tree is simple, just call the method we created:

```
else if (command.equals ("Tree") {
  ATreeNode node = buildTree (f);
```

Once you have your tree created, with a root of node, you need to associate the tree to the `TreeControl`. The `LinkedTreeNode` class—ATreeNode's superclass—has a related class called `LinkedTreeContainer`. The `LinkedTreeContainer` serves as the model of our tree and is associated to the `TreeControl`.

```
TreeControl tc = new TreeControl();
tc.setModel(new LinkedTreeContainer (node));
```

MVC: MODEL/VIEW/CONTROLLER

This is your first introduction to *MVC: Model/View/Controller,* which is used considerably within JBuilder and will be used in capabilities forthcoming in the Java core. The MVC design originated in Smalltalk to help create more reusable interfaces. It is composed of three pieces:

- The *Model* defines the state of the system. In our case, the model is the `LinkedTreeContainer`, consisting of a collection of nodes with children. At a particular instance in time, there is always only one model for the system.

- The *View* is how the user sees the model. In our program it is in the `TreeControl`. However, if we wanted to display the model differently, the model would not change—only our view of it would.

- The *Controller* is how the user interacts with the model. In our program, this too is the `TreeControl`. Because of the close ties between display and interaction, the two pieces are combined.

Two other things worth doing here are to make our tree read-only via the `setEditInPlace` method and to associate an `ActionListener` to the tree. By default, a `TreeControl` allows you to alter the names of the nodes. Without adding renaming capabilities to the program, we want to turn this off. In addition, we need to listen for double-clicking on a node. This action triggers an `ActionEvent`, similar to pressing a button. Therefore, we need to associate an `ActionListener` to the tree too. Thankfully, you do not associate the listener to each node, but to the entire tree.

```
tc.setEditInPlace (false);
tc.addActionListener (this);
```

In order to display the tree, we need to place it into its own window. Similar to our main program, we'll use a `DecoratedFrame`. We need to create it, set its title, add the `TreeControl`, size it, and show it. If you then run the program, enter a directory, such as **\JBuilder**, in the text field and select Tree; you'll see the screen shown in Figure 8.3. After selecting several of the '+'s, you'll see the screen shown in Figure 8.4. We did not need to add any code to open and close the '+' or '-' graphics.

```
DecoratedFrame df = new DecoratedFrame ();
df.setTitle ("Tree for " + node.toString());
df.add (tc, BorderLayout.CENTER);
df.setSize(300, 300);
df.setVisible(true);
```

FIGURE 8.3: The initial Tree screen for the \JBuilder directory

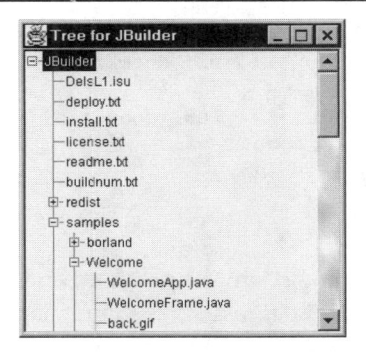

FIGURE 8.4: After opening up various entries for the directory

Handling Selection in the Tree

One thing we started but didn't complete is handling the selection (double-click) of an entry in the `TreeControl`. When the user double-clicks on an entry, the source of the `ActionEvent` generated is the `TreeControl`, and the action command of the `ActionEvent` is the label of the node. Because the node's label isn't sufficient to read a file, we have to get the actual node and ask for the file before we can display it.

To get the selected node, you ask the `TreeControl` via its `getSelection` method. This returns an object that implements the `WritableGraphSelection` interface. You then ask the return object for everything that is selected. In our case there will always be only one selected; however, the functionality supports multiple selections.

The `WritableGraphSelection.getAll` method returns a `GraphLocation` array. `GraphLocation` is again something familiar; it's our node. You can now ask the node for its file and display the appropriate information about it. We can now add the following code to `actionPerformed`. If the node selected is a file, read it. If it is a directory, display a listing of the files within it.

```
if (parm1.getSource() instanceof TreeControl) {
  TreeControl tc = (TreeControl)parm1.getSource();
  WritableGraphSelection sel = tc.getSelection();
  GraphLocation gl[] = sel.getAll();
  for (int i=0;i<gl.length;i++) {
    if (gl[i] instanceof ATreeNode) {
      ATreeNode node = (ATreeNode)gl[i];
      File nodeFile = node.getFile();
      if (nodeFile.isFile()) {
        readFile (pw, nodeFile);
      } else if (nodeFile.isDirectory()) {
        dirFile (pw, nodeFile);
      } else {
        infoFile (pw, nodeFile);
      }
    }
  }
}
```

Now, save and run the program and display a tree. Notice how double-clicking on a node of the tree displays information about the node in the original window. `DirReader.java` contains the whole listing for the application we created in this skill.

DirReader.java

```java
package skill8;

import java.awt.*;
import java.awt.event.*;
import java.io.*;
import borland.jbcl.model.*;
import borland.jbcl.control.*;
import borland.jbcl.layout.*;

class ATreeNode extends LinkedTreeNode {
  File file;
  public ATreeNode(File f) {
    this.file = f;
  }
  public File getFile () {
    return file;
  }
  public String toString() {
    return file.getName();
  }
}

public class DirReader extends DecoratedFrame implements ActionListener {
  BorderLayout borderLayout1 = new BorderLayout();
  TextField input = new TextField();
  TextArea output = new TextArea();

  //Construct the frame
  public DirReader() {
    try {
      jbInit();
    }
    catch (Exception e) {
      e.printStackTrace();
    };
  }

  //Component initialization
  public void jbInit() throws Exception{
    this.setLayout(borderLayout1);
    this.setSize(newDimension(400, 300));
    this.setTitle("Frame Title");
    this.add(input, BorderLayout.NORTH);
    this.add(output, BorderLayout.CENTER);
```

Skill 8 • Accessing Files

```java
      Panel p = new Panel ();
      Button info = new Button ("Info");
      info.addActionListener (this);
      p.add (info);
      Button read = new Button ("Read");
      read.addActionListener (this);
      p.add (read);
      Button dir = new Button ("Dirs");
      dir.addActionListener (this);
      p.add (dir);
      Button tree = new Button ("Tree");
      tree.addActionListener (this);
      p.add (tree);
      this.add (p, BorderLayout.SOUTH);
   }

   public void actionPerformed(ActionEvent parm1) {
      StringWriter sw = new StringWriter();
      PrintWriter pw  = new PrintWriter (sw);
      if (parm1.getSource() instanceof Button) {
         String command = parm1.getActionCommand();
         File f = new File (input.getText());
         if (command.equals ("Info")) {
            infoFile (pw, f);
         } else if (command.equals ("Read")) {
            readFile (pw, f);
         } else if (command.equals ("Dirs")) {
            dirFile (pw, f);
         } else if (command.equals ("Tree")) {
            ATreeNode node = buildTree (f);
            TreeControl tc = new TreeControl();
            tc.setModel(new LinkedTreeContainer (node));
            tc.setEditInPlace (false);
            tc.addActionListener (this);
            DecoratedFrame df = new DecoratedFrame ();
            df.setTitle ("Tree for " + node.toString());
            df.add (tc, BorderLayout.CENTER);
            df.setSize(300, 300);
            df.setVisible(true);
         }
      } else {
         if (parm1.getSource() instanceof TreeControl) {
            TreeControl tc = (TreeControl)parm1.getSource();
            WritableGraphSelection sel = tc.getSelection();
            GraphLocation gl[] = sel.getAll();
            for (int i=0;i<gl.length;i++) {
               if (gl[i] instanceof ATreeNode) {
                  ATreeNode node = (ATreeNode)gl[i];
```

```
            File nodeFile = node.getFile();
            if (nodeFile.isFile()) {
              readFile (pw, nodeFile);
            } else if (nodeFile.isDirectory()) {
              dirFile (pw, nodeFile);
            } else {
              infoFile (pw, nodeFile);
            }
          }
        }
      }
    }
  }
  output.setText (sw.toString());
}
private ATreeNode buildTree (File file) {
  ATreeNode root = new ATreeNode (file);
  if (file.isDirectory()) {
    String files[] = file.list();
    for (int i=0;i<files.length;i++) {
      File newFile = new File (file, files[i]);
      ATreeNode child = buildTree (newFile);
      root.appendChild (child);
    }
  }
  return root;
}
private void readFile (PrintWriter pw, File f) {
  if (f.isFile()) {
    try {
      FileReader fr = new FileReader (f);
      BufferedReader br = new BufferedReader (fr);
      String line;
      while ((line = br.readLine()) != null) {
        pw.println (line);
      }
    } catch (IOException e) {
      pw.println ("Problems reading file");
    }
  } else {
    pw.println ("Not a normal file");
  }
}
private void dirFile (PrintWriter pw, File f) {
  if (f.isDirectory()) {
    String files[] = f.list();
    for (int i=0;i<files.length;i++) {
      pw.println (files[i]);
```

```
      }
    } else {
      pw.println ("Not a directory");
    }
  }
  private void infoFile (PrintWriter pw, File f) {
    pw.println ("canRead() " + f.canRead());
    pw.println ("canWrite() " + f.canWrite());
    pw.println ("exists() " + f.exists());
    pw.println ("getAbsolutePath() " + f.getAbsolutePath());
    try {
      pw.println ("getCanonicalPath() " + f.getCanonicalPath());
    } catch (IOException e) {
      pw.println ("getCanonicalPath() unknown");
    }
    pw.println ("getName() " + f.getName());
    pw.println ("getParent() " + f.getParent());
    pw.println ("getPath() " + f.getPath());
    pw.println ("isAbsolute() " + f.isAbsolute());
    pw.println ("isDirectory() " + f.isDirectory());
    pw.println ("isFile() " + f.isFile());
    pw.println ("lastModified() " + new
 java.util.Date(f.lastModified()));
    pw.println ("length() " + f.length());
  }
}
```

Wow—how's that for reuse? Your program gets to reuse pieces of JBuilder itself. You now also know how to daisy chain parts of `java.io` to exchange data within your Java program. In Skill 9, we'll move into the JavaBeans pieces of JBuilder and start to see how JBuilder isn't just an Integrated Development Environment (IDE) for Java, but a true Rapid Application Development (RAD) tool.

Are You Experienced?

Now you can...

- ☑ display file information
- ☑ use *StringWriter* for temporary storage
- ☑ use *PrintWriter* for easy writing of any data
- ☑ use *FileReader* to read a file
- ☑ use *BufferedReader* to buffer file accesses
- ☑ use *TreeControl* to display a graphical hierarchy
- ☑ describe the Model/View/Controller architecture
- ☑ respond to selections within the *TreeControl*

PART II

Digging into JavaBeans

PROGRAMMERS
C, C, VB, Cobol, exp. Call 534-555-6543 or fax 534-555-6544.

PROGRAMMING
MRFS, Inc. is looking for a Sr. Windows NT developer. Reqs. 3-5 yrs. Exp. In C under Windows, Win95 & NT, using Visual C, Excl. OO design & implementation skills a must. OLE2 & ODBC are a plus. Excl. Salary & bnfts. Resume & salary history to HR, 8779 HighTech Way, Computer City, AR

PROGRAMMERS
Contractors Wanted for short & long term assignments; Visual C, MFC Unix C/C, SQL Oracle Dev elopers PC Help Desk Support Windows NT & NetWareTelecommunications Visual Basic, Access, HTML, CGI, Perl MMI & Co., 885-555-9933

PROGRAMMER
World Wide Web Links wants your HTML & Photoshop skills. Develop great WWW sites. Local & global customers. Send samples & resume to WWWL, 2000 Apple Road, Santa Rosa, CA.

TECHNICAL WRITER
Software firm seeks writer/editor for manuals, research notes, project mgmt. Min 2 years tech. writing, DTP & programming experience. Send resume & writing samples to: Software Systems, Dallas, TX.

TECHNICAL
Software development firm looking for Tech Trainers. Ideal candidates have programming experience in Visual C, HTML & JAVA. Need quick self starter. Call (443) 555-6868 for interview.

TECHNICAL WRITER/
Premier Computer Corp is seeking a combination of technical skills, knowledge and experience in the following areas: UNIX, Windows 95/NT, Visual Basic, on-line help & documentation, and the internet. Candidates must possess excellent writing skills, and be comfortable working in a quality vs. deadline driven environment. Competitive salary. Fax resume & samples to Karen Fields, Premier Computer Corp., 444 Industrial Blvd. Concord, CA. Or send to our website at www.premier.com.

WEB DESIGNER
BA/BS or equivalent programming/multimedia production. 3 years of experience in use and design of WWW services streaming audio and video HTML, PERL, CGI, GIF, JPEG. Demonstrated interpersonal, organization, communication, multi-tasking skills. Send resume to The Learning People at www.learning.com

WEBMASTER-TECHNICAL
BSCS or equivalent, 2 years of experience in CGI, Windows 95/NT, UNIX, C, Java, Perl, Demonstrated ability to design, code, debug and test on-line services. Send resume to The Learning People at www.learning.com

PROGRAMMER
World Wide Web Links wants your HTML & Photoshop skills. Develop great WWW sites. Local & global customers. Send samples

---

ing tools. Experienced in documentation preparation & programming languages (Access, C, FoxPro) are a plus. financial or banking customer service support is required along with excellent verbal & written communication skills with multi levels of end-users. Send resume to KKUP Enterprises, 45 Orange Blvd., Orange, CA.

COMPUTERS
Small Web Design firm seeks indiv w/NT, Webserver & Database management exp. Fax resume to 556-555-4221.

COMPUTER/
Visual C/C, Visual Basic Exp'd Systems Analysts/Programmers for growing software dev. team in Roseburg. Computer Science or related degree preferred. Develop adv. Engineering applications for engineering firm. Fax resume to 707-555-8744.

COMPUTER
Web Master for dynamic SF Internet co. Site. Dev. test, coord, train. 2 yrs prog. Exp. C C, Web C, FTP. Fax resume to Best Staffing 845-555-7722.

COMPUTER PROGRAMMER
Ad agency seeks programmer w/exp. in UNIX/NT Platforms, Web Server, CGI/Perl. Programmer Position avail. on a project basis with the possibility to move into F/T. Fax resume & salary req. to R. Jones 334-555-8332.

COMPUTERS
Programmer/Analyst Design and maintain C based SQL database applications. Required skills: Visual Basic, C, SQL, ODBC, Document existing and new applications. Novell or NT exp. a plus. Fax resume & salary history to 235-555-9935.

GRAPHIC DESIGNER
Webmaster's Weekly is seeking a creative Graphic Designer to design high impact marketing collateral, including direct mail promois. CD-ROM packages, ads and WWW pages. Must be able to juggle multiple projects and learn new skills on the job very rapidly. Web design experience a big plus, technical troubleshooting also a plus. Call 435-555-1235.

GRAPHICS - ART DIRECTOR - WEB-MULTIMEDIA
Leading internet development company has an outstanding opportunity for a talented, high-end Web Experienced Art Director. In addition to a great portfolio and fresh ideas, the ideal candidate has excellent communication and presentation skills. Working as a team with innovative producers and programmers, you will create dynamic, interactive web sites and application interfaces. Some programming experience required. Send samples and resume to: SuperSites, 333 Main, Seattle, WA.

MARKETING
Fast paced software and services provider looking for MARKETING COMMUNICATIONS SPECIALIST to be responsible for its webpage.

PROGRAMMERS
Multiple short term assignments available: Visual C, 3 positions SQL ServerNT Server, 2 positions JAVA & HTML, long term NetWare Various locations. Call for more info. 356-555-3398.

PROGRAMMERS
C, C, VB, Cobol, exp.
Call 534-555-6543
or fax 534-555-6544

PROGRAMMING
MRFS Inc. is looking for a Sr. Windows NT developer. Reqs. 3-5 yrs. Exp. In C under Windows, Win95 & NT, using Visual C, Excl. OO design & implementation skills a must. OLE2 & ODBC are a plus. Excl. Salary & bnfts. Resume & salary history to HR, 8779 HighTech Way, Computer City, AR

PROGRAMMERS/
Contractors Wanted for short & long term assignments; Visual C, MFC Unix C/C, SQL Oracle Developers PC Help Desk Support Windows NT & NetWareTelecommunications Visual Basic, Access, HTML, CGI, Perl MMI & Co., 885-555-9933

PROGRAMMER
World Wide Web Links wants your HTML & Photoshop skills. Develop great WWW sites. Local & global customers. Send samples & resume to WWWL, 2000 Apple Road, Santa Rosa, CA.

TECHNICAL WRITER
Software firm seeks writer/editor for manuals, research notes, project mgmt. Min 2 years tech. writing, DTP & programming experience. Send resume & writing samples to: Software Systems, Dallas, TX.

COMPUTER PROGRAMMER
Ad agency seeks programmer w/exp. in UNIX/NT Platforms, Web Server, CGI/Perl. Programmer Position avail. on a project basis with the possibility to move into F/T. Fax resume & salary req. to R. Jones 334-555-8332.

TECHNICAL WRITER
Premier Computer Corp is seeking a combination of technical skills, knowledge and experience in the following areas: UNIX, Windows 95/NT, Visual Basic, on-line help & documentation, and the internet. Candidates must possess excellent writing skills, and be comfortable working in a quality vs. deadline driven environment. Competitive salary. Fax resume & samples to Karen Fields, Premier Computer Corp., 444 Industrial Blvd. Concord, CA. Or send to our website at www.premier.com.

WEB DESIGNER
BA/BS or equivalent programming/multimedia production. 3 years of experience in use and design of WWW services streaming audio and video HTML, PERL, CGI, GIF, JPEG. Demonstrated interpersonal, organization, communication, multi-tasking skills. Send resume to The Learning People at www.learning.com

WEBMASTER-TECHNICAL
BSCS or equivalent, 2 years of experience in CGI, Windows 95/NT,

---

COMPUTERS
Small Web Design Firm seeks indiv w/NT, Webserver & Database management exp. Fax resume to 556-555-4221.

COMPUTER
Visual C/C, Visual Basic Exp'd Systems Analysts/Programmers for growing software dev. team in Roseburg. Computer Science or related degree preferred. Develop adv. Engineering applications for engineering firm. Fax resume to 707-555-8744.

COMPUTER
Web Master for dynamic SF Internet co. Site. Dev. test, coord., train. 2 yrs prog. Exp. C C, Web C, FTP. Fax resume to Best Staffing 845-555-7722.

COMPUTERS/ QA SOFTWARE TESTERS
Qualified candidates should have 2 yrs exp. performing integration & system testing using automated testing tools. Experienced in documentation preparation & programming languages (Access, C, FoxPro) are a plus. financial or banking customer service support is required along with excellent verbal & written communication skills with multi levels of end-users. Send resume to KKUP Enterprises, 45 Orange Blvd., Orange, CA.

COMPUTERS
Programmer/Analyst Design and maintain C based SQL database applications. Required skills: Visual Basic, C, SQL, ODBC, Document existing and new applications. Novell or NT exp. a plus. Fax resume & salary history to 235-555-9935.

GRAPHIC DESIGNER
Webmaster's Weekly is seeking a creative Graphic Designer to design high impact marketing collateral, including direct mail promo's. CD-ROM packages, ads and WWW pages. Must be able to juggle multiple projects and learn new skills on the job very rapidly. Web design experience a big plus, technical troubleshooting also a plus. Call 435-555-1235.

GRAPHICS - ART DIRECTOR - WEB-MULTIMEDIA
Leading internet development company has an outstanding opportunity for a talented, high-end Web Experienced Art Director. In addition to a great portfolio and fresh ideas, the ideal candidate has excellent communication and presentation skills. Working as a team with innovative producers and programmers, you will create dynamic, interactive web sites and application interfaces. Some programming experience required. Send samples and resume to: SuperSites, 333 Main, Seattle, WA.

COMPUTER PROGRAMMER
Ad agency seeks programmer w/exp. in UNIX/NT Platforms, Web Server, CGI/Perl. Programmer Position avail. on a project basis with the possibility to move into F/T. Fax resume & salary req. to R. Jones 334-555-8332.

PROGRAMMERS / Established
software company seeks programmer. Must be a self-starter, energetic, organized. Must have 2 yrs web experience. Programming plus. Call 985-555-9854.

PROGRAMMERS
Multiple term assignments available: Visual C, 3 positions SQL ServerNT Server, 2 positions JAVA & HTML, long term NetWare Various locations. Call more info. 356-555-3398.

PROGRAMMERS
C, C, VB, Cobol, exp. Call 534-555-6543 or fax 534-555-6544.

PROGRAMMING
MRFS Inc. is looking for a Windows NT developer. Reqs. yrs. Exp. In C under Windows, Win95 & NT, using Visual C, OO design & implementation a must. OLE2 & ODBC are a plus. Excl. Salary & bnfts. Resume salary history to HR, 8779 High Way, Computer City, AR

PROGRAMMERS/
Contractors Wanted for short & long term assignments: Visual C, MFCUnix C/C, Oracle Developers PC Help Support Windows NT & NetWare Telecommunications Visual Basic, Access, HTML, CGI, Perl MMI & 885-555-9933

PROGRAMMER
World Wide Links wants your HTML & Photoshop skills. Develop great WWW Local & global customers. Send samples & resume to WWWL, Apple Road, Santa Rosa, CA.

TECHNICAL WRITER
Software seeks writer/editor for manuals research notes, project mgmt. years tech. writing, DTP & programming experience. Send resume writing samples to: Software Systems, Dallas, TX.

TECHNICAL
Software development firm looking for Tech Trainers, candidates have programming experience in Visual C, HTML & Need quick self starter. Call 555-6868 for interview.

TECHNICAL WRITER
Computer Corp is seeking a combination of technical skills, knowledge and experience in the following areas: UNIX, Windows 95/NT, Basic, on-line help & documentation and the internet. Candidates possess excellent writing skills be comfortable working in a vs. deadline driven environment Competitive salary. Fax resume samples to Karen Fields, Premier Computer Corp., 444 Industrial Concord, CA. Or send to our at www.premier.com

WEB DESIGNER
BA/BS or equivalent programming/multimedia production years of experience in use design of WWW services streaming audio and video HTML, PERL GIF, JPEG. Demonstrated interpersonal, organization, communication multi-tasking skills. Send resume The Learning People at www.learning.com

WEBMASTER-TECHNICAL

SKILL 9

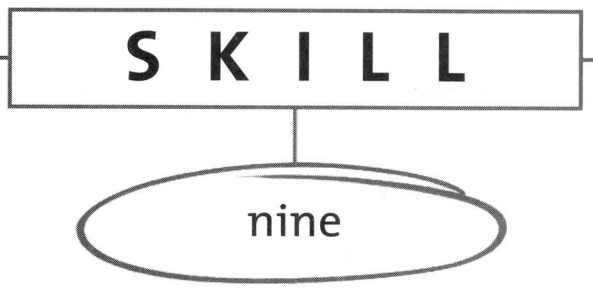

nine

Understanding JavaBeans

- ❑ Explaining bean basics
- ❑ Explaining the IDE's role
- ❑ Using drag-and-drop
- ❑ Changing properties with the Inspector

What's a Bean?

According to Sun, "A *JavaBean* is a reusable software component that can be manipulated visually in a builder tool." A formal definition is all well and good, but what does it mean and what good are beans? Well, the use of reusable components means the software industry is finally maturing. In fields like electrical engineering and manufacturing, products are built from various components. For instance, if you want to build a PC-compatible computer, you don't go off and design a disk controller, graphics controller, and keyboard. You buy the pieces from the component makers and put them together. Now, in software development, you can do the same thing with JavaBeans.

Instead of creating monolithic applications that take two years to develop and are out-of-date before they're even delivered, you play connect-the-beans to create programs from component parts, the beans. With the Internet life cycle running in dog years, you no longer have the luxury of taking your sweet time to deliver a solution to customers. They want it yesterday, and they want it fully tested, or they'll go elsewhere. With JavaBeans, that reality is closer.

What's inside a Bean?

So, what defines a bean, and what makes it work so well with other beans? A bean is defined by its structure. By following a certain set of design rules, a builder tool can discover all it needs to know about a bean.

Beans need to know how to handle events. When something happens, it must be able to react. A bean must be visually configurable, without which a builder tool wouldn't function very well. Beans must also be able to save and restore themselves. This allows each to continue functioning over time, after restarting from a stopped application.

Properties, Methods, and Events

Inside a bean, the first thing to look at is its *properties*. Each property is a named attribute of the bean. A pair of specially named methods reads or sets a property's value. While within a builder tool, a property editor allows the application developer to modify the properties.

Next are *methods*. Methods are just that—they provide the means to manipulate a bean and access properties. A builder tool will have access to all public methods of a bean, or to a subset if you restrict its access.

Finally, there are *events*. Events serve as the notification mechanism between beans. If a bean wants to know when an event happens, it registers itself with the source of the event. Then, when the event happens, the source notifies anyone registered, or listening.

> **NOTE** Skill 12 discusses the specifics of the property and event usage of beans.

Customization and Introspection

When a bean is created, you publish its capabilities. This exposes the names of the properties and events supported. The publishing process is called *customization*. When a bean is reused within a builder, the tool needs to discover what has been published. This discovery process is called *introspection*.

> **NOTE** Skills 13 and 14 explain the introspection and customization processes, respectively.

Persistence

In order for beans to be useful, they need a storage mechanism. If the same bean is reused in twenty-million applications, without *persistence*, the bean will look the same in all twenty-million applications. However, with persistence, you can customize each bean to be different in each of the applications. Then, after the bean has been configured, it can be saved separately for each application.

Skill 15 discusses the details of persistence.

What Does JBuilder Have to Do with All This?

As stated earlier, "A JavaBean is a reusable software component that can be manipulated visually in a builder tool." As its name implies, JBuilder is a builder tool. It helps you both create beans and manipulate them visually. Let's look at the part of JBuilder that we've avoided so far, the UI Designer.

Using the UI Designer

At this point, close all your open projects and create a new application (File ➤ New ➤ Application). Call the project **skill9**, and save it as **C:\skills\skill9\skill9.jpr**. Select Finish. Then, within the Application Wizard, select Next, name the class **ListBuilder**, and select Finish. Now, if you select the `ListBuilder.java` file in the Navigation pane, and the Design tab at the bottom of the Content pane, this will bring up the UI Designer, as shown in Figure 9.1. To the right of the UI Designer is the Inspector window; we'll explain that one shortly. Using the UI Designer, you can drag any component from the palette and drop it into your system.

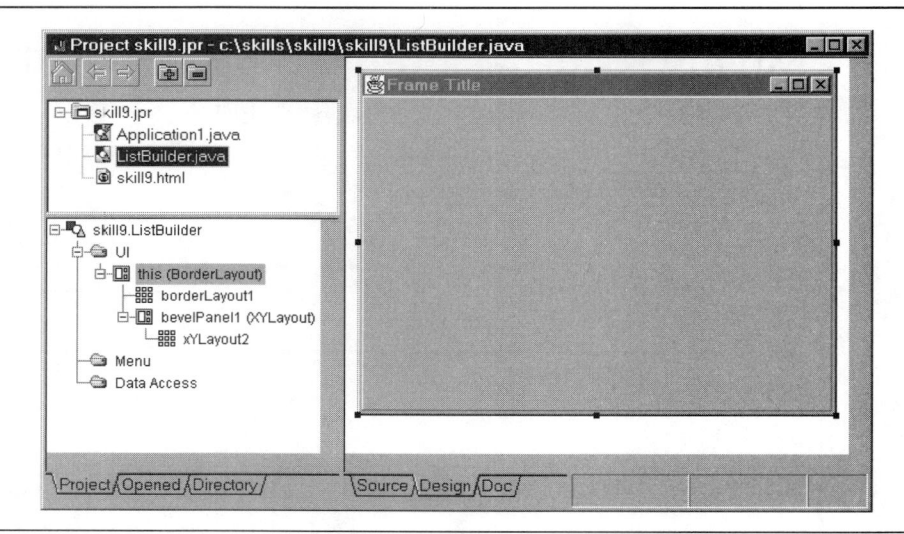

FIGURE 9.1: The UI Designer window, for drag-and-drop screen creation

To the right of the UI Designer window is a floating Inspector window. The Inspector displays the properties and events of the currently selected bean. To toggle between listings, select the appropriate tab at the bottom of the Inspector screen, as shown in Figure 9.2.

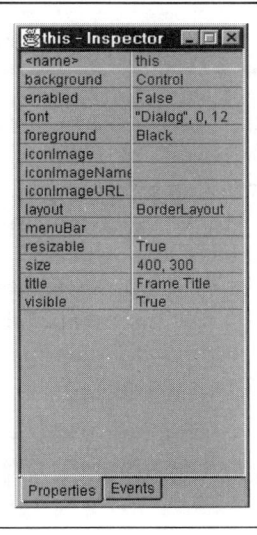

FIGURE 9.2: The Inspector window for a frame

Dragging Components and Dropping Them into Your System

To get a feel for the UI Designer, let's create a program with a `TextField` for input, two `Buttons` that say what to do with the input (add or remove), and a `List` for maintaining an input history list. First, we'll create the screen. Then, we'll add the code to do the work. Figure 9.3 shows the AWT component palette that we'll be using.

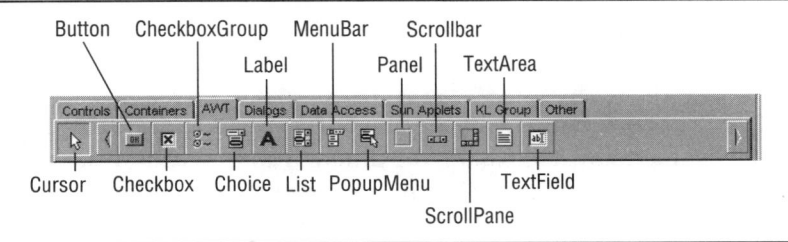

FIGURE 9.3: The AWT component palette

> **TIP** The components on the palette are not necessarily in alphabetical order.

Before dragging anything onto the screen, select the `bevelPanel1 (XYLayout)` entry in the Structure pane. This ensures that what we drag onto the screen will become a part of that grouping. Then, select the TextField icon on the AWT component palette, move the mouse into the highlighted `bevelPanel1`, and select the panel. You have just added a `TextField` to your program. Next, add two `Buttons` and a `List` component from the palette. Don't worry about positioning just yet, we'll do that next. Your UI Designer screen should now look something like Figure 9.4. At this point, if it isn't an exact match, don't worry. We'll fix it up shortly.

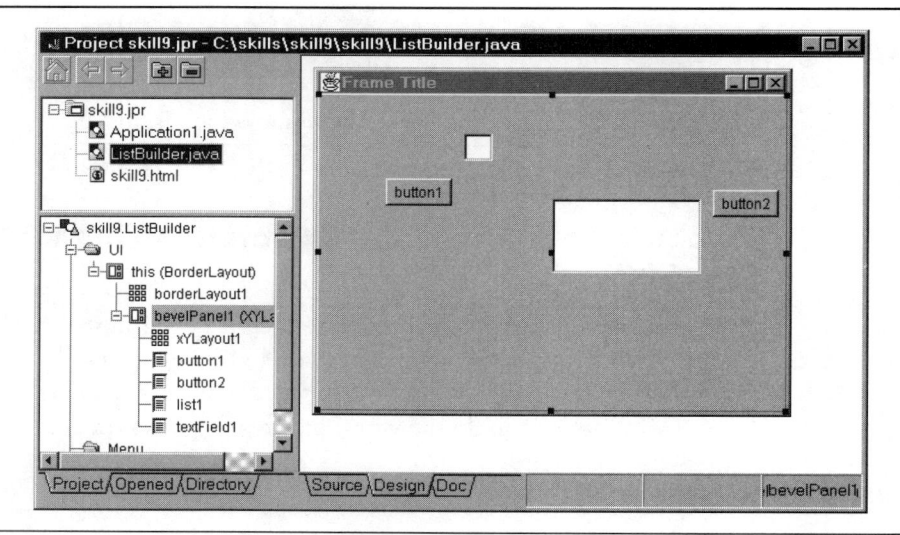

FIGURE 9.4: The initial input screen for our program

Remember the `BorderLayout` layout manager from Skill 6? We're going to use it now to position the different components around the screen. First, select `bevelPanel1 (XYLayout)` again in the Structure pane. If you now look in the Inspector window, on the property tab page, you'll see an entry for layout with XYLayout next to it. If you select XYLayout and change it to `BorderLayout`, we can then start moving everything around.

We want to move the text field to the North quadrant, place the list in the Center, and put the buttons on the two sides—East and West. We also want one button to have a label of Add and the other to have a label of Remove.

Starting with `button1`, select it. Once you've selected the button, move over to the Inspector screen and select that. We can now change the properties and events for the `button1` component. In the Inspector screen, select the label property, and change it to **Add**, and then press Enter to accept the change. Once the label is changed, select the constraints property and change that to **West**.

Now, select `button2`. Change the label to **Remove**, and place `button2` in the **East** quadrant.

Next, select the `TextField`. If you are not sure which component left is the `TextField`, select one and look on the title bar of the Inspector window. It displays the variable name used for the object. `textField1` is the `TextField`. (You can also select the component in the Structure pane.) Place the text field in the **North** quadrant.

Lastly, place the `List` in the **Center** quadrant. The screen setup is now complete and will look like Figure 9.5.

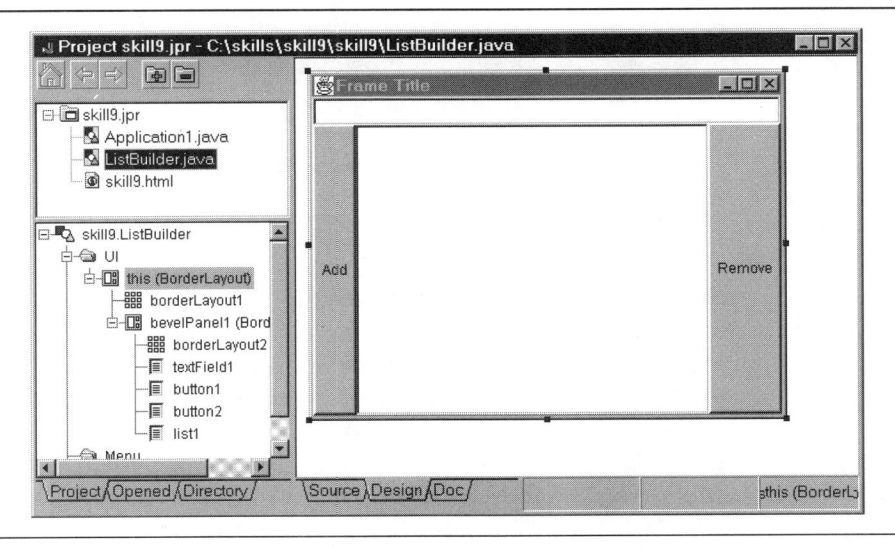

FIGURE 9.5: The final input screen for our program

Bringing the Screen to Life

Now that the screen is all in place, we need to make it work. If the Add button is selected, we get the contents of the `TextField` and add it to the `List`. When Remove is selected, we get the contents of the `TextField` and try to remove it from the `List`. In either case, if nothing is in the `TextField`, nothing is done.

To define the Add button's action, first select Add, and then select the Events tab of the Inspector. This shows all the possible events that could happen to a button, as shown in Figure 9.6. Each entry is for a specific method call. When the event happens, the event's source notifies anyone interested.

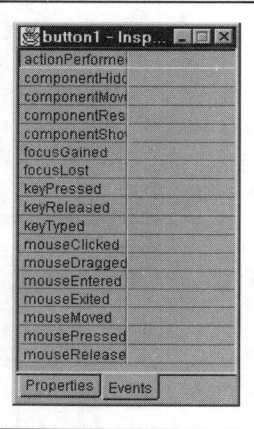

FIGURE 9.6: The Button event list

If you double-click in the right column of one of these events, you can fill in the block of code to perform when the event happens. In the case of the button, the method is `actionPerformed`, the first entry. If you triple-click in the field—once to select and twice to double-click while it's selected—this will place you in the source code of the `Frame1` class. Now you can fill in the appropriate source code. By default, the code added is just the framework of the method. We need to change it, so it gets the contents of the `TextField` and displays it in the `List`, if it isn't empty. The `getText()` method of `TextField` we've seen already, however the `add()` method of `List` is new. Similar to adding a component to a screen, the way to add an object to a `List` is with the `add()` method.

```
void button1_actionPerformed(ActionEvent e) {
    String s = textField1.getText();
```

```
      if (s.length() > 0)
        list1.add (s);
    }
```

Going back to the UI Designer, we can do almost the same for the Remove button. Select the button and triple-click the `actionPerformed` entry again. Here the code is similar, however we use the `remove()` method of `List` to remove an element. If you try to remove an element that isn't present, the `IllegalArgumentException` is thrown. We can check for the exception to not have a message shown in the Console Window.

```
    void button2_actionPerformed(ActionEvent e) {
      String s = textField1.getText();
      if (s.length() > 0)
        try {
          list1.remove (s);
        } catch (IllegalArgumentException iae) {
          // Ignore - not found
        }
    }
```

That's all there is to it. You can now save and compile the program to see how it works. Figure 9.7 shows how it looks when running. The `ListBuilder.java` source follows. At the end of the source code you may notice a few additional classes defined. JBuilder generated these classes.

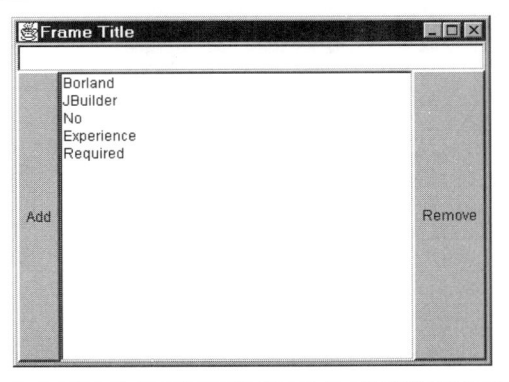

FIGURE 9.7: Executing the program after entering and removing a few entries

ListBuilder.java

```java
package skill9;

import java.awt.*;
import java.awt.event.*;
import borland.jbcl.control.*;
import borland.jbcl.layout.*;

public class ListBuilder extends DecoratedFrame {
  BorderLayout borderLayout1 = new BorderLayout();
  BevelPanel bevelPanel1 = new BevelPanel();
  TextField textField1 = new TextField();
  Button button1 = new Button();
  Button button2 = new Button();
  List list1 = new List();
  BorderLayout borderLayout2 = new BorderLayout();

  //Construct the frame
  public ListBuilder() {
    try {
      jbInit();
    }
    catch (Exception e) {
      e.printStackTrace();
    }
  }

  //Component initialization
  public void jbInit() throws Exception{
    this.setLayout(borderLayout1);
    this.setSize(new Dimension(400, 300));
    this.setTitle("Frame Title");
    button1.setLabel("Add");
    button1.addActionListener(new ListBuilder_button1_actionAdapter(this));
    button2.setLabel("Remove");
    button2.addActionListener(new ListBuilder_button2_actionAdapter(this));
    bevelPanel1.setLayout(borderLayout2);
    this.add(bevelPanel1, BorderLayout.CENTER);
    bevelPanel1.add(textField1, BorderLayout.NORTH);
    bevelPanel1.add(button1, BorderLayout.WEST);
    bevelPanel1.add(button2, BorderLayout.EAST);
    bevelPanel1.add(list1, BorderLayout.CENTER);
  }
```

```
  void button1_actionPerformed(ActionEvent e) {
    String s = textField1.getText();
    if (s.length() > 0)
      list1.add (s);
  }

  void button2_actionPerformed(ActionEvent e) {
    String s = textField1.getText();
    if (s.length() > 0)
      try {
        list1.remove (s);
      } catch (IllegalArgumentException iae) {
        // Ignore - not found
      }
  }
}

class ListBuilder_button1_actionAdapter implements java.awt.event.ActionListener {
  ListBuilder adaptee;

  ListBuilder_button1_actionAdapter(ListBuilder adaptee) {
    this.adaptee = adaptee;
  }

  public void actionPerformed(ActionEvent e) {
    adaptee.button1_actionPerformed(e);
  }
}

class ListBuilder_button2_actionAdapter implements java.awt.event.ActionListener {
  ListBuilder adaptee;

  ListBuilder_button2_actionAdapter(ListBuilder adaptee) {
    this.adaptee = adaptee;
  }

  public void actionPerformed(ActionEvent e) {
    adaptee.button2_actionPerformed(e);
  }
}
```

Congratulations! Now that you have a feel for using drag-and-drop to create your screens, Skill 10 will introduce the Interaction Wizard. Instead of having to manually add the event-handling code, as we did in this skill, the Interaction Wizard will add the code for us.

Are You Experienced?

Now you can...

- ☑ describe what a JavaBean is
- ☑ describe what's inside a bean
- ☑ use the UI Designer
- ☑ change properties with the Inspector
- ☑ add objects to the *List* component

PROGRAMMERS
C, C, VB, Cobol, exp. Call 534-555-6543 or fax 534-555-6544.

PROGRAMMING
MRFS Inc. is looking for a Sr. Windows NT developer. Reqs. 3-5 yrs. Exp. in C under Windows, Win95 & NT, using Visual C. Excl. OO design & implementation skills a must. OLE2 & ODBC are a plus. Excl. Salary & bnfts. Resume & salary history to HR, 8779 HighTech Way, Computer City, AR

PROGRAMMERS
Contractors Wanted for short & long term assignments: Visual C, MFC Unix C/C, SQL Oracle Developers PC Help Desk Support Windows NT & NetWareTelecommunications Visual Basic, Access, HTML, CGI, Perl MMI & Co.. 885-555-9933

PROGRAMMER World Wide Web Links wants your HTML & Photoshop skills. Develop great WWW sites. Local & global customers. Send samples & resume to WWWL, 2000 Apple Road, Santa Rosa, CA.

TECHNICAL WRITER Software firm seeks writer/editor for manuals, research notes, project mgmt. Min 2 years tech. writing, DTP & programming experience. Send resume & writing samples to: Software Systems, Dallas, TX.

TECHNICAL Software development firm looking for Tech Trainers. Ideal candidates have programming experience in Visual C, HTML & JAVA. Need quick self starter. Call (443) 555-6868 for interview.

TECHNICAL WRITER/ Premier Computer Corp is seeking a combination of technical skills, knowledge and experience in the following areas: UNIX, Windows 95/NT, Visual Basic, on-line help & documentation, and the internet. Candidates must possess excellent writing skills, and be comfortable working in a quality vs. deadline driven environment. Competitive salary. Fax resume & samples to Karen Fields, Premier Computer Corp., 444 Industrial Blvd. Concord, CA. Or send to our website at www.premier.com.

WEB DESIGNER
BA/BS or equivalent programming/multimedia production. 3 years of experience in use and design of WWW services streaming audio and video HTML, PERL, CGI, GIF, JPEG. Demonstrated interpersonal, organization, communication, multi-tasking skills. Send resume to The Learning People at www.learning.com.

WEBMASTER-TECHNICAL
BSCS: or equivalent. 2 years of experience in CGI. Windows 95/NT, UNIX, C, Java, Perl. Demonstrated ability to design, code, debug and test on-line services. Send resume to The Learning People at www.learning.com.

PROGRAMMER World Wide Web Links wants your HTML & Photoshop skills. Develop great WWW sites. Local & global customers. Send samples

---

R. Jones 356-555-3398.

ing tools. Experienced in documentation preparation & programming languages (Access, C, FoxPro) are a plus. Financial or banking customer service support is required along with excellent verbal & written communication skills with multi levels of end-users. Send resume to KKUP Enterprises 45 Orange Blvd. Orange, CA.

COMPUTERS Small Web Design firm seeks indiv. w/NT, Webserver & Database management exp. Fax resume to 556-555-4221.

COMPUTER/ Visual C/C, Visual Basic Exp'd Systems Analysts/ Programmers for growing software dev. team in Roseburg. Computer Science or related degree preferred. Develop adv. Engineering applications for engineering firm. Fax resume to 707-555-8744.

COMPUTER Web Master for dynamic SF Internet co. Site Dev., test, coord., train. 2 yrs prog. Exp. C C Web C FTP. Fax resume to Best Staffing 845-555-7722.

COMPUTER PROGRAMMER
Ad agency seeks programmer w/exp. in UNIX/NT Platforms, Web Server, CGI/Perl. Programmer Position avail. on a project basis with the possibility to move into F/T. Fax resume & salary req. to R. Jones 334-555-8332.

COMPUTERS Programmer/Analyst Design and maintain C based SQL database applications. Required skills: Visual Basic, C, SQL, ODBC. Document existing and new applications. Novell or NT exp. a plus. Fax resume & salary history to 235-555-9935.

GRAPHIC DESIGNER
Webmaster's Weekly is seeking a creative Graphic Designer to design high impact marketing collater al, including direct mail promois, CD-ROM packages, ads and WWW pages. Must be able to juggle multiple projects and learn new skills on the job very rapidly. Web design experience a big plus, technical troubleshooting also a plus. Call 435-555-1235.

GRAPHICS - ART DIRECTOR - WEB-MULTIMEDIA
Leading internet development company has an outstanding opportunity for a talented, high-end Web Experienced Art Director. In addition to a great portfolio and fresh ideas, the ideal candidate has excellent communication and presentation skills. Working as a team with innovative producers and programmers, you will create dynamic, interactive web sites and application interfaces. Some programming experience required. Send samples and resume to: SuperSites, 333 Main, Seattle, WA

WEB DESIGNER
BA/BS or equivalent programming/multimedia production. 3 years of experience in use and design of WWW services streaming audio and video HTML, PERL, CGI, GIF, JPEG. Demonstrated interpersonal, organization, communication, multi-tasking skills. Send resume to The Learning People at www.learning.com.

MARKETING
Fast paced software and services provider looking for MARKETING COMMUNICATIONS SPECIALIST to be responsible for its webpage.

PROGRAMMERS Multiple short term assignments available: Visual C, 3 positions SQL ServerNT Server, 2 positions JAVA & HTML, long term NetWare Various locations. Call for more info. 356-555-3398.

PROGRAMMERS
C, C, VB, Cobol, exp.
Call 534-555-6543
or fax 534-555-6544.

PROGRAMMING
MRFS Inc. is looking for a Sr. Windows NT developer. Reqs. 3-5 yrs. Exp. In C under Windows, Win95 & NT, using Visual C. Excl. OO design & implementation skills a must. OLE2 & ODBC are a plus. Excl. Salary & bnfts. Resume & salary history to HR. 8779 HighTech Way, Computer City, AR

PROGRAMMERS/ Contractors Wanted for short & long term assignments: Visual C, MFC Unix C/C, SQL Oracle Developers PC Help Desk Support Windows NT & NetWareTelecommunications Visual Basic, Access, HTML, CGI, Perl MMI & Co.. 885-555-9933

PROGRAMMER World Wide Web Links wants your HTML & Photoshop skills. Develop great WWW sites. Local & global customers. Send samples & resume to WWWL, 2000 Apple Road, Santa Rosa, CA.

TECHNICAL WRITER Software firm seeks writer/editor for manuals, research notes, project mgmt. Min 2 years tech. writing, DTP & programming experience. Send resume & writing samples to: Software Systems, Dallas, TX.

COMPUTER PROGRAMMER
Ad agency seeks programmer w/exp. in UNIX/NT Platforms, Web Server, CGI/Perl. Programmer Position avail. on a project basis with the possibility to move into F/T. Fax resume & salary req. to R. Jones 334-555-8332.

TECHNICAL WRITER Premier Computer Corp is seeking a combination of technical skills, knowledge and experience in the following areas: UNIX, Windows 95/NT, Visual Basic, on-line help & documentation, and the internet. Candidates must possess excellent writing skills, and be comfortable working in a quality vs. deadline driven environment. Competitive salary. Fax resume & samples to Karen Fields, Premier Computer Corp., 444 Industrial Blvd. Concord, CA. Or send to our website at www.premier.com.

WEB DESIGNER
BA/BS or equivalent programming/multimedia production. 3 years of experience in use and design of WWW services streaming audio and video HTML, PERL, CGI, GIF, JPEG. Demonstrated interpersonal, organization, communication, multi-tasking skills. Send resume to The Learning People at www.learning.com.

WEBMASTER-TECHNICAL
BSCS: or equivalent. 2 years of experience in CGI. Windows 95/NT,

---

COMPUTERS Small Web Design firm seeks indiv. w/NT, Webserver & Database management exp. Fax resume to 556-555-4221.

COMPUTER Visual C/C, Visual Basic Exp'd Systems Analysts/ Programmers for growing software dev. team in Roseburg. Computer Science or related degree preferred. Develop adv. Engineering applications for engineering firm. Fax resume to 707-555-8744.

COMPUTER Web Master for dynamic SF Internet co. Site Dev., test, coord., train. 2 yrs prog. Exp. C C Web C FTP. Fax resume to Best Staffing 845-555-7722.

COMPUTERS/ QA SOFTWARE TESTERS Qualified candidates should have 2 yrs exp. performing integration & system testing using automated testing tools. Experienced in documentation preparation & programming languages (Access, C, FoxPro) are a plus. Financial or banking customer service support is required along with excellent verbal & written communication skills with multi levels of end-users. Send resume to KKUP Enterprises, 45 Orange Blvd. Orange, CA.

COMPUTERS Programmer/Analyst Design and maintain C based SQL database applications. Required skills: Visual Basic, C, SQL, ODBC. Document existing and new applications, Novell or NT exp. a plus. fax resume & salary history to 235-555-9935.

GRAPHIC DESIGNER
Webmaster's Weekly is seeking a creative Graphic Designer to design high impact marketing collater al, including direct mail promo's. CD-ROM packages, ads and WWW pages. Must be able to juggle multiple projects and learn new skills on the job very rapidly. Web design experience a big plus, technical troubleshooting also a plus. Call 435-555-1235.

GRAPHICS - ART DIRECTOR - WEB-MULTIMEDIA
Leading internet development company has an outstanding opportunity for a talented, high-end Web Experienced Art Director. In addition to a great portfolio and fresh ideas, the ideal candidate has excellent communication and presentation skills. Working as a team with innovative producers and programmers, you will create dynamic, interactive web sites and application interfaces. Some programming experience required. Send samples and resume to: SuperSites, 333 Main, Seattle, WA

COMPUTER PROGRAMMER
Ad agency seeks programmer w/exp. in UNIX/NT Platforms, Web Server, CGI/Perl. Programmer Position avail. on a project basis with the possibility to move into F/T. Fax resume & salary req. to R. Jones 334-555-8332.

PROGRAMMERS / Established software company seeks program-

COMPUTERS Small Web Design firm seeks indiv. w/NT, Webserver & Database management exp. Fax resume to 556-555-4221.

PROGRAMMERS Multiple short term assignments available: Visual C, 3 positions SQL ServerNT Server, 2 positions JAVA & HTML, long term NetWare Various locations. Call for more info. 356-555-3398.

PROGRAMMERS
C, C, VB, Cobol, exp. Call 534-555-6543 or fax 534-555-6544.

PROGRAMMING
MRFS Inc. is looking for a Sr. Windows NT developer. Reqs. 3 yrs. Exp. In C under Windows Win95 & NT, using Visual C. Ex OO design & implementation sk a must. OLE2 & ODBC are a p Excl. Salary & bnfts. Resume salary history to HR. 8779 HighT Way, Computer City, AR

PROGRAMMERS/ Contract Wanted for short & long term assign ments: Visual C, MFCUnix C/C, S Oracle Developers PC Help De Support Windows NT & NetWa Telecommunications Visual Ba Access, HTML, CGI, Perl MMI & 885-555-9933

PROGRAMMER World Wide W Links wants your HTML & Photosh skills. Develop great WWW si Local & global customers. Send s ples & resume to WWWL, 20 Apple Road, Santa Rosa, CA.

TECHNICAL WRITER Software f seeks writer/editor for manu research notes, project mgmt. M years tech. writing, DTP & progr ming experience. Send resume writing samples to: Softw Systems, Dallas, TX.

TECHNICAL Software developm firm looking for Tech Trainers. Id candidates have programming ex rience in Visual C, HTML & JA Need quick self starter. Call (4 555-6868 for interview.

TECHNICAL WRITER Prem Computer Corp is seeking a com nation of technical skills, knowle and experience in the followi areas: UNIX, Windows 95/NT, Vi Basic, on-line help & documentat and the internet. Candidates m possess excellent writing skills, be comfortable working in a qua vs. deadline driven environm Competitive salary. Fax resume samples to Karen Fields, Pre Computer Corp. 444 Industrial B Concord, CA. Or send to our we at www.premier.com.

WEB DESIGNER
BA/BS or equivalent progr ming/multimedia production. years of experience in use design of WWW services stream audio and video HTML, PERL, GIF, JPEG. Demonstrated inter sonal, organization, communicat multi-tasking skills. Send resum The Learning People at www. ing.com.

WEBMASTER-TECHNIC

SKILL 10

ten

Connecting Beans

- ❑ Using the Interaction Wizard
- ❑ Using the Interaction Wizard Editor
- ❑ Examining the generated source
- ❑ Using the Expression Assistant

Getting Started

In Skill 9, you used the Events page of the Inspector window to select the appropriate event listener method to respond to. While this works perfectly well, it does require you to manually edit the source code to include your event-handling actions. Instead of having to know what methods are for which event listener, Borland's JBuilder comes with a Wizard called the Interaction Wizard. The Wizard helps you connect beans by generating all the code for you, instead of your having to pick event methods within the Inspector.

To connect two beans, the Interaction Wizard requires that you select the event source and event target, followed by the event type and response. After entering any required information for the response, the Wizard generates the code to do the connection. Adding the response source is where the Wizard shines.

In addition to adding the response source, the Interaction Wizard comes with a supporting cast: the Interaction Wizard Editor and Expression Assistant. In order to be more useful, the Interaction Wizard allows you to restrict the list of events and responses for a bean. Then, instead of seeing long lists of infrequently used pieces, you can limit the display to the more frequently used event mechanisms. As a helper to the Interaction Wizard Editor, the Expression Assistant allows you to configure smart defaults to help the bean connector along.

To demonstrate the capabilities of the Wizard, Editor, and Assistant, this skill takes you through the process of connecting two text fields, three buttons, a Choice component (or pull-down list box), and a List component. The second text field displays what is in the first text field but converts the contents to uppercase. The remaining components set the contents of the first text field.

Setting Up the Screen

To set up Skill 10, start up JBuilder, close any open projects, and run the Application Wizard. Within the Project Wizard screen, save the project to **C:\skills\skill10\skill10.jpr** and select Finish. Select Next, and on the second screen of the Application Wizard, name the frame class **Wizard** before selecting Finish again.

After running the Wizard, select Wizard.java in the Navigation pane and select the Design tab on the Contents pane to set up the screen. Now, you can place all the components within the frame:

1. Select bevelPanel1 (XYLayout) in the Structure pane and change the layout property to FlowLayout.

2. Select the AWT tab on the Component palette.
3. Select the `TextField` bean and drop two of them into the frame.
4. Select the `TextField` bean on the left; change the `<name>` property to **first** and the `columns` property to **20**.
5. For the `TextField` bean on the right, change the `<name>` property to **second** and the `columns` property to **20**.
6. Select the `Button` bean from the Component palette and drop three of them into the frame, below the two text fields.
7. Change the label property of the three buttons to **Lower**, **Numbers**, and **Mixed**.
8. Select the `Choice` bean and drop one into the frame at the bottom right.
9. Because the items pseudo-property of `Choice` isn't a real property and it isn't visible in the Inspector, you need to add the different choices in the source code. In the `jbInit` method, add the following lines after the label setting lines for the buttons:

    ```
    choice1.add ("First");
    choice1.add ("Second");
    choice1.add ("Third");
    choice1.add ("Fourth");
    choice1.add ("Fifth");
    ```

10. Go back to the UI Designer. Select the `List` bean and drop one into the frame at the bottom right.
11. In `jbInit` add the following lines right after the previous ones entered in step 9:

    ```
    list1.add ("Cheese");
    list1.add ("Pepperoni");
    list1.add ("Sausage");
    list1.add ("More Cheese");
    list1.add ("Sardines");
    ```

Saving everything at this point and running the program brings up the screen shown in Figure 10.1.

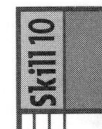

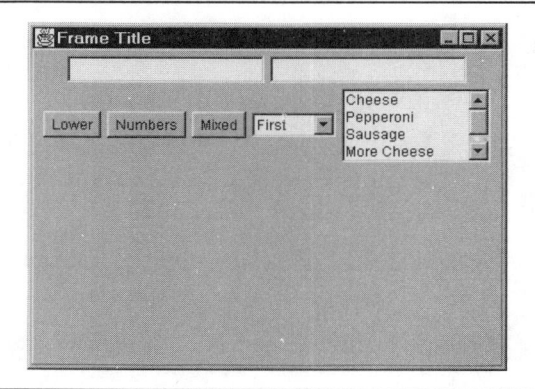

FIGURE 10.1: The initial Wizard screen

> **WARNING** If you've used the Interaction Wizard Editor before doing this skill and modified the initial interaction set, you may experience certain differences in appearance. You'll need to skip ahead to read about the Interaction Wizard Editor to set up the initial interactions. If you ever want to change these interactions outside of JBuilder, they are contained in the file `C:\JBuilder\bin\interactions.ini`.

Making the First Connection

The first connection we'll make is from the first text field to the second text field. Whenever anything is entered in the first text field, either manually or programmatically, the second text field displays the contents of the first field in all uppercase letters. If we didn't have to worry about programmatic content changes, we could just capture keystrokes. However, that isn't sufficient for our case. Text fields also serve as the source for `TextEvent`s. These are the type of events we need to connect the two beans. Java generates the events when the text of the bean has changed. To connect the beans, select Wizards ➤ Interaction Wizard. The wizard will go to the Step 1 of 4 screen if there are multiple windows, or containers, to pick from. Figure 10.2 shows this screen.

For the purposes of our example, the wizard opens to the Step 2 of 4 screen, shown in Figure 10.3, to pick the event source.

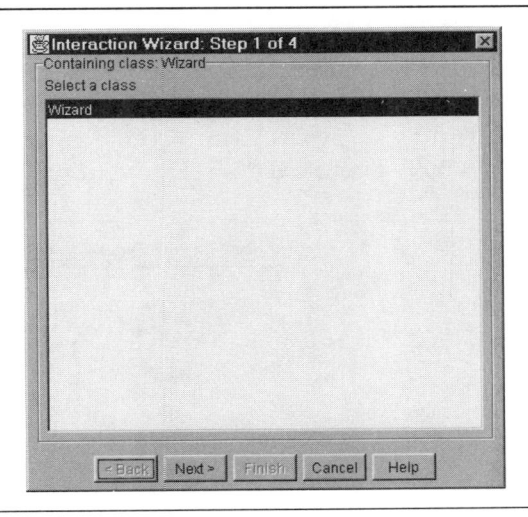

FIGURE 10.2: The unseen Step 1 of 4: Containing class dialog box appears when there are multiple windows, or containers, to pick.

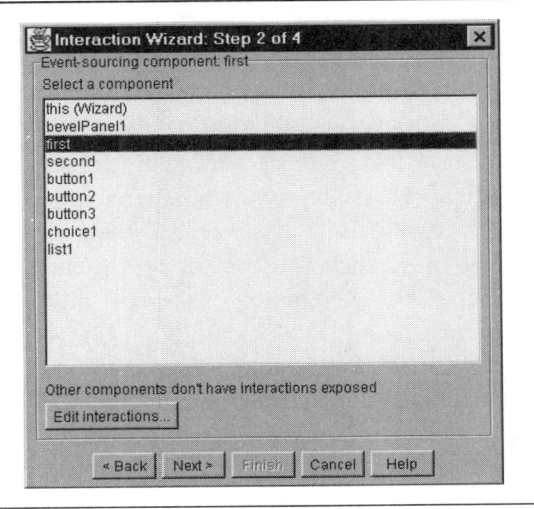

FIGURE 10.3: The Step 2 of 4: Event-Sourcing Component dialog box is the initial dialog box shown for the Interaction Wizard in our example.

To make the connection, it is necessary to pick out the event source from the Event-Sourcing Component dialog box. Here, a list of all the components used with exposed events is displayed. If you need to use a component that has no exposed events, you would need to select Edit Interactions (or Tools ➤ Interaction Wizard Editor) to expose them. Because our event source is `first`, we can select that and then select Next to see Figure 10.4.

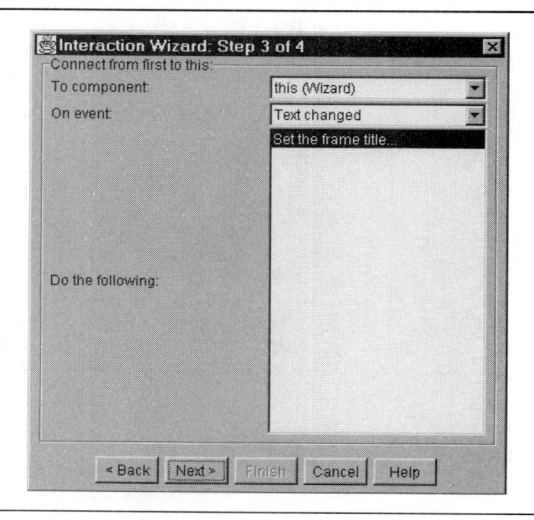

FIGURE 10.4: The Connect From First to This dialog box in the Interaction Wizard is Step 3 of 4.

You'll spend most of your time working in this dialog box when the events and behavior are already exposed properly. If not, you'll be spending more time with the Interaction Wizard Editor, which I'll show you later. Here, you need to select the event destination or target from the To Component pull-down list. You want `second`, so pick that. Notice how the Do the Following list changed based on which target you selected.

After selecting the target, you need to select the action that triggers the event generation from the On Event pull-down list. Here, the text field initially shows `Text changed`, `Got focus`, and `Lost focus` as the available events. By default, the mouse, key, and component events are all not listed. Luckily, we care about when the text is changed, so leave `Text changed` selected for On event.

In the Do the Following list, a list of the exposed actions are shown. From here, you pick what you want to happen when the event source generates the event and notifies the event target. These entries are basically methods that may be called within the event target's class. However, the methods need to be exposed within the Interaction Wizard Editor. Exposing is only available for methods declared `public`. For our example here, when the contents of `first` change, we need to set the text of `second`. Therefore, we need to select Set the Text... and then Next to move on to the final screen in the Interaction Wizard.

> **TIP**
>
> If you find that the behavior you want isn't exposed, you need to cancel out of the Interaction Wizard and start the Interaction Wizard Editor. Selecting Edit Interactions in the Step 2 of 4 screen (shown in Figure 10.3) does not allow you to alter those beans that already expose anything.

The appearance of the final screen varies depending upon the behavior selected in Figure 10.4. There is one line for each parameter in the method being called. Because the `setText` method associated with the Set the text... option only has one parameter, of type `String`, the screen you see is shown in Figure 10.5.

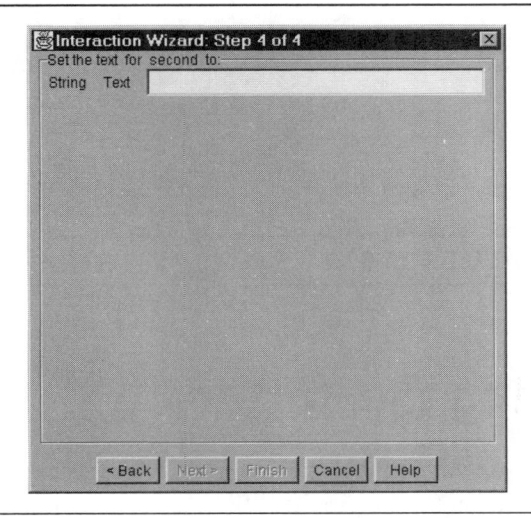

FIGURE 10.5: The Step 4 of 4 screen in the Interaction Wizard, where you configure parameter settings for the event notification

Now, here is where we need to fudge something and correct it later. The Wizard only allows you to enter in *literal expressions,* or constants. Because we want to use the actual contents of `first` and place the value in `second`, we'll have to put in a placeholder. Just enter **0** or anything you'd like, and select Finish.

To correct the behavior, select the new `first_textValueChanged1` method in the Structure pane. Change the contents to get the value of `first`, convert it to uppercase, and set the value of `second` to the new value.

```
void first_textValueChanged1(TextEvent textEvent) {
  String s = first.getText();
  second.setText (s.toUpperCase());
}
```

At this point, you can save and run the application to demonstrate the initial behavior of the program. Typing lowercase into the left text field displays the uppercase text in the right text field. Running the program brings up the screen shown in Figure 10.1 again, as shown below in Figure 10.6.

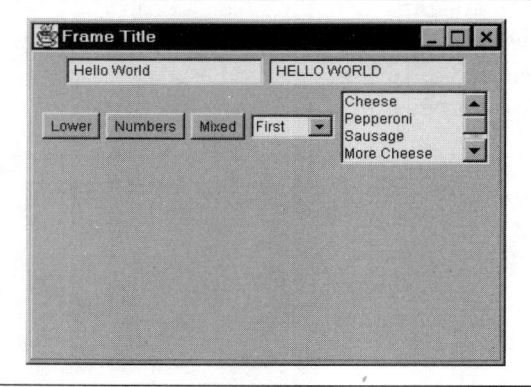

FIGURE 10.6: Running the Wizard program, after the first connection

Connecting the Buttons

For the three buttons we need to do the same thing. When the button is pressed, set the text in the first text field to something. We'll set the `Lower` button to **welcome**; we'll set the `Numbers` button to **555-1212**; then we'll set the `Mixed` button to **HowdY PaRtNeR**. Make sure you enter the exact text shown for each of these.

To set the `Lower` button, follow these steps:

1. Select Wizards ➤ Interaction Wizard.

2. Select button1 and Next.

3. Select first in the To Component pull-down list, Pressed in the On Event pull-down list, and Set the Text in Do the Following list. Then select Next.

4. On the final screen, enter **welcome**—without quotes—and the Finish button.

This generated the appropriate source for the connection:

```
void button1_actionPerformed1(ActionEvent actionEvent) {
   first.setText("welcome");
}
```

For button2, the Numbers button, follow the same steps, but in step 4 set the text to **555-1212**. For button3, the Mixed button, set the text to **HowdY PaRtNeR** in step 4. This added two more methods:

```
void button2_actionPerformed1(ActionEvent actionEvent) {
   first.setText("555-1212");
}

void button3_actionPerformed1(ActionEvent actionEvent) {
   first.setText("HowdY PaRtNeR");
}
```

Again, save and run the program at this point. Notice how the second text field is updated when you either type in the first text field or select a button? This is a result of connecting to the text event, versus a standard keystroke-capturing event.

Connecting the *Choice*

The choice component is the next component to connect. When the user changes the choice value, the new selection is placed in the first text field.

1. Select Wizards ➤ Interaction Wizard.

2. Select choice1 and Next.

3. Select first in the To Component pull-down list, Selected in the On Event pull-down list and Set the Text in the Do the Following list. Then select Next.

4. On the final screen, we need to enter a placeholder, such as **0**, and then select the Finish button.

To correct the behavior, select the new `choice1_itemStateChanged1` method in the Structure pane. Change the contents to get the value of `choice1` and display it. To find the currently selected item of a choice component, use its `getSelectedItem` method.

```
void choice1_itemStateChanged1(ItemEvent itemEvent) {
  String s = choice1.getSelectedItem();
  first.setText(s);
}
```

Save and run the program again to test the added behavior.

Connecting the *List*

For our final component, we need to add two connections. If a list entry is selected once, just display the selected item in the first text field. Then, if a list entry is double-clicked, display the reverse of the selected item in the first text field. This second behavior will require the use of the Interaction Wizard Editor, as the behavior isn't available by default.

The first part is easy; we perform almost the same steps as we did when we set up Choice:

1. Select Wizards ➤ Interaction Wizard.

2. Select `list1` and Next.

3. Select `first` in the To Component pull-down list, `Selected` in the On Event pull-down list and `Set the Text` in the Do the Following list. Then select Next.

4. On the final screen, we need to enter a placeholder, such as **0**, and then select the Finish button.

To correct the behavior, select the new `list1_itemStateChanged1` method in the Structure pane. Change the contents to get the value of `list1` and display it. To find the currently selected item of a list component, use its `getSelectedItem` method.

```
void list1_itemStateChanged1(ItemEvent itemEvent) {
  String s = list1.getSelectedItem();
  first.setText(s);
}
```

> **WARNING** Lists can be in multiselect mode, allowing you to select multiple choices. When this is the case, you need to use `getSelectedItems` to get the array of strings for all the selected choices.

Using the Interaction Wizard Editor

For the last event, we'll need to introduce the Interaction Wizard Editor. Double-clicking on an item in a list generates a different event than single-clicking does. So, we want to do something different. Initially, the Interaction Wizard blocks this event out, hence, we need to enable it. (The JBuilder team configured the initial set of exposed events, based on what they thought would be appropriate.) To enable it, select the class you want to modify in the Structure pane, in this case Wizard, and then select Tools ➤ Interaction Wizard Editor to bring up Figure 10.7.

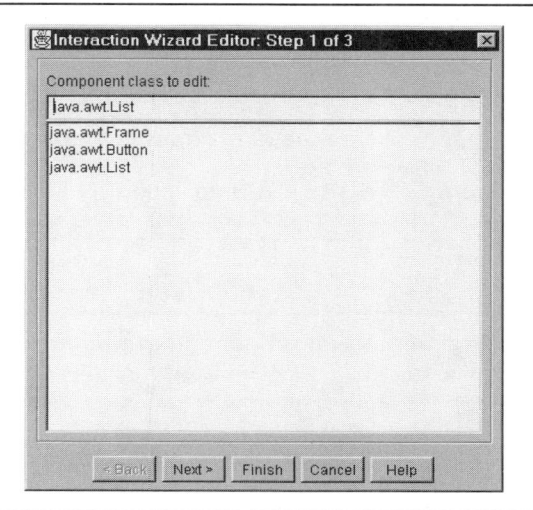

FIGURE 10.7: The initial Interaction Wizard Editor dialog box, Step 1 of 3

TIP If you forgot to select the component first, it is possible that the component to change will not be displayed. You can then either select Cancel and select it, or type in the class name in its input field.

Once the dialog box appears, select the class you want to modify, `java.awt.List`, and then select Next to see Figure 10.8. Here, you'll change what the Interaction Wizard displays for every usage of the `List` class.

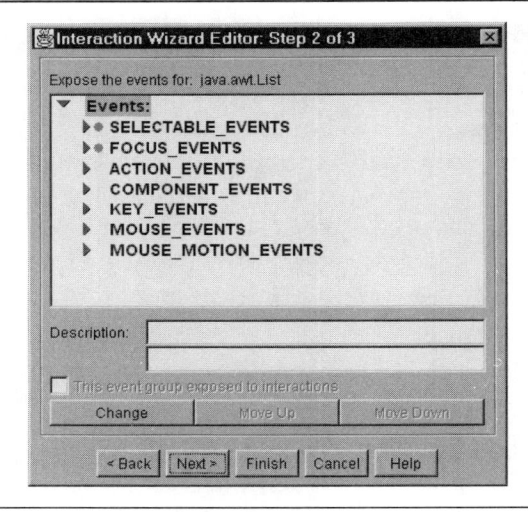

FIGURE 10.8: The Interaction Wizard Editor dialog box for exposing events, Step 2 of 3

TIP Changing the events and methods exposed here will not break any existing code. It only restricts what is displayed within the Interaction Wizard.

The green dots next to SELECTABLE_EVENTS and FOCUS_EVENTS mean that these event sets are available within the Interaction Wizard. Each set may be one or more actual event types. In this case, `selectable` is one event type, while `focus` is two (`got` and `lost`). If you ever forget what event types make up an event set, selecting the triangle on the left will open and close each grouping. Figure 10.9 shows the listing after opening many of the arrows.

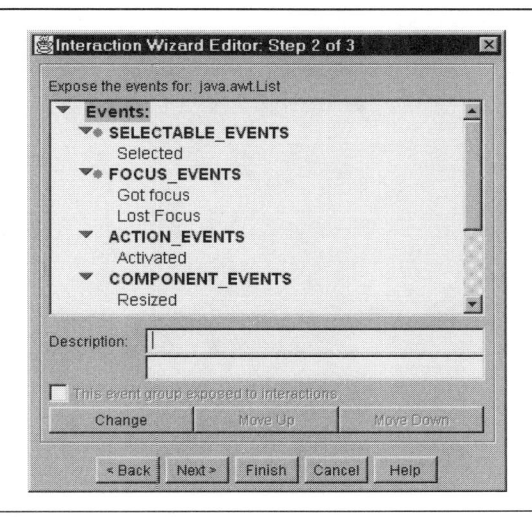

FIGURE 10.9: The Interaction Wizard Editor dialog box with full event sets displayed

Now, we need to expose the ACTION_EVENTS set. To do this, first select the ACTION_EVENTS item, then select the This Event Group Exposed to Interactions toggle, and the green dot will be added.

The other thing we'll change here is the text displayed in the On Event area. The default text of Activated doesn't seem to make as much sense for List. We'll change it to Double-Clicked. To change the event label, open the ACTION_EVENTS set so you see the Activated entry. Select Activated and notice that the Description field is filled in and the Interface line changes to Method. In the Description field, type in **Double-Clicked** and select Change. The event description now changes in the primary screen area, as shown in Figure 10.10.

> **TIP** Any new displayed text should be in past tense, as the Interaction Wizard connects beans after the event happened.

We've exposed the event we needed to, so now we could just select Finish. However, we should look at one more screen. Selecting Next brings up the list of exposed actions. As Figure 10.11 shows, this looks similar to the dialog box shown in Figure 10.10.

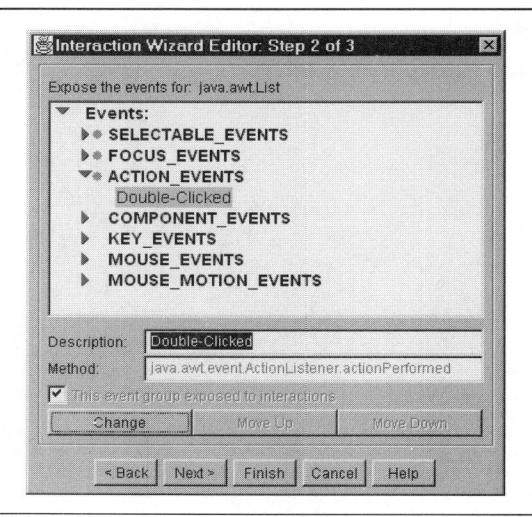

FIGURE 10.10: Changing the exposed event description in the Interaction Wizard Editor

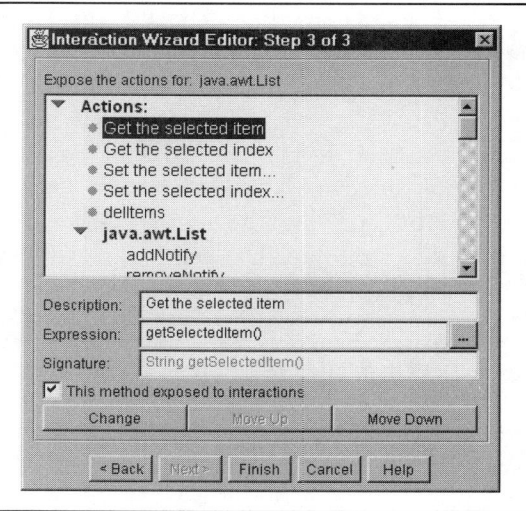

FIGURE 10.11: The Interaction Wizard Editor dialog box for exposing actions, Step 3 of 3

From the Expose the Actions For list, you can pick which methods of the class are available in the Do the Following list in the Interaction Wizard Step 3 of 4 screen. Just as for the events, you can change the description. By default, the description shown is the method name, and you expose individual methods, versus a whole set of them.

Using the Expression Assistant

One big difference in exposing methods is the expression field. When you expose a method that accepts parameters, you can either offer defaults or change a parameter's prompt string. For instance, in Figure 10.11, the (deprecated) `delItems` method of `List` has two parameters. The first is the start position to delete and the second is the ending position. If you wanted to change these, you could find `delItems` at the bottom of the `java.awt.List` methods list, select the This Method Exposed to Interactions toggle to expose it, and then select the "…" at the end of the Expression line to change it. This brings up the Expression Assistant dialog box, shown in Figure 10.12, and the Interaction Wizard UI dialog box, shown in Figure 10.13.

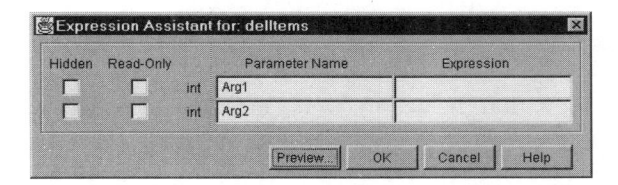

FIGURE 10.12: The Expression Assistant dialog box to support the Interaction Wizard Editor

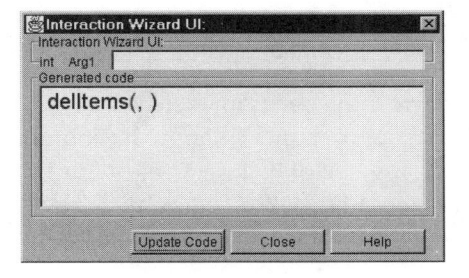

FIGURE 10.13: The Interaction Wizard UI dialog box to support the Expression Assistant shows intermediate results before accepting them.

To change the parameter prompts, change `Arg1` to **start** and `Arg2` to **end** in the Expression Assistant dialog. Selecting OK then changes the prompts for the `List` class only. In this skill, we aren't going to use what we just did. However Figure 10.14 shows the changes to the prompt screen if you were to connect to this method.

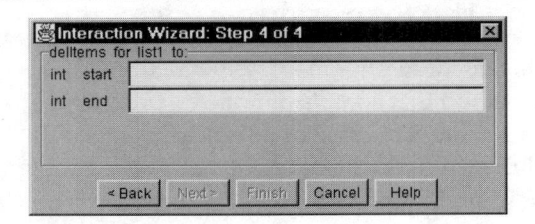

FIGURE 10.14: Connecting to delItems and showing off the new prompts

Returning to the necessary pieces for the Skill, just select Finish and we can finally go back to connecting the list to the text field.

Making the Final Connection

Now that the action event set is available, we can connect our last piece.

1. Select Wizards ➤ Interaction Wizard.

2. Select `list1` and then click the Next button.

3. Select `first` in the To Component pull-down list, `Double-Clicked` in the On Event pull-down list, and `Set the Text` in the Do the Following list. Then select Next.

4. On the final screen, we need to enter a placeholder, such as **0**, and then select the Finish button.

To correct the behavior, select the new `list1_actionPerformed1` method in the Structure pane. Change the contents to get the value of `list1` and display the reverse of it. To reverse a `String`, you need to use a support class, `java.lang.StringBuffer`. It has a `reverse` method. You create an instance of the `StringBuffer` class (`sb1`) and call the constructor, passing your string to it. Then you need another `StringBuffer` to store the reversed string. Once this is done, you can use the `toString` method in `StringBuffer` to get the string and pass it to `setText`.

```
void list1_actionPerformed1(ActionEvent actionEvent) {
  String s = list1.getSelectedItem();
  StringBuffer sb1 = new StringBuffer (s);
  StringBuffer sb2 = sb1.reverse();
  first.setText(sb2.toString());
}
```

> **TIP** A `String` object is a fixed string. It will never change. If you need to change the contents, you need to create a new object. A `StringBuffer` is a growable/changeable string-type object. When you are working with changing text strings, a `StringBuffer` is a more efficient object to use, as it does not require you to constantly create new objects.

With this last connection, our Wizard frame is complete. Save everything and run the new program. Notice how the `List` object now responds to single- and double-clicks differently. Figure 10.15 shows the working program after double-clicking on Sardines in the list. The complete source for `Wizard.java` follows.

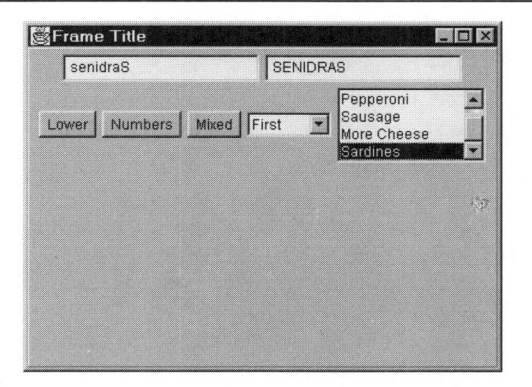

FIGURE 10.15: The final running program after double-clicking on Sardines

Wizard.java

```java
package skill10;

import java.awt.*;
import java.awt.event.*;
import borland.jbcl.control.*;
import borland.jbcl.layout.*;

public class Wizard extends DecoratedFrame {
  BorderLayout borderLayout1 = new BorderLayout();
  BevelPanel bevelPanel1 = new BevelPanel();
  TextField first = new TextField();
  TextField second = new TextField();
  FlowLayout flowLayout1 = new FlowLayout();
  Button button1 = new Button();
  Button button2 = new Button();
  Button button3 = new Button();
  Choice choice1 = new Choice();
  List list1 = new List();

  //Construct the frame
  public Wizard() {
    try {
      jbInit();
    }
    catch (Exception e) {
      e.printStackTrace();
    }
  }

  //Component initialization
  public void jbInit() throws Exception{
    this.setLayout(borderLayout1);
    this.setSize(new Dimension(400, 300));
    this.setTitle("Frame Title");
    first.setColumns(20);
    second.setColumns(20);
    button1.setLabel("Lower");
    button2.setLabel("Numbers");
    button3.setLabel("Mixed");
    choice1.add ("First");
    choice1.add ("Second");
    choice1.add ("Third");
    choice1.add ("Fourth");
    choice1.add ("Fifth");
```

```java
      list1.add ("Cheese");
      list1.add ("Pepperoni");
      list1.add ("Sausage");
      list1.add ("More Cheese");
      list1.add ("Sardines");
      bevelPanel1.setLayout(flowLayout1);
      this.add(bevelPanel1, BorderLayout.CENTER);
      bevelPanel1.add(first, null);
      bevelPanel1.add(second, null);
      bevelPanel1.add(button1, null);
      bevelPanel1.add(button2, null);
      bevelPanel1.add(button3, null);
      bevelPanel1.add(choice1, null);
      bevelPanel1.add(list1, null);
      first.addTextListener(new Wizard_firstTextAdapter1(this));
      button1.addActionListener(new Wizard_button1ActionAdapter1(this));
      button2.addActionListener(new Wizard_button2ActionAdapter1(this));
      button3.addActionListener(new Wizard_button3ActionAdapter1(this));
      choice1.addItemListener(new Wizard_choice1ItemAdapter1(this));
      list1.addItemListener(new Wizard_list1ItemAdapter1(this));
      list1.addActionListener(new Wizard_list1ActionAdapter1(this));
  }

  void first_textValueChanged1(TextEvent textEvent) {
    String s = first.getText();
    second.setText (s.toUpperCase());
  }

  void button1_actionPerformed1(ActionEvent actionEvent) {
    first.setText("welcome");
  }

  void button2_actionPerformed1(ActionEvent actionEvent) {
    first.setText("555-1212");
  }

  void button3_actionPerformed1(ActionEvent actionEvent) {
    first.setText("HowdY PaRtNeR");
  }

  void choice1_itemStateChanged1(ItemEvent itemEvent) {
    String s = choice1.getSelectedItem();
    first.setText(s);
  }
```

```java
  void list1_itemStateChanged1(ItemEvent itemEvent) {
    String s = list1.getSelectedItem();
    first.setText(s);
  }

  void list1_actionPerformed1(ActionEvent actionEvent) {
    String s = list1.getSelectedItem();
    StringBuffer sb1 = new StringBuffer (s);
    StringBuffer sb2 = sb1.reverse();
    first.setText(sb2.toString());
  }
}

// JBUILDER GENERATED ADAPTER CLASS FOR first
class Wizard_firstTextAdapter1 implements java.awt.evert.TextListener {

  Wizard_firstTextAdapter1(Wizard wizard) {
    this.wizard = wizard;
  }
  Wizard wizard;

  public void textValueChanged(TextEvent textEvent) {
    wizard.first_textValueChanged1(textEvent);
  }
}

// JBUILDER GENERATED ADAPTER CLASS FOR button1
class Wizard_button1ActionAdapter1 implements
java.awt.event.ActionListener {

  Wizard_button1ActionAdapter1(Wizard wizard) {
    this.wizard = wizard;
  }
  Wizard wizard;

  public void actionPerformed(ActionEvent actionEvent) {
    wizard.button1_actionPerformed1(actionEvent);
  }
}

// JBUILDER GENERATED ADAPTER CLASS FOR button2
class Wizard_button2ActionAdapter1 implements
java.awt.event.ActionListener {

  Wizard_button2ActionAdapter1(Wizard wizard) {
    this.wizard = wizard;
  }
  Wizard wizard;
```

```java
    public void actionPerformed(ActionEvent actionEvent) {
      wizard.button2_actionPerformed1(actionEvent);
    }
  }

  // JBUILDER GENERATED ADAPTER CLASS FOR button3
  class Wizard_button3ActionAdapter1 implements
  java.awt.event.ActionListener {

    Wizard_button3ActionAdapter1(Wizard wizard) {
      this.wizard = wizard;
    }
    Wizard wizard;

    public void actionPerformed(ActionEvent actionEvent) {
      wizard.button3_actionPerformed1(actionEvent);
    }
  }

  // JBUILDER GENERATED ADAPTER CLASS FOR choice1
  class Wizard_choice1ItemAdapter1 implements java.awt.event.ItemListener
  {

    Wizard_choice1ItemAdapter1(Wizard wizard) {
      this.wizard = wizard;
    }
    Wizard wizard;

    public void itemStateChanged(ItemEvent itemEvent) {
      wizard.choice1_itemStateChanged1(itemEvent);
    }
  }

  // JBUILDER GENERATED ADAPTER CLASS FOR list1
  class Wizard_list1ItemAdapter1 implements java.awt.event.ItemListener {

    Wizard_list1ItemAdapter1(Wizard wizard) {
      this.wizard = wizard;
    }
    Wizard wizard;

    public void itemStateChanged(ItemEvent itemEvent) {
      wizard.list1_itemStateChanged1(itemEvent);
    }
  }
```

```
// JBUILDER GENERATED ADAPTER CLASS FOR list1
class Wizard_list1ActionAdapter1 implements
java.awt.event.ActionListener {

  Wizard_list1ActionAdapter1(Wizard wizard) {
    this.wizard = wizard;
  }
  Wizard wizard;

  public void actionPerformed(ActionEvent actionEvent) {
    wizard.list1_actionPerformed1(actionEvent);
  }
}
```

By now, you should have a good handle on using the Interaction Wizard and Interaction Wizard Editor. With them, it is relatively easy to connect beans and expose various pieces of each. Now, let's move on to adding more beans to the Component palette so you can more easily drag-and-drop your way to the future.

Are You Experienced?

Now you can...

- ☑ connect beans with the Interaction Wizard
- ☑ expose more events and methods with the Interaction Wizard Editor
- ☑ customize exposed events and methods to offer better names
- ☑ use the Expression Assistant
- ☑ work with AWT List and Choice components

PROGRAMMING

C, C, VB, Cobol, exp. Call 534-555-6543 or fax 534-555-6544.

PROGRAMMING

MRFS Inc. is looking for a Sr. Windows NT developer. Reqs. 3-5 yrs. Exp. In C under Windows, Win95 & NT, using Visual C. Excl. OO design & implementation skills a must. OLE2 & ODBC are a plus. Excl. Salary & bnfts. Resume & salary history to HR, 8779 HighTech Way, Computer City, AR

PROGRAMMERS

Contractors Wanted for short & long term assignments; Visual C, MFC Unix C/C, SQL Oracle Dev elop ers PC Help Desk Support Windows NT & NetWareTelecommunications Visual Basic, Access, HTMT, CGI, Perl MMI & Co., 885-555-9933

PROGRAMMER World Wide Web Links wants your HTML & Photoshop skills. Develop great WWW sites. Local & global customers. Send samples & resume to WWWL, 2000 Apple Road, Santa Rosa, CA.

TECHNICAL WRITER Software firm seeks writer/editor for manuals, research notes, project mgmt. Min 2 years tech. writing, DTP & programming experience. Send resume & writing samples to: Software Systems, Dallas, TX.

TECHNICAL Software development firm looking for Tech Trainers, Ideal candidates have programming experience in Visual C, HTML & JAVA. Need quick self starter. Call (443) 555-6868 for interview.

TECHNICAL WRITER / Premier Computer Corp is seeking a combination of technical skills, knowledge and experience in the following areas: UNIX, Windows 95/NT, Visual Basic, on-line help & documentation, and the internet. Candidates must possess excellent writing skills, and be comfortable working in a quality vs. deadline driven environment. Competitive salary. Fax resume & samples to Karen Fields, Premier Computer Corp., 444 Industrial Blvd. Concord, CA. Or send to our website at www.premier.com.

WEB DESIGNER

BA/BS or equivalent programming/multimedia production. 3 years of experience in use and design of WWW services streaming audio and video HTML, PERL, CGI, GIF, JPEG. Demonstrated interpersonal, organization, communication, multi-tasking skills. Send resume to The Learning People at www.learning.com.

WEBMASTER-TECHNICAL

BSCS or equivalent, 2 years of experience in CGI, Windows 95/NT, UNIX, C, Java, Perl. Demonstrated ability to design, code, debug and test on-line services. Send resume to The Learning People at www.learning.com.

PROGRAMMER World Wide Web Links wants your HTML & Photoshop skills. Develop great WWW sites. Local & global customers. Send sam-

---

ing tools. Experienced in documentation preparation & programming languages (Access, C, FoxPro) are a plus. Financial or banking customer service support is required along with excellent verbal & written communication skills with multi levels of end-users. Send resume to KKUP Enterprises, 45 Orange Blvd. Orange, CA.

COMPUTERS Small Web Design firm seeks indiv. w/NT, Webserver & Database management exp. Fax resume to 556-555-4221.

COMPUTER/ Visual C/C, Visual Basic Exp'd Systems Analysts/ Programmers for growing software dev. team in Roseburg. Computer Science or related degree preferred. Develop adv. Engineering applications for engineering firm. Fax resume to 707-555-8744.

COMPUTER Web Master for dynamic SF Internet co. Site, Dev, test, coord, train, 2 yrs prog. Exp. C C Web C FTP. Fax resume to Best Staffing 845-555-7722.

COMPUTER PROGRAMMER

Ad agency seeks programmer w/exp. in UNIX/NT Platforms, Web Server, CGI/Perl. Programmer Position avail. on a project basis with the possibility to move into F/T. Fax resume & salary req. to R. Jones 334-555-8332.

COMPUTERS Programmer/Analyst Design and maintain C based SQL database applications. Required skills: Visual Basic, C, SQL ODBC Document existing and new applications, Novell or NT exp. a plus. Fax resume & salary history to 235-555-9935.

GRAPHIC DESIGNER

Webmaster's Weekly is seeking a creative Graphic Designer to design high impact marketing collateral, including direct mail promos, CD-ROM packages, ads and WWW pages. Must be able to juggle multiple projects and learn new skills on the job very rapidly. Web design experience a big plus, technical troubleshooting also a plus. Call 435-555-1235.

GRAPHICS - ART DIRECTOR - WEB-MULTIMEDIA

Leading internet development company has an outstanding opportunity for a talented, high-end Web Experienced Art Director. In addition to a great portfolio and fresh ideas, the ideal candidate has excellent communication and presentation skills. Working as a team with innovative producers and programmers, you will create dynamic, interactive web sites and application interfaces. Some programming experience required. Send samples and resume to: SuperSites, 333 Main, Seattle, WA

MARKETING

Fast paced software and service provider looking for MARKETING COMMUNICATIONS SPECIALIST to be responsible for its webpage, seminar coordination, and ad place-

---

PROGRAMMERS Multiple short term assignments available: Visual C, 3 positions SQL ServerNT Server, 2 positions JAVA & HTML, long term NetWare Various locations. Call for more info. 356-555-3398.

PROGRAMMERS

C, C, VB, Cobol, exp.
Call 534-555-6543
or fax 534-555-6544.

PROGRAMMING

MRFS Inc. is looking for a Sr. Windows NT developer. Reqs. 3-5 yrs. Exp. In C under Windows, Win95 & NT, using Visual C Excl. OO & implementation skills a must. OLE2 & ODBC are a plus. Excl. Salary & bnfts. Resume & salary history to HR, 8779 HighTech Way, Computer City, AR

PROGRAMMERS/ Contractors Wanted for short & long term assignments; Visual C, MFC Unix C/C, SQL Oracle Developers PC Help Desk Support Windows NT & NetWareTelecommunications Visual Basic, Access, HTMT, CGI, Perl MMI & Co., 885-555-9933

PROGRAMMER World Wide Web Links wants your HTML & Photoshop skills. Develop great WWW sites. Local & global customers. Send samples & resume to WWWL, 2000 Apple Road, Santa Rosa, CA.

COMPUTERS Programmer/Analyst Design and maintain C based SQL database applications. Required skills: Visual Basic, C, SQL, ODBC Document existing and new applications, Novell or NT exp. a plus. Fax resume & salary history to 235-555-9935.

GRAPHIC DESIGNER

Webmaster's Weekly is seeking a creative Graphic Designer to design high impact marketing collateral, including direct mail promo's. CD-ROM packages, ads and WWW pages. Must be able to juggle multiple projects and learn new skills on the job very rapidly. Web design experience a big plus, technical troubleshooting also a plus. Call 435-555-1235.

GRAPHICS - ART DIRECTOR - WEB-MULTIMEDIA

Leading internet development company has an outstanding opportunity for a talented, high-end Web Experienced Art Director. In addition to a great portfolio and fresh ideas, the ideal candidate has excellent communication and presentation skills. Working as a team with innovative producers and programmers, you will create dynamic, interactive web sites and application interfaces. Some programming experience required. Send samples and resume to: SuperSites, 333 Main, Seattle, WA

COMPUTER PROGRAMMER

Ad agency seeks programmer w/exp. in UNIX/NT Platforms, Web Server, CGI/Perl. Programmer Position avail. on a project basis with the possibility to move into F/T. Fax resume & salary req. to R. Jones 334-555-8332.

PROGRAMMERS / Established software company seeks program-

---

ment. Must be a self-starter, energetic, organized. Must have 2 year web experience. Programming a plus. Call 985-555-9854.

PROGRAMMERS Multiple short term assignments available: Visual C, 3 positions SQL ServerNT Server, 2 positions JAVA & HTML, long term NetWare Various locations. Call for more info. 356-555-3398.

PROGRAMMERS

C, C, VB, Cobol, exp. Call 534-555-6543 or fax 534-555-6544.

PROGRAMMING

MRFS Inc. is looking for a Sr. Windows NT developer. Reqs. 3-5 yrs. Exp. In C under Windows, Win95 & NT using Visual C Exc. OO design & implementation skills a must. OLE2 & ODBC are a plus. Excl Salary & bnfts. Resume salary history to HR, 8779 HighTech Way, Computer City, AR

PROGRAMMERS/ Contractors Wanted for short & long term assignments: Visual C, MFCUnix C/C, SQL Oracle Developers PC Help Desk Support Windows NT & NetWare Telecommunications Visual Basic, Access, HTMT, CGI, Perl MMI & Co. 885-555-9933

PROGRAMMER World Wide Web Links wants your HTML & Photoshop skills. Develop great WWW sites. Local & global customers. Send samples & resume to WWWL, 2000 Apple Road, Santa Rosa, CA.

TECHNICAL WRITER Software firm seeks writer/editor for manuals, research notes, project mgmt. Min 2 years tech. writing, DTP & programming experience. Send resume writing samples to: Softwa Systems, Dallas, TX.

TECHNICAL Software development firm looking for Tech Trainers, Ideal candidates have programming experience in Visual C, HTML & JAV. Need quick self starter. Call (44 555-6868 for interview.

TECHNICAL WRITER Premi. Computer Corp is seeking a comb nation of technical skills, knowledg and experience in the followin areas: UNIX, Windows 95/NT, Visu Basic, on-line help & documentatio and the internet. Candidates m. possess excellent writing skills, an be comfortable working in a quali vs. deadline driven environmer Competitive salary. Fax resume samples to Karen Fields. Premi Computer Corp. 444 Industrial Blv Concord, CA. Or send to our websi at www.premier.com.

WEB DESIGNER

BA/BS or equivalent program ming/multimedia production. years of experience in use an design of WWW services stream audio and video HTML, PERL, C GIF, JPEG. Demonstrated interpe sonal, organization, communicatic multi-tasking skills. Send resume The Learning People at www.lear ing.com

WEBMASTER-TECHNICA

SKILL

eleven

Configuring the Palette

- ❑ Adding beans from an archive
- ❑ Adding beans from a package
- ❑ Deleting beans from palette
- ❑ Finding beans

Setting Up the Component Palette

After playing connect-the-beans in the last skill and showing off the various components on the Component palette, this skill will show you how to extend the Component palette so even more beans are available. You'll need to extend the palette because either you've purchased some beans or you've created your own and want to reuse them more easily. If you're experimenting with various beans from the Web and you need to get rid of them, I'll also discuss the extra steps necessary to completely remove them. Finally, I'll wrap up the skill by showing you where to look for more beans.

Adding from an Archive

Let's say you're Wile E. Coyote, and you've just purchased the Acme Bean Collection. You want to add the beans to JBuilder so you can hunt down your nemesis, the Road Runner. Adding a new bean—or an entire set of beans—to JBuilder is as easy as following Wile's blue prints for a road runner trap. Thankfully, with JBuilder, the process always works as expected in the end.

To add beans to JBuilder, the first step is to get the collection, which may involve either downloading from the Web or placing a CD-ROM into the drive. Once you've installed the product, you will probably end up with the beans in either a ZIP file or JAR file.

> **NOTE** JAR files are *Java Archives*. They are similar to ZIP files, but contain something called a manifest that describes the contents of the file. You'll learn more about these in Skill 17.

For this skill, we'll actually use a collection that comes with JBuilder, so you don't have to bother with downloading something off the Internet. Borland has included some Java demos from Sun in the `C:\JBuilder\lib\jbcl.zip` file. Some of these can be found on the Sun Applets tab of the Component palette. We'll add yet another one.

Once you have the collection available, select Tools ➤ Configure Palette to bring up the dialog box shown in Figure 11.1. The first page you'll see is the Pages tab, which shows a list of each tab, or page, on the Component palette.

To add a bean from a ZIP or JAR file, select the Add from Archive tab. You'll see the dialog box shown in Figure 11.2.

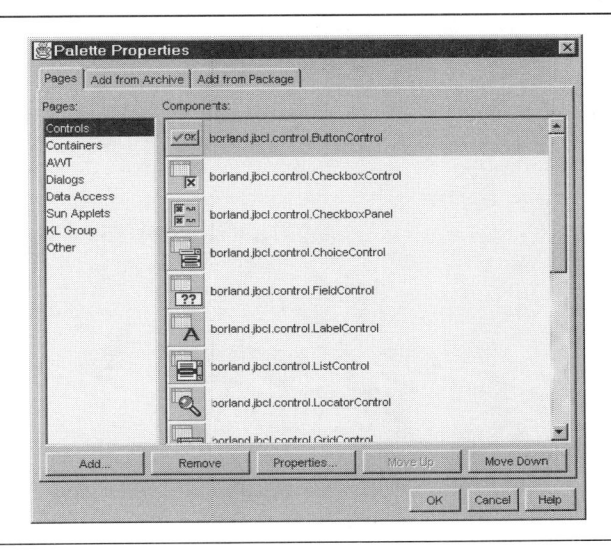

FIGURE 11.1: The Palette Properties dialog box, where you configure the Component palette. From here, you can add, remove, or reorder beans on the palette.

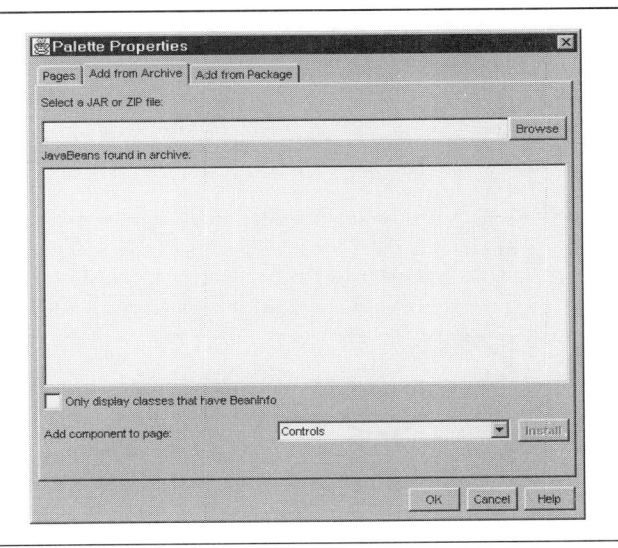

FIGURE 11.2: The Add from Archive tab of the Palette Properties dialog box. From here, you pick an archive, pick a page, and then select the beans to install.

To find the ZIP file we are going to use, select Browse, the `lib` folder, and then the `jbcl.zip` file. Once you select Open, Figure 11.2 will split in two, and you'll see a list of all the packages found in the archive, as well as an area to list beans within each package. The package we'll be using is the first package in the list, so select `borland.jbcl.appletwrappers.arctest`, as shown in Figure 11.3.

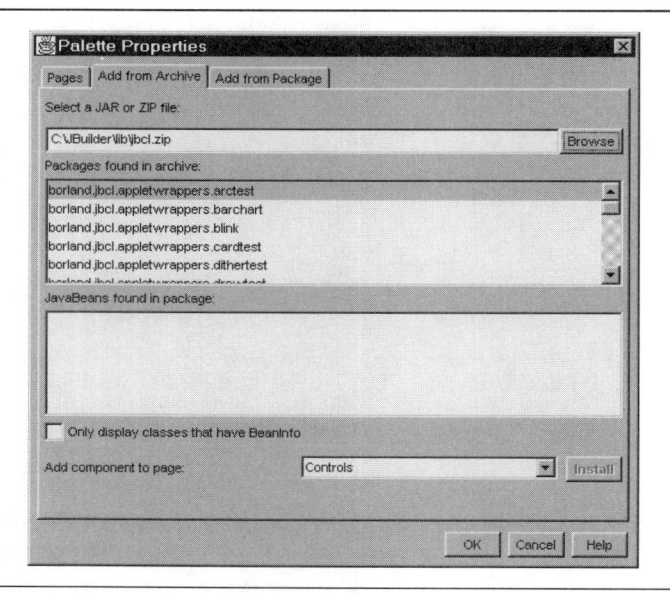

FIGURE 11.3: Picking a bean to install from an archive in the Palette Properties dialog box

> **NOTE** At this point, don't worry about the Only Display Classes That Have Beaninfo checkbox. We'll talk about `BeanInfo` in Skill 13. Basically, it is an optional support class provided to help builder tools understand beans.

Once you've selected the `arctest` package from the list, the `ArcTest` and `ArcTestWrapper` beans show up in the JavaBeans Found in Package list. `ArcTest` happens to be an applet, while `ArcTestWrapper` wraps the applet into a panel that knows when to call the appropriate applet life-cycle methods.

> **NOTE** In order for ArcTest and ArcTestWrapper to appear, you need to select another package first, then reselect arctest.

We want to install the ArcTestWrapper bean, so we select it, choose which page to add it to (Other or Sun Applets is most appropriate) in the Add Component to Page list, and press the Install button. Initially, the only thing that happens is that the Install button becomes unselectable, or disabled. If you look on the Component palette, the new bean isn't added yet. Until you actually select the OK button from the Palette Properties dialog box, no change is made. Once you select OK, you'll find the new bean added to the palette. If we added the palette to the Sun Applets tab of the Component palette, it would look like Figure 11.4.

FIGURE 11.4: The Sun Applets tab of the Component palette with the new ArcTestWrapper bean

> **WARNING** When you add a bean to the palette from an archive, JBuilder copies the entire archive file into the C:\JBuilder\beans directory. This means that you cannot add beans to the palette from two different archives with the same name. You will need to rename one of the archives for this to work.

Adding from a Package

Adding a bean from a package is slightly different from adding one from an archive. For example, JBuilder doesn't duplicate the archive file on disk, but remembers where the package is located when you use the bean. However, other than a couple of labels on the dialog boxes, the dialog boxes look identical. The bean we'll add to the Other tab is the CardFrame we created in Skill 6. As a refresher, Figure 11.5 shows what this looks like.

> **TIP** One thing to remember: although we are demonstrating visual beans, not all beans have to be visual. You can create beans that have no visual representation. When you drop these beans into JBuilder, you will just see the class name.

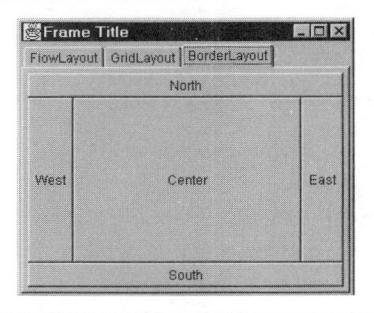

FIGURE 11.5: The CardFrame bean from Skill 6

To add the `CardFrame` bean from the `skill6` package, start by selecting Tools ➤ Configure Palette. Now, instead of selecting the Add from Archive tab, select Add from Package. At this point, you need to select any `.class` file in the package you want to add a bean from. Remember that JBuilder places the `.class` files from its projects under its `myclasses` directory, so select Browse, and then select `myclasses\skill6` and any `.class` file in the directory. Clicking the Open button or double-clicking on a `.class` file lists all the classes in the package, as shown in Figure 11.6.

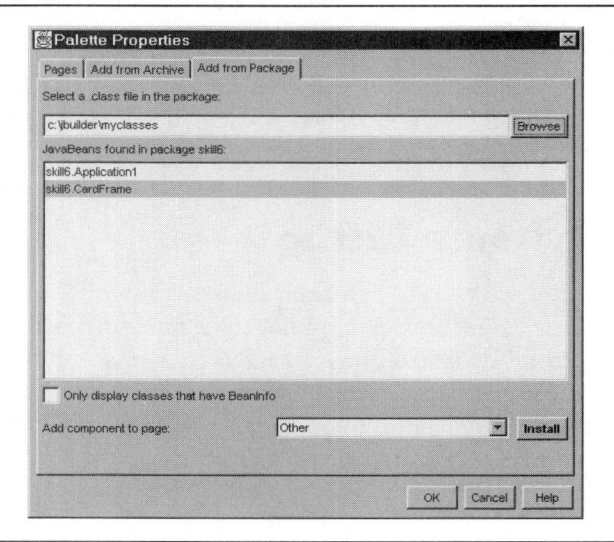

FIGURE 11.6: Picking a bean from a package to install from the Palette Properties dialog box

Just as with adding from an archive, if you select the bean you want to add, the page you want to add it to, and then the Install button, the bean is not added to the Component palette until you select the OK button.

Customizing Palette Entries

One thing you may have noticed when you inserted the `ArcTestWrapper` bean is that it shows a generic icon. By default, when you add a bean, a generic image is displayed. You can change this generic icon in two ways: You can use a `BeanInfo` class that supports your bean and says which icon to display instead. We'll look into this in Skill 13. However, the second way is actually much less work and, as long as you are not distributing your beans across the world, works best for an individual. We'll describe the second way here.

To change the icon of `ArcTestWrapper`, bring up the Palette Properties dialog box again by selecting Tools ➤ Configure Palette, the Sun Applets page, and the `borland.jbcl.appletwrappers.arctest.ArcTestWrapper` component. At this point, if you click the Properties button, the screen shown in Figure 11.7 will pop up.

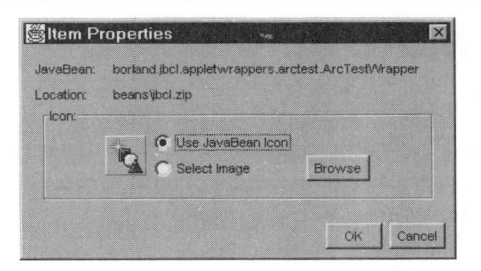

FIGURE 11.7: The Item Properties dialog box where you can change a bean icon

By default, the Use JavaBean Icon option is selected. This causes the bean to use the default icon or the one provided by the supporting `BeanInfo` class when available. To change the image, choose the Select Image option, and then Browse to find an appropriate image. JBuilder automatically starts the search in either the `C:\JBuilder\lib\image32` or the `C:\JBuilder\lib\image16` directory. Each directory contains close to one hundred GIF icons. Which directory you start in depends on your current screen resolution. You can select an image from either directory or one you've created. Once you've selected the image file, select OK on the Item Properties and Palette Properties dialog boxes.

> **TIP**
>
> If you do want to create an icon image, you need to use a program other than JBuilder to create it. Paint Shop Pro is a shareware program available at http://www.visitorinfo.com/software/paint.htm—it supports creating GIF-formatted images.

Removing Beans

Removing a bean from the component palette is straightforward. Just select Tools ➤ Configure Palette, find the bean, and select Remove. There is one catch though; if you added the bean from an archive and you do not want to use the bean in any of your programs, you need to do one more thing. JBuilder creates a copy of the archive file in the `C:\JBuilder\beans` directory. If you are *really* sure you don't want to use the bean package any more, you need to use Explorer to manually delete the file, too. If you forget to delete the file, nothing bad will happen. However, if you find yourself testing lots of beans from various sources, your hard drive will fill up quickly.

Locating More Beans

Now that you know how to integrate new beans into JBuilder, where can you find them? Well, there are several different places to look, each with its own benefits. Instead of listing the specific vendors, I'll just point out some of the component warehouses.

KL Group

To get the first set of beans you don't even have to go anywhere. The JClass family of components from KL Group of Toronto comes with JBuilder. It consists of several AWT-like components and a charting component. While most of the AWT-like components have a similar component within the JBCL controls, you may find the charting one worthwhile. Figure 11.8 lists the JClass components available under the KL Group tab of the Component palette.

You can find the JClass Web site at http://www.klg.com/jclass, and additional support is also available in the JClass Chart Programmer's Reference or JClass Table Programmer's Reference books, under JBuilder's Help ➤ Help Topics menu.

Locating More Beans 217

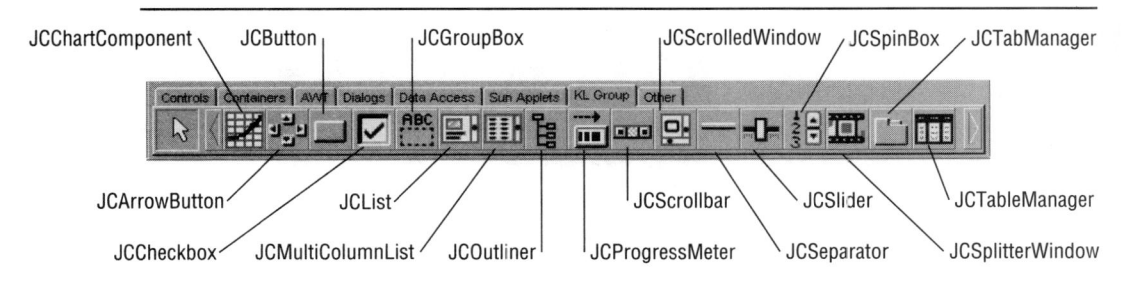

FIGURE 11.8: The KL Group palette of components

Labels on the palette:
- JCChartComponent
- JCButton
- JCGroupBox
- JCScrolledWindow
- JCSpinBox
- JCTabManager
- JCArrowButton
- JCList
- JCScrollbar
- JCSlider
- JCTableManager
- JCCheckbox
- JCMultiColumnList
- JCOutliner
- JCProgressMeter
- JCSeparator
- JCSplitterWindow

> **TIP** While the `JCChartComponent` comes with JBuilder, if you are looking for a good charting package I personally like the chart bean from NetFactory at `http://www.netcharts.com`.

Gamelan

Gamelan is the official directory for Java. In the spring of 1997, Gamelan outgrew its strictly Java origin at `http://www.gamelan.com` and moved on to `http://www.developer.com`, where it has become an online service for all Internet technologies, not just Java. One of these new technologies is JavaBeans, and you can locate their bean listings at `http://javabeans.developer.com`. Figure 11.9 shows the entry screen, which always gives you some current beans news, too.

> **NOTE** *Gamelan* (pronounced *Gamma-lahn*) is an Indonesian word referring to a musical orchestra. It originates from the island of Java.

The Coffee Grinder

Another place worth checking for beans calls itself "The Coffee Grinder." This site is dubbed "A haven for JavaBeans developers" and markets some commercially available beans. In addition to the beans, you'll also find links to various beans-related FAQs (Frequently Asked Questions), newsgroups, and magazine articles. The URL is `http://TrevorHarmon.com/coffeegrinder/index.html`, and Figure 11.10 shows The Coffee Grinder home page.

218 Skill 11 • Configuring the Palette

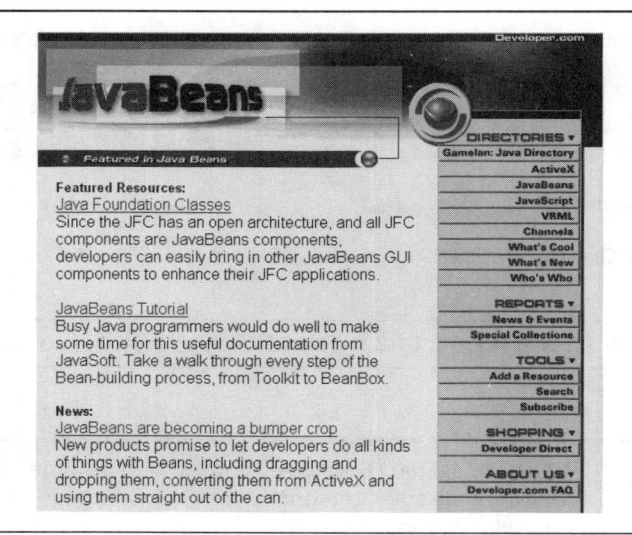

FIGURE 11.9: Developer.com's JavaBeans listing screen. Scrolling down the screen shows the search field. (© 1997 Developer.com, located at http://javabeans.developer.com)

FIGURE 11.10: The Coffee Grinder's entryway

Java Applet Rating Service (JARS)

JARS serves as a "best of the web" rating service for Java programs. Among the many things they rate are beans. If you look under their Top 1%, you'll find what their reviewers think are the best beans in the business. You may get lucky and find some that even include source code. The beans listing starts at `http://www.jars.com/listing-JavaBeans.html`, while the JARS home page is shown in Figure 11.11.

FIGURE 11.11: The JARS home page—well organized, but it takes awhile to load

JavaBeans Home

The official home page for JavaBeans itself is `http://splash.javasoft.com/beans/`. From here, you'll find white papers on the technology and some pointers to future bean plans. In addition, you will find Sun's JavaBeans Directory. It serves as a comprehensive directory of JavaBean components. As with all the other listings though, if the bean creator didn't submit their entry you won't find it in any of the listings.

> **NOTE:** Although not a bean collection, JBuilder comes with another library of classes: ObjectSpace's Generic Library for Java (JGL). JGL is a set of reusable data structures and algorithms. For a description, look in the online JGL User Guide and in the samples directory: `C:\JBuilder\samples\objectspace\jgl_samples`.

Now that you know how to add already existing beans to JBuilder, let's look into creating our own. Skill 12 starts the process by looking at the properties and events aspect of bean creation.

Are You Experienced?

Now you can...

- ☑ use the configure palette tool
- ☑ add beans to the component palette
- ☑ remove beans from the component palette
- ☑ customize beans on the component palette
- ☑ fill your hard disk with more beans

PROGRAMMERS
C, C, VB, Cobol, exp. Call 534-555-6543 or fax 534-555-6544.

PROGRAMMING
MRFS Inc. is looking for a Sr. Windows NT developer. Reqs. 3-5 yrs. Exp. In C under Windows, Win95 & NT, using Visual C. Excl. OO design & implementation skills a must. OLE2 & ODBC are a plus. Excl. Salary & bnfts. Resume & salary history to HR, 8779 HighTech Way, Computer City, AR

PROGRAMMERS
Contractors Wanted for short & long term assignments; Visual C, MFC Unix C/C, SQL Oracle Developers PC Help Desk Support Windows NT & NetWareTelecommunications Visual Basic, Access, HTMT, CGI, Perl MMI & Co. 885-555-9933

PROGRAMMER
World Wide Web Links wants your HTML & Photoshop skills. Develop great WWW sites. Local & global customers. Send samples & resume to WWWL, 2000 Apple Road, Santa Rosa, CA.

TECHNICAL WRITER
Software firm seeks writer/editor for manuals, research notes, project mgmt. Min 2 years tech. writing, DTP & programming experience. Send resume & writing samples to: Software Systems, Dallas, TX.

TECHNICAL
Software development firm looking for Tech Trainers. Ideal candidates have programming experience in Visual C, HTML & JAVA. Need quick self starter. Call (443) 555-6868 for interview.

TECHNICAL WRITER /
Premier Computer Corp is seeking a combination of technical skills, knowledge and experience in the following areas: UNIX, Windows 95/NT, Visual Basic, on-line help & documentation, and the internet. Candidates must possess excellent writing skills, and be comfortable working in a quality vs. deadline driven environment. Competitive salary, fax resume & samples to Karen Fields, Premier Computer Corp. 444 Industrial Blvd. Concord, CA. Or send to our website at www.premier.com.

WEB DESIGNER
BA/BS or equivalent programming/multimedia production. 3 years of experience in use and design of WWW services streaming audio and video HTML, PERL, CGI, GIF, JPEG. Demonstrated interpersonal, organization, communication, multi-tasking skills. Send resume to The Learning People at www.learning.com.

WEBMASTER-TECHNICAL
BSCS or equivalent, 2 years of experience in CGI, Windows 95/NT, UNIX, C, Java, Perl. Demonstrated ability to design, code, debug and test on-line services. Send resume to The Learning People at www.learning.com.

PROGRAMMER
World Wide Web Links wants your HTML & Photoshop skills. Develop great WWW sites. Local & global customers. Send samples & resume to WWWL, 2000 Apple Road, Santa Rosa, CA.

PROGRAMMERS
Multiple short term assignments available: Visual C, 3 positions SQL ServerNT Server, 2 positions JAVA & HTML, long term NetWare Various locations. Call for more info. 356-555-3398.

PROGRAMMERS
C, C, VB, Cobol, exp.
Call 534-555-6543
or fax 534-555-6544.

PROGRAMMING
MRFS Inc. is looking for a Sr. Windows NT developer. Reqs. 3-5 yrs. Exp. In C under Windows, Win95 & NT, using Visual C. Excl. OO design & implementation skills a must. OLE2 & ODBC are a plus. Excl. Salary & bnfts. Resume & salary history to HR, 8779 HighTech Way, Computer City, AR

PROGRAMMERS /
Contractors Wanted for short & long term assignments; Visual C, MFC Unix C/C, SQL Oracle Developers PC Help Desk Support Windows NT & NetWareTelecommunications Visual Basic, Access, HTMT, CGI, Perl MMI & Co. 885-555-9933

PROGRAMMER
World Wide Web Links wants your HTML & Photoshop skills. Develop great WWW sites. Local & global customers. Send samples & resume to WWWL, 2000 Apple Road, Santa Rosa, CA.

TECHNICAL WRITER
Software firm seeks writer/editor for manuals, research notes, project mgmt. Min 2 years tech. writing, DTP & programming experience. Send resume & writing samples to: Software Systems, Dallas, TX.

COMPUTER PROGRAMMER
Ad agency seeks programmer w/exp. in UNIX/NT Platforms, Web Server, CGI/Perl. Programmer Position avail. on a project basis with the possibility to move into F/T. Fax resume & salary req. to R. Jones 334-555-8332.

TECHNICAL WRITER
Premier Computer Corp is seeking a combination of technical skills, knowledge and experience in the following areas: UNIX, Windows 95/NT, Visual Basic, on-line help & documentation, and the internet. Candidates must possess excellent writing skills, and be comfortable working in a quality vs. deadline driven environment. Competitive salary. Fax resume & samples to Karen Fields, Premier Computer Corp. 444 Industrial Blvd. Concord, CA. Or send to our website at www.premier.com.

WEB DESIGNER
BA/BS or equivalent programming/multimedia production. 3 years of experience in use and design of WWW services streaming audio and video HTML, PERL, CGI, GIF, JPEG. Demonstrated interpersonal, organization, communication, multi-tasking skills. Send resume to: SuperSites, 333 Main, Seattle, WA

COMPUTER PROGRAMMER
Ad agency seeks programmer w/exp. in UNIX/NT Platforms, Web Server, CGI/Perl. Programmer Position avail. on a project basis with the possibility to move into F/T. Fax resume & salary req. to R. Jones 334-555-8332.

PROGRAMMERS / Established
software company seeks programmers

COMPUTERS
Small Web Design firm seeks indiv. w/NT, Webserver & Database management exp. Fax resume to 556-555-4221.

COMPUTER /
Visual C/C, Visual Basic Exp'd Systems Analysts/Programmers for growing software dev. team in Roseburg. Computer Science or related degree preferred. Develop adv. Engineering applications for engineering firm. Fax resume to 707-555-8744.

COMPUTER
Web Master for dynamic SF Internet co. Site, Dev., test, coord, train. 2 yrs prog. Exp. C C Web C FTP, fax resume to Best Staffing 845-555-7722.

COMPUTERS: QA SOFTWARE TESTERS
Qualified candidates should have 2 yrs exp. performing integration & system testing using automated testing tools. Experienced in documentation preparation & programming languages (Access, C, FoxPro) are a plus. Financial or banking customer service support is required along with excellent verbal & written communication skills with multi levels of end-users. Send resume to KKUP Enterprises, 45 Orange Blvd. Orange, CA.

COMPUTERS
Programmer/Analyst Design and maintain C based SQL database applications. Required skills: Visual Basic, C, SQL, ODBC, Document existing and new applications, Novell or NT exp. a plus. Fax resume & salary history to 235-555-9935.

GRAPHIC DESIGNER
Webmaster's Weekly is seeking a creative Graphic Designer to design high impact marketing collateral, including direct mail promo's. CD-ROM packages, ads and WWW pages. Must be able to juggle multiple projects and learn new skills on the job very rapidly. Web design experience a big plus, technical troubleshooting also a plus. Call 435-555-1235.

GRAPHICS - ART DIRECTOR - WEB-MULTIMEDIA
Leading internet development company has an outstanding opportunity for a talented, high-end Web Experienced Art Director. In addition to a great portfolio and fresh ideas, the ideal candidate has excellent communication and presentation skills. Working as a team with innovative producers and programmers, you will create dynamic, interactive web sites and application interfaces. Some programming experience required. Send samples and resume to: SuperSites, 333 Main, Seattle, WA

COMPUTER PROGRAMMER
Ad agency seeks programmer w/exp. in UNIX/NT Platforms, Web Server, CGI/Perl. Programmer Position avail. on a project basis with the possibility to move into F/T. Fax resume & salary req. to R. Jones 334-555-8332.

PROGRAMMERS
Multiple short term assignments available: Visual C, 3 positions SQL ServerNT Server, 2 positions JAVA & HTML, long term NetWare Various locations. Call more info. 356-555-3398.

PROGRAMMERS
C, C, VB, Cobol, exp. Call 534-555-6543 or fax 534-555-6544.

PROGRAMMING
MRFS Inc. is looking for a Sr. Windows NT developer. Reqs. 3-5 yrs. Exp. In C under Windows, Win95 & NT, using Visual C. Excl. OO design & implementation skills a must. OLE2 & ODBC are a plus. Excl. Salary & bnfts. Resume & salary history to HR, 8779 HighTech Way, Computer City, AR

PROGRAMMERS /
Contractors Wanted for short & long term assignments; Visual C, MFCUnix C/C, SQL Oracle Developers PC Help Desk Support Windows NT & NetWare Telecommunications Visual Basic, Access, HTMT, CGI, Perl MMI & Co. 885-555-9933

PROGRAMMER
World Wide Web Links wants your HTML & Photoshop skills. Develop great WWW sites. Local & global customers. Send samples & resume to WWWL, 2000 Apple Road, Santa Rosa, CA.

TECHNICAL WRITER
Software firm seeks writer/editor for manuals, research notes, project mgmt. Min 2 years tech. writing, DTP & programming experience. Send resume to: Software Systems, Dallas, TX.

TECHNICAL
Software development firm looking for Tech Trainers. Ideal candidates have programming experience in Visual C, HTML & JAVA. Need quick self starter. Call (443) 555-6868 for interview.

TECHNICAL WRITER
Premier Computer Corp is seeking a combination of technical skills, knowledge and experience in the following areas: UNIX, Windows 95/NT, Visual Basic, on-line help & documentation, and the internet. Candidates must possess excellent writing skills, and be comfortable working in a quality vs. deadline driven environment. Competitive salary, fax resume & samples to Karen Fields, Premier Computer Corp. 444 Industrial Blvd. Concord, CA. Or send to our website at www.premier.com.

WEB DESIGNER
BA/BS or equivalent programming/multimedia production. 3 years of experience in use and design of WWW services streaming audio and video HTML, PERL, CGI, GIF, JPEG. Demonstrated interpersonal, organization, communication, multi-tasking skills. Send resume to The Learning People at www.learning.com.

WEBMASTER-TECHNICAL

SKILL twelve

12

Creating Beans: Events/Properties

- ❏ Creating your first bean
- ❏ Explaining the delegation event model
- ❏ Creating new events
- ❏ Making the bean triangular
- ❏ Creating simple properties
- ❏ Creating indexed properties
- ❏ Creating bound properties
- ❏ Creating constrained properties

Creating New Beans

So far, you've gotten a feel for using some of the existing beans. Starting in this chapter, and continuing in the following three chapters, I'll explain the different pieces necessary to create your own beans. You don't need all the chapters to create simple beans. However, as the complexity of a bean increases, you may want to provide more pieces so the bean user has an easier time. After we look at how to do the different pieces ourselves, we'll look at JBuilder's BeansExpress to see how JBuilder helps automate some of these tasks.

To demonstrate where we are going, let's start by creating a simple bean. This bean will be a basic blue box. Wherever you place the bean, you'll see a blue box on the screen. First, close any open projects. Then, create a new project in **C:\skills\skill12\skill12.jpr** with the Project Wizard. Do not run the Application Wizard yet, as we aren't creating an application; we're creating a bean.

After creating the project, create a new class with the New Class Wizard, select File ➤ New, and then double-click the Class icon on the New tab, as shown in Figure 12.1.

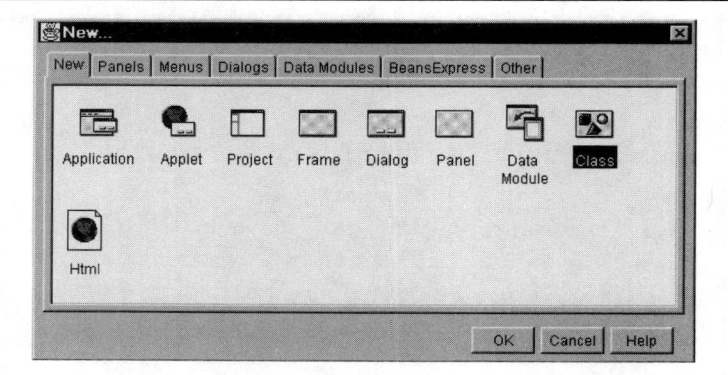

FIGURE 12.1: Creating a new class with the Class Wizard

This brings up the New Object dialog box, as shown in Figure 12.2. There are no specific naming requirements for beans, so we'll enter a class name of **BlueBox**. Because we are creating a visual bean, in the Extends text box we need to enter **java.awt.Component** to extend it. If the bean wasn't visual, such as for a data structure, you could just leave the Extends field as `java.lang.Object`. The Public checkbox is already selected, as is the Generate Default Constructor checkbox, so just select the OK button to have the class generated.

FIGURE 12.2: The New Object dialog box, for creating new classes

> **TIP** All beans must be public classes and must have a no argument constructor. The no argument constructor is considered the default constructor.

In order to have the bean be one big blue area, we need to override the `paint` method. Using the Override Methods Wizard, select the `paint (Graphics)` method under the `java.awt.Component` list, and select OK. To make the bean blue, we need to change the color and draw a filled rectangle of the appropriate size. Just add the highlighted lines to the `paint` method:

```
public void paint(Graphics parm1) {
  super.paint( parm1);
  parm1.setColor (Color.blue);
  Dimension d = getSize();
  parm1.fillRect (0, 0, d.width-1, d.height-1);
}
```

> **TIP** The width of the bean's area is `getSize().width`. However, because the width starts at 0, the last spot is `width-1`. It is the same for height.

At this point our bean is done. Save and compile it to make sure everything is okay. We can't run the program yet because the bean hasn't been used. In order to make it usable by another program, it is best to just drop it into the Component palette.

Adding Our First Bean to the Palette

As we learned in the last skill, select Tools ➤ Configure Palette to bring up the Palette Properties dialog box, as shown in Figure 12.3.

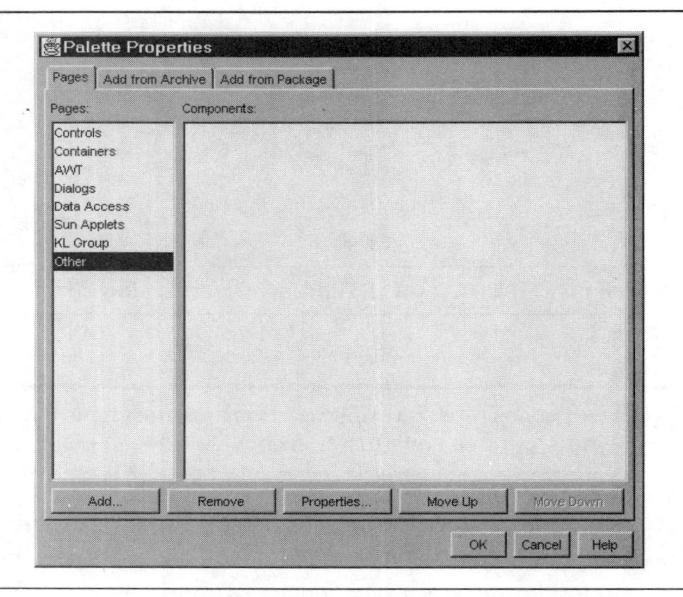

FIGURE 12.3: A view of the Palette Properties dialog box for adding and removing components from the palette

To add the new `BlueBox` bean to the Other tab, select Other in the Pages column, and then select the Add from Package tab. From here, we need to browse to the location where the compiled `BlueBox.class` file is, so select the Browse button. By default, JBuilder places all of your classes under the `myclasses` directory, so select it. Because we are working in `skill12`, select the `skill12` directory. Finally, you should see the `BlueBox.class` file. Double-clicking that file adds the bean to the Palette Properties dialog box, as shown in Figure 12.4.

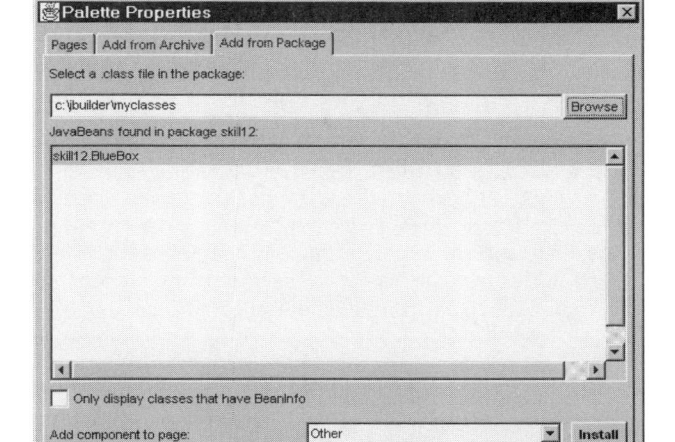

FIGURE 12.4: The Palette Properties dialog box now has the `skill12.BlueBox` bean in its list.

Once the beans in the package are listed, select the bean you want to install—for the purposes of our example, `skill12.BlueBox`, and then press the Install button. The bean will then be installed when you select the OK button.

> **TIP** Be sure to press the Install button before you select OK. If you forget to press the Install button, the bean won't be installed.

> **WARNING** Throughout this skill, we frequently change beans that we've added to the Component palette. Java, and hence JBuilder, doesn't like dynamically changing definitions of classes already loaded. Therefore, if you find the system not picking up recent changes, you may want to exit JBuilder and restart it. If this were necessary, it would probably happen when creating one of the tester programs. I will list all instances when you need to restart JBuilder before continuing.

Using the *BlueBox* Bean

Now it's time to show off our new bean. Let's create a new project to do the testing. Close the `skill12` project, and start up the Application Wizard. In the Project Wizard, we'll name this one **skill12b** and place it in the file **c:\skills\skill12b\skill12b.jpr**. In the Application Wizard, select Next to move to the second screen, name the frame **BlueBoxTester**, and select Finish.

> **TIP** When testing out your beans, it is best to test them from a different project. This provides a more realistic testing environment and verifies that proper access keywords like `private`, `protected`, and `public` were used.

Once you select `BlueBoxTester.java` in the Navigation pane, then select the Design tab in the Contents pane and the Other tab on the Component palette, you can try out the `BlueBox` bean. Select the bean from the Other tab and drop it into the frame. At this point, you don't see the bean there. After you drop the bean into the frame, you need to drag the mouse because we didn't do anything to size the bean. When you drag, you are providing the bean with a desired size. So, select the `BlueBox` again from the palette and place a few more beans into the frame, but drag the mouse a bit. At this point, if you save and run the program, you may end up with a screen that should look similar to the screen shown in Figure 12.5.

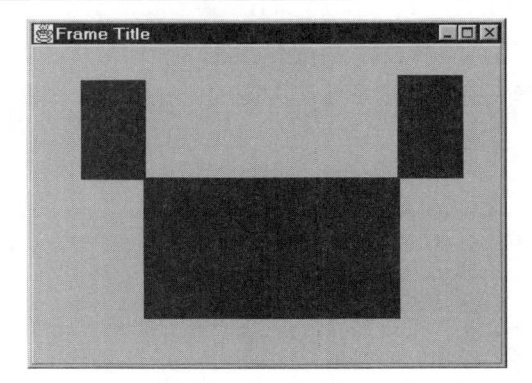

FIGURE 12.5: Running the `BlueBoxTester` after dropping in a few beans. Your screen will probably differ, depending upon the size and placement of the `BlueBox` beans.

> **NOTE** If you have more than one bean on the Other tab and aren't sure which one is the BlueBox, briefly rest your mouse over each bean to see the class name displayed; skill12.BlueBox is the right one for our example.

My BlueBoxTester source follows. Yours will differ slightly, depending upon the number and placement of beans.

BlueBoxTester.java

```java
package skill12b;

import java.awt.*;
import java.awt.event.*;
import borland.jbcl.control.*;
import borland.jbcl.layout.*;
import skill12.*;

public class BlueBoxTester extends DecoratedFrame {
  BorderLayout borderLayout1 = new BorderLayout();
  XYLayout xYLayout2 = new XYLayout();
  BevelPanel bevelPanel1 = new BevelPanel();
  BlueBox blueBox1 = new BlueBox();
  BlueBox blueBox2 = new BlueBox();
  BlueBox blueBox3 = new BlueBox();
  BlueBox blueBox4 = new BlueBox();

  //Construct the frame
  public BlueBoxTester() {
    try {
      jbInit();
    }
    catch (Exception e) {
      e.printStackTrace();
    }
  }

  //Component initialization
  public void jbInit() throws Exception{
    this.setLayout(borderLayout1);
    this.setSize(new Dimension(400, 300));
    this.setTitle("Frame Title");
    bevelPanel1.setLayout(xYLayout2);
```

```
        this.add(bevelPanel1, BorderLayout.CENTER);
        bevelPanel1.add(blueBox1, new XYConstraints(130, 69, -1, -1));
        bevelPanel1.add(blueBox2, new XYConstraints(92, 112, 215, 122));
        bevelPanel1.add(blueBox3, new XYConstraints(40, 29, 55, 86));
        bevelPanel1.add(blueBox4, new XYConstraints(304, 25, 56, 89));
    }
}
```

Introducing Events

As we learned in Skill 9, events serve as the notification mechanism between beans. If a bean wants to know when an event happens, it registers itself with the source of the event. Then, when the event happens, the source notifies anyone registered, or listening. The event itself must be a subclass of `java.util.EventObject`, while the listener implements the `java.util.EventListener` interface. All the AWT events work this way, so implicitly all AWT components are beans. The whole scenario looks something like Figure 12.6.

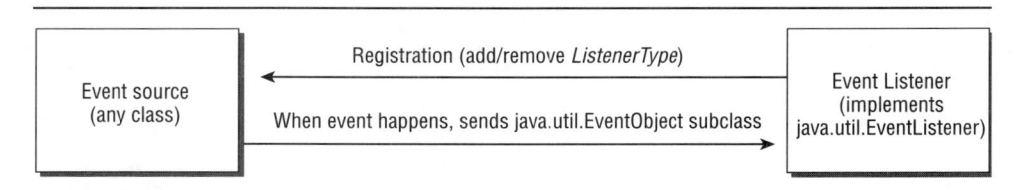

FIGURE 12.6: The Event source, listener, and object cycle

If we wanted to add some event handling to the `BlueBox`, we need to pick an event to generate, and then maintain the listener list. We could create our own event type; however, with all the work the Java team put into creating the AWT event structure, it is much easier just to reuse what they created. For general events, this is usually sufficient. Skill 16 explores creating custom events.

Reopening the `skill12` project, we can add some event handling to the `BlueBox`. The most common event handler to add is for the `ActionEvent` event class. The `ActionEvent` serves as a general event type. We saw it used with a `Button` when it gets selected and with a `TextField` when the user presses Enter while entering text.

In order to process an event within a class, you need to maintain a list of listeners. In the case of the `ActionEvent`, the appropriate listener is `ActionListener`—so add a variable of that type, and initialize it to null:

```
ActionListener actionListener = null;
```

The `ActionListener` class happens to be in the `java.awt.event` package, so we should also import that package. Right after the other import line, add the following line:

```
import java.awt.event.*;
```

So someone can listen for when the event happens, the event source—`BlueBox`—has to add and remove listeners from the `ActionListener` list. The add and remove methods need to be named a certain way for JBuilder, or any bean-connection tool, to find them when you use the UI Designer. The method names always follow the same naming pattern, where you only fill in the specific listener type. The method name patterns, or signatures, follow:

```
public synchronized void addListenerType(ListenerType l)
public synchronized void removeListenerType(ListenerType l)
```

In the case of the `BlueBox` with the `ActionListener`, the methods need to be named `addActionListener` and `removeActionListener`. Naming the methods is the easy part, but now you need to maintain the lists. Thankfully, AWT also provides a support class for this. The class is called `AWTEventMulticaster`, and it has **add** and **remove** methods to help maintain the listener list. As long as you are only reusing the AWT events, you can use the support class to help maintain the listener list.

```
public synchronized void addActionListener (ActionListener l) {
    actionListener = AWTEventMulticaster.add (actionListener, l);
}
public synchronized void removeActionListener (ActionListener l) {
    actionListener = AWTEventMulticaster.remove (actionListener, l);
}
```

Both the **add** and **remove** methods take two parameters, a list and a listener to add or remove. The **add** method always adds the listener, possibly resulting in the same object listening multiple times, while the **remove** method only removes the listener if it is in the list.

> **NOTE** The methods are synchronized so two threads do not try to update the listener list simultaneously.

Notifying Listeners

At this point, our `BlueBox` bean maintains the listener list fine. There is only one problem—it doesn't notify the listeners. To complete the process, the bean needs to notify them. Before we describe what activates the notification, let's create a method to notify the listeners. With the help of the `AWTEventMulticaster` support class, the method is rather simple. If there are multiple listeners, the support class handles the looping through the listener list. If there are no listeners, nothing needs to happen.

```java
public void notifyActionListeners() {
  if (actionListener != null) {
    ActionEvent e = new ActionEvent (this, ActionEvent.ACTION_PERFORMED, "");
    actionListener.actionPerformed(e);
  }
}
```

> **NOTE** There is no magic to the name of this method, unlike the add and remove listener method names.

No matter what event you are handling, the list variable, `add`/`remove` methods, and notification code is identical. The only thing that might change is the listener type and the creation of the specific event object sent to all the listeners. The only thing different is what triggers the notification to happen. In the case of the blue box, we'll have it notify the listeners when the user clicks the mouse within it.

> **TIP** Keep in mind that a click is when the mouse doesn't move between press and release.

In order for the blue box to respond to mouse clicks, it needs to implement the `MouseListener` interface. Using the Implement Interface Wizard, select the java.awt.event.MouseListener interface and select OK. Now, once you find the newly added mouseClicked method, you can have it call notifyActionListeners:

```
public void mouseClicked(MouseEvent parm1) {
  notifyActionListeners();
}
```

The last step before we have a new and improved blue box, which notifies anyone listening for action, is to add the MouseListener to the BlueBox bean itself. In the constructor, add the listener:

```
public BlueBox() {
  addMouseListener (this);
}
```

Now, you can save and recompile BlueBox. It isn't necessary to add it again to the palette as it is already there. However, you do need to restart JBuilder before you can test it.

The complete source for BlueBox follows:

BlueBox.java

```
package skill12;

import java.awt.*;
import java.awt.event.*;

public class BlueBox extends Component implements MouseListener {

  ActionListener actionListener = null;

  public BlueBox() {
    addMouseListener (this);
  }

  public void paint(Graphics parm1) {
    super.paint( parm1);
    parm1.setColor (Color.blue);
    Dimension d = getSize();
    parm1.fillRect (0, 0, d.width-1, d.height-1);
  }
  public synchronized void addActionListener (ActionListener l) {
    actionListener = AWTEventMulticaster.add (actionListener, l);
  }
  public synchronized void removeActionListener (ActionListener l) {
    actionListener = AWTEventMulticaster.remove (actionListener, l);
  }
```

```
  public void notifyActionListeners() {
    if (actionListener != null) {
      ActionEvent e = new ActionEvent (this, ActionEvent.ACTION_PERFORMED, "");
      actionListener.actionPerformed(e);
    }
  }

  public void mouseClicked(MouseEvent parm1) {
    notifyActionListeners();
  }

  public void mousePressed(MouseEvent parm1) {
  }

  public void mouseReleased(MouseEvent parm1) {
  }

  public void mouseEntered(MouseEvent parm1) {
  }

  public void mouseExited(MouseEvent parm1) {
  }
}
```

Creating a New Tester

We can now create a new test program to try out the new and improved `BlueBox`. Closing the `skill12` project, run the Application Wizard again, create a **skill12c** project in **c:\skills\skill12c\skill12c.jpr**, and name the frame class **BlueBoxActionTester**.

We'll have a blue box and a text field on the screen. When the user selects the blue box, the text field will display `I've been hit`. Select `BlueBoxActionTester.java` in the Navigation pane and then select the Design tab in the Content pane to set up the screen.

To place the blue box on the screen, select the Other tab of the Component palette. Then, select the blue box and drop it into the frame, dragging the mouse to size it.

Next, select the AWT tab of the Component palette and select the `TextField` bean. This should be the last icon on the right. Just drop this one onto the screen. On the Inspector screen, change the column property to **20** to make sure we can see the entire message.

To register the frame as a listener for the BlueBox, double-click the BlueBox within the UI Designer. This is the same as selecting the Events tab on the Inspector and double-clicking in the actionPerformed method as we've done in the past. This places us in the Source pane to fill in the event-handling code. Just call the setText method of textField1 with the appropriate string, I've been hit.

```
void blueBox1_actionPerformed(ActionEvent e) {
  textField1.setText ("I've been hit");
}
```

Saving and running the program now demonstrates the BlueBox bean and its action listener. Figure 12.7 shows the program in action. Here is the source of the testing program.

```
package skill12c;

import java.awt.*;
import java.awt.event.*;
import borland.jbcl.control.*;
import borland.jbcl.layout.*;
import skill12.*;

public class BlueBoxActionTester extends DecoratedFrame {
  BorderLayout borderLayout1 = new BorderLayout();
  XYLayout xYLayout2 = new XYLayout();
  BevelPanel bevelPanel1 = new BevelPanel();
  BlueBox blueBox1 = new BlueBox();
  TextField textField1 = new TextField();

  //Construct the frame
  public BlueBoxActionTester() {
    try {
      jbInit();
    }
    catch (Exception e) {
      e.printStackTrace();
    }
  }

  //Component initialization
  public void jbInit() throws Exception{
    this.setLayout(borderLayout1);
    this.setSize(new Dimension(400, 300));
    this.setTitle("Frame Title");
    blueBox1.addActionListener(new BlueBoxActionTester_blueBox1_actionAdapter(this));
```

```
    textField1.setColumns(20);
    bevelPanel1.setLayout(xYLayout2);
    this.add(bevelPanel1, BorderLayout.CENTER);
    bevelPanel1.add(blueBox1, new XYConstraints(48, 89, 148, 83));
    bevelPanel1.add(textField1, new XYConstraints(177, 194, -1, -1));
  }

  void blueBox1_actionPerformed(ActionEvent e) {
    textField1.setText ("I've been hit");
  }

}

class BlueBoxActionTester_blueBox1_actionAdapter implements
java.awt.event.ActionListener {
  BlueBoxActionTester adaptee;

  BlueBoxActionTester_blueBox1_actionAdapter(BlueBoxActionTester adaptee) {
    this.adaptee = adaptee;
  }

  public void actionPerformed(ActionEvent e) {
    adaptee.blueBox1_actionPerformed(e);
  }
}
```

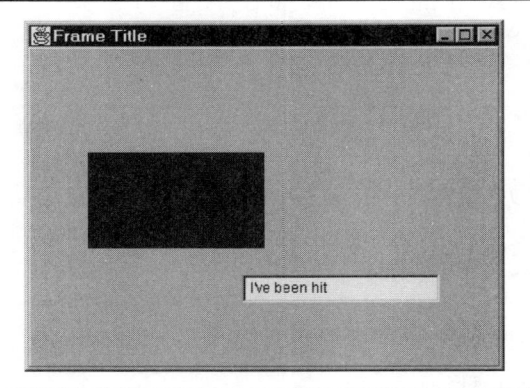

FIGURE 12.7: The BlueBoxActionTester in action after selecting the BlueBox.

Making a Blue Triangle

Creating new beans that are rectangular doesn't involve much work: define how to draw it, maintain your event lists, and determine when to generate the events. Then, whenever the event happens, notify the event-listener lists. If the event has to do with mouse clicks, the click can happen anywhere within the bean. If you want to restrict where the click triggers the event, you have to do a little extra work. Let's covert the blue box to a blue triangle so you can see what I mean.

Close project `skill12c` and reopen `skill12`. Create a new class with the Class Wizard and call it **BlueTriangle**. Have it extend **BlueBox** since we are just going to customize it a little. Instead of duplicating all the functionality of `BlueBox` in `BlueTriangle`, we're going to inherit it and change the undesirable behavior. Click OK.

The essential difference between the `BlueBox` and `BlueTriangle` is the painting. For the triangle, we need to define a `Polygon` that contains the different points of the triangle. Then, we can rely on the `drawPolygon` of `Graphics` method to draw it.

A `Polygon` is another class of AWT. You use it to describe closed figures through a series of points. Our `Polygon` will have three points for the triangle. They could be anywhere within the bean, but we'll use the top-left, bottom-left, and bottom-right corners.

Override the `paint(Graphics)` method using the Override Methods Wizard. We don't want to call the super class's (`BlueBox`'s) `paint` method because then we would still have a blue box drawn, so remove the `super.paint` method call. To declare a polygon, place three points in it and draw it:

```
public void paint(Graphics parm1) {
  parm1.setColor (Color.blue);
  Dimension d = getSize();
  Polygon p = new Polygon ();
  p.addPoint (0, 0);
  p.addPoint (0, d.height-1);
  p.addPoint (d.width-1, d.height-1);
  parm1.fillPolygon (p);
}
```

> **NOTE** The reason we have to size the triangle each time is that the screen, and hence the component, may have been resized.

At this point, the `BlueTriangle` would work exactly like the `BlueBox`, except it would look a little different. For the functionality to be distinct—so only selecting the actual triangle triggers the action event—you need to override the `contains` method of `Component`. By default, `contains` always returns `true`. If we change `contains` to only return `true` while over the triangle, we've accomplished our mission. Thankfully, `Polygon` has a `contains` method, too. Because it reports if a point is within the polygon, we only need to return what it returns.

Using the Overrides Method Wizard select Component's `contains (int, int)` method and select OK. Moving the polygon creation code out of `paint` and into a shared helper routine, `getTriangle` results in the following completed source.

BlueTriangle.java

```java
package skill12;

import java.awt.*;
import java.awt.event.*;

public class BlueTriangle extends BlueBox {

  public BlueTriangle() {
  }

  private Polygon getTriangle() {
    Dimension d = getSize();
    Polygon p = new Polygon ();
    p.addPoint (0, 0);
    p.addPoint (0, d.height-1);
    p.addPoint (d.width-1, d.height-1);
    return p;
  }

  public boolean contains(int parm1, int parm2) {
    Polygon p = getTriangle();
    return p.contains (parm1, parm2);
  }

  public void paint(Graphics parm1) {
    parm1.setColor (Color.blue);
    Polygon p = getTriangle();
    parm1.fillPolygon (p);
  }
}
```

At this point, save and compile `BlueTriangle`. Once it is error free, add it to the Component palette next to the `BlueBox` by following these steps:

1. Select Tools ➤ Configure Palette.
2. Select the Add from Package tab.
3. Select the Browse button.
4. Double-click the `myclasses` folder.
5. Double-click the `skill12` folder
6. Double-click any `.class` file.
7. Back on the Palette Properties screen, select `skill12.BlueTriangle`.
8. Select Other in the Add Component To Page text box.
9. Select the Install button.
10. Select OK.

The `BlueTriangle` is now on the Component palette.

Updating the New Tester

If we close project `skill12` and reopen `skill12c`, we can add a `BlueTriangle` to the test program. Select `BlueBoxActionTester` in the Navigation pane, and then select the Design tab in the Contents pane and the Other tab on the Component palette. Next, pick the `BlueTriangle` from the Component palette and place it in the frame, making sure to drag the mouse when dropping it in. You should now see the blue triangle on the screen. If you save and run the program at this point, you'll see the screen shown in Figure 12.8.

After quitting the program, return to the UI Designer. Now, if you double-click on the triangle, you'll make the frame listen for action events within the `BlueTriangle`. Like the `BlueBox`, we'll just change the text in the text field, this time to `I'm not square`:

```
void blueTriangle1_actionPerformed(ActionEvent e) {
    textField1.setText ("I'm not square");
}
```

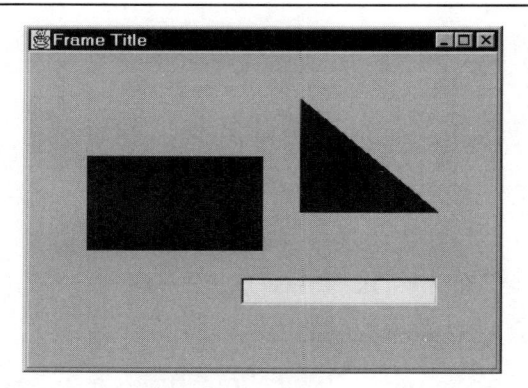

FIGURE 12.8: The `BlueBoxActionTester` with a blue box and a blue triangle.

If you save everything and run the program again, you'll notice that when you click the mouse on the blue triangle, the text changes; when you click in the gray area—within the boundary rectangle, the text does not change.

Introducing Properties

As we learned in Skill 9, a property is a named attribute of the bean. A pair of specially named methods reads or sets a property's value. While within a builder tool, a property editor allows the application developer to modify the properties. In JBuilder, this property editor is called the Inspector.

There are four types of properties:

- Simple
- Indexed
- Bound
- Constrained

Working with Simple Properties

As the name might imply, *simple properties* are the simplest to work with. A simple property is defined by a set of routines—one called `set` and one called `get`.

The rest of the method signature defines the property name and datatype. The `set` routine allows someone to change the property value, while the `get` routine allows one to retrieve the value.

```
public DataType getPropertyName ()
public void setPropertyName (DataType value)
```

An obvious property to add to our `BlueBox` is a color. Instead of always being blue, we can add a color property. Then, when someone uses the bean, they can define what color they want the bean to be.

Close project `skill12c` and reopen `skill12`. Create a new class with the Class Wizard and call it **Box**. Have Box extend **BlueBox**, since we are just going to customize it a little. Select OK. Just as we did with **BlueTriangle**, instead of duplicating all the functionality of `BlueBox`, we're going to inherit it and change the undesirable behavior.

1. Add an instance variable to save the value of the new color:

    ```
    private Color color = Color.blue;
    ```

2. Override `paint` and draw with the new color:

    ```
    public void paint(Graphics parm1) {
      parm1.setColor (color);
      Dimension d = getSize();
      parm1.fillRect (0, 0, d.width-1, d.height-1);
    }
    ```

3. Add a `setColor` method:

    ```
    public final void setColor (Color c) {
      color = c;
      repaint();
    }
    ```

4. Add a `getColor` method:

    ```
    public final Color getColor () {
      return color;
    }
    ```

5. Don't forget to import `java.awt.*`, as you are using its `Graphics` class.

    ```
    import java.awt.*;
    ```

> **NOTE** The name of the property added is Color. Its name arrives from the set/get method names, not the instance variable name.

Box.java

```java
package skill12;

import java.awt.*;

public class Box extends BlueBox {

  private Color color = Color.blue;

  public void Box () {
  }

  public final void setColor (Color c) {
    color = c;
    repaint();
  }

  public final Color getColor () {
    return color;
  }

  public void paint(Graphics parm1) {
    parm1.setColor (color);
    Dimension d = getSize();
    parm1.fillRect (0, 0, d.width-1, d.height-1);
  }
}
```

> **NOTE** From an object-oriented perspective, this hierarchy is backwards. BlueBox should subclass Box because it is a specialization. However, we created BlueBox first, so for this example, we just have to live with it.

Now, save and compile the bean, and add it to the component palette. When you add it to the test program you created in skill12c using the UI designer as we did with the other beans, then if you look at the Inspector you'll see a property named color available, as shown in Figure 12.9.

FIGURE 12.9: The Inspector for Box with the Color property available

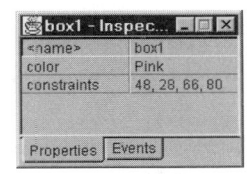

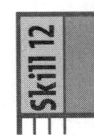

NOTE If the datatype of a property is *boolean*, the name of the get routine can have a prefix of `is`, instead of `get`. For instance, for a property called `active` of type boolean, the `set` routine would be `setActive`, and the get routine would be `isActive`.

Working with Indexed Properties

An *indexed property* is for properties that can hold an array of values within a single property. When creating your own properties to be indexed, there are four methods you need to define:

```
public void setPropertyName (DataType[] list)
public void setPropertyName (DataType element, int position)
public DataType[] getPropertyName ()
public DataType getPropertyName (int position)
```

An example of an indexed property is the `items` property of the `borland.jbcl.control.ListControl` class, where each item displayed in the list is an entry in the indexed property. There isn't an obvious indexed property for our `Box`, so we won't try to force the issue.

Working with Bound Properties

Bound properties are for when you want property changes to propagate from bean to bean to bean. For instance, if we have ten box beans on a screen and we want each to be the same color, then we should make the `color` property a *bound* property and register each box as interested when the property changes. Then, only one color change can propagate out to the other beans, keeping the color consistent. However, there has to be a way to change the color property at run time.

In order to make this work, let's change the `color` property of Box to be bound. For every class with a bound property, the same code needs to be added:

1. Create a property-change listener list. The `java.beans` package has a support class for this called `PropertyChangeListener`. The listener list name can be anything.

   ```
   import java.beans.*;
   ...
   private PropertyChangeSupport changes =
     new PropertyChangeSupport (this);
   ```

2. Create add/remove listener methods. Fortunately these methods are just like the event listener add/remove methods. The `PropertyChangeSupport` class has add/remove methods we can call.

   ```
   public void addPropertyChangeListener (PropertyChangeListener p) {
     changes.addPropertyChangeListener (p);
   }
   public void removePropertyChangeListener (PropertyChangeListener p)
   {
     changes.removePropertyChangeListener (p);
   }
   ```

3. Modify the `set` method to notify the listeners.

   ```
   public final void setColor (Color c) {
     Color oldColor = color;
     color = c;
     changes.firePropertyChange ("color", oldColor, color);
     repaint();
   }
   ```

> **TIP** It isn't necessary to check if the color actually changed. The `firePropertyChange` method does this for us.

Two things to point out here. First, the `firePropertyChange` method passes along the name of the property that changed. This means that any listener needs to check the name before it can react to the event.

> **TIP**
> You should pass the empty string ("") as the first parameter to firePropertyChange when you don't want to tell a listener which property changed. This needs to be treated as if every property changed.

Second, it passes both the old and new value. This means that you have to save the old value before you change it. The notification happens after the property value has changed. For prior notification, see "Working with Constrained Properties."

At this point, save and compile the Box so we can test it.

> **TIP**
> You'll need to exit JBuilder and restart to test at this point.

Testing of Bound Properties

For our test program, let's place three box components on the screen and bind each color property to the color of the first box. Then, if the user clicks the first bean, the boxes all turn red; if they click the second bean, they go white; and if they click the third bean, they go blue.

Create a new application with the Application Wizard within project skill12c and name the frame **TriBoxer**. At this point, hop over to the UI Designer and drop in three boxes. Remember to size them when you place them there.

Next, select the first box, and go to the Event tab of the Inspector. As Figure 12.10 shows, the last event is the method, propertyChange for property change listening. Select it, and double-click in the Method Name area to create the listener's method. Here we have to check that we have the right property, and then pass along the change to box2 and box3.

```
void box1_propertyChange(PropertyChangeEvent e) {
  if (e.getPropertyName().equals ("color")) {
    Color newColor = (Color)e.getNewValue();
    box2.setColor (newColor);
    box3.setColor (newColor);
  }
}
```

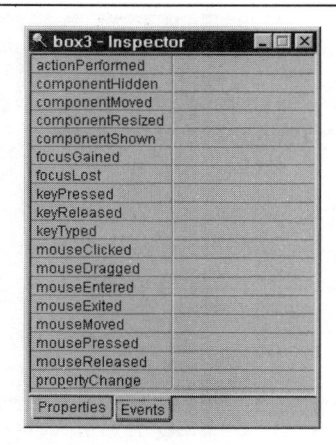

FIGURE 12.10: The Event Inspector screen for the Box bean.

Now, any change of the `color` property in box1 will propagate to box2 and box3. In order to demonstrate something, we have to add an action listener for each of the three boxes. Double-click on each box to add the appropriate source:

```
void box1_actionPerformed(ActionEvent e) {
  box1.setColor (Color.red);
}

void box2_actionPerformed(ActionEvent e) {
  box1.setColor (Color.white);
}

void box3_actionPerformed(ActionEvent e) {
  box1.setColor (Color.blue);
}
```

Now, if you save, compile, and run the program as you click on each box, you'll notice the color change propagating all around. Bound properties become very powerful as the number of listeners increase. Figure 12.11 shows one possible screen setup. Depending on where you placed things, yours will probably look different. The complete source of the test program follows.

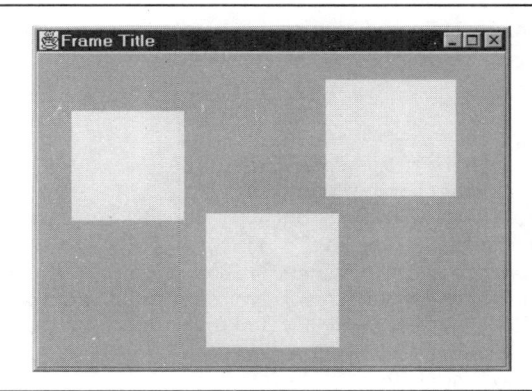

FIGURE 12.11: TriBoxer test program with color property bound between boxes

> **TIP** To run TriBoxer, make sure you select Application2 in the Navigation pane, before selecting the Run icon.

```
package skill12c;

import java.awt.*;
import java.awt.event.*;
import borland.jbcl.control.*;
import borland.jbcl.layout.*;
import skill12.*;
import java.beans.*;

public class TriBoxer extends DecoratedFrame {
  BorderLayout borderLayout1 = new BorderLayout();
  XYLayout xYLayout2 = new XYLayout();
  BevelPanel bevelPanel1 = new BevelPanel();
  Box box1 = new Box();
  Box box2 = new Box();
  Box box3 = new Box();

  //Construct the frame
  public TriBoxer() {
    try {
      jbInit();
    }
```

```java
      catch (Exception e) {
        e.printStackTrace();
      }
    }

    //Component initialization
    public void jbInit() throws Exception{
      this.setLayout(borderLayout1);
      this.setSize(new Dimension(400, 300));
      this.setTitle("Frame Title");
      box3.addActionListener(new TriBoxer_box3_actionAdapter(this));
      box2.addActionListener(new TriBoxer_box2_actionAdapter(this));
      box1.addActionListener(new TriBoxer_box1_actionAdapter(this));
      box1.addPropertyChangeListener(new TriBoxer_box1_propertyChangeAdapter(this));
      bevelPanel1.setLayout(xYLayout2);
      this.add(bevelPanel1, BorderLayout.CENTER);
      bevelPanel1.add(box1, new XYConstraints(28, 50, 95, 96));
      bevelPanel1.add(box2, new XYConstraints(140, 139, 112, 116));
      bevelPanel1.add(box3, new XYConstraints(240, 23, 110, 102));
    }

    void box1_propertyChange(PropertyChangeEvent e) {
      if (e.getPropertyName().equals ("color")) {
        Color newColor = (Color)e.getNewValue();
        box2.setColor (newColor);
        box3.setColor (newColor);
      }
    }

    void box1_actionPerformed(ActionEvent e) {
      box1.setColor (Color.red);
    }

    void box2_actionPerformed(ActionEvent e) {
      box1.setColor (Color.white);
    }

    void box3_actionPerformed(ActionEvent e) {
      box1.setColor (Color.blue);
    }
}

class TriBoxer_box1_propertyChangeAdapter implements
java.beans.PropertyChangeListener{
  TriBoxer adaptee;
```

```java
  TriBoxer_box1_propertyChangeAdapter(TriBoxer adaptee) {
    this.adaptee = adaptee;
  }

  public void propertyChange(PropertyChangeEvent e) {
    adaptee.box1_propertyChange(e);
  }
}

class TriBoxer_box1_actionAdapter implements java.awt.event.ActionListener {
  TriBoxer adaptee;

  TriBoxer_box1_actionAdapter(TriBoxer adaptee) {
    this.adaptee = adaptee;
  }

  public void actionPerformed(ActionEvent e) {
    adaptee.box1_actionPerformed(e);
  }
}

class TriBoxer_box2_actionAdapter implements java.awt.event.ActionListener {
  TriBoxer adaptee;

  TriBoxer_box2_actionAdapter(TriBoxer adaptee) {
    this.adaptee = adaptee;
  }

  public void actionPerformed(ActionEvent e) {
    adaptee.box2_actionPerformed(e);
  }
}

class TriBoxer_box3_actionAdapter implements java.awt.event.ActionListener {
  TriBoxer adaptee;

  TriBoxer_box3_actionAdapter(TriBoxer adaptee) {
    this.adaptee = adaptee;
  }

  public void actionPerformed(ActionEvent e) {
    adaptee.box3_actionPerformed(e);
  }
}
```

Working with Constrained Properties

Constrained properties take bound properties one level further. When the `set` method of a property is called, the bean asks anyone interested if the new value is okay before changing the actual value. If it isn't appropriate, the listener can reject the change, and the original change request will be aborted. What frequently happens next is the constrained property is also bound, so anyone interested in successful property changes will be notified.

Similar to bound properties, for every constrained property, the same code needs to be added. Here we'll make the color property of `Box` constrained:

1. Create a property change listener list. The `java.beans` package has a support class for this called `VetoableChangeSupport`. The listener list name can be anything.

   ```
   private VetoableChangeSupport vetoes = new VetoableChangeSupport (this);
   ```

2. Create `add`/`remove` listener methods:

   ```
   public void addVetoableChangeListener (VetoableChangeListener v) {
     vetoes.addVetoableChangeListener (v);
   }
   public void removeVetoableChangeListener (VetoableChangeListener v) {
     vetoes.removeVetoableChangeListener (v);
   }
   ```

3. Modify the `set` method to notify the listeners. Here, the method can now throw an exception:

   ```
   public final void setColor (Color c)
       throws PropertyVetoException {
     Color oldColor = color;
     vetoes.fireVetoableChange ("color", oldColor, c);
     color = c;
     changes.firePropertyChange ("color", oldColor, color);
     repaint();
   }
   ```

If someone rejects the color change, an exception is thrown and the line `color=c;` is never reached. At this point, save and compile the `Box` so we can test it.

> **TIP** You'll need to exit JBuilder and restart to test at this point.

Testing of Constrained Properties

Now, if we want to veto any changes to the color red, we can attach a vetoable listener to box1 by selecting `vetoableChange` in the Inspector and defining it like this:

```
void box1_vetoableChange(PropertyChangeEvent e) throws
PropertyVetoException{
  if (e.getPropertyName().equals ("color")) {
    Color newColor = (Color)e.getNewValue();
    if (newColor.equals (Color.red))
      throw new PropertyVetoException("I hate red", e);
  }
}
```

In addition, because `setColor` throws an exception now, anywhere it's called you'll have to add a `try/catch` block. The complete source follows:

TriBoxer.java

```
  package skill12c;

import java.awt.*;
import java.awt.event.*;
import borland.jbcl.cortrol.*;
import borland.jbcl.layout.*;
import skill12.*;
import java.beans.*;

public class TriBoxer extends DecoratedFrame {
  BorderLayout borderLayout1 = new BorderLayout();
  XYLayout xYLayout2 = new XYLayout();
  BevelPanel bevelPanel1 = new BevelPanel();
  Box box1 = new Box();
  Box box2 = new Box();
  Box box3 = new Box();

  //Construct the frame
  public TriBoxer() {
    try {
      jbInit();
    }
    catch (Exception e) {
      e.printStackTrace();
    }
  }
```

```java
//Component initialization
public void jbInit() throws Exception{
  this.setLayout(borderLayout1);
  this.setSize(new Dimension(400, 300));
  this.setTitle("Frame Title");
  box1.addVetoableChangeListener(new TriBoxer_box1_vetoableChangeAdapter(this));
  box3.addActionListener(new TriBoxer_box3_actionAdapter(this));
  box2.addActionListener(new TriBoxer_box2_actionAdapter(this));
  box1.addActionListener(new TriBoxer_box1_actionAdapter(this));
  box1.addPropertyChangeListener(new TriBoxer_box1_propertyChangeAdapter(this));
  bevelPanel1.setLayout(xYLayout2);
  this.add(bevelPanel1, BorderLayout.CENTER);
  bevelPanel1.add(box1, new XYConstraints(28, 50, 95, 96));
  bevelPanel1.add(box2, new XYConstraints(140, 139, 112, 116));
  bevelPanel1.add(box3, new XYConstraints(240, 23, 110, 102));
}

void box1_propertyChange(PropertyChangeEvent e) {
  if (e.getPropertyName().equals ("color")) {
    Color newColor = (Color)e.getNewValue();
    try {
      box1.setColor (newColor);
      box2.setColor (newColor);
      box3.setColor (newColor);
    } catch (PropertyVetoException pve) {
      System.out.println ("Unable to change");
    }
  }
}

void box1_actionPerformed(ActionEvent e) {
  try {
    box1.setColor (Color.red);
  } catch (PropertyVetoException pve) {
    System.out.println ("Unable to change");
  }
}

void box2_actionPerformed(ActionEvent e) {
  try {
    box1.setColor (Color.white);
  } catch (PropertyVetoException pve) {
    System.out.println ("Unable to change");
  }
}
```

```java
  void box3_actionPerformed(ActionEvent e) {
    try {
      box1.setColor (Color.blue);
    } catch (PropertyVetoException pve) {
      System.out.println ("Unable to change");
    }
  }

  void box1_vetoableChange(PropertyChangeEvent e) throws PropertyVetoException{
    if (e.getPropertyName().equals ("color")) {
      Color newColor = (Color)e.getNewValue();
      if (newColor.equals (Color.red))
        throw new PropertyVetoException("I hate red", e);
    }
  }
}

class TriBoxer_box1_propertyChangeAdapter implements
java.beans.PropertyChangeListener{
  TriBoxer adaptee;

  TriBoxer_box1_propertyChangeAdapter(TriBoxer adaptee) {
    this.adaptee = adaptee;
  }

  public void propertyChange(PropertyChangeEvent e) {
    adaptee.box1_propertyChange(e);
  }
}

class TriBoxer_box1_actionAdapter implements java.awt.event.ActionListener{
  TriBoxer adaptee;

  TriBoxer_box1_actionAdapter(TriBoxer adaptee) {
    this.adaptee = adaptee;
  }

  public void actionPerformed(ActionEvent e) {
    adaptee.box1_actionPerformed(e);
  }
}

class TriBoxer_box2_actionAdapter implements java.awt.event.ActionListener{
  TriBoxer adaptee;

  TriBoxer_box2_actionAdapter(TriBoxer adaptee) {
    this.adaptee = adaptee;
  }
```

```java
    public void actionPerformed(ActionEvent e) {
      adaptee.box2_actionPerformed(e);
    }
}

class TriBoxer_box3_actionAdapter implements java.awt.event.ActionListener {
  TriBoxer adaptee;

  TriBoxer_box3_actionAdapter(TriBoxer adaptee) {
      this.adaptee = adaptee;
  }

  public void actionPerformed(ActionEvent e) {
      adaptee.box3_actionPerformed(e);
  }
}

class TriBoxer_box1_vetoableChangeAdapter implements
java.beans.VetoableChangeListener {
  TriBoxer adaptee;

  TriBoxer_box1_vetoableChangeAdapter(TriBoxer adaptee) {
      this.adaptee = adaptee;
  }

  public void vetoableChange(PropertyChangeEvent e) throws PropertyVetoException{
      adaptee.box1_vetoableChange(e);
  }
}
```

Congratulations on making your way through Skill 12! You've made your way through the first of four important skills for creating beans. Now that you're able to add events and properties to beans, let's move on to Skill 13, where you'll learn about customization. Customization allows someone who is reusing your beans to configure them more easily.

Are You Experienced?

Now you can...

- ☑ create beans
- ☑ add events to beans
- ☑ make visible beans nonrectangular
- ☑ add simple, indexed, bound, and constrained properties to beans
- ☑ handle bound and constrained properties

PROGRAMMERS
C, C, VB, Cobol, exp. Call 534-555-6543 or fax 534-555-6544.

PROGRAMMING
MRFS Inc. is looking for a Sr. Windows NT developer. Reqs. 3-5 yrs. Exp. In C under Windows, Win95 & NT, using Visual C. Excl. OO design & implementation skills a must. OLE2 & ODBC are a plus. Excl. Salary & bnfts. Resume & salary history to HR, 8779 HighTech Way, Computer City, AR

PROGRAMMERS
Contractors Wanted for short & long term assignments: Visual C, MFC Unix C/C, SQL Oracle Dev elop ers PC Help Desk Support Windows NT & NetWareTelecommunications Visual Basic, Access, HTML, CGI, Perl MMI & Co., 885-555-9933

PROGRAMMER
World Wide Web Links wants your HTML & Photoshop skills. Develop great WWW sites. Local & global customers. Send samples & resume to WWWL, 2000 Apple Road, Santa Rosa, CA.

TECHNICAL WRITER
Software firm seeks writer/editor for manuals, research notes, project mgmt. Min 2 years tech. writing, DTP & programming experience. Send resume & writing samples to: Software Systems, Dallas, TX.

TECHNICAL
Software development firm looking for Tech Trainers. Ideal candidates have programming experience in Visual C, HTML & JAVA. Need quick self starter. Call (443) 555-6868 for interview.

TECHNICAL WRITER
Premier Computer Corp is seeking a combination of technical skills, knowledge and experience in the following areas: UNIX, Windows 95/NT, Visual Basic, on-line help & documentation, and the internet. Candidates must possess excellent writing skills, and be comfortable working in a quality vs. deadline driven environment. Competitive salary. Fax resume & samples to Karen Fields, Premier Computer Corp. 444 Industrial Blvd. Concord, CA. Or send to our website at www.premier.com.

WEB DESIGNER
BA/BS or equivalent programming/multimedia production. 3 years of experience in use and design of WWW services streaming audio and video HTML, PERL, CGI, GIF, JPEG. Demonstrated interpersonal, organization, communication, multi-tasking skills. Send resume to The Learning People at www.learning.com.

WEBMASTER-TECHNICAL
BSCS or equivalent. 2 years of experience in CGI, Windows 95/NT, UNIX, C, Java, Perl. Demonstrated ability to design, code, debug and test on-line services. Send resume to The Learning People at www.learning.com.

COMPUTER PROGRAMMER
Ad agency seeks programmer w/exp. in UNIX/NT Platforms, Web Server, CGI/Perl. Programmer Position avail. on a project basis with the possibility to move into F/T. Fax resume & salary req. to R. Jones 334-555-8332.

COMPUTERS Programmer/Analyst
Design and maintain C based SQL database applications. Required skills: Visual Basic, C, SQL, ODBC. Document existing and new applications, Novell or NT exp. a plus. Fax resume & salary history to 235-555-9935.

GRAPHIC DESIGNER
Webmaster's Weekly is seeking a creative Graphic Designer to design high impact marketing collateral, including direct mail promois, CD-ROM packages, ads and WWW pages. Must be able to juggle multiple projects and learn new skills on the job very rapidly. Web design experience a big plus, technical troubleshooting also a plus. Call 435-555-1235.

GRAPHICS - ART DIRECTOR - WEB-MULTIMEDIA
Leading internet development company has an outstanding opportunity for a talented, high-end Web Experienced Art Director. In addition to a great portfolio and fresh ideas, the ideal candidate has excellent communication and presentation skills. Working as a team with innovative producers and programmers, you will create dynamic, interactive web sites and application interfaces. Some programming experience required. Send samples and resume to: SuperSites, 333 Main. Seattle, WA.

MARKETING
Fast paced software and services provider looking for MARKETING COMMUNICATIONS SPECIALIST to be responsible for its webpage.

COMPUTERS
Small Web Design firm seeks indiv. w/NT, Webserver & Database management exp. Fax resume to 556-555-4221.

COMPUTER
Visual C/C, Visual Basic Exp'd Systems Analysts/ Programmers for growing software dev. team in Roseburg. Computer Science or related degree preferred. Develop adv. Engineering applications for engineering firm. Fax resume to 707-555-8744.

COMPUTER Web Master
for dynamic SF Internet co. Site. Dev., test, coord., train, 2 yrs prog. Exp. C C Web C, FTP. Fax resume to Best Staffing 845-555-7722.

COMPUTERS: QA SOFTWARE TESTERS
Qualified candidates should have 2 yrs exp performing integration & system testing using automated testing tools. Experienced in documentation preparation & programming languages (Access, C, FoxPro) are a plus. Financial or banking customer service support is required along with excellent verbal & written communication skills with multi levels of end-users. Send resume to KKUP Enterprises, 45 Orange Blvd. Orange, CA.

PROGRAMMERS
Multiple short term assignments available: Visual C, 3 positions SQL ServerNT Server. 2 positions JAVA & HTML, long term NetWare Various locations. Call for more info. 356-555-3398.

GRAPHIC DESIGNER
Webmaster's Weekly is seeking a creative Graphic Designer to design high impact marketing collateral, including direct mail promo's. CD-ROM packages, ads and WWW pages. Must be able to juggle multiple projects and learn new skills on the job very rapidly. Web design experience a big plus, technical troubleshooting also a plus. Call 435-555-1235.

SKILL

thirteen

Creating Beans: Introspection

- ❑ Understanding introspection
- ❑ Looking into reflection
- ❑ Examining the `BeanInfo` interface
- ❑ Working with property and event set descriptors

Introducing Introspection

Skill 9 described introspection as the process of discovering information about a bean. The bean-connection tool, JBuilder, does this to decide what to show in the Inspector window when using the UI Designer. By default, JBuilder lists a property for each set of set*PropertyName* and get*PropertyName* methods. Under the Inspector's Event tab, JBuilder lists the methods for each event listener defined by a pair of add*EventType*Listener and remove*EventType*Listener methods. JBuilder examines the bean class file for all the different methods. For each pair that follows the appropriate naming pattern, a property or event is defined. This inspection process is called *introspection*.

In this skill, we'll see how introspection works and look into the `BeanInfo` interface to define what is sent back. Unless you override the default behavior, `BeanInfo` uses reflection to inspect.

Introducing Reflection

By default, bean introspection uses the `java.lang.reflect` package to discover and use bean information. To demonstrate how reflection works, let's create a program that displays a `DecoratedFrame` instance, and prompts for a command in a text field. There will be three actions supported:

1. `bigger` —to make the frame bigger by 10%
2. `smaller` —to make the frame smaller by 5%
3. *anything else* —the program checks to see if the command is a predefined `Color`. If so, it changes the background color of the frame; otherwise, it does nothing.

This program sounds rather simple and could be done completely without reflection. However, the way we are going to create this program will demonstrate the magic that JBuilder needs to perform to work with classes it never knew about when Borland created it.

Let's start by creating the basics of the program; then we'll talk about reflection and add in all the magic. Close any open projects in JBuilder, and run the Application Wizard. Save the project in **C:\skills\skill13\skill13.jpr**, and on the second page of the Application Wizard, name the class **Lookup**, and select Finish. Go into the UI Designer for Lookup.java, and drop in a TextField from the AWT tab on the Component palette. The screen is almost done. Change the layout manager of bevelPanel1 to **BorderLayout**, and set the constraints of textField1 to the **North** quadrant to make sure that you will see any input when it is entered.

Now, if we add a bigger and smaller method, we can show you how to use reflection.

```
public void bigger() {
  Dimension d = getSize();
  int width = (int)(d.width * 1.1);
  int height = (int)(d.height * 1.1);
  setSize (width, height);
}
public void smaller() {
  Dimension d = getSize();
  int width = (int)(d.width * .95);
  int height = (int)(d.height * .95);
  setSize (width, height);
}
```

At this point, we could add an action listener to the text field: if the input is **bigger**, call the bigger method, and if it is **smaller**, call the smaller method. Instead, we're going to use reflection to locate a method with the name entered and call it indirectly.

When working with reflection, the first class you need to know about is the Class class. Every instance of a class has a Class associated with it. Class holds the keys for unlocking access to the properties and methods of a class instance. There are two ways to get the Class instance associated with a specific class:

> getClass This method is a part of the java.lang.Object class, so everyone inherits it from there.
>
> ClassName.class When you specify the .class filename associated with a class, you gain access to the Class associated with the class—in this case, ClassName.

Once you have a Class, you can discover its variables and methods, among many other pieces of information. Table 13.1 describes just some of this information.

TABLE 13.1: Some of the Methods of Class

Method Name	Description
`Field[] getDeclaredFields()`	Gets list of variables declared within class
`Field getDeclaredField (String)`	Gets specific variable, if declared in class
`Field[] getFields()`	Gets list of declared variables and inherited ones
`Field getField (String)`	Gets specific variable, if declared locally or inherited
`Method[] getDeclaredMethods()`	Gets list of methods declared within class
`Method getDeclaredMethod(String, Class[])`	Gets specific method, if declared in class
`Method[] getMethods()`	Gets list of declared methods and inherited ones
`Method getMethod (String)`	Gets specific method, if declared locally or inherited

Notice that there is no mention of properties or events here, only of methods and fields. In the Lookup program, we'll need to find the method `bigger` or `smaller`, so we should ask `getDeclaredMethod` to see if the method exists for the user's input. Because `bigger` and `smaller` do not require arguments, the second parameter can be `null`. Otherwise, you would have to create an array of the different argument class types and pass that along as the second parameter.

Once you have a specific `Method`, you can use its methods to find out about itself. To do the equivalent of a method call, the `Method` method to call is `invoke`. Putting this all together, we can now add an action listener for the text field. If you double-click on the text field, JBuilder makes the connection. Then, you need to add the appropriate action, shown here:

```
import java.lang.reflect.*;
...
void textField1_actionPerformed(ActionEvent e) {
  String command = e.getActionCommand();
  Class c = getClass();
  try {
    Method m = c.getDeclaredMethod (command, null);
    m.invoke (this, null);
  } catch (NoSuchMethodException ex) {
    System.out.println ("Invalid input");
  } catch (Exception ex) {
    System.out.println ("Invoke error");
  }
}
```

Introducing Reflection   261

Because of the *anything else* case mentioned earlier in the chapter, we are interested if the `NoSuchMethodException` is thrown by `getDeclaredMethod`. We'll have to add something to find the color. However, we don't need to differentiate between the different exceptions that `invoke` throws; hence the second `catch` block is generic.

At this point, if you save and run `Looker`, you can enter **bigger** or **smaller** into the text field, and press Enter to resize the screen. Figure 13.1 shows one possible screen. If you look in the console window after entering an invalid name, you'll see `Invalid input`.

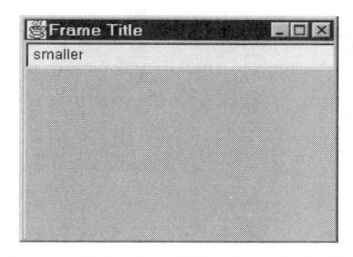

FIGURE 13.1: The Looker class screen after inputting smaller and bigger a few times

Adding the Color-Handling Code

The final thing we need to add to the program is the ability to enter a string, such as **red**, into the input field. Keep in mind that the `Color` class has 13 predefined color constants. If the user enters one of those, we want to change the background color. To see if it exists, there are five steps involved. Within the `textfield1_actionPerformed` method in the `catch (NoSuchMethodException ex)` block, follow these steps:

1. Get an instance of the `Color` class.

   `Class c2 = Color.class;`

2. Check to see if it has a field of the input string.

   `Field f = c2.getDeclaredField (command);`

3. Get the value. Although we are getting a static variable of `Color`, the `get` method requires an instance of the class. Also, it is necessary to cast the return value of `get` to the appropriate class.

   `Color color = (Color)f.get (Color.white);`

4. Use it to set the background of the bevel panel.

   ```
   bevelPanel1.setBackground (color);
   ```

5. Add appropriate exception handling by placing this in a `try`/`catch` block.

   ```
   try {
   … // Above four lines here
   } catch (NoSuchFieldException ex2) {
     System.out.println ("Invalid input");
   } catch (IllegalAccessException ex2) {
     System.out.println ("Access violation");
   }
   ```

Now, you can save and run the program, shown in its entirety in `Lookup.java`. In addition to entering **bigger** or **smaller** to resize the window, you can enter any of the following colors to change the background of the bevel panel:

red	pink
orange	yellow
green	cyan
blue	magenta
black	white
gray	lightGray
darkGray	

Lookup.java

```
package skill13;

import java.lang.reflect.*;
import java.awt.*;
import java.awt.event.*;
import borland.jbcl.control.*;
import borland.jbcl.layout.*;

public class Lookup extends DecoratedFrame {
  BorderLayout borderLayout1 = new BorderLayout();
  BevelPanel bevelPanel1 = new BevelPanel();
  TextField textField1 = new TextField();
  BorderLayout borderLayout2 = new BorderLayout();
```

```java
//Construct the frame
public Lookup() {
  try {
    jbInit();
  }
  catch (Exception e) {
    e.printStackTrace();
  }
}

//Component initialization
public void jbInit() throws Exception{
  this.setLayout(borderLayout1);
  this.setSize(new Dimension(400, 300));
  this.setTitle("Frame Title");
  textField1.setColumns(20);
  textField1.addActionListener(new Lookup_textField1_actionAdapter(this));
  bevelPanel1.setLayout(borderLayout2);
  this.add(bevelPanel1, BorderLayout.CENTER);
  bevelPanel1.add(textField1, BorderLayout.NORTH);
}

public void bigger() {
  Dimension d = getSize();
  int width = (int)(d.width * 1.1);
  int height = (int)(d.height * 1.1);
  setSize (width, height);
}

public void smaller() {
  Dimension d = getSize();
  int width = (int)(d.width * .95);
  int height = (int)(d.height * .95);
  setSize (width, height);
}

void textField1_actionPerformed(ActionEvent e) {
  String command = e.getActionCommand();
  Class c = getClass();
  try {
    Method m = c.getDeclaredMethod (command, null);
    m.invoke (this, null);
```

```
      } catch (NoSuchMethodException ex) {
        try {
          Class c2 = Color.class;
          Field f = c2.getDeclaredField (command);
          Color color = (Color)f.get (Color.white);
          bevelPanel1.setBackground (color);
        } catch (NoSuchFieldException ex2) {
          System.out.println ("Invalid input");
        } catch (IllegalAccessException ex2) {
          System.out.println ("Access violation");
        }
      } catch (Exception ex) {
        System.out.println ("Invoke error");
      }
    }
  }
}

class Lookup_textField1_actionAdapter implements
java.awt.event.ActionListener {
  Lookup adaptee;

  Lookup_textField1_actionAdapter(Lookup adaptee) {
    this.adaptee = adaptee;
  }

  public void actionPerformed(ActionEvent e) {
    adaptee.textField1_actionPerformed(e);
  }
}
```

Although this program doesn't demonstrate all the capabilities of reflection, it does show what JBuilder does to support the Inspector window.

Using the *BeanInfo* Introspector

With JavaBeans, a support class does all the reflection lookups. Instead of using the low-level methods in `java.lang.reflect`, JBuilder asks a class called the `Introspector` for the information associated with a bean. Then, working through an interface named `BeanInfo`, JBuilder can find out about the properties and methods of a bean. By providing one level of indirection for the inspection, you, the bean creator, can restrict what JBuilder sees. Table 13.2 shows what is available through the `BeanInfo` interface.

TABLE 13.2: The BeanInfo interface

Method Name	Description
getAdditionalBeanInfo	Allows a bean to have multiple BeanInfo objects
getBeanDescriptor	Gets a bean's BeanDescriptor
getDefaultEventIndex	Gets index of default event
getDefaultPropertyIndex	Gets index of default property
getEventSetDescriptors	Gets array of EventSetDescriptor objects
getIcon	Gets bean's icon
getMethodDescriptors	Gets array of MethodDescriptor objects
getPropertyDescriptors	Gets array of PropertyDescriptor objects

To demonstrate how the Introspector works for JBuilder, let's create a new program that has a button and text area. When the button is selected, all of its method names are listed in the text area. Let's close any open projects and run the Application Wizard. Save the project in **c:\skills\skill13b\skill13b.jpr** and name the frame class **Inspect**.

To set up the screen, go into the UI Designer for `Inspect.java`. Here, we want to change `bevelPanel1` so it has a layout of **BorderLayout**, with a `Button` in the **North** and a `TextArea` in the **Center**.

If you double-click the button, we can then add an action event handler. In Skill 8, we learned how to use a `StringWriter` to buffer input into a `TextArea`. We'll do the same thing here.

1. Get a `PrintWriter` to print to:

    ```
    StringWriter sw = new StringWriter ();
    PrintWriter pw = new PrintWriter (sw);
    ```

2. Get the `BeanInfo` for the button. Here we get the class for the button; then ask the Introspector for its `BeanInfo`.

    ```
    BeanInfo bi = Introspector.getBeanInfo (button1.getClass());
    ```

3. Get the `MethodDescriptors` for the bean:

    ```
    MethodDescriptor[] md = bi.getMethodDescriptors();
    ```

4. Loop through each, printing out the name. Instead of printing out each name, you could get the specific `Method` with `getMethod` and `invoke` it. Then, you are running methods without *having* to know method names at all.

   ```
   for (int i=0;i<md.length;i++)
     pw.println (md[i].getName());
   ```

5. Display the results in the `TextArea`.

   ```
   String s = sw.toString();
   textArea1.setText (s);
   ```

6. Since the `Introspector` can throw an `IntrospectionException` when getting bean info, place the source from steps 2 through 5 within a `try/catch` block that catches the `IntrospectionException`.

After adding the exception-handling code, the entire source for the action of the button follows:

```
void button1_actionPerformed(ActionEvent e) {
  StringWriter sw = new StringWriter ();
  PrintWriter pw = new PrintWriter (sw);
  try {
    BeanInfo bi = Introspector.getBeanInfo (button1.getClass());
    MethodDescriptor[] md = bi.getMethodDescriptors();
    for (int i=0;i<md.length;i++)
      pw.println (md[i].getName());
  } catch (IntrospectionException ex) {
    pw.println ("Error inspecting");
  }
  String s = sw.toString();
  textArea1.setText (s);
}
```

7. Also, don't forget to import the `java.io` and `java.beans` packages:

   ```
   import java.io.*;
   import java.beans.*;
   ```

If you run the program and press the button, the screen shown in Figure 13.2 will appear.

To see where JBuilder uses this functionality, select Tools ➤ Interaction Wizard Editor, select `java.awt.Button`, and then select Next twice. Now, if you select the little triangles next to the classes, you'll see all the method names Inspect just displayed. As Figure 13.3 shows, JBuilder thankfully sorts the methods alphabetically.

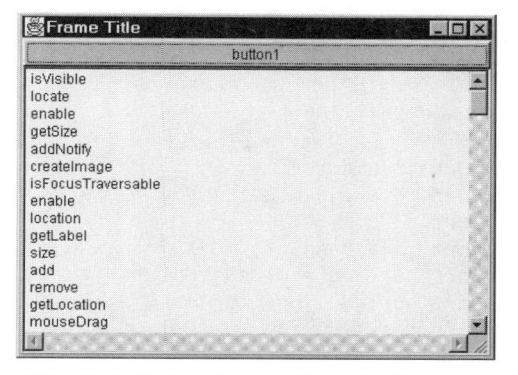

FIGURE 13.2: The Inspect program inspecting the button

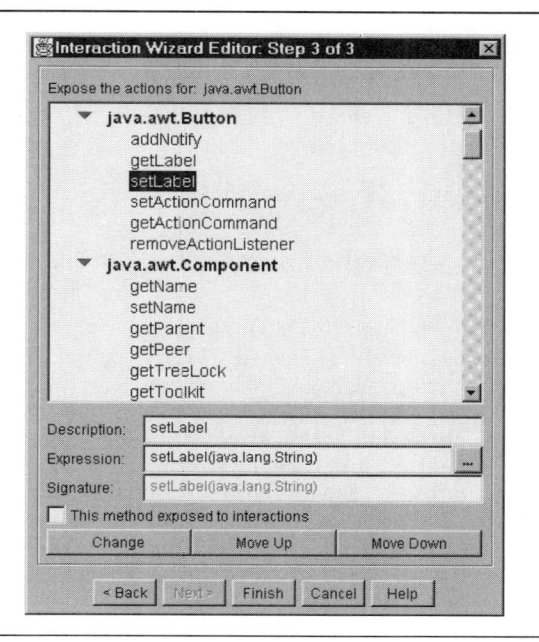

FIGURE 13.3: The Interaction Wizard Editor showing off where JBuilder uses the Introspector

The complete source for `Inspect.java` follows.

Inspect.java

```java
package skill13b;

import java.awt.*;
import java.awt.event.*;
import java.io.*;
import java.beans.*;
import borland.jbcl.control.*;
import borland.jbcl.layout.*;

public class Inspect extends DecoratedFrame {
  BorderLayout borderLayout1 = new BorderLayout();
  BevelPanel bevelPanel1 = new BevelPanel();
  Button button1 = new Button();
  TextArea textArea1 = new TextArea();
  BorderLayout borderLayout2 = new BorderLayout();

  //Construct the frame
  public Inspect() {
    try {
      jbInit();
    }
    catch (Exception e) {
      e.printStackTrace();
    }
  }

  //Component initialization
  public void jbInit() throws Exception{
    this.setLayout(borderLayout1);
    this.setSize(new Dimension(400, 300));
    this.setTitle("Frame Title");
    button1.setLabel("button1");
    button1.addActionListener(new Inspect_button1_actionAdapter(this));
    bevelPanel1.setLayout(borderLayout2);
    this.add(bevelPanel1, BorderLayout.CENTER);
    bevelPanel1.add(button1, BorderLayout.NORTH);
    bevelPanel1.add(textArea1, BorderLayout.CENTER);
  }

  void button1_actionPerformed(ActionEvent e) {
    StringWriter sw = new StringWriter ();
    PrintWriter pw = new PrintWriter (sw);
    try {
```

```
      BeanInfo bi = Introspector.getBeanInfo (button1.getClass());
      MethodDescriptor[] md = bi.getMethodDescriptors();
      for (int i=0;i<md.length;i++)
        pw.println (md[i].getName());
    } catch (IntrospectionException ex) {
      pw.println ("Error inspecting");
    }
    String s = sw.toString();
    textArea1.setText (s);
  }
}

class Inspect_button1_actionAdapter implements
java.awt.event.ActionListener {
  Inspect adaptee;

  Inspect_button1_actionAdapter(Inspect adaptee) {
    this.adaptee = adaptee;
  }

  public void actionPerformed(ActionEvent e) {
    adaptee.button1_actionPerformed(e);
  }
}
```

> **TIP** You can easily change this program to look at the PropertyDescriptor list for the button or the EventSetDescriptor list. The methods to get the appropriate list are getPropertyDescriptors and getEventSetDescriptors, respectively.

Overriding *BeanInfo*

Now that you've seen how to use reflection and how JBuilder uses BeanInfo, it's time to override the default behavior. When you ask the Introspector for the BeanInfo for a class, it first looks for a specific supporting class. The supporting class is the name of the bean, followed by BeanInfo. Therefore, if we had a bean called MyButton, the BeanInfo for it would be in MyButtonBeanInfo. Then, if MyButtonBeanInfo isn't found, the Introspector goes off and uses the default behavior.

To demonstrate this, let's create a subclass of Button. We only want it to have one property—the label—and one event set—action. Let's close any open projects and create a new project by running the Project Wizard—not the Application Wizard.

Save the project in **c:\skills\skill13c\skill13c.jpr**. Next, run the Class Wizard to create the **MyButton** class, have it extend **java.awt.Button**, uncheck the Generate Default Constructor toggle, but leave Public checked, and select OK. We now have our complete `MyButton` class, which we're going to create a `BeanInfo` object for.

MyButton.java

```
package skill13c;

import java.awt.*;
public class MyButton extends Button {
}
```

To implement the `BeanInfo` interface, you could subclass `java.lang.Object` and define each method of the interface yourself. However, this requires lots of unnecessary work; we only want to customize some behavior, in this case the event set and property descriptors. The `java.beans` package provides a support class called `SimpleBeanInfo`. If you subclass this, you only have to override the pieces to provide your specific behavior.

So, run the Class Wizard again: call the class **MyButtonBeanInfo**, extend **java.beans.SimpleBeanInfo**, uncheck the Generate default constructor toggle, but leave Public checked, and select OK.

Limiting Properties

To limit the available properties of a bean, it is necessary to override the `getPropertyDescriptors` method. This method returns a `PropertyDescriptor` array, with one entry for each available property.

To create a single `PropertyDescriptor`, the constructor requires the property name and the bean `Class` object. Once you have a single `PropertyDescriptor`, you need to place it in an array and return the array. Because the constructor might throw an `IntrospectionException` (for when the property isn't available), the entire source code needs to be in a `try/catch` block, returning `null` on error.

```
public PropertyDescriptor[] getPropertyDescriptors() {
  try {
    PropertyDescriptor pd = new PropertyDescriptor ("label",
      MyButton.class);
    PropertyDescriptor[] pds = {pd};
    return pds;
```

```
      } catch (IntrospectionException ex ) {
        return null;
      }
    }
```

Limiting Events

Limiting the available event sets of a bean is similar to limiting properties. You start by overriding the `getEventSetDescriptors` method. This method returns an `EventSetDescriptor` array, with one entry for each available event.

To create a single `EventSetDescriptor`, the constructor requires the bean `Class` object, the event set name, the listener type, and listener method name. Again, once you have the one `EventSetDescriptor`, you need to place it in an array, and return the array. Because the constructor might throw an `IntrospectionException` (when the event set isn't available), the source needs to be in a `try/catch` block, returning `null` on error.

```
public EventSetDescriptor[] getEventSetDescriptors() {
  try {
    EventSetDescriptor ed = new EventSetDescriptor (
        MyButton.class, "action", ActionListener.class, "actionPerformed");
    EventSetDescriptor[] eds = {ed};
    return eds;
  } catch (IntrospectionException ex ) {
    return null;
  }
}
```

Since the ActionListener class is in the `java.awt.event` package, you also need to import `java.awt.event.*`. At this point, you can save and compile everything. When working with `BeanInfo` classes, the smart dependency checker of JBuilder doesn't know about the association between `MyButton` and `MyButtonBeanInfo`. Therefore, it is best to always select the Rebuild icon, instead of Build, to compile the bean and bean info classes.

MyButtonBeanInfo.java

```
package skill13c;

import java.beans.*;
import java.awt.event.*;
public class MyButtonBeanInfo extends SimpleBeanInfo {
  public PropertyDescriptor[] getPropertyDescriptors() {
```

```
      try {
        PropertyDescriptor pd = new PropertyDescriptor ("label", MyButton.class);
        PropertyDescriptor[] pds = {pd};
        return pds;
      } catch (IntrospectionException ex ) {
        return null;
      }
    }
    public EventSetDescriptor[] getEventSetDescriptors() {
      try {
        EventSetDescriptor ed = new EventSetDescriptor (
            MyButton.class, "action", ActionListener.class, "actionPerformed");
        EventSetDescriptor[] eds = {ed};
        return eds;
      } catch (IntrospectionException ex ) {
        return null;
      }
    }
  }
```

To test the bean, we need to add `MyButton` to the Component palette. Select Tools ➤ Configure Palette to bring up the Palette Properties window. Then, select Other in the Pages column, and select Add From Package. From here, we need to browse to the location where the compiled `MyButton.class` file is, so select the Browse button. Select `myclasses`, then `skill13c`, because that is the directory we're working in. Finally, you should see the `MyButton.class` file. Double-clicking that file adds the bean to the Palette Properties dialog box. Once the `skill13c.MyButton` bean is listed, select `skill13c.MyButton`, and press the Install button. When you select the OK button, the bean will then be installed.

> **NOTE** Whenever you recompile a `BeanInfo` class for a bean on the Component palette, you'll need to exit out of JBuilder and restart it. This allows JBuilder to reload the `BeanInfo`. Also, be very careful of typos in `BeanInfo` as a wrong method name will still compile.

Showing Off *MyButton*

At this point, we could create a really complex program that uses `MyButton` and demonstrates it only has one property and one event. However, for us, we'll just reopen the `skill13b` project and drop a `MyButton` onto the Inspect screen. Now, if you look in the Inspector, you'll notice only one property, `label`, as shown in Figure 13.4, as well as only one event, as shown in Figure 13.5. The constraints property has to do with the bean container, not the bean itself. The <name> property is the variable name used within the current program. So, neither of these can be hidden.

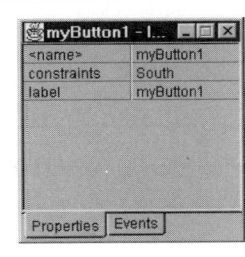

FIGURE 13.4: The Inspector's property screen without all the normal properties of `Button`. All beans have a name, while the constraints property is for the container.

FIGURE 13.5: The Introspector's event screen without all the normal events of `Button`

While this may have seemed like a lot of work just to hide some properties or events, this work tends to be necessary when you specialize beans. Instead of having a be-all, do-all bean, if you limit the functionality to only what is used, the connect-the-beans process becomes much easier as unnecessary pieces are hidden away.

You've now seen how JBuilder uses reflection and the Introspector to dig inside the beans and how you can restrict that through `BeanInfo`. In Skill 14, we'll move on to customizing how properties will be shown to the bean developer.

Are You Experienced?

Now you can...

- ☑ use reflection to discover class information
- ☑ invoke methods that weren't known at compile time
- ☑ use the Introspector
- ☑ examine a bean's *BeanInfo*
- ☑ customize a bean's properties and event sets

PROGRAMMERS
C, C, VB, Cobol, exp. Call 534-6543 or fax 534-555-6544.

PROGRAMMING
MRFS Inc. is looking for a Sr. Windows NT developer. Reqs. 3-5 yrs. Exp. In C under Windows, Win95 & NT, using Visual C, Excl. OO design & implementation skills a must. OLE2 & ODBC are a plus. Excl. Salary & bnfts. Resume & salary history to HR, 8779 HighTech Way, Computer City, AR

PROGRAMMERS
Contractors Wanted for short & long term assignments: Visual C, MFC Unix C/C, SQL Oracle Dev elop ers PC Help Desk Support Windows NT & NetWareTelecommunications Visual Basic, Access, HTML, CGI, Perl MMI & Co., 885-555-9933

PROGRAMMER World Wide Web Links wants your HTML & Photoshop skills. Develop great WWW sites. Local & global customers. Send samples & resume to WWWL, 2000 Apple Road, Santa Rosa, CA.

TECHNICAL WRITER Software firm seeks writer/editor for manuals, research notes, project mgmt. Min 2 years tech. writing, DTP & programming experience. Send resume & writing samples to: Software Systems, Dallas, TX.

TECHNICAL Software development firm looking for Tech Trainers. Ideal candidates have programming experience in Visual C, HTML & JAVA. Need quick self starter. Call (443) 555-6868 for interview.

TECHNICAL WRITER / Premier Computer Corp is seeking a combination of technical skills, knowledge and experience in the following areas: UNIX, Windows 95/NT, Visual Basic, on-line help & documentation, and the Internet. Candidates must possess excellent writing skills and be comfortable working in a quality vs. deadline driven environment. Competitive salary. Fax resume & samples to Karen Fields, Premier Computer Corp., 444 Industrial Blvd. Concord, CA. Or send to our website at www.premier.com

WEB DESIGNER
BA/BS or equivalent programming/multimedia production. 3 years of experience in use and design of WWW services streaming audio and video HTML, PERL, CGI, GIF, JPEG. Demonstrated interpersonal, organization, communication, multi-tasking skills. Send resume to The Learning People at www.learning.com.

WEBMASTER-TECHNICAL
BSCS or equivalent, 2 years of experience in CGI, Windows 95/NT, UNIX, C, Java, Perl. Demonstrated ability to design, code, debug and test on-line services. Send resume to The Learning People at www.learning.com.

COMPUTER PROGRAMMER
Ad agency seeks programmer w/exp. in UNIX/NT Platforms, Web Server, CGI/Perl. Programmer Position avail. on a project basis with the possibility to move into F/T. Fax resume & salary req. to R. Jones 334-555-8332.

COMPUTERS Programmer/Analyst Design and maintain C based SQL database applications. Required skills: Visual Basic, C, SQL, ODBC, Document existing and new applications. Novell or NT exp. a plus. Fax resume & salary history to 235-555-9935.

GRAPHIC DESIGNER
Webmaster's Weekly is seeking a creative Graphic Designer to design high impact marketing collateral including direct mail promos, CD-ROM packages, ads and WWW pages. Must be able to juggle multiple projects and learn new skills on the job very rapidly. Web design experience a big plus, technical troubleshooting also a plus. Call 435-555-1235.

GRAPHICS - ART DIRECTOR - WEB-MULTIMEDIA
Leading internet development company has an outstanding opportunity for a talented, high-end Web Experienced Art Director. In addition to a great portfolio and fresh ideas, the ideal candidate has excellent communication and presentation skills. Working as a team with innovative producers and programmers, you will create dynamic, interactive web sites and application interfaces. Some programming experience required. Send samples and resume to: SuperSites, 333 Main, Seattle, WA.

MARKETING
Fast paced software and services provider looking for MARKETING COMMUNICATIONS SPECIALIST to be responsible for its webpage, seminar coordination, and ad placement. Must be a self-starter, energetic, organized. Must have 2 yrs web experience. Programming plus. Call 985-555-9854

PROGRAMMERS Multiple short term assignments available: Visual C, 3 positions SQL ServerNT Server, 2 positions JAVA & HTML, long term NetWare Various locations. Call for more info. 356-555-3398.

COMPUTERS Small Web Design firm seeks indiv. w/NT, Webserver & Database management exp. Fax resume to 556-555-4221.

COMPUTER Visual C/C, Visual Basic Exp'd Systems Analysts/ Programmers for growing software dev. team in Roseburg. Computer Science or related degree preferred. Develop adv. Engineering applications for engineering firm. Fax resume to 707-555-8744.

COMPUTER Web Master for dynamic SF Internet co. Site, Dev., test, coord., train, 2 yrs prog. Exp. C C, Web C, FTP. Fax resume to Best Staffing 845-555-7722.

COMPUTERS/ QA SOFTWARE TESTERS Qualified candidates should have 2 yrs exp. performing integration & system testing using automated testing tools. Experienced in documentation preparation & programming languages (Access, C, FoxPro) are a plus. Financial or banking customer service support is required along with excellent verbal & written communication skills with multi levels of end-users. Send resume to KKUP Enterprises, 45 Orange Blvd. Orange, CA.

SKILL fourteen

Creating Beans: Customization

- ❑ Making the ShapeBox bean
- ❑ Using property editors for customization
- ❑ Implementing text property editors
- ❑ Implementing selection property editors
- ❑ Implementing a custom property editor

Getting Started

In this skill, we're going to create a bean that draws one of four shapes within its available area: a circle, oval, square, or rectangle. By itself, that doesn't sound too complicated. The class has one property, four constants for the different shapes, and a `paint` routine.

A problem arises, though, when the bean user wants to change the shape property. How do they change it? If the property was saved internally as an integer, the user might have to type **0** for an oval, **1** for a circle, **2** for a rectangle, or **3** for a square. But how do they know what value is for what shape? Instead, it would be better if they could just enter in the string describing the shape they wanted to draw. A pull-down list where they can pick one of the available shapes is even better. Because the list is limited, why let them enter an invalid shape? Or, even better than that is to show the shapes graphically—let the user see the shape they are about to draw. All these options, whether integer input, string input, pull-down list, or graphic are handled by offering a *property editor* to the builder tool. This skill shows you how to create each of these options.

Creating the *ShapeBox*

At this point, start JBuilder, close any open projects, and run the New Project Wizard. Save the project to **c:\skills\skill14\skill14.jpr** and select Finish. Next, use the New Class Wizard to create the **ShapeBox** class, which subclasses **java.awt.Component**. Leaving the Public and Generate default constructor toggles checked creates the beginning of our new bean.

```
package skill14;

import java.awt.*;
public class ShapeBox extends Component {

  public ShapeBox() {
  }
}
```

Now, there are three steps to perform: add constants for the different shapes we support, add a property to save the current shape, and draw the component. Here, we'll look at what is involved in each step.

1. Define the constants:
   ```
   public static final int OVAL = 0;
   public static final int CIRCLE = 1;
   public static final int RECTANGLE = 2;
   public static final int SQUARE = 3;
   ```

2. Add a shape property. Remember to repaint the screen after changing the value. Here, we aren't doing any error checking. When we paint, we will assume an invalid value is the default OVAL.
   ```
   private int shape = OVAL;
   public void setShape (int s) {
      shape = s;
      repaint();
   }
   public int getShape () {
     return shape;
   }
   ```

3. Draw the shape. Here's where we determine which shape the user wanted and draw it. In the case of a circle or square, we need to make sure the height and width are identical. Just so it looks better, leave a little room around the edges.
   ```
   public void paint (Graphics g) {
     Dimension dim = getSize();
     int min = Math.min (dim.width, dim.height);
     switch (shape) {
       case CIRCLE:
         g.drawOval (2, 2, min-4, min-4);
         break;
       case RECTANGLE:
         g.drawRect (2, 2, dim.width-4, dim.height-4);
         break;
       case SQUARE:
         g.drawRect (2, 2, min-4, min-4);
         break;
       case OVAL:
       default:
         g.drawOval (2, 2, dim.width-4, dim.height-4);
         break;
     }
   }
   ```

That's our whole bean. At this point, save your class, compile the bean, and add it to the Other tab of the Component palette.

1. Select Tools ➤ Configure Palette.
2. Select the Add from Package tab.
3. Select the Browse button.
4. Double-click the `myclasses` folder.
5. Double-click the `skill14` folder.
6. Double-click the `ShapeBox.class` file.
7. Back on the Palette Properties screen, select `skill14.ShapeBox`.
8. Select Other in the Add Component To Page text box.
9. Select the Install button.
10. Select OK.

The ShapeBox is now on the Component palette. The entire source code follows in ShapeBox.java.

ShapeBox.java

```
package skill14;

import java.awt.*;
public class ShapeBox extends Component {

  public static final int OVAL = 0;
  public static final int CIRCLE = 1;
  public static final int RECTANGLE = 2;
  public static final int SQUARE = 3;

  private int shape = OVAL;

  public ShapeBox() {
  }
  public void setShape (int s) {
    shape = s;
    repaint();
  }
```

```
      public int getShape () {
        return shape;
      }
      public void paint (Graphics g) {
        Dimension dim = getSize();
        int min = Math.min (dim.width, dim.height);
        switch (shape) {
          case CIRCLE:
            g.drawOval (2, 2, min-4, min-4);
            break;
          case RECTANGLE:
            g.drawRect (2, 2, dim.width-4, dim.height-4);
            break;
          case SQUARE:
            g.drawRect (2, 2, min-4, min-4);
            break;
          case OVAL:
          default:
            g.drawOval (2, 2, dim.width-4, dim.height-4);
            break;
        }
      }
    }
```

Using the Default Property Editor

Now that we have our bean with the single property of type int, we can test the bean to see how JBuilder presents the property to the developer or bean user. Close the skill14 project and run the Application Wizard. Create the new project as **c:\skills\skill14b\skill14b.jpr**, and on the second page of the Application Wizard, name the frame class **ShapeFrame**.

Once the Wizard does its magic, we can add a ShapeBox to the program. Select ShapeFrame.java and open the UI Designer. Change the bevelPanel1 layout property to **BorderLayout**, place a ShapeBox bean in the frame, and make sure the constraints place the ShapeBox in the **Center** quadrant. At this point, your AppBrowser window will look like the screen shown in Figure 14.1.

If you select shapeBox1 in the Structure pane and look in the Inspector window, you'll notice that the shape property is set to 0. Figure 14.2 shows the Inspector window.

282 Skill 14 • Creating Beans: Customization

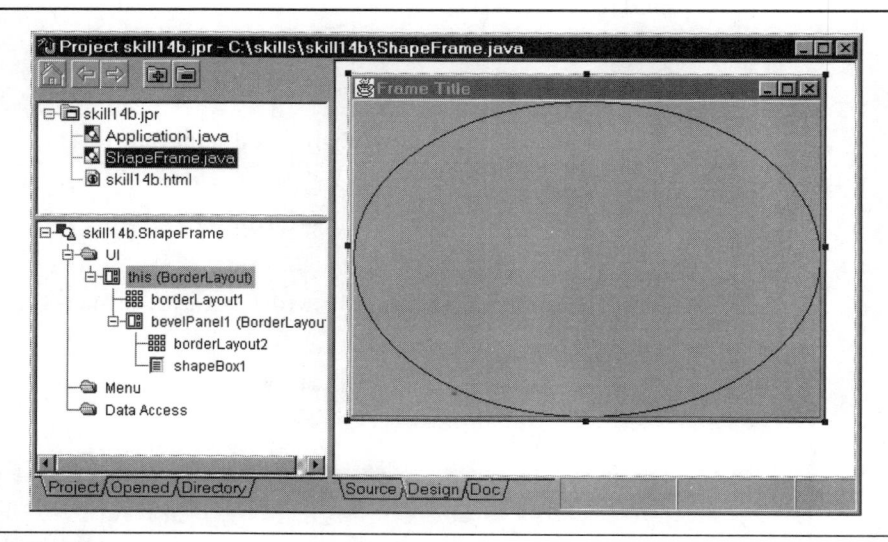

FIGURE 14.1: The AppBrowser window with a ShapeBox drawn in a frame

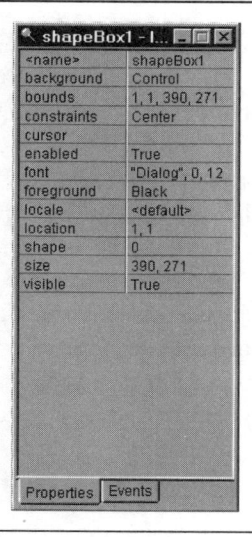

FIGURE 14.2: The Inspector window for a ShapeBox

In order to know what the zero means, we have to go back to the ShapeBox.java source and see that 0 is an oval, 1 is a circle, 2 is a rectangle, and 3 is a square. If you change the shape property to 1, 2, or 3, you will notice that the box changes to the appropriate shape. Saving and running the application draws the appropriate shape within the ShapeFrame, as seen in Figure 14.3.

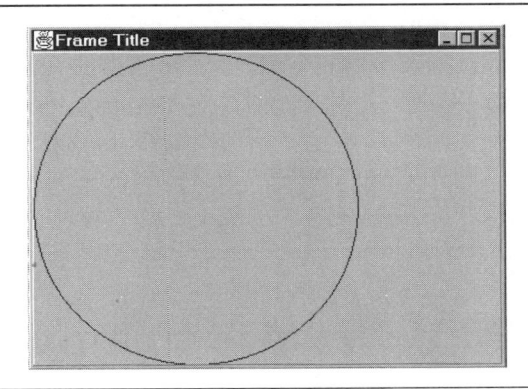

FIGURE 14.3: A ShapeFrame with a ShapeBox shape property of 1 for a circle

Here, JBuilder automatically generated the entire source code of ShapeFrame.java.

ShapeFrame.java

```java
package skill14b;

import java.awt.*;
import java.awt.event.*;
import borland.jbcl.control.*;
import borland.jbcl.layout.*;
import skill14.*;

public class ShapeFrame extends DecoratedFrame {
  BorderLayout borderLayout1 = new BorderLayout();
  BevelPanel bevelPanel1 = new BevelPanel();
  BorderLayout borderLayout2 = new BorderLayout();
  ShapeBox shapeBox1 = new ShapeBox();

  //Construct the frame
  public ShapeFrame() {
    try {
      jbInit();
```

```
      }
      catch (Exception e) {
        e.printStackTrace();
      }
    }

    //Component initialization
    public void jbInit() throws Exception{
      this.setLayout(borderLayout1);
      this.setSize(new Dimension(400, 300));
      this.setTitle("Frame Title");
      shapeBox1.setShape(1);
      bevelPanel1.setLayout(borderLayout2);
      this.add(bevelPanel1, BorderLayout.CENTER);
      bevelPanel1.add(shapeBox1, BorderLayout.CENTER);
    }
}
```

Getting Shape Names as Input

One problem with the previous example arises if you don't know what value is used for which shape. In this simple example, you can easily try out the different numbers to get the values. What would happen though if the developer used numbers like 83,214,243; 187; 381,028,934; and 1,348,744 for the different shapes? Unless these values were well documented somewhere, before you were able to guess 187 to get the first shape you would have probably given up.

There is one alternative. When JBuilder can't find the source code, it looks at the class file to get a best guess of its contents. The process of examining the compiled class file to regenerate source is called *decompiling*. If JBuilder couldn't find the ShapeBox.java source file, it would generate the following listing:

```
// JBuilder API Decompiler STUB SOURCE generated from class file
// Mon Jul 21 11:38:55 EDT 1997
// - implementation of methods is not available

package skill14;

// approximate imports
import java.awt.Graphics;
import java.awt.Component;

public class ShapeBox extends Component {
  // fields
  public static final int OVAL;
  public static final int CIRCLE;
```

```
public static final int RECTANGLE;
public static final int SQUARE;
private int shape;

public ShapeBox() {
  // CONSTRUCTOR implementation not available
}

public void setShape(int p0) {
  // implementation not available
}

public int getShape() {
  // implementation not available
}

public void paint(Graphics p0) {
  // implementation not available
}
}
```

> **TIP** While the Content pane is showing source, double-click on a variable in the Structure pane to find the source file for the variable's class. If the source file can't be found, JBuilder will decompile the class's definition file (.class file).

While the source may look impressive, it still doesn't display the values for the shape constants. Returning to the skill14 project, we need to make some changes. What we need to do is add a property editor to the ShapeBox. The nice thing about property editors, or any other bean-related support files, is you never need to change the original bean. The support classes are only necessary when designing screens, so when the developer who is connecting the beans is done, they do not need to deliver the support classes to their users. This keeps the deliverable size to a minimum. These next three sections will show you how to implement and use the property editor to prompt the developer for the shape name, versus the shape value.

Creating the Property Editor

The first class we need to create when adding a property editor to the ShapeBox will be called ShapeEditor. Because the property name is *shape* and because beans require property editors to end with the name *Editor*, the property editor class is already named for us. New property editor classes need to extend the java.beans.PropertyEditorSupport class or, more specifically, implement the java.beans.PropertyEditor interface. So, run the New Class Wizard, name your class **ShapeEditor** and have it extend **java.beans.PropertyEditorSupport**. Leaving just the Public toggle selected, press OK to create the class framework.

> **TIP** By extending the PropertyEditorSupport class, you only have to override the default behavior you want to change, similar to the SimpleBeanInfo class covered in the last skill.

Providing a property editor for a primitive datatype requires the setValue and getValue methods to be overridden. These methods convert the Object that the Inspector provides from an Object to the primitive datatype, and vice versa. This allows the Inspector to always work with objects. There are three things to do here:

1. Define a variable of the appropriate primitive datatype:

   ```
   protected int shape;
   ```

2. In the getValue method, return the variable as an Object, via the appropriate wrapper class:

   ```
   public Object getValue () {
     return (new Integer (shape));
   }
   ```

3. In the setValue method, set the variable by converting it via the appropriate wrapper class. Also, because you've now changed the property value, you need to notify any registered property listeners. (Remember bound properties from Skill 12? This is where they are actually notified.) The PropertyEditorSupport class already manages the listener list. To notify the listeners, just call the method firePropertyChange:

   ```
   public void setValue (Object o) {
     shape = ((Integer)o).intValue();
     firePropertyChange();
   }
   ```

The remaining methods you need to override depend upon the input support you want to offer. In this first case, we are going to let the bean user input text strings of oval, circle, rectangle, or square. Therefore, we also need to override setAsText and getAsText by following these steps.

1. The `getAsText` method returns the current property setting as a text string. So, based upon the current value of shape, return an appropriate string:

   ```
   public String getAsText () {
     switch (shape) {
       case ShapeBox.CIRCLE:
         return "Circle";
       case ShapeBox.RECTANGLE:
         return "Rectangle";
       case ShapeBox.SQUARE:
         return "Square";
       case ShapeBox.OVAL:
       default:
         return "Oval";
     }
   }
   ```

2. The `setAsText` method works in the reverse direction. Given a text string, set the internal property variable. The method can throw an `IllegalArgumentException` if the input is invalid, or it can use a default setting. Also, as with `setValue`, you need to notify property-change listeners via `firePropertyChange`.

   ```
   public void setAsText (String s) throws IllegalArgumentException {
     if (s.equalsIgnoreCase ("Circle")) {
       shape = ShapeBox.CIRCLE;
     } else if (s.equalsIgnoreCase ("Square")) {
       shape = ShapeBox.SQUARE;
     } else if (s.equalsIgnoreCase ("Rectangle")) {
       shape = ShapeBox.RECTANGLE;
     } else { // Oval - default
       shape = ShapeBox.OVAL;
     }
     firePropertyChange();
   }
   ```

And that is all there is to creating a property editor. The following is the complete source for the `ShapeEditor.java` file which supports text input of a property. Before we can use it, however, we need to tell the bean about it via a `BeanInfo` class.

```
package skill14;

import java.beans.*;
public class ShapeEditor extends PropertyEditorSupport {

  protected int shape;
```

```java
      public void setValue (Object o) {
        shape = ((Integer)o).intValue();
        firePropertyChange();
      }
      public Object getValue () {
        return (new Integer (shape));
      }
      public String getAsText () {
        switch (shape) {
          case ShapeBox.CIRCLE:
            return "Circle";
          case ShapeBox.RECTANGLE:
            return "Rectangle";
          case ShapeBox.SQUARE:
            return "Square";
          case ShapeBox.OVAL:
          default:
            return "Oval";
        }
      }
      public void setAsText (String s) throws IllegalArgumentException {
        if (s.equalsIgnoreCase ("Circle")) {
          shape = ShapeBox.CIRCLE;
        } else if (s.equalsIgnoreCase ("Square")) {
          shape = ShapeBox.SQUARE;
        } else if (s.equalsIgnoreCase ("Rectangle")) {
          shape = ShapeBox.RECTANGLE;
        } else { // Oval - default
          shape = ShapeBox.OVAL;
        }
        firePropertyChange();
      }
    }
```

Creating the *BeanInfo*

Now that we have a property editor for the shape property of the ShapeBox, we need to create a ShapeBoxBeanInfo. This works similarly to the limiting properties example in the last skill. Using the New Class Wizard create a class named **ShapeBoxBeanInfo** which subclasses **java.beans.SimpleBeanInfo**, without the default constructor but with public accessibility, and then override the getPropertyDescriptors method. As in the last class, we need to return a

`PropertyDescriptor` array that describes each property we need to list and customize. Then, for each property that you want a property editor for, you call the `setPropertyEditorClass` method to associate the editor class. This results in the following `ShapeBoxBeanInfo.java` class:

ShapeBoxBeanInfo.java

```
package skill14;

import java.beans.*;
public class ShapeBoxBeanInfo extends SimpleBeanInfo {

  public PropertyDescriptor[] getPropertyDescriptors() {
    try {
      PropertyDescriptor pd1 = new PropertyDescriptor ("shape",
        ShapeBox.class);
      pd1.setPropertyEditorClass (ShapeEditor.class);
      return new PropertyDescriptor[] {pd1};
    } catch (Exception e) {
      return null;
    }
  }
}
```

Now, save everything and rebuild the project to make sure it compiles successfully.

WARNING Before you can use a property editor, whether new or modified, you need to exit out of JBuilder and restart it. This ensures that the UI Designer retrieves the updated `BeanInfo` and the Inspector sees the updated `PropertyEditor`. If you forget, you won't see the changes.

Using the Property Editor

Now that we have a property editor, we can reopen the `skill14b` project and use it. Return to the UI Designer for `ShapeFrame` and select `shapeBox1` to see an updated Inspector window, as shown in Figure 14.4.

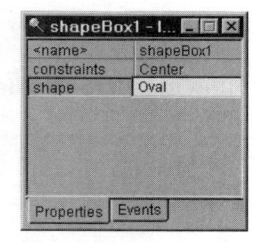

FIGURE 14.4: The Inspector window for a ShapeBox with a property editor for the shape property

Now if you select the property, you can change the setting to **Oval**, **Circle**, **Rectangle**, or **Square**.

> **TIP** If you type in **sQuArE**, it knows you mean Square, and if you type in **Diamond**, it creates an Oval because that is the default.

Converting the Property Editor to a Selection List

Now that the bean user can type in **Oval**, **Circle**, **Rectangle**, or **Square**, we've alleviated the problem of knowing what value to type for each shape. However, there is only a fixed set of values, so why not just display them and let the bean user pick? To display them, we have to return to the property editor to override the getTags method in PropertyEditorSupport (ShapeEditor is our subclass).

The getTags method returns an array of strings, representing the complete list of possible choices. Then, when the developer tries to change the property, they'll see the drop-down list you created using the following source.

```
public String[] getTags () {
   return new String[] {"Oval", "Circle", "Square", "Rectangle"};
}
```

After adding the above method to ShapeEditor.java, saving the change, and recompiling, the ShapeBox bean user will see the updated property editor.

Using the Selection List

After exiting out of JBuilder and returning to the skill14b project, you can now try out the updated editor. After returning to the ShapeFrame UI Designer, and selecting shapeBox1, the Inspector shows off the new shape-property editor, as seen in Figure 14.5.

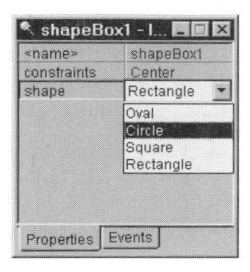

FIGURE 14.5: The Inspector window for a ShapeBox with a pull-down list shown for the property editor of the shape property

Creating a Custom Property Editor

In most cases, textual input or a drop-down list is sufficient to describe a property so a bean user can set the value. However, what do you do when you need something more complicated? For instance, when you try to set a property that is of type Font, a window pops up where you can select the different attributes of a single property, as shown in Figure 14.6.

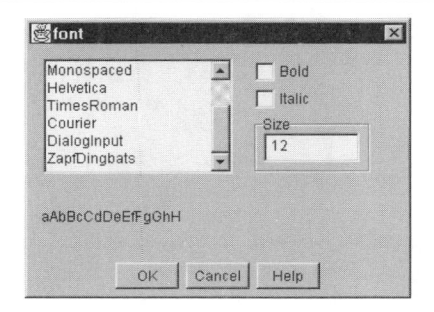

FIGURE 14.6: The custom editor for a Font property

This is what's called a *custom editor*. To create a custom editor, you need to override the `supportsCustomEditor` and `getCustomEditor` methods in `ShapeEditor`, among other things. To convert `ShapeEditor` to use a custom editor, follow these four steps:

1. Delete the `setAsText` and `getTags` methods. You no longer need to show the list of shapes or set the property from a text string. We leave the `getAsText` method because we want to display the property as a text string; we just don't want to allow input as one.

2. Override the `supportsCustomEditor` method to return `true`. By default, `supportsCustomEditor` returns `false`. Because we are providing a custom editor, it needs to return `true`.

   ```
   public boolean supportsCustomEditor() {
     return true;
   }
   ```

3. Override the `getCustomEditor` method and return an instance of the custom editor. We'll call it `ShapeCustomEditor`. You also need to save a reference in a class variable to the editor outside the method, so you can access the variable that it will need to store the property setting. And since it returns a `Component`, you'll need to import `java.awt.*`.

   ```
   import java.awt.*;
   ...
   private ShapeCustomEditor editor;
   public Component getCustomEditor() {
     if (editor == null)
       editor =  new ShapeCustomEditor(shape);
     return editor;
   }
   ```

4. Update `getValue` and `setValue` to access this property setting within the custom editor, if it exists.

   ```
   public void setValue (Object o) {
     shape = ((Integer)o).intValue();
     if (editor != null)
        editor.shape = shape;
     firePropertyChange();
   }
   public Object getValue () {
     if (editor != null)
        shape = editor.shape;
     return (new Integer (shape));
   }
   ```

That's all that is necessary for the updated property editor. You should save the changes, but you can't compile yet because we need to create the `ShapeCustomEditor` class.

ShapeEditor.java

```java
package skill14;

import java.awt.*;
import java.beans.*;
public class ShapeEditor extends PropertyEditorSupport {

  protected int shape;
  private ShapeCustomEditor editor;

  public void setValue (Object o) {
    shape = ((Integer)o).intValue();
    if (editor != null)
       editor.shape = shape;
    firePropertyChange();
  }
  public Object getValue () {
    if (editor != null)
       shape = editor.shape;
    return (new Integer (shape));
  }
  public String getAsText () {
    switch (shape) {
      case ShapeBox.CIRCLE:
        return "Circle";
      case ShapeBox.RECTANGLE:
        return "Rectangle";
      case ShapeBox.SQUARE:
        return "Square";
      case ShapeBox.OVAL:
      default:
        return "Oval";
    }
  }
  public boolean supportsCustomEditor() {
    return true;
  }

  public Component getCustomEditor() {
    if (editor == null)
      editor = new ShapeCustomEditor(shape);
    return editor;
  }
}
```

Creating the *ShapeCustomEditor*

You may have noticed that the `getCustomEditor` method returns a `Component`. This means that a custom editor can be any `Component`, or subclass. In our case, we want to display four `ShapeBox` objects, one for each type, so we'll use a `Container`. If the user selects a shape, that shape becomes the one to use as the property value. Because we need to use the component we want to customize, it is easier to create most of this by hand, instead of with the UI Designer.

1. Using the New Class Wizard, create a class called **ShapeCustomEditor** that subclasses **java.awt.Container**. Make sure the Public and Generate default constructor toggles are checked before selecting OK.

2. Add the property `shape` that we used previously in the `ShapeEditor`. We don't want anyone to access the shape outside the package, so don't add an access modifier like `private`, `protected`, or `public`. The `private` modifier wouldn't let `ShapeEditor` see it.

   ```
   int shape;
   ```

3. Add a constructor that accepts a single integer parameter, which is the initial shape setting.

   ```
   public ShapeCustomEditor (int shape) {
   ```

   Make sure the parameter is valid.

   ```
   if ((shape < 0) | (shape > 3))
     shape = 0;
   this.shape = shape;
   ```

   Change the layout manger to a 2 component wide by 2 component high grid.

   ```
   GridLayout gridLayout1 = new GridLayout(2, 2);
   this.setLayout(gridLayout1);
   ```

   Add four `ShapeBox` components—one for each shape, and add a `MouseListener` to each because we'll need to track mouse events to determine which shape is selected.

   ```
   ShapeBox shapeBox1 = new ShapeBox();
   shapeBox1.setShape (ShapeBox.OVAL);
   shapeBox1.addMouseListener (this);
   this.add(shapeBox1);
   ShapeBox shapeBox2 = new ShapeBox();
   shapeBox2.setShape (ShapeBox.CIRCLE);
   shapeBox2.addMouseListener (this);
   ```

```
      this.add(shapeBox2);
      ShapeBox shapeBox3 = new ShapeBox();
      shapeBox3.setShape (ShapeBox.RECTANGLE);
      shapeBox3.addMouseListener (this);
      this.add(shapeBox3);
      ShapeBox shapeBox4 = new ShapeBox();
      shapeBox4.setShape (ShapeBox.SQUARE);
      shapeBox4.addMouseListener (this);
      this.add(shapeBox4);
    }
```

4. In the default constructor, call the other constructor with a setting of zero:

   ```
   public ShapeCustomEditor () {
     this (0);
   }
   ```

5. Use the Implement Interface Wizard and select the java.awt.event.MouseListener interface. This will add the five methods of the interface to the class:

   - mouseClicked
   - mouseEntered
   - mouseExited
   - mousePressed
   - mouseReleased

6. In the mouseReleased method, set the editor's shape setting to the shape of the component selected:

   ```
   public void mouseReleased(MouseEvent parm1) {
     ShapeBox sb = (ShapeBox)parm1.getComponent();
     shape = sb.getShape();
   }
   ```

7. Lastly, override the getPreferredSize method to give the editor a size. This method says how big you want the custom editor to be. If you don't provide it, it will have a size of zero.

   ```
   public Dimension getPreferredSize () {
     return new Dimension (200, 100);
   }
   ```

That is the entire custom editor which is shown in the ShapeCustomEditor.java source below. One thing worth noting, which you may or may not have noticed, is that there is no OK or Cancel button here. The system automatically adds these buttons. Now, you can save your program and rebuild the entire package to make sure everything is compiled.

ShapeCustomEditor.java

```java
package skill14;

import java.awt.*;
import borland.jbcl.control.*;
import java.awt.event.*;
import borland.jbcl.layout.*;
public class ShapeCustomEditor extends Container implements MouseListener{
  int shape;

  public ShapeCustomEditor () {
    this (0);
  }

  public ShapeCustomEditor (int shape) {
    if ((shape < 0) | (shape > 3))
      shape = 0;
    this.shape = shape;
    GridLayout gridLayout1 = new GridLayout(2, 2);
    this.setLayout(gridLayout1);
    ShapeBox shapeBox1 = new ShapeBox();
    shapeBox1.setShape (ShapeBox.OVAL);
    shapeBox1.addMouseListener (this);
    this.add(shapeBox1);
    ShapeBox shapeBox2 = new ShapeBox();
    shapeBox2.setShape (ShapeBox.CIRCLE);
    shapeBox2.addMouseListener (this);
    this.add(shapeBox2);
    ShapeBox shapeBox3 = new ShapeBox();
    shapeBox3.setShape (ShapeBox.RECTANGLE);
    shapeBox3.addMouseListener (this);
    this.add(shapeBox3);
    ShapeBox shapeBox4 = new ShapeBox();
    shapeBox4.setShape (ShapeBox.SQUARE);
    shapeBox4.addMouseListener (this);
    this.add(shapeBox4);
  }

  public Dimension getPreferredSize () {
    return new Dimension (200, 100);
  }
```

```java
    public void mouseClicked(MouseEvent parm1) {
      //TODO: implement this  java.awt.event.MouseListener method;
    }

    public void mousePressed(MouseEvent parm1) {
      //TODO: implement this  java.awt.event.MouseListener method;
    }

    public void mouseReleased(MouseEvent parm1) {
      ShapeBox sb = (ShapeBox)parm1.getComponent();
      shape = sb.getShape();
    }

    public void mouseEntered(MouseEvent parm1) {
      //TODO: implement this  java.awt.event.MouseListener method;
    }

    public void mouseExited(MouseEvent parm1) {
      //TODO: implement this  java.awt.event.MouseListener method;
    }
}
```

Using the Custom Editor

At this point, exit out of JBuilder and launch it again to make sure you get the new property editor. Reopen the skill14b project, and try to set the shape property in the Inspector. Instead of being able to type into the field, you'll notice three dots. Selecting the three dots will bring up the custom editor, as shown in Figure 14.7.

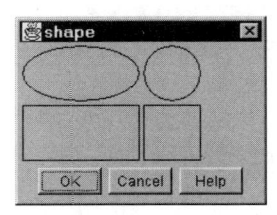

FIGURE 14.7: The custom editor dialog box for the shape property

Here, if you click on a shape and select OK, the ShapeBox changes within the frame. If you click on a shape and select Cancel, nothing happens. Because of the way we set up the ShapeBox, there is no visual clue that you actually selected the button. In the custom editor, you could do something like have the system beep (call the `beep` method of `Toolkit`) to add an auditory clue. However, no visual clue can be shown without changing the bean.

> **LOOKING BEYOND PROPERTY EDITORS**
>
> Customization isn't just for property editors. If you need to set multiple properties simultaneously, a property editor isn't the way to go. It only permits you to set a single property, and you cannot look at any other bean properties. To alleviate this situation, a bean can have something called a *customizer*. Once you create a customizer, the bean user can use it to configure multiple properties within the bean. Unfortunately, JBuilder doesn't support them at design-time, so they won't be described.
>
> If you are interested in learning more about them, see the tutorial offered at `http://splash.javasoft.com/beans/resources.html`.

Now that you've made your way through customizing beans, the next skill describes serialization and what you need to know about it when creating beans. It's the last major area this book will cover in the bean-development arena. For more about beans, see *Mastering JavaBeans* from Sybex.

Are You Experienced?

Now you can...

- ☑ create property editors
- ☑ accept text strings for integer properties
- ☑ display pick-lists to choose property settings
- ☑ create custom property editors for more complex operations

PROGRAMMERS
C, C, VB, Cobol, exp. Call 534-555-6543 or fax 534-555-6544.

PROGRAMMING
MRFS Inc. is looking for a Sr. Windows NT developer. Reqs. 3-5 yrs. Exp. in C under Windows, Win95 & NT, using Visual C. Excl. OO design & implementation skills a must. OLE2 & ODBC are a plus. Excl. Salary & bnfts. Resume & salary history to HR, 8779 HighTech Way, Computer City, AR

PROGRAMMERS
Contractors Wanted for short & long term assignments: Visual C, MFC Unix C/C, SQL Oracle Developers PC Help Desk Support Windows NT & NetWareTelecommunications Visual Basic, Access, HTMT, CGI, Perl MMI & Co., 885-555-9933

PROGRAMMER World Wide Web Links wants your HTML & Photoshop skills. Develop great WWW sites. Local & global customers. Send samples & resume to WWWL, 2000 Apple Road, Santa Rosa, CA.

TECHNICAL WRITER Software firm seeks writer/editor for manuals, research notes, project mgmt. Min 2 years tech. writing, DTP & programming experience. Send resume & writing samples to: Software Systems, Dallas, TX.

TECHNICAL, Software development firm looking for Tech Trainers. Ideal candidates have programming experience in Visual C, HTML & JAVA. Need quick self starter. Call (443) 555-6868 for interview.

TECHNICAL WRITER/ Premier Computer Corp is seeking a combination of technical skills, knowledge and experience in the following areas: UNIX, Windows 95/NT, Visual Basic, on-line help & documentation, and the internet. Candidates must possess excellent writing skills, and be comfortable working in a quality vs. deadline driven environment. Competitive salary. Fax resume & samples to Karen Fields, Premier Computer Corp, 444 Industrial Blvd. Concord, CA. Or send to our website at www.premier.com.

WEB DESIGNER
BA/BS or equivalent programming/multimedia production. 3 years of experience in use and design of WWW services streaming audio and video HTML, PERL, CGI, GIF, JPEG. Demonstrated Interpersonal, organization, communication, multi-tasking skills. Send resume to The Learning People at www.learning.com

WEBMASTER-TECHNICAL
BSCS or equivalent, 2 years of experience in CGI, Windows 95/NT, UNIX, C, Java, Perl. Demonstrated ability to design code, debug and test on-line services. Send resume to The Learning People at www.learning.com.

PROGRAMMER World Wide Web Links wants your HTML & Photoshop skills. Develop great WWW sites. Local & global customers. Send samples

ing tools. Experienced in documentation preparation & programming languages (Access, C, FoxPro) are a plus. Financial or banking customer service support is required along with excellent verbal & written communication skills with multi levels of end-users. Send resume to KKUP Enterprises, 45 Orange Blvd. Orange, CA.

COMPUTERS Small Web Design firm seeks indiv. w/NT, Webserver & Database management exp. Fax resume to 556-555-4221.

COMPUTER/ Visual C/C, Visual Basic Exp'd Systems Analysts/ Programmers for growing software dev. team in Roseburg. Computer Science or related degree preferred. Develop adv. Engineering applications for engineering firm. Fax resume to 707-555-8744.

COMPUTER. Web Master for dynamic SF Internet co. Site. Dev. test, coord. train. 2 yrs prog. Exp. C C. Web C, FTP. Fax resume to Best Staffing 845-555-7722.

COMPUTER PROGRAMMER
Ad agency seeks programmer w/exp. in UNIX/NT Platforms. Web Server, CGI/Perl. Programmer Position avail. on a project basis with the possibility to move into F/T. Fax resume & salary req. to R. Jones 334-555-8332.

COMPUTERS Programmer/Analyst Design and maintain C based SQL database applications, Required skills: Visual Basic, C, SQL, ODBC. Document existing and new applications. Novell or NT exp. a plus. Fax resume & salary history to 235-555-9935.

GRAPHIC DESIGNER
Webmaster's Weekly is seeking a creative Graphic Designer to design high impact marketing collateral, including direct mail promo's, CD-ROM packages, ads and WWW pages. Must be able to juggle multiple projects and learn new skills on the job very rapidly. Web design experience a big plus, technical troubleshooting also a plus. Call 435-555-1235.

GRAPHICS - ART DIRECTOR - WEB-MULTIMEDIA
Leading internet development company has an outstanding opportunity for a talented, high-end Web Experienced Art Director. In addition to a great portfolio and fresh ideas, the ideal candidate has excellent communication and presentation skills. Working as a team with innovative producers and programmers, you will create dynamic, interactive web sites and application interfaces. Some programming experience required. Send samples and resume to: SuperSites, 333 Main. Seattle, WA

MARKETING
Fast paced software and services provider looking for MARKETING COMMUNICATIONS SPECIALIST to be responsible for its webpage.

PROGRAMMERS Multiple short term assignments available: Visual C. 3 positions SQL ServerNT Server, 2 positions JAVA & HTML, long term NetWare. Various locations. Call for more info. 356-555-3398.

PROGRAMMERS
C, C, VB, Cobol, exp.
Call 534-555-6543
or fax 534-555-6544.

PROGRAMMING
MRFS Inc. is looking for a Sr. Windows NT developer. Reqs. 3-5 yrs. Exp. in C under Windows, Win95 & NT, using Visual C. Excl. OO design & implementation skills a must. OLE2 & ODBC are a plus. Excl. Salary & bnfts. Resume & salary history to HR, 8779 HighTech Way, Computer City, AR

PROGRAMMERS/ Contractors Wanted for short & long term assignments: Visual C, MFC Unix C/C, SQL Oracle Developers PC Help Desk Support Windows NT & NetWareTelecommunications Visual Basic, Access, HTMT, CGI, Perl MMI & Co., 885-555-9933

PROGRAMMER World Wide Web Links wants your HTML & Photoshop skills. Develop great WWW sites. Local & global customers. Send samples & resume to WWWL, 2000 Apple Road, Santa Rosa, CA.

TECHNICAL WRITER Software firm seeks writer/editor for manuals, research notes, project mgmt. Min 2 years tech. writing, DTP & programming experience. Send resume & writing samples to: Software Systems, Dallas, TX.

COMPUTER PROGRAMMER
Ad agency seeks programmer w/exp. in UNIX/NT Platforms. Web Server, CGI/Perl. Programmer Position avail. on a project basis with the possibility to move into F/T. Fax resume & salary req. to R. Jones 334-555-8332.

TECHNICAL WRITER Premier Computer Corp is seeking a combination of technical skills, knowledge and experience in the following areas: UNIX, Windows 95/NT, Visual Basic, on-line help & documentation, and the internet. Candidates must possess excellent writing skills, and be comfortable working in a quality vs. deadline driven environment. Competitive salary. Fax resume & samples to Karen Fields, Premier Computer Corp, 444 Industrial Blvd. Concord, CA. Or send to our website at www.premier.com.

WEB DESIGNER
BA/BS or equivalent programming/multimedia production. 3 years of experience in use and design of WWW services streaming audio and video HTML, PERL, CGI, GIF, JPEG. Demonstrated Interpersonal, organization, communication, multi-tasking skills. Send resume to The Learning People at www.learning.com

WEBMASTER-TECHNICAL
BSCS or equivalent, 2 years of experience in CGI, Windows 95/NT,

COMPUTERS Small Web Design firm seeks indiv. w/NT, Webserver & Database management exp. Fax resume to 556-555-4221.

COMPUTER Visual C/C, Visual Basic Exp'd Systems Analysts/ Programmers for growing software dev. team in Roseburg. Computer Science or related degree preferred. Develop adv. Engineering applications for engineering firm. Fax resume to 707-555-8744.

COMPUTER Web Master for dynamic SF Internet co. Site. Dev. test, coord., train. 2 yrs prog. Exp. C C. Web C, FTP. Fax resume to Best Staffing 845-555-7722.

COMPUTERS: QA SOFTWARE TESTERS Qualified candidates should have 2 yrs exp. performing integration & system testing using automated testing tools. Experienced in documentation preparation & programming languages (Access, C, FoxPro) are a plus. Financial or banking customer service support is required along with excellent verbal & written communication skills with multi levels of end-users. Send resume to KKUP Enterprises, 45 Orange Blvd. Orange, CA.

COMPUTERS Programmer/Analyst Design and maintain C based SQL database applications, Required skills: Visual Basic, C, SQL, ODBC. Document existing and new applications, Novell or NT exp. a plus. Fax resume & salary history to 235-555-9935.

GRAPHIC DESIGNER
Webmaster's Weekly is seeking a creative Graphic Designer to design high impact marketing collateral, including direct mail promo's, CD-ROM packages, ads and WWW pages. Must be able to juggle multiple projects and learn new skills on the job very rapidly. Web design experience a big plus, technical troubleshooting also a plus. Call 435-555-1235.

GRAPHICS - ART DIRECTOR - WEB-MULTIMEDIA
Leading internet development company has an outstanding opportunity for a talented, high-end Web Experienced Art Director. In addition to a great portfolio and fresh ideas, the ideal candidate has excellent communication and presentation skills. Working as a team with innovative producers and programmers, you will create dynamic, interactive web sites and application interfaces. Some programming experience required. Send samples and resume to: SuperSites, 333 Main. Seattle, WA

COMPUTER PROGRAMMER
Ad agency seeks programmer w/exp. in UNIX/NT Platforms. Web Server, CGI/Perl. Programmer Position avail. on a project basis with the possibility to move into F/T. Fax resume & salary req. to R. Jones 334-555-8332.

PROGRAMMERS / Established software company seeks programmers

PROGRAMMERS Multiple term assignments available. C. 3 positions SQL ServerNT S 2 positions JAVA & HTML. long NetWare. Various locations. Ca more info. 356-555-3398.

PROGRAMMERS
C, C, VB, Cobol, exp. Call 534 6543 or fax 534-555-6544.

PROGRAMMING
MRFS Inc. is looking for a Windows NT developer. Reqs yrs Exp. in C under Win Win95 & NT, using Visual C OO design & implementation a must. OLE2 & ODBC are a Excl. Salary & bnfts. Resu salary history to HR, 8779 Hi Way, Computer City, AR

PROGRAMMERS/ Contr Wanted for short & long term a ments. Visual C, MFCUnix C/C Oracle Developers PC Help Support Windows NT & Ne Telecommunications, Visual Access, HTML, CGI, Perl MMI 885-555-9933

PROGRAMMER World Wide Links wants your HTML & Phot skills. Develop great WWW Local & global customers. Sen ples & resume to WWWL, Apple Road, Santa Rosa, CA.

TECHNICAL WRITER Softwa seeks writer/editor for ma research notes, project mgmt years tech. writing, DTP & pr ming experience. Send res writing samples to: Sc Systems, Dallas, TX.

TECHNICAL Software develo firm looking for Tech Trainers candidates have programming rience in Visual C, HTML Need quick self starter, Call 555-6868 for interview.

TECHNICAL WRITER Computer Corp is seeking a nation of technical skills, know and experience in the fo areas: UNIX, Windows 95/NT Basic, on-line help & docume and the internet. Candidate possess excellent writing ski be comfortable working in a vs. deadline driven envir Competitive salary Fax re samples to Karen Fields, Computer Corp, 444 Industri Concord, CA. Or send to our at www.premier.com.

WEB DESIGNER
BA/BS or equivalent pr ming/multimedia product years of experience in u design of WWW services st audio and video HTML, PE GIF, JPEG. Demonstrated sonal, organization, commu multi-tasking skills. Send re The Learning People at w ing.com.

WEBMASTER-TECHN

SKILL 15

fifteen

Creating Beans: Serialization

- ❑ Defining persistence
- ❑ Creating a timer
- ❑ Working with transient data
- ❑ Saving the transient data's state
- ❑ Restoring program state

Learning about Persistence

One important bean characteristic is the ability to save the current state of the bean. This means that if a program exits, when it restarts, all the characteristics, or *properties*, of the beans used will be restored to the state they were in when the program exited. In the case of a program's interface, this is fairly easy to do—just recreate the interface from scratch. However, what if the user can change the state of part of the application and you need to restore that when the program restarts? How do you go about saving that extra bit of information? This skill goes through the steps necessary to save a bean's state. We call this characteristic *persistence*, as it allows the state of the bean to persist beyond the lifetime of the bean.

In this skill, we'll show you what you need to do to make sure your beans can persist. Persistence uses Java's *serialization API,* which allows any Java object, not just beans, to be converted to a stream of bytes that can be saved to disk or transferred over the Internet. We'll start by creating a program that displays a counter. Using multithreading, we'll let the user start and stop the counter's operation, as well as enable the saving and restoring of a counter to disk. Saving basically stores the current value of the counter and whether or not the counter is enabled, while restoring restores this state.

Creating the Interface

To create the program, close any open projects and run the Application Wizard. Save the project in **c:\skills\skill15\skill15.jpr**, and then on the second page of the Application Wizard, name the Frame class **Counter**, and select Finish. The program we create will have a label in the Center area and six buttons in the South quadrant. The buttons will be Start, Stop, Reset, Load, Save, and Close. To create this, do the following steps:

1. Select `Counter.java` in the Navigation pane.
2. Select the Design tab in the Contents pane so you can drop the components onto the screen.
3. Select `bevelPanel1(XYLayout)` in the Structure pane and delete it.
4. Select the AWT tab on the Component palette.
5. Select the `Panel` bean and drop it into the Contents pane. Set its constraints property to **South** in the Inspector.

6. Select the Label bean and drop it into the Contents pane. Set its constraints property to **Center**, alignment property to **1** (which is centered), and its text property to **0**. Also, change the font property to a **24 point**, **Bold**, **Serif** font so it appears larger.

7. Select panel1 in the Structure pane and the Button bean from the Component palette. Then place six buttons within the Panel.

8. Change the label property of each button, from left to right they should be **Start**, **Stop**, **Reset**, **Load**, **Save**, and **Close**, although the actual order doesn't really matter.

At this point, save everything and run your program. Running your program will bring up the screen shown in Figure 15.1.

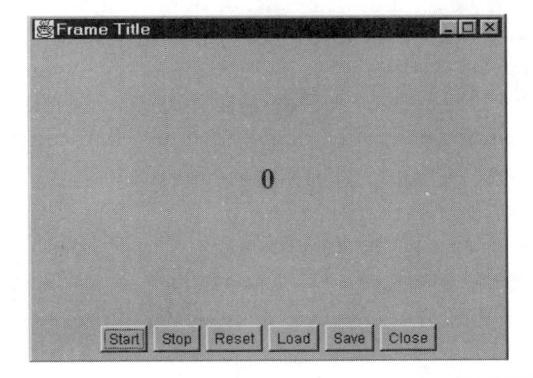

FIGURE 15.1: The initial screen for the Counter program

Making the Counter Count

To get our counter going, we need to define the functionality of three of the buttons: Start, Stop, and Reset. We'll do the Close button, too, to close the window.

Defining the Close Button

Because close is the easiest, we'll do that one first. Double-click the button you've labeled Close, and JBuilder adds an adapter to handle the button selection event. Within this method, have the program hide the window and dispose it. We don't want to call System.exit because we want to allow multiple windows to be opened later when we support save and restore. So, add the following three lines to the method JBuilder just created:

```
System.out.println ("Close");
this.setVisible(false);
this.dispose();
```

> **TIP** It is good practice to hide a frame before disposing it, so you don't watch the different pieces of the screen disappear. What dispose does is release all the resources that the frame uses, including the frame itself.

Defining the Start Button

Next, we'll define the Start button. First, we need to initialize the counter to zero and start a new thread to increment it. A different thread needs to do the incrementing so the screen is still responsive to someone selecting a button. So, go to the UI Designer panel and double-click the Start button; JBuilder will add another event-handling method. We'll then add these lines to our source:

```
System.out.println ("Start");
resetCounter();
t = new Thread (this);
t.start();
```

This in turn requires us to add an instance variable of type Thread to the class:

```
Thread t;
```

The parameter to the Thread constructor must implement the Runnable interface. Therefore, our class needs to implement the Runnable interface in order to be the parameter to the constructor. Selecting the Implement Interface Wizard, the java.lang.Runnable interface, and the OK button, adds the run method to your program. In run, we need to loop forever, constantly updating the counter:

```
public void run() {
  while (t != null) {
    incrementCounter();
    try {
      t.sleep (50);
    } catch (InterruptedException e) {
    }
  }
}
```

50 serves as the millisecond delay between updates. You can increase or decrease this amount to change the update speed.

The `resetCounter` and `incrementCounter` methods are separated for two reasons. First, updating the counter variable is a two-step operation: change the value and then update the label. You don't want to do only one operation before the other, with the counter value changing between steps. Second, because there are multiple threads running, you don't want one thread to interrupt the operations of another. All access to the counter variable needs to be protected.

Finally, add an instance variable, `count`, for the counter, and define the two helper methods as `synchronized`. This ensures that only one thread accesses the new instance variable at all times. The `validate` call is necessary to force the screen to update the display of the components contained within it. Otherwise, the window would only update itself when it thought it needed to. This is similar to calling `repaint` with graphics-related programs.

```
int count;
private synchronized void incrementCounter () {
  count++;
  label1.setText ("" + count);
  validate();
}
private synchronized void resetCounter () {
  count = 0;
  label1.setText ("" + count);
  validate();
}
```

Defining the Reset and Stop Buttons

Because we did so much work for the Start button, we can reuse some of it for these two buttons. For the Reset button, we need to reset the counter to zero. After double-clicking the button in the UI Designer, add the following source to the new method where JBuilder places you:

```
System.out.println ("Reset");
resetCounter();
```

For Stop, we need to stop the thread. The method to permanently stop a thread is `stop`. (The `suspend` method will temporarily suspend a thread's running, while `resume` resumes it.) In addition to stopping the thread, we need to make sure that the old thread's memory is freed up by setting the instance variable to `null` because `start` creates a new thread. If we didn't do this, the system wouldn't free the memory until we created a new thread.

```
System.out.println ("Stop");
t.stop();
t = null;
```

Now, the Counter program is fully functional—from a counting standpoint. If you save everything and run the program you can select Start, Stop, and Reset to see the program at work. Select Close when you are done to stop it. The screen shown in Figure 15.2 looks the same as the one shown in Figure 15.1, except that it has a different number.

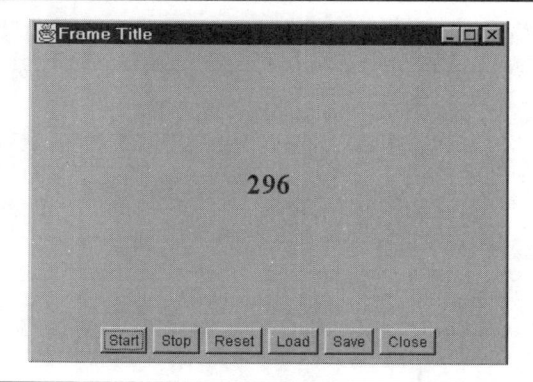

FIGURE 15.2: A working screen in the Counter program

Enabling Save and Load

Now that the program is working, we would like to be able to save it so when we read it back in, the counter value is where it was when we saved it, and the thread is running if it was running when saved. To support saving, there are two steps involved.

First, your class needs to implement the `java.io.Serializable` interface. There are no methods in the interface. It just serves as a flag that says the class can be saved, or *serialized*. Selecting the Implement Interface Wizard, the `java.io.Serializable` interface, and the OK button adds the appropriate definition to your program.

Then there is the second step. For the actual serialization to occur, just implementing the interface isn't enough. Because serialization saves state, every instance variable of the class must also implement the `Serializable` interface. If your class has any class variables defined with the `static` keyword, they are not saved, as they do not define the state of a specific instance of the class.

> **TIP** Because methods aren't state, they are not saved. This means that when a saved class needs to be restored, you still need the `.class` file associated with it.

The process of determining if each variable is serializable gets easier with practice. You learn about the problem cases fairly quickly, and the rest just falls into place. The classes tend to fall into three groups:

- Primitive variables (such as `int`, `float`, and `boolean`) are automatically serializable. There is nothing special that needs to be done. If all your instance variables are primitives or are classes that have only primitive instance variables, just implementing the interface is sufficient.

- Classes that describe non-platform-specific information are automatically serializable. Because the classes do not depend on the run-time environment specifics, they tend to depend only on primitive variables. These classes may include data structures, AWT components, and lots of things in between. For instance, an AWT `Label` component is defined by its text label and alignment, plus some inherited things from `Component`. Although the `Label` component may appear and behave differently on different platforms, it is still defined by a set of primitive variables and by classes that are defined by primitive variables.

- The third set of variables is the problem child of the group. These are instance variables for classes that describe platform-specific information. For instance, `java.io.FileDescriptor` is not serializable. It describes a specific open file on the running system. Saving this information doesn't make sense because when you restore a class that has a `FileDescriptor` instance variable, the original value has possibly changed. You can save a `java.io.File` object, which when used with a `java.io.FileInputStream`, creates the current descriptor. However, on its own a `FileDescriptor` is not serializable.

> **NOTE:** The two classes used most frequently that are not serializable are Image and Thread. For an Image, you just save the URL or filename of the image and reread it. For a Thread, we'll see what to do shortly.

Now that we know about the `Serializable` interface and the fact that `Thread` isn't serializable, how can we make our `Counter` class `Serializable` even though it contains an instance variable that isn't? Well, Java has a keyword, `transient`, that tells the serialization process to not save an instance variable. Every instance variable that isn't `Serializable` must be flagged with the `transient` keyword. Therefore, we add that to our `Thread` variable declaration:

```
transient Thread t;
```

Now, because the parent class, `DecoratedFrame`, is a bean, it is serializable. In addition, our only other instance variable is `count` and it's an `int`, so `Counter` is serializable. One might think we're done here; however, we still haven't saved the actual state of the thread. How will we know if it was running when it was saved? To save this piece of information, we need to add another instance variable of type `boolean`. Then when the `Counter` is read in, you can check the variable to restore the state of the thread.

```
boolean isRunning;
```

Whenever the state of the thread changes, you need to update `isRunning` to reflect it. To update for starting:

```
System.out.println ("Start");
resetCounter();
t = new Thread (this);
t.start();
isRunning = true;
```

And to update for stopping:

```
System.out.println ("Stop");
t.stop();
isRunning = false;
t = null;
```

With a quick change in `run`, we're almost to the point where the only thing we'll need to do is save and restore:

```
public void run() {
  while ((t != null) && isRunning) {
```

```
      incrementCounter();
      try {
        t.sleep (50);
      } catch (InterruptedException e) {
        // Ignore
      }
    }
  }
}
```

Resetting the Thread State on Reading

When a class is saved, or serialized, the saving process looks for a `writeObject` method within any class it serializes. On the *deserializing,* or reading side, the method the system looks for is `readObject`. These two methods offer the opportunity to customize the saving and restoring. The methods are optional, but if you need to create one, you have to create both.

Saving the thread state doesn't require anything special. We've already flagged the variable as transient, which means the `Thread` instance variable won't be saved. To do the default saving behavior, we call the `defaultWriteObject` method of the `ObjectOutputStream` parameter that is passed to `writeObject`.

```
private void writeObject (ObjectOutputStream oos) throws IOException {
  System.out.println ("Write object");
  oos.defaultWriteObject();
}
```

Reading is another story. In order for the thread to have its state restored, a new `Thread` needs to be created if `isRunning` is `true` when the class is reread. To do the actual reading, we call the `defaultReadObject` method of the `ObjectInputStream` parameter passed to `readObject`. Then, if `isRunning` is set, we create and start the thread.

```
private void readObject (ObjectInputStream ois) throws
ClassNotFoundException, IOException {
  System.out.println ("Read object");
  ois.defaultReadObject();
  if (isRunning) {
    t = new Thread (this);
    t.start();
  }
}
```

> **NOTE** The readObject and writeObject methods can throw exceptions during the serialization process for various reasons, such as if the class definition cannot be found, instance variables cannot be serializable, or disk space is an issue. These methods should not worry about the exceptions and should just pass them along to the caller that is doing the saving or restoring. Then, the callers can handle the exceptions as they see fit.

This same restoration pattern is used for the other classes that have instance variables that aren't serializable. Save the state in something that is serializable, and then restore it based on the setting.

Restoring the Adapters

You might think that everything to restore is done at this point; however, there is one minor problem. All the AWT components and JBCL controls flag their event listener lists as `transient` and don't save them at all. Because it isn't known beforehand if the listeners are themselves serializable, a conservative approach was taken to not save any of them. This means you have to manually recreate the internal listeners when you restore the bean. This just adds another step to the restore process. If you move the `addActionListener` methods out of the `jbInit` method and into their own procedure, you can call this procedure both in `jbInit` and within `readObject`, after the `defaultReadObject` call, but before the thread is started.

```
private void setupAdapters () {
   button1.addActionListener(new Counter_button1_actionAdapter(this));
   button4.addActionListener(new Counter_button4_actionAdapter(this));
   button5.addActionListener(new Counter_button5_actionAdapter(this));
   button6.addActionListener(new Counter_button6_actionAdapter(this));
}
```

> **NOTE** Your buttons might be numbered in a different order so make sure you save the right four adapters. Eventually you will save all six, but we've only connected four buttons so far.

Once we have `readObject` and `writeObject` done, we can move on to the actual saving and restoring. Normally, the saving and restoring process is done outside the class definition by whoever is reusing the bean. In this particular case, we want `Counter` to save itself.

Setting Up the Save Button

Because of all the work we've done already, the saving process is going to be really easy. The only thing new to introduce is the `ObjectOutputStream` class that you saw briefly above. It works similarly to the `FileReader` and `StringWriter` classes seen in Skill 8, but works with objects instead of characters. When you create an `ObjectOutputStream`, you need to give it another stream to actually save things in. Then, for any object you want to write to the stream, you call the `writeObject` method of `ObjectOutputStream`. In turn, the `ObjectOutputStream` writes all the non-transient instance variables of the class you told it to write. If any of those instance variables is itself a class, it recursively saves it too, until the only things left are primitive variables.

> **NOTE** ObjectOutputStream is smart enough to know if it has already written a class out to its stream. So, if there is a circular reference to something already written, it will not rewrite it.

So, if you double-click on the Save button, you can add the following source to the event handler.

```
System.out.println ("Save");
try {
  FileOutputStream fos = new FileOutputStream ("Counter.ser");
  ObjectOutputStream oos = new ObjectOutputStream (fos);
  oos.writeObject(this);
  oos.close();
} catch (IOException ex) {
  System.out.println ("Unable to save");
  ex.printStackTrace();
}
```

Also, move the code to connect the new adapter out of `jbInit` into `setupAdapters`:

```
button2.addActionListener(new Counter_button2_actionAdapter(this));
```

And import the `java.io` package:

```
import java.io.*;
```

> **TIP** Serialized classes should be saved in files that have the .ser extension.

Enabling Restoration

The final step involved is to fill in the event for the Restore button. Reading involves an `ObjectInputStream`, which is just the opposite of an `ObjectOutputStream`—you read objects from it.

Double-clicking the Restore button in the UI Designer allows us to add the following event-handling code. After restoring the Counter from the file, just call the `show` method so multiple Counter frames will be visible. We always save to the same file, so you can only remember one at a time.

```java
System.out.println ("Load");
try {
  FileInputStream fis = new FileInputStream ("Counter.ser");
  ObjectInputStream ois = new ObjectInputStream (fis);
  Counter ct = (Counter)ois.readObject();
  ois.close();
  ct.show();
} catch (Exception ex) {
  System.out.println ("Unable to load");
  ex.printStackTrace();
}
```

Again, you need to move the code to connect the new adapter out of `jbInit` into `setupAdapters`. We should now have all six connections in `setupAdapters`, and none in `jbInit`:

```java
private void setupAdapters () {
  button1.addActionListener(new Counter_button1_actionAdapter(this));
  button2.addActionListener(new Counter_button2_actionAdapter(this));
  button3.addActionListener(new Counter_button3_actionAdapter(this));
  button4.addActionListener(new Counter_button4_actionAdapter(this));
  button5.addActionListener(new Counter_button5_actionAdapter(this));
  button6.addActionListener(new Counter_button6_actionAdapter(this));
}
```

At this point, you can finally save and compile everything. Assuming you've typed everything in correctly, you can try out all the buttons when you run the program. After running the program, then saving and restoring several counters, your screen will look something like the one shown in Figure 15.3. You can also save a counter, exit the program, restart the program, and load the saved version to demonstrate persistence. If you look in the Console Window, you'll see the different `println` messages, showing when each action occurred.

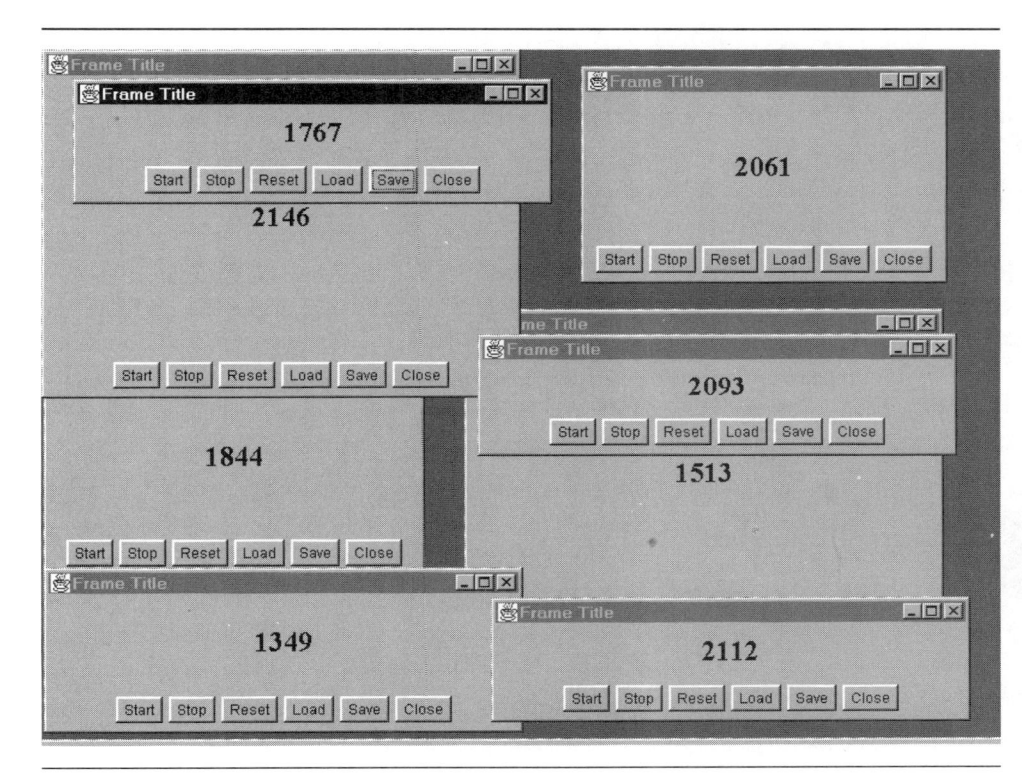

FIGURE 15.3: Multiple running counters after saving and restoring

> **TIP** When you show the saved screen, it is placed at the same position as when it was saved, on top of the existing screen. You'll need to move it to see both screens.

The complete source code is shown below.

Counter.java

```
package skill15;

import java.awt.*;
import java.awt.event.*;
import java.io.*;
```

Skill 15 • Creating Beans: Serialization

```java
import borland.jbcl.control.*;
import borland.jbcl.layout.*;
import java.lang.Runnable;
import java.io.Serializable;

public class Counter extends DecoratedFrame implements Runnable, Serializable{
  BorderLayout borderLayout1 = new BorderLayout();
  Panel panel1 = new Panel();
  Label label1 = new Label();
  Button button1 = new Button();
  Button button2 = new Button();
  Button button3 = new Button();
  Button button4 = new Button();
  Button button5 = new Button();
  Button button6 = new Button();
  transient Thread t;
  int count;
  boolean isRunning;

  //Construct the frame
  public Counter() {
System.out.println ("constructor");
    try {
      jbInit();
    }
    catch (Exception e) {
      e.printStackTrace();
    }
  }

  //Component initialization
  public void jbInit() throws Exception{
    System.out.println ("jbInit");
    this.setLayout(borderLayout1);
    this.setSize(new Dimension(400, 300));
    this.setTitle("Frame Title");
    label1.setText("0");
    button1.setLabel("Close");
    button2.setLabel("Save");
    button3.setLabel("Load");
    button4.setLabel("Reset");
    button5.setLabel("Stop");
    button6.setLabel("Start");
    setupAdapters();
    label1.setFont(new Font("Serif", 1, 24));
    label1.setAlignment(1);
```

```
    this.add(panel1, BorderLayout.SOUTH);
    panel1.add(button6, null);
    panel1.add(button5, null);
    panel1.add(button4, null);
    panel1.add(button3, null);
    panel1.add(button2, null);
    panel1.add(button1, null);
    this.add(label1, BorderLayout.CENTER);
}

private void setupAdapters () {
    button1.addActionListener(new Counter_button1_actionAdapter(this));
    button2.addActionListener(new Counter_button2_actionAdapter(this));
    button3.addActionListener(new Counter_button3_actionAdapter(this));
    button4.addActionListener(new Counter_button4_actionAdapter(this));
    button5.addActionListener(new Counter_button5_actionAdapter(this));
    button6.addActionListener(new Counter_button6_actionAdapter(this));
}

void button1_actionPerformed(ActionEvent e) {
    System.out.println ("Close");
    this.setVisible(false);
    this.dispose();
}

void button6_actionPerformed(ActionEvent e) {
    System.out.println ("Start");
    resetCounter();
    t = new Thread (this);
    t.start();
    isRunning = true;
}

public void run() {
    while ((t != null) && isRunning) {
        incrementCounter();
        try {
            t.sleep (50);
        } catch (InterruptedException e) {
        }
    }
}
private synchronized void incrementCounter () {
    count++;
    label1.setText ("" + count);
    validate();
}
```

```java
private synchronized void resetCounter () {
  count = 0;
  label1.setText ("" + count);
  validate();
}

void button4_actionPerformed(ActionEvent e) {
  System.out.println ("Reset");
  resetCounter();
}

void button5_actionPerformed(ActionEvent e) {
  System.out.println ("Stop");
  t.stop();
  isRunning = false;
  t = null;
}

private void readObject (ObjectInputStream ois) throws
    ClassNotFoundException, IOException {
  System.out.println ("Read object");
  ois.defaultReadObject();
  setupAdapters();
  if (isRunning) {
    t = new Thread (this);
    t.start();
  }
}

private void writeObject (ObjectOutputStream oos) throws IOException {
  System.out.println ("Write object");
  oos.defaultWriteObject();
}

void button2_actionPerformed(ActionEvent e) {
  System.out.println ("Save");
  try {
    FileOutputStream fos = new FileOutputStream ("Counter.ser");
    ObjectOutputStream oos = new ObjectOutputStream (fos);
    oos.writeObject(this);
    oos.close();
  } catch (IOException ex) {
    System.out.println ("Unable to save");
    ex.printStackTrace();
  }
}
```

```
    void button3_actionPerformed(ActionEvent e) {
      System.out.println ("Load");
      try {
        FileInputStream fis = new FileInputStream ("Counter.ser");
        ObjectInputStream ois = new ObjectInputStream (fis);
        Counter ct = (Counter)ois.readObject();
        ois.close();
        ct.show();
      } catch (Exception ex) {
        System.out.println ("Unable to load");
        ex.printStackTrace();
      }
    }
  }

class Counter_button1_actionAdapter implements java.awt.event.ActionListener {
  Counter adaptee;

  Counter_button1_actionAdapter(Counter adaptee) {
    this.adaptee = adaptee;
  }

  public void actionPerformed(ActionEvent e) {
    adaptee.button1_actionPerformed(e);
  }
}

class Counter_button6_actionAdapter implements java.awt.event.ActionListener {
  Counter adaptee;

  Counter_button6_actionAdapter(Counter adaptee) {
    this.adaptee = adaptee;
  }

  public void actionPerformed(ActionEvent e) {
    adaptee.button6_actionPerformed(e);
  }
}

class Counter_button4_actionAdapter implements java.awt.event.ActionListener {
  Counter adaptee;

  Counter_button4_actionAdapter(Counter adaptee) {
    this.adaptee = adaptee;
  }
```

```java
    public void actionPerformed(ActionEvent e) {
      adaptee.button4_actionPerformed(e);
    }
}

class Counter_button5_actionAdapter implements java.awt.event.ActionListener {
  Counter adaptee;

  Counter_button5_actionAdapter(Counter adaptee) {
    this.adaptee = adaptee;
  }

  public void actionPerformed(ActionEvent e) {
    adaptee.button5_actionPerformed(e);
  }
}

class Counter_button2_actionAdapter implements java.awt.event.ActionListener {
  Counter adaptee;

  Counter_button2_actionAdapter(Counter adaptee) {
    this.adaptee = adaptee;
  }

  public void actionPerformed(ActionEvent e) {
    adaptee.button2_actionPerformed(e);
  }
}

class Counter_button3_actionAdapter implements java.awt.event.ActionListener {
  Counter adaptee;

  Counter_button3_actionAdapter(Counter adaptee) {
    this.adaptee = adaptee;
  }

  public void actionPerformed(ActionEvent e) {
    adaptee.button3_actionPerformed(e);
  }
}
```

This skill only scratches the surface of what is possible with serialization in Java. It's an important skill to grasp when creating new beans. The *Mastering JavaBeans* book from Sybex describes some of the more advanced serialization topics. However, this skill describes what is sufficient for most capabilities.

Together with the last three skills, you should now be able to create some pretty nifty beans with lots of properties and events that can be customized and serialized. In the next skill, we'll look at JBuilder's Beans Express to automate some of the tasks we just learned about.

Are You Experienced?

Now you can...

- ☑ describe the serialization process
- ☑ save and restart classes, retaining state information beyond the user interface
- ☑ work with *ObjectInputStream* and *ObjectOutputStream*
- ☑ override the default object behavior for saving and restoring

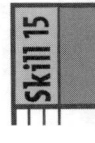

PROGRAMMING

C, C, VB, Cobol, exp. Call 534-555-6543 or fax 534-555-6544.

PROGRAMMING
MRFS Inc. is looking for a Sr. Windows NT developer. Reqs. 3-5 yrs. Exp. In C under Windows, Win95 & NT, using Visual C. Excl. OO design & implementation skills a must. OLE2 & ODBC are a plus. Excl. Salary & bnfts. Resume & salary history to HR, 8779 HighTech Way, Computer City, AR

PROGRAMMERS
Contractors Wanted for short & long term assignments: Visual C, MFC Unix C/C, SQL Oracle Developers PC Help Desk Support Windows NT & NetWareTelecommunications Visual Basic, Access, HTMT, CGI, Perl MMI & Co.. 885-555-9933

PROGRAMMER
World Wide Web Links wants your HTML & Photoshop skills. Develop great WWW sites. Local & global customers. Send samples & resume to WWWL, 2000 Apple Road, Santa Rosa, CA.

TECHNICAL WRITER
Software firm seeks writer/editor for manuals, research notes, project mgmt. Min 2 years tech. writing, DTP & programming experience. Send resume & writing samples to: Software Systems, Dallas, TX.

TECHNICAL
Software development firm looking for Tech Trainers. Ideal candidates have programming experience in Visual C, HTML & JAVA. Need quick self starter. Call (443) 555-6868 for interview.

TECHNICAL WRITER/
Premier Computer Corp is seeking a combination of technical skills, knowledge and experience in the following areas: UNIX, Windows 95/NT, Visual Basic, on-line help & documentation, and the internet. Candidates must possess excellent writing skills, and be comfortable working in a quality vs. deadline driven environment. Competitive salary. Fax resume & samples to Karen Fields, Premier Computer Corp. 444 Industrial Blvd. Concord, CA. Or send to our website at www.premier.com.

---

ing tools. Experienced in documentation preparation & programming languages (Access, C, FoxPro) are a plus. financial or banking customer service support is required along with excellent verbal & written communication skills with multi levels of end-users. Send resume to KKUP Enterprises, 45 Orange Blvd. Orange, CA.

COMPUTERS
Small Web Design firm seeks indiv. w/NT, Webserver & Database management exp. Fax resume to 556-555-4221.

COMPUTER/
Visual C/C, Visual Basic Exp'd Systems Analysts/ Programmers for growing software dev. team in Roseburg. Computer Science or related degree preferred. Develop adv. Engineering applications for engineering firm. Fax resume to 707-555-8744.

COMPUTER
Web Master for dynamic SF Internet co. Site. Dev. test, coord, train. 2 yrs prog. Exp. C C, Web C, FTP. Fax resume to Best Staffing 845-555-7722.

COMPUTER PROGRAMMER

Ad agency seeks programmer w/exp. in UNIX/NT Platforms. Web Server. CGI/Perl. Programmer Position avail. on a project basis with the possibility to move into F/T. Fax resume & salary req. to R. Jones 334-555-8332.

COMPUTERS
Programmer/Analyst Design and maintain C based SQL database applications. Required skills: Visual Basic, C, SQL, ODBC. Document existing and new applications, Novell or NT exp. a plus. Fax resume & salary history to 235-555-9935.

GRAPHIC DESIGNER
Webmaster's Weekly is seeking a creative Graphic Designer to design high impact marketing collateral, including direct mail promo's, CD-ROM packages, ads and WWW pages. Must be able to juggle multiple projects and learn new skills on the job very rapidly. Web design experience a big plus, technical troubleshooting also a plus. Call 435-555-1235.

GRAPHICS - ART DIRECTOR - WEB-MULTIMEDIA
Leading internet development company has an outstanding opportunity for a talented, high-end Web Experienced Art Director. In addition to a great portfolio and fresh ideas, the ideal candidate has excellent communication and presentation skills. Working as a team with innovative producers and programmers, you will create dynamic, interactive web sites and application interfaces. Some programming experience required. Send samples and resume to: SuperSites, 333 Main, Seattle WA.

MARKETING
Fast paced software and services provider looking for MARKETING COMMUNICATIONS SPECIALIST to be responsible for its webpage. seminar coordination and ad place-

---

PROGRAMMERS
Multiple short term assignments available: Visual C. 3 positions SQL ServerNT Server. 2 positions JAVA & HTML, long term NetWare Various locations. Call for more info. 356-555-3398.

PROGRAMMERS
C, C, VB, Cobol, exp.
Call 534-555-6543
or fax 534-555-6544

PROGRAMMING
MRFS Inc. is looking for a Sr. Windows NT developer. Reqs. 3-5 yrs. Exp. In C under Windows, Win95 & NT. using Visual C. Excl. OO design & implementationskills a must. OLE2 & ODBC are a plus. Excl. Salary & bnfts, Resume & salary history to HR, 8779 HighTech Way, Computer City, AR

PROGRAMMERS/
Contractors Wanted for short & long term assignments: Visual C, MFC Unix C/C, SQL Oracle Developers PC Help Desk Support Windows NT & NetWareTelecommunications Visual Basic, Access, HTMT, CGI, Perl MMI & Co., 885-555-9933

PROGRAMMER
World Wide Web Links wants your HTML & Photoshop skills. Develop great WWW sites. Local & global customers. Send samples & resume to WWWL, 2000 Apple Road, Santa Rosa, CA.

TECHNICAL WRITER
Software firm seeks writer/editor for manuals, research notes, project mgmt. Min 2 years tech. writing, DTP & programming experience. Send resume & writing samples to: Software Systems, Dallas, TX.

COMPUTER PROGRAMMER

Ad agency seeks programmer w/exp. in UNIX/NT Platforms, Web Server, CGI/Perl. Programmer Position avail. on a project basis with the possibility to move into F/T. fax resume & salary req. to R. Jones 334-555-8332.

TECHNICAL WRITER
Premier Computer Corp is seeking a combination of technical skills, knowledge and experience in the following areas: UNIX, Windows 95/NT, Visual Basic, on-line help & documentation, and the internet. Candidates must possess excellent writing skills, and be comfortable working in a quality vs. deadline driven environment. Competitive salary. Fax resume & samples to Karen Fields, Premier Computer Corp. 444 Industrial Blvd. Concord, CA. Or send to our website at www.premier.com.

WEB DESIGNER
BA/BS or equivalent programming/multimedia production. 3 years of experience in use and design of WWW services streaming audio and video HTML, PERL, CGI, GIF, JPEG. Demonstrated interpersonal, organization, communication, multi-tasking skills. Send resume to: The Learning People at www.learning.com

WEBMASTER-TECHNICAL
BSCS or equivalent, 2 years of experience in CGI, Windows 95/NT,

---

COMPUTERS
Small Web Design Firm seeks indiv. w/NT, Webserver & Database management exp. fax resume to 556-555-4221.

COMPUTER
Visual C/C. Visual Basic Exp'd Systems Analysts/ Programmers for growing software dev. team in Roseburg. Computer Science or related degree preferred. Develop adv. Engineering applications for engineering firm. Fax resume to 707-555-8744.

COMPUTER
Web Master for dynamic SF Internet co. Site. Dev. test, coord., train. 2 yrs prog. Exp. C C, Web C, FTP. Fax resume to Best Staffing 845-555-7722.

COMPUTERS/ QA SOFTWARE TESTERS
Qualified candidates should have 2 yrs exp. performing integration & system testing using automated testing tools. Experienced in documentation preparation & programming languages (Access, C, FoxPro) are a plus. Financial or banking customer service support is required along with excellent verbal & written communication skills with multi levels of end-users. Send resume to KKUP Enterprises, 45 Orange Blvd. Orange, CA.

COMPUTERS
Programmer/Analyst Design and maintain C based SQL database applications. Required skills: Visual Basic, C, SQL, ODBC. Document existing and new applications. Novell or NT exp. a plus. Fax resume & salary history to 235-555-9935.

GRAPHIC DESIGNER
Webmaster's Weekly is seeking a creative Graphic Designer to design high impact marketing collateral, including direct mail promo's, CD-ROM packages, ads and WWW pages. Must be able to juggle multiple projects and learn new skills on the job very rapidly. Web design experience a big plus, technical troubleshooting also a plus. Call 435-555-1235.

GRAPHICS - ART DIRECTOR - WEB-MULTIMEDIA
Leading Internet development company has an outstanding opportunity for a talented, high-end Web Experienced Art Director. In addition to a great portfolio and fresh ideas, the ideal candidate has excellent communication and presentation skills. Working as a team with innovative producers and programmers, you will create dynamic, interactive web sites and application interfaces. Some programming experience required. Send samples and resume to: SuperSites, 333 Main, Seattle, WA.

COMPUTER PROGRAMMER
Ad agency seeks programmer w/exp. in UNIX/NT Platforms, Web Server, CGI/Perl. Programmer Position avail. on a project basis with the possibility to move into F/T. Fax resume & salary req. to R. Jones 334-555-8332.

PROGRAMMERS / Established
software company seeks program-

PROGRAMMERS
Multiple sh term assignments available: Vis C. 3 positions SQL ServerNT Ser 2 positions JAVA & HTML, long te NetWare Various locations. Call more info. 356-555-3398.

PROGRAMMERS
C, C, VB, Cobol, exp. Call 534-5 6543 or fax 534-555-6544.

PROGRAMMING
MRFS Inc. is looking for a Windows NT developer. Reqs. yrs. Exp. In C under Windo Win95 & NT. using Visual C. OO design & implementation s a must. OLE2 & ODBC are a Excl. Salary & bnfts. Resume salary history to HR, 8779 High Way, Computer City, AR

PROGRAMMERS/ Contrac
Wanted for short & long term as ments: Visual C, MFCUnix C/C, Oracle Developers PC Help D Support Windows NT & Netw Telecommunications Visual B Access, HTMT, CGI, Perl MMI & 885-555-9933

PROGRAMMER
World Wide Links wants your HTML & Photos skills. Develop great WWW Local & global customers. Send ples & resume to WWWL, Apple Road, Santa Rosa, CA.

TECHNICAL WRITER
Software seeks writer/editor for man research notes, project mgmt. M years tech. writing, DTP & prog ming experience. Send resume writing samples to: Soft Systems, Dallas, TX.

TECHNICAL
Software develop firm looking for Tech Trainers, candidates have programming e rience in Visual C, HTML & Need quick self starter. Call 555-6868 for interview.

TECHNICAL WRITER
Pre Computer Corp is seeking a co nation of technical skills, know and experience in the folio areas: UNIX, Windows 95/NT, Basic, on-line help & document and the internet. Candidates possess excellent writing skills be comfortable working in a q vs. deadline driven environ Competitive salary. Fax resu samples to Karen Fields, Pr Computer Corp. 444 Industrial Concord, CA. Or send to our w at www.premier.com.

WEB DESIGNER
BA/BS or equivalent prog ming/multimedia productio years of experience in use design of WWW services str audio and video HTML, PERL GIF, JPEG. Demonstrated int sonal, organization, communi multi-tasking skills. Send resu The Learning People at www ing.com

WEBMASTER-TECHNI

SKILL 16

sixteen

Using the BeansExpress Wizards

- ❑ Using BeansExpress
- ❑ Looking at the `OkCancelBean`
- ❑ Creating new beans with the New Bean Wizard
- ❑ Creating new bean events with the New Bean Event Wizard
- ❑ Creating `BeanInfo` with the Bean Info Wizard

Learning about BeansExpress

BeansExpress is part of JBuilder Professional. It adds a new tab to the Object Gallery (File ➤ New) that presents five Wizards. Two of the Wizards, OK Cancel Bean and DB Bean, offer complete sample beans that you can examine. The other three, New Bean, Bean Info, and New Event Bean, help you create new beans. In this skill, we'll look at the OK Cancel Bean Wizard and the three Wizards used to create new beans. Since the last four skills looked at the various parts of beans—Properties/Events, Customization, Introspection, and Persistence—this skill concentrates on the specifics of the BeansExpress Wizards.

Examining the *OKCancelBean*

The OkCancelBean demonstrates how to properly create *compound* bean components for use within JBuilder. By compound, we mean beans that contain other beans, where you add the combined object to the component palette. Although the OkCancelBean contains something special to function properly within JBuilder's UI Designer, the bean will work properly within other tools, provided the necessary Java class files are available.

To show what we mean here, let's create an OkCancelBean, and place it on the Component palette. Before creating it, close any open projects and run the Project Wizard. Enter the project file as **c:\skills\skill16\skill16.jpr** and select Finish. To create the bean's source, select File ➤ New ➤ the BeansExpress tab ➤ OK Cancel Bean ➤ OK. This adds OkCancelBean.java to the project with the following source (without the initial comments):

OkCancelBean.java

```java
package skill16;

import java.awt.*;
import java.awt.event.*;
import borland.jbcl.layout.*;
import borland.jbcl.control.*;
import borland.jbcl.view.*;
import borland.jbcl.util.BlackBox;

public class OkCancelBean extends BeanPanel implements BlackBox{
  // Use these constants in the event listener.
  public final static String OK_EVENT = "OkEvent";
```

```java
public final static String CANCEL_EVENT = "CancelEvent";
public final static String HELP_EVENT = "HelpEvent";

private BorderLayout borderLayout1 = new BorderLayout();
private Panel panel1 = new Panel();
private FlowLayout flowLayout1 = new FlowLayout();
private Button ok = new Button();
private Button cancel = new Button();
private Button help = new Button();

public OkCancelBean() {
  try {
    jbInit();
  }
  catch (Exception e) {
    e.printStackTrace();
  }
}

public void jbInit() throws Exception{
  ok.setLabel("   OK   ");
  ok.addActionListener(new OkCancelBean_ok_actionAdapter(this));
  cancel.setLabel("Cancel");
  cancel.addActionListener(new OkCancelBean_cancel_actionAdapter(this));
  help.setLabel(" Help ");
  help.addActionListener(new OkCancelBean_help_actionAdapter(this));
  panel1.setLayout(flowLayout1);
  this.setLayout(borderLayout1);
  this.add(panel1, BorderLayout.CENTER);
  panel1.add(ok, null);
  panel1.add(cancel, null);
  panel1.add(help, null);
}

// The action listener for this bean should check the ActionEvent
// to determine which button was pressed.
// The Help button could be handled entirely inside this bean
// if desired.
void ok_actionPerformed(ActionEvent e) {
  //Args: event source,event ID, event command
  processActionEvent(new ActionEvent(this,ActionEvent.ACTION_PERFORMED,OK_EVENT));
}
void cancel_actionPerformed(ActionEvent e) {
  processActionEvent(new ActionEvent(this,ActionEvent.ACTION_PERFORMED,CANCEL_EVENT));
}
```

```java
    void help_actionPerformed(ActionEvent e) {
      processActionEvent(new ActionEvent(this,ActionEvent.ACTION_PERFORMED,HELP_EVENT));
    }
}

class OkCancelBean_ok_actionAdapter implements java.awt.event.ActionListener {
  OkCancelBean adaptee;

  OkCancelBean_ok_actionAdapter(OkCancelBean adaptee) {
    this.adaptee = adaptee;
  }

  public void actionPerformed(ActionEvent e) {
    adaptee.ok_actionPerformed(e);
  }
}

class OkCancelBean_cancel_actionAdapter implements java.awt.event.ActionListener {
  OkCancelBean adaptee;

  OkCancelBean_cancel_actionAdapter(OkCancelBean adaptee) {
    this.adaptee = adaptee;
  }

  public void actionPerformed(ActionEvent e) {
    adaptee.cancel_actionPerformed(e);
  }
}

class OkCancelBean_help_actionAdapter implements java.awt.event.ActionListener {
  OkCancelBean adaptee;

  OkCancelBean_help_actionAdapter(OkCancelBean adaptee) {
    this.adaptee = adaptee;
  }

  public void actionPerformed(ActionEvent e) {
    adaptee.help_actionPerformed(e);
  }
}
```

The OK Cancel Bean is a panel with three buttons on it: OK, Cancel, and Help. Within the UI Designer, the panel looks like Figure 16.1.

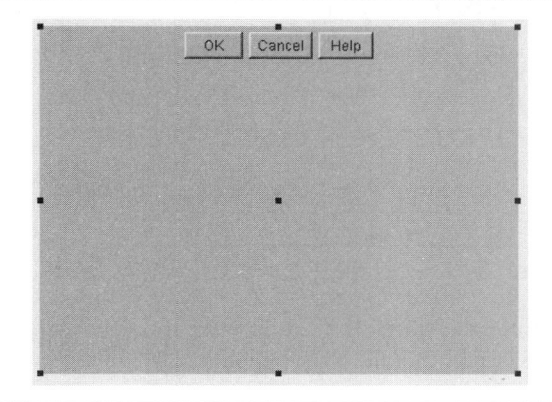

FIGURE 16.1: Showing off the OkCancelBean in the UI Designer

There are three things to notice in the source code though:

- The bean extends `BeanPanel`. When you create a bean with multiple sub-components within it, you need to group them together somehow. Using `java.awt.Panel` is the natural way; however, Borland improved on this somewhat and created `borland.jbcl.view.BeanPanel`. It does some internal management of events that makes your life easier.

- After registering an action listener with the `OkCancelBean`, the bean will send notification if any of the buttons are selected. The other thing that `BeanPanel` does is maintain the action listener list for you. This means all the components within it share the event listener list and if you are only interested in one of the buttons being selected, you have to test to see which one generated the event.

- The bean implements `BlackBox`. The `borland.jbcl.util.BlackBox` interface is like `java.io.Serializable`. There are no methods to it, and its only purpose is to notify the tool to exhibit a particular behavior when appropriate. Unlike `Serializable`, `BlackBox` is a JBuilder specific behavior. Someone else using the bean in a different tool may or may not exhibit the same behavior. So what is that behavior? Well, when the bean is used in the UI Designer, it acts as a single object. You would not be able to add additional beans to this bean. You can only interact with the object, `BeanPanel` in this case, as a whole.

Adding the Bean to the Palette

At this point, save and compile the class. Once that has completed, add the bean to the Component palette. To do all this, follow these steps:

1. Select File ➤ Save All.
2. Select Build ➤ Make "OkCancelBean.java".
3. Select Tools ➤ Configure Palette.
4. Choose the Add from Package tab.
5. Click the Browse button, select `myclasses\skill16\OkCancelBean.class`, and then click the OK button.
6. Select `skill16.OkCancelBean` in the JavaBeans Found in Package list.
7. Select Other from the Add Component to Page pull-down list.
8. Click the Install button and then the OK button.

The `OkCancelBean` should now be on the Other tab of the Component palette.

Using the *OkCancelBean*

To test this out, let's create an application with the Application Wizard. Staying in the skill16 package, run the Application Wizard, enter a Frame class name of **OkTester**, and then select Finish. To drop the bean into the program, select `OkTester.java` in the Navigation pane and the Design tab at the bottom of the Contents page. Then, select the Other tab on the Component palette before selecting `OkCancelBean`, and dropping it into the screen. Now, your design screen should look like Figure 16.2.

In Figure 16.2, you'll notice that the entire `OkCancelBean` area is selected. To demonstrate the difference in implementing the `BlackBox` interface, let's remove the clause from the class. Select `OkCancelBean.java` in the Navigation pane and `BlackBox` in the Structure pane. This moves the source to the appropriate line. Place `implements BlackBox` within `/* */` comment tags like so:

```
public class OkCancelBean extends BeanPanel /* implements BlackBox */ {
```

Then save and recompile the class, by selecting File ➤ Save All and Build ➤ Make "OkCancelBean.java".

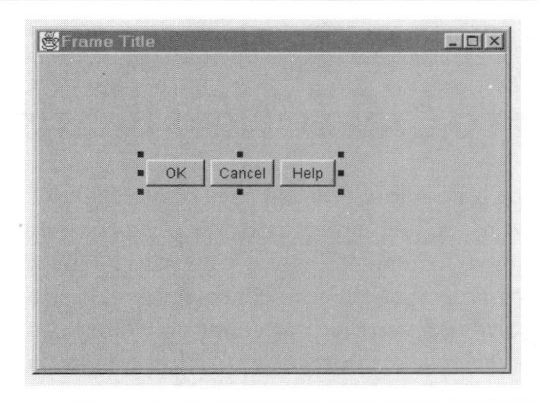

FIGURE 16.2: The OkCancelBean within a frame when OkCancelBean implements BlackBox

To see the new behavior of OkCancelBean within the UI Designer, you need to exit out of JBuilder and restart it. Because JBuilder automatically reopens the last opened project, the work to see the new behavior is minimal. Just go back to the UI Designer for OkTester.java and select the OkCancelBean. Some changes you'll notice are the Inspector allows you to change the layout constraint and you can drop additional beans into the OkCancelBean. Figure 16.3 shows the results of dropping the BlackBox interface, changing the layout to GridLayout, and adding two more buttons.

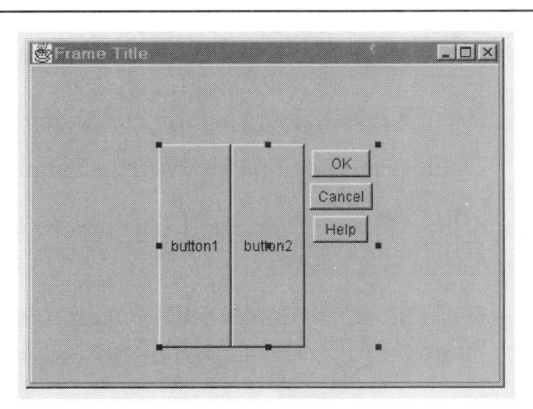

FIGURE 16.3: The OkCancelBean without implementing the BlackBox interface

At this point, you can either fix the OkCancelBean so it implements BlackBox again, or if you don't plan on using it, remove it from the Component palette.

Working to Create New Beans and Bean Events

Besides providing an example of the complete bean, BeansExpress offers three Wizards to help you create new beans or the pieces necessary for them. The bean we'll create will have a Yes and No button. When the Yes button is selected, a yes-type YesNoEvent will be generated. When the No button is selected, a no-type YesNoEvent will be generated. Our bean will also extend the BeanPanel class because BeanPanel already manages the ActionEvent type. Lastly, we'll add a BeanInfo support class that designates an icon to display when the bean is on the Component palette. After creating the bean, we'll place it on the Component palette and use it in a program.

Using the New Bean Wizard

The first thing we need to do is create the new bean. We'll keep it in the skill16 package we're currently working in. In the last four skills, we created the new bean by hand. Here we'll use the New Bean Wizard in BeansExpress. Select File ➤ New, the BeansExpress tab, and double-click on New Bean. This adds the file NewBean.java to the Navigation pane.

The Wizard doesn't prompt for a bean name, so you have to manually change it after creating it. To rename the bean, you have to rename the file and replace any reference to the class name, NewBean, within it. To rename the file:

1. Select NewBean.java in the Navigation pane.
2. Select File ➤ Rename to bring up the Save As dialog box.
3. Enter **YesNoBean.java** in the File Name text box.
4. Select the Save button.

To rename the class:

1. Select Search ➤ Replace to bring up the Replace Text dialog box, seen in Figure 16.4.

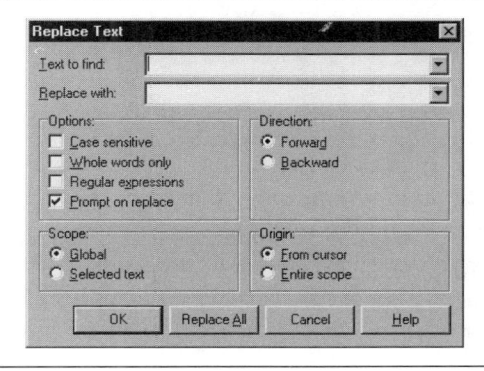

FIGURE 16.4: The Replace Text dialog box, where you can perform search and replace operations

2. In the Text to Find text box, enter **NewBean**.
3. In the Replace with text box, enter **YesNoBean**.
4. Make sure Prompt on Replace and Global are selected in the Replace Text dialog box.
5. Select Replace All. Because Prompt to Replace is selected, you are prompted at each occurrence to change NewBean:
   - At public class NewBean..., select Yes to replace.
   - At the constructor public NewBean(), select Yes to replace.

As with the OkCancelBean, this class subclasses BeanPanel and implements BlackBox. That means that we can use the UI Designer to add components to the bean; however, users of the bean will not be able to modify the content. To add our Yes and No buttons to the bean, go into the design mode for the class and add two buttons:

1. Select the Design tab at the bottom of the Contents pane.
2. Select bevelPanel1 (XYLayout) in the Structure pane.
3. Change the layout property to FlowLayout as this will size and position the buttons more effectively.
4. Select the AWT tab on the Component palette.
5. Select the Button bean and place two of them within the panel.

6. Select the button on the left and change the <name> property to yes and the label property to Yes.

7. Select the other button on the right and change its <name> property to no and the label property to No.

Visually, our bean is done, so you should save it now; however, before we can add the event handling, we need to create the appropriate event classes. Also, if you look in the bean source, you'll notice a property named example. We're not going to worry about bean properties in this skill, as there is no special support for them in BeansExpress. Review Skill 12 for information on working with properties though. Let's move on to creating the event classes.

Using the New Bean Event Wizard

Now that we have the basic bean, we should create the events for selecting the Yes and No buttons. Selecting File ➤ New ➤ BeansExpress Tab ➤ New Event Bean, and then OK brings up the Paste Snippet dialog box, shown in Figure 16.5, where you configure the new event. Enter **YesNoEvent** in the Your Class field and select OK.

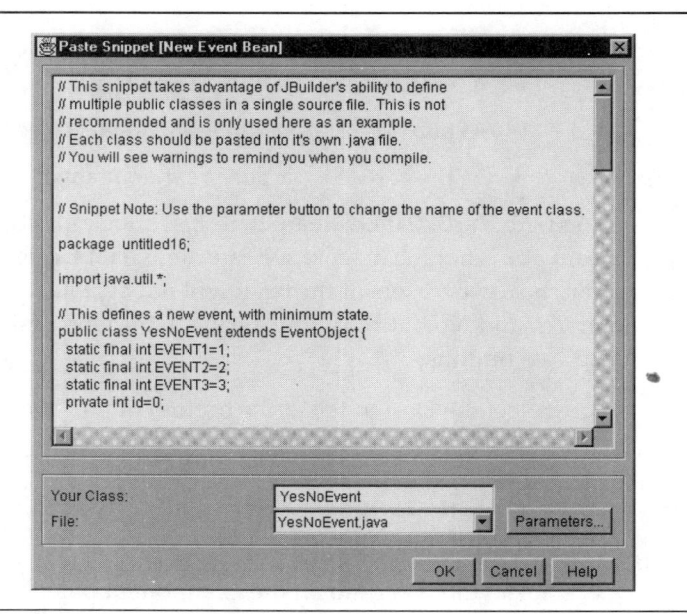

FIGURE 16.5: The Paste Snippet dialog box for the New Event Bean BeansExpress Wizard

This adds a new file, `YesNoEvent.java`, to the Navigation pane. However, within this file, we need to move several pieces around. The first thing we'll move is the `YesNoEventListener`. Every event type needs to have a listener interface. The interface describes what methods the listener class needs to implement in order to be notified when the event happens. The New Event Bean Wizard creates an initial listener class, but we need to move it into its own file and define our own method names.

To move the `YesNoEventListener` to its own file, you need to create an empty class file to place it in. To create the file, select File ➤ Open/Create. In the File Name field enter **YesNoEventListener.java**, and then select the Add to Project toggle on the bottom left, and select Open.

Once JBuilder creates the file, you need to copy the class definition from `YesNoEvent.java` into `YesNoEventListener.java`:

1. Select `YesNoEvent.java` in the Navigation pane.

2. Highlight the `YesNoEventListener` class description:

   ```
   // This defines a listener interface for the set of events that
   // are generated by YesNoEvent
   public interface YesNoEventListener extends EventListener {
     public void event1(YesNoEvent e);
     public void event2(YesNoEvent e);
     public void event3(YesNoEvent e);
   }
   ```

3. Select Edit ➤ Cut to place the contents on the clipboard.

4. Select `YesNoEventListener.java` to switch back to the original file.

5. Select Edit ➤ Paste to place the contents there.

6. Add these two lines to the top of the source code:

   ```
   package skill16;
   import java.util.*;
   ```

Once we've copied the contents over, we need to define the actual listener interface. An event listener interface is the set of methods that can be called when an event happens. In the case of the `YesNoEvent`, two things can cause the event to happen, so the interface should have only two methods. We'll call these methods **yesHappened** and **noHappened** and replace the three automatically generated methods. The following is a list of the final `YesNoEventListener.java` source.

YesNoEventListener.java

```
package skill16;
import java.util.*;

// This defines a listener interface for the set of events that
// are generated by YesNoEvent
public interface YesNoEventListener extends EventListener {
  public void yesHappened(YesNoEvent e);
  public void noHappened(YesNoEvent e);
}
```

Fixing Up *YesNoEventExampleBean*

The next thing to move around is YesNoEventExampleBean in YesNoEvent.java. This class contains the source code necessary for a class to listen for the event and to notify any listeners when the event happens. Since the YesNoBean serves as the event source for the YesNoEvent, we need to move part of the YesNoEventExampleBean class definition into the YesNoBean class definition, and then get rid of the rest.

In YesNoEvent.java, find the YesNoEventExampleBean definition at the bottom of the source. Highlight the entire class description and cut it out of the file with Edit ➤ Cut. Select the YesNoBean.java file and paste the source at the end of the source code with Edit ➤ Paste.

As with the YesNoEventListener, you need to fix a few things once you've copied the source. Delete the following:

- The closing } from the original class definition of YesNoBean
- The public class YesNoEventExampleBean line
- The YesNoEventExampleBean constructor
- The testYesNoEvent method

The code below shows the different lines that you are deleting:

```
}
// This is an example of a non-visual Bean that fires the new events
public class YesNoEventExampleBean {
  YesNoEventExampleBean() {
  }
  ...
// A test method to fire all 3 example events
```

```
public void testYesNoEvent () {
  processYesNoEvent (new YesNoEvent (this, YesNoEvent.EVENT1));
  processYesNoEvent (new YesNoEvent (this, YesNoEvent.EVENT2));
  processYesNoEvent (new YesNoEvent (this, YesNoEvent.EVENT3));
}
```

Now, there is one thing to add here; just as we did with `YesNoEventListener`, we need to import the `java.util` package. The class is already in the `skill16` package, so adding that line isn't necessary. Instead, add the following line where the other packages are imported:

```
import java.util.*;
```

Finishing Up the *YesNoEvent*

We'll make some more changes in `YesNoBean` soon, but for now, let's go back to `YesNoEvent.java` to finish things up there.

You'll notice there are three lines that declare EVENT1, EVENT2, and EVENT3. These are for the different states of the event. For us, we only need two of them, but instead of calling them EVENT1 and EVENT2, we'll name them YES and NO. So, replace these three lines:

```
static final int EVENT1=1;
static final int EVENT2=2;
static final int EVENT3=3;
```

with:

```
static final int YES=1;
static final int NO=2;
```

This actually is all there is to `YesNoEvent.java`. The final source for this is shown next.

YesNoEvent.java

```
package skill16;
import java.util.*;

// This defines a new event, with minimum state.
public class YesNoEvent extends EventObject {
  static final int YES=1;
  static final int NO=2;
  private int id=0;
```

```
    public int getID() {return id;};

    YesNoEvent(Object source,int i) {
      super(source);
      id=i;
      }
}
```

Finishing Up the *YesNoBean*

Now that we've wrapped up YesNoEventListener and the YesNoEvent, we can finalize the YesNoBean. Before we add any new code, let's fix up some old stuff. The processYesNoEvent method is for processing each state of the event. Because we've changed the three states to two states, we need to change this method. Basically, just delete the handling for EVENT3 and rename the case tag for EVENT1 to **YES** and EVENT2 to **NO**. Also, change the method called from event1 to the method in YesNoEventListener, **yesHappened**, and from event2, **noHappened**. This results in the following method definition for processYesNoEvent:

```
    protected void processYesNoEvent(YesNoEvent e) {
      switch (e.getID()) {
        case YesNoEvent.YES:
          for (int i=0; i<listenerList.size(); i++)
            //Send event to all registered listeners
            ((YesNoEventListener)listenerList.elementAt(i)).yesHappened(e);
          break;
        case YesNoEvent.NO:
          for (int i=0; i<listenerList.size(); i++)
            //Send event to all registered listeners
            ((YesNoEventListener)listenerList.elementAt(i)).noHappened(e);
          break;
      }
    }
```

Now we can modify the event firing code placed there by the New Bean Wizard:

```
public static final String EXAMPLE_EVENT = "ExampleEvent";
protected void fireExampleActionEvent() {
  //Args:  event source,event ID, event command
  processActionEvent(new ActionEvent(this,ActionEvent.ACTION_PERFORMED, EXAMPLE_EVENT));
}
```

We should now change the EXAMPLE_EVENT variable name to **YES_EVENT**, with a setting of **"Yes"** and add a **NO_EVENT** with a setting of **"No"**.

```
    public static final String YES_EVENT = "Yes";
    public static final String NO_EVENT  = "No";
```

Then, we should change `fireExampleActionEvent` to both fire action events and yes and/or no events, which was our original goal. We'll actually make this two methods, one for each:

```
protected void fireYesEvents() {
  //Args:   event source,event ID, event command
  processActionEvent(new ActionEvent(this, ActionEvent.ACTION_PERFORMED, YES_EVENT));
  processYesNoEvent(new YesNoEvent(this, YesNoEvent.YES));
}
protected void fireNoEvents() {
  //Args:   event source,event ID, event command
  processActionEvent(new ActionEvent(this, ActionEvent.ACTION_PERFORMED, NO_EVENT));
  processYesNoEvent (new YesNoEvent(this, YesNoEvent.NO));
}
```

Once you've added these two methods and deleted `fireExampleActionEvent`, we can hook up the event firing to the buttons. Before switching over to the UI Designer, you should compile everything first to make sure you made no errors. Double-click the Yes button to add the `yes_actionPerformed` method. Have it call **fireYesEvents()**. For the No button, double-click and have `no_actionPerformed` call **fireNoEvents()**.

At this point, save everything and recompile. The bean is complete and the source for `YesNoBean` follows.

YesNoBean.java

```
package  skill16;

import java.awt.*;
import java.awt.event.*;
import java.util.*;
import borland.jbcl.layout.*;
import borland.jbcl.control.*;
import borland.jbcl.view.*;
import borland.jbcl.util.BlackBox;

public class YesNoBean extends BeanPanel implements BlackBox{
  BevelPanel bevelPanel1 = new BevelPanel();
  BorderLayout borderLayout1 = new BorderLayout();

  public YesNoBean() {
    try {
      jbInit();
    }
    catch (Exception e) {
```

```java
      e.printStackTrace();
  }
}

public void jbInit() throws Exception{
  yes.setActionCommand("yes");
  yes.addActionListener(new YesNoBean_yes_actionAdapter(this));
  yes.setLabel("Yes");
  no.setActionCommand("no");
  no.addActionListener(new YesNoBean_no_actionAdapter(this));
  no.setLabel("No");
  bevelPanel1.setLayout(flowLayout1);
  this.setLayout(borderLayout1);
  this.add(bevelPanel1, BorderLayout.CENTER);
  bevelPanel1.add(yes, null);
  bevelPanel1.add(no, null);
}

// Example properties
private String example = "Example1";

public void setExample(String s) {
  example=s;
}
public String getExample(){
  return example;
}

// Example event
public static final String YES_EVENT = "Yes";
public static final String NO_EVENT  = "No";
FlowLayout flowLayout1 = new FlowLayout();
Button yes = new Button();
Button no = new Button();
protected void fireYesEvents() {
  //Args:   event source,event ID, event command
  processActionEvent(new ActionEvent(this, ActionEvent.ACTION_PERFORMED, YES_EVENT));
  processYesNoEvent(new YesNoEvent(this, YesNoEvent.YES));
}
protected void fireNoEvents() {
  //Args:   event source,event ID, event command
  processActionEvent(new ActionEvent(this, ActionEvent.ACTION_PERFORMED, NO_EVENT));
  processYesNoEvent (new YesNoEvent(this, YesNoEvent.NO));
}

// The add/remove methods provide the signature for the IDE to recognize
// these events and show them in the event list
public synchronized void addYesNoEventListener(YesNoEventListener l) {
```

```
    listenerList.addElement(l);
  }
  public synchronized void removeYesNoEventListener(YesNoEventListener l){
    listenerList.removeElement(l);
  }

  // A single process method keeps all event dispatching in one place.
  // Separate processEVENT1, processEVENT2, etc methods could also be used.
  protected void processYesNoEvent(YesNoEvent e) {
    switch (e.getID()) {
      case YesNoEvent.YES:
        for (int i=0; i<listenerList.size(); i++)
          //Send event to all registered listeners
          ((YesNoEventListener)listenerList.elementAt(i)).yesHappened(e);
        break;
      case YesNoEvent.NO:
        for (int i=0; i<listenerList.size(); i++)
          //Send event to all registered listeners
          ((YesNoEventListener)listenerList.elementAt(i)).noHappened(e);
        break;
    }
  }

  private Vector listenerList = new Vector();

  void yes_actionPerformed(ActionEvent e) {
    fireYesEvents();
  }

  void no_actionPerformed(ActionEvent e) {
    fireNoEvents();
  }
}

class YesNoBean_yes_actionAdapter implements java.awt.event.ActionListener {
  YesNoBean adaptee;

  YesNoBean_yes_actionAdapter(YesNoBean adaptee) {
    this.adaptee = adaptee;
  }

  public void actionPerformed(ActionEvent e) {
    adaptee.yes_actionPerformed(e);
  }
}

class YesNoBean_no_actionAdapter implements java.awt.event.ActionListener {
  YesNoBean adaptee;
```

```
YesNoBean_no_actionAdapter(YesNoBean adaptee) {
    this.adaptee = adaptee;
  }

  public void actionPerformed(ActionEvent e) {
    adaptee.no_actionPerformed(e);
  }
}
```

Testing Out the *YesNoBean*

Now that the YesNoBean is complete, you should add it to the Component palette. Follow these steps:

1. Select Tools ➤ Configure Palette.
2. Select the Add from Package tab.
3. Select the Browse button.
4. Select myclasses\skill16\YesNoBean.class.
5. Select skill16.YesNoBean from the list of beans in the package.
6. Select Other from the Add Component to Page pull-down list.
7. Select the Install button.
8. Select OK for the bean to be installed.

To use the YesNoBean, return to the OkTester.java entry in the Navigation pane. Delete the OkCancelBean it currently uses and drop in a YesNoBean. Here's how:

1. Select the Design tab at the bottom of the Contents pane.
2. Select the OkCancelBean on the screen.
3. Press the **Del** key to delete it.
4. Select the Other tab on the Component palette.
5. Select the YesNoBean and place it into the frame.

The design area will now look like Figure 16.6.

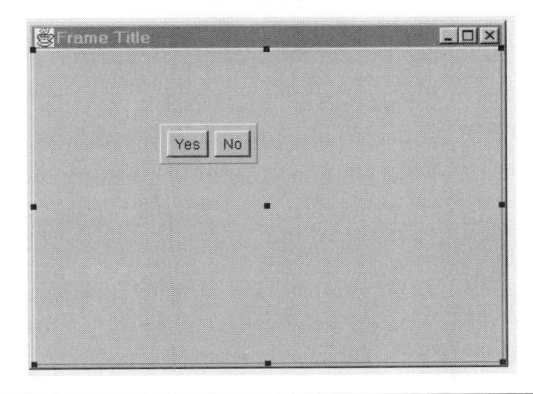

FIGURE 16.6: The design area of OkTester with a YesNoBean added

If you look in the Events tab of the Inspector window for the YesNoBean, you'll notice the two YesNoEventListener methods included—yesHappened and noHappened, as shown in Figure 16.7.

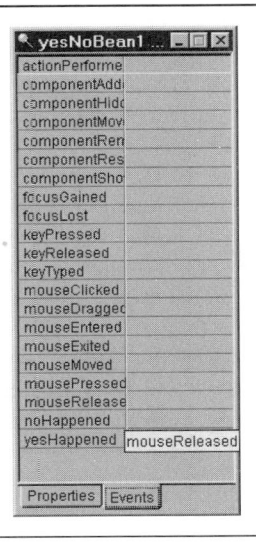

FIGURE 16.7: The Events tab of YesNoBean Inspector

Now, to actually have the `OkTester` do something, we should add an appropriate `System.out.println` statement to the `actionPerformed`, `yesHappened`, and `noHappened` events. Double-click in each entry in the Inspector's window and add an appropriate `System.out.println` statement that shows which method you are in:

```
void yesNoBean1_actionPerformed(ActionEvent e) {
  System.out.println ("Action Event");
}

void yesNoBean1_noHappened(YesNoEvent e) {
  System.out.println ("No Event");
}

void yesNoBean1_yesHappened(YesNoEvent e) {
  System.out.println ("Yes Event");
}
```

Now if you save, compile, and run the program, you can select the different buttons to print the messages. If you then look in the Console Window, you'll see that both the `ActionEvent` and `YesNoEvent` events are generated for each button with the appropriate listener methods getting called. The final `OkTester.java` source follows.

OkTester.java

```
package skill16;

import java.awt.*;
import java.awt.event.*;
import borland.jbcl.control.*;
import borland.jbcl.layout.*;
import skill16.*;

public class OkTester extends DecoratedFrame {
  BorderLayout borderLayout1 = new BorderLayout();
  XYLayout xYLayout2 = new XYLayout();
  BevelPanel bevelPanel1 = new BevelPanel();
  YesNoBean yesNoBean1 = new YesNoBean();

  //Construct the frame
  public OkTester() {
    try {
      jbInit();
    }
```

```
      catch (Exception e) {
        e.printStackTrace();
      }
    }

    //Component initialization
    public void jbInit() throws Exception{
      this.setLayout(borderLayout1);
      this.setSize(new Dimension(400, 300));
      this.setTitle("Frame Title");
      yesNoBean1.addYesNoEventListener(new OkTester_yesNoBean1_yesNoEventAdapter(this));
      yesNoBean1.addActionListener(new OkTester_yesNoBean1_actionAdapter(this));
      bevelPanel1.setLayout(xYLayout2);
      this.add(bevelPanel1, BorderLayout.CENTER);
      bevelPanel1.add(yesNoBean1, new XYConstraints(105, 64, -1, -1));
    }

    void yesNoBean1_actionPerformed(ActionEvent e) {
      System.out.println ("Action Event");
    }

    void yesNoBean1_noHappened(YesNoEvent e) {
      System.out.println ("No Event");
    }

    void yesNoBean1_yesHappened(YesNoEvent e) {
      System.out.println ("Yes Event");
    }
}

class OkTester_yesNoBean1_actionAdapter implements java.awt.event.ActionListener{
  OkTester adaptee;

  OkTester_yesNoBean1_actionAdapter(OkTester adaptee) {
    this.adaptee = adaptee;
  }

  public void actionPerformed(ActionEvent e) {
    adaptee.yesNoBean1_actionPerformed(e);
  }
}

class OkTester_yesNoBean1_yesNoEventAdapter implements skill16.YesNoEventListener{
  OkTester adaptee;
```

```
  OkTester_yesNoBean1_yesNoEventAdapter(OkTester adaptee) {
    this.adaptee = adaptee;
  }

  public void noHappened(YesNoEvent e) {
    adaptee.yesNoBean1_noHappened(e);
  }

  public void yesHappened(YesNoEvent e) {
    adaptee.yesNoBean1_yesHappened(e);
  }
}
```

Adding *BeanInfo* to Display an Image

Now that we have a working bean, we can customize the bean by adding some `BeanInfo` to display an image on the Component palette. The Bean Info Wizard of BeansExpress assists here. If you double-click on the Wizard, the Paste Snippet [Bean Info] dialog box is displayed, as shown in Figure 16.8.

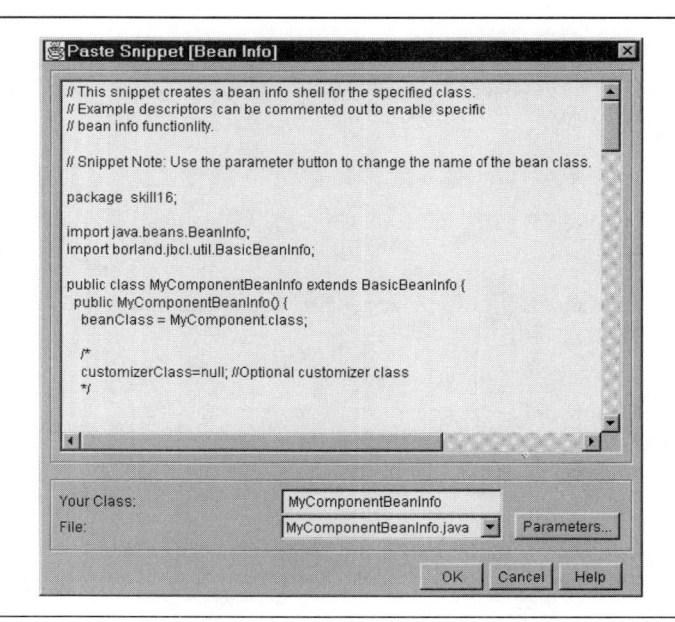

FIGURE 16.8: The initial dialog box shown after running the Bean Info Wizard of BeansExpress

Once this is displayed, you need to select the Parameters button to customize it. This shows the dialog box in Figure 16.9, which prompts for the name of the `BeanInfo` class and bean class. Enter **YesNoBeanBeanInfo** and **YesNoBean**, as shown, before selecting OK on both screens.

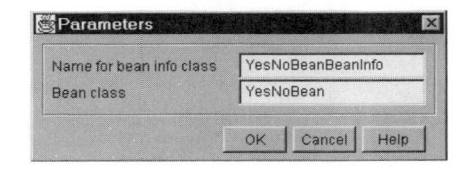

FIGURE 16.9: The Snippet's Parameters dialog box for the Bean Info Wizard

The source that this Wizard generates is initially full of comments. Similar to working with the `BeanInfo` in the earlier skills, you set an instance variable in the constructor and override some methods. JBuilder provides a `BasicBeanInfo` support class that does the actual overriding of the methods. It's your job to just set the appropriate instance variables within its constructor. Initially, most of the instance variables that you can set are commented out. There is one, `methodNames`, that should be, but isn't. You should find this line and comment it out by placing // at the beginning of it.

To set the icon for the bean on the Component palette, there are four variables at the very bottom of `YesNoBeanBeanInfo.java`: `iconColor16x16`, `iconColor32x32`, `iconMono16x16`, and `iconMono32x32`. You can provide a separate icon image for each or just pick one. If multiple icons are available, the size and color model that is chosen depends on the user's screen resolution. For this skill, we'll use a 32×32 image file that comes with JBuilder as our icon. The `C:\JBuilder\lib\image32` directory is where you will find the images for the JBuilder beans. We'll use the `blink.gif` file located there as our icon.

> **NOTE** Normally, we would use the `borland.jbcl.util.ImageLoader` class to load the image. However, a method doesn't seem to exist that will load an image without a `Component` subclass parameter. Since we are working in the `YesNoBeanBeanInfo` class, and not `YesNoBean`, we unfortunately cannot use `ImageLoader` to help in loading.

To have the `YesNoBean` show an icon image on the palette, set the `iconMono32x32` variable to an instance of `Image` for the `blink.gif` file. To load the file follow these steps:

1. Import the `java.net`, `java.io`, `java.awt`, and `java.awt.image` packages. Their support is necessary to load the image.

   ```
   import java.net.*;
   import java.io.*;
   import java.awt.*;
   import java.awt.image.*;
   ```

2. Use the following source to load the `blink.gif` file. Instead of copying the file out of the JBuilder directory, and putting it in the directory where the `YesNoBeanBeanInfo.class` file is, we are relying on where JBuilder keeps the images.

   ```
   try {
     URL url = getClass().getResource("../../lib/image32/blink.gif");
     Toolkit tk = Toolkit.getDefaultToolkit();
     iconColor32x32 = tk.createImage((ImageProducer) url.getContent());
   } catch (IOException ex) {
     iconColor32x32 = null;
   }
   ```

> **NOTE** The `Class.getResource` method looks for the file parameter relative to the class file location—`YesNoBeanBeanInfo.class` in this case. The `Toolkit.createImage` method creates the image from the contents of the URL. If the resource file isn't found, an `IOException` is thrown. If you copy `blink.gif` from `C:\JBuilder\lib\image32\blink.gif` to `C:\JBuilder\myclasses\skill16\blink.gif`, the getResource parameter would just be `blink.gif`. If we were to be delivering the YesNoBean to someone else, the image file should be relocated.

At this point, save everything and compile; use Build ➤ Rebuild Project "skill16.jpr" to ensure everything gets compiled. The completed bean info source follows:

YesNoBeanBeanInfo.java

```
package skill16;

import java.net.*;
import java.io.*;
import java.awt.*;
```

```java
import java.awt.image.*;
import java.beans.BeanInfo;
import borland.jbcl.util.BasicBeanInfo;

public class YesNoBeanBeanInfo extends BasicBeanInfo {
  public YesNoBeanBeanInfo() {
    beanClass = YesNoBean.class;

    /*
    customizerClass=null; //Optional customizer class
    */

    /**
     * The event information for your JavaBean.
     * Format:  {{"EventSetName", "EventListenerClass", "AddMethod",
     *     "RemoveMethod"}, ...}
     * Example: {{"ActionListener", "java.awt.event.ActionListener",
     *     "addActionListener", "removeActionListener"}, ...}
     */
    /*
    eventSetDescriptors = new String[][] {
      {"ActionListener", "java.awt.event.ActionListener", "addActionListener",
        "removeActionListener"},
    };
    */

    /**
     * The names of each event set's listener methods.
     * Format:  {{"listener1Method1", "listener1Method2", "listener1Method3",
     *     ...}, ...}
     * Example: {{"actionPerformed"}, ...}
     */
    /*
    eventListenerMethods = new String[][] {
      {"actionPerformed"},
    };
    */

    /**
     * The index of the default event for your JavaBean.
     */
    defaultEventIndex = -1;

    // Property Info

    /**
     * The property information for your JavaBean.
```

```
 * Format:  {{"PropertyName", ""PropertyDescription", "ReadMethod",
     "WriteMethod"}, ...}
 * Example: {{"fontSize", "Get the font size (points)", "getFontSize",
     setFontSize"}, ...}
 */
/*
String[][] propertyDescriptors = new String[][] {
  {"fontSize", "Get the font size (points)", "getFontSize", "setFontSize"},
};
*/

/**
 * The index of the default property for your JavaBean.
 */
defaultPropertyIndex = -1;

// Method Info

/**
 * The method names (non-properties) for your JavaBean.
 * Format:  {"method1", "method2", "method3", ...}
 * Example: {"fillRect", "eraseRect", "close", "open"}
 */
//methodNames = new String[] {"fillRect", "eraseRect", "close", "open"};

/**
 * The method parameters for each of your JavaBean's methods.
 * Format:  {{"method1Parameter1", "method1Parameter2", ...}, ...}
 * Example: {{"java.awt.Graphics", "java.awt.Rectangle", ...}, ...}
 */
/*
methodParameters = new String[][] {
  {"java.awt.Graphics", "java.awt.Rectangle"},
};
*/

// Icon Info

/**
 * A 16x16 color icon for your JavaBean.
 */
iconColor16x16 = null;

/**
 * A 32x32 color icon for your JavaBean.
 */
try {
  URL url = getClass().getResource("../../lib/image32/blink.gif");
```

```
      Toolkit tk = Toolkit.getDefaultToolkit();
      iconColor32x32 = tk.createImage((ImageProducer) url.getContent());
    } catch (IOException ex) {
      iconColor32x32 = null;
    }

    /**
     * A 16x16 monochromatic icon for your JavaBean.
     */
    iconMono16x16 = null;

    /**
     * A 32x32 monochromatic icon for your JavaBean.
     */
    iconMono32x32 = null;

    // Additional Info

    /**
     * Any additional BeanInfo for this JavaBean.
     */
    /*
    additionalBeanInfo = new BeanInfo[0];
    */
  }
}
```

Seeing the Icon

Once you've added the icon to the `YesNoBeanBeanInfo` class and compiled it, you need to exit out of JBuilder and reenter to have the Component palette show the new information. Once you reenter, look on the Other tab of the Component palette, and you'll see the image as shown in Figure 16.10. The nice part about using the `BeanInfo` class to provide an icon image is when you package up your beans for others to reuse, the icons automatically appear. Using JBuilder's Configure Palette options works only for a specific copy of JBuilder.

FIGURE 16.10: Checking out the icon image associated with the YesNoBeanBeanInfo class

You've now worked your way through the various Wizards of BeansExpress and seen what you can automate. What you do by hand, as we did in the last four skills, and what you rely on the Wizards for is entirely up to you. In addition, as JBuilder matures, you can expect even more capabilities added into BeansExpress. Now that you can create all these beans, let's move on to Skill 17 where I'll show you how to deploy them.

Are You Experienced?

Now you can...

- ☑ create new beans with the help of the New Bean Wizard
- ☑ create new event types with the New Bean Event Wizard
- ☑ associate icons to beans with the Bean Info Wizard

PART III

Advanced Skills

PROGRAMMERS

C, C, VB, Cobol, exp.
Call 534-555-6543
or fax 534-555-6544.

PROGRAMMING

MRFS Inc. is looking for a Sr. Windows NT developer. Reqs. 3-5 yrs. Exp. In C under Windows, Win95 & NT, using Visual C. Excl. OO design & implementation skills a must. OLE2 & ODBC are a plus. Excl. Salary & bnfts. Resume & salary history to HR, 8779 HighTech Way, Computer City, AR

PROGRAMMERS/
Contractors Wanted for short & long term assignments; Visual C, MFC Unix C/C, SQL Oracle Developers PC Help Desk Support Windows NT & NetWareTelecommunications Visual Basic, Access, HTMT, CGI, Perl MMI &, Co., 885-555-9933

PROGRAMMER World Wide Web Links wants your HTML & Photoshop skills. Develop great WWW sites. Local & global customers. Send samples & resume to WWWL, 2000 Apple Road, Santa Rosa, CA.

TECHNICAL WRITER Software firm seeks writer/editor for manuals, research notes, project mgmt. Min 2 years tech. writing, DTP & programming experience. Send resume & writing samples to: Software Systems, Dallas, TX.

TECHNICAL Software development firm looking for Tech Trainers, Ideal candidates have programming experience in Visual C, HTML & JAVA. Need quick self starter. Call (443) 555-6868 for interview.

TECHNICAL WRITER/ Premier Computer Corp is seeking a combination of technical skills, knowledge and experience in the following areas: UNIX, Windows 95/NT, Visual Basic, on-line help & documentation, and the Internet. Candidates must possess excellent writing skills, and be comfortable working in a quality vs. deadline driven environment. Competitive salary. Fax resume & samples to Karen Fields, Premier Computer Corp., 444 Industrial Blvd., Concord, CA. Or send to our website at www.premier.com.

WEB DESIGNER
BA/BS or equivalent programming/multimedia production. 3 years of experience in use and design of WWW services streaming audio and video HTML, PERL, CGI, GIF, JPEG. Demonstrated interpersonal, organization, communication, multi-tasking skills. Send resume to The Learning People at www.learning.com.

WEBMASTER-TECHNICAL
BSCS or equivalent. 2 years of experience in CGI, Windows 95/NT, UNIX, C, Java, Perl. Demonstrated ability to design, code, debug and test on-line services. Send resume to The Learning People at www.learning.com.

PROGRAMMER World Wide Web Links wants your HTML & Photoshop skills. Develop great WWW sites. Local & global customers. Send samples & resume to WWWL, 2000 Apple Road, Santa Rosa, CA.

---

ing tools. Experienced in documentation preparation & programming languages (Access, C, FoxPro) are a plus. Financial or banking customer service support is required along with excellent verbal & written communication skills with multi levels of end-users. Send resume to KKUP Enterprises, 45 Orange Blvd. Orange, CA.

COMPUTERS Small Web Design firm seeks indiv. w/NT, Webserver & Database management exp. Fax resume to 556-555-4221.

COMPUTER/ Visual C/C, Visual Basic Exp'd Systems Analysts/ Programmers for growing software dev. team in Roseburg. Computer Science or related degree preferred. Develop adv. Engineering applications for engineering firm. Fax resume to 707-555-8744.

COMPUTER Web Master for dynamic SF Internet co. Site. Dev., test, coord., train. 2 yrs prog. Exp. C C Web C, FTP. Fax resume to Best Staffing 845-555-7722.

COMPUTER PROGRAMMER

Ad agency seeks programmer w/exp. in UNIX/NT Platforms, Web Server, CGI/Perl. Programmer Position avail. on a project basis with the possibility to move into F/T. Fax resume & salary req. to R. Jones 334-555-8332.

COMPUTERS Programmer/Analyst Design and maintain C based SQL database applications, Required skills: Visual Basic, C, SQL, ODBC. Document existing and new applications, Novell or NT exp. a plus. Fax resume & salary history to 235-555-9935.

GRAPHIC DESIGNER
Webmaster's Weekly is seeking a creative Graphic Designer to design high impact marketing collateral, including direct mail promo's, CD-ROM packages, ads and WWW pages. Must be able to juggle multiple projects and learn new skills on the job very rapidly. Web design experience a big plus, technical troubleshooting also a plus. Call 435-555-1235.

GRAPHICS - ART DIRECTOR - WEB-MULTIMEDIA
Leading internet development company has an outstanding opportunity for a talented, high-end Web Experienced Art Director. In addition to a great portfolio and fresh ideas, the ideal candidate has excellent communication and presentation skills. Working as a team with innovative producers and programmers you will create dynamic, interactive web sites and application interfaces. Some programming experience required. Send samples and resume to: SuperSites, 333 Main, Seattle, WA.

MARKETING
Fast paced software and services provider looking for MARKETING COMMUNICATIONS SPECIALIST to be responsible for its webpage, seminar coordination, and ad place-

---

PROGRAMMERS Multiple short term assignments available: Visual C, 3 positions SQL ServerNT Server, 2 positions JAVA & HTML, long term NetWare Various locations. Call for more info. 356-555-3398.

PROGRAMMERS

C, C, VB, Cobol, exp.
Call 534-555-6543
or fax 534-555-6544.

PROGRAMMING
MRFS Inc. is looking for a Sr. Windows NT developer. Reqs. 3-5 yrs. Exp. In C under Windows, Win95 & NT, using Visual C. Excl. OO design & implementation skills a must. OLE2 & ODBC are a plus. Excl. Salary & bnfts. Resume & salary history to HR, 8779 HighTech Way, Computer City, AR

PROGRAMMERS/ Contractors Wanted for short & long term assignments: Visual C, MFC Unix C/C, SQL Oracle Developers PC Help Desk Support Windows NT & NetWareTelecommunications Visual Basic, Access, HTMT, CGI, Perl MMI & Co., 885-555-9933

PROGRAMMER World Wide Web Links wants your HTML & Photoshop skills. Develop great WWW sites. Local & global customers. Send samples & resume to WWWL, 2000 Apple Road, Santa Rosa, CA.

TECHNICAL WRITER Software firm seeks writer/editor for manuals, research notes, project mgmt. Min 2 years tech. writing, DTP & programming experience. Send resume & writing samples to: Software Systems, Dallas, TX.

COMPUTER PROGRAMMER
Ad agency seeks programmer w/exp. in UNIX/NT Platforms, Web Server, CGI/Perl. Programmer Position avail. on a project basis with the possibility to move into F/T. Fax resume & salary req. to R. Jones 334-555-8332.

TECHNICAL WRITER Premier Computer Corp is seeking a combination of technical skills, knowledge and experience in the following areas: UNIX, Windows 95/NT, Visual Basic, on-line help & documentation, and the Internet. Candidates must possess excellent writing skills, and be comfortable working in a quality vs. deadline driven environment. Competitive salary. Fax resume & samples to Karen Fields, Premier Computer Corp., 444 Industrial Blvd., Concord, CA. Or send to our website at www.premier.com.

WEB DESIGNER
BA/BS or equivalent programming/multimedia production. 3 years of experience in use and design of WWW services streaming audio and video HTML, PERL, CGI, GIF, JPEG. Demonstrated interpersonal, organization, communication, multi-tasking skills. Send resume to The Learning People at www.learning.com.

WEBMASTER-TECHNICAL
BSCS or equivalent. 2 years of experience in CGI, Windows 95/NT,

---

COMPUTERS Small Web Design firm seeks indiv. w/NT, Webserver & Database management exp. Fax resume to 556-555-4221.

COMPUTER Visual C/C, Visual Basic Exp'd Systems Analysts/ Programmers for growing software dev. team in Roseburg. Computer Science or related degree preferred. Develop adv. Engineering applications for engineering firm. Fax resume to 707-555-8744.

COMPUTER Web Master for dynamic SF Internet co. Site. Dev., test, coord., train. 2 yrs prog. Exp. C C Web C, FTP. Fax resume to Best Staffing 845-555-7722.

COMPUTERS/ QA SOFTWARE TESTERS Qualified candidates should have 2 yrs exp. performing integration & system testing using automated testing tools. Experienced in documentation preparation & programming languages (Access, C, FoxPro) are a plus. Financial or banking customer service support is required along with excellent verbal & written communication skills with multi levels of end-users. Send resume to KKUP Enterprises, 45 Orange Blvd. Orange, CA.

COMPUTERS Programmer/Analyst Design and maintain C based SQL database applications, Required skills: Visual Basic, C, SQL, ODBC. Document existing and new applications, Novell or NT exp. a plus. Fax resume & salary history to 235-555-9935.

GRAPHIC DESIGNER
Webmaster's Weekly is seeking a creative Graphic Designer to design high impact marketing collateral, including direct mail promo's, CD-ROM packages, ads and WWW pages. Must be able to juggle multiple projects and learn new skills on the job very rapidly. Web design experience a big plus, technical troubleshooting also a plus. Call 435-555-1235.

GRAPHICS - ART DIRECTOR - WEB-MULTIMEDIA
Leading internet development company has an outstanding opportunity for a talented, high-end Web Experienced Art Director. In addition to a great portfolio and fresh ideas, the ideal candidate has excellent communication and presentation skills. Working as a team with innovative producers and programmers you will create dynamic, interactive web sites and application interfaces. Some programming experience required. Send samples and resume to: SuperSites, 333 Main, Seattle, WA.

COMPUTER PROGRAMMER
Ad agency seeks programmer w/exp. in UNIX/NT Platforms, Web Server, CGI/Perl. Programmer Position avail. on a project basis with the possibility to move into F/T. Fax resume & salary req. to R. Jones 334-555-8332.

PROGRAMMERS / Established software company seeks program-

---

ment. Must be a self-starter, energetic, organized. Must have 2 y web experience. Programming plus. Call 985-555-9854.

PROGRAMMERS Multiple term assignments available: V C, 3 positions SQL ServerNT Se 2 positions JAVA & HTML, long NetWare Various locations. Ca more info. 356-555-3398.

PROGRAMMERS
C, C, VB, Cobol, exp. Call 534-6543 or fax 534-555-6544.

PROGRAMMING
MRFS Inc. is looking for a Windows NT developer. Reqs. yrs. Exp. In C under Wind Win95 & NT, using Visual C. OO design & implementation a must. OLE2 & ODBC are a Excl. Salary & bnfts. Resum salary history to HR, 8779 Hig Way, Computer City, AR

PROGRAMMERS/ Contra Wanted for short & long term ments; Visual C MFCUnix C/C, Oracle Developers PC Help Support Windows NT & Net Telecommunications Visual Access, HTMT, CGI, Perl MMI 885-555-9933

PROGRAMMER World Wide Links wants your HTML & Photo skills. Develop great WWW Local & global customers. Send ples & resume to WWWL, Apple Road, Santa Rosa, CA.

TECHNICAL WRITER Software seeks writer/editor for ma research notes, project mgmt. years tech. writing, DTP & pro ming experience. Send resu writing samples to: So Systems, Dallas, TX.

TECHNICAL Software develo firm looking for Tech Trainers, candidates have programming rience in Visual C, HTML & Need quick self starter. Call 555-6868 for interview.

TECHNICAL WRITER P Computer Corp is seeking a c nation of technical skills, know and experience in the foll areas: UNIX, Windows 95/NT, Basic, on-line help & documen and the Internet. Candidates possess excellent writing skill be comfortable working in a vs. deadline driven enviro Competitive salary. Fax resu samples to Karen Fields, P Computer Corp., 444 Industria Concord, CA. Or send to our w at www.premier.com.

WEB DESIGNER
BA/BS or equivalent pr ming/multimedia producti years of experience in us design of WWW services stre audio and video HTML, PER GIF, JPEG. Demonstrated in sonal, organization, commu multi-tasking skills. Send res The Learning People at www ing.com.

WEBMASTER-TECHN

SKILL 17

seventeen

Delivering Programs

- ❑ Creating the program to deliver
- ❑ Using the Deployment Wizard
- ❑ Running from an archive

Scooping Ice Cream

In this skill, we're going to put together some of the earlier skills to create a program that you can give away. The program we create is going to be an ice-cream order that serves either one, two, or three scoops of vanilla, chocolate, or strawberry ice cream. We'll create the program as an applet, package it up with the Deployment Wizard, and then run it outside of JBuilder. The end result will look like the screen shown in Figure 17.1.

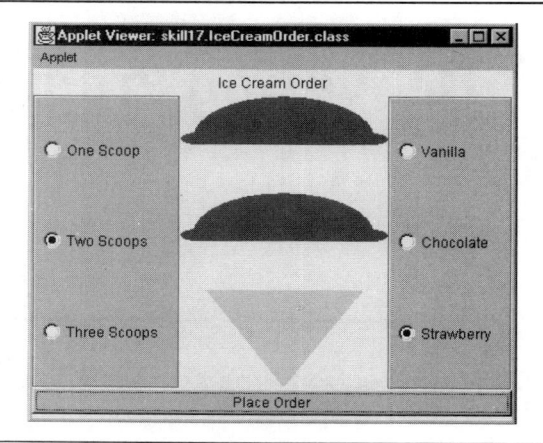

FIGURE 17.1: The Ice Cream Order program that we will create

Creating the Applet

We'll use the Applet Wizard to create the applet with two parameters. One parameter, scoops, will be the default number of scoops selected. The other parameter, flavor, will be the default flavor selected. Close any open projects and run the Applet Wizard. Save the project to **c:\skills\skill17\skill17.jpr**. In the first dialog box of the Applet Wizard, name the class **IceCreamOrder**, and select Next. In the second dialog box, create the two parameters as shown in Table 17.1 and Figure 17.2, then select Finish.

TABLE 17.1: IceCreamOrder Parameter Settings

Name	Type	Description	Variable	Default
scoops	int	Count	scoops	3
flavor	String	Default Flavor	flavor	Vanilla

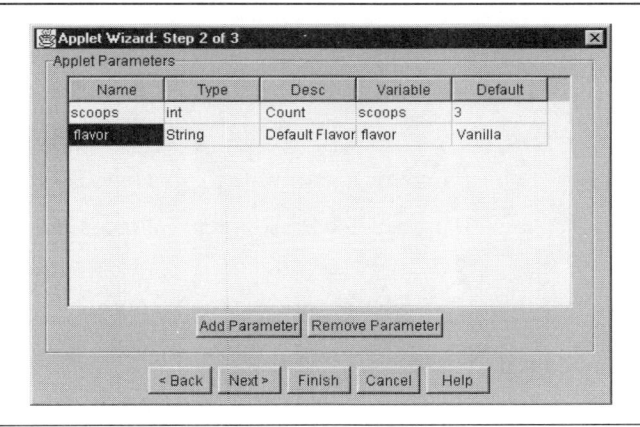

FIGURE 17.2: Setting the IceCreamOrder Parameter Settings in the Applet Wizard

Once JBuilder generates the initial program, select `IceCreamOrder.java` and go into the UI Designer. From here, we need to describe the screen:

1. Change the layout property of the applet to `BorderLayout`, as we are going to position objects around the different quadrants of the screen.

2. Place and center a `Label` in the north quadrant. The contents of the `Label` should be `Ice Cream Order`. Here are the steps to follow:

    - Select the AWT tab on the Component palette.
    - Select the `Label` bean from the palette.
    - Drop it onto the top of the screen.
    - Change its constraints property to **North**.

> **TIP**: If you happen to drop the component in the proper area of the screen, you won't have to reset the constraints property.

- Change its text property to **Ice Cream Order**.
- Change its alignment property to **1**. An alignment of 0 is left-justified. An alignment of 1 is centered, while an alignment of 2 is right-justified.

3. Place a `Button` in the south quadrant with a label of **Place Order**.
   - Select the `Button` bean from the palette.
   - Drop it onto the bottom of the screen.
   - Change its constraints property to **South**.
   - Change its label property to **Place Order**.

4. Add the scoop `CheckboxPanel` to the west quadrant, with choices of `One Scoop`, `Two Scoops`, and `Three Scoops`.
   - Select the Controls tab on the Component palette.
   - Select the `CheckboxPanel` bean from the palette.
   - Drop it onto the left side of the screen.
   - Make sure its constraints property is **West**.
   - Set the labels property to **One Scoop**, **Two Scoops**, and **Three Scoops**, with each label on a separate line. To do this, select the `labels` property and once the button with "…" appears, click it, enter one label per line, and select OK.
   - Set the grouped property to **true**, so only one can be selected.
   - Change the <name> property to **scoopList** to give it more meaning.

5. Add the flavors `CheckboxPanel` to the east quadrant with choices of `Vanilla`, `Chocolate`, and `Strawberry`.
   - Select the `CheckboxPanel` bean from the palette.
   - Drop it onto the right side of the screen.
   - Make sure its constraints property is **East**.

- Set the labels property to **Vanilla**, **Chocolate**, and **Strawberry**, with each label on a separate line.
- Set the grouped property to **true**, so only one can be selected.
- Change the name property to **flavorList** to give it more meaning

At this point, if you save everything and run the program, you'll see the screen shown in Figure 17.3.

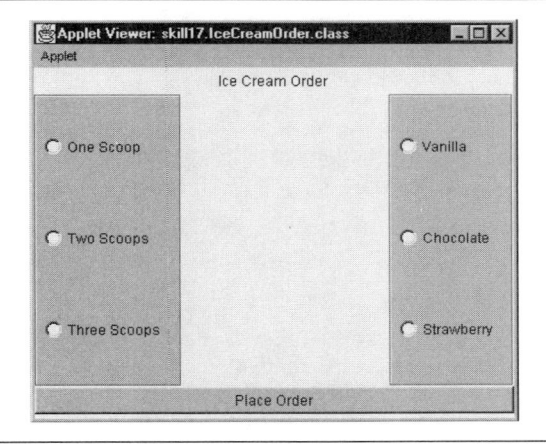

FIGURE 17.3: The initial IceCreamOrder program screen

Using the Parameters

Now that we have the general screen setup done, we should check the parameter settings to set the default selections in the on-screen lists. The `scoopList` needs to be set with the `scoops` variable, and the `flavorList` needs to be set with the `flavor` variable. If you look in the `init` method, you'll remember that JBuilder automatically adds the code to set the variables from the HTML parameters:

```
public void init() {
  try { scoops = Integer.parseInt(this.getParameter("scoops", "3"));
  } catch (Exception e) { e.printStackTrace(); }
  try { flavor = this.getParameter("flavor", "Vanilla");
  } catch (Exception e) { e.printStackTrace(); }
  try { jbInit();
  } catch (Exception e) { e.printStackTrace(); }
}
```

For `scoopList`, we are using the integer variable `scoops` to set its initial value. We can either check for a valid value of one, two, or three and then use it, or use it and then check for any problems. If we go the latter route, using an invalid `scoops` amount throws `ArrayIndexOutOfBoundsException`. If we place our source within a `try/catch` block at the end of `jbInit`, the following source will set the `scoopList` to the appropriate value. If the value is invalid, the default, `Three Scoops` (whose array index has a value of 2), will be selected.

```
try {
  scoopList.setSelectedIndex (scoops-1);
} catch (ArrayIndexOutOfBoundsException e) {
  scoopList.setSelectedIndex (2);
}
```

For `flavorList`, we are using the string variable `flavor` to set its initial value. We can either check for a valid value of Vanilla, Chocolate, or Strawberry and then use it, or just use the value. Because trying to set the label to an invalid label doesn't throw an exception, we need to set the label to the default first, to ensure something is selected after the operation.

```
flavorList.setSelectedLabel ("Vanilla");
flavorList.setSelectedLabel (flavor);
```

The complete `jbInit` follows. JBuilder automatically generated most of this source:

```
//Component initialization
  public void jbInit() throws Exception{
    this.setSize(new Dimension(400, 300));
    label1.setAlignment(1);
    label1.setText("Ice Cream Order");
    button1.setLabel("Place Order");
    scoopList.setGrouped(true);
    scoopList.setLabels(new String[] {"One Scoop", "Two Scoop", "Three Scoop"});
    flavorList.setGrouped(true);
    flavorList.setLabels(new String[] {"Vanilla", "Chocolate", "Strawberry"});
    this.setLayout(borderLayout1);
    this.add(label1, BorderLayout.NORTH);
    this.add(button1, BorderLayout.SOUTH);
    this.add(scoopList, BorderLayout.WEST);
    this.add(flavorList, BorderLayout.EAST);
```

```
try {
  scoopList.setSelectedIndex (scoops-1);
} catch (ArrayIndexOutOfBoundsException e) {
  scoopList.setSelectedIndex (2);
}
flavorList.setSelectedLabel ("Vanilla");
flavorList.setSelectedLabel (flavor);
}
```

Creating the Scoop

Before we add the action for selecting the button, let's create our ice-cream scoop and cone. Instead of just drawing them directly to the screen, we'll create them to be components just like the AWT components. When you create new AWT components, you usually find the nearest AWT component and subclass it. In the case of an ice-cream scoop, there really isn't an appropriate one, so you just create a subclass of java.awt.Component.

Using the New Class Wizard, create a class called **Scoop** that subclasses **java.awt.Component**. Uncheck the Public and Generate default constructor toggles, as the class will only be used within this package once we publish the program. After selecting OK, your source file should look pretty empty:

```
package skill17;

import java.awt.*;
class Scoop extends Component {
}
```

Before the scoop of ice cream can be drawn, we need to know the color and shape to draw. We can add a constructor to get the color and override the paint method to define its shape.

There are three steps involved in drawing the scoop:

1. Draw the main scoop, leaving room to the sides and below to crunch up some ice cream near the cone.

2. On each side, draw a half circle off to the side to provide the edges of our crunch zone.

3. Then, fill in the rest between it with a rectangle.

The completed source file follows in Scoop.java.

Scoop.java

```java
package skill17;

import java.awt.*;
class Scoop extends Component {
  Color color;
  public Scoop (Color c) {
    color = c;
  }
  public void paint (Graphics g) {
    Dimension dim = getSize();
    int halfHeight = dim.height/2;
    int heightEdge = dim.height/8;
    int widthEdge  = dim.width/8;
    g.setColor (color);
    g.fillArc (widthEdge/2, 0, dim.width-widthEdge, dim.height-heightEdge, 0, 180);
    g.fillArc (0, halfHeight-heightEdge, widthEdge, heightEdge, 90, 180);
    g.fillArc (dim.width-widthEdge, halfHeight-heightEdge, widthEdge, heightEdge, 90, -180);
    g.fillRect (widthEdge/2, halfHeight-heightEdge, dim.width-widthEdge, heightEdge);
  }
}
```

Creating the Cone

Creating the ice-cream cone is even easier than the scoop. Here, we use the New Class Wizard to create a class named **Cone** that subclasses **java.awt.Component**. Again, uncheck the Public and Generate default constructor toggles. Here, we just have to override the `paint` method to draw the cone in the allotted area. We'll draw the cone as a filled triangle. The complete source follows in Cone.java.

Cone.java

```java
package skill17;

import java.awt.*;
class Cone extends Component {
  public void paint (Graphics g) {
    g.setColor (Color.yellow);
    Dimension dim = getSize();
    int halfWidth  = dim.width/2;
```

```
        int heightEdge = dim.height/8;
        int widthEdge  = dim.width/8;
        Polygon p = new Polygon();
        p.addPoint (widthEdge, 0);
        p.addPoint (halfWidth, dim.height);
        p.addPoint (dim.width-widthEdge, 0);
        g.fillPolygon (p);
      }
    }
```

Adding Action

Now that we've defined our ice-cream pieces, we can add the source for how to use them. Some people may find it better to do this step first, then define the scoop and cone. Which way you do it is entirely up to you. To add the button's action handler, select `IceCreamOrder.java` and return to the UI Designer. From here, if you double-click on the Place Order button, JBuilder adds an event adapter and places you back into the source code of the new `button1_actionPerformed` method.

In this method, we need to find out what flavor of ice cream the patron wants, determine what color that flavor is, find out how many scoops they want, create a scoop for each, add a cone, and place it on the screen. Here are the specifics:

1. To find out what flavor they want, just ask `flavorList`:

    ```
    String flavor = flavorList.getSelectedLabel();
    ```

2. To find out what color that flavor is, add a supporting method to do the work:

    ```
    Color determineFlavorColor (String flavor) {
      Color c;
      if (flavor.equals ("Chocolate")) {
        c = new Color (210, 105, 30);
      } else if (flavor.equals ("Vanilla")) {
        c = new Color (250, 235, 215);
      } else if (flavor.equals ("Strawberry")) {
        c = new Color (255, 20, 147);
      } else {
        c = Color.black;
      }
      return c;
    }
    ```

> **TIP**
> To find what colors to use for the different flavors, X-Windows/Unix systems maintain a list of color names and their corresponding red-green-blue values. The list is available with the showrgb command. If you do not have access to an X-Windows system, there are at least two places on the Web where you can see the list: http://www.dsinclair.com/resources/rgb.txt.html shows just the list, while http://eies.njit.edu/~kevin/rgb.txt.html also shows a sample of each color.

3. Call that supporting method in button1_actionPerformed.

   ```
   Color c = determineFlavorColor (flavor);
   ```

4. To find out how many scoops they want, just ask scoopList. Remember to add one to the position returned, since it is a zero-based list.

   ```
   int count = scoopList.getSelectedIndex() + 1;
   ```

5. Group the scoops into a Panel on the screen when you create them. The layout manager of this panel should be GridLayout so they appear one on top of another. The number of rows is the number of scoops, plus one for the cone.

   ```
   Panel p = new Panel(new GridLayout (count+1, 1));
   for (int i=0;i<count;i++) {
     Scoop scoop = new Scoop(c);
     p.add (scoop);
   }
   Cone cone = new Cone();
   p.add (cone);
   ```

6. Place the scoop and cone on the screen and update the display.

   ```
   add(p, BorderLayout.CENTER);
   validate();
   ```

   If we stopped there, our program would work okay the first time it ran. However, the old cone isn't removed from the screen before the next one is added. To do this properly, you need to add three steps.

7. Create a new instance variable for the class, as this variable will need to save the component to be removed between each scooping out of ice cream.

   ```
   Component lastAdded = null;
   ```

8. Before we add the new ice-cream cone to the screen, we need to remove the previous one, if it exists:

   ```
   if (lastAdded != null)
     remove (lastAdded);
   ```

9. And lastly, we need to retain a reference to the ice-cream cone just added:

   ```
   lastAdded = p;
   ```

Once all that is put together, it gives us the following method definition:

```
void button1_actionPerformed(ActionEvent e) {
   String flavor = flavorList.getSelectedLabel();
   Color c = determineFlavorColor (flavor);
   int count = scoopList.getSelectedIndex() + 1;
   Panel p = new Panel(new GridLayout (count+1, 1));
   for (int i=0;i<count;i++) {
     Scoop scoop = new Scoop(c);
     p.add (scoop);
   }
   if (lastAdded != null)
     remove (lastAdded);
   Cone cone = new Cone();
   p.add (cone);
   add(p, BorderLayout.CENTER);
   lastAdded = p;
   validate();
}
```

Saving, compiling, and running the program at this point will bring up the applet shown in Figure 17.4.

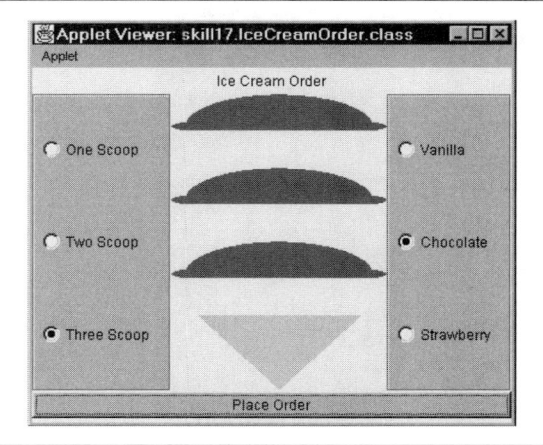

FIGURE 17.4: The IceCreamOrder applet with three scoops of chocolate

Run the program through the ropes a few times by altering the HTML source to change the defaults. The complete source of the applet follows:

IceCreamOrder.java

```
package skill17;

import java.awt.*;
import java.awt.event.*;
import java.applet.*;
import borland.jbcl.layout.*;
import borland.jbcl.control.*;

public class IceCreamOrder extends Applet {
  boolean isStandalone = false;
  int scoops;
  String flavor;
  BorderLayout borderLayout1 = new BorderLayout();
  Label label1 = new Label();
  Button button1 = new Button();
  CheckboxPanel scoopList = new CheckboxPanel();
  CheckboxPanel flavorList = new CheckboxPanel();
  Component lastAdded = null;

  //Get a parameter value
  public String getParameter(String key, String def) {
    return isStandalone ? System.getProperty(key, def) :
      (getParameter(key) != null ? getParameter(key) : def);
  }

  //Construct the applet
  public IceCreamOrder() {
  }

  //Initialize the applet
  public void init() {
    try {
      scoops = Integer.parseInt(this.getParameter("scoops", "3"));
    } catch (Exception e) {
      e.printStackTrace();
    }
    try {
      flavor = this.getParameter("flavor", "Vanilla");
    } catch (Exception e) {
      e.printStackTrace();
    }
```

```java
    try {
      jbInit();
    } catch (Exception e) {
      e.printStackTrace();
    }
  }

  //Component initialization
  public void jbInit() throws Exception{
    this.setSize(new Dimension(400, 300));
    label1.setAlignment(1);
    label1.setText("Ice Cream Order");
    button1.setLabel("Place Order");
    button1.addActionListener(new IceCreamOrder_button1_actionAdapter(this));
    scoopList.setGrouped(true);
    scoopList.setLabels(new String[] {"One Scoop", "Two Scoop", "Three Scoop"});
    flavorList.setGrouped(true);
    flavorList.setLabels(new String[] {"Vanilla", "Chocolate", "Strawberry"});
    this.setLayout(borderLayout1);
    this.add(label1, BorderLayout.NORTH);
    this.add(button1, BorderLayout.SOUTH);
    this.add(scoopList, BorderLayout.WEST);
    this.add(flavorList, BorderLayout.EAST);
    try {
      scoopList.setSelectedIndex (scoops-1);
    } catch (ArrayIndexOutOfBoundsException e) {
      scoopList.setSelectedIndex (2);
    }
    flavorList.setSelectedLabel ("Vanilla");
    flavorList.setSelectedLabel (flavor);
  }

  //Get Applet information
  public String getAppletInfo() {
    return "Applet Information";
  }

  //Get parameter info
  public String[][] getParameterInfo() {
    String pinfo[][] =
    {
      {"scoops", "int", "Scoops"},
      {"flavor", "String", "Deafult Flavor"},
    };
    return pinfo;
  }
```

```java
  void button1_actionPerformed(ActionEvent e) {
    String flavor = flavorList.getSelectedLabel();
    Color c = determineFlavorColor (flavor);
    int count = scoopList.getSelectedIndex() + 1;
    Panel p = new Panel(new GridLayout (count+1, 1));
    for (int i=0;i<count;i++) {
      Scoop scoop = new Scoop(c);
      p.add (scoop);
    }
    if (lastAdded != null)
      remove (lastAdded);
    Cone cone = new Cone();
    p.add (cone);
    add(p, BorderLayout.CENTER);
    lastAdded = p;
    validate();
  }

  Color determineFlavorColor (String flavor) {
    Color c;
    if (flavor.equals ("Chocolate")) {
      c = new Color (210, 105, 30);
    } else if (flavor.equals ("Vanilla")) {
      c = new Color (250, 235, 215);
    } else if (flavor.equals ("Strawberry")) {
      c = new Color (255, 20, 147);
    } else {
      c = Color.black;
    }
    return c;
  }
}

class IceCreamOrder_button1_actionAdapter implements java.awt.event.ActionListener {
  IceCreamOrder adaptee;

  IceCreamOrder_button1_actionAdapter(IceCreamOrder adaptee) {
    this.adaptee = adaptee;
  }

  public void actionPerformed(ActionEvent e) {
    adaptee.button1_actionPerformed(e);
  }
}
```

Creating an Archive

Once you have the applet completed, it's time to package it up to run in a browser outside of JBuilder. JBuilder's Deployment Wizard is responsible for this. Using this Wizard, you select what you want to deploy, and the Wizard finds any dependencies to make sure you deliver a complete package. If you select Wizards ➤ Deployment Wizard, you'll see the dialog box shown in Figure 17.5.

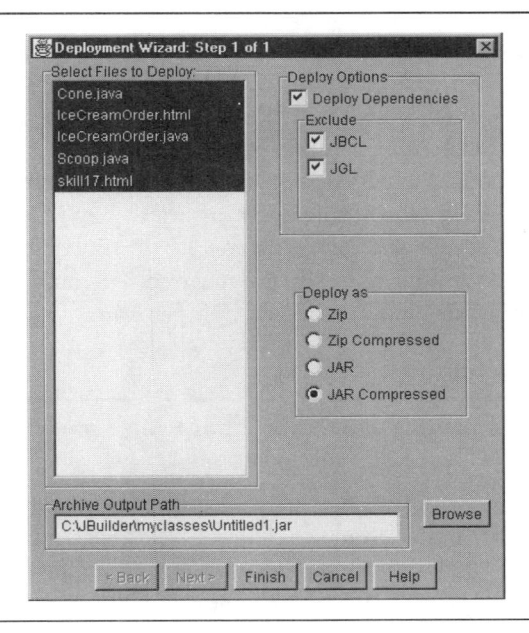

FIGURE 17.5: The Deployment Wizard dialog box; from here, you pick which files you want to send out, along with a structure and name.

> **WARNING** With the exception of Sun's HotJava browser, the browsers in general release—Internet Explorer from Microsoft and Navigator/Communicator from Netscape—do not support Java 1.1. Until such a time when they are fully supported, it isn't recommended to deliver applets created from JBuilder. JBuilder can create Java 1.0 applets that you can deliver; however there is no way to tell JBuilder to only use Java 1.0 features. The burden is placed on the developer to use only the earlier capabilities. Delivering JBuilder applications does not have this restriction as there is no browser dependency.

The files we want to deploy are the class files associated with `Cone.java`, `IceCreamOrder.java`, and `Scoop.java`, so we can uncheck `skill17.html` and `IceCreamOrder.html`. Press the Ctrl key and the mouse button to unselect an option. The `IceCreamOrder.html` file can be used to run the applet once deployed; however, you do not want to bundle it with the applet, as it cannot be used from within the bundle.

With the Deploy Dependencies toggle selected, the Wizard finds any classes that these classes depend on. If you know that the computer you are delivering your program to already has the JBCL and JGL packages, you don't need to send them along. Otherwise, you should uncheck the Exclude JBCL and Exclude JGL options to ensure your archive is complete. Unchecking these does not automatically include all of the two packages; the Wizard will just extend its dependency checker to these packages as well.

The Deploy As option determines the format of what JBuilder creates. The Zip and JAR formats are supported. The JAR format adds a manifest file to the Zip file. If you do not specify your own manifest file (one that ends with `.mf`), JBuilder automatically creates one. The only time you need to create your own manifest file is when you are delivering files that will be used within another builder tool.

NOTE For a full description of JAR files and the manifest file specification, see http://java.sun.com/products/jdk/1.1/docs/guide/jar/index.html.

The final field in the dialog box shown in Figure 17.5 is the Archive Output Path. The only requirement here is that the filename extension matches the Deploy As toggle. If you are deploying as a Zip file, the file must end with `.zip`. If you are deploying as a JAR file, the filename must end with `.jar`. If you try to save an archive with the wrong extension, you'll see a screen pop up, like the one shown in Figure 17.6.

FIGURE 17.6: The error message received when saving to the wrong filename extension

If you enter **c:\skills\order.jar** in the Archive Output Path text box, uncheck the JBCL and JGL options, select JAR Compressed as the Deploy As format, and select the three `.java` files. When you select Finish, JBuilder will bundle up your classes into the archive.

> **TIP** If you deploy the same package multiple times, you are prompted to overwrite the manifest file that JBuilder creates for you. As long as you didn't customize it outside of JBuilder, just select Yes when asked to overwrite.

Running *IceCreamOrder* from *order.jar*

To test the applet outside of JBuilder, we need to use the command-line tools of the Java Development Kit. By using JBuilder, this is what you normally get to avoid. However, for testing purposes, it is the only alternative until the most frequently used browsers support Java 1.1.

To bring up a command window, select the Windows Start menu ➤ Run to bring up Figure 17.7. Then enter **cmd** for Windows NT 4—or **command** for Windows 95—and press Enter to bring up the command window, as shown in Figure 17.8.

Once you have the command window open, follow the steps below to set up everything to run the applet.

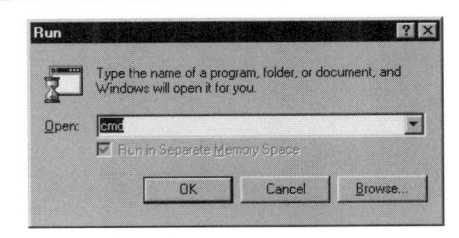

FIGURE 17.7: The Run dialog box, where you type the name of a program for Windows to run

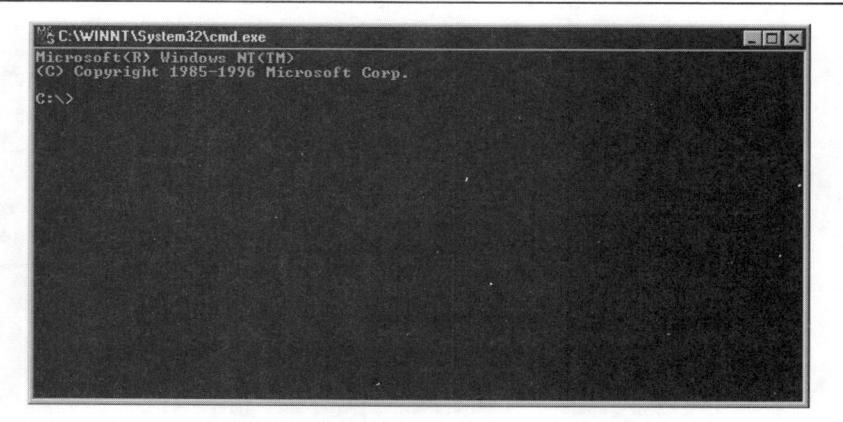

FIGURE 17.8: A windows command window

1. Temporarily set the CLASSPATH environment variable to include Java's `classes.zip` file.

    ```
    set CLASSPATH=c:\JBuilder\java\lib\classes.zip
    ```

2. Place the Java utilities in your PATH environment variable.

    ```
    set PATH=C:\JBuilder\java\bin;%PATH%
    ```

3. To make sure that this is set up correctly, run the following command. It should display `JDK1.1.2Borland` or something similar. If it doesn't, the CLASSPATH and PATH variables aren't correct, and you'll need to reset them.

    ```
    java -version
    ```

4. Create the HTML applet loader file. We'll use the `c:\skills` directory because that is where the `order.jar` file is. After you type everything below, enter Ctrl+Z to finish creating the `start.html` file. The `archive` parameter specifies the `.jar` file for the applet's files.

    ```
    cd \skills
    copy con: start.html
    <APPLET
      code="skill17.IceCreamOrder.class"
      width=400
      height=300
    ```

```
            archive="order.jar"
        >
        </APPLET>
```

5. Use the `appletviewer` program to show the applet. This brings up Figure 17.9, which shows the applet running.

    ```
    appletviewer start.html
    ```

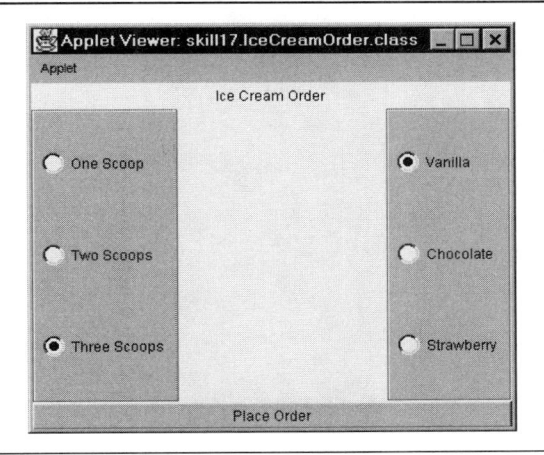

FIGURE 17.9: The IceCreamOrder applet with defaults for the parameters: three scoops of vanilla. Once you select Place Order, you'll see the scoops.

NOTE If you happen to have the Java Development Kit (JDK) already installed on your system, you can start with step four above.

TIP Packaging up applications works in the same way as applets. However, to run an application, its archive file needs to be added to the CLASSPATH. Then you just run the program with the `java` or `jre` command.

Congratulations! You've now successfully created an applet and packaged it up in an archive. Put it on your Web site to show off what you've done or send it to your friends via e-mail. The `order.jar` file is only a little over 40K because it only contains the necessary pieces for the applet to run. Now let's move on to learn how to use menus within your Java programs.

Are You Experienced?

Now you can...

- ☑ create new components
- ☑ package programs in archives with the Deployment Wizard
- ☑ run JBuilder-generated programs outside of JBuilder

356-555-3398.

PROGRAMMING
C, C, VB, Cobol, exp. Call 534-555-6543 or fax 534-555-6544.

PROGRAMMING
MRFS Inc. is looking for a Sr. Windows NT developer. Reqs. 3-5 yrs. Exp. In C under Windows, Win95 & NT, using Visual C. Excl. OO design & implementation skills a must. OLE2 & ODBC are a plus. Excl. Salary & bnfts. Resume & salary history to HR, 8779 HighTech Way, Computer City, AR

PROGRAMMERS
Contractors Wanted for short & long term assignments: Visual C, MFC Unix C/C, SQL Oracle Dev elop ers PC Help Desk Support Windows NT & NetWare Telecommunications Visual Basic, Access, HTMT, CGI, Perl MMI & Co., 885-555-9933

PROGRAMMER
World Wide Web Links wants your HTML & Photoshop skills. Develop great WWW sites. Local & global customers. Send samples & resume to WWWL, 2000 Apple Road, Santa Rosa, CA.

TECHNICAL WRITER
Software firm seeks writer/editor for manuals, research notes, project mgmt. Min 2 years tech. writing, DTP & programming experience. Send resume & writing samples to: Software Systems, Dallas, TX.

TECHNICAL
Software development firm looking for Tech Trainers. Ideal candidates have programming experience in Visual C, HTML & JAVA. Need quick self starter. Call (443) 555-6868 for interview.

TECHNICAL WRITER/
Premier Computer Corp is seeking a combination of technical skills, knowledge and experience in the following areas: UNIX, Windows 95/NT, Visual Basic, on-line help & documentation, and the Internet. Candidates must possess excellent writing skills, and be comfortable working in a quality vs. deadline driven environment. Competitive salary. Fax resume & samples to Karen Fields, Premier Computer Corp. 444 Industrial Blvd. Concord, CA. Or send to our website at www.premier.com.

WEB DESIGNER
BA/BS or equivalent programming/multimedia production. 3 years of experience in use and design of WWW services streaming audio and video HTML, PERL, CGI, GIF, JPEG. Demonstrated Interpersonal, organization, communication, multi-tasking skills. Send resume to The Learning People at www.learning.com

WEBMASTER-TECHNICAL
BSCS or equivalent, 2 years of experience in CGI, Windows 95/NT, UNIX, C, Java, Perl. Demonstrated ability to design code, debug and test on-line services. Send resume to The Learning People at www.learning.com.

PROGRAMMER
World Wide Web Links wants your HTML & Photoshop skills. Develop great WWW sites.

---

ing tools. Experienced in documentation preparation & programming languages (Access, C, FoxPro) are a plus. Financial or banking customer service support is required along with excellent verbal & written communication skills a must with multi levels of end-users. Send resume to KKUP Enterprises, 45 Orange Blvd. Orange, CA.

COMPUTERS
Small Web Design Firm seeks indiv. w/NT, Webserver & Database management exp. Fax resume to 556-555-4221.

COMPUTER/
Visual C/C, Visual Basic Exp'd Systems Analysts/Programmers for growing software dev. team in Roseburg. Computer Science or related degree preferred. Develop adv. Engineering applications for engineering firm. Fax resume to 707-555-8744.

COMPUTER
Web Master for dynamic SF internet co. Site, Dev, test, coord, train. 2 yrs prog. Exp. C C, Web C, FTP. Fax resume to Best Staffing 845-555-7722.

COMPUTER PROGRAMMER
Ad agency seeks programmer w/exp. in UNIX/NT Platforms, Web Server, CGI/Perl. Programmer Position avail. on a project basis with the possibility to move into F/T. Fax resume & salary req. to R. Jones 334-555-8332.

COMPUTERS
Programmer/Analyst Design and maintain C based SQL database applications, Required skills: Visual Basic, C, SQL, ODBC, Document existing and new applications. Novell or NT exp. a plus. Fax resume & salary history to 235-555-9935.

GRAPHIC DESIGNER
Webmaster's Weekly is seeking a creative Graphic Designer to design high impact marketing collater al, including direct mail promo's, CD-ROM packages, ads and WWW pages. Must be able to juggle multiple projects and learn new skills on the job very rapidly. Web design experience a big plus, technical troubleshooting also a plus. Call 435-555-1235.

GRAPHICS - ART DIRECTOR - WEB-MULTIMEDIA
Leading internet development company has an outstanding opportunity for a talented, high-end Web Experienced Art Director. In addition to a great portfolio and fresh ideas, the ideal candidate has excellent communication and presentation skills. Working as a team with innovative producers and programmers, you will create dynamic, interactive web sites and application interfaces. Some programming experience required. Send samples and resume to: SuperSites, 333 Main, Seattle, WA.

MARKETING
Fast paced software and services provider looking for MARKETING COMMUNICATIONS SPECIALIST to be responsible for its webpage.

PROGRAMMERS
Multiple short term assignments available: Visual C, 3 positions SQL ServerNT Server, 2 positions JAVA & HTML, long term NetWare Various locations. Call for more info. 356-555-3398.

PROGRAMMERS
C, C, VB, Cobol, exp.
Call 534-555-6543
or fax 534-555-6544.

PROGRAMMING
MRFS Inc. is looking for a Sr. Windows NT developer. Reqs. 3-5 yrs. Exp. In C under Windows, Win95 & NT, using Visual C. Excl. OO design & implementation skills a must. OLE2 & ODBC are a plus. Excl. Salary & bnfts. Resume & salary history to HR, 8779 HighTech Way, Computer City, AR

PROGRAMMERS/
Contractors Wanted for short & long term assignments: Visual C, MFC Unix C/C, SQL Oracle Developers PC Help Desk Support Windows NT & NetWareTelecommunications Visual Basic, Access, HTMT, CGI, Perl MMI & Co., 885-555-9933

PROGRAMMER
World Wide Web Links wants your HTML & Photoshop skills. Develop great WWW sites. Local & global customers. Send samples & resume to WWWL, 2000 Apple Road, Santa Rosa, CA.

TECHNICAL WRITER
Software firm seeks writer/editor for manuals, research notes, project mgmt. Min 2 years tech. writing, DTP & programming experience. Send resume & writing samples to: Software Systems, Dallas, TX.

COMPUTER PROGRAMMER
Ad agency seeks programmer w/exp. in UNIX/NT Platforms, Web Server, CGI/Perl. Programmer Position avail. on a project basis with the possibility to move into F/T. Fax resume & salary req. to R. Jones 334-555-8332.

TECHNICAL WRITER
Premier Computer Corp is seeking a combination of technical skills, knowledge and experience in the following areas: UNIX, Windows 95/NT, Visual Basic, on-line help & documentation, and the Internet. Candidates must possess excellent writing skills, and be comfortable working in a quality vs. deadline driven environment. Competitive salary. Fax resume & samples to Karen Fields, Premier Computer Corp. 444 Industrial Blvd. Concord, CA. Or send to our website at www.premier.com.

WEB DESIGNER
BA/BS or equivalent programming/multimedia production. 3 years of experience in use and design of WWW services streaming audio and video HTML, PERL, CGI, GIF, JPEG. Demonstrated Interpersonal, organization, communication, multi-tasking skills. Send resume to The Learning People at www.learning.com

WEBMASTER-TECHNICAL
BSCS or equivalent, 2 years of experience in CGI, Windows 95/NT,

---

COMPUTERS
Small Web Design Firm seeks indiv. w/NT, Webserver & Database management exp. Fax resume to 556-555-4221.

COMPUTER
Visual C/C, Visual Basic Exp'd Systems Analysts/Programmers for growing software dev. team in Roseburg. Computer Science or related degree preferred. Develop adv. Engineering applications for engineering firm. Fax resume to 707-555-8744.

COMPUTER
Web Master for dynamic SF internet co. Site, Dev, test, coord, train. 2 yrs prog. Exp. C C, Web C, FTP. fax resume to Best Staffing 845-555-7722.

COMPUTERS/ QA SOFTWARE TESTERS
Qualified candidates should have 2 yrs. exp. performing integration & system testing using automated testing tools. Experienced in documentation preparation & programming languages (Access, C, FoxPro) are a plus. Financial or banking customer service support is required along with excellent verbal & written communication skills with multi levels of end-users. Send resume to KKUP Enterprises, 45 Orange Blvd. Orange, CA.

COMPUTERS
Programmer/Analyst Design and maintain C based SQL database applications, Required skills: Visual Basic, C, SQL, ODBC, Document existing and new applications. Novell or NT exp. a plus. Fax resume & salary history to 235-555-9935.

GRAPHIC DESIGNER
Webmaster's Weekly is seeking a creative Graphic Designer to design high impact marketing collater al, including direct mail promo's, CD-ROM packages, ads and WWW pages. Must be able to juggle multiple projects and learn new skills on the job very rapidly. Web design experience a big plus, technical troubleshooting also a plus. Call 435-555-1235.

GRAPHICS - ART DIRECTOR - WEB-MULTIMEDIA
Leading internet development company has an outstanding opportunity for a talented, high-end Web Experienced Art Director. In addition to a great portfolio and fresh ideas, the ideal candidate has excellent communication and presentation skills. Working as a team with innovative producers and programmers, you will create dynamic, interactive web sites and application interfaces. Some programming experience required. Send samples and resume to: SuperSites, 333 Main, Seattle, WA.

COMPUTER PROGRAMMER
Ad agency seeks programmer w/exp. in UNIX/NT Platforms, Web Server, CGI/Perl. Programmer Position avail. on a project basis with the possibility to move into F/T. Fax resume & salary req. to R. Jones 334-555-8332.

PROGRAMMERS / Established
software company seeks program-

---

seminar coordination, and ad placement. Must be a self-starter, energetic, organized. Must have 2 yrs web experience. Programming a plus. Call 985-555-9854.

PROGRAMMERS
Multiple short term assignments available: Visual C, 3 positions SQL ServerNT Server, 2 positions JAVA & HTML, long term NetWare Various locations. Call more info. 356-555-3398.

PROGRAMMERS
C, C, VB, Cobol, exp. Call 534-555-6543 or fax 534-555-6544.

PROGRAMMING
MRFS Inc. is looking for a Windows NT developer. Reqs. yrs. Exp. In C under Windows, Win95 & NT, using Visual C. OO design & implementation a must. OLE2 & ODBC are a p Excl. Salary & bnfts. Resume salary history to HR, 8779 HighTech Way, Computer City, AR

PROGRAMMERS
Contract Wanted for short & long term assignments: Visual C, MFCUnix C/C, SQL Oracle Developers PC Help D Support Windows NT & NetW Telecommunications Visual B Access, HTMT, CGI, Perl MMI & 885-555-9933

PROGRAMMER
World Wide Links wants your HTML & Photos skills. Develop great WWW s Local & global customers. Send s ples & resume to WWWL, 2 Apple Road, Santa Rosa, CA.

TECHNICAL WRITER
Software seeks writer/editor for manu research notes, project mgmt. years tech. writing, DTP & pro ming experience. Send resu writing samples to: Soft Systems, Dallas, TX.

TECHNICAL
Software develop firm looking for Tech Trainers. candidates have programming e rience in Visual C, HTML & J Need quick self starter. Call (555-6868 for interview.

TECHNICAL WRITER
Pre Computer Corp is seeking a co nation of technical skills, knowl and experience in the follo areas: UNIX, Windows 95/NT, Basic, on-line help & document and the Internet. Candidates possess excellent writing skills, be comfortable working in a q vs. deadline driven environ Competitive salary. Fax resu samples to Karen Fields, Pr Computer Corp. 444 Industrial Concord, CA. Or send to our we at www.premier.com.

WEB DESIGNER
BA/BS or equivalent pro ming/multimedia productio years of experience in use design of WWW services stre audio and video HTML, PERL GIF, JPEG. Demonstrated Int sonal, organization, communie multi-tasking skills. Send resu The Learning People at www. ing.com.

WEBMASTER-TECHNI

SKILL

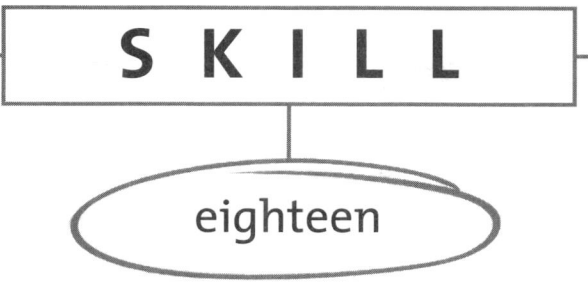

eighteen

Working with Menus

- ❏ Working with an About Box
- ❏ Working with the Menu Designer to create menus
- ❏ Changing colors with the `ColorChooser`
- ❏ Changing fonts with the `FontChooser`

Getting Started

No doubt, you've used the menus in Microsoft Windows programs. With JBuilder, creating them is a snap with the help of the Menu Designer. In this skill, let's create a program that allows us to change the font and color of some displayed text. We'll also have a pop-up window appear to display information about our program.

To start the skill, close any open projects with File ➤ Close All. Next, use the Application Wizard to create a new project and set up the application framework. In the Project Wizard, enter **c:\skills\skill18\skill18.jpr** in the File field, and then select Finish. On the first screen of the Application Wizard, select Next. On the second screen, enter **MenuTester** in the Class field, and then select Generate Menu Bar and Generate About Box. Then select Finish and let JBuilder do its thing. At this point, if you save and run everything you will see the screen shown in Figure 18.1.

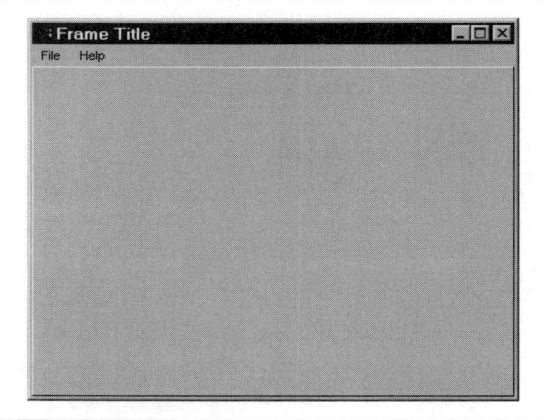

FIGURE 18.1: The initial screen, with default menu setup. You'll find Exit under the File menu and About under the Help menu.

Before we do anything with the menus, let's add a `Label` to the screen. We'll use this label later with the menus to change the font and color of the text displayed. We also want to change the layout manager to almost anything besides

XYLayout because the label size changes when the font changes. To do this, perform the following steps:

1. Select `MenuTester.java` in the Navigation pane.
2. Select the Design tab at the bottom of the Content pane.
3. Select `this (BorderLayout)` in the Structure pane.
4. Change the size property to **300, 200** to reduce the dimensions from within the Inspector window.
5. Select `bevelPanel1 (XYLayout)` in the Structure pane to ensure the label we add is added there. The panel will appear selected in the Content pane.
6. Change the layout property to `BorderLayout` in the Inspector.
7. Select the AWT tab on the Component palette.
8. Select the Label icon on the palette. The icon will appear pressed in.
9. Place the label in the selected panel in the Content pane.
10. To set the text, select the text property in the Inspector window.
11. Type in a short message to display and press Enter. Then enter **Welcome to JBuilder** here.
12. Then change the constraints property of the label to `Center`.

After adding the label to the screen and rerunning the application, your program will look like Figure 18.2. The reason we added the label in the middle of the screen is we're going to change the height when we change the font later.

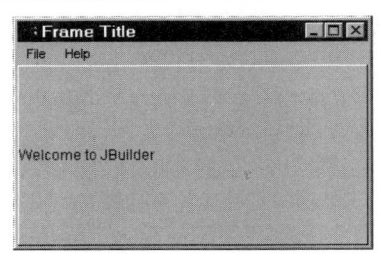

FIGURE 18.2: The screen with the new label

Using an About Box

An About Box is a pop-up window that usually displays information about the name and version of the current program. In JBuilder, for example, if you select Help ➤ About, the screen shown in Figure 18.3 appears.

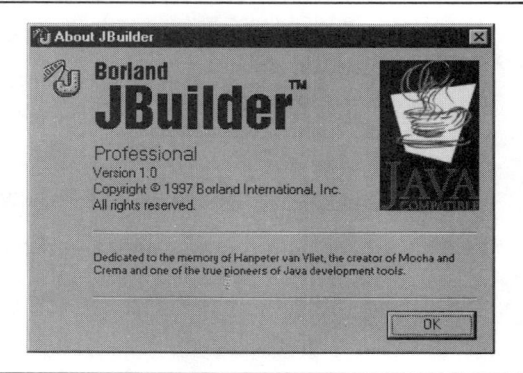

FIGURE 18.3: The JBuilder About box

For our program, the Application Wizard already added the Help and About menu items, as well as the initial About box. We just have to configure the box. To see the initial About box, as seen in Figure 18.4, run the program and select Help ➤ About.

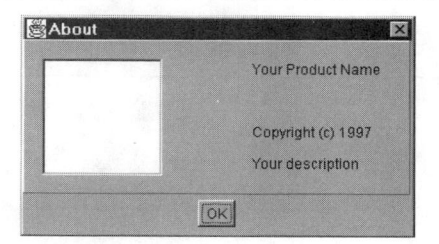

FIGURE 18.4: The initial About box configuration

You will notice that the information you entered in the Project Wizard is displayed here. The white box on the left represents an area for an image. This is usually a logo specific to the product or company. There is no way to enter an image filename in the Wizard screens. The right side includes the title from the Project Wizard, followed by a version number—currently empty, a copyright message with the current year, and the description—again from the Wizard.

To customize the information, you have to manually edit the source. We'll just add a version number for it to display. If you scroll the Structure pane down, you'll see an entry of `MenuTester_AboutBox`. The four text settings shown are the variables `copyright`, `comments`, `product`, and `version`. We'll just provide a version number. Select `version` to move the Content pane to the variable's declaration and change the setting with the following source code:

```
String version = "1.0";
```

> **TIP**
> If you want to show an image, look for the line `imageControl1.setImageName("")` in the `jbInit()` method. Change the quoted string to the filename of a GIF, JPEG, or XBM image file. If the image dimensions are too large or too small, the size will be scaled to fit within the designated area.

At this point, after saving everything with File ➤ Save All, you can run the program again. If you select Help ➤ About, you'll see the screen shown in Figure 18.5.

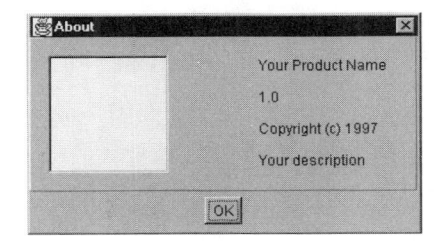

FIGURE 18.5: The About box we just created. The area in the left that looks like a TextArea is for an image file.

Using the Menu Designer

Now that our program displays a message on the screen, we, the developers, can change the font and color of the displayed text through the Inspector or directly in the source code. In order to change the font and color at run time, we need to provide some programmatic way for the user to change things. We can do this by adding menu items.

JBuilder has a nice and easy way to create menus graphically; it's called the Menu Designer. To access the Menu Designer for `MenuTester`, select `MenuTester.java` in the Navigation pane and the Design tab at the bottom of the Content pane. Then, double-click on the `menuBar1` entry in the Structure pane. The Menu Designer then appears in the Content pane, as shown in Figure 18.6.

> **NOTE** Only a Frame in Java can have pull-down menus. There is no built-in support for creating your own pull-down menus within applets. However, any Java component can have a pop-up menu, commonly activated by pressing the right mouse button in a Microsoft Windows platform. See the online User's Guide for usage instructions.

Once the Designer appears, you can select File or Help to see the entries under each menu. For the functionality we want to add—changing the color or font of the label—we'll create another pull-down menu instead of adding to the existing ones. To create another pull-down menu, double-click in the gray box to the right of Help. Here we enter a label for our menu—we'll use **Edit**—and then press Enter.

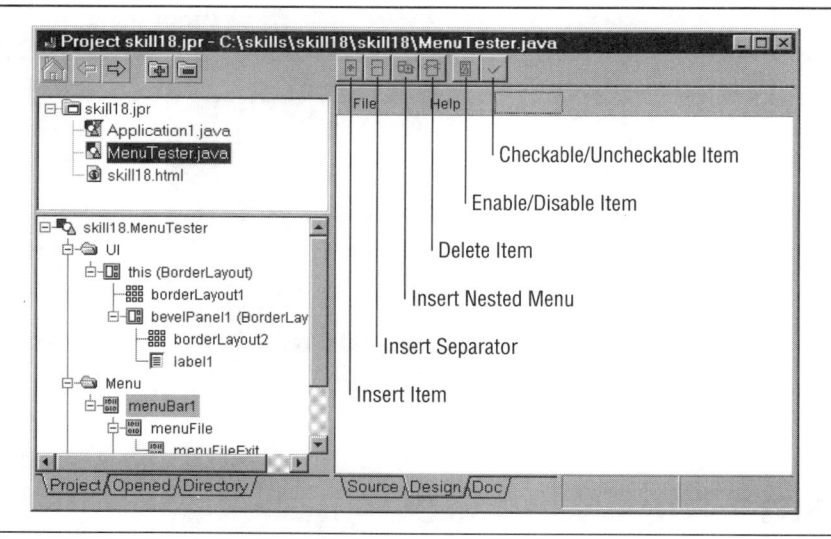

FIGURE 18.6: The JBuilder Menu Designer

Once the Edit menu appears, you can select it and drag it between the File and Help menus. At any point in time, you can just rearrange the order of entries by dragging and dropping.

Now that we have the pull-down menu, we need to add items to it. We want to add one to support changing color and another for changing font. We'll also add two more things. At some point in the future, you may want to support changing the text of the displayed label. Since this functionality isn't available now, we can add it, but it shouldn't be selectable by a user. Then, once you've finished this book, you can come back, add the code, and enable the menu item. We'll also add what's called a *separator*. A separator is an unselectable line that appears on menus for decorative purposes. We'll place future functionality below the separator.

To add the four entries, follow these steps:

1. First double-click within the box below Edit, type **Color**, and press Enter.

2. Then double-click under Color, type **Font**, and press Enter.

3. Before we enter the last menu item, we need to add the separator. To add the separator, use the Separator icon on the Menu Designer toolbar, as shown in Figure 18.6. Click that toolbar icon now to add the separator, then drag below the Font label.

4. For the last entry, Text, there are two steps involved:

   - Double-click under the last entry, type **Text**, and press return. This creates the label.

   - To make it unselectable—or *disabled*—select the Text menu item. Once chosen, if you select the Enable/Disable Item button on the toolbar, the `enabled` property changes to `false`, and the menu item appears grayish.

After you save everything and run the program, the Edit menu shown here appears.

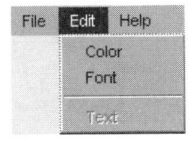

Adding the *ColorChooser*

Just having the Edit menu doesn't do much for our program functionality-wise. In order for a menu item to do anything, you have to add an event-handler routine. For the Color menu item, we want to support changing the color of the displayed message. There are four steps involved here. The first three are the same for all menu items; the last one varies depending on what type of item you're adding:

1. From the Menu Designer, select the menu item—Color in our case.
2. In the Inspector window for the item, select the Events tab.
3. In the only event-handling routine shown—`actionPerformed`, double-click in the right column. This automatically adds the framework for the event handling and places you directly in the source code for the event-handling method, shown here.

   ```
   void menuItem1_actionPerformed(java.awt.event.ActionEvent e) {

   }
   ```

4. Define the specific actions to be performed when the user selects the item.

Customizing the *ColorChooser*

Now we get to customize. In the case of changing colors, JBuilder provides a support class called `ColorChooser`. You can use the same class in your program that JBuilder offers to you when you need to change the color of a property in the Inspector. Figure 18.7 shows the `ColorChooser` for a foreground property.

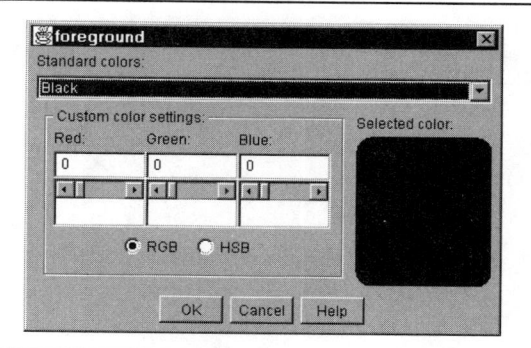

FIGURE 18.7: Changing the foreground property with a `ColorChooser`

To provide a chooser for our program, we can add the code ourselves, or drop one into the program and let JBuilder do the work for us. Dropping is a little different with this component. `ColorChooser` happens to be a stand-alone window, so it won't appear within our main window when we drop it. To drop the chooser, return to design mode for the main program, not the menu. In the Navigation pane, select `MenuTester.java`; in the Content pane, select the Design tab; in the Structure pane, double-click `this (BorderLayout)` to highlight the main program window back in the Content pane. Once selected, we can drop in a `ColorChooser`. On the Component palette, select the Dialogs tab. There are four entries there— a `Filer`, `ColorChooser`, `FontChooser`, and `Message`. Select the `ColorChooser` on the palette and drop it into the Content pane. You'll now notice a new folder, `Other`, in the Structure pane, where `colorChooser1` is now located.

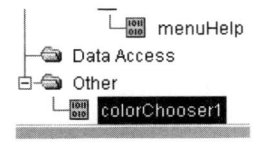

Once there is a `ColorChooser` for us to use, we can fill in the `menuItem1_actionPerformed` method. Return to the source panel of the Content pane and select the `menuItem1_actionPerformed` entry in the Structure pane. This is how the chooser works:

- Either programmatically or with the Inspector, you associate the chooser with a `Frame` and set the title.
- You tell it the current color of the object to change.
- You show the chooser to the user.
- You get its response.

Now, let's get down to specifics:

1. Because `ColorChooser` is a type of `dialog box` or pop-up window, a `Frame` must be associated with it. So, set the frame associated with the chooser:

    ```
    colorChooser1.setFrame (this);
    ```

2. Set the title of the chooser to show the user what you are expecting them to change:

   ```
   colorChooser1.setTitle ("Change Color");
   ```

3. Get current color of object to change. The label is the color we are changing.

   ```
   colorChooser1.setValue (label1.getForeground ());
   ```

4. Show the chooser:

   ```
   colorChooser1.show();
   ```

5. Check the results. If `getValue` returns `null`, the user pressed Cancel.

   ```
   Color c = colorChooser1.getValue();
   if (c != null)
     label1.setForeground(c);
   ```

If you save everything here and run the program, you can change the color of the `Welcome to JBuilder` message. If you picked Yellow, you would see Figure 18.8.

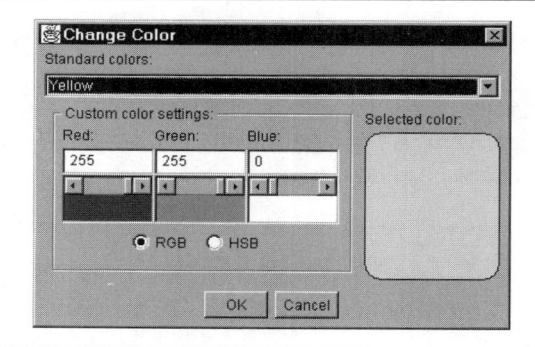

FIGURE 18.8: The JBuilder `ColorChooser` after someone picked Yellow

TIP The pull-down menu of the `ColorChooser` provides a list of 13 predefined color constants, like red and blue, along with 26 colors that are coordinated with your Desktop color scheme. This second set of colors has names like HighlightText and Scrollbar. If you are trying to draw something to coordinate with the standard Desktop, for example to create your own menus, you need to know what color to use. If you hard-code gray menus with black text and a user has configured the Lilac display appearance, your menu will look out of place because it isn't lilac.

Adding a *FontChooser*

The final piece to add to our program is a way to change the font of the message. Just as JBuilder provides a support class for changing colors, there is one for changing fonts, `FontChooser`. As Figure 18.9 shows, you use the same font selection mechanism as the Inspector.

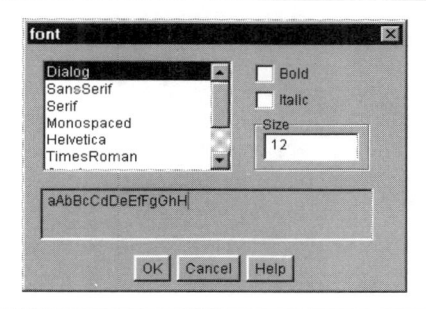

FIGURE 18.9: Changing the font property with a FontChooser

The four steps involved here are pretty much the same ones followed with the `ColorChooser`:

1. From the Menu Designer, select the menu item—Font in our case.
2. In the Inspector window for the item, select the Event tab.
3. In the only event-handling routine shown—`actionPerformed`, double-click in the right column. This automatically adds the framework for the event handling and places you directly in the source code for the event-handling method, shown here.

   ```
   void menuItem2_actionPerformed(java.awt.event.ActionEvent e) {

   }
   ```
4. Define the specific actions to be performed when the user selects the item.

Customizing the *FontChooser*

Now we get to customize it. Drop in a `FontChooser` from the Dialogs tab of the Component palette just like you did a `ColorChooser`. To drop the chooser, return to design mode for the main program, not the menu. In the Navigation pane, select `MenuTester.java`; in the Content pane, select the Design tab; in the Structure pane, select `this (BorderLayout)` to highlight the main program window back in the Content pane. Once selected, we can drop in a `FontChooser`. On the Component palette, the Dialogs tab should already be selected. There are four entries there—a `Filer`, `ColorChooser`, `FontChooser`, and `Message`. Select the `FontChooser` on the palette and drop it into the Content pane. The `ColorChooser` now has company in the `Other` folder.

Other than a few minor changes for the datatype, the source is nearly identical to the color changing code.

1. Because `FontChooser` is a type of dialog box, there must be a `Frame` associated with it. So, set the frame associated with the chooser:

    ```
    fontChooser1.setFrame (this);
    ```

2. Set the title of the chooser to show the user what you are expecting them to change:

    ```
    fontChooser1.setTitle ("Change Font");
    ```

3. Get current font of object to change. The font of the label is what we are changing.

    ```
    fontChooser1.setValue (label1.getFont());
    ```

4. Show the chooser:

    ```
    fontChooser1.show();
    ```

5. Check the results. If `getValue` returns `null`, the user pressed Cancel.

    ```
    Font f = fontChooser1.getValue();
    if (f != null)
      label1.setFont(f);
    ```

We have now completed all the tasks in the skill. If you save and run the program, you can change the color and the font of the label, as well as display an About box under the Help menu. Also, notice that JBuilder automatically placed code to handle the File ➤ Exit menu. Figure 18.10 shows the label with a white, 32-point, bold-italics Serif font.

FIGURE 18.10: Fully functional program, after changing font to 32-point, bold-italics Serif font.

The listing for the entire program follows. Notice how little source we actually typed in ourselves.

MenuTest.java

```
package skill18;

import java.awt.*;
import java.awt.event.*;
import borland.jbcl.control.*;
import borland.jbcl.layout.*;

public class MenuTester extends DecoratedFrame {
  BorderLayout borderLayout1 = new BorderLayout();
  BevelPanel bevelPanel1 = new BevelPanel();
  MenuBar menuBar1 = new MenuBar();
  Menu menuFile = new Menu();
  MenuItem menuFileExit = new MenuItem();
  Menu menuHelp = new Menu();
  MenuItem menuHelpAbout = new MenuItem();
  BorderLayout borderLayout2 = new BorderLayout();
  Label label1 = new Label();
  Menu menu1 = new Menu();
  MenuItem menuItem1 = new MenuItem();
  MenuItem menuItem2 = new MenuItem();
  MenuItem menuItem3 = new MenuItem();
  ColorChooser colorChooser1 = new ColorChooser();
  FontChooser fontChooser1 = new FontChooser();
```

```java
//Construct the frame
public MenuTester() {
  try {
    jbInit();
  }
  catch (Exception e) {
    e.printStackTrace();
  }
}

//Component initialization
public void jbInit() throws Exception{
  this.setLayout(borderLayout1);
  this.setSize(new Dimension(300, 200));
  this.setTitle("Frame Title");
  menuFile.setLabel("File");
  menuFileExit.setLabel("Exit");
  menuFileExit.addActionListener(new MenuTester_menuFileExit_ActionAdapter(this));
  menuHelp.setLabel("Help");
  menuHelpAbout.setLabel("About");
  label1.setText("Welcome to JBuilder");
  menu1.setLabel("Edit");
  menuItem1.setLabel("Color");
  menuItem1.addActionListener(new MenuTester_menuItem1_actionAdapter(this));
  menuItem2.setLabel("Font");
  menuItem2.addActionListener(new MenuTester_menuItem2_actionAdapter(this));
  menuItem3.setEnabled(false);
  menuItem3.setLabel("Text");
  menuHelpAbout.addActionListener(new MenuTester_menuHelpAbout_ActionAdapter(this));
  bevelPanel1.setLayout(borderLayout2);
  menuFile.add(menuFileExit);
  menuHelp.add(menuHelpAbout);
  menuBar1.add(menuFile);
  menuBar1.add(menu1);
  menuBar1.add(menuHelp);
  this.setMenuBar(menuBar1);
  this.add(bevelPanel1, BorderLayout.CENTER);
  bevelPanel1.add(label1, BorderLayout.CENTER);
  menu1.add(menuItem1);
  menu1.add(menuItem2);
  menu1.addSeparator();
  menu1.add(menuItem3);
}

//File | Exit action performed
public void fileExit_actionPerformed(ActionEvent e) {
  System.exit(0);
}
```

Adding a *FontChooser* 389

```
    //Help | About action performed
    public void helpAbout_actionPerformed(ActionEvent e) {
      MenuTester_AboutBox dlg = new MenuTester_AboutBox(this);
      Dimension dlgSize = dlg.getPreferredSize();
      Dimension frmSize = getSize();
      Point loc = getLocation();
      dlg.setLocation((frmSize.width - dlgSize.width) / 2 + loc.x, (frmSize.height -
        dlgSize.height) / 2 + loc.y);
      dlg.setModal(true);
      dlg.show();
    }

    void menuItem1_actionPerformed(ActionEvent e) {
      colorChooser1.setFrame (this);
      colorChooser1.setTitle ("Change Color");
      colorChooser1.setValue (label1.getForeground ());
      colorChooser1.show();
      Color c = colorChooser1.getValue();
        if (c != null)
          label1.setForeground(c);
    }

    void menuItem2_actionPerformed(ActionEvent e) {
      fontChooser1.setFrame (this);
      fontChooser1.setTitle ("Change Font");
      fontChooser1.setValue (label1.getFont());
      fontChooser1.show();
      Font f = fontChooser1.getValue();
        if (f != null)
          label1.setFont(f);
    }
}

class MenuTester_menuFileExit_ActionAdapter implements ActionListener {
  MenuTester adaptee;

  MenuTester_menuFileExit_ActionAdapter(MenuTester adaptee) {
    this.adaptee = adaptee;
  }

  public void actionPerformed(ActionEvent e) {
    adaptee.fileExit_actionPerformed(e);
  }
}

class MenuTester_menuHelpAbout_ActionAdapter implements ActionListener {
  MenuTester adaptee;
```

```
    MenuTester_menuHelpAbout_ActionAdapter(MenuTester adaptee) {
      this.adaptee = adaptee;
    }

    public void actionPerformed(ActionEvent e) {
      adaptee.helpAbout_actionPerformed(e);
    }
}

class MenuTester_AboutBox extends Dialog implements ActionListener {
  Panel panel1 = new Panel();
  BevelPanel bevelPanel1 = new BevelPanel();
  MenuTester_InsetsPanel insetsPanel1 = new MenuTester_InsetsPanel();
  MenuTester_InsetsPanel insetsPanel2 = new MenuTester_InsetsPanel();
  MenuTester_InsetsPanel insetsPanel3 = new MenuTester_InsetsPanel();
  Button button1 = new Button();
  ImageControl imageControl1 = new ImageControl();
  Label label1 = new Label();
  Label label2 = new Label();
  Label label3 = new Label();
  Label label4 = new Label();
  BorderLayout borderLayout1 = new BorderLayout();
  BorderLayout borderLayout2 = new BorderLayout();
  FlowLayout flowLayout1 = new FlowLayout();
  GridLayout gridLayout1 = new GridLayout();
  String product = "Menu Tester";
  String version = "1.0";
  String copyright = "Copyright (c) 1997";
  String comments = "Welcome";

  public MenuTester_AboutBox(Frame parent) {
    super(parent);
    try {
      jbInit();
    }
    catch (Exception e) {
      e.printStackTrace();
    }
    pack();
  }

  void jbInit() throws Exception{
    this.setTitle("About");
    setResizable(false);
    panel1.setLayout(borderLayout1);
    bevelPanel1.setLayout(borderLayout2);
    insetsPanel2.setLayout(flowLayout1);
    insetsPanel2.setInsets(new Insets(10, 10, 10, 10));
```

Adding a FontChooser

```java
      gridLayout1.setRows(4);
      gridLayout1.setColumns(1);
      label1.setText(product);
      label2.setText(version);
      label3.setText(copyright);
      label4.setText(comments);
      insetsPanel3.setLayout(gridLayout1);
      insetsPanel3.setInsets(new Insets(10, 60, 10, 10));
      button1.setLabel("OK");
      button1.addActionListener(this);
      imageControl1.setImageName("");
      insetsPanel2.add(imageControl1, null);
      bevelPanel1.add(insetsPanel2, BorderLayout.WEST);
      this.add(panel1, null);
      insetsPanel3.add(label1, null);
      insetsPanel3.add(label2, null);
      insetsPanel3.add(label3, null);
      insetsPanel3.add(label4, null);
      bevelPanel1.add(insetsPanel3, BorderLayout.CENTER);
      insetsPanel1.add(button1, null);
      panel1.add(insetsPanel1, BorderLayout.SOUTH);
      panel1.add(bevelPanel1, BorderLayout.NORTH);
      pack();
   }

   public void actionPerformed(ActionEvent e) {
      if (e.getSource() == button1) {
      setVisible(false);
      dispose();
      }
   }
}

class MenuTester_InsetsPanel extends Panel {
   protected Insets insets;

   public Insets getInsets() {
      return insets == null ? super.getInsets() : insets;
   }

   public void setInsets(Insets insets) {
      this.insets = insets;
   }

}

class MenuTester_menuItem1_actionAdapter implements java.awt.event.ActionListener {
   MenuTester adaptee;
```

```
  MenuTester_menuItem1_actionAdapter(MenuTester adaptee) {
    this.adaptee = adaptee;
  }

  public void actionPerformed(ActionEvent e) {
    adaptee.menuItem1_actionPerformed(e);
  }
}

class MenuTester_menuItem2_actionAdapter implements java.awt.event.ActionListener {
  MenuTester adaptee;

  MenuTester_menuItem2_actionAdapter(MenuTester adaptee) {
    this.adaptee = adaptee;
  }

  public void actionPerformed(ActionEvent e) {
    adaptee.menuItem2_actionPerformed(e);
  }
}
```

Congratulations! You should now have a good feel for how to set up menus within your Java programs in JBuilder. In the next skill, we'll look at how to add toolbars to our Java applications to make the programs even more user friendly.

Are You Experienced?

Now you can...

- ☑ **create menus**
- ☑ **create an About box**
- ☑ **handle menu-item events**
- ☑ **use the *ColorChooser***
- ☑ **use the *FontChooser***

PROGRAMMERS
C, C, VB, Cobol, exp. Call 534-555-6543 or fax 534-555-6544.

PROGRAMMING
MRFS Inc. is looking for a Sr. Windows NT developer. Reqs. 3-5 yrs. Exp. in C under Windows, Win95 & NT, using Visual C. Excl. OO design & implementation skills a must. OLE2 & ODBC are a plus. Excl. Salary & bnfts. Resume & salary history to HR, 8779 HighTech Way, Computer City, AR

PROGRAMMERS
Contractors Wanted for short & long term assignments; Visual C, MFC Unix C/C, SQL Oracle Developers PC Help Desk Support Windows NT & NetWareTelecommunications Visual Basic, Access, HTMT, CGI, Perl MMI & Co., 885-555-9933

PROGRAMMER World Wide Web Links wants your HTML & Photoshop skills. Develop great WWW sites. Local & global customers. Send samples & resume to WWWL 2000 Apple Road, Santa Rosa, CA.

TECHNICAL WRITER Software firm seeks writer/editor for manuals, research notes, project mgmt. Min 2 years tech. writing, DTP & programming experience. Send resume & writing samples to: Software Systems, Dallas, TX.

TECHNICAL Software development firm looking for Tech Trainers. Ideal candidates have programming experience in Visual C, HTML & JAVA. Need quick self starter. Call (443) 555-6868 for interview.

TECHNICAL WRITER/ Premier Computer Corp is seeking a combination of technical skills, knowledge and experience in the following areas: UNIX, Windows 95/NT, Visual Basic, on-line help & documentation, and the internet. Candidates must possess excellent writing skills, and be comfortable working in a quality vs. deadline driven environment. Competitive salary. Fax resume & samples to Karen Fields, Premier Computer Corp., 444 Industrial Blvd. Concord, CA. Or send to our website at www.premier.com.

WEB DESIGNER
BA/BS or equivalent programming/multimedia production. 3 years of experience in use and design of WWW services streaming audio and video HTML, PERL, CGI, GIF, JPEG. Demonstrated interpersonal, organization, communication, multi-tasking skills. Send resume to The Learning People at www.learning.com.

WEBMASTER-TECHNICAL
BSCS or equivalent, 2 years of experience in CGI, Windows 95/NT, UNIX, C, Java, Perl. Demonstrated ability to design, code, debug and test on-line services. Send resume to The Learning People at www.learning.com.

PROGRAMMERS Multiple short term assignments available: Visual C, 3 positions SQL ServerNT Server, 2 positions JAVA & HTML, long term NetWare Various locations. Call for more info. 356-555-3398.

PROGRAMMERS
C, C, VB, Cobol, exp.
Call 534-555-6543
or fax 534-555-6544

PROGRAMMING
MRFS Inc. is looking for a Sr. Windows NT developer. Reqs. 3-5 yrs. Exp. in C under Windows, Win95 & NT, using Visual C. Excl. OO design & implementation skills a must. OLE2 & ODBC are a plus. Excl. Salary & bnfts. Resume & salary history to HR, 8779 HighTech Way, Computer City, AR

PROGRAMMERS/ Contractors Wanted for short & long term assignments; Visual C, MFC Unix C/C, SQL Oracle Developers PC Help Desk Support Windows NT & NetWareTelecommunications Visual Basic, Access, HTMT, CGI, Perl MMI & Co., 885-555-9933

PROGRAMMER World Wide Web Links wants your HTML & Photoshop skills. Develop great WWW sites. Local & global customers. Send samples & resume to WWWL 2000 Apple Road, Santa Rosa, CA.

TECHNICAL WRITER Software firm seeks writer/editor for manuals, research notes, project mgmt. Min 2 years tech. writing, DTP & programming experience. Send resume & writing samples to: Software Systems, Dallas, TX.

COMPUTER PROGRAMMER
Ad agency seeks programmer w/exp. in UNIX/NT Platforms, Web Server, CGI/Perl. Programmer Position avail. on a project basis with the possibility to move into F/T. Fax resume & salary req. to R. Jones 334-555-8332.

TECHNICAL WRITER Premier Computer Corp is seeking a combination of technical skills, knowledge and experience in the following areas: UNIX, Windows 95/NT, Visual Basic, on-line help & documentation, and the internet. Candidates must possess excellent writing skills, and be comfortable working in a quality vs. deadline driven environment. Competitive salary. Fax resume & samples to Karen Fields, Premier Computer Corp., 444 Industrial Blvd. Concord, CA. Or send to our website at www.premier.com.

WEB DESIGNER
BA/BS or equivalent programming/multimedia production. 3 years of experience in use and design of WWW services streaming audio and video HTML, PERL, CGI, GIF, JPEG. Demonstrated interpersonal, organization, communication, multi-tasking skills. Send resume to The Learning People at www.learning.com.

MARKETING
Fast paced software and services provider looking for MARKETING COMMUNICATIONS SPECIALIST to be responsible for its webpage, seminar coordination and ad placement.

COMPUTERS Small Web Design Firm seeks indiv w/NT, Webserver & Database management exp. fax resume to 556-555-4221.

COMPUTER Visual C/C, Visual Basic Exp'd Systems Analysts/Programmers for growing software dev. team in Roseburg. Computer Science or related degree preferred. Develop adv. Engineering applications for engineering firm. Fax resume to 707-555-8744.

COMPUTER Web Master for dynamic SF Internet co. Site Dev, test, coord, train. 2 yrs prog. Exp. C C Web C, FTP. Fax resume to Best Staffing 845-555-7722.

COMPUTERS/ QA SOFTWARE TESTERS Qualified candidates should have 2 yrs exp. performing integration & system testing using automated testing tools. Experienced in documentation preparation & programming languages (Access, C, FoxPro) are a plus. Financial or banking customer service support is required along with excellent verbal & written communication skills with multi levels of end-users. Send resume to KKUP Enterprises, 45 Orange Blvd. Orange, CA.

COMPUTERS Programmer/Analyst Design and maintain C based SQL database applications. Required skills: Visual Basic, C, SQL, ODBC, Document existing and new applications, Novell or NT exp. a plus. Fax resume & salary history to 235-555-9935.

GRAPHIC DESIGNER
Webmaster's Weekly is seeking a creative Graphic Designer to design high impact marketing collateral including direct mail promo's, CD-ROM packages, ads and WWW pages. Must be able to juggle multiple projects and learn new skills on the job very rapidly. Web design experience a big plus, technical troubleshooting also a plus. Call 435-555-1235.

GRAPHICS - ART DIRECTOR - WEB-MULTIMEDIA
Leading internet development company has an outstanding opportunity for a talented, high-end Web Experienced Art Director. In addition to a great portfolio and fresh ideas, the ideal candidate has excellent communication and presentation skills. Working as a team with innovative producers and programmers; you will create dynamic, interactive web sites and application interfaces. Some programming experience required. Send samples and resume to: SuperSites, 333 Main St. Seattle, WA.

COMPUTER PROGRAMMER
Ad agency seeks programmer w/exp. in UNIX/NT Platforms, Web Server, CGI/Perl. Programmer Position avail. on a project basis with the possibility to move into F/T. Fax resume & salary req. to R. Jones 334-555-8332.

PROGRAMMERS / Established software company seeks programmers with extensive Windows NT

COMPUTERS Small Web Design firm seeks indiv w/NT, Webserver & Database management exp. fax resume to 556-555-4221.

PROGRAMMERS
C, C, VB, Cobol, exp. Call 534-555-6543 or fax 534-555-6544.

PROGRAMMING
MRFS Inc. is looking for a Windows NT developer. Reqs. yrs. Exp. in C under Win Win95 & NT using Visual C OO design & implementation a must, OLE2 & ODBC are Excl. Salary & bnfts. Resum salary history to HR, 8779 Hig Way, Computer City, AR

PROGRAMMERS/ Contr Wanted for short & long term a ments: Visual C, MFCUnix C/C Oracle Developers PC Help Support Windows NT & Ne Telecommunications Visual Access, HTMT, CGI, Perl MMI 885-555-9933

PROGRAMMER World Wid Links wants your HTML & Pho skills. Develop great WWW Local & global customers. Se ples & resume to WWWL Apple Road, Santa Rosa, CA.

TECHNICAL WRITER Softwa seeks writer/editor for m research notes, project mgmt years tech. writing, DTP & pr ming experience. Send res writing samples to: S Systems, Dallas, TX.

TECHNICAL Software deve firm looking for Tech Trainer candidates have programmi rience in Visual C, HTML & Need quick self starter. Ca 555-6868 for interview.

TECHNICAL WRITER Computer Corp is seeking a nation of technical skills, kn and experience in the fo areas: UNIX, Windows 95/N Basic, on-line help & docume and the internet. Candidate possess excellent writing sk be comfortable working in a vs. deadline driven envir Competitive salary. Fax re samples to Karen Fields, Computer Corp., 444 Industr Concord, CA. Or send to our at www.premier.com.

WEB DESIGNER
BA/BS or equivalent p ming/multimedia produc years of experience in design of WWW services s audio and video HTML, P GIF, JPEG. Demonstrated sonal, organization, comm multi-tasking skills. Send r The Learning People at www ing.com.

WEBMASTER-TECH

SKILL 19

nineteen

Creating a Toolbar

- ❑ Creating toolbars
- ❑ Getting filenames as input
- ❑ Using a GroupBox to label an area
- ❑ Using a status line for messages
- ❑ Displaying an image on a button

Working with Toolbars

Now that your Java applications can have menus, it's time to add the toolbars. It's not that your applications are incomplete without them; it's just that most current applications have them, just look at JBuilder.

In this skill, we'll create a program that prompts the user for a filename and, if it is an image, displays the file within a button. Any messages to the user will appear along a status bar, while the prompting is done with Open and Close buttons from a toolbar. To make things a little prettier, we'll place the button within an area that displays the filename selected.

As with the other skills, we'll start by closing any open projects and run through the Application Wizard. Save the project in the **c:\skills\skill19\skill19.jpr** file and press Finish. In the Application Wizard's dialog boxes, press Next to leave the first screen with the default settings. On screen two, name the class **ToolbarTester** and then select the Generate Tool Bar and Generate Status Bar options within the Frame Style area of the screen. Select Finish to have the Wizard generate the code framework. To see what we've generated this time, save everything and run it; you'll see the screen shown in Figure 19.1.

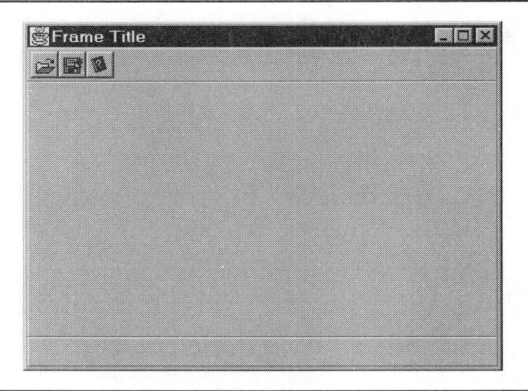

FIGURE 19.1: The initial screen with the default toolbar buttons—Open/File, Close/Save, and Help. The status bar is at the bottom of the screen.

> **NOTE** You'll quickly notice there isn't a way to quit the application. If you double-click in the top-left corner of the window title, or if you click on the close window button in the upper-right-hand corner, it will close.

As in the last skill, we'll do some general housekeeping first, before we add any functionality. We need to adjust the screen size, remove the Help icon from the toolbar, and change the container within the center quadrant of the screen.

First, we'll adjust the screen size:

1. Select `ToolbarTester.java` in the Navigation pane.
2. Select the Design tab at the bottom of the Content pane.
3. Select `this (BorderLayout)` in the Structure pane.
4. Change the size property to **400, 200**. The screen size is now set.

Now we need to remove the Help icon:

1. Select the toolbar in the UI Designer, or select `buttonBar` in the Structure pane.
2. To drop a button from the toolbar, select the labels property.
3. Then, select ... next to the labels property to edit the (unseen) button labels.
4. Delete the `Help` line and select OK.
5. Next, select the `imageNames` property and ... next to the property setting.
6. Delete the `help.gif` line from the list of images and select OK.

Finally, we can change the center quadrant container:

1. First, we need to delete the current one. Select `bevelPanel1 (XYLayout)` in the Structure pane.
2. Press the Delete key to remove it.
3. Next, select the Containers tab on the Component palette.
4. The second component is what's called a `GroupBox`. You'll see an area for a label within its border. Select it.

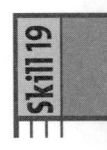

5. Drop it into the Center area of the UI Designer by pressing the mouse button there.

6. In the Inspector, change its constraints to Center if it is anything other than Center.

7. Because we don't want a static label for our example, clear out the label property. Later, we'll make the label the file we are opening.

8. Change the layout property to `BorderLayout`.

At this point, if you save and run the program, you will see the screen shown in Figure 19.2.

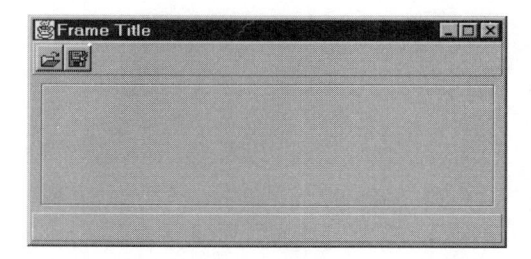

FIGURE 19.2: The new screen after the general housekeeping tasks have been performed

Selecting a Toolbar Button

The toolbar generated by the Application Wizard is a `ButtonBar`. The `ButtonBar` contains a series of buttons, displaying all images, all text, or both images and text.

> **TIP** If you change the buttonType property to have a value of TextOnly, the buttons will have text labels. If the property has a value of TextAndImage, the buttons will contain both text and image labels. The default value of ImageOnly is for images.

The nice part about a `ButtonBar` is you only need to associate one listener for all the buttons on the bar. If we bring up the Events panel in the Inspector, we only need to define one `actionPerformed` method. Selecting the `actionPerformed` method and double-clicking in the right column (three clicks in all), brings us into the Source panel of the Contents pane to define the button-selection handler. An empty handler, `buttonBar_actionPerformed`, was already created by the Application Wizard. We're only going to fill it in.

In our event handler, first we need to determine which button the user selected. For the `ButtonBar`, the text label for the button pressed is the action command of the button. This is part of the `ActionEvent` sent to the `actionPerformed` method. Once you get that, you can determine which button the user pressed.

```
String command = e.getActionCommand();
```

Now, the two default labels for a toolbar are `File` and `Close`. `Help` is the third, but we deleted that one. We just need to add code to check for each. We use the `equals` method of the `String` class to compare. For the `File` command, just call `openIt`. For the `Close` command, just call `closeIt`. We'll fill in these methods later. The necessary code for this is as follows:

```
if (command.equals ("File")) {
  openIt();
} else if (command.equals ("Close")) {
  closeIt();
}
```

Setting the Status Bar

Now we want to display on the status bar at the bottom of the screen the command selected when the user clicked a particular button. We'll add this to the `actionPerformed` method. The status bar is mostly just a label in the South quadrant. In Skill 5, we learned to change the label contents with the `setText` method. So, before going off to perform the command's operation, change the `statusBar` text. We change the message first because the command may provide its own messages. If we changed our message last, the user would miss the command's message:

```
statusBar.setText (command + " selected.");
```

The complete `actionPerformed` method follows, along with empty *stubs* for `openIt` and `closeIt`. If you run the program now, when you select a button on the toolbar, you'll see on the status bar a message describing the button selected. If you select the File button, you'll see the screen shown in Figure 19.3.

> **NOTE** A stub is a method with no body. It satisfies the compiler's need for completeness and leaves space for you to define the method later.

```
void buttonBar_actionPerformed(java.awt.event.ActionEvent e) {
  String command = e.getActionCommand();
  statusBar.setText (command + " selected.");
  if (command.equals ("File")) {
    openIt();
  } else if (command.equals ("Close")) {
    closeIt();
  }
}
void openIt() {
}
void closeIt() {
}
```

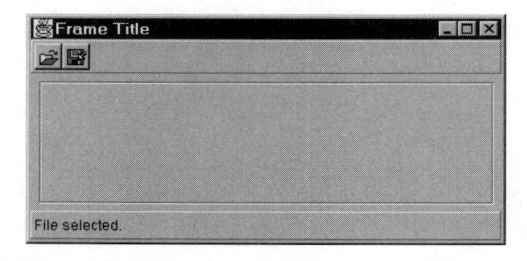

FIGURE 19.3: Showing the status bar after the Open button was selected

> **TIP** Just as the toolbar here is a `ButtonBar`, you can use a `ButtonBar` anywhere in your program. It is found under the Controls tab of the Component palette.

Picking Files

The first stub we'll define is `openIt`. In `openIt`, we need to get the name of an image file to display from the user. We don't have any place to actually display the image yet, but we'll at least get the filename first. Once the user selects a file, we'll display the name as the label in the `GroupBox` and display the full path in the status bar.

The way to prompt for a file from the user is with the help of a `Filer`. This is the standard file-selection window or Open dialog box, specific to the user's platform. On a Windows NT and Windows 95 platform, it looks like Figure 19.4. However, a Unix user sees the Motif file-selection window and a Mac user sees theirs.

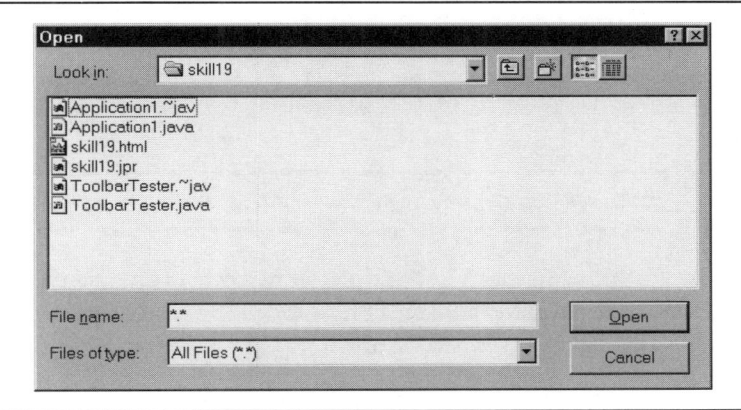

FIGURE 19.4: The Open dialog box in a Windows NT 4 system

In order to use a `Filer` in the `openIt` method, we need to drop it into our program. The `Filer` can be found on the Component palette on the Dialogs tab. To add the `Filer`, select it, select the Design tab on the Contents pane, and then press the mouse button anywhere in the Contents pane. Like the `ColorChooser` and `FontChooser` from the last skill, the `Filer` is a separate window and is added to the Others folder in the Structure pane. Once there, we can use it.

Like `ColorChooser` and `FontChooser`, `Filer` needs to be associated with a `Frame` before it can be used. Again, our program is a subclass of `Frame`, so you can set the frame of the `Filer` to `this` in the `openIt` method.

```
filer1.setFrame (this);
```

There are two modes for `Filer`: load and save. Functionally, there is little difference between the two. However, the mode does set the label of a button on the window. There are constants for the two modes as part of the `FileDialog` class. `FileDialog.LOAD` is load mode, while `FileDialog.SAVE` is save mode. The default mode happens to be load, but we'll set it anyway.

```
filer1.setMode (FileDialog.LOAD);
```

We can limit which names appear in the `Filer` with a `FilenameFilter`. A `FilenameFilter` allows us to create a custom filter. To appear in the `Filer`, filenames must pass the criteria we provide. However, although the property is there, Java doesn't support this feature, so we can't use it. If we want to limit the files listed to a specific filename mask (like `*.java` for all Java source files), we can specify it with the `setFile` method. Although this works, the user can still change the mask if they want.

```
filer1.setFile ("*.gif");
```

> **NOTE** Java can display `.gif`, `.jpg`, `.jpeg`, and `.xbm` images.

Now all that's left to do is show the `Filer`. The method that causes the `Filer` to pop up on the screen is `show`. Once the window is shown, the user must select something or press Cancel.

```
filer1.show();
```

The `getFile` method returns the specific filename the user selected. To designate that the user pressed Cancel, it returns `null`. Otherwise, you can combine `getFile`'s results with `getDirectory` to get the full path of the filename selected.

```
String filename = filer1.getFile();
if (filename != null) {
  String path = filer1.getDirectory() + filename;
}
```

At this point, we would normally show the file in some form. However, we haven't added anything to the program to show the image on. For now, let's tell the `GroupBox` the filename for its label and the status bar the full path, so the user can see what they selected. Add the following within the `if`-block:

```
groupBox1.setLabel(filename);
statusBar.setText (path + " selected.");
```

If you save and run the program now, after selecting a file, you will see Figure 19.5, assuming you pick the `ToolbarTester.java` file. The complete source for `openIt` follows.

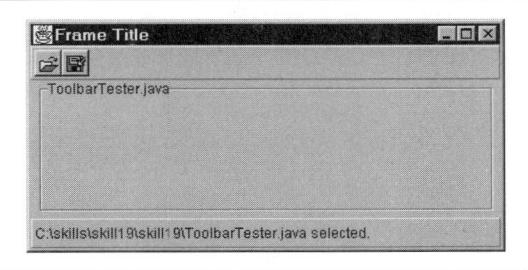

FIGURE 19.5: The current program, with messages for the ToolbarTester.java source file

```
void openIt() {
  filer1.setFrame (this);
  filer1.setMode (FileDialog.LOAD);
  filer1.setFile ("*.gif");
  filer1.show();
  String filename = filer1.getFile();
  if (filename != null) {
    String path = filer1.getDirectory() + filename;
    groupBox1.setLabel(filename);
    statusBar.setText (path + " selected.");
  }
}
```

Showing the Image

Now we want the application to display the file if it's an image file. For this, we'll use a `ButtonControl`. The `ButtonControl` component allows us to have text or an image on a button. It functions similarly to the Java `Button` class and can be found on the Controls tab of the Component palette. The reason we are using a `ButtonControl` to display the image is an image file needs somewhere to be drawn. We could either create our own drawing component for this or just reuse an existing one.

To drop this into the `GroupBox`, select `groupBox1 (BorderLayout)` in the Structure pane, and then select the `ButtonControl` from the Component palette. Next, drop the component into the center of the screen. If the constraints property is not `Center`, change it in the Inspector. Also, because we don't want any text on the button, delete the `label` property settings. If we didn't delete the label, it would appear to the right of the button, space permitting.

At this point, we just have it display the image, by adding one line to `openIt`:

```
void openIt() {
  filer1.setFrame (this);
  filer1.setMode (FileDialog.LOAD);
  filer1.setFile ("*.gif");
  filer1.show();
  String filename = filer1.getFile();
  if (filename != null) {
    String path = filer1.getDirectory() + filename;
    buttonControl1.setImageName(path);
    groupBox1.setLabel(filename);
    statusBar.setText (path + " selected.");
  }
}
```

Saving and running the program now allows us to display the image. Assuming we pick a valid image file, you'll see an image in the button. The image displayed in my application is shown in Figure 19.6. If you select an invalid file, there is no error.

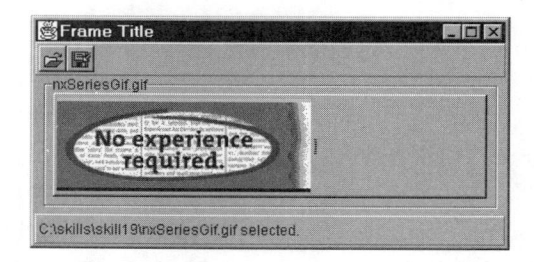

FIGURE 19.6: Displaying an image in the ToolbarTester program

NOTE If the image file is too tall, the program displays the middle of the image. If the file is too wide, it displays the left side of the image.

Closing Up

When the user selects the Close button on the toolbar, we want our application to remove the image from the button and change the label for the GroupBox. To remove the image from the button, just set the image filename to the empty string (""). The same thing is necessary for the label.

```java
void closeIt() {
  buttonControl1.setImageName("");
  groupBox1.setLabel("");
}
```

Now, rerun the program; once you load an image into the button, you can clear it out by pressing the Close button. The complete source for ToolbarTester.java follows.

ToolbarTester.java

```java
package skill19;

import java.awt.*;
import java.awt.event.*;
import borland.jbcl.control.*;
import borland.jbcl.layout.*;

public class ToolbarTester extends DecoratedFrame {
  BorderLayout borderLayout1 = new BorderLayout();
  ButtonBar buttonBar = new ButtonBar();
  StatusBar statusBar = new StatusBar();
  GroupBox groupBox1 = new GroupBox();
  BorderLayout borderLayout2 = new BorderLayout();
  Filer filer1 = new Filer();
  ButtonControl buttonControl1 = new ButtonControl();

  //Construct the frame
  public ToolbarTester() {
    try {
      jbInit();
    }
    catch (Exception e) {
      e.printStackTrace();
    }
  }
```

```java
//Component initialization
public void jbInit() throws Exception{
  this.setLayout(borderLayout1);
  this.setSize(new Dimension(400, 200));
  this.setTitle("Frame Title");
  buttonBar.setButtonType(ButtonBar.IMAGE_ONLY);
  buttonBar.setLabels(new String[] {"File", "Close"});
  buttonControl1.setLabel("");
  buttonControl1.addActionListener(new ToolbarTester_buttonControl1_actionAdapter(this));
  groupBox1.setLayout(borderLayout2);
  buttonBar.addActionListener(new ToolbarTester_buttonBar_actionAdapter(this));
  buttonBar.setImageBase("image");
  buttonBar.setImageNames(new String[] {"openFile.gif", "closeFile.gif"});
  this.add(buttonBar, BorderLayout.NORTH);
  this.add(statusBar, BorderLayout.SOUTH);
  this.add(groupBox1, BorderLayout.CENTER);
  groupBox1.add(buttonControl1, BorderLayout.CENTER);
}

//File | Exit action performed
public void fileExit_actionPerformed(ActionEvent e) {
  System.exit(0);
}

//Help | About action performed
public void helpAbout_actionPerformed(ActionEvent e) {
}

void buttonBar_actionPerformed(ActionEvent e) {
  String command = e.getActionCommand();
  statusBar.setText (command + " selected.");
  if (command.equals ("File")) {
    openIt();
  } else if (command.equals ("Close")) {
    closeIt();
  }
}
void openIt() {
  filer1.setFrame (this);
  filer1.setMode (FileDialog.LOAD);
  filer1.setFile ("*.gif");
  filer1.show();
  String filename = filer1.getFile();
  if (filename != null) {
    String path = filer1.getDirectory() + filename;
    buttonControl1.setImageName(path);
    groupBox1.setLabel(filename);
    statusBar.setText (path + " selected.");
```

```
      }
    }
    void closeIt() {
      buttonControl1.setImageName("");
      groupBox1.setLabel("");
    }

    void buttonControl1_actionPerformed(ActionEvent e) {

    }
}

class ToolbarTester_buttonBar_actionAdapter implements java.awt.event.ActionListener {
  ToolbarTester adaptee;

  ToolbarTester_buttonBar_actionAdapter(ToolbarTester adaptee) {
    this.adaptee = adaptee;
  }

  public void actionPerformed(ActionEvent e) {
    adaptee.buttonBar_actionPerformed(e);
  }
}

class ToolbarTester_buttonControl1_actionAdapter implements java.awt.event.ActionListener {
  ToolbarTester adaptee;

  ToolbarTester_buttonControl1_actionAdapter(ToolbarTester adaptee) {
    this.adaptee = adaptee;
  }

  public void actionPerformed(ActionEvent e) {
    adaptee.buttonControl1_actionPerformed(e);
  }
}
```

Well, now you can place a toolbar in your program and display images on buttons, among many other things. By now, you should be getting really comfortable within the JBuilder environment. In the next skill, we'll look at some of JBuilder's customization features to help make you even more productive.

Are You Experienced?

Now you can...

- ☑ work with toolbars
- ☑ use a *ButtonBar*
- ☑ show messages on a status bar
- ☑ use a *Filer*
- ☑ label a *GroupBox*
- ☑ display images on a *ButtonControl*

PROGRAMMERS
C, C, VB, Cobol, exp. Call 534-555-6543 or fax 534-555-6544

PROGRAMMING
MRFS Inc. is looking for a Sr. Windows NT developer. Reqs. 3-5 yrs. Exp. in C under Windows, Win95 & NT, using Visual C. Excl. OO design & implementation skills a must. OLE2 & ODBC are a plus. Excl. Salary & bnfts. Resume & salary history to HR, 8779 HighTech Way, Computer City, AR

PROGRAMMERS
Contractors Wanted for short & long term assignments; Visual C, MFC Unix C/C, SQL Oracle Dev elop ers PC Help Desk Support Windows NT & NetWareTelecommunications Visual Basic, Access, HTMT, CGI, Perl MMI & Co. 885-555-9933

PROGRAMMER World Wide Web Links wants your HTML & Photoshop skills. Develop great WWW sites. Local & global customers. Send samples & resume to WWWL, 2000 Apple Road, Santa Rosa, CA.

TECHNICAL WRITER Software firm seeks writer/editor for manuals, research notes, project mgmt. Min 2 years tech. writing, DTP & programming experience. Send resume & writing samples to: Software Systems, Dallas, TX.

TECHNICAL Software development firm looking for Tech Trainers. Ideal candidates have programming experience in Visual C, HTML & JAVA. Need quick self starter. Call (443) 555-6868 for interview.

TECHNICAL WRITER / Premier Computer Corp is seeking a combination of technical skills, knowledge and experience in the following areas: UNIX, Windows 95/NT, Visual Basic, on-line help & documentation, and the Internet. Candidates must possess excellent writing skills, and be comfortable working in a quality vs. deadline driven environment. Competitive salary. Fax resume & samples to Karen Fields, Premier Computer Corp, 444 Industrial Blvd. Concord, CA. Or send to our website at www.premier.com.

WEB DESIGNER
BA/BS or equivalent programming/multimedia production. 3 years of experience in use and design of WWW services streaming audio and video HTML, PERL, CGI, GIF, JPEG. Demonstrated interpersonal, organization, communication, multi-tasking skills. Send resume to The Learning People at www.learning.com.

WEBMASTER-TECHNICAL
BSCS or equivalent, 2 years of experience in CGI, Windows 95/NT, UNIX, C, Java, Perl. Demonstrated ability to design, code, debug and test on-line services. Send resume to The Learning People at www.learning.com.

PROGRAMMER World Wide Web Links wants your HTML & Photoshop skills. Develop great WWW sites. Local & global customers. Send samples...

ing tools. Experienced in documentation preparation & programming languages (Access, C, FoxPro) are a plus. Financial or banking customer service support is required along with excellent verbal & written communication skills with multi levels of end-users. Send resume to KKUP Enterprises, 45 Orange Blvd. Orange, CA.

COMPUTERS Small Web Design firm seeks indiv. w/NT, Webserver & Database management exp. Fax resume to 556-555-4221.

COMPUTER/ Visual C/C Visual Basic Exp'd Systems Analysts/Programmers for growing software dev. team in Roseburg. Computer Science or related degree preferred. Develop adv. Engineering applications for engineering firm. Fax resume to 707-555-8744.

COMPUTER Web Master for dynamic SF Internet co. Site, Dev, test, coord, train, 2 yrs prog. Exp. C C Web C, FTP. Fax resume to Best Staffing 845-555-7722.

COMPUTER PROGRAMMER
Ad agency seeks programmer w/exp. in UNIX/NT Platforms, Web Server, CGI/Perl. Programmer Position avail. on a project basis with the possibility to move into F/T. Fax resume & salary req. to R. Jones 334-555-8332.

COMPUTERS Programmer/Analyst Design and maintain C based SQL database applications. Required skills: Visual Basic, C, SQL, ODBC. Document existing and new applications. Novell or NT exp. a plus. Fax resume & salary history to 235-555-9935.

GRAPHIC DESIGNER
Webmaster's Weekly is seeking a creative Graphic Designer to design high impact marketing collateral, including direct mail promos, CD-ROM packages, ads and WWW pages. Must be able to juggle multiple projects and learn new skills on the job very rapidly. Web design experience a big plus, technical troubleshooting also a plus. Call 435-555-1235.

GRAPHICS - ART DIRECTOR - WEB-MULTIMEDIA
Leading internet development company has an outstanding opportunity for a talented, high-end Web Experienced Art Director. In addition to a great portfolio and fresh ideas, the ideal candidate has excellent communication and presentation skills. Working as a team with innovative producers and programmers, you will create dynamic, interactive web sites and application interfaces. Some programming experience required. Send samples and resume to: SuperSites, 333 Main, Seattle, WA.

MARKETING
Fast paced software and services provider looking for MARKETING COMMUNICATIONS SPECIALIST to be responsible for its webpage,

PROGRAMMERS
Multiple short term assignments available: Visual C, 3 positions SQL ServerNT Server, 2 positions JAVA & HTML, long term NetWare Various locations. Call for more info. 356-555-3398.

PROGRAMMERS
C, C, VB, Cobol, exp. Call 534-555-6543 or fax 534-555-6544

PROGRAMMING
MRFS Inc. is looking for a Sr. Windows NT developer. Reqs. 3-5 yrs. Exp. in C under Windows, Win95 & NT, using Visual C. Excl. OO design & implementation skills a must. OLE2 & ODBC are a plus. Excl. Salary & bnfts. Resume & salary history to HR, 8779 HighTech Way, Computer City, AR

PROGRAMMERS Contractors Wanted for short & long term assignments: Visual C, MFC Unix C/C, SQL Oracle Developers PC Help Desk Support Windows NT & NetWareTelecommunications Visual Basic, Access, HTMT, CGI, Perl MMI & Co. 885-555-9933

PROGRAMMER World Wide Web Links wants your HTML & Photoshop skills. Develop great WWW sites. Local & global customers. Send samples & resume to WWWL, 2000 Apple Road, Santa Rosa, CA.

TECHNICAL WRITER Software firm seeks writer/editor for manuals, research notes, project mgmt. Min 2 years tech. writing, DTP & programming experience. Send resume & writing samples to: Software Systems, Dallas, TX.

COMPUTER PROGRAMMER
Ad agency seeks programmer w/exp. in UNIX/NT Platforms, Web Server, CGI/Perl. Programmer Position avail. on a project basis with the possibility to move into F/T. Fax resume & salary req. to R. Jones 334-555-8332.

TECHNICAL WRITER Premier Computer Corp is seeking a combination of technical skills, knowledge and experience in the following areas: UNIX, Windows 95/NT, Visual Basic, on-line help & documentation, and the Internet. Candidates must possess excellent writing skills, and be comfortable working in a quality vs. deadline driven environment. Competitive salary. Fax resume & samples to Karen Fields, Premier Computer Corp, 444 Industrial Blvd. Concord, CA. Or send to our website at www.premier.com.

WEB DESIGNER
BA/BS or equivalent programming/multimedia production. 3 years of experience in use and design of WWW services streaming audio and video HTML, PERL, CGI, GIF, JPEG. Demonstrated interpersonal, organization, communication, multi-tasking skills. Send resume to The Learning People at www.learning.com.

WEBMASTER-TECHNICAL
BSCS or equivalent, 2 years of experience in CGI, Windows 95/NT,

PROGRAMMERS / Established software company seeks programmer...

COMPUTERS
Small Web Design firm seeks indiv w/NT, Webserver & Database management exp. Fax resume to 556-555-4221.

COMPUTER Visual C/C Visual Basic Exp'd Systems Analysts/Programmers for growing software dev. team in Roseburg. Computer Science or related degree preferred. Develop adv. Engineering applications for engineering firm. Fax resume to 707-555-8744.

COMPUTER Web Master for dynamic SF Internet co. Site, Dev, test, coord, train, 2 yrs prog. Exp. C C Web C, FTP. Fax resume to Best Staffing 845-555-7722.

COMPUTERS/ QA SOFTWARE TESTERS Qualified candidates should have 2 yrs exp. performing integration & system testing using automated testing tools. Experienced in documentation preparation & programming languages (Access, C, FoxPro) are a plus. Financial or banking customer service support is required along with excellent verbal & written communication skills with multi levels of end-users. Send resume to KKUP Enterprises, 45 Orange Blvd. Orange, CA.

COMPUTERS Programmer/Analyst Design and maintain C based SQL database applications. Required skills: Visual Basic, C, SQL, ODBC. Document existing and new applications. Novell or NT exp. a plus. Fax resume & salary history to 235-555-9935.

GRAPHIC DESIGNER
Webmaster's Weekly is seeking a creative Graphic Designer to design high impact marketing collateral, including direct mail promo's, CD-ROM packages, ads and WWW pages. Must be able to juggle multiple projects and learn new skills on the job very rapidly. Web design experience a big plus, technical troubleshooting also a plus. Call 435-555-1235.

GRAPHICS - ART DIRECTOR - WEB-MULTIMEDIA
Leading internet development company has an outstanding opportunity for a talented, high-end Web Experienced Art Director. In addition to a great portfolio and fresh ideas, the ideal candidate has excellent communication and presentation skills. Working as a team with innovative producers and programmers, you will create dynamic, interactive web sites and application interfaces. Some programming experience required. Send samples and resume to: SuperSites, 333 Main, Seattle, WA.

COMPUTER PROGRAMMER
Ad agency seeks programmer w/exp. in UNIX/NT Platforms, Web Server, CGI/Perl. Programmer Position avail. on a project basis with the possibility to move into F/T. Fax resume & salary req. to R. Jones 334-555-8332.

PROGRAMMERS / Established software company seeks program-

...ment. Must be a self-starter, energetic, organized. Must have 2 years web experience. Programming a plus. Call 985-555-9854.

PROGRAMMERS
Multiple short term assignments available: Visual C, 3 positions SQL ServerNT Server, 2 positions JAVA & HTML, long term NetWare Various locations. Call for more info. 356-555-3398.

PROGRAMMERS
C, C, VB, Cobol, exp. Call 534-555-6543 or fax 534-555-6544

PROGRAMMING
MRFS Inc. is looking for a Sr. Windows NT developer. Reqs. 3-5 yrs. Exp. in C under Windows, Win95 & NT, using Visual C. Excl. OO design & implementation skills a must. OLE2 & ODBC are a plus. Excl. Salary & bnfts. Resume & salary history to HR, 8779 HighTech Way, Computer City, AR

PROGRAMMERS/ Contractors Wanted for short & long term assignments: Visual C, MFCUnix C/C, SQL Oracle Developers PC Help Desk Support Windows NT & NetWare Telecommunications Visual Basic, Access, HTMT, CGI, Perl MMI & Co. 885-555-9933

PROGRAMMER World Wide Web Links wants your HTML & Photoshop skills. Develop great WWW sites. Local & global customers. Send samples & resume to WWWL, 2000 Apple Road, Santa Rosa, CA.

TECHNICAL WRITER Software firm seeks writer/editor for manuals, research notes, project mgmt. Min 2 years tech. writing, DTP & programming experience. Send resume & writing samples to: Software Systems, Dallas, TX.

TECHNICAL Software development firm looking for Tech Trainers. Ideal candidates have programming experience in Visual C, HTML & JAVA. Need quick self starter. Call (443) 555-6868 for interview.

TECHNICAL WRITER Premier Computer Corp is seeking a combination of technical skills, knowledge and experience in the following areas: UNIX, Windows 95/NT, Visual Basic, on-line help & documentation, and the Internet. Candidates must possess excellent writing skills, and be comfortable working in a quality vs. deadline driven environment. Competitive salary. Fax resume & samples to Karen Fields, Premier Computer Corp, 444 Industrial Blvd. Concord, CA. Or send to our website at www.premier.com.

WEB DESIGNER
BA/BS or equivalent programming/multimedia production.

WEBMASTER-TECHNICAL

SKILL 20

twenty

Customizing JBuilder

- ❑ Setting JBuilder project defaults
- ❑ Reconfiguring the Explorer.java association
- ❑ Adding code snippets

Setting the Project Author

Well, you're almost done with the book, and by now, you probably have some strong opinions about the JBuilder interface. In case there are some things you'd like to improve, this chapter should help you set up JBuilder to be user-friendlier. Also, even if you just love everything, this skill will show you some pointers for setting up an even better environment.

You've reached Skill 20, and after you've been introduced to the first tip, you'll probably be very thankful. JBuilder maintains a set of project properties. In fact, you see most of them every time you create a new project. When you use the Project Wizard, JBuilder pops up the dialog box shown in Figure 20.1, asking for a filename for the new project file, as well as a project title, your name, company, and a short description.

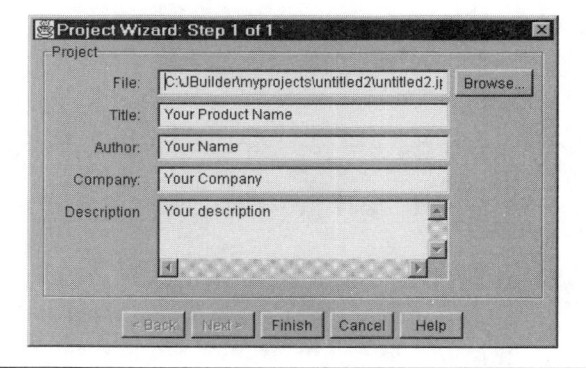

FIGURE 20.1: The Project Wizard, with properties for filename, title, author, company, and description shown

You see the remaining project properties when you create an About box with the Application Wizard. If you select the Generate About box toggle on the second page of the Application Wizard, a screen similar to the one shown in Figure 20.2 will be generated with the help of the project properties.

All in all, there are seven project properties, all shown in Table 20.1.

Setting the Project Author 413

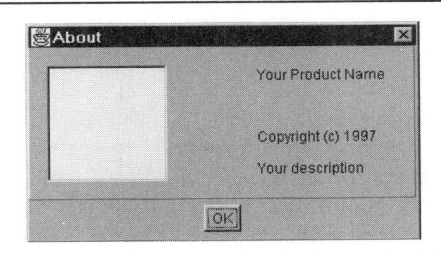

FIGURE 20.2: An About box, with project properties for title, version, copyright, and description shown

TABLE 20.1: The Project Properties and Their Default Settings

Property	Default
jbuilder.projectdefault.DefaultPackage	
jbuilder.projectdefault.Title	Your Product Name
jbuilder.projectdefault.Version	
jbuilder.projectdefault.Author	Your Name
jbuilder.projectdefault.Company	Your Company
jbuilder.projectdefault.Copyright	Copyright (c) 1997
jbuilder.projectdefault.Description	Your description

These setting are stored in a file called `jbuilder.properties` in the `lib` subdirectory under the JBuilder installation directory. If you installed JBuilder in the default installation directory, the full path would be `C:\JBuilder\lib\jbuilder.properties`.

WARNING Since you're about to change the file `C:\JBuilder\lib\jbuilder.properties`, I highly recommend that you back up this file before modifying it. Using Explorer, find the file, right-click on it, and select Copy. Find an appropriate destination directory and then right-click again, and select Paste. If you paste it to the same directory, a second copy is created called `Copy of jbuilder.properties`; otherwise, it retains its original name in the new directory.

From project to project, your name and company aren't going to change much. Unless you are on a system shared by many users, you can edit the properties file and change the appropriate lines in the file. Before editing the file, exit out of JBuilder.

> **WARNING** If you edit this file while JBuilder is open, it will revert to the original settings when you exit out of JBuilder. Also, JBuilder only reads the file when it starts.

Start up your favorite text editor and edit the file `C:\JBuilder\lib\jbuilder.properties`. You will notice the following seven lines in it:

```
jbuilder.projectdefault.DefaultPackage=
jbuilder.projectdefault.Title=Your Product Name
jbuilder.projectdefault.Version=
jbuilder.projectdefault.Author=Your Name
jbuilder.projectdefault.Company=Your Company
jbuilder.projectdefault.Copyright=Copyright (c) 1997
jbuilder.projectdefault.Description=Your description
```

Change the Your Name entry on the author line to be your name. Change the Your Company entry on the company line to be your company.

```
jbuilder.projectdefault.Author=John Zukowski
jbuilder.projectdefault.Company=Sybex
```

Save the file and restart JBuilder. Now, when you create a new project, the new entries for author and company are present, as shown in Figure 20.3. You no longer have to change it for each and every project you create.

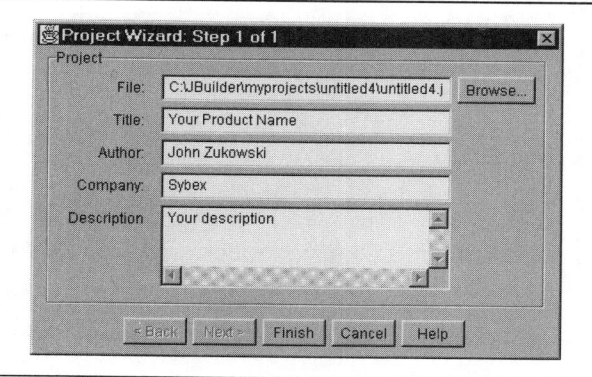

FIGURE 20.3: Creating a project with your own name and company

> **TIP**
>
> The default directory that new projects are created under is the first entry of the Default Source Path list, shown on the IDE Options screen. If you want to change this, add an entry to the beginning. For all the projects related to this book, that would be `c:\skills`. That is why we added `c:\skills` to this in the second skill.

Changing the *.java* Association in Explorer

When you installed JBuilder, it changed the default associations of Explorer so that JBuilder is associated with `.java` and `.jpr` files. If you double-click on a file with either extension, JBuilder either starts up and opens it, or it just opens it if JBuilder is already running.

> **WARNING**
>
> There is a bug in the initial release of JBuilder where this behavior is not implemented correctly. If JBuilder is already open and you double-click on a file with either extension, JBuilder doesn't open anything. The tool only comes to the front of the screen if it isn't iconified. Hopefully, this problem will be rectified by the time you read this.

While `.jpr` is the file extension for JBuilder project files, you can change the Explorer associations fairly easily if you don't want to open JBuilder for Java source (`.java`) files. Instead of opening JBuilder, you may want to open Notepad or your favorite text editor. To change the association to Notepad, follow these eight steps:

1. Start Explorer and select View ➤ Options.
2. Select the File Types tab to bring up the window shown in Figure 20.4.
3. Scroll down to the Java File entry (the list is alphabetical).
4. Select Edit… to see the Edit File Type dialog box, shown in Figure 20.5.

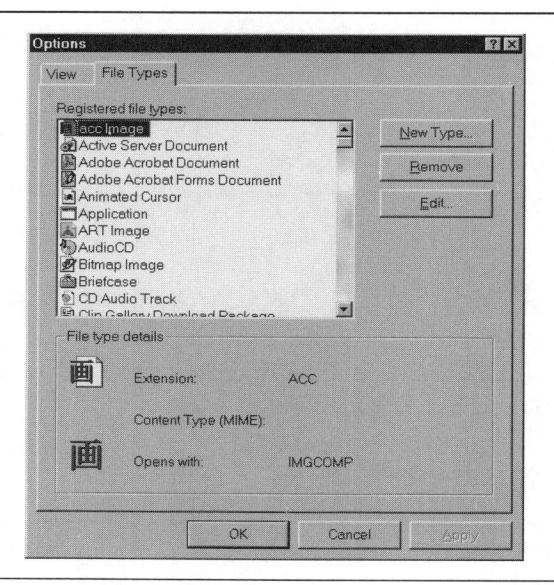

FIGURE 20.4: The Registered File Types list on the File Types tab of the Options dialog box, showing the different file types currently registered

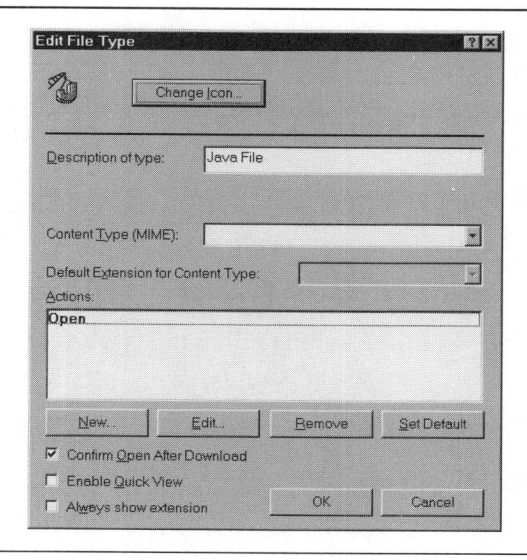

FIGURE 20.5: Editing a file type to change the action associated with it

5. Select Open in the Actions list.
6. Click Edit... to see the Editing Action for Type dialog box, as shown in Figure 20.6.

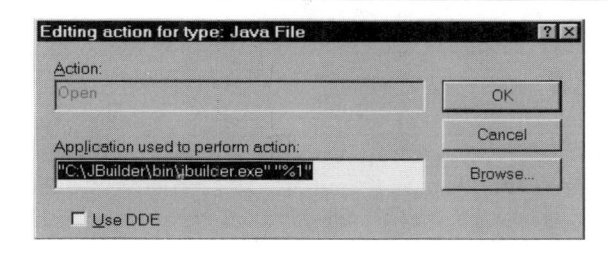

FIGURE 20.6: Picking a new program to use to open a specific file type

7. Select Browse..., find Notepad in `C:\winnt` (for Windows NT) or `c:\Windows` (for Windows 95), and select OK.
8. Select Close twice.

An alternate approach is to add a new Action to the Actions list in the Edit File Type dialog box, so that if you right-click on the file, you can select a new menu item to open the file with either the text editor or JBuilder. To add a new Action, follow the first four steps above and then continue with these:

1. Select New.
2. Enter an Action of **Edit**.
3. Select Browse..., find Notepad in `C:\winnt` (Windows NT) or in `C:\Windows` (Windows 95), and select OK.
4. Select Close twice.

Now, if you double-click on the source file, JBuilder still opens it. However, if you right-click on the file, you can select Edit to open it in Notepad.

Incorporating Your Own Snippets

Are you constantly incorporating the same block of code or class into your programs? Do you frequently hook up a set of components together with the same event-handling code? Wouldn't you just love to add the results of your actions to the Object Gallery that appears when you select File ➤ New, so the connections are already present the next time you need the set? JBuilder lets you do this and even adds its own comment keywords to help customize the files when you select them from the gallery.

Although the Component palette maintains a list of beans you can drop into the UI Designer, the various objects in the Object Gallery tend to be objects that are more complex. (The items under the New tab are the exception here.) While there is nothing that stops you from adding the complex object to the Component palette, when you select an object, or *snippet*, from the gallery, you get a class with the actual source code added to your project. In addition to the ability to customize the source code for your specific purposes, you can create snippets that prompt you for various parameters to customize it. This is done with the *Snippet Language*.

> **TIP** You would want to incorporate a complex object into the Component palette when the only changes necessary can be done through properties and events. By including the source when you use the Object Gallery, every place the source was included would be buggy if there was an error in the source code. If there was an error in the component on the palette, you would fix up the component, and everything would be magically updated.

Understanding the Snippet Language

The language used to define snippets is similar to HTML. There are a set of tags, similar to <APPLET>, <IMG>, or <p>, which may or may not have a closing tag, such as </APPLET>. Each tag has a special meaning and purpose. You specify the tags within Java comment lines.

> **NOTE** Objects appearing in the Object Gallery are defined by files in the snippets directory in the JBuilder installation area. If you are curious how a specific snippet works in the gallery, look there for the source.

Some of the most common tags include the following:

<EXCLUDE>...</EXCLUDE> Lines between these two tags are not placed in the resulting file when the user invokes the snippet code. They allow you to add comments to your snippets.

```
//<EXCLUDE>
//Hello There
//</EXCLUDE>
```

<FILE> The <FILE> tag allows you to specify a filename for the generated code. This can be hard coded to a specific name or specified by a parameter.

```
//<FILE=Foo.java>
```

<TARGET> The <TARGET> tag is for when users will use your snippet to create public classes. To ensure the public class name matches the filename, use this tag. The tag parameter `text` shows a prompt. The `pattern` parameter shows the pattern name that will be searched for to replace the user-specified input. Unless the user enters something else, the initial value provided is used. JBuilder searches everything for the pattern, including quoted strings, and changes the pattern to the value entered.

```
//<Target text="Name of Class" pattern=%class% default=AClass>
```

<PROMPT> The <PROMPT> tag is for parameters that don't necessarily have to do with the class name. If certain settings can be set at run time, this provides the means to update them.

```
//<Prompt text="Height of Panel" pattern=%height% default=250>
```

<PACKAGE> The <PACKAGE> tag ensures the appropriate package line is added to the generated source. Then, the new class will belong to the correct package.

```
//<PACKAGE>
```

All tags are optional. If none are specified, the source generated will be placed in the current project, within a file `UntitledN.java`, where *N* is a one-up number that increases to the next unused number.

If your new snippet only has <EXCLUDE>, <FILE>, and <PACKAGE> tags, you should name the snippet with an extension of `.java`. If your new snippet includes other Snippet Language tags, you should name the file with an extension of `.snippet`. However, there is nothing that requires this naming convention; it just follows the lead that Borland offers with their own snippets.

Creating the Class

The first thing you need to do in order to create a snippet is to create the snippet-to-be class as a normal class. One thing that is nice to have around is a `ScrollBar` with a `TextField` associated with it. When the user moves the scrollbar, the text field displays the value. When the user enters a value in the text field, the scrollbar position changes. We'll also show a `Label` so the user knows what to do.

> **NOTE** While this combination could easily be packaged as a bean and placed on the Component palette, we'll keep it as a snippet.

To create this, close everything and select the Panel icon in the Object Gallery (File ➤ New). This starts up the Project Wizard. Let's enter a project filename of **C:\skills\skill20\skill20.jpr** and select Finish. On the New Panel dialog, just select OK, and eventually `Panel1.java` will be added to the Navigation pane.

Switch over to design mode to set up the screen by selecting the Design tab in the Contents pane. We want to add the scrollbar to the bottom quadrant, with the label and text field next to each other in the top quadrant.

1. First, change the layout manager of the panel to `BorderLayout`.
2. Add a `Panel` from the AWT tab on the Component palette and make it the North quadrant.
3. Add a `Label` to the new `Panel` and change the text property to `Enter amount:`.
4. Add a `TextField` to the new `Panel` and change the `columns` property to **5**. Make sure this is added to the right of the label.
5. Finally, add a `Scrollbar` to the South quadrant and set its orientation to **0**, or horizontal. Also, give it a maximum value of **250**. The specific maximum will be customized later with the snippet.

The user interface is done and should look like Figure 20.7. Now we have to add the interactivity.

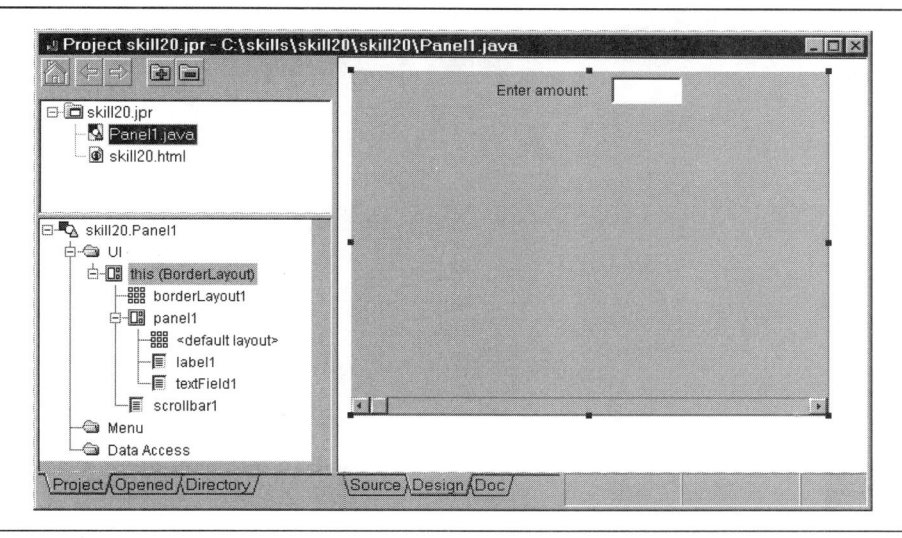

FIGURE 20.7: The initial screen for the program, as shown in the UI Designer

We need to add two event handlers: one for moving the scrollbar and a second for pressing Enter in the text field. With the help of the Interaction Wizard we'll add these, so the system does the hard parts. However, we'll have to customize the generated code because it doesn't do exactly what we want.

For the scrollbar event handling, select Wizards ➤ Interaction Wizard. Select the `scrollbar1` entry and select Next. We want to connect the scrollbar to the text field, so select `textField1` in the To component field. The On Event of Value Changed is already selected, so we just have to select Set the Text under Do the Following, as shown in Figure 20.8.

Selecting Next prompts us to enter a new value for the contents of the text field. Here we want to set it to the event's value. Unfortunately, the Wizard only accepts constants. For now just enter **0**, and we'll fill it in later. After selecting Finish, the first event handler is added.

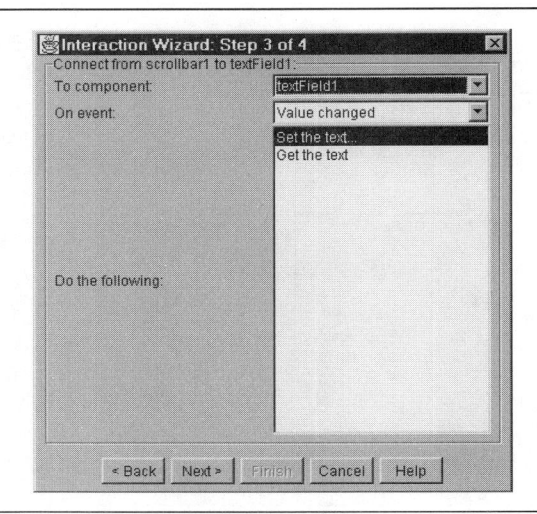

FIGURE 20.8: Step 3 of 4 in the Interaction Wizard, connecting the scrollbar to the text field

Next, we need to add an action handler for the text field. When the user presses Enter, set the scrollbar value to the text field contents. Again, start the Interaction Wizard with Wizards ➤ Interaction Wizard. The source of the event this time is the text field, so select `textField1` and the Next button. The To component is `scrollbar1` this time and our On Event is Activated. But wait, there is no Activated event. By default, Activated isn't available to the Interaction Wizard; you need to turn it on manually. We could use the Text Changed event, but then the scrollbar will jump all around as each digit of a number is entered.

In order to add Activated, we need to open the Interaction Wizard Editor. First, select Cancel to halt the initial operation. Then, select the `TextField` in the UI Designer, and Tools ➤ Interaction Wizard Editor. Select the `java.awt.TextField` entry and select Next. This brings up the screen shown in Figure 20.9, where you select which events to expose.

If you select `ACTION_EVENTS`, the This Event Group Exposed to Interactions toggle becomes enabled. Select the checkbox so it is toggled on. You'll notice a green dot next to the `ACTION_EVENTS` entry. The other events will not appear within the Interaction Wizard now.

Once you select Next, the screen shown in Figure 20.10 appears, and you can configure which methods the event handler can call.

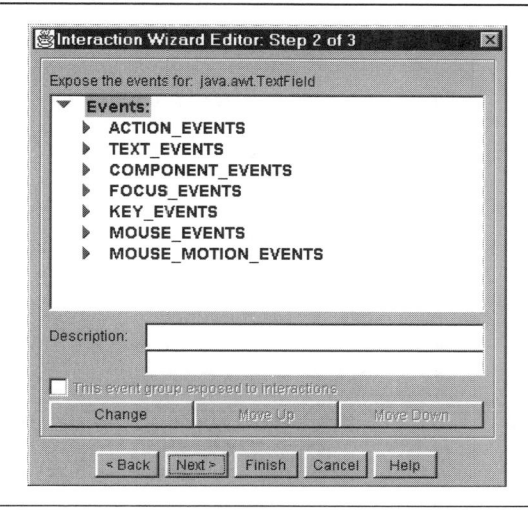

FIGURE 20.9: Configuring the exposed events in the Interaction Wizard Editor

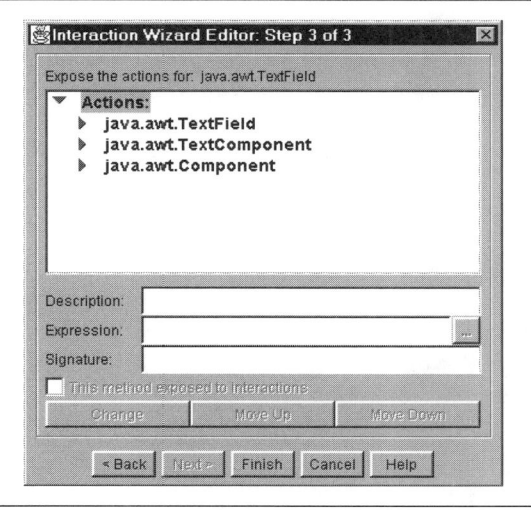

FIGURE 20.10: Exposing actions for a TextField in the Interaction Wizard Editor

Here, we need to get the text value of the `TextField`, so we need to find the `getText` method. This happens to be a method of `TextComponent`, so we select the arrow to the left of `TextComponent` to reveal its method list. Selecting `getText` enables the This Method Exposed to Interactions toggle, which we select. Again, you'll notice the green dot. Now, you can press Finish and go back to the original Interaction Wizard.

Restarting the Interaction Wizard (Wizards ➤ Interaction Wizard) allows us to select `textField1` again and then Next. On the second screen, labeled Step 3 of 4, we need to select `scrollbar1`, so the two can communicate. The Activated event is now available and selected, so we just have to choose Set the Value for the `Scrollbar` and then chose Next. Here, we want to convert the text field's contents to an integer and set the scrollbar. However, the Wizard only works with constants so we just need to fill in something, such as **0**, to generate the source framework that we'll expand momentarily.

Once you select Finish, the second event handler code is added. If you switch back into source mode, you'll see two methods added to `Panel1`: `scrollbar1_adjustmentValueChanged1` and `textField1_actionPerformed1`. These are the two methods we need to customize because the Wizard couldn't quite do everything for us. You'll also notice that two new classes were created: `Panel1_scrollbar1AdjustmentAdapter` and `Panel1_textFieldActionAdapter`. These adapter classes connect the new panel methods to the event handling.

In `scrollbar1_adjustmentValueChanged1`, we need to change the text field value to the new scrollbar setting. The parameter to the method is `AdjustmentEvent`, and it just happens to contain the current setting. Change the current line (`textField1.setText("0");`) to the following:

```
textField1.setText("" + adjustmentEvent.getValue());
```

For `textField1_actionPerformed1`, the same thing holds true. The `ActionEvent` parameter contains the text field setting, which we need to pass along to the scrollbar. Replace its current line (`scrollbar1.setValue(0);`) with the following:

```
scrollbar1.setValue(new
Integer(actionEvent.getActionCommand()).intValue());
```

That's all there is to the panel.

To test the interactions, let's create a test program. Using the Application Wizard, create a frame called **PanelTester**, and select Finish. Change the line that declares the instance variable `bevelPanel1`, as shown here:

```
BevelPanel bevelPanel1 = new BevelPanel();
```

to

```
BevelPanel bevelPanel1 = new Panel1();
```

And delete the line that sets its layout manager in `jbInit`:

```
bevelPanel1.setLayout(xYLayout2);
```

Running the program at this point demonstrates the interactivity between the two components, as shown in Figure 20.11. If you move the scrollbar, the text field value changes. If you enter a new value in the text field, when you press return the scrollbar changes. The source for the `PanelTester` and `Panel1` follows.

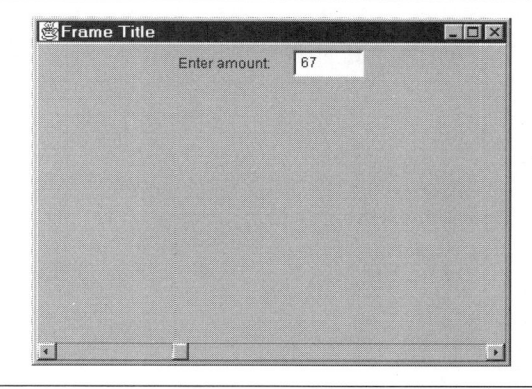

FIGURE 20.11: The Panel1 class with scrollbar and text field connected

> **TIP** Be sure to select `Application1.java` before you select Run, otherwise JBuilder tries to run `PanelTester`, which doesn't have a `main` method.

PanelTester.java

```java
package skill20;

import java.awt.*;
import java.awt.event.*;
import borland.jbcl.control.*;
import borland.jbcl.layout.*;

public class PanelTester extends DecoratedFrame {
  BorderLayout borderLayout1 = new BorderLayout();
  XYLayout xYLayout2 = new XYLayout();
  BevelPanel bevelPanel1 = new Panel1();

  //Construct the frame
  public PanelTester() {
    try {
      jbInit();
    }
    catch (Exception e) {
      e.printStackTrace();
    }
  }

  //Component initialization
  public void jbInit() throws Exception{
    this.setLayout(borderLayout1);
    this.setSize(new Dimension(400, 300));
    this.setTitle("Frame Title");
    this.add(bevelPanel1, BorderLayout.CENTER);
  }
}
```

Panel1.java

```
//Title:         Your Product Name
//Version:
//Copyright:     Copyright (c) 1997
//Author:        John Zukowski
//Company:       Sybex
//Description:   Your description
```

Incorporating Your Own Snippets

```java
package skill20;

import java.awt.*;
import java.awt.event.*;
import borland.jbcl.layout.*;
import borland.jbcl.control.*;

public class Panel1 extends BevelPanel {
  BorderLayout borderLayout1 = new BorderLayout();
  Panel panel1 = new Panel();
  Label label1 = new Label();
  TextField textField1 = new TextField();
  Scrollbar scrollbar1 = new Scrollbar();

  public Panel1() {
    try {
      jbInit();
    }
    catch (Exception e) {
      e.printStackTrace();
    }
  }

  public void jbInit() throws Exception{
    label1.setText("Enter amount:");
    textField1.setColumns(5);
    scrollbar1.setOrientation(0);
    scrollbar1.setMaximum(250);
    this.setLayout(borderLayout1);
    this.add(panel1, BorderLayout.NORTH);
    panel1.add(label1, null);
    panel1.add(textField1, null);
    this.add(scrollbar1, BorderLayout.SOUTH);
    scrollbar1.addAdjustmentListener(new Panel1_scrollbar1AdjustmentAdapter1(this));
    textField1.addActionListener(new Panel1_textField1ActionAdapter1(this));
  }

  void scrollbar1_adjustmentValueChanged1(AdjustmentEvent adjustmentEvent) {
    textField1.setText("" + adjustmentEvent.getValue());
  }

  void textField1_actionPerformed1(ActionEvent actionEvent) {
    scrollbar1.setValue(new Integer(actionEvent.getActionCommand()).intValue());
  }
}
```

```
// JBUILDER GENERATED ADAPTER CLASS FOR scrollbar1
class Panel1_scrollbar1AdjustmentAdapter1 implements
java.awt.event.AdjustmentListener {

  Panel1_scrollbar1AdjustmentAdapter1(Panel1 panel1) {
    this.panel1 = panel1;
  }
  Panel1 panel1;

  public void adjustmentValueChanged(AdjustmentEvent adjustmentEvent) {
    panel1.scrollbar1_adjustmentValueChanged1(adjustmentEvent);
  }
}

// JBUILDER GENERATED ADAPTER CLASS FOR textField1
class Panel1_textField1ActionAdapter1 implements java.awt.event.ActionListener {

  Panel1_textField1ActionAdapter1(Panel1 panel1) {
    this.panel1 = panel1;
  }
  Panel1 panel1;

  public void actionPerformed(ActionEvent actionEvent) {
    panel1.textField1_actionPerformed1(actionEvent);
  }
}
```

Adding the Snippet

Once you've created the class you want to turn into a snippet, you can add it to the Object Gallery. Before you can add it to the Object Gallery, however, you need to customize it, so when you're reusing it from the gallery, it won't always be the same. If you don't want to modify the original version, you should save a copy of the file outside the project directory. The default directory that contains snippet source code is the `snippet` directory under the JBuilder installation directory. So, using Explorer, copy the `Panel1.java` source file to `C:\JBuilder\snippets\MyPanel.snippet`.

Once copied, you need to add the package tag and prompts for class name and maximum scrollbar value. This involves deleting the existing package line, adding these three lines in your own editor:

```
//<PACKAGE>
//<Target text="Name of Class" pattern=%class% default=ScrollPanel>
//<Prompt text="Maximum size" pattern=%max% default=100>
```

and replacing the class name everywhere with the class name prompt:

```
public class %class% extends BevelPanel {
...
public %class%() {
...
Panel1_scrollbar1AdjustmentAdapter1(%class% panel1) {
...
%class% panel1;
...
Panel1_textField1ActionAdapter1(%class% panel1) {
...
%class% panel1;
...
```

Use the max prompt value, too:

```
scrollbar1.setMaximum (%max%);
```

This results in the following snippet source file.

MyPanel.snippet

```
//<PACKAGE>
//<Target text="Name of Class" pattern=%class% default=ScrollPanel>
//<Prompt text="Maximum size" pattern=%max% default=100>

import java.awt.*;
import java.awt.event.*;
import borland.jbcl.layout.*;
import borland.jbcl.control.*;

public class %class% extends BevelPanel {
  BorderLayout borderLayout1 = new BorderLayout();
  Panel panel1 = new Panel();
  Label label1 = new Label();
  TextField textField1 = new TextField();
  Scrollbar scrollbar1 = new Scrollbar();

  public %class%() {
    try {
      jbInit();
    }
    catch (Exception e) {
      e.printStackTrace();
    }
  }
```

```
  public void jbInit() throws Exception{
    label1.setText("Enter amount:");
    textField1.setColumns(5);
    scrollbar1.setOrientation(0);
    scrollbar1.setMaximum(%max%);
    this.setLayout(borderLayout1);
    this.add(panel1, BorderLayout.NORTH);
    panel1.add(label1, null);
    panel1.add(textField1, null);
    this.add(scrollbar1, BorderLayout.SOUTH);
    scrollbar1.addAdjustmentListener(new Panel1_scrollbar1AdjustmentAdapter1(this));
    textField1.addActionListener(new Panel1_textField1ActionAdapter1(this));
  }

  void scrollbar1_adjustmentValueChanged1(AdjustmentEvent adjustmentEvent) {
    textField1.setText("" + adjustmentEvent.getValue());
  }

  void textField1_actionPerformed1(ActionEvent actionEvent) {
    scrollbar1.setValue(new Integer(actionEvent.getActionCommand()).intValue());
  }
}

// JBUILDER GENERATED ADAPTER CLASS FOR scrollbar1
class Panel1_scrollbar1AdjustmentAdapter1 implements
java.awt.event.AdjustmentListener {

  Panel1_scrollbar1AdjustmentAdapter1(%class% panel1) {
    this.panel1 = panel1;
  }
  %class% panel1;

  public void adjustmentValueChanged(AdjustmentEvent adjustmentEvent) {
    panel1.scrollbar1_adjustmentValueChanged1(adjustmentEvent);
  }
}

// JBUILDER GENERATED ADAPTER CLASS FOR textField1
class Panel1_textField1ActionAdapter1 implements java.awt.event.ActionListener {

  Panel1_textField1ActionAdapter1(%class% panel1) {
    this.panel1 = panel1;
  }
  %class% panel1;
```

```
  public void actionPerformed(ActionEvent actionEvent) {
    panel1.textField1_actionPerformed1(actionEvent);
  }
}
```

Once we have the source file set up, save it and return to the JBuilder environment. Select File ➤ New to reopen the Object Gallery. We'll add the snippet to the Other tab, so select that. Once there, right-click over the Gallery and you'll see a pull-down menu with a single entry on it: Add Snippet. Selecting it brings up the Add Snippet dialog box, shown in Figure 20.12.

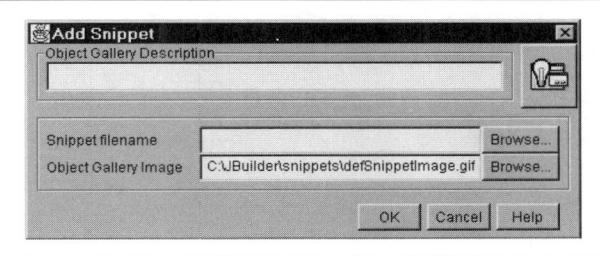

FIGURE 20.12: The Add Snippet dialog box. From here, you can add your own code fragments to the Object Gallery.

In the Object Gallery Description field, enter **Scrolling Panel Prompt** as its name. This name is what you will see when you look in the Gallery. The top-right corner shows you the image-icon that will be displayed in the Gallery. The default icon is the `defSnippetImage.gif` image file. If you want a different icon, select the icon image or select the Browse button next to the Object Gallery Image text box.

> **TIP** The icon for a Gallery entry should be no larger than approximately 40 pixels wide × 50 pixels tall.

Finally, enter **C:\JBuilder\snippets\MyPanel.snippet** into the Snippet filename text box, and select OK. You will now see the new snippet in the Gallery, as shown in Figure 20.13.

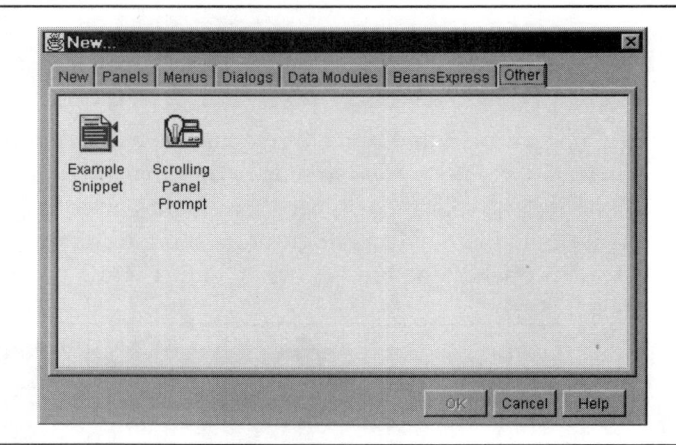

FIGURE 20.13: The Scrolling Panel Prompt added to the Object Gallery

Using the New Snippet

Now, we can reuse our new snippet like all the other ones. Close everything by selecting File ➤ Close All, and start the Application Wizard. In the Project Wizard, call the project **skill20b** and save it to **c:\skills\skill20b\skill20b.jpr**. On the second screen of the Application Wizard, name the frame class **SnippetTester** and select Finish.

Once JBuilder creates the application framework, let's use our new snippet. Select File ➤ New and the Other tab to return to Figure 20.13. If you double-click the Scrolling Panel Prompt entry, you'll get the Paste Snippet dialog box, as shown in Figure 20.14.

To customize the Scrolling Panel Prompt, select Parameters and you'll see the dialog box shown in Figure 20.15. From here, enter a class name of **MyScrollPanel** and a maximum value of **500**. Select OK and watch the contents of the original window change. Select OK again and the snippet will be added to the project as `MyScrollPanel.java`.

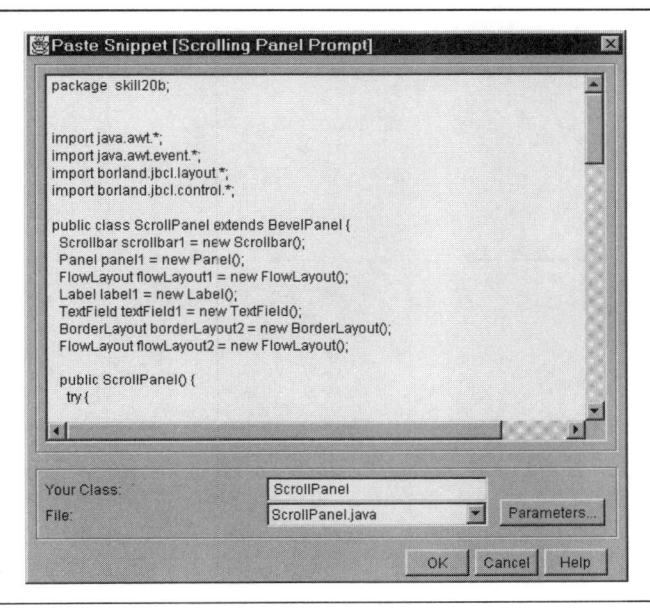

FIGURE 20.14: The Paste Snippet dialog box for a Scrolling Panel Prompt object. From here, you can customize it or just create it with the default settings.

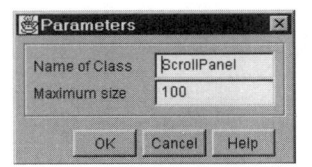

FIGURE 20.15: Selecting Parameters allows you to customize the settings for your specific needs.

Now, we need to change the `SnippetTester` source. Currently, it displays a plain `BevelPanel` in the center quadrant of the screen. Here, we just have to change it to display a `MyScrollPanel`. Select `SnippetTester.java` and change the first line shown here to the second line within its source:

```
BevelPanel bevelPanel1 = new BevelPanel();
```

to

```
BevelPanel bevelPanel1 = new MyScrollPanel();
```

Also, because the `MyScrollPanel` already has a layout manager, the program no longer needs to set the `bevelPanel1` layout manager. Delete the following line from `jbInit`:

```
bevelPanel1.setLayout(xYLayout2);
```

Now, if you save everything and run the program, you'll see Figure 20.16 displayed.

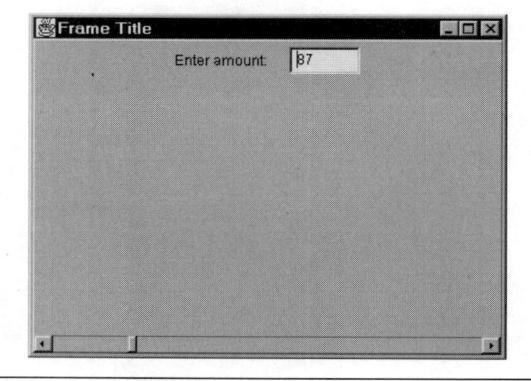

FIGURE 20.16: The complete program with the new snippet added. Enter a value in the text field or move the scrollbar to see the changes.

The complete source for the testing program follows. You'll find the source for `MyScrollPanel` earlier in the skill, with the class name as `ScrollPanel`.

SnippetTester.java

```
package skill20b;

import java.awt.*;
import java.awt.event.*;
import borland.jbcl.control.*;
import borland.jbcl.layout.*;

public class SnippetTester extends DecoratedFrame {
  BorderLayout borderLayout1 = new BorderLayout();
  XYLayout xYLayout2 = new XYLayout();
  BevelPanel bevelPanel1 = new MyScrollPanel();
```

```
//Construct the frame
public SnippetTester() {
  try {
    jbInit();
  }
  catch (Exception e) {
    e.printStackTrace();
  }
}

//Component initialization
public void jbInit() throws Exception{
  this.setLayout(borderLayout1);
  this.setSize(new Dimension(400, 300));
  this.setTitle("Frame Title");
  this.add(bevelPanel1, BorderLayout.CENTER);
}
}
```

With the customizations shown here in this skill, you should become more productive in the JBuilder environment. Two more JBuilder skills worth learning are using the debugger and gaining a better understanding of multithreading. The final skill, Skill 21, explains these last two capabilities.

Are You Experienced?

Now you can...

- ☑ reset the project author and company
- ☑ set up the *.java* file association
- ☑ create your own code snippets
- ☑ incorporate your own snippets into JBuilder

PROGRAMMERS
C, C, VB, Cobol, exp. Call 534-555-6543 or fax 534-555-6544.

PROGRAMMING
MRFS Inc. is looking for a Sr. Windows NT developer. Reqs. 3-5 yrs. Exp. In C under Windows, Win95 & NT, using Visual C. Excl. OO design & implementation skills a must. OLE2 & ODBC are a plus. Excl. Salary & bnfts. Resume & salary history to HR, 8779 HighTech Way, Computer City, AR

PROGRAMMERS
Contractors Wanted for short & long term assignments: Visual C, MFC Unix C/C, SQL Oracle Dev elop ers PC Help Desk Support Windows NT & NetWareTelecommunications Visual Basic, Access, HTMT, CGI, Perl MMI & Co., 885-555-9933

PROGRAMMER World Wide Web Links wants your HTML & Photoshop skills. Develop great WWW sites. Local & global customers. Send samples & resume to WWWL, 2000 Apple Road, Santa Rosa, CA.

TECHNICAL WRITER Software firm seeks writer/editor for manuals, research notes, project mgmt. Min 2 years tech. writing, DTP & programming experience. Send resume & writing samples to: Software Systems, Dallas, TX.

TECHNICAL Software development firm looking for Tech Trainers. Ideal candidates have programming experience in Visual C, HTML & JAVA. Need quick self starter. Call (443) 555-6868 for interview.

TECHNICAL WRITER/ Premier Computer Corp is seeking a combination of technical skills, knowledge and experience in the following areas: UNIX, Windows 95/NT, Visual Basic, on-line help & documentation, and the internet. Candidates must possess excellent writing skills, and be comfortable working in a quality vs. deadline driven environment. Competitive salary. Fax resume & samples to Karen Fields, Premier Computer Corp., 444 Industrial Blvd. Concord, CA. Or send to our website at www.premier.com.

WEB DESIGNER
BA/BS or equivalent programming/multimedia production. 3 years of experience in use and design of WWW services streaming audio and video HTML, PERL, CGI, GIF, JPEG. Demonstrated interpersonal, organization, communication, multi-tasking skills. Send resume to The Learning People at www.learning.com.

WEBMASTER-TECHNICAL
BSCS or equivalent. 2 years of experience in CGI, Windows 95/NT, UNIX, C, Java, Perl. Demonstrated ability to design code, debug and test on-line services. Send resume to The Learning People at www.learning.com.

PROGRAMMER World Wide Web Links wants your HTML & Photoshop skills. Develop great WWW sites. Local & global customers. Send sam-

---

ing tools. Experienced in documentation preparation & programming languages (Access, C, FoxPro) are a plus. Financial or banking customer service support is required along with excellent verbal & written communication skills with multi levels of end-users. Send resume to KKUP Enterprises, 45 Orange Blvd. Orange, CA.

COMPUTERS Small Web Design firm seeks indiv. w/NT, Webserver & Database management exp. Fax resume to 556-555-4221.

COMPUTER/ Visual C/C, Visual Basic Exp'd Systems Analysts/Programmers for growing software dev. team in Roseburg. Computer Science or related degree preferred. Develop adv. Engineering applications for engineering firm. Fax resume to 707-555-8744.

COMPUTER Web Master for dynamic SF Internet co. Site, Dev., test, coord, train, 2 yrs prog. Exp. C C Web C, FTP. Fax resume to Best Staffing 845-555-7722.

COMPUTER PROGRAMMER
Ad agency seeks programmer w/exp. in UNIX/NT Platforms, Web Server, CGI/Perl. Programmer Position avail. on a project basis with the possibility to move into F/T. Fax resume & salary req. to R. Jones 334-555-8332.

COMPUTERS Programmer/Analyst Design and maintain C based SQL database applications. Required skills: Visual Basic, C, SQL, ODBC Document existing and new applications. Novell or NT exp. a plus. Fax resume & salary history to 235-555-9935.

GRAPHIC DESIGNER
Webmaster's Weekly is seeking a creative Graphic Designer to design high impact marketing collateral, including direct mail promo's, CD-ROM packages, ads and WWW pages. Must be able to juggle multiple projects and learn new skills on the job very rapidly. Web design experience a big plus, technical troubleshooting also a plus. Call 435-555-1235.

GRAPHICS - ART DIRECTOR - WEB-MULTIMEDIA
Leading internet development company has an outstanding opportunity for a talented, high-end Web Experienced Art Director. In addition to a great portfolio and fresh ideas, the ideal candidate has excellent communication and presentation skills. Working as a team with innovative producers and programmers, you will create dynamic, interactive web sites and application interfaces. Some programming experience required. Send samples and resume to: SuperSites, 333 Main, Seattle, WA.

MARKETING
Fast paced software and services provider looking for MARKETING COMMUNICATIONS SPECIALIST to be responsible for its webpage, seminar coordination, and ad place-

---

PROGRAMMERS Multiple short term assignments available: Visual C, 3 positions SQL ServerNT Server, 2 positions JAVA & HTML, long term NetWare Various locations. Call for more info. 356-555-3398.

PROGRAMMERS
C, C, VB, Cobol, exp.
Call 534-555-6543
or fax 534-555-6544.

PROGRAMMING
MRFS Inc. is looking for a Sr. Windows NT developer. Reqs. 3-5 yrs. Exp. In C under Windows, Win95 & NT, using Visual C. Excl. OO design & implementation skills a must. OLE2 & ODBC are a plus. Excl. Salary & bnfts. Resume & salary history to HR, 8779 HighTech Way, Computer City, AR

PROGRAMMERS/ Contractors Wanted for short & long term assignments: Visual C, MFC Unix C/C, SQL Oracle Developers PC Help Desk Support Windows NT & NetWareTelecommunications Visual Basic, Access, HTMT, CGI, Perl MMI & Co., 885-555-9933

PROGRAMMER World Wide Web Links wants your HTML & Photoshop skills. Develop great WWW sites. Local & global customers. Send samples & resume to WWWL, 2000 Apple Road, Santa Rosa, CA.

TECHNICAL WRITER Software firm seeks writer/editor for manuals, research notes, project mgmt. Min 2 years tech. writing, DTP & programming experience. Send resume & writing samples to: Software Systems, Dallas, TX.

COMPUTER PROGRAMMER
Ad agency seeks programmer w/exp. in UNIX/NT Platforms, Web Server, CGI/Perl. Programmer Position avail. on a project basis with the possibility to move into F/T. Fax resume & salary req. to R. Jones 334-555-8332.

TECHNICAL WRITER Premier Computer Corp is seeking a combination of technical skills, knowledge and experience in the following areas: UNIX, Windows 95/NT, Visual Basic, on-line help & documentation, and the internet. Candidates must possess excellent writing skills, and be comfortable working in a quality vs. deadline driven environment. Competitive salary. Fax resume & samples to Karen Fields, Premier Computer Corp., 444 Industrial Blvd. Concord, CA. Or send to our website at www.premier.com.

WEB DESIGNER
BA/BS or equivalent programming/multimedia production. 3 years of experience in use and design of WWW services streaming audio and video HTML, PERL, CGI, GIF, JPEG. Demonstrated interpersonal, organization, communication, multi-tasking skills. Send resume to The Learning People at www.learning.com.

WEBMASTER-TECHNICAL
BSCS or equivalent. 2 years of experience in CGI, Windows 95/NT,

---

PROGRAMMERS Multiple short term assignments available: Visual C, 3 positions SQL ServerNT Server, 2 positions JAVA & HTML, long term NetWare Various locations. Call for more info. 356-555-3398.

COMPUTERS Small Web Design firm seeks indiv. w/NT, Webserver & Database management exp. Fax resume to 556-555-4221.

COMPUTER Visual C/C, Visual Basic Exp'd Systems Analysts/Programmers for growing software dev. team in Roseburg. Computer Science or related degree preferred. Develop adv. Engineering applications for engineering firm. Fax resume to 707-555-8744.

COMPUTER Web Master for dynamic SF Internet co. Site, Dev., test, coord, train, 2 yrs prog. Exp. C C Web C, FTP. Fax resume to Best Staffing 845-555-7722.

COMPUTERS/ QA SOFTWARE TESTERS Qualified candidates should have 2 yrs exp. performing integration & system testing using automated testing tools. Experienced in documentation preparation & programming languages (Access, C, FoxPro) are a plus. Financial or banking customer service support is required along with excellent verbal & written communication skills with multi levels of end-users. Send resume to KKUP Enterprises, 45 Orange Blvd. Orange, CA.

COMPUTERS Programmer/Analyst Design and maintain C based SQL database applications. Required skills: Visual Basic, C, SQL, ODBC Document existing and new applications. Novell or NT exp. a plus. Fax resume & salary history to 235-555-9935.

GRAPHIC DESIGNER
Webmaster's Weekly is seeking a creative Graphic Designer to design high impact marketing collateral, including direct mail promo's, CD-ROM packages, ads and WWW pages. Must be able to juggle multiple projects and learn new skills on the job very rapidly. Web design experience a big plus, technical troubleshooting also a plus. Call 435-555-1235.

GRAPHICS - ART DIRECTOR - WEB-MULTIMEDIA
Leading internet development company has an outstanding opportunity for a talented, high-end Web Experienced Art Director. In addition to a great portfolio and fresh ideas, the ideal candidate has excellent communication and presentation skills. Working as a team with innovative producers and programmers, you will create dynamic, interactive web sites and application interfaces. Some programming experience required. Send samples and resume to: SuperSites, 333 Main, Seattle, WA.

COMPUTER PROGRAMMER
Ad agency seeks programmer w/exp. in UNIX/NT Platforms, Web Server, CGI/Perl. Programmer Position avail. on a project basis with the possibility to move into F/T. Fax resume & salary req. to R. Jones 334-555-8332.

PROGRAMMERS / Established software company seeks program-

---

ment. Must be a self-starter, energetic, organized. Must have 2 yrs web experience. Programming plus. Call 985-555-9854.

PROGRAMMERS Multiple term assignments available: Vi C, 3 positions SQL ServerNT Ser 2 positions JAVA & HTML, long t NetWare Various locations. Call more info. 356-555-3398.

PROGRAMMERS
C, C, VB, Cobol, exp. Call 534-6543 or fax 534-555-6544.

PROGRAMMING
MRFS Inc. is looking for a Windows NT developer. Reqs. yrs. Exp. In C under Wind Win95 & NT, using Visual C, OO design & implementation a must. OLE2 & ODBC are a Excl. Salary & bnfts. Resume salary history to HR, 8779 High Way, Computer City, AR

PROGRAMMERS/ Contra Wanted for short & long term as ments, Visual C, MFCUnix C/C, Oracle Developers, PC Help Support Windows NT & NetW Telecommunications Visual Access, HTMT, CGI, Perl MMI & 885-555-9933

PROGRAMMER World Wide Links wants your HTML & Photos skills. Develop great WWW Local & global customers. Send ples & resume to WWWL, 2 Apple Road, Santa Rosa, CA.

TECHNICAL WRITER Software seeks writer/editor for ma research notes, project mgmt. years tech. writing, DTP & pro ming experience. Send resu writing samples to: Sof Systems, Dallas, TX.

TECHNICAL Software develo firm looking for Tech Trainers candidates have programming rience in Visual C, HTML & Need quick self starter. Call 555-6868 for interview.

TECHNICAL WRITER Pr Computer Corp is seeking a co nation of technical skills, know and experience in the foll areas: UNIX, Windows 95/NT, Basic, on-line help & documen and the internet. Candidates possess excellent writing skills be comfortable working in a C vs. deadline driven environ Competitive salary. Fax res samples to Karen Fields, P Computer Corp. 444 Indust Concord, CA. Or send to our w at www.premier.com.

WEB DESIGNER
BA/BS or equivalent pro ming/multimedia producti years of experience in use design of WWW services str audio and video HTML, PER GIF, JPEG. Demonstrated in sonal, organization, commun multi-tasking skills. Send res The Learning People at www. ing.com.

WEBMASTER-TECHN

SKILL

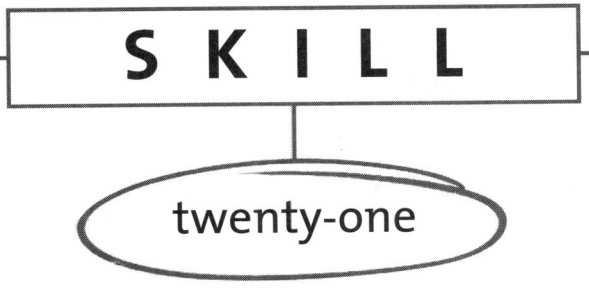

twenty-one

Debugging Multithreaded Programs

- ❑ Working with threads
- ❑ Putting the threads together
- ❑ Stepping through the source
- ❑ Examining variables
- ❑ Modifying variables
- ❑ Setting breakpoints

Exploring the Debugger

Taking a debugger through the ropes is always interesting. You can create a bug-ridden example and demonstrate how to use the debugger to kill the bugs, or create a working example and use the debugger to examine known pieces of a working program. In this skill, we'll do the latter.

The program we'll create will use multiple threads, to show off the debugger's multithreading support. The first thread works as a manufacturer. It produces strings for someone to use. We'll call this thread the *producer*. Next, there is the consumer that uses up the strings manufactured by the producer. We'll call this piece the *consumer*. The last thread works as a buffer. Because the producer and consumer work at different speeds, we need a holding group that stores strings and displays what is currently stored on the screen. We'll call it a *display buffer*. There's one catch in all this—the display buffer has a fixed size. This means that if the producer manufactures strings faster than the consumer uses them, the producer will need to slow down when the buffer is full. This adds *interthread* communication to the picture. Once we create the program, we'll use the debugger to examine the pieces.

At this point, close all your open projects and create a new application. Call the project **skill21**, and save it as **C:\skills\skill21\skill21.jpr**. Select Finish. Then, within the Application Wizard, select Next, name the class **DisplayBuffer**, and select Finish.

Creating the Producer

The first piece to create is the producer. This class will need to work independently of everything else, as its sole purpose is the production of strings. The way we did this in Skill 4 was by implementing the `Runnable` interface, creating a `Thread`, and passing the thread the class that implemented the interface. Once started, the thread did the work within the run method of the implementer. Here's the general framework to set this up:

```
public class foo extends SomeClass implements Runnable {
  …
  public void run() { … }
  …
  public void anyMethod () {
    Thread t = new Thread (this);
    t.start();
    …
  }
}
```

The `Runnable` interface is used for those cases where the class you are working with is a subclass of any other class *besides* `Object`. Because Java doesn't permit extending multiple classes, it needed to provide an alternative way to work with multiple threads. In the case where the direct parent is `Object`, you can change your class to subclass `Thread`. Because `Thread` already implements the `Runnable` interface, you can provide a `run` method directly within the subclass.

Getting back to the producer, its sole job is production; it doesn't do anything else. Therefore, we need to create a `Thread` subclass for the producer to work. To create a new independent class, use the Class Wizard: select File ➤ New, select the New tab, and double-click the Class icon.

This brings up the dialog box shown in Figure 21.1.

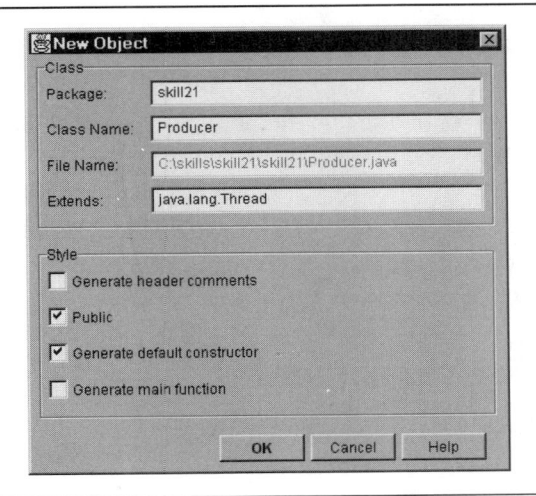

FIGURE 21.1: The New Object dialog box—use this to create new classes in separate files from the main project file.

In the New Object dialog box, enter a class name of **Producer** and fill in the extends field with **java.lang.Thread**. Be sure the Public and Generate default constructor boxes are selected and then select OK. This action adds a new file to the project called `Producer.java`.

There are really only two things to do here. In the constructor, we need to get a buffer to work with. The producer and consumer need to share a buffer, so we maintain the buffer outside the producer class. Then, as with all subclasses of `Thread` and implementers of the `Runnable` interface, we need to define a `run` method to give the class something to do once it's started.

For the constructor, change the default constructor to accept a `DisplayBuffer` parameter. We'll use this as the buffer between the consumer and producer. Also, get a count for the number of items to produce. Once the constructor has these parameters, we need to store them somewhere, so add instance variables `buffer` and `runs` to retain a copy to use later. One more thing that will make our life easier later on is to name the thread. `Thread` has a constructor that accepts a `String` parameter, so call the superclass's constructor and pass along a name, **Producer**:

```java
private DisplayBuffer buffer;
private int runs;
public Producer(DisplayBuffer db, int testRuns) {
  super ("Producer");
  buffer = db;
  runs = testRuns;
}
```

Now on to the `run` method. Here, we just loop for the number of runs requested, generating a new string each time. Instead of complete randomness in the strings generated, we'll pick them out of an array. Initially this looks like the following code, with the added `println` call to show the selected choice:

```java
public void run() {
  String choices[] = {
    "The", "Quick", "Brown", "Fox",
    "Jumped", "Over", "The", "Lazy",
    "Sleeping", "Dog"};
  String choice;
  for (int i=0;i<runs;i++) {
    choice = choices[(int)(Math.random() * choices.length)];
    System.out.println ("Added: " + choice);
  }
}
```

> **NOTE** For those unfamiliar with the sentence "The quick brown fox jumped over the lazy sleeping dog," it is a sentence commonly used in beginning typing classes. It consists of at least one instance of each letter of the alphabet.

To notify the buffer of a new choice, use the add method. We also need to add a delay. Our producer takes time to produce its strings, so we'll add a random delay of under a half-second between runs. This completes our Producer class definition and makes it look like Producer.java.

Producer.java

```java
package skill21;

public class Producer extends Thread {

  private DisplayBuffer buffer;
  private int runs;
  private final static int delay = 500;

  public Producer(DisplayBuffer db, int testRuns) {
    super ("Producer");
    buffer = db;
    runs = testRuns;
  }
  public void run() {
    String choices[] = {
      "The", "Quick", "Brown", "Fox",
      "Jumped", "Over", "The", "Lazy",
      "Sleeping", "Dog"};
    String choice;
    for (int i=0;i<runs;i++) {
      choice = choices[(int)(Math.random() * choices.length)];
      buffer.add(choice);
      System.out.println ("Added: " + choice);
      try {
        sleep ((int)(Math.random() * delay));
      } catch (InterruptedException e) {
        // Ignore
      }
    }
  }
}
```

Notice how the producer doesn't care about the size of the buffer, or whether or not the buffer fills it. It is not the producer's job to worry about that.

Creating the Consumer

Next, we create our consumer. Use the Class Wizard to create a new class. Call it **Consumer** and subclass **java.lang.Thread** again. The main differences here are the use of `remove` to get the string out of the buffer and a different delay speed. After adding all this, `Consumer.java` contains the source code we use to create the consumer.

Consumer.java

```java
public class Consumer extends Thread {

  private DisplayBuffer buffer;
  private int runs;
  private final static int delay = 2000;

  public Consumer(DisplayBuffer db, int testRuns) {
    super ("Consumer");
    buffer = db;
    runs = testRuns;
  }

  public void run() {
    String choice;
    for (int i=0;i<runs;i++) {
      choice = buffer.remove();
      System.out.println ("Got: " + choice);
      try {
        sleep ((int)(Math.random() * delay));
      } catch (InterruptedException e) {
        // Ignore
      }
    }
  }
}
```

Creating the Display Buffer

The `DisplayBuffer` is what makes this whole thing work. In it, there is a buffer. Strings are added to it with `add` and removed with `remove`. The buffer also needs to display the current buffer to the screen. The simplest way to do this is with components. Because `DisplayBuffer` is a frame, just add and remove components from it. We'll use buttons for this. In order for the screen to look somewhat decent, we should change the layout manager to `GridLayout`, with one column and five rows. This keeps the buttons in one column, with space reserved when the number of rows is fewer than five.

To change the layout of the bevel panel, select `DisplayBuffer.java` in the Navigation pane and the Design tab at the bottom of the Content pane. Selecting `bevelPanel1 (XYLayout)` in the Structure pane alters the Inspector's view. Change the layout property to **GridLayout**. The `xyLayout1` entry in the Structure pane should now be `gridLayout1`; select it. In the Inspector, change the columns property to **1** and rows to **5** to complete the screen setup.

Because we'll be using a fixed-size buffer, we need to reserve the space. Then we have to maintain our own positioning within it. The positioning variable will say how many objects are currently in the buffer. In addition, we'll remove a string from the buffer with the positioning variable. The buffer will work as a last-in, first-out structure—the last element added is the next one removed. Add the following instance variables to `DisplayBuffer.java`.

```
private String buffer[] = new String[5];
private int position = 0;
```

Adding to the Buffer

Adding to the buffer seems like the next most logical thing. In the producer, we defined the method to be called **add** which would accept one **String** parameter.

```
public void add (String s)
```

In order to add to the buffer, we have to make sure the buffer isn't full. The buffer is full when the `position` amount is the `buffer` length:

```
while (position == buffer.length);
```

To add the string to the screen, we just create a `Button` and add it:

```
bevelPanel1.add (new Button (s));
```

To add the string to the buffer, we just place it in the buffer and increment the position:

```
buffer[position++] = s;
```

Putting all this together gives us:

```
public void add (String s) {
  while (position == buffer.length);
  bevelPanel1.add (new Button (s));
  buffer[position++] = s;
}
```

While this will work, there are some major flaws with it; the most obvious is the `while` loop. The `while` loop is structured as what's called a *busy-wait loop*. While the system is waiting for some condition to be true, it keeps the CPU busy. We could use the `sleep` method of `Thread` to pause for a short period, but for how long? Instead of trying to sleep for a random amount of time and trying to discover when things have cleared up, there is a `wait` method in `Object` that everyone inherits. This allows you to not use the CPU until someone notifies you, via a method called `notify`.

Also, if there were multiple producers, each may discover that the buffer isn't full and try to place something into it. To remedy this, we need to use the `synchronized` keyword. We first saw this in Skill 4 when we had our scrolling billboard. Here, we want to synchronize the whole method, so that only one producer can run at a time. The `wait` method mentioned above must also be within a try-catch block because it throws the `InterruptedException`. Inside the catch block, we will print out a stack trace and exit the application because we've detected a problem.

The last problem is the call to `add`. Whenever you update the screen, you need to tell the screen to update itself. Otherwise, the screen waits until it discovers that it needs to update itself. Using components, use the `validate` method to force the update. If we were drawing, it would be `repaint`.

Putting all this together results in the following `add` method (the `notify` call is explained in a moment):

```
public synchronized void add (String s) {
  while (position == buffer.length) {
    try {
      wait();
    } catch (InterruptedException e) {
      e.printStackTrace();
      System.exit(1);
    }
  }
  bevelPanel1.add (new Button (s));
  bevelPanel1.validate();
  buffer[position++] = s;
  notify();
}
```

The `notify` call at the bottom is not what notifies the `wait` at the top. We need some way to notify the producer when there is free space in a previously full buffer and to notify the consumer when there is something in a previously empty buffer. The `remove` method has a corresponding `wait` and `notify`. When `remove` frees some space in the buffer, it calls `notify`, which signals the `wait` method of add. Then, the `notify` method of add signals the `wait` method of remove.

Removing from the Buffer

The `Consumer` class defined our `remove` method for us, and had it return the element removed. The primary difference here is the `while` condition; when the position is zero, there is nothing to remove, so wait. To remove an element from the screen, just pass along the position, and then notify the producer there is some free space.

```
public synchronized String remove() {
  while (position == 0) {
    try {
      wait();
    } catch (InterruptedException e) {
      e.printStackTrace();
      System.exit(1);
    }
  }
  bevelPanel1.remove (==position);
  bevelPanel1.validate();
  notify();
  return (buffer[position]);
}
```

NOTE Having both add and remove synchronized means only one will run at a time. The way wait-notify works is when add or remove goes into the wait-state, it gives up its synchronized lock. Then, when it is notified, it won't continue until it gets it again (the notifier relinquishes the synchronized lock first).

The complete `DisplayBuffer` source follows.

DisplayBuffer.java

```
package Threads;

import java.awt.*;
import java.awt.event.*;
import borland.jbcl.control.*;
import borland.jbcl.layout.*;
```

```java
public class DisplayBuffer extends DecoratedFrame {
  BorderLayout borderLayout1 = new BorderLayout();
  BevelPanel bevelPanel1 = new BevelPanel();
  GridLayout gridLayout1 = new GridLayout();
  private String buffer[] = new String[5];
  private int position = 0;

  //Construct the frame
  public DisplayBuffer() {
    try {
      jbInit();
    }
    catch (Exception e) {
      e.printStackTrace();
    }
  }

  //Component initialization
  public void jbInit() throws Exception{
    this.setLayout(borderLayout1);
    this.setSize(new Dimension(400, 300));
    this.setTitle("The Buffer");
    gridLayout1.setColumns(1);
    gridLayout1.setRows(5);
    bevelPanel1.setLayout(gridLayout1);
    this.add(bevelPanel1, BorderLayout.CENTER);
  }
  public synchronized String remove() {
    while (position == 0) {
      try {
        wait();
      } catch (InterruptedException e) {
        e.printStackTrace();
        System.exit(1);
      }
    }
    bevelPanel1.remove (==position);
    bevelPanel1.validate();
    notify();
    return (buffer[position]);
  }
  public synchronized void add (String s) {
    while (position == buffer.length) {
      try {
        wait();
      } catch (InterruptedException e) {
        e.printStackTrace();
```

```
        System.exit(1);
      }
    }
    bevelPanel1.add (new Button (s));
    bevelPanel1.validate();
    buffer[position++] = s;
    notify();
  }
}
```

Putting It All Together

The last thing to do is create the producer and consumer and send them off on their merry way. We do this in the application's constructor in `Application1.java`. First, we need to set up how many strings will run through our buffer and then create the producer and consumer objects in the constructor. We declare a final static `int` to store the number of runs (the final static keywords here tell the compiler that this is a *constant literal* [like C's `#define`]) at the class level. The last thing we'll do in the constructor is create the new objects.

```
private final static int testRuns = 10;
Producer p = new Producer(frame, testRuns);
Consumer c = new Consumer(frame, testRuns);
```

In Skill 4, you learned that the way to start a `Runnable` object is with the `start` method. You do not call the `run` method directly. Calling `start` on a `Runnable` object or `Thread` causes the thread to enter the runnable state. Then, the system's scheduler will look through all the runnable threads and pick one to run.

```
p.start();
c.start();
```

> **NOTE** The scheduler determines the execution order of multiple threads. With one CPU, it picks one thread at a time to run. With multiple CPUs, it can pick many threads, one per CPU. Which thread is picked is dependent on the scheduler.

Putting all this together gives us the following program in `Application1.java`.

Application1.java

```java
package Threads;

public class Application1 {
  boolean packFrame = false;
  private final static int testRuns = 10;

  //Construct the application
  public Application1() {
    DisplayBuffer frame = new DisplayBuffer();
    //Pack frames that have useful preferred size info, e.g. from their layout
    //Validate frames that have preset sizes
    if (packFrame)
      frame.pack();
    else
      frame.validate();
    frame.setVisible(true);
    Producer p = new Producer(frame, testRuns);
    p.start();
    Consumer c = new Consumer(frame, testRuns);
    c.start();
  }

  //Main method
  static public void main(String[] args) {
    new Application1();
  }
}
```

At this point, you can save everything and run it. With the initial settings, the buffer should fill quickly before the consumer has time to pick at it much. You can add more producers and consumers, or change the delay times to see the effect. Figure 21.2 shows one possible screen display, with the buffer partially full. Select View ➤ Execution Log to see the `println` output.

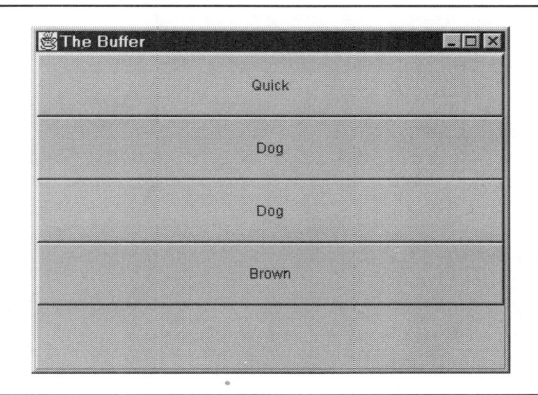

FIGURE 21.2: The `DisplayBuffer` during the producer's and consumer's run

Debugging

Now that we have a program to look at, let's jump over to the debugger. A debugger helps you find problems in your source code. The first stage of debugging is adding `System.out.println` lines throughout your code, to check on the state of the system at certain places. Instead of having to change the source, you can use a debugger and ask it what the system state is.

To start the debugging process do one of the following:

- Press F9
- Select Run ➤ Debug "Application1"
- Select the Debug icon on the toolbar
- Right-click on `Application1.java` and select Debug.

This turns the AppBrowser into a debugger (see Figure 21.3). When you run a program in debug mode, it stops at the first executable line of code.

> **TIP** If the debugger isn't starting, select File ➤ Project Properties and check the Include Debug Information compiler option.

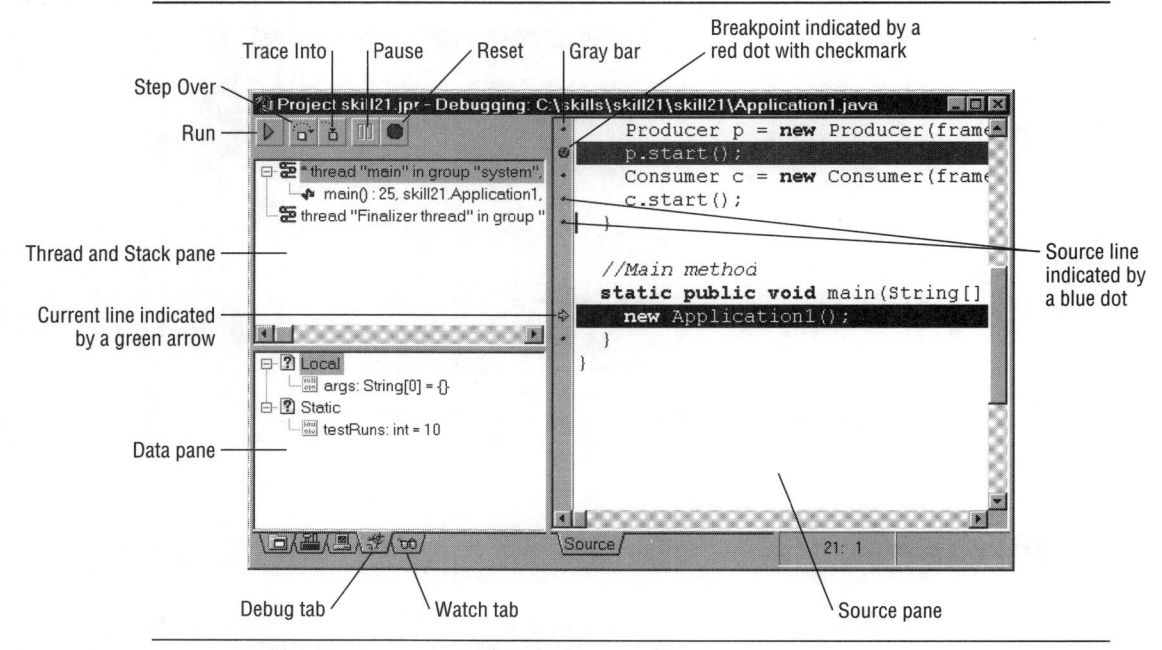

FIGURE 21.3: The AppBrowser in debug mode

When running in debug mode, the Thread and Stack pane (top-left pane) displays the list of threads running, along with what they are running, via a *call stack*. The Data pane (bottom-left pane) shows the data variables currently visible, and the Source pane (the right side of the window) shows the source.

On the left side of the Source pane, you'll see a gray vertical bar. In this bar, blue dots indicate source lines and a green arrow indicates the currently executing line, while comment lines are blank. A red dot with a checkmark indicates a *breakpoint*, a place where you've told the debugger to stop.

Selecting the Run icon causes the program to run from the current location until something causes it to stop. The Step Over icon lets you avoid going through every single line within a method. Trace Into allows you to single-step through the source—into every method where the source is available. If you want to avoid stepping into some libraries, you can turn off whole packages by selecting View ➤ Loaded Classes. When the debugger is not running, you will see Figure 21.4. When the debugger is running, you see Figure 21.5.

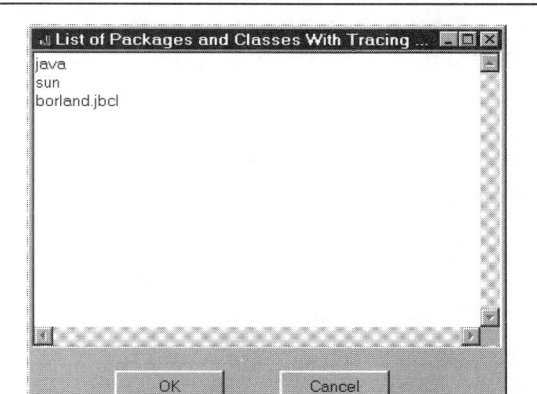

FIGURE 21.4: The List of Packages and Classes With Tracing Disabled dialog box. Enter one package or class per line to avoid tracing.

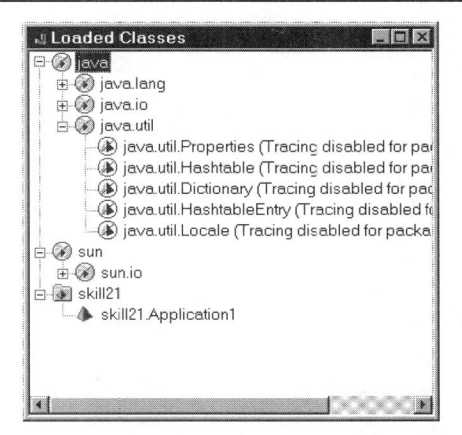

FIGURE 21.5: When the debugger is running, this is the window you'll see; it shows the specific classes that are loaded. You can individually turn off classes with source.

To pause a program while it's running, select the Pause icon; selecting the Reset icon stops the program and allows you to rerun it from the beginning.

Stepping Through the Program

Let's work our way into the program a little and then examine a few pieces of it. Select the Trace Into button to enter the `Application1` constructor and then press the Step Over button six times, until the current line of code creates a producer (`Producer p = new Producer(frame, testRuns)`). Now we can look at the Thread and Stack pane, as shown in Figure 21.6.

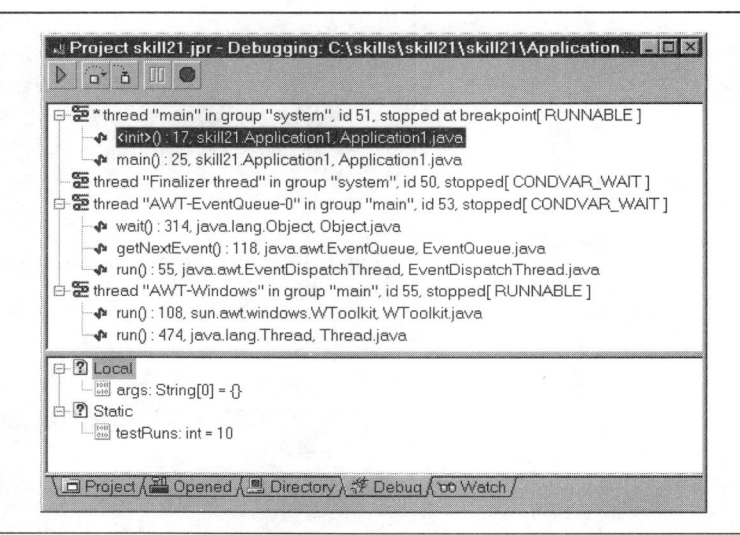

FIGURE 21.6: The Thread and Stack pane, after the program has started

There are four threads listed in this pane. We didn't explicitly create any of these. The first entry is our main program thread; the asterisk to the left indicates it would be running if we didn't stop it. The second entry is the `"Finalizer thread"`. This thread is responsible for garbage collecting or freeing up memory when we no longer need it. The next two, `"AWT-EventQueue-0"` and `"AWT-Windows"` were created when the `DisplayBuffer` frame was created. This shows that the event handling and window refreshing is done in separate threads.

Below the Thread and Stack pane is the Data pane. Here we can look and see that there is initially nothing in the buffer by selecting `frame: skill21 .DisplayBuffer = {...}` and `buffer: String[5] = {...}`. This displays each setting as `null`, as shown in Figure 21.7.

Debugging 453

FIGURE 21.7: The initial Data pane with nothing in the buffer

The next time you press the Trace Into icon, you will be taken into the Producer constructor. If you scroll down a little and select the for loop line, you can press F5 to toggle on a breakpoint. To set the breakpoint, you can also click in the gray bar on the blue dot that shows it is a line of code. The line will turn red. At this point, if you click the Run icon while in the Thread and Stack pane, the program continues and stops at the for loop. If you stop the program and restart, it stops at the for loop.

Examining the Variables

If you press Trace Into again, you're in the loop, and the i variable is now defined. Then look in the Data pane, and you will see i: int = 0, instead of i: int = ???. Another way to examine the value of a variable is with the Evaluate/Modify dialog box. Selecting Run ➤ Evaluate/Modify brings up the dialog box shown in Figure 21.8. Entering **i** in the Expression field and pressing Enter shows a 0 in the Result area.

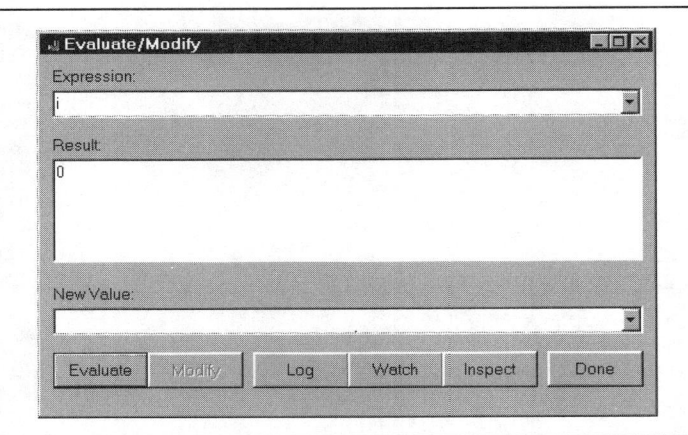

FIGURE 21.8: The Evaluate / Modify dialog box where you can examine variable settings

If what you enter is an array, you can select the Inspect button to examine the contents, as Figure 21.9 shows.

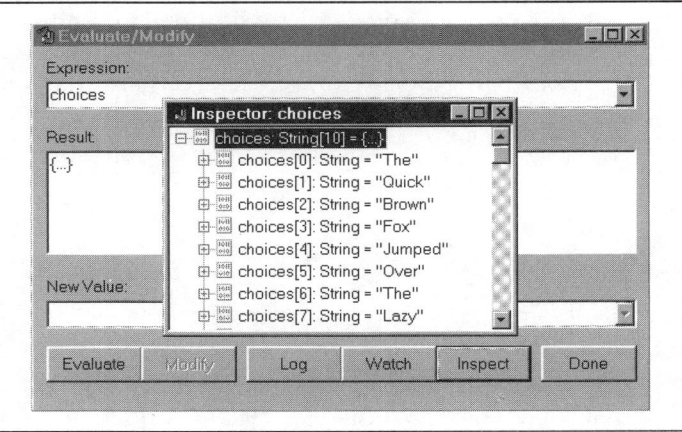

FIGURE 21.9: Inspecting an array variable

If you want to modify the value, the easiest place for this is in the Data pane. If you right-click over a variable with a primitive datatype and select the Modify Value menu choice, you can test out what happens with hard-to-generate test cases. Changing the value of i to **11** would end the producer's life fairly quickly, leaving the consumer waiting for a long time. Figure 21.10 shows the Change Data Value dialog box, which appears after selecting Modify Value.

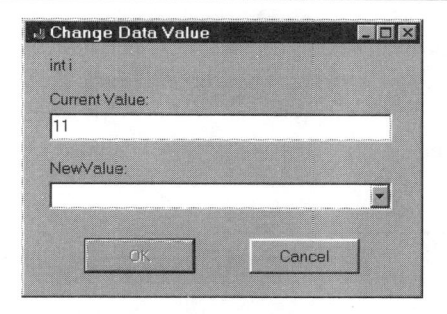

FIGURE 21.10: Modifying the primitive datatype

The Run ➤ Inspect menu choice also allows you to examine a variable in the current execution scope. You'll be prompted for a variable name, as shown in Figure 21.11, before bringing up the Inspector (see Figure 21.9). When you select the menu item, the system automatically enters whatever happens to be under the cursor into the input field.

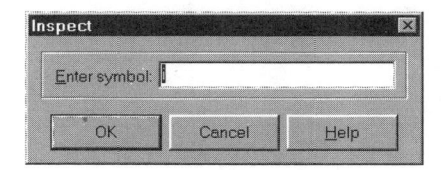

FIGURE 21.11: Inspecting variables some more

Setting Breakpoints

Just using the Step Over and Trace Into buttons can create rather long debugging sessions. There are various ways to improve upon this experience. Pressing F5 on a line of source is one way to set breakpoints we discussed in the section "Stepping through the Program." You can also select a blue dot and turn it into a red checkmark.

The Run ➤ Run to Cursor and Run ➤ Run to End of Methods options will quickly become your favorites though. The Run ➤ Run to Cursor option continues the program up to the line the cursor is currently on. The Run ➤ Run to End of Method option is typically used when you enter a method you think you want to step through, or accidentally step into. If you select it, it will run until the end of the current method.

The most powerful way to set breakpoints though is with the Run ➤ Add Breakpoint menu command. Selecting this command brings up Figure 21.12, where you can enter conditions like `var > 10` in the Condition field, (sets a breakpoint that stops only when `var` is greater than 10). This is great for times when you know a variable is getting an invalid condition, but you don't know exactly why.

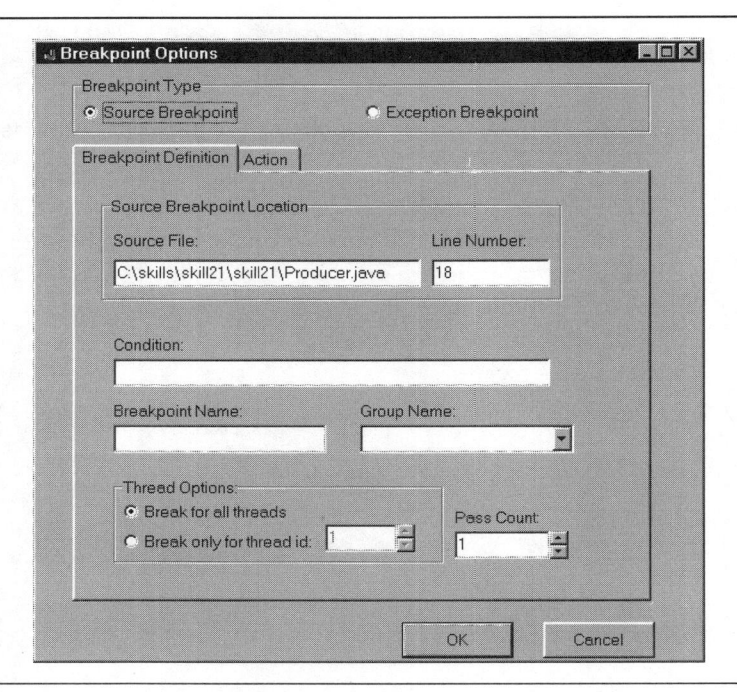

FIGURE 21.12: The Breakpoint Options dialog box, where you can set breakpoints in many different ways

Another nice thing you can do here is set a break point to stop after so many passes. The Pass Count field is for this. If a loop always fails on the 5120 pass, you can set Pass Count to 5115, for example, and manually walk through the last five passes, instead of all 5000. Combining pass counts and conditions adds even more flexibility to setting breakpoints. If var loops from 0 to 49 and you know the program breaks the 100th time through the loop when var > 10, you can enter **var > 10** in the Condition field and **100** in the Pass Count field. Then, the 100th time var is greater than 10, the program stops.

> **NOTE** Unfortunately, you cannot enter a method call in the Condition field. It can only be a variable test.

Selecting the Exception Breakpoint toggle at the top of the Breakpoint Options dialog box allows you to handle even unhandled exceptions, without having the program completely abort. You can check for all exceptions, or just one. Then once you select the Action tab, shown in Figure 21.13, you can perform actions such as enabling breakpoint groups. This allows you to customize the session for frequent pitfalls, but not have to break there all the time.

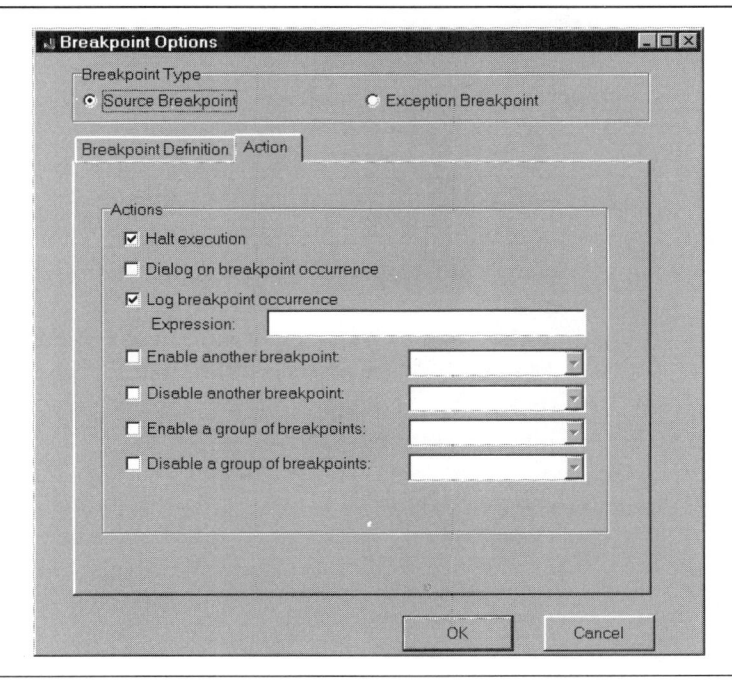

FIGURE 21.13: The Breakpoint Options dialog box with the Actions tab selected

Once you've set all those breakpoints, the last things we'll do are find them, disable them, or delete them. Select View ➤ Breakpoints to bring up the window shown in Figure 21.14.

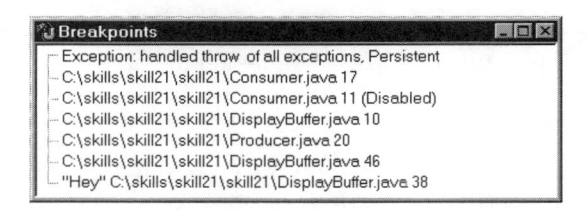

```
Breakpoints
Exception: handled throw of all exceptions, Persistent
C:\skills\skill21\skill21\Consumer.java 17
C:\skills\skill21\skill21\Consumer.java 11 (Disabled)
C:\skills\skill21\skill21\DisplayBuffer.java 10
C:\skills\skill21\skill21\Producer.java 20
C:\skills\skill21\skill21\DisplayBuffer.java 46
"Hey" C:\skills\skill21\skill21\DisplayBuffer.java 38
```

FIGURE 21.14: Find your breakpoints in the Breakpoints window. Right-click in the window for lots of options.

From the Breakpoints window, right-clicking in the window brings up a menu full of choices. You can select Goto Breakpoint to locate the specific source line, Disable or Enable to toggle the state of the exception, while Remove will eliminate the exception from the list, and Options brings up the Breakpoint Options window. The remaining menu choices deal with all breakpoints together, rather than each one separately.

Now, you should run the program a few times, stepping all over the place, to get a good feel for the debugger. Instead of having to add `System.out.println` statements to your programs, you'll be able to use the debugger to help you find your problems much more easily, and in the end it will make you a better Java programmer.

Congratulations! You've reached the end of the skills—but not the end of JBuilder's capabilities. By now, you should have a good base of Java skills and be very comfortable in the JBuilder and JavaBeans world. Explore until your heart's content and become a Java master.

Also, be sure to examine the glossary for more complete definitions of some of the new terms you've seen throughout this book.

Are You Experienced?

Now you can...

- ☑ create threads for multithreaded programs
- ☑ synchronize communications across threads
- ☑ use the JBuilder debugger
- ☑ step through source
- ☑ inspect data variables
- ☑ modify data variables during program execution
- ☑ set breakpoints
- ☑ brag about your JBuilder proficiency

PROGRAMMERS
C, C, VB, Cobol, exp. Call 534-555-6543 or fax 534-555-6544.

PROGRAMMING
MRFS Inc. is looking for a Sr. Windows NT developer. Reqs. 3-5 yrs. Exp. in C under Windows, Win95 & NT, using Visual C. Excl. OO design & implementation skills a must. OLE2 &/ODBC are a plus. Exd. Salary & bnfts. Resume & salary history to HR, 8779 HighTech Way, Computer City, AR

PROGRAMMERS
Contractors Wanted for short & long term assignments. Visual C, MFC Unix C/C, SQL Oracle Developers PC Help Desk Support Windows NT & NetWareTelecommunications Visual Basic, Access, HTMT, CGI, Perl MMI & Co., 885-555-9933

PROGRAMMER World Wide Web Links wants your HTML & Photoshop skills. Develop great WWW sites. Local & global customers. Send samples & resume to WWWL 2000 Apple Road, Santa Rosa, CA.

TECHNICAL WRITER Software firm seeks writer/editor for manuals, research notes, project mgmt. Min 2 years tech. writing, DTP & programming experience. Send resume & writing samples to: Software Systems, Dallas, TX.

TECHNICAL Software developement firm looking for Tech Trainers. Ideal candidates have programming experience in Visual C, HTML & JAVA. Need quick self starter. Call (443) 555-6868 for interview.

TECHNICAL WRITER/ Premier Computer Corp is seeking a combination of technical skills, knowledge and experience in the following areas: UNIX, Windows 95/NT, Visual Basic, on-line help & documentation, and the internet. Candidates must possess excellent writing skills and be comfortable working in a quality vs. deadline driven environment. Competitive salary. Fax resume & samples to Karen Fields, Premier Computer Corp. 444 Industrial Blvd. Concord, CA. Or send to our website at www.premier.com.

WEB DESIGNER
BA/BS or equivalent programming/multimedia production. 3 years of experience in use and design of WWW services streaming audio and video HTML, PERL, CGI, GIF, JPEG. Demonstrated interpersonal, organization, communication, multi-tasking skills. Send resume to The Learning People at www.learning.com

WEBMASTER-TECHNICAL
BSCS or equivalent, 2 years of experience in CGI, Windows 95/NT, UNIX, C, Java, Perl. Demonstrated ability to design code, debug and test on-line services. Send resume to The Learning People at www.learning.com

PROGRAMMER World Wide Web Links wants your HTML & Photoshop skills. Develop great WWW sites. Local & global customers. Send sam-

---

ing tools. Experienced in documentation preparation & programming languages: (Access, C, FoxPro) are a plus. Financial or banking customer service support is required along with excellent verbal & written communication skills with multi levels of end-users. Send resume to KKUP Enterprises, 45 Orange Blvd., Orange, CA.

COMPUTERS Small Web Design firm seeks indiv. w/NT, Webserver & Database management exp. Fax resume to 556-555-4221.

COMPUTER/ Visual C/C, Visual Basic, Exp'd Systems Analysts/Programmers for growing software dev. team in Roseburg. Computer Science or related degree preferred. Develop adv. Engineering applications for engineering firm. Fax resume to 707-555-8744.

COMPUTER Web Master for dynamic SF Internet co. Site. Dev., test, coord., train. 2 yrs prog. Exp. C C Web C, FTP. Fax resume to Best Staffing 845-555-7722.

COMPUTER PROGRAMMER
Ad agency seeks programmer w/exp. in UNIX/NT Platforms, Web Server, CGI/Perl. Programmer Position avail. on a project basis with the possibility to move into F/T. Fax resume & salary req. to R. Jones 334-555-8332.

COMPUTERS Programmer/Analyst Design and maintain C based SQL database applications. Required skills: Visual Basic, C, SQL, ODBC. Document existing and new applications. Novell or NT exp. a plus. Fax resume & salary history to 235-555-9935.

GRAPHIC DESIGNER
Webmaster's Weekly is seeking a creative Graphic Designer to design high impact marketing collateral, including direct mail promos, CD-ROM packages, ads and WWW pages. Must be able to juggle multiple projects and learn new skills on the job very rapidly. Web design experience a big plus, technical troubleshooting also a plus. Call 435-555-1235.

GRAPHICS - ART DIRECTOR - WEB-MULTIMEDIA
Leading internet development company has an outstanding opportunity for a talented, high-end Web Experienced Art Director. In addition to a great portfolio and fresh ideas, the ideal candidate has excellent communication and presentation skills. Working as a team with innovative producers and programmers, you will create dynamic, interactive web sites and application interfaces. Some programming experience required. Send samples and resume to: SuperSites, 333 Main, Seattle, WA.

MARKETING
Fast paced software and services provider looking for MARKETING COMMUNICATIONS SPECIALIST to be responsible for its webpage, seminar coordination, and ad place-

---

PROGRAMMERS Multiple short term assignments available: Visual C, 3 positions SQL ServerNT Server, 2 positions JAVA & HTML, long term NetWare Various locations. Call for more info. 356-555-3398.

PROGRAMMERS
C, C, VB, Cobol, exp.
Call 534-555-6543
or fax 534-555-6544.

PROGRAMMING
MRFS Inc. is looking for a Sr. Windows NT developer. Reqs. 3-5 yrs. Exp. in C under Windows, Win95 & NT, using Visual C. Excl. OO design & implementation skills a must. OLE2 & ODBC are a plus. Excl. Salary & bnfts. Resume & salary history to HR, 8779 HighTech Way, Computer City, AR

PROGRAMMERS/ Contractors Wanted for short & long term assignments: Visual C, MFC Unix C/C, SQL Oracle Developers PC Help Desk Support Windows NT & NetWareTelecommunications Visual Basic, Access, HTMT, CGI, Perl MMI & Co., 885-555-9933

PROGRAMMER World Wide Web Links wants your HTML & Photoshop skills. Develop great WWW sites. Local & global customers. Send samples & resume to WWWL, 2000 Apple Road, Santa Rosa, CA.

TECHNICAL WRITER Software firm seeks writer/editor for manuals, research notes, project mgmt. Min 2 years tech. writing, DTP & programming experience. Send resume & writing samples to: Software Systems, Dallas, TX.

COMPUTER PROGRAMMER
Ad agency seeks programmer w/exp. in UNIX/NT Platforms, Web Server, CGI/Perl. Programmer Position avail. on a project basis with the possibility to move into F/T. Fax resume & salary req. to R. Jones 334-555-8332.

TECHNICAL WRITER Premier Computer Corp is seeking a combination of technical skills, knowledge and experience in the following areas: UNIX, Windows 95/NT, Visual Basic, on-line help & documentation, and the internet. Candidates must possess excellent writing skills, and be comfortable working in a quality vs. deadline driven environment. Competitive salary. Fax resume & samples to Karen Fields, Premier Computer Corp., 444 Industrial Blvd. Concord, CA. Or send to our website at www.premier.com.

WEB DESIGNER
BA/BS or equivalent programming/multimedia production. 3 years of experience in use and design of WWW services streaming audio and video HTML, PERL, CGI, GIF, JPEG. Demonstrated interpersonal, organization, communication, multi-tasking skills. Send resume to The Learning People at www.learning.com

WEBMASTER-TECHNICAL
BSCS or equivalent, 2 years of experience in CGI, Windows 95/NT

COMPUTERS Small Web Design firm seeks indiv. w/NT, Webserver & Database management exp. Fax resume to 556-555-4221.

COMPUTER Visual C/C, Visual Basic Exp'd Systems Analysts/Programmers for growing software dev. team in Roseburg. Computer Science or related degree preferred. Develop adv. Engineering applications for engineering firm. Fax resume to 707-555-8744.

COMPUTER Web Master for dynamic SF Internet co. Site. Dev., test, coord., train. 2 yrs prog. Exp. C C Web C, FTP. Fax resume to Best Staffing 845-555-7722.

COMPUTERS/ QA SOFTWARE TESTERS Qualified candidates should have 2 yrs exp. performing integration & system testing using automated testing tools. Experienced in documentation preparation & programming languages (Access, C, FoxPro) are a plus. Financial or banking customer service support is required along with excellent verbal & written communication skills with multi levels of end-users. Send resume to KKUP Enterprises, 45 Orange Blvd., Orange, CA.

COMPUTERS Programmer/Analyst Design and maintain C based SQL database applications. Required skills: Visual Basic, C, SQL, ODBC. Document existing and new applications. Novell or NT exp. a plus. Fax resume & salary history to 235-555-9935.

GRAPHIC DESIGNER
Webmaster's Weekly is seeking a creative Graphic Designer to design high impact marketing collateral including direct mail promo's. CD-ROM packages, ads and WWW pages. Must be able to juggle multiple projects and learn new skills on the job very rapidly. Web design experience a big plus, technical troubleshooting also a plus. Call 435-555-1235.

GRAPHICS - ART DIRECTOR - WEB-MULTIMEDIA
Leading internet development company has an outstanding opportunity for a talented, high-end Web Experienced Art Director. In addition to a great portfolio and fresh ideas, the ideal candidate has excellent communication and presentation skills. Working as a team with innovative producers and programmers, you will create dynamic, interactive web sites and application interfaces. Some programming experience required. Send samples and resume to: SuperSites, 333 Main, Seattle, WA.

COMPUTER PROGRAMMER
Ad agency seeks programmer w/exp. in UNIX/NT Platforms, Web Server, CGI/Perl. Programmer Position avail. on a project basis with the possibility to move into F/T. Fax resume & salary req. to R. Jones 334-555-8332.

PROGRAMMERS / Established software company seeks program-

GLOSSARY

G

Glossary

a

abstract
Retaining the essential features of some thing, process, or structure. The opposite of *concrete*.

abstract class
A class that contains abstract methods. Abstract classes cannot be instantiated.

abstract function
A function that is declared but not implemented. Abstract functions are used to ensure that subclasses implement the function.

Abstract Window Toolkit (AWT)
The collection of Java classes that allows you to implement platform-independent (hence *abstract*) GUIs.

adapter class
A class, possibly generated by JBuilder, that implements an event listener.

API
See *Application Programming Interface*.

AppBrowser
The primary JBuilder window for developing programs. It consists of three areas, the Navigation pane in the upper left, the Structure pane in the lower left, and the Content pane on the right.

applet
A Java program that runs within the context of a browser and is launched from and appears to be embedded in a Web document.

appletviewer
A JDK utility that displays only Java applets from HTML documents—as opposed to a Web browser—which shows applets embedded in Web documents.

Application Programming Interface (API)
A set of methods, functions, classes, or libraries provided by a language or operating system to help application developers write applications without needing to reinvent low-level functions. All of the standard Java packages combined form the Java Core API. An API can also be an interface to an application that allows other applications to manipulate it from within their own applications.

array
A group of variables of the same type that can be referenced by a common name and an index value. An array is an object with `length` as its public data member holding the size of the array. It can be initialized by a list of comma-separated expressions surrounded by curly braces.

atomic
Indivisible or uninterruptible. In the context of multithreading, an operation (statement, code block, or even an entire method) that cannot be interrupted. Code that accesses composite data structures shared with other threads usually must protect its critical sections by making them atomic.

AWT
See *Abstract Window Toolkit*.

b

base class
The superclass from which other classes can inherit behavior and state.

baseline
The imaginary line text is drawn on.

BDK
See *Beans Development Kit*.

bean
A reusable software component created with a specific naming convention to define the properties and events it understands. It can be manipulated visually in a builder tool.

BeanInfo
A bean support class that defines information about the bean with the same base name.

Beans Development Kit (BDK)
A JavaSoft tool that helps Java developers create reusable components (beans) through the inclusion of introductory documentation, a tutorial, sample Beans, and a test container.

boolean
A variable that can assume only the values `true` or `false`. Booleans can be used to represent things that have a binary state, such as alive/dead, connected/disconnected, same/not the same, open/closed, and so on.

breakpoint
A place where you've told the debugger to stop.

break statement
One of the flow-breaking statements. Without a label, control will be transferred to the statement just after the innermost enclosing loop or `switch` statement. With a label, control will be transferred to the enclosing statement or block of statements carrying the same label.

buffer
An amount of storage set aside to temporarily hold and/or accumulate some information, such as write and read (disk) buffers and frame buffers.

bytecode verifier
Part of Java's security precautions, the bytecode verifier checks that the bytecodes can be executed safely by the Java Virtual Machine (VM).

bytecodes
Compiled Java code. Bytecodes are portable instructions that can be executed by any Java Virtual Machine (VM).

C

case clause
A part of a `switch` statement. The clause consists of the `case` keyword, followed by a constant expression, a colon, and one or more statements. See also *switch statement*.

casting
Explicitly coercing a value from one datatype to another.

CGI
See *Common Gateway Interface*.

class
A description of a specific kind of Java object, including the state (instance variables) and behavior (methods) that are particular to it.

class file
A binary file containing Java bytecodes. The Java compiler generates a class file from source code (`.java` file) for each Java class.

class library
A collection of prefabricated classes that the programmer can use to build applications more rapidly. Java's class library is the Core API. In Java, these are also called *packages*.

class loader
The part of the Java Virtual Machine (VM) that fetches classes from the client file system or from across the network.

class variable
A variable within a class that is available for use by the class itself. Only one copy of the variable exists, and the class variable is unique to all instances of the class within the program.

compiler
A utility that reads the commands in a source file, interprets each command, and creates a new file containing equivalent bytecodes (or in the case of a C compiler, creates a file with native machine code instructions).

Component palette
Part of the JBuilder user interface where reusable beans are displayed for use within your programs.

concrete
Opposite of *abstract*. See also *abstract*.

conditional statement
A statement for selective execution of program segments, such as the `if` and `switch` statements.

constructor
A method that creates an instance of the class to which it belongs and is run when that instance is created.

Content pane
The part of the JBuilder AppBrowser interface that displays varying information based upon which of three modes it is in. A tab at the bottom of the pane determines its mode: source, design, and doc.

continue statement
One of the flow-breaking statements. Without a label, control will be transferred to the point immediately after the last statement in the enclosing loop body. With a label, control will be transferred to the end of the enclosing loop body carrying the same label.

critical section
In the context of multithreaded systems, any section of code that needs to take precautions to avoid corrupting data structures shared with other threads.

d

daisy chaining
The concept of building on a simpler I/O class with something that offers more capabilities.

data hiding
The ability to hide data within a class. Any changes to the hidden data from outside the class, if permitted at all, must be via methods.

Data pane
Within the JBuilder debugger, the screen area where data values are displayed.

datatype
The specific type of data stored in variables; for example, `int` variables hold whole numbers, `char` variables hold individual alphanumeric characters, and `String` variables hold groups of alphanumeric characters.

debugger
A utility that can monitor and suspend execution of a program so the state of the running program can be examined.

default clause
An optional part of a `switch` statement. It consists of the `default` keyword, followed by a colon, and one or more statements. Its statements are executed when none of the other case clauses are satisfied. See also *switch statement*.

default constructor
A constructor that is automatically available to a class that does not define its own constructor. It has no parameters.

deprecated methods
Methods that were supported in previous releases of the Java Development Kit (JDK) but are not the preferred ones in the 1.1 release. Future releases may drop the methods altogether.

design pattern
A reusable, standard approach to a design problem. This approach is different from algorithms in that design patterns address higher-level issues and usually describe solutions in structural/relationship terms.

destructor
A method that is called to delete an object from memory. This method is executed when an object goes out of scope. Java does not support destructors directly.

DNS
See *Domain Name System*.

do statements
One of the loop statements. The loop body is executed once, and then the conditional expression is evaluated. If it evaluates to `true`, the loop body is reexecuted and the conditional expression is retested. It will be repeated until the conditional expression evaluates to `false`.

documentation comment
A comment block that will be used by javadoc to create documentation.

Domain Name System (DNS)
A distributed Internet database that can resolve textual Internet addresses to their real numeric forms. The DNS is organized as a hierarchy with each node responsible for a subset of the Internet host address namespace (hence distributed database).

double buffering
In general, the use of two buffers to allow one buffer to be constructed while the other is being used. Double buffering is used in animation to display one animation frame while the next is being drawn off-screen. Double buffering can also be used in the context of I/O logic to decouple the algorithm's performance from the performance limits of the I/O device (called being *I/O-bound*).

e

else clause
An optional clause for an `if` statement. If the conditional expression of an `if` statement is evaluated to `false`, the statement or block of statements of the `else` clause will be executed.

encapsulation
Embedding both data and code into a single entity.

event
A system-generated object for when something interesting happens. Java components serve as event sources for events such as key presses, mouse clicks, or changes to bean properties.

event-driven programming
Programming that allows the user to control the sequence of operations that the application executes via a graphical user interface (GUI).

exception
An abnormal condition that disrupts normal program flow.

expression
A combination of terms that evaluates to a single data value.

extend
See *subclass*.

f

finalizer
A method that is called immediately before a class is garbage-collected.

flow-breaking statement
A statement for breaking the flow. These include `break`, `continue`, and `return` statements.

flow-control statement
A statement for flow control. These include conditional, loop, and flow-breaking statements.

flushing
Final writing of any output data left in a write buffer. When you close files and streams, their data buffers are flushed automatically (this is one of the reasons to close files and streams).

for statements
One of the loop statements. The initialization part is executed, followed by the evaluation of the conditional expression. If the expression evaluates to `true`, the loop body is executed, followed by the execution of the increment part. This cycle is repeated if the conditional expression evaluates to `true`.

frame
In the context of GUIs, the graphical outline of a window.

g

garbage collection
A feature of automatic memory management that discards unused blocks of memory, freeing the memory for new storage.

GIF
See *Graphics Interchange Format*.

graphical user interface (GUI)
The mouse-driven iconic interface to modern computer operating systems. Also called *windows, icons, menus, and pointer (WIMP)* interface.

Graphics Interchange Format (GIF)
A standard format for storing compressed images.

GUI
See *graphical user interface*.

h

HTML
See *Hypertext Markup Language*.

HTTP
See *Hypertext Transfer Protocol*.

Hypertext Markup Language (HTML)
The language in which Web documents are written. Java applets appear embedded in HTML documents.

Hypertext Transfer Protocol (HTTP)
The application protocol used by the World Wide Web for requesting, transmitting, and receiving Web documents.

i

IDDE
See *Integrated Development and Debugging Environment*.

IDE
See *Integrated Development Environment*.

identifier
A name the programmer gives to a class, variable, or method. Identifiers have restrictions on leading characters.

if statement
One of the two types of conditional statements. It consists of the `if` keyword, followed by a conditional expression enclosed in a pair of parentheses, and a statement (or block of statements) to be executed when the conditional expression evaluates to `true`. It may be followed by an optional `else` clause consisting of the `else` keyword and a statement (or block of statements) to be executed when the conditional expression evaluates to `false`.

inheritance
The ability to write a class that inherits the member variables and member functions (or methods) of another class.

inner classes
Classes that are defined within other classes, much in the way methods are defined within those classes. Inner classes have the same scope and access as other variables and methods defined within the same class. Their existence is hidden from view behind the enclosing class.

Inspector
Part of the JBuilder UI Designer where properties and events are customized for the component selected within the Structure pane.

instance
An instance of a class; in other words, an object.

instance variable
A variable within a class, a new copy of which is available for storage in each instance of that class. Each object of that class has its own copy of the instance variable (as opposed to a class variable).

instantiation
The process of creating an object instance of a class.

Integrated Development and Debugging Environment (IDDE)
The same as an Integrated Development Environment (IDE), but with built-in debugging features; IDDE programs include Borland's JBuilder, Sun's Java WorkShop, and Symantec's Café.

Integrated Development Environment (IDE)
A program that aids in application development by providing a graphical environment that combines all the tools required to write code.

interface
A formal set of method and constant declarations that must be defined by classes that implement it.

interpreter
A utility that reads the commands in a file, and then interprets and executes each command one at a time.

introspection
A mechanism that allows classes to publish the operations and properties they support, and a mechanism to support the discovery of such mechanisms.

j

Java Archive (JAR) file
Like a TAR or ZIP file, a file that holds an aggregate of files. These may be signed by their creator to permit greater access to the user.

JavaBeans API
An API for the creation of reusable components. Through bridges, these Java objects can link with objects created in other languages, including ActiveX, OpenDoc, and several other industry standards. A Java "Bean" is a single reusable software component.

Java Core API
Java's class library. It contains core language features and functions for tasks such as networking, I/O, and graphics.

Java Database Connectivity (JDBC)
Defines a set of Java classes and methods to interface with databases.

Java Developers Kit (JDK)
The set of Java development tools distributed (for free) by Sun Microsystems. The JDK consists mainly of the Core API classes (including their source), a Java compiler (written in Java), and the Java Virtual Machine (VM) interpreter.

Java Virtual Machine (VM)
The system that loads, verifies, and executes Java bytecodes.

JavaScript
A separate programming language loosely related to Java. JavaScript can be coded directly in an HTML document, which makes the JavaScript source code part of the document itself.

JBCL
See *JBuilder Component Library*.

JBuilder Component Library (JBCL)
A package of components included with JBuilder.

JDBC
See *Java Database Connectivity*.

JDK
See *Java Developers Kit*.

JIT compiler
See *Just-In-Time (JIT) compiler*.

JPEG (Joint Photography Engineering Group) file
A compressed graphics file format. JPEG images may be compressed in a *lossy* fashion, which sacrifices image detail for smaller image size, or in a *lossless* method, where information about the image is retained, but the file size increases accordingly.

Just-In-Time (JIT) compiler
A compiler that converts verified bytecodes to native processor instructions before execution and can significantly improve Java application performance.

k

keyword
A word that has a special meaning for the Java compiler, such as a datatype name or a program construct name.

l

LayoutManager
A Java class that handles preprogrammed layout styles for the graphical user interface (GUI) components.

life-cycle methods
Methods, such as `init()`, that you do not call directly—the browser calls them for you.

literal
An actual value, such as 35, or "Hello", as opposed to an identifier, which is a symbol for a value.

loop statement
A statement for the repeated execution of program segments. These include `for`, `while`, and do statements.

m

megabyte (MB)
A megabyte is one million characters of information.

member
The generic term for data or code entities within a class.

member function
See *method*.

member variable
A variable that is part of a class.

Menu designer
The JBuilder interface that allows you to visually create menus.

message
A method call.

method
A function or routine that is part of a class. Also called a *member function*.

multidimensional array
An array of arrays. It can be nonrectangular. A multidimensional array can be initialized by grouping comma-separated expressions with nested curly braces.

multiple inheritance
The ability to write a class that inherits the member variables and methods (member functions) of more than one class. See also *inheritance*. Java does not support multiple inheritance.

multithreading
The means to perform multiple tasks independent of each other.

n

native method
Code that is native to a specific processor. On Windows 95, native methods refer to code written specifically for Intel x86 processors.

Navigation pane
The part of the JBuilder AppBrowser interface that allows you to move through the different parts of the current project or highlighted area.

nesting
The "Russian dolls" effect of repeatedly wrapping or layering entities around other entities. In graphical user interface (GUI) design, widgets are often nested in container widgets, which themselves are nested in bigger containers and so on.

null
A value that means *no object*; can be held by an object variable.

o

object
A reusable software bundle that has characteristics (state) and behavior (methods).

object-oriented programming (OOP)
Programming that focuses on independent objects and their relationships to other objects, rather than using a top-down, linear approach (as with traditional Pascal or C).

object pointer
In C++ and Delphi, an object variable that points to a specific memory location.

object variable
A name for an object. It may refer to an object or be null.

octet
Another term for the eight-bit byte. Used only in the data communications world.

OOP
See *object-oriented programming*.

overloaded functions
Functions defined multiple times, each definition having the same name but accepting different parameters, either in number or type. The compiler knows which function to call based on the parameters it is passed.

p

package
A collection of related classes.

pane
A screen area within JBuilder.

parent class
See *superclass*.

persistence
The ability of a Java object to record its state so it can be reproduced in the future, perhaps in another environment.

persistent object stores
Database-independent, object-oriented storage systems for storing various types of objects, such as video, audio, and graphics.

pixel
Display units on a screen.

polymorphism
The ability of a single object to operate on many different types.

project
A grouping of related files within JBuilder, usually to create a specific application, applet, or bean.

properties
Describe attributes associated with a component in a graphical user interface (GUI), such as color, size, and the string to be used as a label.

r

RAD
See *Rapid Application Development*.

Rapid Application Development (RAD)
A development tool that enables programmers to create sophisticated programs quickly.

reader
Similar to an input stream (used in I/O programming), but the basic unit of data is a Unicode character.

recursive
Self-calling. A recursive method calls itself repeatedly, either directly or indirectly.

rendering
Computer graphics jargon for drawing (used as both a verb and a noun).

return statement
One of the flow-breaking statements. It is used to return control to the caller from within a method or constructor. Before the control is passed back to the caller, all of the `finally` clauses of the enclosing `try` statements are executed, from the innermost `finally` clause to the outermost one.

root class
In general, any class that acts as the superclass for a subhierarchy. An entire inheritance hierarchy, such as Java's, has a single absolute root class: class `Object`.

S

SecurityManager
A Java class that restricts access to files, the network, or other parts of the system for security purposes.

separator
An unselectable line that appears on menus for decorative purposes.

serialization
The process whereby an object records itself by writing out the values that describe its state. *Deserialization* is the process of restoring serialized objects.

signature
A method's unique profile, consisting of its name, argument list, and return type. If two methods with the same name have the slightest difference in their argument lists, they are considered totally unrelated as far as the compiler is concerned.

source file
A text file containing human-readable instructions. A Java source file is a text file written in the Java programming language.

state
An unambiguous, nonoverlapping mode of "being;" for example, the binary states *on* and *off*.

stream
An abstract concept used in the context of I/O programming to represent a linear, sequential flow of bytes of input or output data. A program can read from *input streams* (that is, read the data a stream delivers to it), and write to *output streams* (that is, transfer data to a stream).

streaming
Term used to denote audio, video, and other Internet content that is distributed in real time and does not need to be downloaded.

Structure pane
The part of the JBuilder AppBrowser interface that displays the objects of the current application or object. The items shown in the Structure pane change whenever a different object is selected in the Navigation pane.

stub
A method with no body. It satisfies the compiler's need for completeness and leaves space for you to define the method later.

subclass
A class that descends or inherits (*extends* in Java terminology) from a given class. Subclasses are more specialized than the classes they inherit from.

superclass
A class from which a given class inherits. This can be its immediate parent class or more levels away. Superclasses become more and more generic as you travel up the inheritance hierarchy and, for this reason, can often be abstract.

switch statement
A multiway selection statement. The integer expression is evaluated, and the first `case` clause whose constant expression is evaluated to the same value is executed. The optional `default` clause is executed if there is no `case` clause matching the value. The `break` statement is usually used as the last statement of a `case` clause so the control will not continue on to statements of the next `case` clause.

system property
An attribute defined automatically for the current Java session. For instance, the location of the Java runtime environment is one of the automatic system properties.

t

thread
A single flow of control within a program, similar to a process (or a running program), but easier to create and destroy than a process because less resource management is involved. Each thread must have its own resources, such as the program counter and the execution stack, as the context for execution. However, all threads in a program share many resources, such as memory space and opened files.

Threads and Stack pane
Within the JBuilder debugger, the screen area where the threads are displayed with each call stack.

Tool tip
A pop-up box that describes an item's purpose. It appears when the mouse cursor dwells (rests) over an area designated with a defined tip.

u

UI Designer
The drag-and-drop visual design tool within JBuilder.

Unicode
An International character-mapping scheme (see `http://www.stonehand.com/unicode.html` for more information).

Uniform Resource Locator (URL)
A string that identifies the location of a resource and the protocol used to access it.

untrusted applets
Applets downloaded from a network whose source cannot be traced or trusted. These applets need to be verified before they are executed because they could contain malicious virus programs.

URL
See *Uniform Resource Locator*.

V

Virtual Machine
See *Java Virtual Machine (VM)*.

W

Watch pane
An screen area shown while debugging JBuilder programs. Variables placed within the window are dynamically updated during program execution pauses.

Web browser
A viewer program used by the client machine to display Web documents.

Web site
A set of Web documents belonging to a particular organization. A Web site may share a server machine with other sites or may extend across several machines.

while statements
One of the loop statements. The conditional expression is first evaluated. If it evaluates to `true`, the loop body is executed, and the conditional expression is reevaluated. It will cycle through the testing of the conditional expression and the execution of the loop body until the conditional expression evaluates to `false`.

widgets
From "window gadgets," a generic term for graphical user interface (GUI) elements, such as buttons, scrollbars, radio buttons, text input fields, and so on.

World Wide Web (WWW)
A huge collection of interconnected hypertext documents on the Internet.

writer
Similar to an output stream (used in I/O programming), but the basic unit of data is a Unicode character.

Index

Note to the Reader: Throughout this index **boldfaced** page numbers indicate primary discussions of a topic. *Italicized* page numbers indicate illustrations.

Symbols

& (ampersands)
  in assignment operators, 58
  in bitwise operators, 58
  in logical operators, 57
* (asterisks)
  in assignment operators, 58
  for comments, 54
  for multiplication, 57
  for packages, 65
\ (backslashes), 60
^ (carets), 58
: (colons), 68
{} (curly braces)
  for arrays, 63
  for classes, 62
$ (dollar signs), 56
" (double quotes)
  for parameters, **43–44**
  representing, 60
  for strings, 61
= (equal signs)
  in assignment operators, **58–59**
  for initializing variables, 62
  in relational operators, 57
  for system properties, 47
! (exclamation points), 57
/ (forward slashes)
  in assignment operators, 58
  for comments, 54
  for multiplication, 57
> (greater than signs)
  in assignment operators, 59
  in relational operators, 57
  in shift operators, 58
< (less than signs)
  in assignment operators, 59
  in relational operators, 57
  in shift operators, 58
- (minus signs)
  in assignment operators, 58
  for subtraction, 57
() (parentheses), 56
% (percent signs)
  in assignment operators, 58
  for modulus operation, 57
+ (plus signs)
  for addition, 57
  in assignment operators, 58
; (semicolons), 56
' (single quotes), 60
[] (square brackets), 63
~t (tildes), 58
_ (underscores), 56
| (vertical bars)
  in assignment operators, 58
  in bitwise operators, 58
  in logical operators, 57

a

About Boxes, **378–379**, *378–379*, 412–413, *413*
abs method, 132
absolute URLs, 81
abstract classes, 64, 462
abstract functions, 462
abstract quality, 462
Abstract Window Toolkit (AWT), 18, **96–97**
   buttons, **103–104**, *104*
   component palette for, 175, *175*
   defined, 462
   events, **105–109**
   labels, **97–100**, *98*, *101*
   text fields, **101–102**, *103*
access modifiers, **66**
Action tab, 457, *457*
ActionEvent class, **105–107**, 230
ActionListener interface, 105–106, 231
actionPerformed method
   in ActionListener, 106–107
   in DirReader, 152–157, 162, 164–165
   in HiLo, 110–111
   in MenuTester_AboutBox, 391
   in Tabs, 125
adapter classes, 462
Add from Archive tab, 210–212, *211*
Add from Package tab, 214–215, *214*, 226–227, *227*
add method
   in BorderLayout, 122
   in DisplayBuffer, 443–444, 446–447
   in List, 178
   for objects, 99
Add Snippet dialog box, 431, *431*
Add to Project icon, *11*
Add to Project option, 15
addActionListener method
   in BlueBox, 231, 233
   in Button, 105–106
addition, 57
addKeyListener method, 108
addMouseListener method, 135
addMouseMotionListener method, 137
addPropertyChangeListener method, 244
addVetoableChangeListener method, 250
addYesNoEventListener method, 336–337
adjustmentValueChanged method, 428, 430
ampersands (&)
   in assignment operators, 58
   in bitwise operators, 58
   in logical operators, 57
AND operators
   bitwise, 58
   logical, 57
animation, 141
Animator applet, 141
APIs (Application Programming Interfaces), 462
AppBrowser, **11–13**, *11*
   for debugging, **449–450**, *450*
   defined, 462
appendChild method, 159
Applet class, 75–76
<APPLET> tag, **19–20**
Applet Viewer tool, 83, *83*
Applet Wizard
   for creating applets, **29–32**, *29–32*
   for parameters, **35–37**, *37*
   source code generated by, **32–35**
applets
   creating, **13–16**, *14–16*, **29–32**, *29–32*
   defined, 462
   life-cycle methods in, **79–80**
   parameters for, **35–37**, *37*
   running, **16–17**, *17*, 31–32, *32*
   sound in, **80–83**, *83*
   source code for, **32–35**
   tag for, **19–20**
   untrusted, 474
AppletViewer program, 17, *17*, 371, *371*, 462
Application Programming Interfaces (APIs), 462

Application Wizard
  for creating applications, **37–38**, *39*
  for parameters, **42–50**, *43*, *46*
  source code generated by, **39–42**, *41*
Application1 class, 40, 44–45, 448
Application1.java program, 115, 448
applications
  vs. applets, 13
  creating, **37–38**, *39*
  parameters for, **42–50**, *43*, *46*
  source code for, **39–42**, *41*
Archive Output Path field, 368–369
archives
  Component palette beans from, **210–213**, *211–213*
  creating, **367–371**, *367–371*
arcs, 133
ArcTest bean, 212–213
ArcTestWrapper bean, 212–213, 215
args parameter, 44
ArrayIndexOutOfBoundsException class, 358
arrays
  declaring, **62–63**
  defined, 462
  examining, **454**, *454*
  indexed properties for, 243
  initializing, 63–64
  multidimensional, 63, 470
  size of, 44, 62–63
assignment operators, **58–59**
associations, **415–417**, *416–417*
asterisks (*)
  in assignment operators, 58
  for comments, 54
  for multiplication, 57
  for packages, 65
atomic quality, 463
ATreeNode class, 158–160, 163
.au files, 80
AudioClip interface, 80–82
author setting, **412–415**, *412–414*
AWT. *See* Abstract Window Toolkit (AWT)

AWT tab, 234
awt.toolkit system property, 48
AWTEventMulticaster class, 231

b

\b value, 60
background color, 96
backslashes (\), 60
backspaces, 60
base classes, 22, 463
baselines, 19, 463
BasicBeanInfo class, 343
BDK (Beans Development Kit), 463
Bean Info Wizard, **342–344**
BeanInfo interface, 215, **264–269**, *267*
  defined, 463
  for images, **342–344**
  for input, **288–289**
  overriding, **269–272**
BeanPanel class, 325
beans, 22, **172**
  Component palette for. *See* Component palette
  connecting. *See* connecting beans
  creating, **174–179**, *174–179*, **224–226**, *224–225*
  customizing. *See* customizing
  defined, 463
  events for, **230–240**, *230*, *240*
  instrospection of. *See* introspection
  New Bean Event Wizard for, **330–335**, *330*
  New Bean Wizard for, **328–330**, *328*
  parts of, **172–173**
  properties for, **240–251**, *243*, *246–247*
  serializing. *See* serialization
  sources for, **216–220**, *217–219*
Beans Development Kit (BDK), 463
BeansExpress, **322**
  Bean Info Wizard, **342–344**
  New Bean Event Wizard, **330–335**, *330*
  New Bean Wizard, **328–330**, *328*
  Ok Cancel Bean Wizard, **322–328**, *325*, *327*

beep method, 107, 298
bigger method, 259, 263
Billboard class, 89–91
   creating, **74**, *74*
   overriding methods for, **75–79**, *75*, *77–78*
   sound in, **80–83**
Billboard.java program, 89–91
bitwise operators, **57–58**
black constant, 142
BlackBox interface, 325
blink.gif file, 343–344
blue constant, 142
BlueBox bean
   adding to palette, **226–227**, *226–227*
   creating, **224–226**, *224–225*
   listing for, 233–234
   using, **228–230**, *228*, **234–236**, *236*
BlueBox class, 233–234
BlueBox.java program, 233–234
blueBox1_actionPerformed method, 236
BlueBoxActionTester class, 234–236
BlueBoxActionTester_blueBox1_actionAdapter class, 236
BlueBoxTester class, 229–230
BlueBoxTester.java program, 229–230
BlueTriangle class, **237–240**, *240*
BlueTriangle.java program, 238–239
blueTriangle1_actionPerformed method, 239
boolean datatype, 59–60
   defined, 463
   literals, 60
   for parameters, 30
   properties for, 243
BorderLayout manager, **122–123**, *123*
borland.jbcl.control package, 41
borland.jbcl.util package, 140, 325, 343
bound properties, **243–249**, *246–247*
Box class, 241–243
Box.java program, 242
box1_actionPerformed method, 246, 248, 252
box1_propertyChange method, 245, 248, 252

box1_vetoableChange method, 251, 253
box2_actionPerformed method, 246, 248, 252
box3_actionPerformed method, 246, 248, 253
break statements
   defined, 463
   with switch statements, 68–69
Breakpoint Options dialog box, 456–458, *456–457*
breakpoints, 450, *450*
   defined, 463
   setting, **455–458**, *456–458*
Breakpoints window, 458, *458*
Browse Symbol button, *10*
browser system property, 48
browser.vendor system property, 48
browser.version system property, 48
browsers
   defined, 474
   iconified, 79
BufferedReader class, 154–155
buffers, 438, 466
   adding to, **443–445**
   creating, **442–443**
   defined, 463
   for drawing, **137–141**, *139*
   removing from, **445**
Build ➤ Make command, 16
Build ➤ Make Project command, 31
buildTree method, 165
busy-wait loops, 444
Button button, *175*
Button class, **103–104**, *104*, 266
button1_actionPerformed method
   in Counter, 315
   in IceCreamOrder, 363, 366
   in Inspect, 266, 268–269
   in ListBuilder, 181
button1_actionPerformed1 method, 203
button2_actionPerformed method
   in Counter, 316
   in ListBuilder, 179, 181

button2_actionPerformed1 method, 193, 203
button3_actionPerformed method, 317
button3_actionPerformed1 method, 193, 203
button4_actionPerformed method, 316
button5_actionPerformed method, 316
button6_actionPerformed method, 315
buttonBar_actionPerformed method, 398–400, 406
ButtonBar class, 398–399
buttonControl_actionPerformed method, 407
ButtonControl class, 403
buttons
   connecting, **192–193**
   for Counter class, **303–306**, *306*
buttonType property, 398
byte datatype, 59–60
bytecode verifier, 463
bytecodes, 114, 463

C

call stacks, 450
Can Run Standalone style, 33, 37
cancel_actionPerformed method, 323
canRead method, 150
canWrite method, 150
CardFrame bean, 213–214, *214*
CardLayout manager, 123
carets (^), 58
case clauses, **68–69**, 464
casting, 464
Center quadrant in BorderLayout, 122, *123*
Change Data Value dialog box, 455, *455*
char datatype, 59
   converting to strings, 117
   literals, 60
Character class, 108
Checkbox button, *175*
CheckboxGroup button, *175*
Choice button, *175*
choice components, connecting, **193–194**

choice1_itemStateChanged1 method, 194, 203
choices, switch statements for, **68–69**
Class class, 259–260
Class Definition icons, *12*
class files, 464
   directory for, 17
   in serialization, 307
class libraries, 464
class loaders, 464
class variables, **22**, 464
classes
   abstract, 64, 462
   adapter, 462
   for applets, 29
   base, 22, 463
   declaring, **61–62**
   defined, 464
   deriving, 22
   documentation for, 54, *55*
   extending, 18
   identifiers for, 56
   inner, 468
   instances of, 21
   root, 472
   for snippets, **420–428**, *421–423*, *425*
CLASSPATH environment variable, 48, 370–371
Clone option in Applet Viewer, 83
Close File button, *10*
Close option in Applet Viewer, 83
closeIt method, 399–400, 405, 407
closing
   files, **405**
   projects, 26
CODE option for applets, 20
Coffee Grinder site, **217**, *218*
colons (:), 68
color, 96
   for Box, 241
   in drawing, **141–144**, *144*
   for IceCreamOrder, 361–362

for Lookup, **261–262**
menus for, **382–384**, *382*, *384*
Color class, 130, 142–143, 261
ColorChooser class, **382–384**, *382*, *384*
command-line parameters, **43–47**, *47*
comments, **54**, *55*
  documentation, 465
  for Object Gallery, 418
  in snippets, 418–419
  TODO, 77
Compact setup option, 6
company information for projects, 412–413
compilers
  defined, 464
  Just-In-Time, 469
compiling, 16, 31
complement operator, 58
Component class, 75–76, 96
Component palette, **10–11**, *10*, 175, **210**
  archived beans for, **210–213**, *211–213*
  customizing entries on, **215–216**, *215*
  defined, 464
  icons on, **342–347**, *347*
  new beans for, **226–227**, *226–227*
  removing beans from, **216**
  sources of beans for, **216–220**, *217–219*
componentAdded method, 119, 125
componentRemoved method, 119, 125
components
  adding, **96–97**, *97*
  for beans, **175–177**, *175–177*
  buttons, **103–104**, *104*
  labels, **97–100**, *98*, *101*
  reusable. *See* beans
  text fields, **101–102**, *103*
compound bean components, 322
concrete quality, 464
Condition field, 456–457
conditional statements, 464
  if-else, **67**
  switch, **68–69**

conditions with breakpoints, 456–457
Cone class, 360–361
Cone.java program, 360–361
configuration options, **28**, *28*
  associations, **415–417**, *416–417*
  project settings, **412–415**, *412–414*
Connect From First to This dialog box, *190*
connecting beans, **186**
  button connections in, **192–193**
  choice connections in, **193–194**
  Expression Assistant for, **199–200**, *199–200*
  first connections in, **188–192**, *189–192*
  Interaction Wizard Editor for, **195–199**, *195–198*
  list connections in, **194–195**
  screen setup for, **186–188**, *188*
constants, **60**
constrained properties, **250–251**
constraints for components, 100
Constructor icon, *12*
constructors, 34, 98
  default, 465
  defined, 464
consume method, 108
Consumer class, 438, 442
Consumer.java program, 442
Container class, 75–76, 294
ContainerEvent class, 119
ContainerListener interface, **118–120**
Containing class dialog box, *189*
contains method, 238
Content pane, **11–12**, *11*, 464
continue statements, 464
controllers in MVC, 160
controls, 34–35. *See also* components
converting
  characters to strings, 117
  parameter types, 29–30
  property editor to selection list, **290–291**
  sound files, 80
  strings to integers, 36, 106

coordinates
    for components, 100
    for drawings, 134
    for points, 131
    for strings, 19, *19*
copyright information
    in About Boxes, 379
    in jbuilder.properties, 414
Counter class
    creating, **302–306**, *303*, *306*
    listing, 314–317
    serializing, **306–311**
Counter_button1_actionAdapter class, 317
Counter_button2_actionAdapter class, 318
Counter_button3_actionAdapter class, 318
Counter_button4_actionAdapter class, 317–318
Counter_button5_actionAdapter class, 318
Counter_button6_actionAdapter class, 317
Counter.java program, 313–319
critical sections, 465
curly braces ({})
    for arrays, 63
    for classes, 62
Cursor button, *175*
custom property editors
    creating, **291–297**, *291*
    using, **297–298**, *297*
customizers, 298
customizing
    beans, 173, **278**
        custom property editors for, **291–298**, *291*, *297*
        name input in, **284–290**, *290*
        property editor for, **281–284**, *282–283*
        selection lists for, **290–291**
        ShapeBox for, **278–281**
    Component palette entries, **215–216**, *215*
    JBuilder
        associations, **415–417**, *416–417*
        incorporating snippets, **417–435**
        project settings, **412–415**, *412–414*
cyan constant, 142

d

D for double literals, 60
-D for system properties, 47
daisy chaining, 155, 465
darkGray constant, 142
data hiding, 465
Data pane, 450, *450*, 452, *452–453*, 465
datatypes, **59–60**
    for arrays, 62
    defined, 465
    for parameters, 29–30
Date class, 154
DB Bean, 322
Debug button, *10*
debuggers, 465
debugging, **438**, **449–451**, *450–451*
    breakpoints in, **455–458**, *456–458*
    examining variables, **453–455**, *454–455*
    stepping through programs, **452–453**, *452–453*
declaring
    arrays, **62–63**
    classes, **61–62**
    interfaces, 64
    variables, **62**
decompiling source code, 284
DecoratedFrame class, 41, 161, 258, 308
default clauses, 68–69, 465
default constructors, 225, 465
default projects directories, 14
default property editor, **281–284**, *282–283*
Default Source Path field, 28
default values for system properties, 48
defaultReadObject method, 309–310
defaultWriteObject method, 309
defining threads, **84–88**
defSnippetImage.gif file, 431
Deploy Dependencies option, 368

Deployment Wizard dialog box, **367–369**, *367*
deprecated methods, 465
deriving classes, 22
descriptions
   in About Boxes, 379
   for parameters, 30
   for projects, 412–413
design patterns, 465
Design tab, 228
Destination Directory field, 7
destroy method, **80**, 82–83, 90
destructors, 465
determineFlavorColor method, 361, 366
digital signatures, 150
directories
   for .class files, 17
   graphical display of, **158–161**, *161*
   for installation, 7
   listing, **157**
   for packages, 65
   for projects, 14, 415
   system properties for, 49
dirFile method, 165–166
DirReader class, 150, 158–159
   for file selection, **162**
   for graphical directory displays, **158–161**, *161*
   listing of, 163–166
   for listing directories, **157**
   for reading files, **154–157**
   for retrieving filenames, **151–154**
DirReader.java program, 163–166
disabled menu items, 381
disks
   images from, **140–141**
   sector size on, 6
   space requirements for, **4–6**, *5*
DisplayBuffer class, 438
   adding to buffers in, **443–445**
   creating buffers in, **442–443**
   listing, 446–447
   removing from buffers in, **445**
DisplayBuffer.java program, 443, 445–447
displayImage method, 140
displaying
   directories, **158–161**, *161*
   images, **140–141**, 150, **403–404**, *404*
dispose method, 304
DNS (Domain Name System), 466
do loops, **68**, 465
Doc tab, 54
documentation comments, 54, *55*, 465
dollar signs ($), 56
Domain Name System (DNS), 466
double buffering, **137–141**, *139*, 466
double datatype, 59
   literals, 60
   for parameter types, 30
double quotes (")
   for parameters, **43–44**
   representing, 60
   for strings, 61
drag and drop for beans, **175–177**, *175–177*
draw3DRect method, 133
drawArc method, 133
drawImage method, 138
drawing, **130**
   buffers for, **137–141**, *139*
   color in, **141–144**, *144*
   mouse events in, **133–137**
   with paint, **130–132**
Drawing class, 144–146
Drawing.java program, 144–146
drawOval method, 133
drawPolygon method, 237
drawRect method, 133
drawRoundRect method, 133
drawString method, 78

e

East quadrant in BorderLayout, 122, *123*
Edit File Type dialog box, 415–417, *416*
editing
   jbuilder.properties file, 414
   properties. *See* property editors
Editing Action for Type dialog box, 417
eies.njit.edu site, 362
else clauses, **67**, 466
Enable/Disable Item button, 381
encapsulation, 466
encryption keys, 150
ending points for drawings, 134
environment. *See* Integrated Development Environment (IDE)
Environment Options dialog box, **28**, *28*
equal signs (=)
   in assignment operators, **58–59**
   for initializing variables, 62
   in relational operators, 57
   for system properties, 47
equals method, 399
errors
   compilation, 16, *16*
   exception handling, **69–71**
Evaluate/Modify dialog box, 453–454, *454*
event-driven programming, 466
Event-Sourcing Component dialog box, *189*, 190
EventListener interface, 230
EventObject class, 230
events, **105**
   action, **105–107**
   in beans, 173, **230–240**, *230*, *240*
   in connecting beans, 196–197
   defined, 466
   in Inspector, 178
   keyboard, **108–109**
   limiting, **271**
   listeners for, **232–233**
   mouse, **133–137**

Events tab, 178
EventSetDescriptor class, 269, 271
examining variables, **453–455**, *454–455*
Exception Breakpoint option, 457
exception handling, **69–71**
exceptions, 466
exclamation points (!), 57
<EXCLUDE> tags, 418–419
Execution Log, 47, 49
exists method, 150
exit method, 303
Expression Assistant, 186, **199–200**, *199–200*
expressions, 56, 466
extending classes, 18

f

F for float literals, 60
\f value, 60
factorial problems, 159
File class, 150
File ➤ Close All command, 13, 26
file.encoding system property, 48
file.encoding.pkg system property, 48
File ➤ New command, 26, 29
File ➤ New Project command, 26
File ➤ Open/Create command, 13, 15–16, 331
File Open/Create dialog box, 13–15, *14–15*
File ➤ Project Properties command, 449
File ➤ Save All command, 31
File ➤ Save command, 16–17
file.separator system property, 48
<FILE> tags, 419
File Types tab, 415, *416*
FileDialog class, 401
fileExit_actionPerformed method
   in MenuTester, 388
   in ToolbarTester, 406
FilenameFilter class, 402

Filer class, 401–402
FileReader class, 154–155
files
  associating, **415–417**, *416–417*
  closing, **405**
  displaying directories, **158–161**, *161*
  filenames for, **151–154**, *154*
  information for, **150–151**
  listing directories, **157**
  reading, **154–157**, *157*
  selecting, **162**, **400–403**, *401*, *403*
fill3DRect method, 133
fillArc method, 133
fillOval method, 133
fillRect method, 131
fillRoundRect method, 133
finalizer methods, 466
finally blocks, **70–71**
Find button, *10*
fireNoEvents method, 335–336
firePropertyChange method, 244–245, 286–287
fireVetoableChange method, 250
fireYesEvents method, 335–336
first_textValueChanged1 method, 192, 203
flashing in drawings, **137–141**, *139*
float datatype, 59
  literals, 60
  for parameter types, 30
flow control, **66–67**
  defined, 466
  do loops, **68**
  exception handling, **69–71**
  if-else, **67**
  for loops, **68**
  switch statements, **68–69**
  while loops, **67–68**
FlowLayout manager, **116–118**, *117–118*
flushing, 466

folders for installation, 7
FontChooser class, **385–387**, *385*, *387*
fonts
  menus for, **385–387**, *385*, *387*
  setting, 96
for loops, 44, **68**, 467
foreground color, 96
foreground property, 382, *382*
form feeds, 60
forward slashes (/)
  in assignment operators, 58
  for comments, 54
  for multiplication, 57
Frame1 class, 41–42, 45–46
Frame1.java program, 45–47
frames, 380, 467
"friendly" access modifier, 66
functions. *See also* methods
  abstract, 462
  overloaded, 471

g

gadgets. *See* components
Gamelan site, **217**, *218*
garbage collection, 467
GB (gigabytes), 6
Generate About Box option, 376, 412
Generate Default Constructor option, 225, 270
Generate Menu Bar option, 376
Generate Standard Methods option, 74, 82
Generate Status Bar option, 396
Generate Tool Bar option, 396
Generic Library for Java, 220
geographic regions, system property for, 49
getAbsolutePath method, 151
getAction method, 399
getActionCommand method, 103–104, 156
getAdditionalBeanInfo method, 265

getAll method, 162
getAppletInfo method, 35
  in Billboard, 91
  in Drawing, 145
  in HiLo, 110
  in IceCreamOrder, 365
getAsText method, 286–288, 293
getAudioClip method, **80–82**
getBackground method, 96
getBeanDescriptor method, 265
getCanonicalPath method, 151
getChild method, 119
getClass method, 259
getCodeBase method, 81
getColor method, 241–242
getCustomEditor method, 292–293
getDeclaredField method, 260
getDeclaredFields method, 260
getDeclaredMethod method, 260–261
getDeclaredMethods method, 260
getDefaultEventIndex method, 265
getDefaultPropertyIndex method, 265
getDocumentBase method, 81
getEventSetDescriptors method, 265, 269, 272
getExample method, 336
getField method, 260
getFields method, 260
getFile method
  in ATreeNode, 158, 163
  in Filer, 402
getFont method, 96
getForeground method, 96
getGraphics method, 138
getIcon method, 265
getID method, 334
getInsets method, 391
getLabel command, 104
getMethod method, 260, 266
getMethodDescriptors method, 265
getMethods method, 260

getName method, 151
getNextNumber method, 105, 109
getParameter method, 36
  in Billboard, 89
  in Drawing, 144
  in HiLo, 109
  in IceCreamOrder, 364
getParameterInfo method, 35
  in Billboard, 91
  in Drawing, 145
  in HiLo, 110
  in IceCreamOrder, 365
getParent method, 151
getPath method, 151
getPreferredSize method, 295–296
getPropertyDescriptors method, 265, 269–270, 288–289
getResource method, 344
getSelectedIndex method, 362
getSelectedItems method, 195
getSelectedLabel method, 361
getSelectedText method, 102
getSelection method, 162
getShape method, 279, 281, 285
getSize method, 225
getTags method, 290
getText method
  in TextComponent, 424
  in TextField, 106, 178
getToolkit method, 107
getTriangle method, 238
getValue method
  in ColorChooser, 384
  in ShapeEditor, 286, 288, 293
GIF (Graphics Interchange Format), 141, 467
gigabytes (GB), 6
Goto Breakpoint option, 458
grammar, 54
graphical displays for directories, **158–161**, *161*
graphical user interfaces (GUIs), 96, 467
Graphics class, 18, 130, 137–138

Graphics Interchange Format (GIF), 141, 467
GraphLocation interface, 158, 162
gray constant, 142
greater than signs (>)
   in assignment operators, 59
   in relational operators, 57
   in shift operators, 58
green constant, 142
GridLayout manager, **120–121**, *121*
GroupBox class, 403–405
guessing game. *See* Hi-Lo guessing game
GUIs (graphical user interfaces), 96, 467

h

hard disks
   images from, **140–141**
   sector size on, 6
   space requirements for, **4–6**, *5*
height
   of applets, 20
   in BorderLayout, 122
   of components, 100
   of text fields, 102
HEIGHT option, 20
help, online, 6
Help ➤ About command, 378–379
help_actionPerformed method, 324
Help ➤ Help Topics command, 216
Help ➤ Java Reference command, 133
Help ➤ Welcome Project (Sample) command, 12
helpAbout_actionPerformed method
   in MenuTester, 389
   in ToolbarTester, 406
helper classes, 62
hexadecimal numbers, 60
Hi-Lo guessing game, 96–97, *97*
   buttons for, **103–104**, *104*
   events in, **105–109**
   labels for, **97–100**, *98*, *101*
   listing for, 109–111
   text fields for, **101–102**, *103*
HiLo class, 109–111
HiLo.java program, 109–111
home directory, system property for, 49
Home icon, *11*, 12
HTML (Hypertext Markup Language), 467
HTML pages, generating, 31, *31*
Hypertext Transfer Protocol (HTTP), 467

i

IceCreamOrder class, **354**, *354*
   actions for, **361–366**, *363*
   applet for, **354–357**, *355*, *357*
   cone for, **360–361**
   creating archive for, **367–371**, *367–371*
   listing for, 364–366
   parameters for, **357–359**
   running from archive, **369–371**, *369–371*
   scoop for, **359–360**
IceCreamOrder_button1_actionAdapter class, 366
IceCreamOrder.java program, 364–366
iconified browsers, 79
icons
   on Component palette, **215–216**, *215*, **342–347**, *347*
   creating, 216
   for snippets, 431
IDDE (Integrated Development and Debugging Environment), 468
IDE. *See* Integrated Development Environment (IDE)
IDE Options dialog box, **28**, *28*
identifiers, **56**, 467
if-else flow control, **67**, 467
IllegalArgumentException class, 179, 287
Image class, 130, 137–138, 308
ImageLoader class, 140, 343
images
   for About Boxes, 379
   for buttons, 398
   displaying, **140–141**, 150, **403–404**, *404*

Implement Interface Wizard, 84–85, *85*
implementing interfaces, 64
Implements interface icon, *12*
Import statement icon, *13*
importing packages, 65
incrementCounter method, 305, 315
incrementing in for loops, 68
indexed properties, **243**
infoFile method, 156, 166
inheritance, 22, 468, 470
init method
   for applets, 34, **79**
   in Billboard, 82
   in Drawing, 138, 145
   in HiLo, 99, 110
   in IceCreamOrder, 357, 364–365
   icon for, *12*
initializing
   arrays, 63–64
   in for loops, 68
   variables, 62
inner classes, 468
input, names in, **284–290**, *290*
Inspect_button1_actionAdapter class, 269
Inspect class, 268–269
Inspect dialog box, 455, *455*
Inspect.java program, 268–269
Inspector, **174**, *175*, 178, 245, *246*, 468
installation, **4–8**, *5*, *7–8*
Installation Notes screen, 6
instance variables, **21**, 468
   for parameters, 30
   in serialization, 307
instances, 21, 468
instantiation, 468
int datatype, 59
   converting strings to, 36, 106
   literals, 60
   for parameter types, 30

Integrated Development and Debugging Environment (IDDE), 468
Integrated Development Environment (IDE), **9**, *9*
   AppBrowser, **11–13**, *11*
   component palette, **10–11**, *10*
   defined, 468
   status messages, **11**
   toolbar, **10**, *10*
Interaction Wizard
   for beans, 186, 188–194, *188–191*, 199–200, *200*
   for snippets, 421–422, *422*, 424
Interaction Wizard Editor
   for beans, 186, 188, 190–191, **195–199**, *195–198*, 266, *267*
   for snippets, 422–424, *423*
Interaction Wizard UI dialog box, 199, *199*
interface keyword, 64
interfaces, **64**, 468
interpreters, 468
interrupt method, 86
interthread communication, 438
introspection, 173, **258**, 468
   BeanInfo inspector for, **264–269**, *267*
   overriding BeanInfo inspector, **269–272**
   and reflection, **258–264**, *261*
IntrospectionException class, 266, 270
Introspector class, 264–266
invoke method, 260
isAbsolute method, 151
isDirectory method, 151
isFile method, 151, 156
Item Properties dialog box, 215, *215*
items property, 243
itemStateChanged method, 205

j

JAR (Java Archive) files, 210, 368, 468
JAR Compressed option, 369
JARS (JAVA Applet Rating Service), **219**, *219*
java.applet package, 75–76

Java Archive (JAR) files, 210, 368, 468
java.awt package, 18, 41, 65, 76
java.awt.event package, 271
java.beans package, 270, 286
java.class.path system property, 48
java.class.version system property, 48
Java Core API, 469
Java Database Connectivity (JDBC), 4, 469
Java Developers Kit (JDK), 369–371, 469
.java extension, **415–417**, *416–417*, 419
java.home system property, 48
java.io package, 150, 306
java.lang package, 65, 85
java.lang.reflect package, 258, 264
java.sun.com site, 368
java.util package, 230
java.vendor system property, 48
java.vendor.url system property, 48
java.version system property, 48
Java Virtual Machine Specification document, 114
Java Virtual Machines (JVMs), 114, 469
Java VM Parameters field, **47**
JavaBeans. *See* beans
JavaBeans API, 468
JavaBeans Component Library (JBCL), 22, 96
javabeans.developer.com site, 217
JavaScript language, 469
JBCL (JavaBeans Component Library), 22, 96
JBCL (JBuilder Component Library), 469
jbcl.zip file, 210, 212
jbInit method, 34
   in Billboard, 90
   in BlueBoxActionTester, 235–236
   in BlueBoxTester, 229–230
   in Counter, 314–315
   in DirReader, 152, 155, 163–164
   in DisplayBuffer, 446
   in Drawing, 136, 145
   in Frame1, 42

   in HiLo, 99–100, 104, 107, 109–110
   in IceCreamOrder, 358–359, 365
   in Inspect, 268
   in ListBuilder, 180
   in Lookup, 263
   in MenuTester, 388
   in MenuTester_AboutBox, 390–391
   in MyPanel, 430
   in OkCancelBean, 323
   in OkTester, 341
   in Panel1, 427
   in PanelTester, 426
   in ShapeFrame, 284
   in SnippetTester, 435
   in Tabs, 116–117, 124–125
   in ToolbarTester, 406
   in TriBoxer, 248, 252
   in Wizard, 187, 202–203
   in YesNoBean, 336
JBuilder Component Library (JBCL), 469
jbuilder.properties file, 413–414
JCChartComponent class, 217
JClass class, 216
JDBC (Java Database Connectivity), 4, 469
JDK (Java Developers Kit), 369–371, 469
JGL library, 220
JPEG (Joint Photography Engineering Group) files, 141, 469
.jpr extension, 14, **415–417**, *416–417*
Just-In-Time (JIT) compilers, 469
JVMs (Java Virtual Machines), 114, 469

k

KB (kilobytes), 6
key-value pairs, 47
keyboard events, **108–109**
KeyListener interface, 108

keyPressed method
    in HiLo, 111
    in KeyListener, 108
keyReleased method
    in HiLo, 111
    in KeyListener, 108
keys for system properties, 47
keyTyped method
    in HiLo, 111
    in KeyListener, 108
keywords, **54–55**, 469
kilobytes (KB), 6
KL Group, **216–217**, *217*

L

L for long literals, 60
Label button, *175*
Label class, 97–98
labels, **97–100**, *98*, *101*
    for buttons, 398
    for group boxes, 404–405
lastModified method, 151, 154
layout management, 33, **114**
    with BorderLayout, **122–123**, *123*
    with ContainerListener, **118–120**
    with FlowLayout, **116–118**, *117–118*
    with GridLayout, **120–121**, *121*
    with TabsetPanel, **114–116**, *115*
LayoutManager class, 75–76, 99, 469
length
    of arrays, 62–63
    of files, 151
    of strings, 61
    of text fields, 101–102
length method
    in File, 151
    in String, 61

less than signs (<)
    in assignment operators, 59
    in relational operators, 57
    in shift operators, 58
libraries. *See* packages
license agreement, 6
life-cycle methods, **79–80**, 469
lightGray constant, 142
limiting
    events, **271**
    properties, **270–271**
line.separator system property, 48
LinkedTreeContainer class, 160
LinkedTreeNode class, 158, 160
List button, *175*
List class, 178–179
list method, 157
List of Packages and Classes With Tracing dialog box, *451*
list1_actionPerformed1 method, 200–201, 204
list1_itemStateChanged1 method, 194–195, 204
ListBuilder class, 174, 180–181
ListBuilder_button1_actionAdapter class, 181
ListBuilder_button2_actionAdapter class, 181
ListBuilder.java program, 180–181
listeners
    adding and removing, **231**
    notifying, **232–233**
    registering, 105, 107–108
listening, 105
listing directories, **157**
lists
    connecting, **194–195**
    selection, **290–291**
literals, **60**
    defined, 469
    for initializing variables, 62
    with Interaction Wizard, 191
load method, 140–141
load mode in Filer, 401

Loaded Classes dialog box, *451*
local variables, **22**
logical operators, **57**
login names, system property for, 49
long datatype, 59
   literals, 60
   for parameter types, 30
Lookup class, 259–264
Lookup.java program, 262–264
Lookup_textField1_actionAdapter class, 264
loop method, 80, 82
loops
   busy-wait, 444
   defined, 470
   do, **68**
   for, **68**
   while, **67–68**

m

magenta constant, 142
main method
   in Application1, 40, 44–45, 448
   icon for, *12*
Make button, *10*
manifest files, 368–369
Math class, 132
math operators, **56–57**
max method, 132
MB (megabytes), 6, 470
member variables, 470
members, 470
Menu Designer, **379–381**, *380*, 470
MenuBar button, *175*
MenuComponent class, 97
menuItem1_actionPerformed method, 383, 389
menuItem2_actionPerformed method, 389
menus, **376–377**, *376–377*
   for About Boxes, **378–379**, *378–379*

   for color, **382–384**, *382*, *384*
   for fonts, **385–387**, *385*, *387*
   Menu Designer for, **379–381**, *380*
MenuTest.java program, 387–392
MenuTester class, 376–377, 387–389
MenuTester_AboutBox class, 390–391
MenuTester_InsetsPanel class, 391
MenuTester_menuFileExit_ActionAdapter class, 389
MenuTester_menuHelpAbout_ActionAdapter class, 389–390
MenuTester_menuItem1_actionAdapter class, 391–392
MenuTester_menuItem2_actionAdapter class, 392
messages, 470
Method icon, *12*
methods, **21**
   in beans, 173
   creating, **63**
   defined, 470
   deprecated, 465
   identifiers for, 56
   life-cycle, **79–80**, 469
   native, 470
   overloading, 36
   overriding, **75–79**, *75*, *77–78*
   in serialization, 307
.mf extension, 368
min method, 132
minus signs (-)
   in assignment operators, 58
   for subtraction, 57
Model/View/Controller design, 160
modification dates for files, 154
modulus operation, 57
mouse events, **133–137**
mouseClicked method
   in BlueBox, 233–234
   in Drawing, 139, 146
   in MouseListener, 134
   in ShapeCustomEditor, 295, 297

mouseDragged method
   in Drawing, 146
   in MouseMotionListener, 136
mouseEntered method
   in BlueBox, 234
   in Drawing, 146
   in MouseListener, 134, 142–143
   in ShapeCustomEditor, 295, 297
mouseExited method
   in BlueBox, 234
   in Drawing, 146
   in MouseListener, 134
   in ShapeCustomEditor, 295, 297
MouseListener interface, 134–135, 232–233, 295
MouseMotionListener interface, 134, **136–137**
mouseMoved method
   in Drawing, 146
   in MouseMotionListener, 136
mousePressed method
   in BlueBox, 234
   in Drawing, 139, 146
   in MouseListener, 134–135
   in ShapeCustomEditor, 295, 297
mouseReleased method
   in BlueBox, 234
   in Drawing, 139, 146
   in MouseListener, 134–135
   in ShapeCustomEditor, 295, 297
-ms option, 47
multidimensional arrays, 63, 470
multifile sequencing, 141
multiline comments, 54
multiple inheritance, 470
multiplication, 57
multiselect list mode, 195
multithreading, **84**, **438**, 470
   combining elements for, **447–448**, *449*
   consumer thread for, **442**
   creating threads in, **88–89**

debugging. *See* debugging
   defining threads in, **84–88**
   display buffer for, **442–447**
   producer thread for, **438–441**, *439*
MVC design, **160**
-mx option, 47
My Computer folder, 4–5, *5*
MyButton class, 270
MyButton.java program, 270
MyButtonBeanInfo class, 271–272
MyButtonBeanInfo.java program, 271–272
myclasses directory, 17
MyPanel.snippet program, 428–431
myprojects directory, 14
MyScrollPanel class, 432

n

\n value, 60
names
   for beans, 224, **328–329**
   for editors, 285
   in input, **284–290**, *290*
   for projects, 14, 412–413
   for snippets, 431
Native method icon, *12*
native methods, 470
Navigation pane, **11–12**, *11*, 470
nesting, 470
New Bean Event Wizard, **330–335**, *330*
New Bean Wizard, **328–330**, *328*
new keyword
   for arrays, 63
   for constructors, 98
   for variables, 62
New Object dialog box, 224–225, *225*, 439, *439*
New tab, 224, *224*
newline characters, 60
Next View icon, *11*

no_actionPerformed method, 337
noHappened method
   in OkTester_yesNoBean1_yesNoEventAdapter, 342
   in YesNoEvent, 331
North quadrant in BorderLayout, 122, *123*
NoSuchMethodException class, 261
NOT operator, 57
notify method, 444
notifyActionListeners method, 232, 234
notifying listeners, **232–233**
null values, 470
NumberFormatException class, 106

O

Object class, 75
Object Gallery, 418, **428–431**, *431–432*
Object instance variable icon, *12*
object-oriented programming (OOP)
   defined, 471
   inheritance in, **22**
   objects in, **21–22**
object pointers, 471
object variables, 471
ObjectInputStream class, 312
ObjectOutputStream class, 311
objects, **21–22**
   defined, 470
   hierarchy of, 75–76
   serializing. *See* serialization
octal numbers, 60
octets, 471
ok_actionPerformed method, 323
OkCancelBean class, **322–328**, *325, 327*
OkCancelBean_cancel_actionAdapter class, 324
OkCancelBean_help_actionAdapter class, 324
OkCancelBean.java program, 322–325
OkCancelBean_ok_actionAdapter class, 324
OkTester class, 338–341
OkTester.java program, 338–342

OkTester_yesNoBean1_actionAdapter class, 341
OkTester_yesNoBean1_yesNoEventAdapter class, 341–342
online help, 6
OOP (object-oriented programming)
   defined, 471
   inheritance in, **22**
   objects in, **21–22**
Open dialog box, 401, *401*
Open/Create dialog box, 13–14, *14*
Open File button, *10*
openIt method, **399–404**, 406–407
operators, **56–59**
Options dialog box, 415, *416*
OR operators
   bitwise, 58
   logical, 57
orange constant, 142
order.jar file
   creating, **367–369**, *367*
   running from, **369–371**, *369–371*
os.arch system property, 48
os.name system property, 48
os.version system property, 49
-oss option, 47
ovals, 133
overloading, 36, 471
Override Inherited Methods dialog box, **75–79**, *75, 77*
Override Methods Wizard, **75–79**, *75, 77–78*
overriding
   BeanInfo inspector, **269–272**
   methods, **75–79**, *75, 77–78*

P

Package declaration icon, *13*
<PACKAGE> tags, 419
packages, 18, **65–66**
   adding beans from, **213–215**, *214*
   for applets, 29, 32
   defined, 471

Pages tab, 210, *211*
paint method, 87, **130–132**
    in Billboard, **76–79**, 91
    in BlueBox, 225, 233
    in BlueTriangle, 237–238
    in Box, 241–242
    in Cone, 360–361
    in Drawing, 138, 143, 145
    in Frame1, 46
    in Scoop, 360
    in ShapeBox, 279, 281
Paint Shop Pro program, 216
Palette Properties dialog box, 210–214, *211–212*, *214*, 226–227, *226–227*
Panel button, *175*
Panel class, 75–76, 325
Panel1 class, 424–427, *425*
Panel1.java program, 426–428
Panel1_scrollbar1AdjustmentAdapter1 class, 428, 430
Panel1_scrollbarAdjustmentAdapter class, 424
Panel1_textField1ActionAdapter1 class, 428, 430–431
Panel1_textFieldActionAdapter class, 424
PanelTester class, 425–426
PanelTester.java program, 426
panes
    in AppBrowser, **11–13**, *11*, 450, *450*
    defined, 471
<PARAM> tags, 30–31, 36
parameters
    for applets, **29–30**, *30*, **33–37**, *37*
    for applications, **42–50**, *43*, *46*
    for BeanInfo, 343, *343*
    command-line, **43–47**, *47*
    for IceCreamOrder, **357–359**
Parameters dialog box, 42, *43*, 343, *343*
parentheses (), 56
parseInt method, 36–37, 106
Pass Count field, 456–457
Paste Snippet dialog box, 330, *330*, 432, *433*
Paste Snippet [Bean Info] dialog box, 342–343, *342*

PATH environment variable, 370
path.separator system property, 49
paths
    for archives, 368–369
    configuration options for, **28**, *28*
Pause button, *450*, 451
percent signs (%)
    in assignment operators, 58
    for modulus operation, 57
permissions, 150
persistence, 173, 471. *See also* serialization
persistent object stores, 471
pink constant, 142
pixels, 19, 471
play method, 80
plus signs (+)
    for addition, 57
    in assignment operators, 58
Point class, 131
Polygon class, 237
polymorphism, 471
PopupMenu button, *175*
position of components, 100
preferred height
    in BorderLayout, 122
    in text fields, 102
Previous View icon, *11*
Primitive method icon, *12*
println method
    in debugging, 449
    in PrintWriter, 153
PrintWriter class, 153
private access modifier, 66
processYesNoEvent method, 334, 337
Producer class, **438–441**, *439*
Producer.java program, 441
Product Notes, 8
programs, stepping through, **452–453**, *452–453*
Project Wizard, **26–28**, *26–28*, 412–414, *412*, *414*

projects
  closing, 26
  creating, **13–16**, *14–16*, **26–28**, *26–28*
  defined, 471
  properties for, **412–415**, *412–414*
  <PROMPT> tags, 419
properties
  in beans, 172, **240–251**, *243*, *246–247*
  bound, **243–249**, *246–247*
  constrained, **250–251**
  defined, 471
  indexed, **243**
  limiting, **270–271**
  for projects, **412–415**, *412–414*
  simple, **240–243**, *243*
  system, 38, **47–50**, 473
property editors, 278, **281–284**, *282–283*
  converting to selection lists, **290–291**
  creating, **285–288**
  custom, **291–298**, *291*, *297*
  using, **289–291**, *291*
propertyChange method, 249, 253
PropertyChangeListener interface, 244
PropertyChangeSupport class, 244
PropertyDescriptor arrays, 269–270, 289
PropertyEditorSupport class, 286, 290
protected access modifier, 66
public access modifier, 66
public classes, 62
pull-down menus, 380–381

q

quadrants in BorderLayout, **122–123**, *123*
Quick Start Guide, 12
Quit option in Applet Viewer, 83

r

\r value, 60
random method, 119
rapid application development (RAD) environment, 4, 471
read-only TextFields, 101
readers, 472
readFile method, 165
reading files, **154–157**, *157*
readLine method, 156–157
readObject method, 309–310, 316
Rebuild button, *10*
rectangles, 131–132, *132*
recursive algorithms, 159, 472
red constant, 142
Redo button, *10*
reflection, **258–264**, *261*
registering listeners, 105, 107–108
relational operators, **57**
Reload option in Applet Viewer, 83
remainder operation, 57
Remove from Project icon, *11*
remove method
  in DisplayBuffer, 445–446
  in List, 179
removeActionListener method, 231, 233
removeVetoableChangeListener method, 250
removeYesNoEventListener method, 337
removing Component palette items, **216**
renaming beans, **328–329**
rendering, 472
repaint method, 86, 135, 140, 444
Replace button, *10*
Replace Text dialog box, 328–329, *329*
Reset button, *450*, 451
resetCounter method, 305, 316
Restart option in Applet Viewer, 83
restoring serialization, **312–313**, *313*

return characters, 60
return statements, 63, 472
reusable components. *See* beans
reverse method, 200–201
reversing strings, 200–201
root classes, 472
rounded-cornered rectangles, 133
Run ➤ Add Breakpoint command, 456
Run button, *10*, 32, *450*
Run ➤ Debug command, 449
Run ➤ Evaluate/Modify command, 453
Run ➤ Inspect command, 455
run method, 84–85
   in Billboard, 91
   in Consumer, 442
   in Counter, 304, 315
   in Producer, 440–441
Run ➤ Parameters command, 42
Run ➤ Run Applet command, 17, 31–32
Run ➤ Run to Cursor command, 455
Run ➤ Run to End of Method command, 455–456
Runnable interface, 84–85, 438–439
running applets, **16–17**, *17*, 31–32, *32*
runtime exceptions, 71
runtime parameters, **29–30**, *30*, **33–37**, *37*

S

Save File button, *10*
save mode in Filer, 401
Save Project button, *10*
saving
   bean state. *See* serialization
   projects, 16
scheduler, 447
Scoop class, 359–360
Scoop.java program, 360
Scrollbar button, *175*

ScrollBar class, 420, 424
scrollbar1_adjustmentValueChanged1 method
   in MyPanel, 430
   in Panel1, 424, 427
scrolling text applet
   creating, **74**, *74*
   overriding methods for, **75–79**, *75*, *77–78*
   sound in, **80–83**
ScrollPane button, *175*
Search Again button, *10*
Search ➤ Replace command, 328
sector size, 6
security in applets, 13
SecurityManager class, 472
Select Destination Location window, 7
Select Image option, 215
Select Setup Type window, 6
selecting
   files, 162, **400–403**, *401*, *403*
   toolbar buttons, **398–399**
selection lists, converting property editor to, **290–291**
semicolons (;), 56
Send Run Output to Execution Log option, 47
separators, 381, 472
.ser extension, 311
Serializable interface, 306–307
serialization
   Counter class for, **302–306**, *303*, *306*
   defined, 472
   enabling, **306–311**
   listing for, 313–319
   restoring, **312–313**, *313*
setActionCommand method, 103–104
setAsText method, 286–288
setBackground method, 96
setColor method, 143, 241–242, 244
setDrawingColor method, 142, 146
setEchoChar method, 102
setEditable method, 101
setEditInPlace method, 160

setEndPoint method, 131, 135, 146
setExample method, 336
setFile method, 402
setFont method, 96
setForegroundColor method, 96
setFrame method, 383
setImageName method, 379
setInsets method, 391
setLabel command, 104
setMessage method, 45–46
setPropertyEditorClass method, 289
setShape method, 279–280, 285
setSize method, 118–119
setStartPoint method, 131, 146
setText method
   in Label, 107, 399
   in TextArea, 153
   in TextField, 102
setTitle method
   in ColorChooser, 384
   in FontChooser, 386
setup, **6–8**, *7–8*
Setup Is Complete dialog box, 8, *8*
setupAdapters method, 310, 312, 315
setValue method
   in ColorChooser, 384
   in FontChooser, 386
   in ShapeEditor, 286, 288, 293
ShapeBox class
   creating, **278–281**
   property editor for, **281–284**, *282–283*
   shape names in, **284–290**, *290*
ShapeBox.java program, 280–281
ShapeBoxBeanInfo class, 288–289
ShapeBoxBeanInfo.java program, 289
ShapeCustomEditor class, **292–298**
ShapeCustomEditor.java program, 296–297
ShapeEditor class, **285–288**
ShapeEditor.java program, 287–288, 293

ShapeFrame class, 281–284
ShapeFrame.java program, 283–284
shift operators, 58
short datatype, 59
   literals, 60
   for parameter types, 30
showrgb command, 362
signatures
   digital, 150
   method, 472
simple properties, **240–243**, *243*
SimpleBeanInfo class, 270
single quotes ('), 60
size
   of applets, 19–20
   of applications, 38
   of arrays, 44, 62–63
   of beans, 225, 228
   of components, 100
   of datatypes, **59–60**
   of disk sectors, 6
   of text fields, 101–102
Skills directory, 26–28
slashes (/)
   in assignment operators, 58
   for comments, 54
   for multiplication, 57
sleep method, 86, 444
smaller method, 259, 263
.snippet extension, 419
snippets, **417–418**
   adding to Object Gallery, **428–431**, *431–432*
   class for, **420–428**, *421–423, 425*
   snippet language for, **418–419**
   using, **432–435**, *433–434*
snippets directory, 418, 428
SnippetTester class, 432–435
SnippetTester.java program, 434–435
sound in applets, **80–83**, *83*
Sound Ring site, 81

source files
  for applets, **32–35**
  for applications, **39–42**, *41*
  creating, 15–16
  decompiling, 284
  defined, 472
  documentation from, 54, *55*
  examining, **18–20**, *19*
Source pane, 450, *450*
Source tab, 16
sources of events, 105
South quadrant in BorderLayout, 122, *123*
SoX tool, 80
spaces for parameters, 43
splash.javasoft.com site, **219**, 298
square brackets ([]), 63
-ss option, 47
stand-alone applications, 37–38
start method, **79**, 82
  in Billboard, 90
  for threads, 88, 447
Start option in Applet Viewer, 83
starting points for drawings, 134
statements, 56
states, 472
static variables in serialization, 307
status bar, setting, **399–400**, *400*
status messages, **11**
Step Over button, 450, *450*
stepping through programs, **452–453**, *452–453*
stop method, **80**
  in AudioClip, 80, 82
  in Billboard, 90
  in Counter, 306
  for threads, 88
Stop option in Applet Viewer, 83
streaming, 472
streams, 472

String class, 61
  importing, 65
  vs. StringBuffer, 201
StringBuffer class, 200–201
strings, **61**
  converting characters to, 117
  converting to integers, 36, 106
  coordinates of, 19, *19*
  for parameters, 29–30, **43–44**
  reversing, 200–201
StringWriter class, **153–154**
Structure pane, **11–13**, *11*, 473
stubs, 399, 473
subclasses, 22, 473
subtraction, 57
Superclass icon, *12*
superclasses, 22, 473
supportsCustomEditor method, 292–293
switch statements, **68–69**, 473
synchronized blocks, **86–87**, 444–445
syntax
  access modifiers, 66
  arrays, **62–63**
  classes, **61–62**
  comments, **54**
  datatypes, **59–60**
  flow control, **66–69**
  identifiers, **56**
  interfaces, **64**
  keywords, **54–55**
  literals, **60**
  methods, **63**
  operators, **56–59**
  packages, **65–66**
  strings, **61**
  variables, **62**
system properties, 38, **47–50**, 473
system threads, 84

t

\t value, 60
tab characters, 60
tabbed property sheets, **114–116**, *115*
Tabs class, 124–125
Tabs.java program, 115, 124–125
TabsetPanel class, **114–116**, *115*
tags
  in applets, 19–20, 30–31
  in snippet language, **418–419**
<TARGET> tags, 419
terminating conditions in for loops, 68
testing
  beans, **228–230**, *228*, **234–236**, *236*, **239–240**, *240*
  bound properties, **245–247**, *246–247*
  constrained properties, **251**
  YesNoBean class, **338–340**, *339*
testYesNoEvent method, 333
text fields, **101–102**, *103*
text labels, 98, 398
TextArea button, *175*
TextArea class, 151–152
TextComponent class, 424
TextField button, *175*
TextField class, **101–102**, *103*, 151–152, 420–424, *423*
textField1_actionPerformed method
  in Lookup, 260–261, 263–264
  in Panel1, 427
textField1_actionPerformed1 method
  in MyPanel, 430
  in Panel1, 424
textValueChanged method, 204
This Event Group Exposed to Interactions option, 197
this keyword, 86, 138
This Method Exposed to Interactions option, 199
Thread and Stack pane, 450, *450*, 452, *452*, 473
Thread class, 84, 308, 439

threads, 79, 473. *See also* multithreading
  creating, **88–89**
  defining, **84–88**
three-dimensional rectangles, 133
throws keyword, 70
tildes (~t), 58
time zones, system property for, 49
titles
  for HTML pages, 31
  for projects, 412–413
//TODO comments, 77
tool tips, 10, 473
toolbars, **10**, *10*, **396–398**, *396*, *398*
  for closing files, **405**
  for displaying images, **403–404**, *404*
  listing for, 405–407
  selecting buttons on, **398–399**
  for selecting files, **400–403**, *401*, *403*
  status bar for, **399–400**, *400*
ToolbarTester class, 396, 405–407
ToolbarTester_buttonBar_actionAdapter class, 407
ToolbarTester_buttonControl1_actionAdapter class, 407
ToolbarTester.java program, 405–407
Toolkit class, 107, 298
Tools ➤ Configure Palette command, 210, 214–216
Tools ➤ IDE Options command, 28
Tools ➤ Interaction Wizard Editor command, 195, 266
toString method
  in ATreeNode, 158, 163
  in StringBuffer, 201
  in StringWriter, 153
Trace Into button, 450, *450*
transient variables in serialization, 308
TreeControl class, 150, 158, 160, 162
TrevorHarmon.com site, 217
triangle bean, **237–240**, *240*
TriBoxer class, 245–248, *247*, 251–253

TriBoxer_box1_actionAdapter class, 249, 253
TriBoxer_box1_propertyChangeAdapter class, 248–249, 253
TriBoxer_box1_vetoableChangeAdapter class, 254
TriBoxer_box2_actionAdapter class, 249, 253–254
TriBoxer_box3_actionAdapter class, 249, 254
TriBoxer.java program, 251–254
trigonometric functions, 132
try / catch blocks, **70–71**
Typical setup option, 6

u

UI Designer, **174**, *174–175*, 473
underscores (_), 56
Undo button, *10*
Unicode character set, 56, 474
Uniform Resource Locators (URLs), 80–81, 474
untrusted applets, 474
update method, 140, 146
URLs (Uniform Resource Locators), 80–81, 474
Use JavaBean Icon option, 215
user.dir system property, 49
user.home system property, 49
user.language system property, 49
user.name system property, 49
user.region system property, 49
user threads, 84
user.timezone system property, 49

v

validate method, 305, 444
values for system properties, 47
variables, **21–22**
　class, 464
　declaring, **62**
　examining, **453–455**, *454–455*
　in for loops, 68
　identifiers for, 56
　member, 470
　object, 471
　in serialization, 307–308
vendors, system property for, 48
-version option, 47
versions
　in About Boxes, 379
　system properties for, 48–49
vertical bars (|)
　in assignment operators, 58
　in bitwise operators, 58
　in logical operators, 57
vetoableChange method, 254
VetoableChangeSupport class, 250
View ➤ Breakpoints command, 458
View ➤ Loaded Classes command, 450
View ➤ Toolbar command, 10
views in MVC, 160
visibility, access modifiers for, **66**
void return type, 63
volume control support, 107

w

wait method, 444
waitForImage method, 141
Watch pane, 474
.wav files, 80
Web browsers, 474
Web sites, 474
Welcome to JBuilder Setup window, 6, 7
West quadrant in BorderLayout, 122, *123*
while loops, **67–68**, 474
white constant, 142
widgets, 474. *See also* components

width
  of applets, 20
  of beans, 225
  of components, 100
  of text fields, 101–102
WIDTH option, 20
Wizard class, 186, 202–203
Wizard_button1ActionAdapter1 class, 204
Wizard_button2ActionAdapter1 class, 204–205
Wizard_button3ActionAdapter1 class, 205
Wizard_choice1ItemAdapter1 class, 205
Wizard_firstTextAdapter1 class, 204
Wizard.java program, 202–206
Wizard_list1ActionAdapter1 class, 206
Wizard_list1ItemAdapter1 class, 205
Wizards ➤ Deployment Wizard command, 367
Wizards ➤ Implement Interface command, 85
Wizards ➤ Override Methods command, 75
working directory, system property for, 49
World Wide Web (WWW), 474
WritableGraphSelection interface, 162
writeObject method, 309–311, 316
writers, 474
www.developer.com site, 217, *218*
www.dsinclair.com site, 362
www.jars.com site, 219, *219*
www.javasoft.com site, 114, 141
www.klg.com site, 216
www.netcharts.com site, 217
www.nidlink.com site, 81
www.spies.com site, 80
www.unicode.org site, 56
www.visitorinfo.com site, 216

x

x for hexadecimal numbers, 60
x-position in coordinate system, 19, *19*
XBM file format, 141
XOR operator, 58
XYConstraints class, 100
XYLayout class, 99–100

y

y-position in coordinate system, 19, *19*
yellow constant, 142
yes_actionPerformed method, 337
yesHappened method
  in OkTester_yesNoBean1_yesNoEventAdapter, 342
  in YesNoEvent, 331
YesNoBean class, **335–340**, *339*
YesNoBean.java program, 335–338
YesNoBean_no_actionAdapter class, 337–338
YesNoBean_yes_actionAdapter class, 337
yesNoBean1_actionPerformed method, 340–341
yesNoBean1_noHappened method, 340–341
yesNoBean1_yesHappened method, 340–341
YesNoBeanBeanInfo class, 343–347
YesNoBeanBeanInfo.java program, 344–347
YesNoEvent class, 330–331, 333–334
YesNoEvent.java program, 331–334
YesNoEventExampleBean class, **332–333**
YesNoEventListener interface, 331–332
YesNoEventListener.java program, 331–332

Z

zero-based arrays, 44
zeros for octal numbers, 60
zip files
  for archives, 368
  Component palette beans from, **210–213**, *211–213*

JAVA BOOKS FROM SYBEX

Java® is a revolution. For 30 years the computer world has had scores of incompatible programming languages and operating systems. Now Java, a simple yet powerful language, lets programmers write code that will run on every computer hooked to the Internet or an intranet, whether they're running Windows, Unix, Macintosh OS, or anything else.

Java is the language of the future, and Sybex provides the tools that let you master that language.

Java 1.1: No experience required
Steven Holzner
ISBN: 0-7821-2083-0, $34.99
CD included

The ABCs of JavaScript
Lee Purcell, Mary Jane Mara
ISBN: 0-7821-1937-9, $29.99

Mastering Visual J++
Steven Holzner
ISBN: 0-7821-2041-5, $39.99
CD included

Visual J++1.1: No experience required
Steven Holzner
ISBN: 0-7821-2078-4, $29.99

Mastering Java 1.1
Laurence Vanhelsuwé, Ivan Phillips, Goang-Tay Hsu, Eric Ries, and John Zukowski
ISBN: 0-7821-2070-9, $49.99
CD included

Java 1.1 Developer's Handbook
Philip Heller, Simon Roberts, with Peter Seymour and Tom McGinn
ISBN: 0-7821-1919-0, $59.99
CD included

SYBEX

SYBEX BOOKS ON THE WEB!

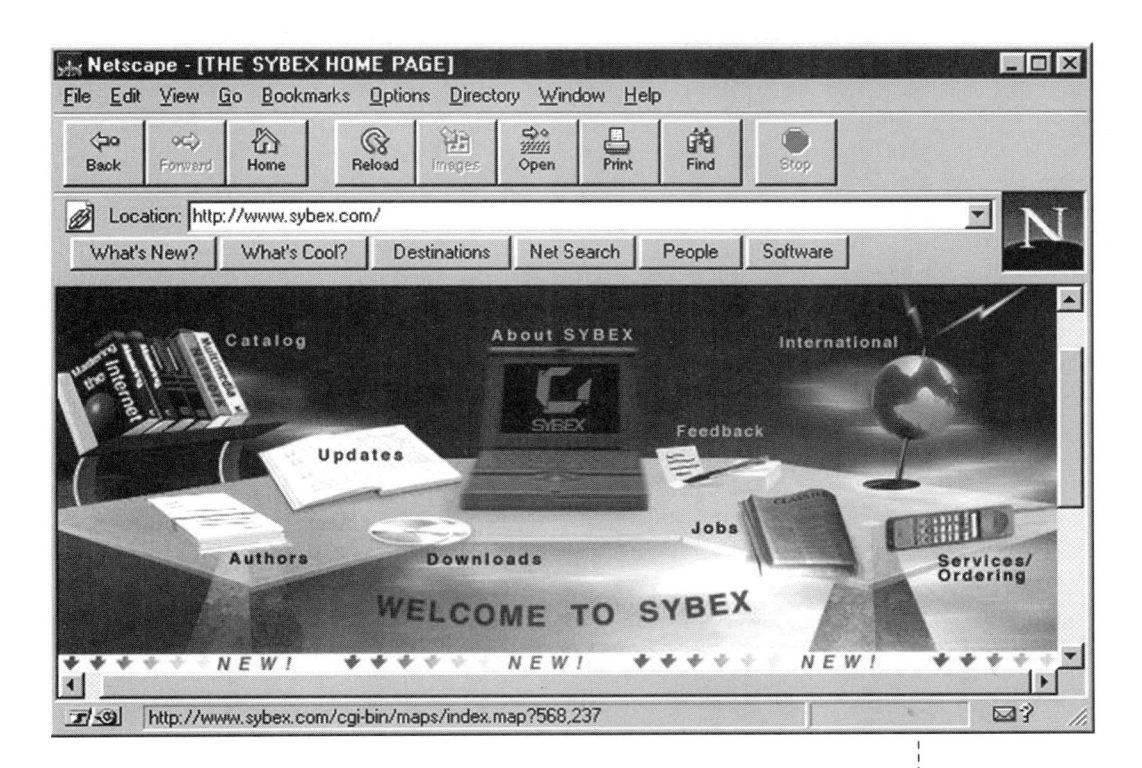

Presenting a truly dynamic environment that is both fun and informative.

- download useful code
- e-mail your favorite Sybex author
- preview a book you might want to own
- find out about job opportunities at Sybex
- order books
- learn about Sybex
- discover what's new in the computer industry

http://www.sybex.com

SYBEX Inc. • 1151 Marina Village Parkway • Alameda, CA 94501 • 510-523-8233

The JBuilder Component Palette

Controls [package borland.jbcl.control]

ButtonControl	CheckboxControl	CheckboxPanel
ChoiceControl	FieldControl	LabelControl
ListControl	LocatorControl	GridControl
ImageControl	NavigatorControl	ButtonBar
ShapeControl	StatusBar	TabsetControl
TextAreaControl	TextFieldControl	TreeControl

Containers [package borland.jbcl.control]

BevelPanel	GroupBox	SplitPanel	TabsetPanel	

AWT [package java.awt]

Button	Checkbox	CheckboxGroup	Choice
Label	List	MenuBar	PopupMenu
Panel	Scrollbar	ScrollPane	TextArea
TextField			

Dialogs [package borland.jbcl.control]

Filer	ColorChooser	FontChooser	Message